# Glass Construction Manual

SCHITTICH
STAIB

BALKOW
SCHULER
SOBEK

BIRKHÄUSER – PUBLISHERS FOR ARCHITECTURE
BASEL · BOSTON · BERLIN

EDITION DETAIL
MÜNCHEN

The original German edition of this book was conceived and developed by
*DETAIL*, Review of Architecture.

Authors:

Christian Schittich
Dipl.-Ing., architect, Chief Editor of the journal *DETAIL*

Gerald Staib
Prof. Dipl.-Ing., freelance architect,

Chair of Building Structures and Design, Dresden Technical University

Dieter Balkow
Dipl.-Ing., publicly appointed independent expert for glass in buildings and daylighting
Director of the Swiss Institute for Glass in Building, Zurich

Matthias Schuler
Dipl.-Ing., Managing Partner of Transsolar Energietechnik, Stuttgart

Werner Sobek
Prof. Dr.-Ing.,
Head of the Institute for Lightweight Structures, Stuttgart University

Assistants:

Eckhard Helfrich, Dipl.-Ing.; Mathias Kutterer, Dipl.-Ing.; Anja Witte;
Silke Brumm, Dipl.-Ing.; Friedemann Kik, Dipl.-Ing.; Friedrich Sick, Dipl.-Ing.; Peter Voit, Dipl.-Ing.


Published by:
Institut für internationale Architektur-Dokumentation GmbH, Munich
Editorial services:
Christian Schittich, Dipl.-Ing.; Sonja Brandl, Dipl.-Ing.; Susanne Funk M. A., Cornelia Hilpert M. A.
Drawings: Sabine Drey, Dipl.-Ing.

Translators (German/English):
Peter Green, Dipl. Arch., Munich/London (Part 4)
Gerd Söffker, Philip Thrift, Hanover (Parts 1 – 3)

A CIP catalogue record for this book is available from the Library of Congress,
Washington, D.C., USA

Deutsche Bibliothek – Cataloging-in-Publication Data

Glass Construction Manual / [Hrsg.: Institut für Internationale Architektur-Dokumentation GmbH,
München.]
Balkow ... [Red.: Christian Schittich ... Transl. (German/Engl.) Peter Green (part 4); Gerd Söffker,
Philip Thrift (parts 1–3). Zeichn.: Sabine Drey]. – Basel; Boston; Berlin : Birkhäuser, 1999
Dt. Ausg. u.d.T.: Glasbau-Atlas
ISBN 3-7643-6077-1 (Basel ...)
ISBN 0-8176-6077-1 (Boston)

This book is also available in a German language edition (ISBN 3-7643-5944-7).

© 1999  Birkhäuser – Publishers for Architecture, P.O. Box, 133, CH-4010 Basel, Switzerland
Printed on acid-free paper produced from chlorine-free pulp. TCF ∞

Printed in Germany
ISBN 3-7643-6077-1
ISBN 0-8176-6077-1

9 8 7 6 5 4 3 2

# Contents

# Preface

Hardly any other building material can match the current immense popularity of glass among architects and engineers. Glass has witnessed a long period of evolution in architecture – from the solid, plain wall to the see-through and light-permeable outer skin.

A material that gives us the chance to erect transparent, open and seemingly weightless buildings alters the correlation between interior and exterior, the relationship between humankind, space, light and nature. It is not difficult to understand why glass has such a high priority as an architectural medium.

The property of being able to "capture" the warmth of the sun within the building was still a major problem at the beginning of the 20th century as new structural solutions were being explored and the desire arose to reach beyond the confining walls of our constructions. Today we have many different options available for the intelligent control and admission of the right amount of light and heat into our buildings. And glass is being increasingly used as a loadbearing element by the structural engineer – considerably reducing the proportion of bulky supporting construction.

Glass has very recently been given an enormous innovative boost. We are now in the position to comply with the stringent demands of fire protection and safety. The latest thin-film coatings render possible low-emission and solar-control glasses which at the same time permit optimum transparency. And yet other technologies can make glass alternately translucent or transparent, or – by way of holograms or liquid crystals – turn it into an information medium.

These diverse innovations lead to an enormous thirst for information among architects and engineers.

This book is intended to quench that thirst. The aim of the Glass Construction Manual is to present the multifarious aesthetic and engineering possibilities presented by glass as a building material. Following on in the tradition of such "construction manuals" from Edition Detail, this book also takes an overall look at the subject. Basics such as the properties of glass, its loadbearing behaviour, thermal, acoustic and fire aspects, glass as an energy provider and a systematic selection of fixing details and construction forms are all covered here.

The first part deals with the history of glass and illustrates all the applications of the material from its earliest beginnings right up to the present day.

The final section contains examples intended to show, above all, the interaction of aesthetics and engineering. The projects selected are not just those where vast expanses of glazing and technical innovations are prominent but also everyday solutions, such as the integration of elementary windows in a wall of timber or exposed clay facing bricks.

It remains to hope that this book will contribute to a better practical and theoretical understanding of this multipurpose material, perhaps even to inspiring architects and engineers in their daily duties.

The Authors

# Part 1 · Glass in architecture

# From the origins to classical modernism

**Gerald Staib**

### The main stages in the manufacture of glass – a historical perspective

The word glass is derived from glaza, the Germanic term meaning "amber", "glare" or "shimmer". The glass jewellery the Romans imported closely resembled amber and was consequently named as such. In Latin, amber is *glesum* or *glaesum*. The Romans, on the other hand, referred to glass as *vitrum*, providing the root for the French expressions *vitre* for window pane and *verre* for glass.

#### Origins in Mesopotamia and Egypt
It is still uncertain where the manufacture of glass originated. An ash discovered by chance when copper was smelted or when clay vessels were fired was used to glaze ceramics from early times. Articles showing evidence of this and dating back to the 5th century BC have been found in Mesopotamia, while others from the early 4th century BC were excavated in Egypt. When the tombs of Egyptian pharaohs were opened, greenish glass beads that stemmed from around 3500 BC came to light. This marks the beginning of what could be referred to as intentional glass manufacture. From the middle of the 2nd century BC, rings and small figures, which had been produced using bowls as casting moulds, began to appear. The core-wound technique also allowed the production of small glasses, vases, etc. from the viscous, opaque melt. A sand core containing clay was fixed to a rod, dipped in the molten glass and turned around its own axis to create a thick "glass thread" that adhered to it. This was subsequently rolled into a suitable shape on a flat surface and the core removed after cooling. The oldest blueprint for glass appears on clay tablets in the great library of the Assyrian king Ashurbanipal (668–626 BC) in Nineveh. The inscriptions in cuneiform read: "Take 60 parts of sand, 180 parts of ash from marine plants, 5 parts of chalk – and you will obtain glass". In principle, this is still correct today (see "Composition", p. 61).

#### The Syrian blowing iron
Only after the invention of the blowing iron around 200 BC by Syrian craftsmen in the Sidon region did it become possible to produce thin-walled hollow vessels in a wide variety of shapes. The gaffer (blower) gathers

1.1.1

molten glass on the end of a 1.5 m hollow rod and blows this into a thin-walled vessel.

#### The Roman age
Excavations have revealed that glass was first used as part of the building envelope in villas at Pompeii and Herculaneum, and at public baths. These panes were installed either without a frame or were given a bronze or wood surround; they measured approx. 300 x 500 mm and were between 30 and 60 mm thick. Although cylinder sheet glass was known at this time, these panes were cast and drawn: a viscous paste was first poured onto a framed table sprinkled with sand and then stretched by drawing it with iron hooks. As far as the weathered fragments discovered can indicate, this Roman window glass seems to have been a bluish green and not particularly transparent.

#### The Middle Ages
With the Romans, this technique of glass production also spread to northern Alpine regions. After the period of migration, the Roman tradition was first revived by the Merovingian Franks. Objects preserved from the early Middle Ages include mastos vessels, drinking horns and claw beakers. These

1.1.1 Glass "claw beaker", Lower Franconia, 6th century, Mainfränkisches Museum, Würzburg, Germany
1.1.2 Smelting glass, engraving from *De re metallica*, 12 books on mining and metallurgy, Georgius Agricola (1494–1555), Basel, 1557

utensils continued to be produced right into the high Middle Ages, although glass production now revolved more and more around the building of churches and monasteries. The largest glassworks were located in forested areas and along rivers, i.e. wherever there was an abundance of wood, to provide energy and potash, and water, for cooling and transporting the sand. When the supply of wood in the vicinity was depleted, the glassworks moved on. Deforestation became critical, and glass-making was prohibited in many areas. Coal did not replace wood as a fuel until the 18th century, finally marking the end of forest glassworks.

#### Blown cylinder sheet glass and crown glass
The two most important production techniques since the early Middle Ages, the blown cylinder sheet and crown glass processes, remained the basis of glass production until the late 19th and early 20th century. While flat glass had been produced

1.1.2

using a blowing iron in the cylinder process in the 1st century AD, the method of producing crown glass was not discovered until the 4th century AD. It was again Syrian craftsmen who developed both processes and disseminated these during their travels in the north.

In both the crown glass and blown cylinder glass processes, a blob of molten glass is drawn off with a blowing iron, preformed into a round shape and blown into a "balloon", which is continually reheated to keep it ductile for shaping.

In the blown cylinder sheet glass process, primarily applied in Lorraine and along the River Rhine, the balloon was shaped into a

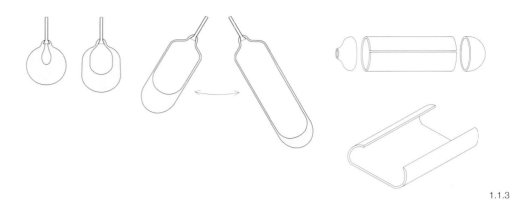

1.1.3

1.1.4

cylinder, as long and thin-walled as possible, by blowing, swinging and rolling it on a table. A dampened iron pin, later a diamond, was used to cut off both ends and slit open the stress-relieved, cooled cylinder lengthwise before it was reheated in the flattening furnace and bent into a flat pane. The dimensions of the cylinder, and consequently of the pane, were limited only by the power of the blower's lungs! Cylinders measured a maximum of 2 m long with a diameter of 300 mm.

To produce crown glass, the bubble of glass was "stuck" to the iron plate on the glass-maker's pontil (iron rod) and the blowing iron cracked off; the hole was enlarged to form a rim. This bell-shaped object was again reheated and rotated at speed to form a disc. As it was uneven, the glass-maker cut this "crown" glass into smaller rectangles, rhombuses or hexagons, depending on its quality. The thick centre, the bull's-eye, and smaller panes were sold as bull's-eye panes without being cut again. In contrast to cylinder glass, the crown glass process produced more even, purer and more lustrous surfaces as the glass did not come into contact with the rough, hot floor of the furnace. This method was still applied until the mid-19th century, particularly in Normandy – presumably the reason it is called *verre de France* – and in England.

### Venice

Between the 15th and 17th centuries, the city of Venice was the major producer of glass bowls, drinking vessels and mirrors (panes of flat glass backed with an amalgam of tin and mercury), which were primarily exported to Germany and France. The success of Venetian glass was due to its extraordinary purity and absence of colour, achieved by adding the ash of a marine plant as well as manganese and white arsenic as decolourizing agents.

### 17th/18th century

The glass boom in the 17th century – glass was no longer sold solely to churches and monasteries but also to dealers in the cities for glazing palaces and houses – and the glass monopoly held by Venice motivated glass-makers to seek new methods of production. In 1687 the Frenchman Bernard Perrot developed a vital innovation, the cast glass process, in which the glass melt was poured onto a smooth, preheated copper table and pressed into a pane by a water-cooled metal roller. The thickness of the pane depended on the height of the surround. The pane, far more even in comparison to previous processes, was subsequently ground with sand and water and polished with a paste made from iron oxide. These so-called *grandes glaces* or "plate" glass panes measured up to 1.20 x 2 m and were able to be produced in better quality with less manpower, leading to a reduction in costs. The true breakthrough, however, came with the invention of a casting and rolling method, the Bicheroux process, by Max Bicheroux in 1919 (see "Early 20th century", p. 11).

Despite this, window glass continued to be an expensive material, partly because both sides had to be polished. Glass was so precious at the end of the 18th century that coach drivers, for instance, replaced the glass panes in their carriages by wickerwork at the end of the day. In England, tenants removed the window glass when they moved house as it did not constitute part of the fixed furnishings.

### Industrialization

Considerable progress was made in all realms of glass production in the 19th century. In 1856 Friedrich Siemens patented an improved version of the melting furnace; this rationalized operations and halved the amount of fuel required. It boosted efficiency in production and prices declined. The blown cylinder sheet glass process similarly experienced major development: in 1839 the Chance brothers succeeded in adapting the cutting, grinding and polishing of the blown cylinder to reduce breakage and improve the surface finish. With the advent of this process in 1850–51 it became possible to produce the enormous number of glass panes for the construction of the Crystal Palace in just a few months. Around the turn of the century, the American, John H. Lubbers, developed a mechanical process to combine blowing and drawing. In the melting tank, the top of a cylinder was connected to a compressed air supply and slowly drawn out vertically with the preheated compressed air flowing continually. With this process it now became possible to obtain lengths of 12 m and diameters of 800 mm. However, before the pane could be produced, the "detour" via cutting and forming the cylinder was still necessary. One particular difficulty was turning the cylinder into a horizontal position.

### Early 20th century
Machine-made, brilliant glass panes did not become possible until 1913, when Emile Fourcault of Belgium succeeded in drawing these directly out of the glass melt. In this process a nozzle made of fired clay was immersed in the molten glass, which flowed out through a slit, was gripped by iron tongs and, while being cooled, drawn vertically upwards, like "honey". Slight undulations across the sheets caused by the drawing process proved to be a problem. For this reason, window glass, apart from very small panes, was installed with the undulations running horizontally.

In America, Irving Colburn patented a similar method in 1905 called the Libbey-Owens process. In this method the glass was not drawn vertically through a nozzle like with Fourcault, but gradually turned over a polished nickel-alloy roller into the horizontal plane, cooled to hand-hot in a 60 m cooling

channel and then cut to size. The glass sheet measured 2.5 m across and thicknesses, between 0.6 and 20 mm, were defined by the speed of drawing: faster drawing produced thinner sheets. The glass needed for the Crystal Palace could have been produced in just two days using this method! The process, applied by the Pittsburgh Plate Glass Company since 1928, combined the advantages of the two methods above, thus further boosting the speed of production. As the three processes were improved, polished plate glass with its high production costs became more and more obsolete.

In 1919 Max Bicheroux succeeded in taking a vital step in the production of cast glass. The production process, previously split up into several stages, was now concentrated in one continuous rolling mill: the glass melt left the crucible in portions and passed through two cooled rollers to form a glass ribbon. The hot glass was cut into panes and transported into cooling furnaces on rolling tables. Panes measuring 3 x 6 m were now possible. Since the beginning of this century, experiments have also been made with flowing glass, initially without success, however, until Alastair Pilkington developed the float-glass process during the 1950s, which today still forms the basis of glass production (see "Float glass", p. 62).

### The glass block or the translucent wall
Glass slabs for unrestricted foot traffic had existed since the mid-19th century. Thaddeus Hyatt had laid them, framed in metal, in pavements in England to admit light into basements. However, another 30 years were to pass before a glass product with sufficient light transmission could be developed as bricks for walls. The invention by Gustave Falconnier of France ushered in the mass production of hand-blown glass bricks that were produced from 1886 in oval and hexagonal form. Despite their restricted loadbear-

ing capacity and problems with condensation, these products enjoyed extreme popularity with architects like Hector Guimard, Auguste Perret and Le Corbusier, among others.

The "Prism glass" of the Luxfer-Prismen Company brought more light into interiors from 1899 onwards. Light was able to be directed into rooms by these 100 x 100 mm solid bricks formed inside like prisms and enclosed in narrow metal frames – a principle still in use today. In 1907 the "reinforced concrete glass blocks" of Friedrich Keppler appeared. Lateral grooves in the block, which is 40 to 65 mm thick, interlocked with the reinforced concrete cames. This made it possible to install large slab constructions with high load-carrying capacity and light transmission. Bruno Taut applied this technique to the walls and roof of his "Glass Pavilion" at the Deutsche Werkbund Exhibition in Cologne in 1914.

The "Nevada brick" (200 x 200 x 40 mm) produced by Saint-Gobain marked a further milestone. Demonstrated in buildings by Le Corbusier and Pierre Chareau, this "glass brick" gained worldwide popularity.

In addition to these solid bricks pressed in moulds, Luxfer and Siemens developed the hollow glass brick in the old German *Reichsformat* (250 x 125 x 96 mm) that was laid with the open side down.

In the 1930s the Owens Illinois Glass Corporation succeeded in producing a brick consisting of two halves pressed together under heat and pressure, like those with which we are familiar today.

1.1.3   The production of blown cylinder sheet glass
1.1.4   The production of crown glass, engraving from *Encyclopédie* by Diderot and d'Alembert, 1773
1.1.5   The production of polished plate glass, engraving from *Encyclopédie* by Diderot and d'Alembert, 1773
1.1.6   ditto

1.1.5

1.1.6

1.1.7

1.1.8

## The traditional house

The traditional domestic house has largely developed independently of prevailing architectural styles or principles. Individual, distinctive styles have emerged, moulded by the particular features of the location, the landscape and the climate, local resources, techniques and traditions; solutions to mostly age-old problems that today have again become highly topical with the significance of architecture and environmental technology.

Each part of such a house expresses a necessity, has a definite function and, consequently, its place and value; this in turn generates its form and its dimension.

One example of this is the outer wall: The windows are not large, the opening vents are indeed very small. In houses employing the old method of log construction, the opening is derived from the height of the stacked logs. In rubble masonry, it is limited by the loadbearing capacity of the stone used.

In this age there was a lack of time and leisure to remain in these rooms during the day. Daylight was essential for work, and this was normally conducted outdoors. The opening in the outer wall could be considered more of a weak spot: it had to contend with the wind and the weather, with dangers approaching from outside, for maintaining a sheltered interior climate during harsh winters. From region to region, various locally available materials were used to close openings, e.g. thin, scraped hides, animal bladders, canvas and similar materials, as glass remained very expensive until a much later date. The materials were additionally oiled or greased to make them water-repellent and as windproof as possible. Depending on the tradition and prosperity of the inhabitants, the materials were attached to hinged or sliding frames, the windows now consisting of both fixed and movable elements.

This "weak spot" in the wall consequently has a series of difficult requirements to fulfil: On the one hand, there is the desire for an "opening" to admit some light and air into the interior, and on the other, for "protection" from the wind, the weather and similar unpleasantries. In many regions the structure of the "window" displays an existential link for some people between inside and outside, forming a very special element in the design of their houses. It becomes a focal point in the façade and is emphasized by colour or by particular hand-crafted adornments; decorated frames and facings establish a transition from opening/window to wall. Particularly expressed in these traditional windows is how the "opening" on the threshold between outside and inside developed into a sculpted, gradated zone of transition. On the outside, the window box with flowers: ornamental, but frequently also a "filter" when looking out or in, shutters to keep out wind and weather, the sun, brightness and dangers outside, often integrated with adjustable slits that admit a filtered light and permit an exchange of air.

On the inside: curtains – mostly allowing some light to pass but also reducing the glare of the sun and significant for the overall appearance of the window from outside – soften the hard character of the window from the inside and embellish the room. A window sill also often appears with flowers or other utensils.

This all illustrates the "value" the element "window" has for mankind. However, it also shows how mankind is able to develop a differentiated apparatus with the most simple materials and means and – taking the particular features of the location into account – to be able to control the effects of the environment via filters, barriers and dividers to make indoor living viable.

The "traditional window" illustrates how each problem and need succeeds in finding its particular material, its technique and its solution.

1.1.9

1.1.7   Window of an old stone house, Ticino
1.1.8   Window of a farmhouse, Westphalia, Germany,
        Westfalia Open-air Museum, Detmold
1.1.9   Traditional wooden window, Bhaktapur, Nepal
1.1.10  Window of a Swiss farmhouse

1.1.10

1.1.11

## The Gothic cathedral – "God is light"

The Gothic cathedral marked the centre of the medieval town, symbolizing the power of the bishop and the chapter house as well as the sovereign, and the ambition of towns in this age. Spiritual and worldly power, and especially the dissemination of religious faith, the essence of the medieval world, are revealed in this edifice – the "church in Heaven's image".

The compact style of Romanesque architecture gave way to a structural skeleton of linear beams and columns: the load of the vault flows diagonally into ribs and is carried by shafts, piers and flying buttresses. The wall developed into a multi-tiered structure of piers and arches. The spaces created were filled with large, coloured tracery windows. The interior was opened up to the light. The coloured glass in the windows transformed light into something sacred and beautiful.

The light played on the interior stonework to enhance it as something special: "...pervaded by a new light, the almighty work shines in splendour".

The glass window became a filter between interior and exterior, between God and man. It transformed the rays of the sun into a mystical medium.

The painted glass, joined together by lead cames to form complex coloured areas, recounted episodes from the Holy Scriptures, of God and man, recounted history and the future, and also portrayed the church's patrons.

The intention to create a bright space illuminated by coloured light was derived from Abbot Suger (1081–1151) of Saint-Denis. During the rebuilding of the choir in the abbey church (1141–44) it became possible for the first time to conceive a ground plan and window disposition that would set off the peristyle columns of the sanctuary with a band of light. According to Suger, all visible things are "material images" that ultimately reflect light as the "divine light of God". The more precious "material light" is, the more it is able to convey "divine light". "The blind spirit attains truth through what is material, and when he perceives the light, he re-emerges from his former oblivion", is what Suger had inscribed on the portal of Saint-Denis in 1134.

Architecture and light created a space of spiritualization and dematerialization.

1.1.11 Chartres Cathedral, rose window in the north transept, c.1240
1.1.12 Abbey church of the Order of Saint Benedict in Neresheim, Germany, Balthasar Neumann, begun in 1745
1.1.13 Galerie des Glaces in the Palace of Versailles, Jules Hardouin-Mansart, Charles Le Brun, 1678–84

## Baroque – attempting to admit the light

Baroque architecture was essentially concerned with the rhythmic movement and vivid immediacy of space, focussed and extended to infinity.

Light played a special role in this respect. The diffuse, mystic light of the Gothic cathedral had been superseded by bright sunlight streaming in through ample window and door openings. Light to create space, but also light as a means of dissolving the limits of space. In the interaction with painting and plasterwork, with light church walls – the abbey church by Balthasar Neumann in Neresheim (begun in 1745) deserves special mention here – and mirrors in palaces, space loses its material character; it expands into infinity, the walls begin to dissolve and dematerialize. The solid outer wall separating interior and exterior fades into the background. Architecture and nature, inside and outside, merge to become one. The achievements manifested in the baroque buildings of this age were to gain more and more significance. The increasing trend towards opening up architecture prompted a huge demand for glass. The mushrooming glass industry in the north was still working with traditional methods at this time and with the inherent disadvantages of the crown glass and blown cylinder sheet glass processes. With the casting and rolling method, which first appeared in 1688, larger and almost pure panes of glass became possible, heralding the era of the *grandes glaces*. These were combined in a remarkable way with mirrors, familiar since antiquity, but still made of bronze and copper with a polished surface and coated with silver or platinum. Convex mirrors had been produced since the 13th century and backed by lead or terne metal. Venetian mirrors, coated with an amalgam, had been known since the late 15th century and continued to be produced in this way into the 19th century. The Galerie des Glaces (1678–84) at the Palace of Versailles by Jules Hardouin-Mansart and Charles Le Brun is an exemplary display of how glass can be combined with mirrors. The façade of the long transverse wing overlooking the gardens comprises a long repetitive series of arched windows which almost dissolve the wall, transforming it into a mere frame. These openings reappear on the opposite internal wall as mirrors (divided into individual elements measuring 600 x 900 mm). The reflections of nature, the trees and the clouds are continued in the white and coloured marble walls. In the light streaming through the large openings, the reflections in the mirrors and the iridescent materials, the room itself seems almost to melt away completely.

1.1.12

1.1.13

1.1.14

1.1.15

1.1.14  Kammerzell House, Strasbourg, 1589
1.1.15  Town house, Langemarkt 14, Gdansk, 1609–17

## The town house – the external wall becomes a permeable structure

The architecture of the town house generally featured a heavy, solid envelope. The openings were small, frequently tiny, and were normally divided into two sections: an upper part for admitting light, permanently closed by thin, scraped animal hides and other materials that allowed light to enter, and a lower part with wooden shutters that could be opened. The whole window was often closed by the shutters during the winter and by gratings in the summer.

Wooden frames with round panes mounted on lead cames began to appear only very gradually. Glass, however, remained rare and precious and was employed, apart from in palaces, almost exclusively in the construction of churches and monasteries. The Gothic era saw openings increasing in size with pointed arch windows clustered in groups, not only evident in churches. In principle, it was difficult to break through the wall, to produce large openings in heavy stone architecture as the properties of natural stone and brick relied on carrying loads exclusively in compression. It was totally different in the case of timber-frame construction. Here, a clear distinction in the structure between loadbearing and non-loadbearing elements made the areas between the members available for openings. Within this grid of horizontal and vertical lines, it now became possible to string together a series of narrow windows separated by the timber posts, forming an early style of continuous strip window. This generous breakdown and composition of the façades for town halls, guild-halls and, later, domestic houses became characteristic of the flourishing towns of the 16th century. In stone architecture too, attempts were made to open up the wall as far as possible. As houses were built very close together – Dutch towns illustrate this feature very well – the outer wall could be reduced to a fine skeleton of just a few loadbearing elements and filled in with large windows despite the masonry style. The generous openings to the front allowed light to penetrate into the deep, narrow rooms. The external wall was thus no longer a hard division between inside and outside, it now became an element of the transition; private and public spheres merged. The modelling of this zone looks back on a long tradition, particularly in the Netherlands. Tax levies on glass and windows in England since the early 17th century, and in France on doors and windows, led to the development of different forms for the outer wall.

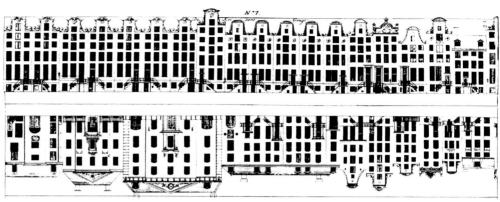

1.1.16

1.1.17 Jan Vermeer, "Street in Delft", c.1657/58, oil on canvas, 543 x 440 mm, Rijksmuseum, Amsterdam

1.1.16 Façades of two terraces on Heerengracht, Amsterdam, 18th century engraving
1.1.17 Jan Vermeer, "Street in Delft", c.1657/58, oil on canvas, 543 x 440 mm, Rijksmuseum, Amsterdam

## The traditional Japanese house

The climatic conditions prevailing in this group of islands, the abundance of wood as a building material, the risk of earthquakes and the strong adherence to cultural and religious traditions have produced a type of house in Japan that has followed the same rules for centuries.

The open plan, the bond with the garden, the lightweight, opening elements reaching up to the ceiling and the full length of the wall had a great influence on modernist architects like Frank Lloyd Wright and Bruno Taut.

The traditional Japanese house is a house made of wood, bamboo, frequently clay for the walls, paper to fill in the sliding elements and straw floors; a skeleton construction with lightweight, mostly sliding wall units. All parts of the house, the wooden constructions, the wall elements and the sliding doors, the arrangement and dimensions of the rooms, the size of the straw mats etc. are all defined exactly. Each part relates to the other – a very early form of dimensional coordination and standardization.

As the climate normally requires a high degree of permeability, the skeleton construction allows the walls, spanned with paper and transmitting light, to become sliding doors. Structure and building envelope are clearly demarcated. Consequently, the openings in this house are not holes in the wall, but part of the wall. Combined with the generous overhang of the roof, providing protection from sun and rain, and the surrounding veranda, the large sliding walls (*shoji*) on the inner side of the veranda, the room side, form a deep zone of transition. When these "walls" are open, garden and interior are linked by the veranda to create an extended living space.

Sliding shutters made completely of wood, later with glass panels too, and fitted to the outer side of the veranda form a sort of "double-leaf" external wall providing greater protection from the cold. Sheets and bamboo blinds are hung up to cut out the glare of the sun. An "outer wall" ensues that can be adapted to a whole range of situations and, in this way, is able to offer the most diverse interaction between inside and outside.

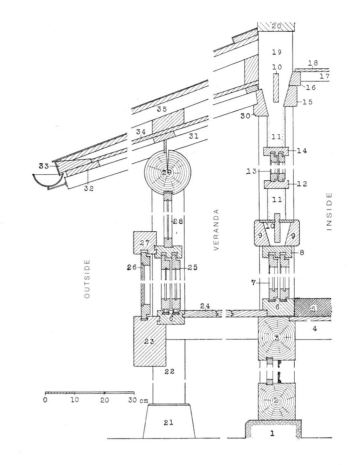

1.1.18

1.1.18 Part of a drawing for a Japanese domestic house, typical construction details
1.1.19 Katsura Imperial Villa, Kyoto, Japan, 17th century

1.1.19

# Iron – reaching for the light

Up until the 18th century, architecture was chiefly defined by the natural resources available. Buildings were made of stone, clay and wood. Architectural form was defined by the properties of these materials and the limited strength of humans. As stones and clay could only accommodate compressive loads, solid walls and vaults predominated. In contrast, wood appeared in architecture either as a skeleton (framework method) or as a solid construction (using logs).

In the quest for new building materials, iron was discovered at an early stage. Yet it was not able to be used as an independent material for construction until the late 18th century when coke was recognized as suitable for smelting iron ore, subsequently leading to better quality iron in larger quantities.

Industrial production, boosted by technical improvements to the steam engine, the mechanical loom and the ability to produce cast iron, now finally blossomed. Iron, with its higher load-carrying capacity, its far superior performance to the materials employed previously, and its ability to accommodate tensile loads far better than any material used up until then, opened up totally new horizons for both building methods and architectural design. The forces previously borne by solid stone walls were now concentrated in a slender skeleton (first cast iron, later mainly wrought iron) of columns and beams; interiors now became unobstructed, extended and could be shaped in many ways. With this, the wall lost its loadbearing function and could be replaced by a glass skin to admit the light. Rooms, hardly "confined" any longer, became larger and brighter.

During the course of the enormous social, structural and industrial upheavals of the 19th century, numerous new tasks for architecture arose, e.g. market halls, department stores, railway stations etc. The buildings illustrated here are just a few representative examples.

## The large glass dome

Vaulted or domed constructions made of stone as well as waffle floors or open roof constructions with artistic wood carvings were methods of covering large, grand interiors.

The passage of light through a dome was initially defined by the inherent character of this construction and was only possible through the apex (Pantheon) or through smaller openings at the base of the dome (Hagia Sophia). Vaults could now be broken down into practically immaterial, supporting structures according to the principle of the timber plank roofs of the 16th century and filled, first with metal sheets and later with glass. Large, bright interiors flooded with light emerged.

One of the earliest constructions of this kind was the dome over the Halle au Blé in Paris. Between 1763 and 1769, a flour and corn exchange was erected here and a roof of timber planks added in 1783. This burned down in 1803. The cast-iron replacement by the architect François Joseph Bélanger and the engineer François Brunet was glazed only at the apex. During its conversion to form the Bourse de Commerce (1888–89), the dome was again replaced, but this time by the first completely glazed, wrought-iron construction, designed by Henri Blondel (see figure on p. 7).

## The department store

As the supply of consumer goods continued to rise, there was a need for spacious and well-lit rooms where goods could be displayed and sold "under one roof". This requirement could be ideally met by iron frame construction and the large roofs with extensive glazing that this made possible. The department stores of America and England in the first half of the 19th century, with façades comprising prefabricated cast elements, and later the pure iron frames of the department stores of Paris, mark major milestones in the development of framed buildings utilizing iron structures and glass infill panels.

The first department store to have a complete iron frame was the "Magasin Bon Marché" (1876) in Paris by Louis-Auguste Boileau and Gustave Eiffel. Although the Parisian authorities had permitted exposed iron construction since 1870, this building was still "faced" with stonework. An example of a consistent iron frame visible from the outside with large areas of glazing was the "La Samaritaine" building (1905) by Frantz Jourdain.

## The arcade

Covered shopping streets look back on a long tradition. The arcade, a glass-covered public thoroughfare flanked by shops, workshops and restaurants, with apartments and offices above, is a characteristic trait of 19th century architecture. From the 1820s, a common feature was the continuous, normally pitched glass roof. The minimal framing ensured maximum daylighting; the glass panes were often imbricated and laid with a small clearance to allow hot air to escape. The Galerie d'Orléans (1828–30, demolished in 1935) in Paris by Pierre François Fontaine had a lasting impact on the future development of the arcade. It was the first to be completely covered by an iron-and-glass construction. Its volume, the pitched glazed roof and the interior façades were to be copied many times.

## The railway station

The task of building railway stations also heralded many innovations in structural engineering. Vast roofs spanned over multiple bays. The translucent or transparent roofs with their mostly very filigree frameworks brought openness and lightness to these urban railway structures.

Whereas the arched form was more popular in England, the truss along the lines of the Wiegmann-Polonceau system predominated in France. The development of this intricate spanning construction, consisting of metal sheets and simple sections, whose form is primarily derived from the structure, was the province of the engineer. The solid, representative "style architecture" for the railway station to enable it to blend with the city was the responsibility of the architect. For the Gare d'Austerlitz (1843–47) in Paris, a hall of 51 x 280 m was covered with intricate trussed girders using the Polonceau system. Extensive glazing to the roof, front and sides enhanced the lightness of the building. Wide, brightly lit, seemingly boundless space is the outcome. These constructions reduced to only a few elements did not remain without criticism. Official architectural attitudes evoked the opinion of it appearing to be "more stimulating than safe and reliable".

The modernity of these engineered constructions for the coming and going of the puffing iron horse on the one hand, and the palatial, representative architecture of the platform concourse as a transition to the concept of the townscape on the other, typically reflect the conflict in the architecture of this period.

England, the home of the railway, held a spearhead position in inventing halls and the space deriving from these. One example is Paddington Station in London (1854) by Isambard Kingdom Brunel and Matthew Digby Wyatt. It is one of the first wrought-iron constructions with curved ribs. A statement accompanying the design published in The Builder in the year of completion made it clear that the intention was to avoid any reworking of existing styles and to attempt to design the building in accordance with its structural function and the properties of the materials employed.

1.1.20

1.1.21

1.1.22

1.1.23

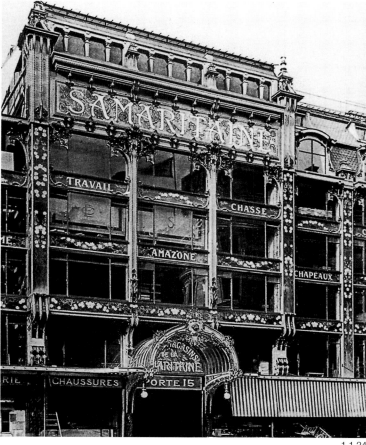

1.1.24

**The palm house**

The principles of iron architecture in the 19th century developed with this genre, initially with cast iron and later with wrought iron. The prefabrication and dimensional coordination of many identical parts; the shaping of enclosed space to be as transparent as possible; the technology of glass, its method of production and connection to the loadbearing elements – all combined to give architecture a totally new identity.

In the 15th century, when plants were brought home after the first voyages of discovery, special buildings were erected to house them. These were initially "wooden sheds" that were set up around the plants in winter, the so-called "removable orange houses". These were followed by the orangery with walls on three sides until the autonomous "palm house" style evolved, made completely of iron and glass.

A space enclosed by a glass cover with its own internal climate independent of the seasons (later aided by steam heating) characterizes the palm house as the most consistent and innovative architecture in glass and iron of the 19th century.

The basic rules were simple and precise: to achieve maximum heat and light, the material elements had to be reduced to a minimum

and remain free of stylistic or architectural requirements. The major pioneering work was carried out by the Englishmen John Claudius Loudon and Sir Joseph Paxton. Loudon created "intelligent" forms for the outer skin to accommodate the trajectory of the sun (the "ridge-and-furrow" roof). Apart from structural engineering innovations, Paxton also introduced sophisticated heating and ventilation systems to counteract the climatic difficulties arising with such large expanses of glass in these "houses".

The "Palm House", and the "Crystal Palace" (1851) in London based on its principles, questioned the conventional perceptions of space which were characterized by mass and opening – space without limits arose. The clear, minimal iron constructions and the open space paved the way for modern architecture. Each element had a clear function which defined its material and form. "There is nothing there that cannot be immediately understood down to the last detail" (Alfred Gotthold Meyer, 1907).

The Palm House (1844–48), at the Royal Botanical Gardens in Kew, London, designed by Richard Turner and Decimus Burton, followed both the principle of the curvilinear envelope and the shell. The glass enclosure of space and framework lie in one plane. The

arched segments consist of wrought-iron double-T beams (228 x 50 mm), the curved glass panes (241 x 972 mm) are imbricated and puttied. The cast and wrought-iron construction measuring approximately 110 m long rises up from a one-metre-high stone plinth integrating ventilation louvres. A heating system below ground provides warmth: even when outside temperatures fall below zero, it is possible to maintain 27 °C inside. The whole glazed roof was originally green and could be purchased at a relatively "reasonable" price as the tax levies on windows in England were abolished in 1845.

1.1.20 Palm House in Bicton Gardens, Devon, England, presumably by John Claudius Loudon, 1818–38
1.1.21 Palm House in the Royal Botanic Gardens (now Kew Gardens), London, Richard Turner, Decimus Burton, 1844–48
1.1.22 Claude Monet, interior view of Gare Saint-Lazare, "Arrival of a train", 1877, 820 x 1010 mm, Fogg Art Museum, Harvard University Art Museums, Cambridge, Massachusetts
1.1.23 Passage Jouffroy, Paris, 1847
1.1.24 La Samaritaine department store, Paris, Frantz Jourdain, 1906–07

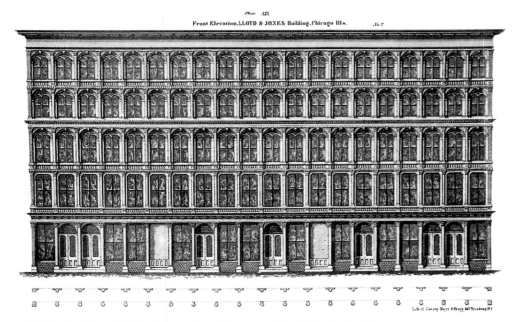

1.1.25 Lloyd and Jones Building, Chicago, Daniel Badger and John M. Van Osdel, 1856

## From wall to skin – releasing the external wall from its loadbearing function

The emergence of iron as a construction material during the industrial revolution and the invention of the iron frame opened up a whole new scope for devising the external elevation.

The process of dissolving and dematerializing the façade is directly coupled to relieving it more and more of its loadbearing function. The ability of the frame to concentrate loads from the floors directly in beams and columns laid the foundation for opening up the wall until, ultimately, just a glass skin could be hung in front of the frame as a "boundary" between inside and outside. The steps in the development of this process are briefly outlined here:

In England, the nucleus of the industrial revolution, countless spinning mills went up in flames towards the end of the 18th century. As a result of this, the multistorey timber-frame constructions – surrounded by solid walls with few openings – were replaced by cast iron ones, also allowing the increasingly larger and heavier production machines to be accommodated. While timber floor beams were retained when converting a mill in

1.1.26 The Crystal Palace, Hyde Park, London, Joseph Paxton, 1851

1792, just a few years later Benyon, Bage & Marshall erected one of the first cast-iron frames with columns and beams on a 2.65 m grid for a cotton spinning mill near Shrewsbury (1796–97). The building was also an early example of progress in the series production of building components.

Iron was introduced as a construction material in the USA in the first half of the 19th century.

The engineer James Bogardus replaced the masonry outer wall of a five-storey factory in 1848 by prefabricated columns and spandrel panels made of cast iron. This prefabricated system unfolded new structural scope for the design of the building envelope. The façade was no longer a solid surface with perforations, but a frame filled in with glass. This system was now frequently applied to office buildings and department stores as it allowed both an expanse of wide, light openings on the office floors and spacious shop windows on the ground floor previously reserved for the solid stone foundation.

When the Crystal Palace was erected for the Great Exhibition in 1851 in London, the prefabricated system of building with components reached a transient climax. The

design competition preceding this and attracting 245 entrants produced no satisfactory result. The Exhibition committee had envisaged a building made of individual parts that could be dismantled and reused later. The gardener Joseph Paxton, who had already practised his innovative spirit on many a greenhouse, submitted a feasible design in cooperation with Fox, Henderson & Co. without even being asked, and obtained the commission. The first exposition building made of iron and glass was erected. A building that was revolutionary with its economical construction, with the organization of production, supply and assembly, particularly considering the extremely short erection period of only nine months for the three-storey exhibition palace measuring 564 m long and 40 m high.

This was only made possible by prefabricating and standardizing the components. The one basic module for the whole construction was the glass pane of 1220 x 250 mm. A construction grid of approx. 7.32 m was derived from this. It was divided along the outer walls into three sections that were filled with wooden windows, timber panels and ventilation louvres. The dimensional coordination was transferred to the third dimension too with the utmost consistency.

Despite varying loads on equally tall supports, only two types of column were employed in the two storeys which varied only in the thickness of the internal walls and thus allowed uniform assembly. Similarly, the girders, despite their various effective spans, retained the same web depths. The roof areas constructed according to the ridge-and-furrow principle and mounted on valley girders and purlins, were glazed from purpose-built glazier's cradles; 270,000 standardized glass panes could thus be installed in piece work.

The individual components were prefabricated by the respective companies, transported to the building site and assembled in situ. As attention was paid to designing a simple solution for joining the elements, assembly and dismantling progressed very quickly. The early involvement of engineers and the manufacturers in the planning process had an impact on both the production method and procedures and contributed to the smooth, quick erection of this gigantic glass palace.

The result was a distinct, structural form: all components were self-explanatory, showed how they functioned and what they achieved. However, the solar radiation caused high temperatures inside the glass building and awnings had to be fitted as temporary protection from the sun.

The greatest impact of this glass structure was generated by its space. It was a unique kind of space no longer framed and defined by dense, sealed walls; it was a large, open, light, atmospheric space with a blurred border between inside and outside.

Alfred Gotthold Meyer expressed his personal emotions in his book on iron constructions in 1907:

"This huge space possessed something liberating. One felt secure inside, yet without inhibitions. The awareness of gravity, one's own physical confines, was lost... yet the portion of atmosphere in which we find ourselves in the Crystal Palace, is 'cut out' of the total space; the 'barrier' placed between us and the landscape is almost 'unreal', but it still exists."

Growing populations, rural-urban drift and the increasing shortage of building land in the conurbations, e.g. New York, Chicago, pushed the number of storeys upwards. Serious fires in Chicago in 1871 and 1874 destroyed large numbers of timber houses but also clearly demonstrated the weaknesses of unprotected iron construction. An immense building boom ensued. Based on

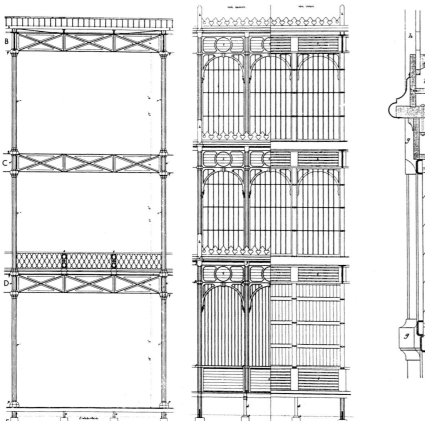
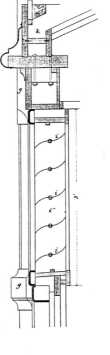

1.1.27

1.1.28

1.1.27 The Crystal Palace, Hyde Park, London, Joseph Paxton, 1851, façade details
1.1.28 The Crystal Palace, vent detail

1.1.29

1.1.30

1.1.31

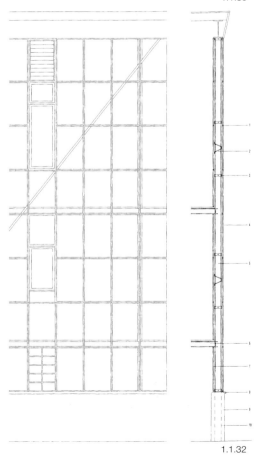

1.1.32

the essential building technology already available, the invention of the electric safety elevator (Otis, 1852) and the fire-protected steel frame, the first generation of skyscrapers emerged designed by architects of the so-called Chicago School (Burnham, Holabird & Roche, Jenney, Root, Sullivan). The "external wall", however, was treated in quite different ways by each architect: preferences varied from the loadbearing masonry wall with perforated façade (the heavy external wall thickens to 1 m or more at the ground) to the wall carrying just its own weight to structural steel frames with infill panels.

The Carson, Pirie & Scott department store (1899–1904) by Louis Henry Sullivan is characteristic of the Chicago School. Here a strict network of horizontal and vertical lines continued the clarity of the loadbearing structure to define the outer wall. The large and broad "Chicago windows" on the uppermost floors incorporated thin metal frames, while the remaining windows were framed by a narrow terracotta decoration. This corresponded to Sullivan's view that the exterior of a building should express its inner structure and function, that there should be a relationship between content and outer form ("form follows function"). The lowest two shop-window storeys were lavishly adorned with cast-iron Art Nouveau plates to provide the noble appearance desired. Sullivan regarded the representative character of a building to be one of its major functions.

Sullivan's department store marked the end of this significant stylistic and constructive direction in Chicago which was succeeded by an eclectic Beaux Arts movement less interested in the relationships between form, structure and content, preferring the "pure form".

Georges Chedanne's "Le Parisien" building (1903–05) for a publishing house in Paris followed the formal tradition of French department stores, documenting the status of structural steelwork on the continent at that time. The whole method of construction can be gleaned from the outer wall: loadbearing and infill elements, with Art Nouveau features applied to imply the paths of the forces. The open plan layout brings flexibility into the outlines of the inner structure.

1.1.29 Carson Pirie Scott, Chicago, Louis H. Sullivan, 1899–1904
1.1.30 "Le Parisien", Paris, Georges Chedanne, 1903–05
1.1.31 Steiff works, Giengen, 1903–11
1.1.32 Steiff works, Giengen, façade elevation and section
1.1.33 Fagus works, Alfeld an der Leine, Walter Gropius, 1911

Façades taken over almost totally by glass appeared for the first time on industrial buildings, promoted by scientific findings purporting the positive physical and psychological effect of daylight, air and sunshine, and which could be applied to factory buildings for the benefit of productivity. An early example of this is the eastern façade of the Margarethe Steiff GmbH factory in Giengen, Germany. Although the architect remains unknown, Richard Steiff, grandson of the company's founder, is thought to have had a significant hand in the design. The double-leaf façade made of translucent glass panels that extend over three storeys is divided so that the inner leaf is positioned between the floor and ceiling of each storey, while the other runs continuously past the front of the framework. The main columns stand in the cavity, and coupled windows are placed at regular intervals. Curtains were hung on the inside to attempt to moderate problems with heat accumulation.

In cooperation with Adolf Meyer, Walter Gropius finally succeeded in mounting a glass curtain wall on the front of an industrial building for a factory producing shoe lasts in Alfeld an der Leine, Germany (Fagus works, 1911–25). This took the form of a thin, transparent skin without any kind of loadbearing function – a fact which is clearly evident.

To achieve this, Gropius omitted the corner columns, allowing the glass walls to spread across the three storeys and join up, lending even more lightness to the façade. "The role of the wall is now only to ward off rain, cold and heat" (Gropius). To satisfy the fire-protection authority, metal sheets backed by bricks were integrated in the spandrel panels. The façade consists of a steel frame made of standard sections suspended from each floor. In the first few years, curtains and then blinds were attached to the inside to regulate the climate (heat gain in summer, loss in winter) and create an acceptable working environment.

1.1.33

## The destruction of the box – the fluent transition between inside and outside

A significant motor in the development of modern architecture was the iron, concrete and glass construction of the 19th century. Another was the growing dissolution of the traditional, solid cubic building. Frank Lloyd Wright referred to it as "the destruction of the box". The clear limits between inside and outside defined by loadbearing walls were being broken up. Columns, walls, glazing and large overhanging eaves detached themselves from the closed configuration of the cube and became autonomous elements. The division between interior and exterior space was transformed into flowing, open space.

The architecture of Frank Lloyd Wright initiated this process and followed it consistently. This "dissolving" was influenced by various artistic movements at the beginning of the 20th century; for example, expressionism, cubism, Russian constructivism and suprematism, futurism, etc. Traditional rules and forms lost their validity. The cubists, for example, reduced images to simple geometric forms via a process of analytical dissection. The constructivists and suprematists eliminated all content from the surface and reduced pictorial elements to a minimum: beams and planes combined into a composition of few colours. Many of the works displayed astonishing parallels with architectural designs (e.g. Theo van Doesburg's Composition XIII, 1914, and Mies van der Rohe's draft for a country house in brick, 1923).

The houses Frank Lloyd Wright designed and constructed in the first four decades of the 20th century are an exemplary documentation of the shift towards a new, objective perception of space. Characteristic of these constructions is how they blend into the landscape, extend over an open plan and break the object down into individual elements, "opening up" the house to nature and interweaving interior and exterior space. Also influenced by the traditional Japanese house, Wright transformed the basic elements of the American home into a new architectural vocabulary. The extensive masonry hearth in the centre now anchored the house to the spot; the space around it was freely formed yet organized and opened out onto the surrounding landscape. Partitions flowed successively into horizontal and vertical planes: wide cantilevered roofs, freestanding brick and natural stone walls and columns, expanses of windows and glazed doors reaching to the ceiling. All elements are in balanced "dynamic equilibrium". An early example of this is the house of Ward W. Willit in Highland Park, Illinois (1902–03). Wright attached particular impor-

1.1.34

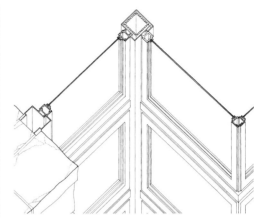

1.1.35

tance to utilizing the materials in a way sensitive to their organic composition: "in the nature of the materials". Among the materials he preferred – stone, wood, glass, reinforced concrete – glass is the most precious as it can generate a new relationship between mankind and nature.

"I suppose as a material we may regard it as crystal – thin sheets of air in air to keep air out or keep it in. And with this sense of it, we can think of uses to which it might be put as various and beautiful as the frost-designs upon the pane of glass itself. Glass and light – two forms of the same thing!"

He did not use glass without glazing bars "invisibly", as Mies did, but initially in small configurations with inlaid, coloured panes in lead frames; later more generously, but still with glazing bars to create an awareness of the "boundary" between inside and outside – from protected space to the freedom of nature – with colours and textures.

A key work displaying the integration of nature and architecture is "Fallingwater", Pennsylvania (1935/36). Wide terraces hovering far out over the rocks and a waterfall create open, fluent space. The materials are sensitively applied, exploiting their nature: reinforced concrete for the cantilevered planes, steel for the delicate glaz-

1.1.36

ing bars in the glazed corners, wood in the construction of large openings to the terraces, sedimentary rock for the walls and floors in the living area. Nothing more is left of the house as a "box". The principle of spatial freedom as Frank Lloyd Wright interpreted it in architecture was also taken up by a Dutch group of artists, "De Stijl", established in 1917 and strongly influenced by cubism. The principles of isolating surfaces summarised by neo-plasticism defined architecture as the free interplay of intersecting planes, a principle consistently implemented in Schröder House, Utrecht (1924), by Gerrit Rietveld. In contrast to the houses of Wright, the major priority here is not harmony with the landscape nor the use

1.1.34 House of William R. Heath, Buffalo, New York, Frank Lloyd Wright, between 1900 and 1909, glass window
1.1.35 House of Edgar J. Kaufmann, "Fallingwater", Bear Run, Pennsylvania, Frank Lloyd Wright, 1935/36, detail of a glazed corner
1.1.36 House of Edgar J. Kaufmann, "Fallingwater", Bear Run, Pennsylvania, living room
1.1.37 House of Edgar J. Kaufmann, "Fallingwater", Bear Run, Pennsylvania, plan of entrance level
1.1.38 House of Ward W. Willit, Highland Park, Illinois, Frank Lloyd Wright, 1902–03, plan of first floor
1.1.39 Schröder House, Utrecht, Gerrit Rietveld, 1924
1.1.40 House of Edgar J. Kaufmann, "Fallingwater", Bear Run, Pennsylvania, 1935/36

1.1.39

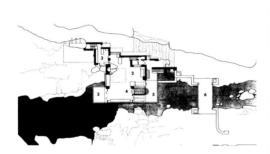

1.1.37

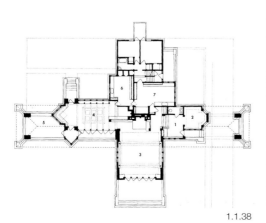

1.1.38

1.1.40

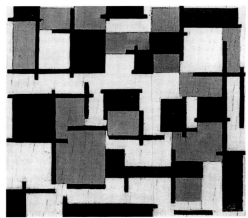

1.1.41

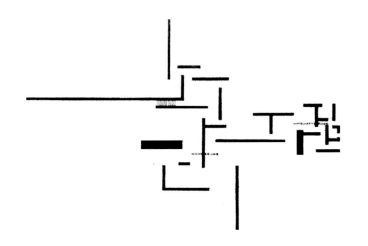

1.1.42

of the material. The impact of this house radiates through its form and colour, through lines, planes and free-flowing zones of space. The elements are interwoven to form a dynamic whole. The formal aspect has become detached from earlier contexts. The house as an ordinary box with perforations was also rejected by Mies van der Rohe. His draft for a country house in brick (1924) only contains an ensemble of freestanding walls. The cubic space, the division between "outer wall" and "inner wall", no longer exists. Constructed space and natural space belong together. For Mies, nature took on a more profound meaning and became part of a larger whole.

Mies was able to put his ideas of modern architecture into practice in pure form for the 1929 world exposition in Barcelona. A "house" consisting of planes, i.e. plates, of various materials with various structures. In line with its function, architecture was reduced to individual elements. The columns bear the roof plate; the wall plates, relieved of their loadbearing functions and consequently made of glass or precious, thin natural stone, divide and define the rooms.

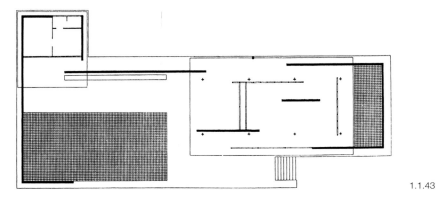

1.1.43

1.1.44

1.1.41 Theo van Doesburg, Composition XIII, 1918, oil/wood, 290 x 300 mm, Stedelijk Museum, Amsterdam

1.1.42 Draft for a country house in brick, Ludwig Mies van der Rohe, 1923

1.1.43 German Pavilion at the 1929 world exposition in Barcelona, Ludwig Mies van der Rohe, 1929, plan

1.1.44 German Pavilion at the 1929 world exposition in Barcelona

1.1.45 Exhibition pavilion at Deutscher Werkbund Exhibition in Cologne, 1914, Bruno Taut, working drawing of dome, reinforced concrete lattice

1.1.46 Exhibition pavilion at the Deutscher Werkbund Exhibition in Cologne, 1914, Bruno Taut, glass staircase

## Creating visions with glass – "Without a glass palace, life becomes a burden"

As the *Deutscher Werkbund* looked towards forms deriving from utilization and the new industrial scope, the members of 'Die Gläserne Kette' (The Glass Chain), founded in 1919 and influenced by expressionism, turned away from industry. Under the guidance of Bruno Taut in the post-war years when the building industry was in a period of stagnation, the architects searched for a way of creating fantastic visions of a new world, a better community and their symbols through art.

Glass is of vital significance in these visions. *Glasarchitektur*, a work published in 1914 by the poet Paul Scheerbart, one of the pioneers of expressionism, provided a blueprint for the group. In the book, he describes a world no longer determined by the mass and imperviousness of brick, but of openness and lightness, of steel and glass.

"We mostly live in enclosed rooms. These form the environment that gives rise to our culture. In a way, our culture is a product of our architecture. In order to raise our culture to a higher level, we are forced, whether we like it or not, to change our architecture. And this will be possible only if we free the rooms in which we live of their enclosed character. This, however, we can only do by introducing a glass architecture, which admits the light of the sun, of the moon, and of the stars into the rooms, not only through a few windows, but through as many walls as feasible, these to consist entirely of glass – of coloured glass. The new environment we produce in this way has to bring us a new culture."

In his work, Scheerbart also makes very definite proposals for the economically feasible use of glass. Considering the single-glazed glasshouses in Dahlem, he pleads for double glazing that would "devour" less coal (*Glasarchitektur I*). And, as if he had been able to look decades into the future: "As air is one of the worst conductors of heat, the double glass wall is an essential condition for all glass architecture."

"The walls can be one metre apart – or even farther... To install radiators or heaters would not be advisable in most cases as too much heat or cold would escape into the atmosphere." (*Glasarchitektur IV*)

In his opinion, the "window" would disappear, and only walls of glass would exist. Visions that Mies and Le Corbusier proposed and in some cases implemented a few years later.

For the group of architects around Bruno Taut, glass was less significant on account of its potential to save energy or its optical transparency; it was far more a symbol of "flowing, graceful, angular, sparkling..." qualities. They saw glass in a Gothic sense, as a symbol of purity and of death.

Taut summarised his Utopias in papers: his *Alpine Architektur* published in 1917/18 was conceived as an anti-war manifesto, and in 1919 *Stadtkrone* [citadel] described a place for a new society. A garden city, whose centre was marked by a glass "Stadtkrone" just like the Gothic cathedrals of medieval towns. Magnificent architecture and a new "pleasing" city were to arise.

An early version of the "Stadtkrone" was embodied in the exhibition pavilion at the 1914 Deutscher Werkbund Exhibition in Cologne which Taut built for the Luxfer-Prismen syndicate – in the spirit of a Gothic cathedral, as he said – a shimmering, fabulous building, demonstrating the scope glass offered at that time.

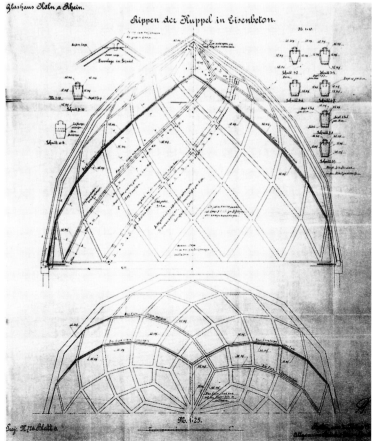

1.1.45

1.1.46

1.1.47

1.1.48

He wrote about this: "As author Paul Scheerbart envisaged, and it is dedicated to him, it is meant to break up the far too 'bonded' perceptions of space in today's architecture and provide an impetus for the effects glass embodies to enter the world of architecture," but additionally to show "what glass can achieve to improve our feeling for life".
The circular building on 14 reinforced concrete columns with the intermediate bays filled by Luxfer glass bricks supports a lattice dome with a diameter of 8.70 m and a height of 1.65 m. The infill to the lattice formed by 120 x 200 mm vault ribs has a three-layered shell. The inner layer consists of Luxfer prisms laid using Keppler's reinforced concrete glass blocks with lightweight reinforced concrete ribs (see "The glass block or the translucent wall", p. 11). The dome was glazed normally on the outside but coloured panes were inserted in the intermediate layer. Even the floors, walls and stairs are all made from glass bricks.

At this time, Mies van der Rohe was very close to "expressionist" architecture, but was tending more in another direction. He wanted to exploit the possibilities, techniques, structures and materials available and try to develop a building "evolving from inside" by rational methods. Full of admiration for the steel frames under construction in Chicago, he commented on the subsequent "concealing" of this framework: "When the fronts are infilled with masonry, it (the constructive idea) will be obscured by a senseless and trivial jumble of forms and thus totally destroyed."
In his skyscraper projects for Berlin in 1921 (a 20 storey high-rise building on a prismatic plan) and in 1922 (a 30 storey high-rise building on a polygonal plan) he tried to apply this notion. The idea was to construct the complete outer wall of a multistorey office building solely from glass for the first time. This, however, never came about.
In contrast to 20 years earlier in the Chicago projects, glass was now slipped like a "skin" over the building's underlying steel structure that only consisted of columns and floor slabs. Mies called it "skin and bones architecture". He developed this form using models in order to investigate how light, with its mirror effects and reflections, could be integrated into the structure. In the journal *Frühlicht*, the mouthpiece of the Glass Chain, Mies demanded an attempt be made "to design the form from the essence of the new function. The new constructive principle of these buildings will then clearly be mani-

fested if glass is used for the outer walls relieved of the loads. The use of glass does compel us to go new ways."

1.1.47 Hans Scharoun, watercolour, 1919, Akademie der Künste, Berlin
1.1.48 "Glass Skyscraper" project for Berlin, Mies van der Rohe, 1921
1.1.49 Villa Savoye, Paris, Le Corbusier, 1931

## Light, air, sunshine – "the house machine"

At the beginning of the 20th century architects tried, in different ways but with a common goal, to create a new architecture, an architecture that, freed from the appended ornamentation of the previous century and liberated from the constraints of building traditions, would express itself with the potential offered by industry, technology and new materials. Furthermore, they tried to conceive housing which, although not exactly spacious, was indeed inexpensive and, in contrast to the inhuman ghettos of industrial conurbations, offered great flexibility and a decent standard of comfort. An open architecture providing the population with light, air and sunshine.

Sigfried Giedion expressed it in 1929 in "Liberated Living":

"BEAUTIFUL is a house that matches our awareness of life. This awareness demands LIGHT, AIR, MOVEMENT; SPACE.

BEAUTIFUL is a house that rests with ease, that can adapt to all the conditions of the terrain.

BEAUTIFUL is a house that allows us to live among the skies and the trees.

BEAUTIFUL is a house that instead of shadow (window frames) has light (walls of glass).

BEAUTIFUL is a house whose rooms never give rise to a feeling of CONFINEMENT. BEAUTIFUL is a house whose charm consists of the interaction of well-accomplished functions."

Le Corbusier was an instrumental force in creating this new architecture. On the one hand, in his role as an advocate for a formal, aesthetic architecture "by means of shapes which stand in a certain relationship to one another... such that they are clearly revealed in light"; architecture as harmony, as poetry. On the other, in the role of an architect exploiting the opportunities presented by industry and building technology. In 1926 he drew up his "cinq points d'une architecture nouvelle":

1. The "pilotis" elevating the mass off the ground.
2. The free plan, achieved through the separation of the loadbearing columns from the walls subdividing the space.
3. The free façade, the corollary of the free plan in the vertical plane.
4. The long, horizontal sliding window or "fenêtre en longueur".
5. The roof garden restoring the area of ground covered by the house.

With his Villa Savoye of 1931 Le Corbusier created a new type of house. All five points were applied here; poetic, fluent spaces are the result, in three dimensions as well as in two. This was intended to signal a new beginning. Like Mies he accords importance to the construction, but more in the sense of an underlying framework creating scope for other elements.

Le Corbusier contributed to the further development of the "external wall" with the "fenêtre en longueur" and "pan de verre". The size of the opening, freed from its loadbearing role, could be arranged at will. Like most of his colleagues, he underestimated the problem of overheating caused by large panes devoid of any shading. Around 1929 he recognized that the many functions fulfilled by a solid wall – thermal insulation, heat storage, privacy, sound insulation and sunshading – could not all be transferred to a glass wall, which indeed had to be supplemented with important "external wall functions".

The first attempts to solve these problems by technical means, e.g. via ventilation of the interior – the "réspiration exacte" or the "mur neutralisant" (in which warm or cool air to suit the season was blown into the cavity of the double glazing) – failed. The first effective answer was to affix external

1.1.49

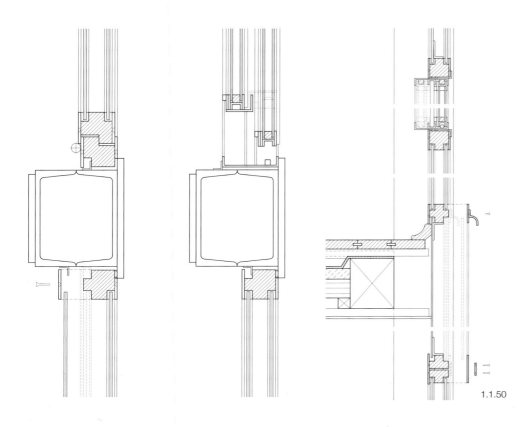

1.1.50

awnings (e.g. Immeuble Clarté, Geneva) and the "brise-soleil" borrowed from traditional Arabian architecture (mashrabya) but converted to a larger format. At the Salvation Army Home (1932–33), attempts to seal the glass skin completely in order to stabilize the internal climate by means of the ventilation led to the building first becoming habitable after the addition of opening lights and, later, the "brise-soleil" in front of these. Consequently, the functions of the outside wall, taken over en bloc from the solid wall, had been split into individual components which received their materiality and form from the task they had to perform. The external wall became a differentiated layer. Egon Eiermann demonstrated this in exemplary fashion in his works of the 1950s and later.

Another example of this provided by Le Corbusier is the aforementioned multi-occupancy block "Immeuble Clarté" in Geneva (1930–32). This residential building has a structural steel framework and a large-format glass façade (pan de verre) between the columns, with spandrel panels of polished wired glass. The façade construction comprises a timber core protected by iron sheeting screwed to both sides. To achieve a continuous façade plane, the ends of the floor slabs are also disguised by glass – fastened by cover strips. To admit light into the internal staircase, the landings and treads are made from glass bricks.

One of the most important industrial buildings of the 20th century is the van Nelle tobacco factory in Rotterdam (1926–30) by the architects Johannes Andreas Brinkman, Lodewijk Cornelis van der Vlugt and Mart Stam. The fine tracery of the expansive glass wall consists of a steel lattice which glazes the upper two-thirds of each storey. The lower third is clad inside and out in iron sheeting with 30 mm torfoleum between. The staircases are fully glazed, with the panes attached from the outside. Lath blinds like those found in greenhouses are included for controlling the incoming solar radiation. This was a structure of which Le Corbusier said, "The serenity of the place is total. Everything is open to the outside... [It is] a creation of the modern age." This factory building is probably the most convincing specimen of constructivist architecture.

One milestone of modern architecture is the open-air school in Amsterdam by Johannes Duiker (1930), with its open terraces and bright classrooms flooded with light. The generously proportioned glass enclosure seems to "span" without support from spandrel to floor slab. Long cantilevering beams enable the corners of the building to remain

1.1.51

unobstructed and so emphasize the lightness of the whole structure.

The Maison Dalsace in Paris (1928–32) by Pierre Chareau and Bernard Bijovet, which was quickly nicknamed "Maison de Verre", is an impressive example of a building conceived around the needs of the individual rooms, the result then being made visible on the exterior (Fig. 1.1.54, p. 34). It is distinguished by large, translucent walls of glass bricks and an extraordinarily thorough design of all constructional and partitioning elements. All the parts of this house, whether hand-crafted or prefabricated by machine, are suited to their respective purpose. The large space is zoned, but not dissected, by offset levels at different heights and space-defining components like sliding doors and columns. It is lit via huge three-storey-high walls, predominantly of glass bricks, on the garden and courtyard elevations. The problem of getting light into the narrow building set back into the inner court led to this steel frame solution with large, glazed façades. The apertures are confined to a few variously sized windows. Saint-Gobain produced and delivered the bricks but, owing to lack of experience with such a size of structure, refused to accept any responsibility for the walls built using their bricks! To reduce the load from the courses of bricks, a steel structure was erected and the glass bricks used as infills (4 x 6 "Nevada bricks" each 200 x 200 x 40 mm). There are a few opening and fixed lights in clear glass as well.

Le Corbusier had introduced the term "machine à habiter" in an article in *Esprit Nouveau* in 1921. His understanding of the term was a product produced using prefabricated parts. Chareau's glasshouse was planned and accomplished in this sense.

1.1.52

1.1.50 Immeuble Clarté, Geneva, Le Corbusier, 1932, horizontal/vertical section, fixed glazing and sash window
1.1.51 Immeuble Clarté, Geneva
1.1.52 Amsterdam Open-air School, Johannes Duiker, 1930
1.1.53 Van Nelle tobacco factory, Rotterdam, Johannes Andreas Brinkmann and Lodewijk Cornelis van der Vlugt with Mart Stam, 1926–30
1.1.54 Maison de verre, Pierre Chareau, 1931–32

1.1.53

1.1.54

# Glass architecture in the second half of the 20th century

**Christian Schittich**

## Transparency and translucency – the glazed skin comes alive

The great glasshouses, glazed railway stations and passages flooded with light erected during the 19th century are impressive specimens of glass architecture. But at the time of their construction they were isolated examples in the urban landscape, marginal rather than dominant. The expressionism of the early part of the 20th century experimented freely with glass and individual architects sketched fabulous visions of glass crystals. It was the classical modernism of the 1920s and 1930s that brought us the first private houses with large expanses of glass. But these too were at first prototypes of the avant-garde. The real breakthrough in glass architecture did not arrive until after the Second World War. The interaction of economic, technological and stylistic factors now contributed to the rapid spread of the use of glass as a building material. Towering, glazed office blocks became fashionable as company headquarters – at a time when more and more multinational groups were emerging and an enormous building boom prevailed in war-torn Europe. Glass curtain walls became the status symbol of confident companies and the silhouette of glass towers the sign of a prosperous city. The invention of the float glass process revolutionized the manufacture of glass and the development of innovative sealants also contributed much. Considerable impetus came from America, which had become home to many of Europe's avant-garde emigrants during the years of the Third Reich, including Bauhaus directors Walter Gropius and Ludwig Mies van der Rohe.

In 1938 Mies became head of the Armour (from 1940 the Illinois) Institute of Technology in Chicago, where he was given the task of designing the new university campus. This and his many other American projects gave him the opportunity to implement some of the ideas he had already formulated earlier in Europe. Steel and glass, plus the occasional use of facing brickwork, were the dominant materials.

The evolutionary process is detectable in Mies' IIT projects. While the Mineral and Metal Research Building (1942) still exhibits façade infills flush with the supporting structure, the three buildings erected on the campus in 1945 and 1946 make use of a secondary frame system and continuous H-section façade columns extending over several storeys, thus establishing the typical Mies style which was later imitated many times. The climax is the Crown Hall for the Faculty of Architecture (1956).

The roof of the building is suspended from exposed steel frames. This creates an interior unobstructed by columns, merely divided by freestanding partition walls. The building envelope consists of 6 mm plate glass between steel stanchions which extend the full storey height of 8.20 m. Mies used both clear and sand-blasted translucent glass in a pane format of 3 x 3.50 m.

Crown Hall is a successful example of the highly articulate effect that can be accomplished through a strict but carefully detailed glass-and-steel cube. However, it also illustrates the typical Mies formalism in which function always played a subordinate role: the bright ground floor is an exhibition hall arranged as a sweeping space; offices and students' work-rooms are located in the poorly lit basement. And the theory of the continuity of the space from interior to exterior so exalted by Mies is severely impaired in this example through his use of opaque glass – motivated by aesthetic concerns – for the bottom third of the façade, i.e. at eye level.

Mies had proposed a far more radical use of glass a few years earlier (1944) in his design (not built) for the Library and Administration Building on the IIT campus. Here, panes of 5.50 x 3.60 m without intermediate glazing bars were intended to alternate with masonry infills.

1.2.1 Crown Hall, Illinois Institute of Technology, Chicago, Ludwig Mies v. d. Rohe, 1956

1.2.2

1.2.3

1.2.4

## The dream of the glass house

The most radical use of glass during the 1940s is to be found in a number of private houses. Owing to their relatively small dimensions and modesty in terms of design and construction, these offered ideal opportunities for experimentation. One of the most rational culminations of purist glass architecture is Farnsworth House in Plano, Illinois, by Mies van der Rohe. The concept is reminiscent of the Barcelona Pavilion with its fluent room transitions. Large expanses of glass supported by slender steel angles create the continuity of the space from interior to exterior. The surroundings, a virtually untouched landscape near a small river, form the backdrop to residential life – awakening associations with the traditional Japanese house. Raised clear of the ground on eight steel columns, two plates form the floor and the roof and define the volume. Four more columns support the terrace in front of the house. Farnsworth House with its idealized space – only defined by horizontal planes – and the consummate minimalization of the construction quickly became an icon of modern architecture. However, it was also a product of the limited knowledge of building science in that period as well as the lack of understanding for energy and environmental issues. The minimalistic detailing was soon paid for in terms of massive damage to the building fabric soon after being occupied.

In another, at its time visionary, design, Mies went one step further and omitted window frames altogether. Only the entrance to the "50 by 50 House" of 1951 was to be denoted by metal sections.

The Glass House (1949) designed by Philip Johnson, friend and pupil of Mies, is not unrelated to Farnsworth House but at the same time demonstrates its autonomy. The transparent cube without overhanging eaves is an extravagant example of an open-plan house: the solid core is limited to one integral cylinder containing wet cell and fireplace. The only other fixed installation is the line of kitchen units. Any further inclusion would ruffle the order. Sleeping and living zones are merely demarcated, the functions subservient to the architect's aesthetic ambitions. In contrast to Farnsworth House, this glass box is surrounded not by untamed nature but by a precisely sculpted park. But the main differences lie in the details. Johnson uses window frames on the façade which, seen from outside, conceal the load-bearing construction – apart from the four corner columns. The glass façades form a genuine envelope. Both of these houses are the products of highly individual architectural ideas of space and aesthetics which give short shrift to the needs of their occupants.

This period saw a great many glazed villas built in America, with far less dogmatic claims. For instance, Richard Neutra's desert houses, the first of which was built in California in 1946, symbolize an architectural language aimed at a high standard of living, embracing a successful synthesis between an unrestricted bond with the exterior and preservation of the private, internal sphere. It embodies sensible glass architecture in which transparency is not an end in itself.

Charles and Ray Eames' design for their own house at Pacific Palisades near Los Angeles (1949) contrasts with those of Mies and Johnson. It was built within the scope of an experimental housing programme initiated by the journal *Arts and Architecture*, whose aim was the development of modern housing using contemporary, prefabricated components. Charles and Ray Eames primarily made use of standard small-format steel windows, which results in a dense grid on the external walls – the antithesis of the sweeping tracts of glass of Mies and Johnson. In the living zone the glass panes of the rectangular windows alternate between transparent and translucent. The latter, intended to retain some privacy for the occupants, lead to theatrical effects after dark as the blurred outlines of objects at different distances from the façade appear more or less mysterious. The solid infills between the dark steel glazing bars are picked out in bright primary colours – red, blue, yellow – and awaken associations with the paintings of Mondrian. The studio wall has large areas of wired glass.

Although the house was intended to demonstrate the potential of prefabricated building components, the architects were unable to use such articles exclusively. Numerous items had to be specially fabricated – a time-consuming process. Even the installation of the ready-made windows and their connection to the steel structure required an incredible amount of manual welding. Like Farnsworth House, Eames House is first and foremost an architectural statement and an experiment which ignores the physics of buildings. Substantial damage to the fabric of the structure came to light soon after the house was occupied.

Marilyn and John Neuhart, in their book about the house, report that large quantities of water penetrated the flat roof during heavy rain and besides soaking the curtains led to virtually unserviceable floors. But like the house designed by Mies, this damage cannot diminish the importance of this house for the architecture of the 20th century.

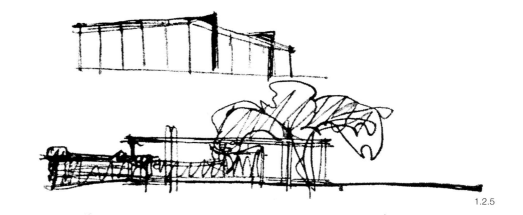

1.2.5

1.2.6

## Glass skyscrapers and curtain walls

Glass-and-steel towers best characterize the work of Mies van der Rohe in America. More or less contemporary with Farnsworth House are his first skyscrapers, on Lake Shore Drive, Chicago (1951). The two 26-storey stern square blocks employ the steel "double-T" façade section he developed for the IIT; however, these are only added externally as the building authorities insisted on a concrete casing to the loadbearing steel columns. The sections emphasize the notion of "reaching for the sky", the verticality of the structure. The entire outer skin is glass, with spandrel bands and aluminium frames flush with the panes. The façades of Mies' American skyscrapers re-interpret the concept of the curtain wall, the origins of which date back to the very beginning of the 20th century. His achievement is the aesthetization of this type of building, and function plays second fiddle to formal aspects. The curtain wall spread rapidly across post-war America. In contrast to Europe, the large architectural practices had already acquired a way of thinking thoroughly influenced by that of industry and the creation of prestige company headquarters in city centres became a significant architectural mission. One of the first curtain walls on a high-rise office block was the work of Pietro Belluschi.

He gave the Equitable Savings and Loan Building (1947) in Portland, Oregon, a smooth, virtually flush outer skin consisting of green insulating glass, aluminium and marble. However, the façade still seems heavy in optical terms, with little differentia-

tion. Another early but more convincing curtain wall design for a skyscraper was that of the Skidmore, Owings & Merrill (SOM) practice, which they conceived for the Lever Building in New York (completed in 1952). A consistent, delicate network of polished stainless steel frame sections clothes the façade, which appears completely detached from the loadbearing structure – there being only discrete connections to transfer the wind loads. The sections, reduced to the absolute minimum size, frame the blue-green shimmering, semi-reflective glass. The solid spandrel panels, clad with the same blue-green glass, are hardly noticeable. Of course, such lightness is only feasible with fixed single glazing. The consequence is a building sealed on all sides, with no opening lights; it only functions with mechanical ventilation and air-conditioning. The Lever Building also shows the aesthetic effect of coloured glass which simultaneously curtails the solar radiation entering through the windows. It was also one of the first skyscrapers to include a permanent roof-mounted cradle for cleaning and maintaining the glass façade.

Just a few hundred metres away, diagonally opposite the Lever Building, is a tower from Mies van der Rohe, the Seagram Building (1958) on New York's Park Avenue. The curtain walls of the two buildings could hardly be more dissimilar. While the design by SOM favours maximum delicacy with a flush outer skin, the Mies scheme aims at a sculpted form. Contrary to his previous works in Chicago, the dissecting members are placed not in front of but within the plane of the glass and are empha-

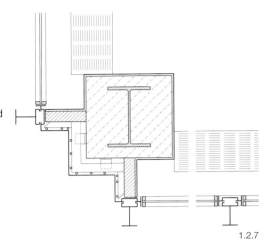

1.2.7

sized by the shadows of the joints. The sections used are no longer mass-produced standard articles but instead expensive special fabrications made from bronze. This enabled Mies to influence the cross-section: he enlarged the exposed flange in order to lend it more weight in optical terms. The windows are devoid of any glazing bars between floor and ceiling, thus achieving a resolute vertical emphasis in the façades. Iron oxide and selenium are added to the glass melt to give the panes their gold-brown hue. This leads to a structure which is no longer transparent and lightweight but massive. This edifice, the most significant of his skyscrapers actually built, bears little resemblance to the towering glass monuments of his bold visions of the 1920s. The transparency he had originally striven to attain seems to be less important now. The once crystalline or elegantly curving struc-

1.2.8

1.2.9

1.2.10

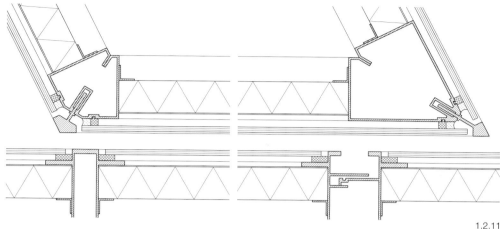

1.2.11

tures had given way to strict quadrilateral containers. Mies was now utterly convinced that the external appearance of a building should be lucid, with the main focus of attention being devoted to choice of materials and careful detailing. He was obsessed with the perfection of certain formal aspects and his architectural language fits neither the location nor the task in hand. Housing and offices all came out of the same mould; the architectural language of his New York skyscrapers was later applied in a similar vein to projects in Chicago and Toronto. This attitude encouraged the imitation of his buildings worldwide. But with this reproduction on a large scale we lose not only originality but also the attention to detail. The outcome is characterless off-the-shelf architecture.

Driven by the international style, these glazed boxes spread throughout the world at a frightening pace until the beginning of the 1970s. The office building became a prime assignment in the building industry and the grid glass curtain wall a symbol. The emergence of uniform, smooth curtain walls was kindled by the advance of anonymous investment architecture. What had originally been a creative, elegant elevational treatment degenerated to become a monotonous covering. Glass architecture was now established on an international level but the aesthetic visions of expressionism and early modernism – from the facets of playful light of Scheerbart's poetry or the visionary sketches of Taut and Mies van der Rohe – had been all but lost along the way. Criticism of the impoverishmnet of the architectural language was becoming louder and louder.

### Structural sealant glazing and container architecture

The method of fixing external glazing by means of loadbearing silicone (structural sealant glazing) which started to appear in the mid-1960s in the USA, as well as other innovative fixing techniques, rendered it possible to clad roofs and walls with a uniformly smooth skin. All conceivable geometrical forms could now be enclosed with unswerving regularity. This was a tempting idea at a time when criticism of identical, right-angled cubes was growing and architectural semantics was gaining ground again. The ensuing formal eclecticism satisfied the desires of many investors and owners for unmistakable, proclamatory buildings. One drastic example of this approach is the Pacific Design Center in Los Angeles, by Cesar Pelli and Victor Gruen, the first phase of which was completed in 1976. It is an elongated, tall structure which reminds

1.2.12

1.2.13

the observer of an oversized ornamental moulding cut off at random. The roof and walls, curves and slopes of this steel structure are wrapped in a uniform curtain wall of shimmering blue glass. From the outside the functions are completely hidden, neither staircase nor showrooms are evident. The unchanging envelope with its stereotyped grid leads to a loss of all sense of scale; the only aid to orientation is the surrounding small-scale suburban development into which the building has been implanted without any feeling for urban affinity. The first phase – 67 000 m$^2$ of retail and showroom space, quickly dubbed the "blue whale" by the local inhabitants – was later joined by a green pyramid and a red cylinder, both employing a similar construction. All three structures look like sealed containers with arbitrary shapes which do not reveal anything of their inner workings to the outside world.

The convention of enclosing everything in a uniform glass skin soon became especially fashionable for American skyscrapers, where architects and developers tried to place an unmistakable mark on the skyline of a city with their ideas, as erratic as they were striking. The resulting specimens can only be imagined in American-style cityscapes.

1.2.14

In Dallas, Ieoh Ming Pei and Henry Cobb designed what is now the First Interstate Bank Tower (1983–86). In line with their importance and financial power, the owners wanted an impressive, sculpted form which would also be the tallest building in the city. The 220 m tower is clad in an identical grid of blue-green reflective glass. Even though the building dates from the mid-1980s the design brief still called for single glazing and full air-conditioning – a peculiarly US phenomenon. The windows can only be opened for cleaning via an ingenious mechanism specially developed for this purpose.

Like the curtain walls of the 1950s and 1960s, the office and commercial buildings enshrouded in structural sealant glazing are rarely actually transparent. Their outer skins comprise coloured and reflective glasses which, although they lead to interesting lighting effects, do not permit a view through during the hours of daylight. The effects of semi-transparency – the simultaneous awareness of the glazed surface and the indistinct internal layout beyond – as Mies had proposed in his early sketches or Gropius had implemented on the façades of the Bauhaus way back in the 1920s, are nowhere to be found.

And the view out is normally only possible via a strip of windows. Great areas of the façade remain impenetrable and the view through the windows of solar-control glass is limited anyway. Nevertheless, criticism concentrated on the lack of scale in these bland containers, the emblems of a transient fashion. Answers emerged from the likes of Norman Foster and Richard Rogers, architects who use the structure to shape their buildings (Hong Kong & Shanghai Bank, Lloyd's Building, London), and the post-modernists. In Northern and Central Europe, the increasing awareness of energy aspects led to façades broken up by protruding sunshades or blinds. And the trend away from coloured glass reflects the desire to save on the electricity for artificial lighting.

But the use of structural sealant glazing has not remained confined to commercial structures. Philip Johnson and John Burgee clad the Crystal Cathedral (1980) in Garden Grove near Los Angeles entirely in polished glass. The design is based on the idea of a crystalline building glistening like a jewel in the sun. In the hot climate and relentless sunshine of southern California the idea of using polished glass is not at all inappropriate: the silver-metallized panes only allow a fraction of the radiation to pass but the naturally ventilated interior remains sufficiently bright. On the other hand, the desired crystalline effect is only apparent under certain lighting conditions. The regular grid of the smooth façade makes the religious function of the building difficult to discern from the outside. But the vast interior, capable of accommodating 3000 people, is imposing, encircled by the delicate steelwork of the structure and the sky visible on all sides through the glass. The church in Garden Grove is one of a handful of buildings of its time in which a covering of coloured, mirrored glass encloses a single, magnificent and undivided space and where the technique of structural sealant glazing enables an uninterrupted transparency from inside to outside.

1.2.15

## Daylight and darkness – glass and light

Transparent or reflective building envelopes are the characteristics of glass architecture. However, the even illumination of the interior by way of large expanses of glass hardly leads to an intensive perception of light. More dramatic effects are brought about by the contrast between light and dark, which can be achieved by means of small window apertures and narrow slits in the walls. The position of these has a decisive influence on the spatial quality, on the awareness of depth, on the contours. The use of coloured glasses can achieve supplementary effects, as the churches of the Middle Ages or the windows of the Art Nouveau period can illustrate in an impressive manner. Le Corbusier used coloured glass in the south façade of the pilgrimage church at Notre-Dame-du-Haut in Ronchamp. The wall is perforated by openings of different sizes, creating an intrusive, mystical atmosphere in an interior kept intentionally dim. In addition, he separated roof and external wall by a bright, narrow, strip of light.

Tadao Ando too uses light to great effect in his designs. Like Le Corbusier he employs narrow, glazed openings again and again to demarcate building components and generate a feeling of depth. Using simple means he has been able to create one of his most invasive scenes in the small Protestant chapel in Ibaraki, Japan, which deserves its epithet "The Church of the Light". Upon entering the unadorned, box-like building of fair-faced concrete, the visitor's gaze is inevitably drawn to the cross of blazing sunlight behind the altar. Although the slit is only 200 mm wide, the great contrast between light and dark reinforces the effect.

1.2.16

1.1.14   Crystal Cathedral, Garden Grove, California, Philip Johnson and John Burgee, 1980, detail of façade
1.1.15   Crystal Cathedral, Garden Grove, California
1.2.16   Pilgrimage church at Notre-Dame-du-Haut, Ronchamp, Le Corbusier, 1951
1.2.17   Church of the light, Ibaraki, Japan, Tadao Ando, 1987–89

1.2.17

1.2.18

## The new transparency – glass as a symbol

The criticism of glass architecture that was voiced in the 1970s was not directed solely at the stereotyped grid-like façades. Triggered by the two oil crises, the energy issue now took the spotlight overnight. Whereas up until that time it was still considered advanced to be able to generate any imaginable climate by means of energy-guzzling machinery within a building sealed on all sides, most Western nations now began to adopt rigorous legislation to force consumers into using resources wisely. The all-glass façade was thrown into question and the humble window identified as an energy leak. This temporary rejection of glass forced the industry to act. A great bout of research activity led to the development of more effective insulating and solar-control glasses, an immense innovative boost was initiated.

Coloured and mirrored glasses were now much less in demand; the clear, transparent varieties had taken centre stage. At the same time, progress was made on the structural side too. Both phenomena had a permanent effect on architecture: real transparency could now be achieved on a wider scale. It was not long before glass architecture became popular again and today there is hardly a prestige project that is not characterized by this material to some extent. The orthogonal, single-colour elevations of the late 1960s no longer satisfy optical tastes. The new status objects draw attention to themselves by way of concise but sometimes even extravagant forms often derived from the construction.

Like a reptile, Nicholas Grimshaw's magnificent terminal slithers alongside London's old Waterloo station amid a densely developed neighbourhood (see pp. 304–309). Rafael Viñoly has given the Tokyo Forum an unmistakable countenance in the form of a giant glass lens. Norman Foster too is using glass for the dome called for by the politicians over the Reichstag in Berlin. An elaborate glass trade fair hall in Leipzig is intended to symbolize what is allegedly an upturn in the fortunes of Germany's eastern federal states. Two of the most widely discussed glass structures which brought this material to the notice of the general public were erected at the end of the 1980s in Paris within the scope of the "Grands Projets de l'Etat" during the era of President Mitterand. Like so many before him, I. M. Pei was captivated by the idea of the glazed crystal as he conceived the entrance pyramid for the Louvre in the course of reorganizing the museum. However, none of his predecessors had been able to realize their dreams with a comparable input of funds and technology; nothing was too expensive for this prestige monument – the new symbol of the Louvre.

1.2.19

To avoid distracting reflections and hence achieve maximum transparency, the architect demanded absolutely flat surfaces from the engineers and manufacturers involved. For this purpose a particularly level, extra-clear glass was developed and the supporting steelwork – which like the structure of a crystal exhibits no visible difference between primary and secondary members – was fabricated with exceptional precision. However, when viewed from inside, the lightness which all had tried so hard to achieve is only visible from certain angles. Looked at from other angles the relatively high proportion of steelwork dominates. In urban terms the unequivocal geometrical assemblage of hard, reflective materials sends a clear message, and is already an intrinsic part of the Parisian cityscape. Despite vehement criticism initially, this contemporary monument has now been accepted by the public and is regarded as an attraction in its own right by the tourists – a proof of acceptance that few icons of modern architecture have been awarded.

In the National Library of France, completed in 1997, Dominique Perrault has used glass, hard and transparent, primarily in a symbolic way: it represents wisdom, technical progress and the spirit of a great nation. Four crystalline towers celebrate the book as a cultural medium. However, functional inconsistencies have led to disputes about the building's merit: while the majority of the books are stored on the transparent upper floors, those using the library are accommodated in dark, artificially lit reading rooms! Despite this situation, Perrault's library is a fascinating structure that demonstrates in impressive manner the significance of glass for a contemporary prestige project. Günter Behnisch is trying to symbolize totally different values with his use of glass. For him glass is the material which best satisfies the claims of democracy. His transparent Bundestag (1993, see pp. 234–241) is open to all citizens at least in visual terms and hence permits the symbolical control of the elected representatives of the people. But the visual link with the landscape, the Rhine, plays an important role as well. Despite all the security stipulations the architect succeeded in creating a transparent parliament in two senses. Glass just a few centimetres thick provides what was in the past the province of massive walls: protection against weather, noise, intruders, attack and fire.

1.2.20

1.2.18   Central Entrance Hall, New Leipzig Trade Fair,
         von Gerkan, Marg + Partner, 1996
1.2.19   Tokyo Forum, Tokyo, Rafael Viñoly, 1997
1.2.20   Bibliothèque Nationale François Mitterand, Paris,
         Dominique Perrault, 1997
1.2.21   Louvre Pyramid, Paris, Ieoh Ming Pei, 1990

1.2.21

## Translucency and reflection

The creative use of glass on the façade is not confined to softening the outer skin or setting accents by means of reflections. As long ago as the 1920s there had been attempts to prompt an awareness of the material properties of glass by way of intentional reflections, as the sketches of Bruno Taut and others show. Pierre Chareau's Maison de Verre of 1931 has a dazzling envelope of glass bricks which in the confines of an inner court guarantees optimum lighting while preserving privacy (Fig. 1.1.54, p. 34). The aesthetic possibilities of translucent walls, allowing the passage of light while remaining non-transparent, i.e. brought about by the material properties themselves, are exploited to the full here. The small opening lights of clear glass represent a deliberate contrast. Many of the glass structures of the following decades no longer exhibit these features; their coloured or reflective façades are dull by comparison. However, since the 1980s, translucency too has been gaining ground alongside transparency. Besides the dematerialization brought about by glass, divulging the physical density and reality of this, basically, transparent material has now become a central theme. A multitude of new products and

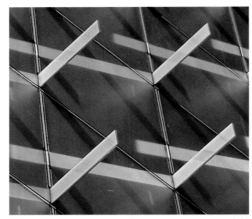

1.2.22

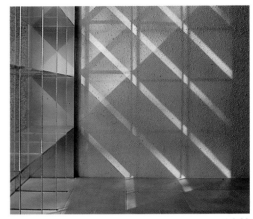

1.2.23

processes have provided the foundation for this.

The possibilities of acid etching, sand-blasting, screen printing and coating with holograms or dichroic films invite experimentation. Many architects are again becoming aware that working with glass means designing with light, indeed, that this transparent, reflective material allows the nuances of changing light conditions to be rendered visible.

A number of impressive settings exploiting this principle have been realized by the artist and architect James Carpenter. In two

windows he designed in 1985–87 for a chapel in Indianapolis he makes intelligent and striking use of the possibilities of dichroic coatings made from various metal oxides which split the light into its spectral colours by way of interference phenomena and either transmit or reflect it, depending on the angle of incidence. The resulting constantly changing colours animate the otherwise plain white interior in dramatic fashion – glass opens up three-dimensional, dynamic opportunities.

Other architects employ acid-etched or sand-blasted panes to make their buildings

1.2.24

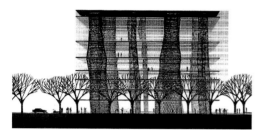

1.2.25

appear weightless and luminous under certain lighting conditions. A number of recent museum projects have skilfully combined this effect with an ingenious illumination of the interior. The Goetz Art Gallery in Munich (1994) by Herzog & de Meuron is a detached building placed in a park-like garden. Two opaque bands of green glass encircle the building, separated from the birchwood cladding panels. As the light changes, the building too varies from solid, two-dimensional object to transparent, floating volume. The glazing to the ground floor is at the same time the clerestory light to the

basement. This plain cuboid does not appear sterile; on the contrary, it seems sensual, light and graceful.

The "Kunsthaus Bregenz" (Bregenz Art Gallery, 1997) by Peter Zumthor represents a successful synthesis of solid concrete structure and glazed outer skin. Translucent but not transparent, it alters its appearance depending on viewing angle, time of day and lighting conditions. Sometimes it sparkles or shines and reflects the sun's rays, sometimes it appears inert and opaque. The acid-etched glass panes of the identical façades without plinth or cornice are laid around the building like a protective envelope. An ingenious system of intermediate floors and glass ceilings enables daylight entering via the façades to be used to illuminate the interior. Against the light the edge of the roof appears to float like an illuminated crown; contours dissolve, the transition to the sky becomes diffuse.

A similar, albeit more extreme version of dematerialization and dissolution of the building outline was proposed by Jean Nouvel in his competition entry for the Tour Sans Fins in Paris La Défense (1989). His tower, substantial and firmly rooted to the earth at the base, was intended to rapidly melt away into an airy construction as it rose higher. Nouvel proposed to use silk-screen printing on his

glass, the pattern becoming denser towards the apex and so reproducing more and more nuances of colour. At the same time this evaporative character was to be achieved by different types of glass at the various levels.

Playing with differing grades of transparency is the intention of Toyo Ito in his Mediathek project in Sendai. Printing and foil coatings as well as the use of water will achieve different degrees of transparency and translucency. Newly developed thermotropic materials will also be employed. Richard Rogers created a translucent envelope for the Lloyd's Building in London (1986) by using a specially produced, textured cast glass.

1.2.22  Dichroic Light Field, New York,
        James Carpenter, 1994
1.2.23  Sweeny Chapel, Christian Theological Seminary,
        Indianapolis, Indiana, James Carpenter
        Architect: Edward L. Barnes, New York,
        1985–87, model photo
1.2.24  Goetz Art Gallery, Munich,
        Herzog & de Meuron, 1994
1.2.25  Mediathek projekt in Sendai, Japan, Toyo Ito
1.2.26  Lloyd's Building, London, Richard Rogers,
        1982–86, detail of façade
1.2.27  Bregenz Art Gallery, Peter Zumthor, 1997,
        façade

1.2.26

1.2.27

## The façade as a display – the glazed skin comes alive

The opportunities of enamel coatings and screen printing, as well as the possibility of integrating thin films containing liquid crystals or holograms between the panes of laminated units, are increasing, finding acceptance among architects. Media façades with moving pictures, superimposed lettering, printed information and changing colours are the result. Consequently, the external envelope is turned into a display conveying information or content, or simply insipid advertising. Jean Nouvel has provided plenty of inspiration in this field. His prize-winning competition design for the DuMont Schauberg publishing house (1990) employs an external envelope covering transparent planes which reveal their presence through the effects of depth and backlighting, reflections and mirages. The glass façades manifest themselves by way of printed letters and signs and turn the building itself into a symbol of its function as a media operation.
In his succeeding projects for the Mediapark in Cologne (1990), the Euralille shopping centre (1995) and the Lafayette department store in Berlin (1996), Nouvel makes use of the latest information technologies in order to turn the façade into a "screen". He abandons the traditional façade divided up by columns and windows and replaces it with technically produced images and graphic characters. The outer skin becomes pure packaging, decoration. Nouvel interprets his façades as mirror images of our world overflowing with information, although he too contributes to this vast flood of images. This is a new kind of embellishment.

Printed patterns and lettering are met with more frequently than moving pictures. Besides their decorative functions, such printing can serve to provide shade or privacy. Sometimes though it is no more than the name of the owner in oversize letters purely for publicity purposes. Nouvel's reflective Cartier warehouse near Fribourg is the most sensational example of this. A more subtle approach is demonstrated by Kazuyo Sejima from Japan on the Kinbasha Pachinco Parlor in Ibaraki (1993) and Basel-based architects Jacques Herzog and Pierre de Meuron on their SUVA Insurance Building in Basel (1993, see Fig. 1.2.66, p. 57). Besides advertising, the printing on both buildings serves to create a semi-transparency and hence a skilful unfolding of the glass as a material. In the Japanese example the play of light and shadow brought about by the giant letters lends form to the rooms behind the façade, whereas in the Swiss case the thousands of tiny letters are only legible from close up and produce a sort of veiling effect.

1.2.28

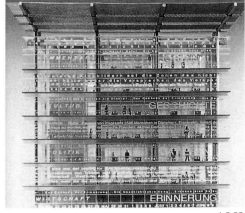

1.2.29

1.2.30

1.2.31

KINBASHA KINBASHA KINBASHA KINBASHA KINBASHA KINBASHA

1.2.32

1.2.33

1.2.34

# Developments in glass construction

Recent decades have witnessed enormous strides taking place in the field of glass construction. The longing for dematerialization and transparency – an essential ingredient of modern architecture – leads to the material taking on more and more loadbearing functions. At the same time, improved adhesives have enabled designers to increase the proportion of glass in façades. The growing power of the computer renders possible new methods of calculation and – in the case of complex pane geometries – enables the cutting of the glass to be controlled directly. Nevertheless, the material has still not been adequately researched and many of the applicable standards and directives lag behind the current level of knowledge or are inadequate. Therefore, innovative applications usually require costly tests in order to verify the initial calculations.

The possibility of prestressing glass to form toughened safety glass, practised by the French company Saint-Gobain since 1929, and the manufacture of laminated glass, patented by Edouard Benedictus in 1909, are essential prerequisites for today's glass constructions. Both types were originally developed for use in vehicles.

Another major step was the invention of the float process in 1955 by Alastair Pilkington. This method, in which the glass pane is formed by floating the melt on a bath of liquid tin (see p. 62), revolutionized the manufacture of good-quality glass and large formats.

## Curtain walls

The modern curtain wall originated around the middle of the 20th century in America. Crucial to its development, besides aesthetic and architectural factors, was, above all, economics. At that time labour was more expensive in America than it was in Europe and so there was a trend towards prefabrication in the building industry.

The majority of the curtain walls customary during that period involved fitting the glazing and solid infills to a supporting framework of posts and rails attached to the primary structure. Façades of actual glazing elements, like on the Alcoa Building in Pittsburgh (1955, architects: Harrison & Abramovitz), were still rare.

One of the most influential curtain walls of that time was the delicate skin of SOM's Lever Building in New York (see p. 38). The supporting framework of loadbearing rolled steel sections was concealed behind folded stainless steel sheet. Putty was still used to attach the fixed single glazing. To check the spread of fire, the authorities – like in all US cities – required a narrow strip of concrete masonry behind the curtain wall, either in the area of each spandrel panel or just below each floor slab. This was not visible from outside.

The state of the art in façade construction in the Europe of the mid-1950s is demonstrated by the Jespersen office block (1955) in Copenhagen. Visually, Arne Jacobsen's delicate façades owe much to the Lever Building: like in that example, a fine network of metal sections lend texture to the surface and the spandrel panels are filled with green glass. However, the supporting structure of the façades, with their chunky squared timber, is more reminiscent of the work of craftsmen. Jacobsen's building already employs insulating glass and the relatively bulky glazing beads are painted green to match the softly reflective panes. Just a few years later he was able to use a factory-made curtain wall in his main work, the SAS Building (1958–60) in the centre of the Danish capital.

### Sealing profiles made from synthetic rubber

One of the first totally prefabricated curtain walls was that on the General Motors Technical Center in Warren, Michigan, near Detroit (1949–56). This is a masterpiece, in formal terms too, from the Finnish-American architect Eero Saarinen. As the building is not in a city centre location, a solid panel near the ceiling is adequate – no heavy masonry like on the Lever Building. The joints are sealed in a very special way: befitting a building for the automotive industry, Saarinen used synthetic, permanently elastic rubber profiles (neoprene) like those that had been common in vehicles for a long time. More or less at the same time, SOM incorporated this, for the construction industry, new material in their design for the arrivals terminal at New York's Idlewild international airport (1955–57). However, the principles of the two concepts differ in the way they seal the façade and retain the glass. At Idlewild press-fit clamping angles exert pressure on the neoprene seals (Fig. 1.2.39, p. 49) – a method that did not prove to be effective and was soon abandoned; but the General Motors Technical Center does not require any press-fit metal retainers. In this case the sealing lip is distorted upon inserting the glass pane and subsequently secured by inserting an extra wedge profile (Fig. 1.2.40, p. 49). Permanently elastic synthetic rubber seals quickly found widespread favour in the building industry and since the mid-1960s have been a regular feature of façade technology. Neoprene seals were first used in

1.2.28  Vreeburg cinema, Utrecht, Gerrit Rietveld, 1934–36
1.2.29  DuMont Schauberg publishing house, Cologne, Jean Nouvel, competition entry, 1990
1.2.30  Euralille shopping centre, France, Jean Nouvel, 1995
1.2.31  Pfaffenholz Sport Center, St Louis, France, Herzog & de Meuron, 1993, detail of façade
1.2.32  Kinbasha Casino, Ibaraki, Japan, Kazuyo Sejima, 1993, elevation
1.2.33  Cartier warehouse, Fribourg, Switzerland, Jean Nouvel, detail of façade
1.2.34  Kinbasha Casino, Ibaraki, Japan, Kazuyo Sejima, 1993, façade
1.2.35  Jespersen office block, Copenhagen, Arne Jacobsen, 1955, design sketch

1.2.35

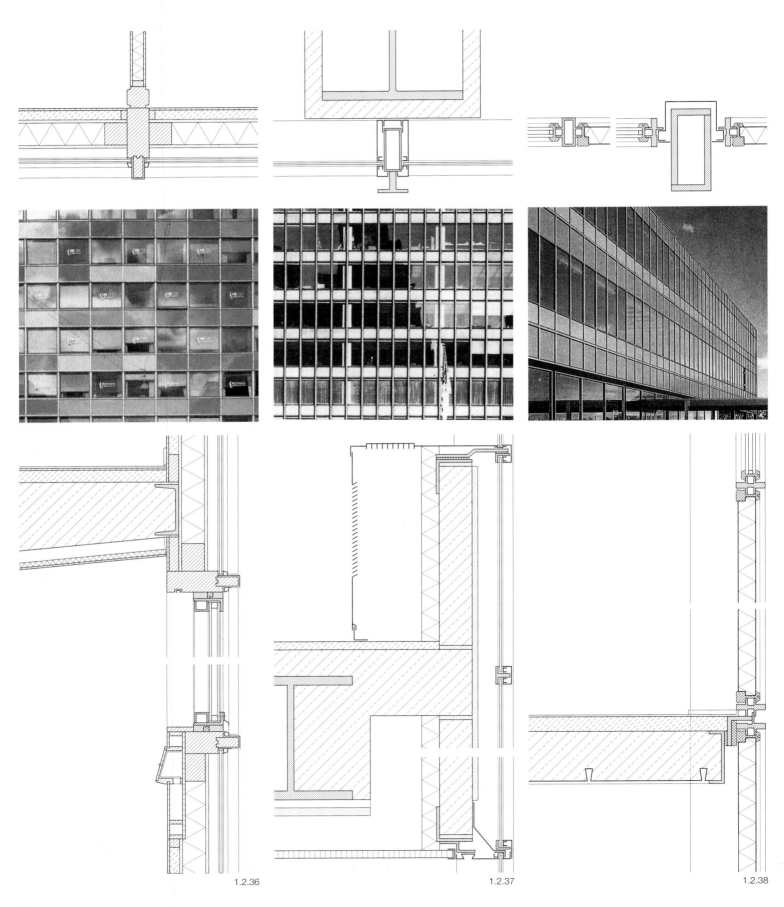

1.2.36

1.2.37

1.2.38

Germany in 1962. This year also marks the introduction of the first façade profiles with a thermal break (National House in Frankfurt, BASF Building in Ludwigshafen).

**Glazing with integral profiles**

Various glazing systems employing integral synthetic rubber profiles appeared on the American market during the 1960s. Besides acting as seals, these profiles also fixed the glass panes to the frame construction. These systems came about as the result of trying to replace manual work on site by a higher degree of prefabrication. Norman Foster used such profiles for the first time in 1970 on a two-storey building at the Fred Olsen Amenity Centre in the Port of London. The fully glazed façades of this building are distinguished by their exceptional delicacy and dematerialization, a feature which was to be recalled later in the identical methods used for the external skin of the IBM Technical Park (1975–80).

**Structural sealant glazing**

The introduction of synthetic seals led to trials involving silicone adhesives to enable the glass to be glued directly to the frame. This work started around 1960 in the USA and the first application on a façade came in 1963. The silicone was no longer just a seal to prevent the ingress of the weather but instead also carried some of the self-weight of the panes and transferred the wind pressure and suction acting on the glazing back to the supporting construction. It became a significant loadbearing component in the façade. This technique quickly established itself in the USA and had a permanent influence on the American skyscraper architecture of the 1970s and 1980s (see p. 39). Utterly smooth façades and roofs without a hint of any contour were now feasible. To conceal the supporting construction as well as floor slabs and spandrel panels, coloured and reflective glasses were used at first almost without exception. The rational integration of opening lights remained unsolved for a long time. This fact led to structural sealant glazing façades being reserved for air-conditioned office blocks at first. In Germany the first such façades were on the Rosenthal office building in Selb in 1986/87 and, roughly at the same time, on the Neoplan distribution centre in Stuttgart. The stipulations of the building authorities in Germany – like in some other European countries – have severely limited the potential for these façades.

1.2.36   Jespersen office block, Copenhagen, Arne Jacobsen, 1955, façade and façade horizontal/vertical sections
1.2.37   Lever Building, New York, Skidmore, Owings & Merrill, 1952, façade and façade horizontal/vertical sections
1.2.38   General Motors Technical Center, Warren, Michigan, Eero Saarinen, 1949–56, façade and façade horizontal/vertical sections
1.2.39   Idlewild airport, New York, Skidmore, Owings & Merrill, 1955–57, façade detail
1.2.40   General Motors Technical Center, Warren, Michigan, Eero Saarinen, 1949–56 façade detail
1.2.41   Fred Olsen Amenity Centre, London, Norman Foster, 1968–72, façade detail
1.2.42   IBM Technical Park, Greenford, England, Norman Foster, 1975–80

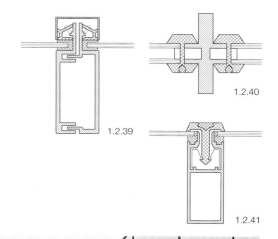

1.2.40

1.2.39

1.2.41

1.2.42

## Suspended glazing and point fixings

Instead of inserting glass panes into the building fabric, the idea of suspending them from above and so avoiding the risk of deflection was investigated by the Frankfurt-based entrepreneur Otto Hahn during the 1950s. In 1956 his company proposed such a solution for the showroom windows of a car dealer in Vienna (Steyer, Daimler, Puch) which, however, was not implemented. The first applications of what had in the meantime become a fully fledged glazing system were in 1964 on the Wilhelm Lehmbruck Museum in Duisburg (architect: Manfred Lehmbruck) and in 1960/63 on the entrance foyer to Broadcasting House in Paris (architect: Henri Bernard). Here, the glass panes (approx. 4 m high) are stiffened to resist bending stresses by means of glass fins attached with adhesive. The panes of glass are held by clamps fitted into articulated bearings. These ensure that the loads are distributed evenly via the separate suspension points.

The principle of suspended glazing quickly became popular although its use for insulating glass remained less attractive because the manufacturing process did not yet permit large pane sizes.

Suspended glazing underwent a further development in 1971–75 with Norman

1.2.43

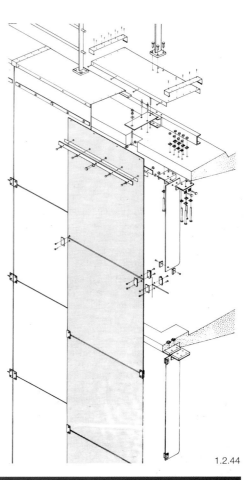

1.2.44

1.2.43    Project for a glass tower in Berlin on a polygonal plan, Mies v. d. Rohe, 1922
1.2.44    Offices for Willis, Faber & Dumas, Ipswich, Norman Foster, 1971–75, façade detail
1.2.45    Offices for Willis, Faber & Dumas, Ipswich
1.2.46    Renault Centre, Swindon, Norman Foster, 1982, detail of glass fixing
1.2.47    Renault Centre, Swindon

1.2.45

Foster's design – in conjunction with the UK glass manufacturer Pilkington – for the offices of Willis, Faber & Dumas in Ipswich. Each pane on this building is clamped to its neighbour above using "patch" fittings. Like a chain mail coat, the three-storey façade hangs from the roof slab, stiffened against wind loads by internal glass fins suspended from the floor slabs and extending halfway down each storey. The building is an impressive illustration of how constructional innovations, sensibly implemented, can be used to realize an inspired idea. The continuous, reflective glass façade of this building gives it an intangible quality which responds to the mature surroundings of the old quarter of Ipswich by reflecting them in the façade. As the flat panes of glass are arranged at different angles as they follow the curved contours, they refract the light differently, producing exciting effects. The informal layout follows the line of the plot and at the same time is an ideal solution to the open-plan offices so prevalent at that time. Fifty years after Mies van der Rohe's futuristic vision of a glass tower, Norman Foster had successfully executed such a construction, albeit freely interpreted and on a smaller scale. Mies' sketches include polygonal walls and in his model of the project we can see the suspension system he had already devised.

The technical innovation of the Willis, Faber & Dumas project was in suspending a series of several panes of glass. They are clamped together by means of patch fittings which project beyond the plane of the glazing. The next major step forward in all-glass façades was to be the shifting of the fixings into the plane of the glazing itself. This system was again the result of a collaboration between Foster and Pilkington and led to the planar system, first used on the Renault Centre in Swindon (1982). The single glazing of this building is not suspended but screwed to a supporting frame of posts and rails.

A simultaneously suspended and trussed glass façade with flush discrete fixings was successfully achieved in 1986 on the large greenhouses of the Musée de Sciences et de l'Industrie at Parc La Villette, Paris (Fig. 1.2.48, p. 52). The brief presented by architect Adrien Fainsilber to the glazing design team of Peter Rice, Martin Francis and Ian Ritchie called for maximum transparency. As, however, unlike Foster's building in Ipswich, there were no floor slabs to absorb the horizontal forces, the engineers developed a suspended façade which was fixed with individual, flush-fitting bolts and provided with a system of cable trusses to carry the wind loads, the first of its kind. The glass acts structurally because the tension cables gain their stability from being fixed to the glass panes. The panes of glass, each 2 m

1.2.46

square and 12 mm thick, are suspended at the top by prestressed steel springs. In order to avoid stresses in the panes and to be able to calculate the forces with greater accuracy, the individual fixings include an articulated head which lies exactly in the plane of the glazing. In the following years, Rice, Francis and Ritchie (RFR) continued to develop and vary the principle of suspended and trussed glass façades by way of a number of different projects.

The H-shaped, articulated four-point connector used at La Villette was soon replaced by an X-shaped assembly with just one articulated joint at the centre of the X. One decisive factor, apart from aesthetic considerations, was the realization that glass walls joined with silicone are relatively rigid, so the risk of racking of the entire wall is rather low.

RFR managed to incorporate an essentially dematerialized and particularly delicate glass façade on an otherwise mediocre office and commercial building in Avenue Montaigne, Paris (architects: Epstein, Glaimann & Vidal, 1993). The glass wall separates the semicircular south-facing atrium from the adjacent internal court. The supporting structure consists of a series of cable trusses with radial anchors to the respective floor slabs. This arrangement, made possible by the geometry of the building, enabled the use of a particularly fine network of cables and panes 3.80 m high! To make the façade appear even lighter and to satisfy the architects' wish that the half-cylinder should be reflected in the glass and so create the illusion of a whole cylinder, the point fixings were attached to the outside of the façade. Therefore, the inside face is a completely smooth glass surface. The individual fixings are connected to the tension cables via stainless steel rods which penetrate the glazing at the intersection of every

1.2.47

four panes, the corners of which are trimmed to accommodate this detail.
The first use of a trussed façade employing insulating glass was in 1990 on a bank in Montgermont near Rennes (architects: Odile Decq and Benoît Cornette). The special feature of this is the fact that the continuous 120 m long façade uses single glazing for the entrance foyer and insulating glass for the office wing. To be able to use the same type of fixing for both, RFR adapted the fixing with the articulated head in the plane of the glazing to fit the insulating glass. The holes in the finished glazing units had to line up exactly and that proved troublesome. This was compounded by the fact that three-ply laminated glass was required at certain places. A slender structure of steel 2 m in front of the façade stabilizes this against wind forces and at the same time serves as a support framework for the roller blinds.

## Glazed nets

At the end of the 1980s the Stuttgart-based engineers Schlaich, Bergermann & Partner first created delicate glass roof constructions by developing shell structures, i.e. surfaces curved in two planes, over a distended structure of separate linear members. The primary grid of these structures consists of a square mesh of flat bars which can be moulded into virtually any shape by altering the 90° squares of the original mesh to a rhomboid form. This permits loadbearing structures curved in two planes that can follow any contour. Prestressed, continuous cables take on the function of diagonals to triangulate the net and hence make it stable. A special feature of these nets is the members that make up the square mesh: these also serve to support the glazing directly (merely a strip of EPDM between). The omission of secondary glazing bars fitted to the main structure, as is normally the case, leads not only to cost-savings but to optimum transparency.
One of the first and still one of the most outstanding examples of this technique, which Jörg Schlaich has used to great effect, even being able to roof-over irregular plan

shapes, is that of the roof to the courtyard of the Hamburg City History Museum (architects: von Gerkan, Marg & Partner, 1990, see pp. 316–319). In a successful synthesis of engineering and architectural skill, a seemingly weightless, net-like roof now complements the old facing brickwork of Fritz Schumacher without impairing the appearance of the old buildings. This triumphant combination of old and new leads to a high aesthetic quality. At the same time Schlaich and Bergermann covered a leisure pool in Neckarsulm with insulating glass. In contrast to the panes used for the museum in Hamburg, these are bent like a dome.

## Glazed cable-lattice façades

Jörg Schlaich has erected seemingly lightweight glass walls on the 40 m wide x 25 m high atrium gables of Hotel Kempinski at Munich airport (architect: Helmut Jahn; see "Glazed cable or cable-lattice façades", p. 111). The impressive dematerialization of the façade is achieved through highly prestressed horizontal cables anchored to the adjoining wings of the hotel. The panes of glass are clamped to the cables via corner plates.

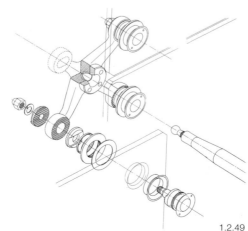

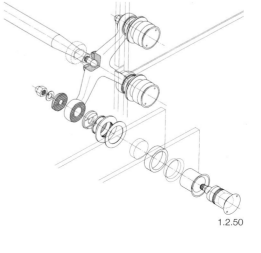

1.2.48

1.2.49

1.2.50

## Glass construction subjected to tension and compression – all-glass buildings

The constant striving for maximum transparency and for the dissolution of façades and roofs inevitably led to the attempt to erect all-glass buildings without loadbearing metal parts. Therefore, it comes as no surprise to discover that numerous architects and engineers have experimented in this field in recent years. Here too, the enormous progress made in glass technology as well as the growing understanding of how glass behaves structurally were indispensable prerequisites.

Nevertheless, the feasibility of many innovations can only be ascertained by practical trials. Therefore, numerous new ideas have been initially studied on small or temporary structures which do not represent long-term risks and whose construction and behaviour is easy to determine.

### Loadbearing glass walls

For the two Dutchmen Jan Benthem and Mels Crouwel, the house of one of the partners (Almere, 1984), initially conceived only as a temporary home, offered them the chance to experiment with unconventional ideas. In terms of space and design it is a re-interpretation of Mies' Farnsworth House (see p. 36): the interior of the raised struc-

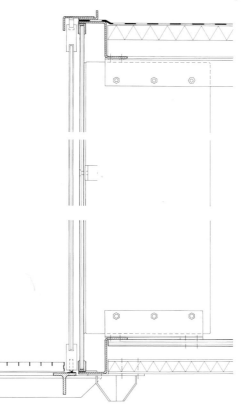

ture is defined merely by way of two horizontal plates – floor and roof. In constructional terms it is inspired by another Mies project, the "50 by 50 House": enclosed on all sides by frameless glass façades which accommodate compressive forces and carry some of the load of the roof of insulated trapezoidal sheeting. Internal glass fins stiffen the 2.50 m high, 12 mm thick panes of toughened safety glass.

The Sonsbeek sculpture pavilion by Benthem & Crouwel, erected two years later, also includes loadbearing all-glass walls but this time adds a horizontal glass roof (with minimum camber to drain rainwater) supported by steel girders. Like with the earlier house, small metal corner fixings are used to hold the panes and the glass walls are

1.2.48  Greenhouses at the Musée de Sciences et de l'Industrie, Parc La Villette, Paris, Adrien Fainsilber and Rice, Francis, Ritchie, 1986, overall view and four-point glass support
1.2.49  Offices, Avenue Montaigne, Paris, Epstein, Glaimann, Vidal and Rice, Francis, Ritchie, 1993, overall view and four-point glass support
1.2.50  Banque Populaire de l'ouest et de l'Armorique, Montgermont, Odile Decq, Benoît Cornette and Rice, Francis, Ritchie, 1990, overall view and four-point glass support
1.2.51  Sculpture pavilion, Sonsbeek, Benthem & Crouwel, 1986, façade section
1.2.52  Sculpture pavilion, Sonsbeek

1.2.51

1.2.52

stiffened by glass fins. The low thermal and moisture loads as well as the fact that the pavilion was only designed as a temporary shelter rendered possible this unusually high degree of transparency.

**All-glass constructions**
The two British engineers Laurence Dewhurst and Tim Macfarlane made an attempt to reduce the metal content to zero by developing a glass-glass mortise and tenon joint inspired by traditional timber construction. This achievement enabled architect Rick Mather to create the first really all-glass construction – a conservatory extension to a house in Hampstead, London (1992). Walls and roof are all transparent but in addition the columns and beams to the monopitch roof are made from three-ply laminated glass with PVB interlayers, so that if a pane breaks, the loadbearing capacity of the member remains guaranteed. Even the edge seal to the insulating glass, normally aluminium, utilizes narrow glass strips glued between the 10 mm panes.

A similar construction measuring 5.70 x 11 m in plan and with an almost horizontal roof was designed by the architectural practice Design Antenna in cooperation with Tim Macfarlane for the extension to an existing museum in Kingswinford, England. It is the largest all-glass construction built to date (see pp. 282–285). However, plans for a larger glass cube are already on the drawing board of the same architects: the Museum of British Glass in London should be ready to open in 2001.

Despite the fascination, all-glass buildings will remain predominantly small one-offs hardly able to shake off their experimental character. In many applications, in housing above all, complete transparency is often undesirable anyway, and even the integra-

1.2.53

tion of mechanical sunshading – usually indispensable – is very involved if conflicts with the aims of the design are to be avoided.

**Glass beams and columns in more heavily loaded structures**
There have also been attempts very recently to employ glass for more heavily loaded structures. Glass beams subjected to bending were used in a horizontal glass roof over the Louvre workshops in Paris (Jérôme Brunet and Eric Saunier, 1994). As the glass roof is at the same level as a courtyard open to the public, it had to be assumed that

despite screening by way of water and planting, the glass could be subjected to the load of several persons simultaneously. The design loads for a surface subjected to unrestricted foot traffic are correspondingly high and so the construction could not be as light as the smaller structures in the Netherlands and England mentioned above. Furthermore, the laminated glass beams, spanning about 4.60 m, had to be placed in rather bulky steel joist hangers. Nevertheless, the transparency and the clear view of the sky were hardly impeded.

The foyer to the local authority offices in Saint-Germain-en-Laye (1996) provided the setting for Brunet and Saunier's first loadbearing glass columns under an extensive roof in a permanently occupied office environment. Their inclusion was only possible after performing comprehensive loading tests in which the ability of the glass to carry enormous compressive forces was impressively demonstrated. The columns have a cruciform cross-section in order to overcome the problem of buckling. However, as the problem of fire protection in particular remains unsolved (encasing glass members defeats the very object of their existence), such glass columns will continue to be isolated cases whose main purpose is to prove what is technically feasible.

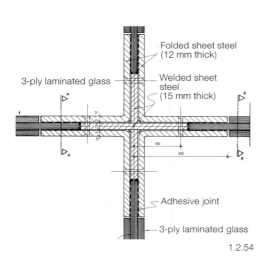

3-ply laminated glass

Folded sheet steel (12 mm thick)

Welded sheet steel (15 mm thick)

Adhesive joint

3-ply laminated glass

1.2.54

1.2.55

# Glass and energy

As the public at large became aware of the energy crisis following in the wake of the oil crises of the 1970s, there was a brief setback to the use of glass. The large expanses of glazing of that period did indeed cause tremendous heat losses in winter and overheated interiors in summer, necessitating energy-guzzling air-conditioning plants for heating and cooling. Furthermore, the coloured or reflective solar-control glasses obstructed the admission of daylight and led to more electricity being consumed to power artificial lighting. However, as no-one happily dispenses with the positive benefits of glass – above all its transparency and translucency – the need for a new glass architecture was obvious. We had to take a fresh look at what had long been known – the use of glass to capture solar energy.

## The development of passive solar architecture

The greenhouse effect, the principle behind the passive use of solar energy (see "The consequence: the 'greenhouse effect'", p. 114), had already been proved and scientifically studied back in the 18th century by the Swiss physicist Horace Bénédict de Saussure. His use of solar energy was initially confined to greenhouses and conservatories.

In 1932 the City Surveyor of Berlin, Martin Wagner, built one of the first passive houses of modern times. It was intended as a prototype for a whole series and resulted from a competition initiated by Wagner in 1931 and entitled "The growing house". The building is enclosed by thermal buffer spaces under sloping glass; these spaces provide protection against bad weather and reduce heat losses. In the following years the notion of utilizing solar energy with the help of glass and mass thermal storage was implemented, mostly for sanatoria. One outstanding example is the Sanatorium in Paimio by Alvar Aalto (1933).

The breakthrough in insulating glass also took place in the 1930s as glass was used for the first time in great quantities (for residential property as well). The principle had been patented in the USA as long ago as 1865. In Germany Sicherheitsglas GmbH of Kunzendorf/Niederlausitz was granted a German patent for its double-pane with glued edge seal. Like the safety glasses, the first applications were in vehicles – high-speed railway rolling stock to be exact – to prevent the windows fogging and icing-up. "Thermopane", an insulating glass with soldered edge seal, was patented in the USA in 1938 and appeared on the German market in 1954.

One important pioneering construction in modern solar architecture was built in 1948 in Dover, Massachusetts: Peabody House, designed by Telkes and Raymond Peabody, generated 80% of its heating requirement from solar energy. It exhibits the typical features of a passive solar house, e.g. a fully glazed southern façade and carefully designed heat storage system filled with mirabilite.

In England in 1961 the architect A. E. Morgan erected the prototype of a flexible double-leaf façade which reacted to external influences. This comprised two glass walls at a spacing of 600 mm. Plates positioned behind these control the admission of solar radiation and the heating for the interior. They are black on one side and coated with polished aluminium on the other, and are rotated as required. The heat is stored in solid concrete slabs. This building, which even during a severe winter needs no other form of heating, is an impressive demonstration of the possibilities of properly implemented passive solar measures.

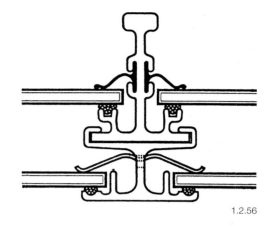

1.2.56

1.2.53  Extension to a private house, Hampstead, Rick Mather and Dewhurst Macfarlane, 1992, all-glass construction, mortise and tenon joint
1.2.54  Local authority offices, Saint-Germain-en-Laye, Brunet & Saunier, 1996, detail of glass column
1.2.55  Local authority offices, Saint-Germain-en-Laye
1.2.56  Insulating glass patent, Henry Hope & Sons, 1950s
1.2.57  Private house in Regensburg, Thomas Herzog, 1978–79

1.2.57

Morgan's school building exploits ideas from Le Corbusier, who had developed a flexible double-leaf façade which reacted to external climatic influences, the "mur neutralisant", as early as 1931 for the Cité de Refuge in Paris.

During the 1950s Felix Trombe worked out the principle of a mass storage wall placed directly behind a large glass façade. In this case the glass was used neither to admit daylight nor to provide a view out; it functioned purely as a heat trap for solar radiation penetrating it to heat up a black-painted mass storage wall. In 1961 Felix Trombe and Jacques Michel utilized the principle, by now patented, in a solar house situated in the French Pyrenées. They employed insulating glass placed in front of a black-painted clay brick wall. In winter the hot air flowed into the living quarters behind the wall via slits in the wall top and bottom. The upper part of the glazing was opened in summer to allow the solar heat gains to escape. By the end of the 1960s more and more architects and building owners had realized the need to be economical with energy resources. The Club of Rome presented its research report "The limits to growth" in 1972, which drew acute awareness to the energy crisis. The two oil crises followed soon afterwards. For the first time, numerous innovative solar buildings appeared, many of them private houses which presented ideal conditions for realizing conventional as well as less conventional concepts. In Germany Thomas Herzog designed two unorthodox detached houses, triangular in section, one in Regensburg (1979) and one in Munich (1982), with sloping, fully glazed south elevations. A similar conception was realized in Warmbronn by Frei Otto and Rob Krier in their passive-energy house of 1969. Dieter Schempp and his group, LOG ID, experimented with "green" solar architecture, based on the greenhouse system, in which a well-insulated solid building is integrated. The conservatory which thus ensues is provided with subtropical flora to regulate the climate. All the new passive-energy designs are distinguished from the Trombe version by their much higher standard of living and involvement.

## Polyvalent walls and intelligent façades

Towards the end of the 1970s Mike Davies, with the Richard Rogers Partnership, elaborated on a glass study for the Pilkington company in England. The visions he thereby formulated for a modern building envelope were summarised in the report "Notes on the Future of Glass" (1979) which he later published in a much heeded article "A Wall for all Seasons" (1981). He developed the notion of a dynamic wall responding to occupants' needs, serving as sunshade or thermal insulation, reflecting heat energy off the building or allowing it to enter, alternating between open and closed. One important source for Davies was the alternative architecture scene of the 1960s and 1970s where in south-western America various architects had experimented with ecological housing having outer walls which responded to the ambient conditions. The technology of Steve Baer's own house consists of a well-insulated multi-layer wall of glass, barrels filled with water to store the heat and unburnt clay bricks in conjunction with solar collectors and wind power. Although the individual elements are straightforward, indeed rather primitive, in engineering terms, their combined effect is extraordinary. Baer's house is an impressive demonstration of how the building envelope can adapt to suit the varying ambient conditions and the changing needs of the occupants. Mike Davies refined this concept by proposing the use of the latest technology. He refers to liquid crystals, laser beams and holograms as well as the solar cells of space capsules and sunglasses which darken in the sunshine.

His polyvalent wall is intended to abolish the difference between opaque and transparent, as his wall can take on both properties. It provides a dynamic control for the flow of energy in both directions to suit internal and external conditions, a dynamic regulator for light and shade throughout the building. The main components in his wall are phototropic or thermotropic glasses, the skin-thin functional coatings of which respond flexibly to changing environments.

Various manufacturers in Europe and Japan soon began to test coatings with variable properties, which led to working prototypes in the early 1980s. However, their wide use in the construction industry has yet to emerge, one decisive factor being their high cost. Just recently there seems to have been something of a breakthrough: since 1993 switchable glasses have been marketed in useful sizes and at reasonable prices for internal applications, and since 1995 adaptable electrochromic materials for external use.

The work of Mike Davies quickly led to the term "intelligent glass façade". However, in practice the "intelligence" of a façade is often coupled with particularly complex technology.

## The double-leaf façade

External walls that respond dynamically are predominantly constructed with two leaves.

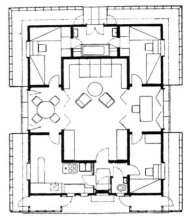

1.2.58

1.2.59

1.2.60

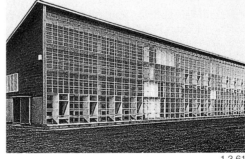

1.3.61

1.2.62

1.2.63

micron

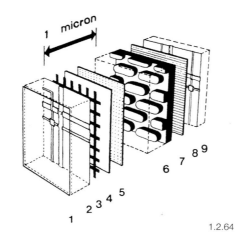

1.2.64

However, double-leaf façades can also function as simple heat buffers without additional technology. Apart from that, they have the advantage of being able to integrate effective uncomplicated sunshading which is protected from the wind.

One of the first modern double-leaf façades was designed by the US practice Hellmuth, Obata & Kassabaum for the Occidental Chemical Center in Niagara Falls (1980). A decisive factor here was the idea of creating a transparent but at the same time energy-conscious building. Extensive testing led to a construction consisting of double glazing for the outer leaf, single glazing for the inner. Between the leaves there are adjustable louvre blinds automatically controlled by solar cells. There are no ventilation openings to the outside.

Richard Rogers employed a fundamentally different approach for the Lloyd's Building in London. The double-leaf façade of storey-high prefabricated elements is designed as an exhaust-air system: hot air from the interior is extracted via the luminaires and channelled via a special connecting nozzle near the upper façade rail into the 75 mm cavity. Near the bottom of the window it is drawn in again and fed back to the air-conditioning plant. This method improves the thermal insulation of the façade during the cold months and creates pleasant temperatures in the vicinity of the windows.

In 1994 Herzog & de Meuron placed a new glass façade around the existing SUVA Building in Basel in order to improve its physical properties. At the same time they gave a visual coherence to the heterogeneous building fabric and lent it a contemporary appearance. The double-leaf façades popular in current high-rise architecture enable individual office windows to be opened despite the great heights and strong winds; this is an important feature in addition to those already mentioned. The Commerzbank in Frankfurt and the RWE Tower in Essen (see pp. 266–273) are just two examples. Another is the Debis head-

1.2.65

1.2.66

1.2.67

1.2.68

1.2.69

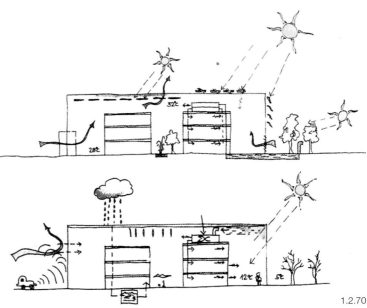

1.2.70

quarters at Potsdamer Platz in Berlin; the south and west elevations of this 21-storey office block by Renzo Piano, completed in 1998, are clad in two leaves of active glass elements – a total of 3400 m². The inner leaf is insulating glass, the outer is made up of pivoting louvres. The double-leaf façade makes a passive contribution to the building's needs and is an important component in the total energy concept. The glass louvres remain closed in the cold winter months, trapping a layer of air which is heated up by incident solar radiation. In warmer weather the chance to open up a large part of the façade ensures adequate through-ventilation and night-time cooling.

### Geodesic shells – man-made spaces under glass

The construction of great domes which encompass whole neighbourhoods and render possible a pleasant autonomous microclimate unaffected by the weather outside has long been one of humankind's dreams, above all in cold, wet regions. This idea is carried to the extreme in the great covered leisure landscapes of Japan, where bathing in the sea or skiing on artificial snow is possible all year round. However, the associated artificial climates are extremely costly and wasteful in terms of energy. Buckminster Fuller initiated, by contrast, undeniably ecological ideas as well when he sketched out his utopian geodesic domes in the 1960s, designed to shelter whole city districts.

The Bell Telephone Corporation Research Laboratories, Holmdel, New Jersey, (1957–62) by Eero Saarinen could be considered an early form of geodesic shell, albeit on a more modest scale than that of Fuller. A box of polished glass over 200 m long encloses the separate buildings inside. Geodesic shells have very recently become topical again owing to the distinctive potential, the new forms of construction and, primarily, the better thermal insulation and solar-control properties of glass. In Nicholas Grimshaw's Eden Project the shells are intended to render possible certain climatic zones in a botanic garden, for cultivating plants and displaying these to the public. Owing to the weight, this astoundingly airy design with its long spans will use not glass but a new type of transparent foil. At the training academy in Herne by Françoise-Hélène Jourda and Gilles Perraudin, currently under construction, a huge 75 x 175 m glasshouse protects the buildings and creates a controlled, almost Mediterranean climate. The glasshouse is not heated and produces a varied transitionary zone between inside and outside. Two long timber buildings are placed inside the shell. Some of the glass-covered railway station designs admitting plenty of daylight which have been proposed for various German cities recently could also be regarded as geodesic shells of a kind.

1.2.69 Project for a geodesic dome over New York city, Buckminster Fuller, early 1960s
1.2.70 Training academy, Herne, Jourda & Perraudin, 1998, climate study for a typical summer's day (top) and winter's day (bottom)
1.2.71 Eden Project, St Austell, Cornwall, Nicholas Grimshaw

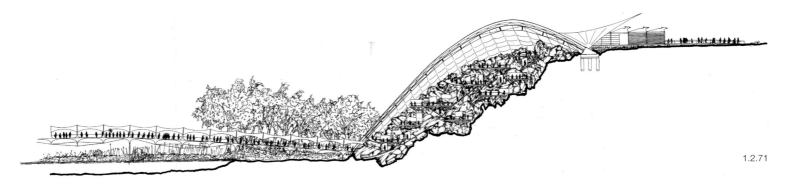

1.2.71

# Part 2 · Principles

# Glass as a building material

**Dieter Balkow**

### Glass – a definition

Glass is a uniform material, a solidified liquid. The molecules are in a completely random order and do not form a crystal lattice. That is why glass is transparent. As it consists of a combination of various bonds, there is no chemical formula. Glass does not have a melting point but instead, upon applying heat, gradually changes from a solid state to a plastic-viscous and finally to a liquid state. In comparison to many other crystals, whose properties depend on the direction in which they are measured, glass exhibits amorphous isotropy, i.e. the properties are not dependent on direction. The general physical properties of glass are given in Tab. 2.1.1.

The glass used today for building purposes is a soda-lime-silica glass. During its production the raw materials are heated to such a high temperature that they become viscous before they are cooled down. This high viscosity coupled with the subsequent cooling leaves the ions and molecules no chance to arrange themselves. Silicate and oxygen cannot form a crystalline structure, in other words the disorderly molecular status is "frozen".

Glass consists of an irregular three-dimensional network of the elements silicon (Si) and oxygen (O) ($SiO_4$ tetrahedra) with cations contained in the interstices. If glass is heated to 800 – 1100 °C and this temperature maintained for a while, then a process known as devitrification begins. This produces silicon crystals which are leached out from the glass mass, an effect which leads to milky, opaque glass.

Natural glass, e.g. obsidian, is produced as a result of volcanic activity. It is formed by the intense heat in the Earth's core and is ejected by the energy of volcanic eruptions. In earlier times, natural glass was used as jewellery, for vessels or for other everyday articles.

### Methods of manufacture

About 5000 years ago the Mesopotamians discovered that when heated together (1400 °C), silicon, lime, sodium carbonate, potassium carbonate and metal oxides could be worked into a glassy mass. But this method was extremely complicated and so glass remained a coveted, rare commodity.

The first written record of a recipe is found on a clay tablet from the Assyrian king Ashurbanipal, dated c. 650 BC.

Flat glass panes were already being produced by casting during the time of the Romans, as well as blown cylinder sheet glass. By the 14th century the crown glass method allowed bull's-eye glasses to be produced for the first time without a rim around the circumference.

Improvements in the 18th century led to the first large panes produced by the blown cylinder sheet glass process.

The Englishman Alastair Pilkington developed the float glass method in the 1950s. The viscous glass melt is passed over a bath of molten tin, floating on the level surface. Owing to the surface tensions together with the viscosities of the glass melt and the molten tin, the liquid glass forms a layer 6 mm thick. The temperature of the molten tin on the inlet side is 1000 °C, on the outlet side 600 °C. After leaving the bath the glass is slowly cooled in a carefully controlled process – to ensure no residual stresses – before being cut to size. (See "The main stages in the manufacture of glass", p. 9.)

### Composition

The glass produced these days is made up as shown in Tab. 2.1.2. Besides those listed here, small proportions of other substances may be introduced in order to influence properties and colour. The manufacture of body-tinted glass requires the addition of minimal amounts of suitable additives; these do not however alter the mechanical strength.

### Durability

Soda-lime-silica glass is generally resistant to acids and alkaline solutions. Likewise, the surface is sufficiently hard (scratch hardness 6 – 7 on the Mohs scale). This property describes the scratch resistance of the glass surface. Therefore, sharp, hard objects, e.g. small sand particles in cleaning water, can cause hairline cracks on the surface if adequate care is not taken when cleaning.

If a film of water remains standing on a glass surface for a long time, leachings form. The bond between the silicon and the oxygen in the water is stronger than that to the components in the lattice interstices in

2.1.1  General physical properties of glass

| Property | Symbol | Value with units |
|---|---|---|
| Density at 18°C | $\rho$ | 2500 kg/m³ |
| Hardness | | 6 units on the Mohs scale |
| Modulus of elasticity | E | $7 \times 10^{10}$ Pa |
| Poisson's ratio | $\mu$ | 0.2 |
| Specific heat capacity | c | $0.72 \times 10^3$ J/(kg × K) |
| Average coefficient of thermal expansion | $\alpha$ | $9 \times 10^{-6}$ K⁻¹ |
| Thermal conductivity | $\lambda$ | 1 W/(m × K) |
| Average refractive index in the visible range of wavelengths 380 – 780 nm | n | 1.5 |

2.1.2  Composition of glass

| | | |
|---|---|---|
| Silicon dioxide | ($SiO_2$) | 69% – 74% |
| Calcium oxide | (CaO) | 5% – 12% |
| Sodium oxide | ($Na_2O$) | 12% – 16% |
| Magnesium oxide | (MgO) | 0% – 6% |
| Aluminium oxide | ($Al_2O_3$) | 0% – 3% |

This composition has been standardized for Europe in EN 572 Part 1.

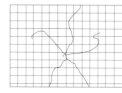

2.1.3  Fracture pattern of a float glass pane

2.1.4  Fracture pattern of a wired glass pane

**2.1.5    Float glass is available in these thicknesses**

| Glass thickness | Tolerance |
|---|---|
| 2, 3, 4, 5, 6 mm | ± 0.2 mm |
| 8, 10, 12 mm | ± 0.3 mm |
| 15 mm | ± 0.5 mm |
| 19, 25 mm | ± 1.0 mm |

The properties of clear and body-tinted float glass are stipulated in European standard EN 572 Part 2.

**2.1.6    Light transmittance values for float and drawn sheet glass**

| Glass thickness | Min. value |
|---|---|
| 3 mm | 0.88 |
| 4 mm | 0.87 |
| 5 mm | 0.86 |
| 6 mm | 0.85 |
| 8 mm | 0.83 |
| 10 mm | 0.81 |
| 12 mm | 0.79 |
| 15 mm | 0.76 |
| 19 mm | 0.72 |
| 25 mm | 0.67 |

**2.1.7    Drawn sheet glass is available in these thicknesses**

| Glass thickness | Tolerance |
|---|---|
| 2, 3, 4 mm | ± 0.2 mm |
| 5, 6 mm | ± 0.3 mm |
| 8 mm | ± 0.4 mm |
| 10 mm | ± 0.5 mm |
| 12 mm | ± 0.6 mm |

Drawn sheet glass is covered in Europe by EN 572 Part 4

**2.1.8    Patterned glass is available in these thicknesses**

| Glass thickness | Tolerance |
|---|---|
| 3, 4, 5, 6 mm | ± 0.5 mm |
| 8 mm | ± 0.8 mm |
| 10 mm | ± 1.0 mm |

Patterned glass is covered in Europe by EN 572 Part 5

**2.1.9    Borosilicate glass is available in these thicknesses**

| Glass thickness | Tolerance |
|---|---|
| 3, 4 , 5, 6.5 , 7.5 mm | - 0.4 / + 0.5 mm |
| 9, 11, 13, 15 mm | - 0.9 / + 1.0 mm |

**2.1.10    Main constituents of borosilicate glass**

| | | |
|---|---|---|
| Silicon dioxide | $(SiO_2)$ | 70% – 87% |
| Boron oxide | $(B_2O_3)$ | 7% – 15% |
| Sodium oxide | $(Na_2O)$ | 1% – 8% |
| Potassium oxide | $(K_2O)$ | 1% – 8% |
| Aluminium oxide | $(Al_2O_3)$ | 1% – 8% |

the glass, i.e. to sodium, calcium and magnesium ions. This means that these form solutions with the water more quickly. In the minute quantity of water in the film the alkaline concentration rises and attacks the residual acidic lattice, leading to corrosion of the glass surface.

Such attacks on the glass surface do not normally occur on windows and façades unless water cannot drain from a horizontal surface.

Leachings from glass are also caused by contact with mineral plasters, wet concrete or extremely alkaline cleaning agents.

## Types of glass

### Float glass

Today float glass is the most widely used type of glass and is produced by way of the float process described above (Fig. 2.1.11). The industrial process makes it possible to produce large quantities of high-quality clear glass with virtually flat surfaces in thicknesses from 2 to 19 mm (Tab. 2.1.5). Modern float glass plants turn out approx. 600 t of glass 4 mm thick each day. Maximum ribbon sizes of 3.2 x 6.0 m are then available for further processing (see EN 572 Part 2).

Float glass can be coloured during the manufacturing process; the light transmittance values alter accordingly.

By choosing the raw materials carefully, e.g. lower amounts of $Fe_2O_3$, it is possible to reduce or even virtually eliminate the natural green tint of float glass. In such cases the glass is almost colourless and is designated low-iron or clear-white glass. The thermal fatigue resistance is about 30 °C (max. 40 °C). If temperature zones are present across the glass surface, the differences

between which lie in this range, the glass can fracture. The warm zone tries to expand but is prevented from doing so by the cold one. Stresses build up which can lead to breakage, especially if this difference is to a covered edge. The fracture pattern of float glass can be seen in Fig. 2.1.3 (p. 61).

### Drawn sheet glass

There are still a few drawn sheet glass plants producing very thin to (in some cases) thick glass. These use either the vertical method (invented by Emile Fourcault in 1902) or the horizontal method (Libby-Owens, 1906).

Drawn sheet glass and float glass have the same chemical composition as well as the same general physical properties. Nevertheless, in comparison to float glass, drawn sheet glass exhibits slight waves and "batter" in the surface perpendicular to the direction of drawing. These are sometimes visible when looking through the glass, in any case in the distorted reflection.

The light transmittance values for drawn sheet and float glass are shown in Tab. 2.1.6.

The fracture pattern of drawn sheet glass is identical with that of float glass (Fig. 2.1.3, p. 61). The thicknesses available are given in Tab. 2.1.7.

### Patterned or rolled glass

In the manufacture of patterned or rolled glass (Fig. 2.1.12), the liquid glass melt, like an overflowing bath, is fed between one or more pairs of rollers to give it a characteristic surface texture as required. Therefore, the glass can be given two smooth surfaces, one smooth and one textured surface or two textured sides depending on the design of the roller or table surfaces.

Rolled glasses are translucent – they cannot

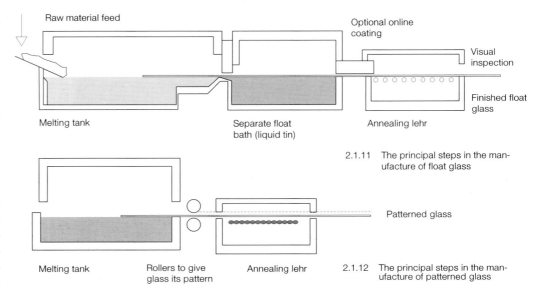

2.1.11    The principal steps in the manufacture of float glass

2.1.12    The principal steps in the manufacture of patterned glass

reproduce the transparency of float or drawn sheet. The various surface textures scatter the light to varying degrees. This enables interiors to be provided with natural lighting while maintaining privacy. Certain surface textures can direct the light in a specific direction, e.g. to brighten the ceiling of a room.

The thermal fatigue resistance for patterned or rolled glass is, like for float glass, about 30 °C (max. 40 °C). The fracture pattern of this type of glass is identical with that of float glass (Fig. 2.1.3, p. 61).

It is possible to insert a wire mesh into the glass while it is still liquid. This is then known as wired patterned glass or, with two smooth surfaces, simply as wired glass. The thermal fatigue resistance of this glass is about 20 K. The fracture pattern of wired glass is shown in Fig. 2.1.4 (p. 61). The thicknesses available are given in Tab. 2.1.8.

The physical properties of patterned and float glass are identical. The ultimate bending strength lies slightly below that of float glass because of the surface pattern.

### Borosilicate glass

This glass contains approx. 7 – 15% boron oxide. In comparison to drawn sheet and float glass, the coefficient of thermal expansion is lower and so the thermal fatigue resistance is considerably higher. It has a high resistance to alkaline solutions and acids.

These days, borosilicate glass can be manufactured like drawn sheet and float glass or like rolled and cast glass. It is used where high thermal fatigue resistance is necessary, e.g. for fire protection. The relevant processing and installation directives must be strictly adhered to.

The fracture pattern of borosilicate glass is identical with that of float glass (Fig. 2.1.3, p. 61). The thicknesses available, main constituents and light transmittance values of borosilicate glass are given in tables 2.1.9, 2.1.10, 2.1.13 and 2.1.14.

### Glass ceramics

Modern methods also render it possible to produce materials with controlled crystallization. These are no longer glasses as such but instead can exhibit a partial or complete microcrystalline structure, while remaining perfectly transparent.

Glass ceramics are produced just like float, drawn sheet or rolled glass. They can be coloured by adding further substances. The fracture pattern of glass ceramics is basically the same as that of float glass (Fig. 2.1.3, p. 61). Glass ceramics are hardly used in the construction industry but are popular as, for example, cooker hobs.

The thicknesses and composition of glass ceramics are listed in tables 2.1.15 and 2.1.16, the general physical properties in Tab. 2.1.17 (p. 64).

### Polished wired glass

Polished wired glass is a clear soda-lime-silica glass whose surfaces have been polished and made parallel. This glass is produced by casting and then polished. A spot-welded wire mesh is inserted during the manufacture. All the nodes of the mesh are welded (EN DIN 572 Part 1).

Wired glass is produced in nominal thicknesses of 6 and 10 mm. The minimum thicknesses are 6 and 7.4 mm respectively, the maximum thicknesses 9.1 and 10.9 mm. The maximum dimensions are 1650 – 3820 mm long x 1980 mm wide.

Tolerances and possible defects are listed and reviewed in EN DIN 572 Part 3. According to DIN 18361 polished wired glass is not a safety glass and possesses no safety properties. It is mainly used for aesthetic reasons, as a G30 fire-resistant glass in certain, limited, situations and as a fragment-bonding glass for roof glazing with maximum spans < 1.0 m or in vertical glazing 1.8 – 2.0 m above the floor, i.e. remote from circulation areas.

The fracture pattern of polished wired glass is shown in Fig. 2.1.4 (p. 61).

### Channel shaped glass

Channel shaped glass is a profiled glass element with textured surfaces which are produced by casting. After leaving the melting tank, a narrower, even more malleable ribbon of glass is passed over moulds so that the edges are bent upwards at 90°. The finished glass element has a U-shape and is supplied in long pieces (Fig. 2.1.8, p. 64). The dimensions and composition of channel shaped glass are specified in European standard EN 572 Part 6.

Channel shaped glass is installed without transoms and is popular not only for industrial applications. It may be erected as single-skin systems, as single-skin "sheet piling" systems or as double-skin systems. The fracture pattern corresponds with that of float glass with narrow dimensions (Fig. 2.1.3, p. 61).

Channel shaped glass can also be produced with a wire mesh insert like wired glass.

As a rule the channel shaped glass is installed according to the "push-in" system. Here, the glass is slipped into a 50 mm deep frame profile and set into a min. 20 mm deep rebate at the bottom. The glass edge cover should be at least 20 mm at the top and 12 mm at the bottom. These glass edge cover dimensions are necessary to

#### 2.1.13 General physical properties of borosilicate glass

| Property | Symbol | Value with unit |
|---|---|---|
| Density at 18°C | $\rho$ | 2200 – 2500 kg/m³ |
| Hardness | | 6 units on the Mohs scale |
| Modulus of elasticity | E | $6 - 7 \times 10^{10}$ Pa |
| Poisson's ratio | $\mu$ | 0.2 |
| Specific heat capacity | c | $0.8 \times 10^3$ J/(kg × K) |
| Average coefficient of thermal expansion | $\alpha$ | Class 1: $(3.1 - 4.0) \times 10^{-6}$ K⁻¹ Class 2: $(4.1 - 5.0) \times 10^{-6}$ K⁻¹ Class 3: $(5.1 - 6.0) \times 10^{-6}$ K⁻¹ |
| Thermal conductivity | $\lambda$ | 1 W/(m × K) |
| Average refractive index in the visible range of wavelengths 380 – 780 nm | n | 1.5 |

#### 2.1.14 Light transmittance values for borosilicate glass

| Glass thickness | Min. value |
|---|---|
| 3 mm | 0.90 |
| 4 mm | 0.90 |
| 5 mm | 0.90 |
| 6 mm | 0.89 |
| 7 mm | 0.89 |
| 8 mm | 0.89 |
| 10 mm | 0.88 |
| 15 mm | 0.84 |

#### 2.1.15 Glass ceramics are available in these thicknesses

| Glass thickness | Tolerance |
|---|---|
| 3, 4 mm | ± 0.2 mm |
| 5, 6 mm | ± 0.3 mm |
| 7, 8 mm | ± 0.4 mm |

#### 2.1.16 Composition of glass ceramics

| | | |
|---|---|---|
| Silicon dioxide | ($SiO_2$) | 50% – 80% |
| Aluminium oxide | ($Al_2O_3$) | 15% – 27% |
| Lithium oxide | ($Li_2O$) | 0% – 5% |
| Zinc oxide | ($ZnO$) | 0% – 5% |
| Titanium dioxide | ($TiO_2$) | 0% – 5% |
| Zirconium dioxide | ($ZrO_2$) | 0% – 5% |
| Magnesium oxide | ($MgO$) | 0% – 8% |
| Calcium oxide | ($CaO$) | 0% – 8% |
| Barium oxide | ($BaO$) | 0% – 8% |
| Sodium oxide | ($Na_2O$) | 0% – 2% |
| Potassium oxide | ($K_2O$) | 0% – 5% |
| others | | |

2.1.17 General physical properties of glass ceramics

| Property | Symbol | Value with unit |
|---|---|---|
| Density at 18°C | $\rho$ | 2500–2600 kg/m³ |
| Hardness (Knoop) | $HK_{01/20}$ | 600–750 |
| Modulus of elasticity | $E$ | $9 \times 10^{10}$ Pa |
| Poisson's ratio | $\mu$ | 0.2 |
| Specific heat capacity | $c$ | $0.8–0.9 \times 10^3$ J/(kg × K) |
| Average coefficient of thermal expansion | $\alpha$ | 0 |
| Thermal conductivity | $\lambda$ | 1.5 W/(m × K) |
| Average refractive index in the visible range of wavelengths 380–780 nm | $n$ | 1.5 |

2.1.18 Channel shaped glass

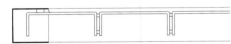

A Single-skin

The standard method of installation is based on the "push-in" principle, i.e. the channel shaped glass elements are slipped into the upper 50 mm deep frame profile and adjusted via the 20 mm deep lower frame profile.

B Single-skin "sheet piling" (internal wall)

The glass edge cover is:
top ≥ 20 mm
bottom ≤ 12 mm

C Double-skin

The depth of construction depends on the type of channel shaped glass selected.

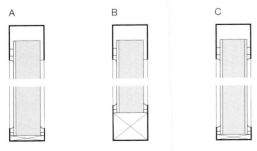

For further packing or seals or other constructional components as required by the application, please refer to the latest edition of the respective manufacturer's literature.

2.1.19 Different installation methods for channel shaped glass

ensure the stability of the wall as a whole. In the double-skin system further packing or seals or other constructional components should be included as directed by the manufacturer. The double-skin system achieves a better standard of thermal insulation (Fig. 2.1.19). Unlike insulating glass, the cavity formed by the channel sections is not hermetically sealed and dehumidified but instead contains air at a corresponding relative humidity. The construction of channel shaped glass elements is similar to that for double glazed or coupled window systems. Like with these latter window types, to avoid the occurrence of condensation as the moist air cools, an opening to the drier outside air should be provided. This vapour-pressure equalization goes a long way towards preventing condensation problems.

### Glass blocks

Glass blocks are hollow glass units. Their production involves melting a quantity of glass and cooling it to approx. 1200 °C. This doughy mass is subsequently moulded into shells. Two shells are required for each block: they are pressed together and the contact faces reheated in such a way that they fuse together.

Further cooling brings about a partial vacuum of about 30% in this airtight internal void and hence an intensive negative pressure. Condensation is impossible in an intact block.

The two outer, exposed surfaces may be smooth or textured. Glass blocks are produced in certain sizes and are covered by European standard EN 1051. Walls of glass blocks are specified by European draft standard prEN 12725 (in Germany DIN 18175 for glass blocks, DIN 4242 for building components made from these).

Glass blocks can be coloured and the surfaces decorated in the most diverse ways. The special form of the glass block enables it to be used as an artistic element.

Walls of glass blocks meeting fire-resistance classes G60 and G120 are also possible. Manufacturers can provide corresponding building authority approval certificates on request. The wall construction must match the specification in the approval documentation exactly. Floors of glass blocks are possible for unrestricted access situations.

### Coatings for glass

Many different coatings are now available for glass. The techniques are being constantly improved and – in line with the demands of the market – adapted to meet differing requirements. It is therefore not possible to give details of coating structures that are not related to a particular manufacturer (Fig. 2.1.20). A coating can be applied to the outside, the inside or between the panes depending on the type, structure or composition of the coating. Manufacturers can provide details of strength, durability and possible applications.

European draft standard prEN 1096 Parts 1 – 4 defines and classifies various applications in terms of coating durability. The coatings undergo tests and are subject to monitoring during production, taking all framework conditions into account, in order to assess the serviceability of the coatings.

The classes are as follows:

Class A
The coating is applied to the outermost glass surface and is directly subjected to the effects of the weather.

Class B
The coating is applied to the outer glass pane but on the surface not directly subjected to the effects of the weather. Such coated glass may be used as single glazing.

Class C
The coating is only applied within the cavity of an insulating glass unit. The glass shall be transported in special packaging and can only be treated directly before further processing.

Class D
The coating is only applied within the cavity and the glass shall be made up into an insulating glass unit immediately after coating. Not suitable for single glazing.

Class S
The coated surface may be used internally or externally and is suitable for special circumstances (e.g. display windows).

All coated glasses can be processed further to form insulating or laminated safety glass units. Some coatings can also withstand the thermal processes required to produce curved, toughened or heat-strengthened glass.

### Online coating

During the production of float glass a metal oxide is spread over the upper surface of the glass while it is still hot. As a result the coating becomes firmly bonded to the glass. Glasses coated in this way can provide better solar control by using a metal oxide that reflects solar radiation or can enhance the thermal insulation by using a tin oxide coating that reduces emissions. These latter glasses coated online achieve an emittance of approx. 13%. This corresponds to insulating glass having a 12 mm cavity and 95% argon gas filling with a thermal transmittance (U-value) of 1.8 W/m². If the coating is open to the air and soiled, then the emittance is altered. The durability of the surface of such a coating is roughly equal to that of a glass surface. The emittance of a normal glass surface is over 90%.

### Offline coating

#### *Magnetron sputtering*

This is a physical coating process. After production and cutting to size, the glass is coated with oxides, e.g. metal oxides, using the magnetron sputtering method. This involves the acceleration of free electrons in an electric field which then collide with gas molecules. These then take on a positive charge and, accelerated by the electric field, bombard a negatively charged cathode, which is provided with the coating material. Particles are thrown off by the impacts and these attach themselves to the surface of the glass. This process repeats millions of times. Glass passing through the coating plant is thus continuously coated on one side. The durability of such coatings depends on the type of material applied and has not yet reached that of float glass itself or online coatings. It is the aim of the glass industry to match the durability of the coatings to that of the glass surfaces.

Glasses coated by means of magnetron sputtering can usually only be left outside for a limited period (approx. three months). Accordingly, such coatings are only employed on surfaces within the cavity of an insulating glass unit in order to be protected from moisture too.

However, these coatings may be safely washed in suitable washing plants within the prescribed storage time.

The high-vacuum method still used in some plants today involves bombarding a metal (e.g. gold) with electrons in a high vacuum. Metal or oxide atoms are thrown off and attach themselves to glass surfaces standing in autoclaves. Glasses coated in this way must undergo further processing without delay.

#### *Evaporization*

The first gold coatings were produced by this physical coating technique. The material to be evaporized is heated so that it condenses on the glass surface.

This method has been superseded by magnetron sputtering.

#### *Sol-gel process*

This is a chemical coating process in which the glass is dipped in a liquid. In doing so the metal compounds adhere to the glass surfaces and edges. They are then converted to the corresponding oxides by heating. Solar-control glasses or those with a low degree of reflectance can be produced in this way.

## Surface treatments

### Enamelling

This involves first applying a coloured ceramic layer to the glass surface and then baking it into the glass during the manufacture of toughened or heat-strengthened glass.

The layer of enamel can also be sprayed on or applied by silk-screen printing.

### Acid etching

The surfaces of glass panes can be given a matt finish by acid etching. The degree of matt finish is determined by the length of time the acid is in contact with the surface. Patterns and pictures can be etched into the surface by masking certain areas. The more intense the etching process, the greater is the roughness of the glass surface; transparency diminishes as roughness increases, so light passing through is scattered and the view through the glass is obscured. The contours of objects behind the glass are clearly recognizable when they are directly adjacent the glass but become more diffuse the further they are from the glass. Etched panes may be curved or toughened but the advice of the manufacturer should be sought.

### Sand-blasting

Glass surfaces can also be sand-blasted to achieve a matt finish. Again, this roughens the glass surface and the optical effects are very similar to those obtained by way of acid etching. Sand-blasted panes become translucent and patterns or pictures can be included by masking certain areas. Subsequent processing must be agreed with the manufacturer.

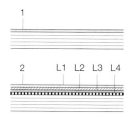

Layer 1: Protective layer
e.g. $SnO_2$, ZnO
Layer 2: Active layer
e.g. NiCr, $TiO_2$
Layer 3: Active layer
e.g. Ag
Layer 4: Bonding layer
e.g. $SnO_2$, ZnO

1 Pyrolytic layer bonded directly to the glass

2 Magnetron layers for thermal insulation or solar control

2.1.20  Coated glass

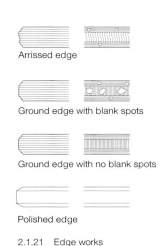

Arrissed edge

Ground edge with blank spots

Ground edge with no blank spots

Polished edge

2.1.21   Edge works

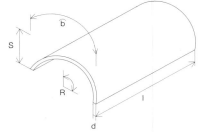

b   development (arc length)
S   rise
R   radius (inner skin)
l   length/width
d   thickness of panel element

2.1.22   Designations for a curved pane

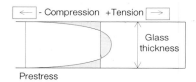

Prestress

2.1.23   Stress distribution in toughened safety glass

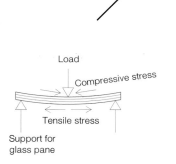

2.1.24   Stress distribution in the glass surface upon
         loading

Moist surfaces or those which have been in
contact with grease or cleaning agents can
impair the optical qualities of a pane. Optical
variations can be induced depending on the
direction of wiping when cleaning the glass.

## Edge works

The edges of glass may be finished in a
variety of ways (Fig. 2.1.21). The normal cut
edge represents the simplest form. Such
edges are used wherever the edge of the
glass is placed in a frame and there is no
danger of being injured by the sharp edge.
Other types of edges are obtained by
means of grinding and polishing. Toughened safety glass is given a small arris to
both sides in order to remove the sharp
edges. DIN 1249 Part 12 describes the individual edge forms, likewise European standard prEN 12150 for thermally toughened
safety glass.
An edge cut exactly to size may exhibit
blank spots in the cross-section of the edge
because in such cases it is the dimension
that is important. But a polished table top,
for example, should have a perfect edge,
while the dimension – cut to a tolerance of
0.5 mm, for instance – is unimportant,
although if several panes meet, the dimension is critical.
Special ground finishes are also possible on
the edge, e.g. for mirrors. The edge treatment must be agreed upon placing an
order; reference samples may need to be
produced.

## Thermally treated glass

### Curved glass

Flat panes of glass may be subsequently
curved. In doing so the pane must be heated beyond its transformation point, i.e. the
glass changes from the solid to the "soft"
state (640 °C). The "doughy" glass is laid or
pressed in the form and then allowed to cool
down so that it is free from residual stresses. The bending tolerances resulting from
the bending procedure must be taken into
account depending on the size, shape and
thickness of the glass.
Curved panes can be allowed to cool down
normally or they can be subsequently pre-

stressed. Likewise, curved glass can be
used for laminated (safety) glass.
Glass producers should be consulted with
respect to the dimensions possible; these
very much depend on the production furnaces available but also the shape. Length,
width, bending radius and rise are all critical
(the latter two can refer to the inside or outside surface) (Fig. 2.1.22). Due to their
shape, curved panes are less flexible than
flat ones and so are less able to deform
under load. Frames for such curved panes
shall make allowance for the bending tolerances. Therefore, a suitable gauge (taking
account of tolerances) should be fabricated
for assembly purposes. Curved panes
should always be installed with tape and
sealing. Shaped glazing can introduce additional loads into the panes – depending on
bending radius and tolerances – and these
could damage any sealing.

### Thermally toughened safety glass

This type of glass is generally called toughened (or tempered) safety glass.
The flat glass pane is heated to its transformation point (min. 640 °C). Once the entire
glass mass has reached this temperature it
is suddenly quenched in blasts of cold air.
Other types of cooling are also possible
(Fig. 2.1.25). As a result the surfaces cool
faster and contract quicker than the core of
the glass. This creates additional compressive stresses in the surfaces which make the
glass stronger (Fig. 2.1.23). The ultimate
bending strength increases, likewise the
thermal fatigue resistance, which lies
around 200 K.
When loaded, the surface of toughened
safety glass can accommodate higher tensile forces – due to the prestress – than
glass cooled in the normal way. Fracture
can occur once the prestress has been
exceeded (Fig. 2.1.24).
If toughened safety glass is overloaded,
then it fractures and breaks into numerous
small pieces whose edges are generally
blunt. The minimum number of dice and
their size within a counting field of
50 x 50 mm are defined for a test pane lying
on a flat surface and not subjected to any
additional stresses.
Toughened glass is classed as a safety glass
because of its higher ultimate bending

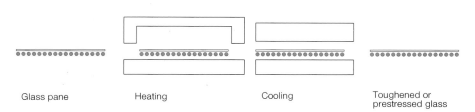

Glass pane          Heating          Cooling          Toughened or
                                                      prestressed glass

2.1.25   The principal steps in the manufacture of toughened glass

strength and its fracture pattern. The glass particles reduce the risk of injury.

Toughened safety glasses cannot be worked any further, e.g. drilled or ground, afterwards. These glasses are covered by European draft standard prEN 12150 or its predecessor DIN 1249 Part 12. The minimum number of dice is greater in the European draft standard than in the DIN standard (Tab. 2.1.26 and Fig. 2.1.27).

Glass can contain inclusions invisible to both the naked eye and the microscope. Nevertheless, these survive the manufacturing process and can lead to fracture at a much later date. If nickel sulphide is present in the glass, providing an energy source causes the nickel sulphide to expand, leading to sudden fracture of the glass. Although NiS impurities are rare in practice, toughened safety glass should be given an additional thermal treatment if the glass will be subjected to extreme temperatures once incorporated in a façade. This is also stipulated for particular applications in DIN 18516 Part 4, and a separate European standard is being drawn up for this situation. It should be noted, however, that this effect is statistically very rare. Toughened safety glass usually fractures as a result of outside influences, damage to the pane or faulty construction not suited to the particular application.

The high ultimate bending strength of toughened safety glass means that it can resist the impact of persons without breaking, something that normal glass cannot do. However, the fixings for the glazing must be capable of taking this load.

The performance as a safety glass can be tested by means of the pendulum impact test to DIN 52337 (soft and hard impact). The test with a soft impact body, a sack filled with lead shot and weighing 45 kg, is intended to simulate the impact of a person, with the impact speed determined by the drop height (prEN 12600). The glass never fails the test with a hard impact body, a 10 kg wooden bulb with a metal ring (see "Laminated safety glass", p. 68). The thickness of the glass should be at least 6 mm, depending on the size of pane, for all constructions in which safety is a relevant factor.

### Heat-strengthened glass

Glass is designated as heat-strengthened when the surface stress is just high enough to ensure that only radial fractures from edge to edge occur upon breakage. There should also be no large, independent fracture islands in the pane.

Heat-strengthened glass and its fracture pattern are specified and defined in European draft standard prEN 1863 "Heat-strengthened glass". The production of heat-strengthened glass is similar to that of thermally toughened glass in that the glass is heated and then cooled with air. However, the cooling takes place more slowly and so the compressive stresses that build up at the surfaces are lower than those in toughened safety glass.

The main difference between these two types of glass lies in their totally different fracture patterns. Heat-strengthened glass has a higher ultimate bending strength than float glass and a better thermal fatigue resistance (100 K, float glass approx. 40 K). But heat-strengthened glass is not classed as a safety glass.

When used as a single pane, heat-strengthened glass should be framed on all four sides in order to exploit its special fracture characteristics. It can be used in laminated (safety) glass, where its fracture properties and somewhat higher ultimate bending strength (compared to float glass) are useful. If heat-strengthened glass is employed in conjunction with a bonding foil, then larger pieces form once the glass is broken. The damaged unit will most likely remain in its fixings as two thermally toughened safety glass panes in laminated safety glass which disintegrates into tiny fragments.

Heat-strengthened glasses cannot be worked any further, e.g. drilled or ground, afterwards.

A schematic presentation of the surface stresses of float, thermally strengthened and heat-strengthened glass is shown in Fig. 2.1.28. The fracture pattern of this type of glass can be seen in Fig. 2.1.29.

### Chemically strengthened glass

Both flat and curved glass may be strengthened by chemical means. The chemical prestressing of a glass pane is realized by ionic exchange. To do this, the glass is immersed in a hot molten salt. The smaller sodium ions in the glass surface are exchanged for the larger ions in the molten salt, which leads to compressive stresses at the surface. However, the strengthened zone is not very deep.

The immersion procedure also strengthens the edges of the pane. Chemically strength-

| 2.1.26 | Minimum number of fragments for toughened safety glass | | |
|---|---|---|---|
| Made from | Nominal thickness (d) in mm | Min. number of fragments |
| Float and | 3 | 15 |
| window | 4 – 12 | 40 |
| glass | 15 – 19 | 30 |
| Rolled glass | 4 – 10 | 30 |

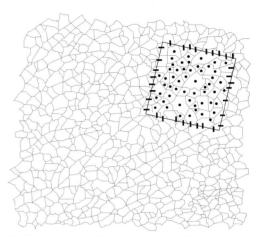

2.1.27 Counting field mask for a fractured thermally prestressed test pane to prEN 12150, showing central and non-central fragments.

Surface stress

Thermally toughened glass
Fracture pattern: small dice

Undefined range

Heat-strengthened glass
Fracture pattern: radial cracks from edge to edge

Undefined range

Float glass
Fracture pattern: normal glass with sharp splinters

2.1.28 Surface stresses of float, thermally toughened and heat-strengthened glass

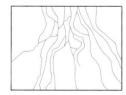

2.1.29 Fracture pattern of heat-strengthened glass

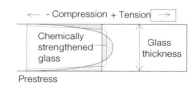

← - Compression + Tension →

Chemically strengthened glass | Glass thickness

Prestress

2.1.30 Stress distribution in chemically strengthened glass compared to thermally toughened glass

1   Glass
2   Interlayer/foil

2.1.31   The structure of laminated (safety) glass

ened glass exhibits a high resistance to mechanical and thermal loads.
Its fracture behaviour corresponds to that of float glass. The ultimate bending strength is in the region of 200 N/mm$^2$.
Chemically strengthened glass may be cut. However, a cut edge only has the strength of normal glass.
Chemically strengthened glass is included in European draft standard prEN 12337. See Fig. 2.1.30 for the stress distribution in chemically strengthened glass and how it compares to thermally strengthened glass.

## Laminated glass

Laminated glass is a glass unit that consists of at least two panes and one intermediate layer, whereby the panes are bonded to the intermediate layer in the manufacturing process.
Laminated glass is defined in European standard EN 12337 Part 3. The permissible tolerances for the thickness and dimensions of units as well as possible defects are specified in this standard.
The bonding of the glass fragments to the interlayer in laminated (safety) glass is checked by means of tests to EN 12337 Part 5.
Laminated glass without safety features can be used for sound insulation or decorative purposes. Here, the interlayer can be made from casting resins as well as other organic or inorganic compounds. However, there are intermediate layers which cover both functions (see "Laminated safety glass" below).
Tolerances for the thickness and dimensions of units arise out of the structure of the intermediate layer and the number of panes of glass.
The glass units shall be resistant to moisture and solar radiation, i.e. their mechanical and optical properties should not alter as a result of being subjected to a specified radiation or a defined moisture load. Special laminated glasses can be produced with interlayers whose properties can be changed upon the application of a voltage. This enables a glass unit to be alternately transparent or translucent but in both cases allowing the passage of light (Fig. 2.3.58, p. 132). Further developments in this sector are conceivable.

## Laminated safety glass

Laminated safety glass consists of at least two panes and one intermediate layer firmly bonded between these (Fig. 2.1.31). Laminated safety glass is defined in European standard EN 12337 Part 2, which also lists permissible tolerances for thicknesses and dimensions of units as well as possible defects.
This is a safety glass – the fragments are held together upon fracture. Notwithstanding, the glass must also fulfil certain requirements, e.g. regarding impact loads. The pendulum impact test in DIN 52337 (soft impact with high mass) is used for tests. A European standard (prEN 12600) is also being drawn up for this test which simulates the impact of a person on the glass. The soft impact body currently used is a leather sack filled with lead shot and weighing 45 kg. The weight is based on the assumption that if a person collides with the glass approx. 60% of the mass acts on the glass. The height from which the sack is dropped (potential energy = g x h) corresponds to the impact velocity, the drop heights of 300, 450, 700 and 1200 mm representing the running speeds of 9, 11, 14 and 18 km/h respectively. This allows the type and thickness of the glass to be accurately selected for each application.
For example, glass at the end of a corridor should be able to withstand the impact of a person running fast, i.e. corresponding to a large drop. A narrow balcony on the other hand need not be designed for such a fast speed. Therefore, it is possible to use a type of glass that can be tested with the impact body falling from a lower height. A drop height of 700 mm has established itself in practice. Nevertheless, distinctions must be made between the individual applications. A drop height of 1200 mm may also be used for testing balustrade constructions and their glasses.
The sack of lead shot is replaced in European standard prEN 12600 by two smaller car tyres, one on top of the other. The mass of the impact body may yet be increased by about 5 kg in order to take account of the increasing average weight of the European population.
PVB (polyvinyl butyral) foil, suitable casting resins or other organic or inorganic mater-

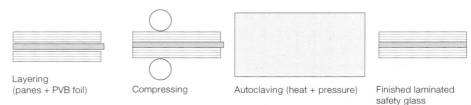

Layering
(panes + PVB foil)

Compressing

Autoclaving (heat + pressure)

Finished laminated safety glass

2.1.32   The principal steps in the manufacture of laminated safety glass with PVB interlayer

ials may be used as the intermediate layer provided that, in conjunction with the glass, the necessary safety requirements are satisfied.

The glass units must be stable with respect to solar radiation. Their mechanical and optical properties should not alter during or after being subjected to radiation or a defined moisture load. When using a PVB interlayer, the foil is placed between the panes and the whole unit pressed together in an autoclave under the action of heat and pressure (Fig. 2.1.32).

The bond at the edge of a laminated safety glass with a PVB interlayer can suffer if subjected to moisture permanently. As the foil is initially very dry, it can absorb humidity and hence weaken the bond at the edge. Therefore, like with insulating glass, the edges must be set in a glass rebate which permits vapour-pressure equalization and prevents permanent humidity. Nevertheless, this effect cannot be entirely ruled out in the long term. Even during transport and storage, care must be taken to ensure that the edges are protected from excess moisture. However, this is only an optical defect and has no effect on the function of the unit as a whole.

The bonding of the glass fragments to the interlayer in laminated (safety) glass is tested using the methods laid down in EN 12337 Part 5.

Casting resin can be introduced between the panes in several ways. Multi-ply components cure by themselves or under the action of UV radiation. Special care is required at the edges when using casting resin. The softeners in sealing materials can penetrate the edge cover strips, seep into the resin and attack this chemically.

**Anti-vandal, anti-intruder and bullet-resistant glazing**

Owing to its ability to bond glass fragments together and its structure comprising individual panes with foil in between, laminated safety glass is ideal for providing protection against attacks with blunt objects or projectiles for a certain length of time.

Throwing stones at glass or striking it with an axe is a combination of large mass and low velocity, whereas a bullet from a gun is a combination of small mass and high velocity, acting on a small area of glass. These concepts must be considered when choosing both glass and foil. When specifying such panes it is essential to remember that the actual glass properties of the window can only be realized if the construction complies with the requirements and is matched to the glass.

To provide effective protection against intruders, a window must be designed in such a way that it cannot be levered out en

bloc or the panes removed without damaging the glass. External glazing bars should not be used. The recommendations of draft German standard DIN V 19054 and draft European standards prEN 1522 and 1523 should be observed.

*Anti-vandal glazing*

These glass units, classified as type "A", are intended to prevent stones thrown at them from penetrating the glass. This property is tested by dropping a 4.11 kg steel ball three times in succession onto the glass from various heights. DIN 52290 Part 4 describes the test. The classifications A1, A2 and A3 refer to the drop heights of 3.5, 6.5 and 9.5 m respectively and are awarded depending on whether or not the ball penetrates the glass. What this means in practice is that glazing at ground floor level should be chosen to provide a high anti-vandal protection level, indeed even anti-intruder protection, while for upper floors a lower level of protection is sufficient, owing to the diminishing impact energy of a stone which is thrown. Laminated safety glass, including several layers of foil or a suitable resin, can give the glass unit an appropriate degree of resistance.

*Anti-intruder glazing*

These glass units, classified as type "B", are intended to prevent an opening larger than 400 x 400 mm being smashed in the glass with an axe in a short space of time. This property is tested in accordance with DIN 52290 Part 3 or prEN 356.

The classification depends on the time taken to produce an opening 400 x 400 mm.

A long-handled axe fitted to a machine simulates the attack conditions and provides objective, comparable test results. In the glass/foil or glass/resin combinations the elastic intermediate layers are held together and protected by the glass. The elasticity of the whole system allows the glass unit to absorb the shock of the impacts.

| 2.1.33 Explosion-resistant glasses | | |
| Class | Max. overpressure $p_r$ of reflected shock wave (bar + 5 %) | Duration $t_0$ of over-pressure phase (ms) |
| --- | --- | --- |
| D 1 | 0.5 | 12 |
| D 2 | 1.0 | 10 |
| D 3 | 2.0 | 8 |

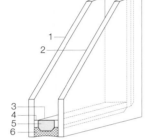

1 Outer pane
2 Inner pane
3 Metal spacer
4 Sealing level (butyl seal)
5 Desiccant
6 Sealing level (polysulphide seal)

2.1.34   Edge seal for insulating glass

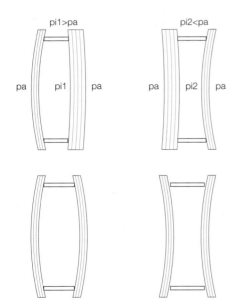

2.1.35   The effect of differing and equal glass thick-nesses on insulating glass units as a result of air pressure fluctuations

*Bullet-resistant glazing*
These glass units are classified as type "C". A bullet fired from a pistol or rifle produces a very small mass acting with a high velocity on a small impact area. Crucial to the protective function of the glass in this instance is its mass and not its elasticity. Consequently, bullet-resistant glazing units contain a high proportion of glass. DIN 52290 Part 2 and prEN 356 stipulate the test procedures which provide comparable results. The classification is based on the type of weapon and ammunition used.
Maximum security is achieved when the projectile does not penetrate the glass and no splinters of glass are flung off from the rear face of the glass unit. According to the theory of elastic impact, the impact energy is transmitted through the material and released at the other end. Additional layers of glass, preferably thermally or chemically strengthened, as well as protective films or plastic layers can prevent this spalling of fragments. Such glass is designated "zero-spall"; glasses in which fragments are ejected from the rear of the unit by the force of a projectile are called "limited/unlimited spall" as appropriate.
For such a window or façade to offer effective resistance, the frame must also comply with the same or a higher specification.

*Explosion-resistant glazing*
These glass units are classified as type "D" and are intended to protect against attacks from outside using explosive devices. Laminated safety glass can be used in such circumstances.
Testing the properties of the glazing is covered by DIN 52290 Part 5, which assumes a spherical pressure wave acting perpendicular to the glass. The new European standard prEN 1099 with its three classes E1, E2 and E3 is comparable with DIN 52290 Part 5. The classifications D1, D2 and D3 to DIN 52290 Part 5 depend on the maximum overpressure of the reflected shock wave for a prescribed duration of the overpressure phase (Tab. 2.1.33). The elastic property of glass, especially laminated safety glass, makes itself noticeable here. Of course, the frame holding the glass must be suitably designed and fixed to the masonry or façade. During the test the glass is held at the edges by the test rig with a pressure of $14\pm3$ N/cm$^2$.

*Alarm glass*
Fine silver wires can be placed within the make-up of the laminated safety glass. If the glass is penetrated or even subjected to severe deformations, breaking one of these wires will cause a circuit to be interrupted and an alarm signal to be triggered. The "Ohmic resistance of a pane" depends on its dimensions. The same effect can be achieved when thermally toughened glass is provided with a conductive loop in one corner. If the glass is damaged, then the conductive pane is interrupted. The position of the connecting cable must be carefully planned and incorporated so that the drainage of the rebate is not hindered and the connection to the glass cannot become wet. Therefore, it is best to incorporate the loop at the top.

### Heated glass
Heated glass can be produced by applying a conductive coating to the surface of the glass or by placing a fine wire within the make-up of the laminated (safety) glass. With the coating method the size of the pane determines the electrical resistance and hence the heating capacity. With the wire method the heating capacity can be determined through appropriate design of the series/parallel circuit for the electrical conductor.

## Insulating glass

### General
Insulating glass consists of at least two separate panes kept apart by spacers fitted around the edge. These days, the first seal is located between the spacers and the panes of glass; this prevents moisture from entering the cavity between the panes. In addition, another seal is positioned behind the spacers and between the panes; this serves as a secondary seal and as an adhesive, keeping the panes and spacers joined together (Fig. 2.1.34). The spacers contain an adsorbent substance that dehumidifies the cavity, which is hermetically sealed against the outside air. This reduces the dew point of the enclosed air to below -30 °C. The sealing systems prevent an exchange of gases between the cavity and the outside air and the ingress of moisture into the cavity. If the seals are damaged and moisture enters the cavity, then the relative humidity in the cavity rises as soon as the desiccant is saturated. When the air cools to below the dew point, this damp air condenses; we say the pane is "fogged" or "steamed up". The dissimilar moisture contents of the cavity air and the outside air give rise to a high vapour-pressure gradient. Therefore, it is necessary to fabricate insulating glass

units with the utmost care and, once installed, to make sure that the rebate is not packed full of sealant but instead remains free of sealant and dry, achieved by way of a functioning vapour-pressure equalization and drainage arrangement. Permanent humidity must be avoided at all costs. The edge seal of an insulating glass unit, if not made from silicone, must be protected against solar radiation. Panes which are not fitted into a rebate will need to be given an enamel or other type of coating in order to provide the necessary shading for the sealing system. Edge seal systems employing silicones should not be used with cavities filled with, for example, argon, krypton and xenon as well as $SF_6$, because the permeability of silicone is too high for these gases. Care in the production and installation of insulating glass units, e.g. rebate free of sealant, adequate vapour-pressure equalization (no permanent dampness) and no additional, undefined mechanical loads on the edge seal, will result in service lives of 30 years or even longer.

The air pressure in the cavity corresponds to the atmospheric pressure prevailing at the time of manufacture. After installation, when the atmospheric pressure rises beyond that in the cavity, both panes are pressed inwards; when the outside pressure drops, the panes bulge outwards (Fig. 2.1.35). These movements can be readily perceived as distortions. Special attention should be given to this "pumping" action when designing large panes with reflective properties. Merely optimizing the glass thicknesses in line with structural requirements is not enough to cope with this effect. Current methods of calculating the glass thickness distribute the loads over both panes. The result of this is that the panes can be thinner, and hence the stiffnesses lower and the pumping movements greater. One tried-and-tested remedy is to make the outer pane, e.g. the one with the reflective coating, thicker and the inner one thinner. The adequacy of the latter must be proved by calculation. Optimizing the glass thickness does not simply mean selecting the thinnest pane but, on the contrary, employing glass thicknesses which are matched to the many different physical phenomena that may be expected. More than ever before, the knowledge of specialists, who understand the interaction of these phenomena, is

crucial for today's applications and combinations. Here too, the rule is that not everything that can be produced may be used everywhere without restrictions.

**Edge seals for insulating glass units**
Fig. 2.1.34 shows the customary edge seal detail of an insulating glass unit. Other systems are also currently available:

*All-glass edge seal*
In the past the usual way of creating an all-glass edge seal was to weld together the edges of the spaced panes and fill the cavity with dry air. This created a rigid edge seal. The all-glass edge seal might well become popular again with the development of "vacuum insulating glass", in which a cavity of just 0.2 mm is sufficient.

*Butyl edge seal with stiffening*
The stiffened butyl edge seal has been around for over 20 years. The spacer here is not a tubular profile but instead a thin metal strip placed perpendicular to the glass. The butyl seal with integral adsorbent is positioned around the strip to soak up the moisture in the cavity. The metal strip too acts as a cavity seal. Another sealant is added to provide mechanical strength (Fig. 2.1.36).

*Butyl edge seal without stiffening*
The solid butyl edge seal, in use for over 25 years, has been undergoing something of a comeback of late. The butyl with integral adsorbent is injected hot into the edge. A second vapour barrier is applied to the outside of the seal. This edge seal is always black (Fig. 2.1.37). The sealant on its own provides a stable edge.

**Physical properties**
The physical properties of insulating glass are determined from measurements and calculations and are subject to the customary fluctuations encountered in production. The make-up of the glass and the thickness, perhaps with coatings, have a decisive influence. The figures specified should always be treated with a certain amount of caution.

*Thermal insulation*
The thermal insulation effect of insulating glass comprising float glass panes is mainly dependent on the cavity and its filling, and in the case of coated float glass on the type of coating.

*Thermal transmittance value (U-value)[1]*
The thermal transmittance value (U-value) of an insulating glass unit consisting of two float glass panes and a 12 mm cavity is 3.0 $W/m^2K$. If the cavity is enlarged to 20 mm, then the value drops to 2.8 $W/m^2K$.

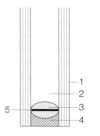
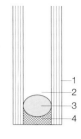

2.1.36 Butyl edge seal with stiffening

2.1.37 Butyl edge seal without stiffening

Insulating glass with soft edge

1 Glass pane
2 Cavity
3 Butyl spacer (1st seal) with integral adsorbent
4 2nd seal and adhesive
5 Metal insert for stability

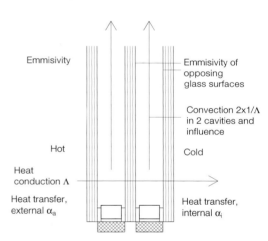

2.1.38 Physical relationships of the U-value for an insulating glass unit with two cavities

[1] The thermal transmittance value U for an insulating glass is determined by the following individual physical phenomena:
· convection in the cavity (1/ L)
· thermal conduction through the glass (d/ l)
· radiation exchange between the surfaces of the panes (in 1/ L – dependent on the emissivity of the coatings used)
· thermal transmission between glass and outside/ inside air ($a_a$, $a_i$)

$$1/k = 1/a_i + d/l + 1/L + 1/a_a$$

With two cavities, 1/L and 1/U become larger but the U-value smaller. The thermal insulation is better.

2.1.39   U-values of various insulating glass units

| Description of insulating glass made from float glass | Cavity with air filling | | Thermal transmittance value U-value W/m²K |
|---|---|---|---|
| 2-ply (1 cavity) | 6 mm < cavity ≤ | 8 mm | 3.4 |
| 2-ply (1 cavity) | 8 mm < cavity ≤ | 10 mm | 3.2 |
| 2-ply (1 cavity) | 10 mm < cavity ≤ | 16 mm | 3.0 |
| 2-ply (1 cavity) | 20 mm < cavity ≤ | 100 mm | 2.8 |
| 3-ply (2 cavities) | 6 mm < cavity ≤ | 8 mm | 2.4 |
| 3-ply (2 cavities) | 8 mm < cavity ≤ | 10 mm | 2.2 |
| 3-ply (2 cavities) | 10 mm < cavity ≤ | 16 mm | 2.1 |

The above values are taken from DIN 4108 Part 4 Tab. 3.

Emissivity of opposing glass surfaces

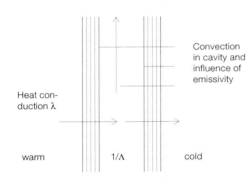

2.1.40   Physical relationships of the U-value for insulating glass

Sound insulation index R (dB)

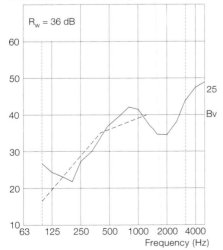

2.1.41   Weighted scale
Sound insulation plotted against frequency for an 8-16-6 air-filled insulating unit with $R_w$ = 36 dB

Dividing the cavity into two separate ones interrupts the convection and so reduces the energy transport. But the convection that occurs with greater spacings reduces the thermal insulation effect.

The U-value of an insulating glass unit consisting of three float glass panes and two 8 mm cavities is 2.4 W/m²K. If each cavity is enlarged to 12 mm, the value drops to 2.2 W/m²K (Figs 2.1.38, p. 72, and 2.1.39). Instead of the middle pane, a suitable foil with additional sunshading can be used to divide up the cavity.

Combinations of thermal insulation coatings and gas fillings can result in U-values of approx. 0.5 – 0.8 W/m²K. Crucial in such instances is the figure used for the emissivity and the influence of the gas filling. Calculations should only be carried out based on EN 673 in order to obtain corresponding comparative results. The possible effects on the building or the interior must be looked at separately.

*Convection – energy transport in a gaseous medium*
Owing to the different temperatures of the two panes and the cavity, the air in the cavity begins to circulate. This results in a flow of energy from the hot to the cold pane. This thermal transport is designated $1/\Lambda$. It can be reduced by filling the cavity with a gas having a lower thermal conductance.

*Thermal conduction – energy transport within a body*
Different temperatures in the boundary layers of a body give rise to an energy transport from the hot to the cold side. The thermal transport through the glass is designated $\lambda$. This specifies how much thermal energy is transported through a material when the temperature difference between the boundary layers is 1 K. The unit is W/mK. It is not possible to reduce the thermal transport without changing the composition of the glass (Fig. 2.1.40).

*Radiation portion*
Two opposing surfaces also exchange energy by way of radiation. Decisive here is the temperatures and the natures of their surfaces. The radiation takes place according to the Stephan-Boltzmann Law. An untreated glass surface reradiates almost all the absorbed energy. The emissivity is very high, about 96%. Coatings can be applied to the glass in order to reduce the radiation portion; such coatings can reduce the emissivity to just 3 – 12%.

*Heat transfer*
The thermal absorption capacity and the circulation of the air causes another energy transport at the glass/air boundary (internal and external). Projecting or recessed corners can have a local influence on the energy transport, so-called heat-sink effects.

**Sound insulation**
*General*
The sound insulation index $R_w$ (expressed in decibels, dB) is still an integral description of a theoretical measured value, of the sound insulation to DIN 52210 as well as the new EN 20717 Part 1. To determine the values, weighted scales are available for all building materials and components. The sound insulation R of the component to be tested is measured over the frequency range 100 – 3200 Hz in one-third octave bands and compared with the required curve according to a prescribed method. This value can prove excellent for monolithic building materials but is inadequate in practice for insulating glass units with small cavities.

The sound insulation qualities of a single-skin wall are determined by its mass. The heavier it is, the better it is as a sound insulator. A single pane 8 mm thick has an $R_w$ value of 32 dB, a single pane 15 mm thick an $R_w$ value of 35 dB.

In an insulating glass unit consisting of two or three separate panes with cavities in between, the glass does not act alone as a mass but instead as an oscillating mass-spring-mass system with a natural frequency and a resulting sound insulation value. This fact is demonstrated by the dramatic reduction in sound insulation of insulating glass units at certain frequencies. Fig. 2.1.41 shows the sound insulation curve of an insulating glass unit and the clear dip at approx. 200 Hz.

Gas fillings, e.g. $SF_6$, alter the sound velocity as well as the "spring effect", depending on the frequency. The partial sound insulation increases for higher frequencies as the insulating effect diminishes for lower frequencies. So although the actual $R_w$ value of a gas-filled insulating glass unit rises, the sound insulation characteristic in the low-frequency range – critical for traffic noise – decreases. This would be perceived as "loud" indoors.

In order that this effect is taken into account, the new European standard EN 20717 Part 1 has introduced glass correction factors for different noise sources (see "Glass correction factors" below).

The sound insulation index $R_w$ of an insulating glass unit consisting of two panes each 4 mm thick and an air-filled cavity of 12 mm is about 30 dB. One 4 mm and one 6 mm pane separated by a 16 mm air-filled cavity is slightly better at 33 dB.

Combinations of laminated and laminated safety glasses can sometimes improve the $R_w$ value, depending on the bonding of the individual panes (resin or foil). It must be remembered that laminated glass made from two 4 mm panes does not behave like one 8 mm pane but instead like two 4 mm panes separated by a layer. The bond should be as "soft" as possible.

The intensity of sound, i.e. the noise level, is specified in dB(A) for traffic noise. The (A) suffix describes the frequency-related distribution of the noise intensity which best resembles traffic noise.

*Glass correction factors*
The sound insulation behaviour of glass, especially insulating glass units with cavities, does not increase linearly like a monolithic wall over the frequencies 100 – 3200 Hz, the range interesting in acoustic terms. Instead, there are significant dips in the range 125 – 250 Hz which depend on the cavity. However, the noise to be attenuated depends on the sources. For example, fast rail traffic exhibits a higher intensity in the upper frequency range above 800 Hz, while the intensity of noise generated by road traffic is high in the range 100 – 500 Hz and then almost constant above this. Road surfacing, the vehicle mix and the speeds all play a decisive role. A goods vehicle approaching a traffic light exhibits a high intensity in the low-frequency range 100 – 300 Hz. The sound insulation of the glass combination remains, however, relatively constant. Changes to the cavity arising from air pressure and temperature fluctuations (Fig. 2.1.35, p. 70) alters the sound insulation behaviour by ±1 to ±2 dB. If the glass combination exhibits a dip in the low-frequency range at high sound intensities originating outside, the noise level in the building will also be higher in this frequency range.

The sound insulation values of glazing units must be tested and cannot be calculated. Such tests take place under prescribed conditions. In practice the values obtained vary due to, for example, size, installation and the pumping motion of the cavity, meaning that the test figures should be taken as a guide and a tolerance of ±2 dB allowed for. The higher the correction factors C and $C_{tr}$, the greater is the dip in the sound insulation for these special frequencies. For example, an insulating glass unit comprising two

4 mm panes and a 12 mm air-filled cavity has a sound insulation index $R_w$ of 30 dB. With a $C_{tr}$ factor of -3 for traffic noise, the corrected $R_w(C_{tr})$ value is 27 dB; this corresponds to our perception of sound in reality. The combination 4-16-4 with air filling has an $R_w$ value of 36 dB. Taking a $C_{tr}$ factor of -6 for traffic noise, this results in an $R_w(C_{tr})$ value of 30 dB.

For an air-filled 4-20-9 combination with a soft casting resin interlayer, the $R_w$ value is 42 dB. If we then take a $C_{tr}$ factor of -5 for traffic noise, the corrected $R_w(C_{tr})$ value drops to 37 dB.

The correction factors C and $C_{tr}$ are calculated from measurements of the glass units and are an indicator of the dip in sound insulation effect in the low-frequency range. The higher the figure, the greater is the dip, i.e. the lower is the sound insulation for those frequencies.

Cavities filled with $SF_6$ gas result in a steeper rise in the sound insulation curve for the higher frequencies but also a more severe dip around the 150 Hz range. The correction factor is approx. -8 to -10, but can be even higher in certain circumstances; the actual sound insulation value diminishes accordingly, depending on the source. What this means in practice is that an economic and functional optimization can be carried out when the actual noise source is known. The correction factor in EN 20717 Part 1 helps to estimate the real effects.

*Influences of the interior*
The sound penetrating the external envelope as a whole is decisive for the actual internal noise level. The sound is reduced further depending on the interior furnishings, room size and absorbent surfaces. Therefore, we can assume that in modern offices such effects attenuate the incoming noise by an additional 3 – 5 dB.

This fact can be demonstrated by two examples:

Example 1: Traffic noise with average sound level measured externally
$L_m$ = 69 dB(A), sound insulating glazing, gas filling, $R_w$ = 38 dB (Fig. 2.1.42).

Example 2: Traffic noise with average sound level measured externally
$L_m$ = 69 dB(A) but with greater sound intensity distribution in low-frequency range, sound insulating glazing, gas filling, $R_w$ = 38 dB (Fig. 2.1.43).

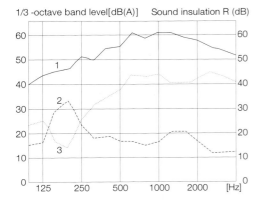

1/3 -octave band level[dB(A)]    Sound insulation R (dB)

1   Intensity distribution of external noise
2   Sound insulation
3   Calculated internal noise level related to frequency

2.1.42   Example 1
         Attenuated traffic noise

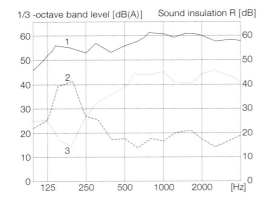

1/3 -octave band level [dB(A)]    Sound insulation R [dB]

1   Intensity distribution of external noise
2   Sound insulation
3   Calculated internal noise level related to frequency

2.1.43   Example 2
         Attenuated bus and goods vehicle noise

With identical sound insulating glazing and equal average external sound levels but different sound intensity distributions across the frequencies, the internal sound level in example 2 will be approx. 7 dB(A) higher than in example 1. So it is vital to investigate the actual noise situation in order to obtain an economic and functional optimization. The relationship between the sound insulation function of a glazing unit and its pane thicknesses and cavity size is not linear. The sound insulation qualities of the glass unit must be matched to the external noise sources.

*Sound insulation of external wall*
The overall sound insulation of the external wall depends on the sound insulating properties of the individual components, their junctions and the resulting flanking paths. Crucial here is the ratio of the areas of the individual components; for instance, a component with poor sound insulation can be compensated for by one with good sound insulation covering a larger area. Leakage paths cannot be eliminated by this method, however. The "components method" in DIN 4109 is a help when adding sound insulation to existing buildings; replacing the windows with others having better sound insulation properties can help to optimize the acoustic situation. The correction factor to EN 20717 Part 1 must be taken into account. Leakage paths at external roller shutter blinds with thin hoods or those only provided for thermal insulation as well as open belt channels must be avoided at all costs.

**Physical parameters of radiation**
The physical parameters of radiation depend on the colour of or coating on the glass being used but also on the distribution of radiation from the sun upon which analyses are based. This distribution can be measured for separate radiation ranges per unit or, and now more than ever before, calculated from the individual data of the panes and layers used. The basis for calculations in Europe is European standard EN 410. Nevertheless, it must be remembered that the results obtained are average values and are the product of the spectral curve of the glass over a specified range of frequencies $d_\lambda$ of the relative "spectral" distribution of the global radiation (direct and diffuse) with the values for 1.42 cm water vapour content and 0.34 cm ozone content (air mass = 1) of the individual glasses. Tolerances in the glass thickness and layers as well as the "green tint" of the glass lead to fluctuations in the values established. A tolerance limit of 2 – 3% either side of the cal-

culated average value can be used. The terrestrial radiation with air mass = 1 for Europe serves as a reference radiation level when calculating physical parameters of radiation, taking the water vapour and ozone figures given above. This was stipulated by the International Commission on Illumination (CIE) in their publication CIE No. 26. This is important when comparing data calculated by means of the various computer programs available which employ differing framework conditions. For instance, the figures obtained can deviate by 5% or more for the same glass just because of the different methods used. The specialist must assess the deviations in terms of their practical significance and be aware of the framework conditions of the computer programs and the glass data because only data ascertained under identical conditions can be compared, or a proper estimate of the error must be carried out.
The actual conditions in practice can differ from the theoretical framework conditions assumed, although this need not have a great influence on the overall effect. With differences of up to approx. (±3%, even ±5%, products can be regarded as equivalent.
A distinction should be made between the following types of solar radiation:

· ultraviolet radiation with wavelengths from 280 to 380 nm,
· visible light with wavelengths from 380 to 780 nm, and
· infrared radiation with wavelengths from 780 to 2500 nm.

Float glass absorbs all wavelengths shorter than approx. 300 nm and longer than 2500 nm.

*Reflected radiation*
This is the proportion of solar radiation that is reflected at the air-glass boundary. It is divided into the total reflected radiation $r_e$ and that in the visible range of wavelengths $r_v$. Reflection always takes place at the boundary of gaseous and solid materials. With coated glass it depends on the side as well because the coating has two boundaries: one with the glass, one with the air. The refractive index at these boundaries is decisive. Consequently, considering one side of the glass can result in a completely different reflection and colour than for the other. This effect must be taken into account if the coatings are to be used in different positions in insulating glass units. The manufacturer must be consulted if coatings are to be used differently to his intentions; for example, whether the coating is to be applied to the

surface of the inner or outer pane facing the cavity (Fig. 2.1.44). The radiation reflected from glass depends on the angle of incidence. However, glass specifications only include information with the angle of incidence at 90° to the glass. One reason for this is that when determining the angle-related reflection values, the polarizing phenomena at the glass and the coatings have to be considered in the measurements. For practical applications this means that for an inclined angle of incidence, the intensity is slightly less than for the perpendicular. To achieve greater accuracy it is not sufficient to apply the physical radiation data as a constant and only consider the irradiation over the whole year related to the angle. In the end the effects that really occur in practice are critical for practical applications.

*Solar direct transmittance*
This is the proportion of incident solar radiation that penetrates the glass or glazing unit. It is divided into the total energy transmission $t_e$ and that in the visible range of wavelengths $t_v$. Like reflected radiation, this too depends on the angle of incidence.

*Solar direct absorbtance*
This is understood to be the proportion of incident solar radiation that is absorbed by the glass. It is divided into the whole range of wavelengths of sunlight $a_e$ and that in the visible range of wavelengths $a_v$.

*Total solar energy transmittance (solar factor)*
This specifies how much solar energy incident on the glass actually penetrates to the inside. It takes into account the proportion that passes through directly and that which penetrates by way of absorption. It can be generally said that the sum of absorption, transmission and reflection is equal to 100 %, i.e. $a_v + t_e + r_v = 100$ %.

*Light transmittance*
This specifies how much radiation in the visible range of wavelengths (380 – 780 nm) passes through the glass, taking into account the luminance sensitivity of the human eye $V_{(\lambda)}$. Critical for the lighting in a room is the daylight factor, a figure which specifies how much daylight is available at any point in a room. The farther the point under consider-ation is from the window, the less light reaches it. Decisive here is how much "sky" can be seen from a particular point.
If necessary, light-redirecting glasses can be employed (see "Redirecting the light", p. 79).

**Low-e glass**

A low-e glass is an insulating glass which has at least one coated surface in the cavity; to achieve the desired U-value it is irrelevant which of these surfaces is coated. The position of the coating can alter the total energy transmittance by about 5%, possibly the perceived colour of the glass or the evenness of the colouring slightly too. The cavities of low-e glazing are usually filled with gas, e.g. argon, krypton, xenon, or mixtures such as krypton/argon and xenon/argon.
The thermal transmittance values are in the region of 1.0 and 2.2. The use of $SF_6$ gas improves the sound insulation and also raises the U-value by approx. 0.3 W/m²K. Triple glazing comprising three panes and two cavities filled with the gases listed above exhibits thermal transmittance values of approx. 0.5 – 0.8 W/m²K. Critical here is that the values are based on calculations to EN 673 and clearly defined basic values for the emissivity of the coatings and the gases used in the cavity. This is the only way to achieve objective, comparable results. The manufacturer is responsible for maintaining the calculated values. Owing to its special properties, each gas has an optimum cavity. EN 673 employs the normal emissivities $\varepsilon_n$ and not the global values for $\varepsilon_n$; the correction factors are given in EN 673. It is important that the underlying figures in the calculations are verified and can be checked.
For passive energy gain, glazing should admit as much solar energy as possible, i.e. exhibit high total energy transmittance g and light transmittance $t_v$ values. The g-value should be in the region of 65%, the $t_v$-value around 60%.
In optical terms, glazing should be identical with standard insulating glass. These days the coatings are virtually colourless and so almost undetectable. Tables 2.1.45 and

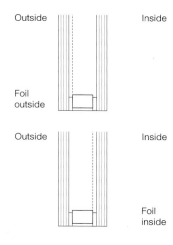

2.1.44  Position of low-e foil in insulating glass

2.1.46 show the relationship between U-value and emissivity for 2- and 3-ply insulating glazing.

## Controlling solar radiation

Controlling solar radiation with glass means preventing some of the solar radiation incident on the glass from entering the interior. There are various ways of achieving this (from outside to inside):

- solar-control glass
- external blinds
- blinds fitted in the cavity
- foil in the cavity
- spun glass (non-woven fabric) between the panes
- internal blinds fitted to the inside of the glazing
- foils attached to the glass
- patterns formed by enamelling and silk-screen printing.

The choice of a solar-control system is always a compromise between minimum energy gain and maximum light use since light is always a component of the total energy.

### Solar-control glass

In contrast to low-e glass, solar-control glass has to prevent as much incident solar radiation as possible from entering the interior. External influences like solar radiation are added to internal heat sources to make up the internal climate. Nevertheless, the light transmittance value should be high in order to admit plenty of daylight.

In addition, solar-control glass also fulfils an aesthetic function. The colour of the reflections as well as the colour of the glass itself can be exploited in the design of a façade. Solar-control glasses should exhibit total energy transmittance values (g) < 50 % and light transmittance values $L(t_v) > 40$ %. In practice, fluctuations in these values amounting to 3 – 5% are irrelevant for the internal environment. Body-tinted glasses absorb more than highly reflective, coated glasses, although these days absorbent coatings too are being employed for solar-control purposes and for coloured effects. The specific values for reflection, colour and hence total energy transmittance for each application depend on which glass surface is coated, while direct transmission, i.e. light transmittance too, remains constant. Values are calculated in accordance with prEN 410 and prEN 673.

2.1.45 Relationship between U-value and emissivity for double insulating glazing

| Emissivity | Thermal transmittance value (U-value) | | | | Total energy transmittance | Light transmittance | Cavity | Element thickness |
|---|---|---|---|---|---|---|---|---|
| | Air [W/m²K] | Argon [W/m²K] | Krypton [W/m²K] | SF₆ [W/m²K] | g-value | τ-value | | |
| $\varepsilon_n = 16\%$ | 2.1 | 1.8 | 1.4 | 2.3 | 72% | 73% | 10 mm | 18 mm |
| | 1.9 | 1.7 | 1.5 | 2.4 | | | 12 mm | 20 mm |
| | 1.7 | 1.5 | 1.5 | 2.4 | | | 16 mm | 24 mm |
| | 1.8 | 1.6 | 1.5 | 2.4 | | | 20 mm | 28 mm |
| $\varepsilon_n = 10\%$ | 2.0 | 1.7 | 1.3 | 2.2 | 66% | 77% | 10 mm | 18 mm |
| | 1.8 | 1.5 | 1.3 | 2.3 | | | 12 mm | 20 mm |
| | 1.6 | 1.4 | 1.3 | 2.3 | | | 16 mm | 24 mm |
| | 1.6 | 1.4 | 1.3 | 2.3 | | | 20 mm | 28 mm |
| $\varepsilon_n = 5\%$ | 1.9 | 1.5 | 1.1 | 2.1 | 59% | 74% | 10 mm | 18 mm |
| | 1.7 | 1.3 | 1.1 | 2.2 | | | 12 mm | 20 mm |
| | 1.4 | 1.2 | 1.1 | 2.2 | | | 16 mm | 24 mm |
| | 1.5 | 1.2 | 1.2 | 2.2 | | | 20 mm | 28 mm |

2.1.46 Relationship between U-value and emissivity for triple glazing

| Emissivity | Thermal transmittance value (U-value) | | | | Total energy transmittance | Light transmittance | Cavity | Element thickness |
|---|---|---|---|---|---|---|---|---|
| | Air [W/m²K] | Argon [W/m²K] | Krypton [W/m²K] | SF₆ [W/m²K] | g-value | τ-value | | |
| $\varepsilon_n = 16\%$ | 1.7 | 1.4 | 1.1 | 1.3 | 54% | 59% | 2 × 6 mm | 24 mm |
| | 1.5 | 1.2 | 0.9 | 1.3 | | | 2 × 8 mm | 28 mm |
| | 1.3 | 1.1 | 0.8 | 1.3 | | | 2 × 10 mm | 32 mm |
| | 1.2 | 1.0 | 0.8 | 1.3 | | | 2 × 12 mm | 36 mm |
| $\varepsilon_n = 10\%$ | 1.7 | 1.3 | 1.0 | 1.2 | 51% | 66% | 2 × 6 mm | 24 mm |
| | 1.4 | 1.1 | 0.8 | 1.2 | | | 2 × 8 mm | 28 mm |
| | 1.2 | 1.0 | 0.7 | 1.2 | | | 2 × 10 mm | 32 mm |
| | 1.1 | 0.9 | 0.6 | 1.2 | | | 2 × 12 mm | 36 mm |
| $\varepsilon_n = 5\%$ | 1.6 | 1.3 | 0.9 | 1.1 | 42% | 60% | 2 × 6 mm | 24 mm |
| | 1.3 | 1.0 | 0.7 | 1.1 | | | 2 × 8 mm | 28 mm |
| | 1.1 | 0.9 | 0.6 | 1.1 | | | 2 × 10 mm | 32 mm |
| | 1.0 | 0.8 | 0.5 | 1.1 | | | 2 × 12 mm | 36 mm |

*Coated/Body-tinted solar-control glass*
Solar-control glazing comprises coated or body-tinted glasses, which in our climate region are used as insulating glass. Minute amounts of additives introduced into the melt give the glass a grey, bronze, green or even blue tint.

The usual methods of coating glass are outlined on pp. 64–65.

The glass surface to which the coating can be applied mainly depends on the nature of the coating. The physical parameters of radiation can be determined according to the principles mentioned above, whereby the coloration and optical consistency of the coating shall be considered besides purely functional aspects.

Only the manufacturer can provide details on the glass surface and position of the coating because only he knows the composition of the coatings, their effects and their durability. Definitions and methods of testing, to determine coating durability, are given in draft European standard prEN 1096 Parts 1–4.

If the coatings are processed with foil or casting resin to form complete units, the new boundary relationships between the coatings and the foil/resin must be taken into account. This applies both to the appearance of the glass and to the physical parameters of radiation. Solar control by means of coatings remains constant and enables consistent, unhindered transparency right across the whole area of the glass. Transmission is reduced by increased absorption or reflection over the entire area.

*Printed solar-control glass*
The transmission of radiation can be reduced by providing some opaque areas (grids). Using silk-screen printing, an opaque pattern can be applied to parts of the glass surface, e.g. by "baking-in" an enamel during the manufacture of toughened safety glass.

Solar control, i.e. reducing the transmission of radiation, is achieved by the glass surface being shaded by the pattern. Thus, only part of the glass pane is transparent and so the area for transmittance of solar radiation is reduced. The solar-control effect depends on the ratio of transparent to opaque areas, including their absorption.

**External shading**
Effective external shading prevents excessive solar energy from even reaching the glass and hence penetrating to the room beyond. Such shades can be adjusted mechanically but they can obstruct the view out and, if the shading effect is too extreme, may necessitate the provision of additional artificial lighting.

External shading must be able to withstand the rigors of wind, snow and moisture and should not cause any additional wind noise. Apart from that, it has to be cleaned and should not be attached to the glazing beads. The fixings for external shading should be joined to the actual façade in such a way that no thermal bridges to the inside are created.

*Fixed shading*
Inclined or horizontal louvres can be arranged in such a way that they shade the transparent areas at a corresponding solar altitude angle. These louvres are usually projecting and can be made of metal, wood, plastic or even glass. Coated glasses, with low transmittance values and sufficiently durable coatings, or body-tinted glasses can be used for this in the form of toughened safety glass or as laminated glass. They are usually rigid but can also be provided as movable louvres. The choice of toughened or laminated safety glass depends on the fixings for the glass as well as the respective additional safety requirements arising from the use of the building.

*Movable external shading*
A movable external shading arrangement enables the shade to be adjusted to suit individual needs. Opaque materials in the form of horizontal shades, translucent fabric blinds and even movable glass elements are all suitable solutions. With horizontal louvres, minimum solar irradiation is achieved when the louvres are arranged in such a way that only indirect radiation can enter the room. However, this can lead to a severely restricted view out and the need to install additional artificial lighting. When using translucent fabric blinds it must be ensured that they are weather- and wind-resistant.

Movable glass elements are placed in front of the windows and are made from body-tinted glass or coated glass with low transmittance. When not in use they remain in front of the spandrel panel and are moved across the windows to provide shade as required. The light transmittance therefore remains commensurate with the transparency.

*Blinds within the cavity of an insulating glass unit*
In this case the shading lies in the plane of the façade. The absorption component is transmitted partly outwards, also partly inwards. A folding or roller blind is placed within the cavity of an insulating glass unit and this can be controlled individually. When in use, it shades the transparent area; when closed, the air in the cavity can be heated up as a result of high absorption caused by solar radiation. Suitable materials must therefore be chosen because addition-

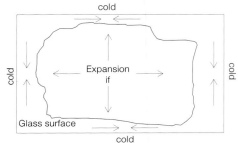

2.1.47   Stresses in glass at points where hot and cold surfaces meet

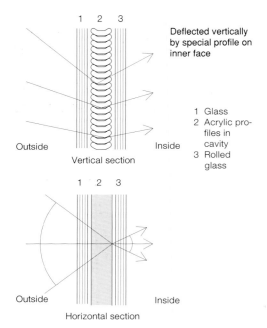

Deflected vertically by special profile on inner face

1 Glass
2 Acrylic profiles in cavity
3 Rolled glass

Outside                                    Inside
Vertical section

Outside                                    Inside
Horizontal section

2.1.48   Light redirecting glass

Angle of incidence 30°

Angle of incidence 60°

2.1.49   Redirecting the light by way of special elements

al thermal loads increase the pressure in the cavity and hence on the panes. In small panes the mechanical stresses in the glass increase, although this can be compensated for in the edge seals or by using pre-stressed panes. In large panes this causes significant bowing which can lead to optical distortion.

In the case of vertical panes, the sunshading is lowered by means of its own weight; with inclined glazing additional mechanisms may need to be incorporated to ensure proper operation.

It is not possible to replace the sunshading in insulating glass without replacing the complete unit. This must be taken into account in the design.

The shading arrangement can consist of a reflective foil, a translucent foil or horizontal louvres. There must be sufficient clearance between the panes and the shading to allow for correct operation even if panes cave inwards as a result of pressure fluctuations in the cavity. A foil blind can heat up severely if it lies in the transparent area when rolled up; the material may be damaged as a result.

*Fixed foils in the cavity*
Reflective foils can be spanned across the cavity. The actual shading facility is placed in the middle of a wide cavity and divides it into two narrow cavities, leading to a lower thermal transmittance value (U-value). The two cavities have to be linked to prevent any differences in pressure. The foils used reflect the solar radiation in a selective manner and so have different colours depending on how they do this. The third surface produces a reflection when viewed from outside.

*Glasses with intermediate layers*
Spun glass, non-woven fabrics, capillary systems or foams can be integrated between the glass panes. The thermal transmittance values and the physical parameters of radiation for the glass unit alter depending on the materials used. Most of these scatter the light depending on their design. The spun glass and non-woven fabrics have a high (diffuse) light transmittance but at the same time reflect the light and so also provide solar-control properties. A

direct view through is not possible. When they are used as rooflights or in roofs, the scattered light can be directed deeper into the interior by reflection, for example, on the ceiling or the walls. Capillary layers and foams can also be employed as "transparent thermal insulation". These have very low U-values (down to approx. 0.3 W/m²K) but still allow the passage of light, albeit diffuse, into the room, leading to an energy gain. The types of glass used are selected according to their application as spandrel panels or as windows in the form of inclined glazing.

**Internal shading**
Internal shading is not subjected to direct external loads. It can only reflect solar radiation back through the glazing; the energy it absorbs remains in the room. An inadequate clearance between pane and shading can lead to a heat build-up which places a thermal load on the panes. As the edges of the panes – covered by the frames – remain cooler, toughened or heat-strengthened glass may well have to be used in order to attain a better thermal fatigue resistance and rule out the possibility of fracture (Fig. 2.1.47).

Internal shading serves more as a form of "glare prevention" to prevent the occupants from being disturbed by direct sunlight.

*Foil attached to the glass*
Reflective or absorbent foils can be glued to the outer surfaces of insulating glass. These change the temperature of the pane directly by way of absorption. Great care is needed when attaching foil to existing windows. Highly absorbent foils which are attached to the inner surfaces can cause a huge build up of heat when subjected to solar radiation (Fig. 2.1.47).

**Antiglare protection**
A diffuse transmitting surface, irrespective of whether it is the glass pane itself or internal/external shading elements, can be used to scatter daylight across the interior. This reduces the great differences in lighting intensity on working surfaces and decreases the physiological glare phenomenon. No persons in the room are subjected to direct sunlight.

### One-way glass

A view through only from one side, e.g. from the outside to the inside, is only possible when looking from the dark side towards the bright side. If the lighting relationship is reversed, then the direction of view also changes. This effect is amplified by additional reflection or absorption. Nevertheless, it is the lighting that determines the direction of view, not the glass.

### Scattering the light

A transparent pane of glass allows a directed beam of light to pass through unaffected. However, owing to their "rough" surfaces, diffusing glasses, or patterned glasses (previously known as cast), scatter the beam of light. The greater the degree of scatter, the more an object behind the glass is obscured. For interiors, a diffusing glass means that the incident light is more or less scattered. The brightness levels are more even and not so dependent on the solar altitude angle. Glasses fitted with spun glass or non-woven fabrics can achieve identical effects.

### Redirecting the light

One simple method of providing more daylight farther away from the windows has been possible for many years using special cast glasses. During production the surfaces undergo extreme shaping so that the light which strikes the first glass surface is deflected towards the next surface in such a way that it shines onto the bright ceiling and from there into the room. A sloping ceiling near the windows can help the light to reach even farther into the interior. Recently, more and more insulating glasses have been developed which enable the light to be redirected to an even greater extent. To do this, curved plastic elements are incorporated which redirect the light up to the ceiling (Figs 2.1.48 and 2.1.49). From there it then radiates deeper into the room. Redirecting insulating glass units are ideal as fanlights because they are designed in such a way that as much sunlight as possible is redirected through the elements regardless of the angle of incidence (Fig. 2.1.50).

### Photovoltaic modules and elements

Solar cells can be installed in the cavity between two glass panes. These then convert the incident solar energy into electrical current. Casting resin is frequently used as a backing material. Either amorphous or crystalline solar cells may be used. The external appearance of the amorphous cells ranges from red and transparent or dark grey to opaque, that of the crystalline cells is blue and opaque with transparent spaces between the cells. The photovoltaic modules are arranged in such a way that they can be processed like conventional glass or insulating glass elements. The degree of efficiency depends on the materials used: 6 – 8% for modules produced using thin-film technology and approx. 10% for silicon mo-dules. New developments are concentrating on a higher degree of efficiency coupled with lower production costs. Photovoltaic modules can be used in the form of curtain walls or cold or warm façades.

### Fire-resistant glass

Each country has its own set of rules and classifications, all of which must be observed. Therefore, European standards on testing and classification are being drawn up with the aim of harmonizing the different approaches. In addition, the passage of radiation is specified separately for glazing. The following classification has therefore been adopted:
R = loadbearing capacity, E = integrity, W = radiation, I = insulation, S = smoke control and C = self-closing (prEN 357 Part 1).

Glass for fire protection purposes is divided into two categories:

G-glass
This type prevents flames and fumes from penetrating for a specified length of time; radiated heat, however, is not contained.

F-glass
This type prevents flames and fumes from penetrating for a specified length of time but also contains the heat radiation produced by the fire.

Doors must be tested separately as fire protection elements together with their associated F-glass. They are awarded a "T" designation with the time of resistance in minutes.
Owing to their structure, most F- and G-glasses satisfy safety criteria too, e.g. acting as safety barriers, in accordance with the pendulum impact test to DIN 52337 (soft impact). The pendulum drop height withstood by the respective type of glass has to be tested for each individual application.
To provide fire protection, fire-resistant glass must be fitted in appropriate frames in conjunction with approved fixing and sealing materials. The complete unit comprising glass and frame is tested to DIN 4102,

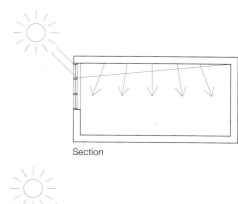

Section

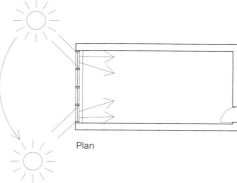

Plan

2.1.50  Distribution of light using redirecting elements in the façade and a reflective ceiling

graded and certified by the Deutsches Institut für Bautechnik. Changes to the materials given in the test report must be specially approved or tested. Inappropriate combinations of materials could lead to smoke and fumes penetrating the barrier, the propagation of the fire or the development of smoke.

Units with F-glass contain substances which absorb energy as the temperature rises and transform without releasing energy.

A critical factor with fire-resistant glazing is how long it withstands the fire; 30, 60, 90 and 120 minutes are the classes of resistance. Until the publication of a uniform European standard, tests in Germany will continue to be performed in accordance with DIN 4102 with its standard time-temperature curve. These tests involve the complete component consisting of frame, seal and glass fitted to the standard aperture in the test furnace. The temperature in the fire chamber rises according to the standard time-temperature curve, reaching 700 °C after 15 min, 825 °C after 30 min, 900 °C after 45 min and 920 °C after 60 min; after 90 min the temperature is just below 1000 °C.

To check the smoke and flame integrity (G-class), a cotton wool pad is held directly behind the glass. This should not ignite spontaneously and there should be no flames. In checking the heat insulation (F-class), the average temperature of the glass on the side not exposed to the fire should not rise more than 140 K above the temperature in the room before the test and at no point on the glass may the maximum temperature rise 180 K above the same initial temperature. In some European countries and for special applications, e.g. ship windows, an additional extinguishing water test must be carried out directly after the fire test. Fire-resistant glasses are produced for both internal and external applications. For the latter it should be ensured that the materials used do not react or change beforehand as a result of absorbing solar radiation or being subjected to low temperatures. Special tests are required for inclined glazing. Certain coatings can also reduce the passage of radiation.

## Combinations of special-function glasses

There are unlimited possibilities for combining the types of glass described here for all manner of applications. The resulting functions must be established in each individual case. Combining functions creates physical relationships which the specialist then has to appraise in order to subsequently select the necessary types of glass according to their properties.

## Applications

Glass is a universal building material. However, rapid developments in the secondary processing of the basic material and the associated increasing number of potential applications make it imperative that we continue researching and establishing physical properties; likewise, exploring the limits for every type of glass and the possible combinations with other materials for the respective applications. In determining the individual physical parameters it is the respective framework conditions which must be observed above all else. In some instances we are taking glass to its limits, i.e. the smallest change in the ambient conditions could lead to failure. So glass should not be treated as an isolated entity, detached from the surrounding construction. It is all too easy to gain the impression that anything that can be manufactured can also be used without constraints.

With the multitude of glass products on the market it takes a specialist to be able to select the best product for a particular application. Only a specialist can estimate how the material will behave in practice based on the given design parameters. Priorities must be stipulated when selecting the glass for a certain situation. It is rare for all demands to be fulfilled. Accordingly, compromises must be made when selecting and combining types of glass.

### Windows and façades
A window in the meaning applied by the building authorities is a component which is not required to fulfil additional requirements such as safety barrier function. Glass is a transparent infill and contributes neither to the stability of the frame nor the construction. If further directives are to be complied with, then these must be taken into account when calculating the glass thickness or selecting the type of glass because the glass is then subjected to additional forces. Windows and façades are positioned vertically in the building envelope and serve to separate interior from exterior.

*Thermal insulation*
High demands are placed on thermal insulation nowadays. In Germany these are defined by the national Thermal Insulation Act. While DIN 4108 stipulates minimum requirements based on physical parameters, the requirements of the Thermal Insulation Act are based on energy-saving aspects.

*Sound insulation*

The sound insulation of a window or façade depends on the frame, glass and installation, but also on the seal between frame and opening light as well as the seal to the surrounding construction. The weakest link determines the effectiveness in this case. Even minute leakage paths have a substantial influence on both the overall sound and thermal insulation. Auxiliary elements such as roller shutter housings and window sills penetrating the construction can have a major effect on the sound insulation. Acoustic bridges are often invisible – but not inaudible! Only careful design and proper workmanship can guarantee success.

*Safety*

Safety requirements, e.g. protection from injury, protection against falling, vandal, intruder and bullet resistance, can be complied with by selecting the right type of glass. Important here is that the frame and the construction are properly matched. The aim of the safety requirement shall be defined.

**Sloping and roof glazing**

Vertical panes are placed in frames on setting blocks which carry the self-weight and service loads, e.g. short-term wind loads, and transfer these to the frame. If the glazing is fitted at an angle, the weight of the glass and loads such as wind and snow are carried via the edges and side frames before being transferred to the supporting structure. This is different from the vertical arrangement and this must be taken into account in the design.

The supports must be adequately elastic and stable so that they can transmit the loads; the edges of the panes must be able to rotate freely. Normal plastic edge tapes as used in vertical glazing cannot be used here. Instead, silicone or EPDM profiles with adequate resilience are required.

# Glass underfoot

Glazing placed at an angle must be cleaned and so needs to be able to support the load of cleaning personnel. However, such loads are not generally allowed for in calculating the glass thickness. Overloading the glass leads to fracture and a serious risk of injury. The glass thickness is normally calculated on the basis of uniformly distributed loads (snow, wind) and not the point loads caused by persons standing or walking on it. Such point loads generate additional stresses in the glass. Even wired glass cannot support such loads.

Panes which need to support the weight of persons must be designed accordingly. We distinguish between two categories here:

**Glass for restricted foot traffic**

In this type of glazing the persons having access to the glass (for maintenance or cleaning purposes) must be fully conversant with safe working procedures. They will not tread on the centres of panes but rather near the edges so that the loads can be transferred directly to the supporting construction and not cause increased deflections in the glass itself. The persons should not carry heavy objects which would cause further additional loads. Safety features to match the severity of the slope must be provided to prevent slipping. Persons may also need to wear safety harnesses; construction law includes provisions on this. Such persons must ascertain what type of glass is involved and must ensure that, for example, there are no sharp stones adhering to the soles of their shoes. If deemed necessary, then an additional 1 kN point load in the centre of the pane can be included when designing the glass. A glass to which broken fragments adhere (e.g. laminated safety glass) should be used and not thermally toughened safety glass.

**Glass for unrestricted foot traffic**

Glazing supported along its edges and intended to carry unrestricted foot traffic must satisfy the same requirements as a normal floor. Therefore, imposed loads of 5 kN/m$^2$ are common; special situations may even presume higher design loads. It must be remembered that once installed, heavy loads may be moved across or even placed on the glass. This applies especially to stairs. Glazing subjected to any kind of foot traffic, restricted or unrestricted, shall consist of laminated safety glass since this, when broken, does not collapse but instead exhibits a residual load-carrying capacity dependent on the support conditions: on two or four sides or at individual points.

The glass thickness necessary is calculated from the load and the applicable permissible ultimate bending strength of the glass under long-term loading. One extra pane at least 6 mm thick should be added on top of the loadbearing laminated safety glass construction to act as a wearing course and to protect it; breakage of this pane should not impair the stability of the overall system. This sacrificial uppermost pane can be provided with enamel or silk-screen printing in order to achieve decorative effects or a non-slip finish (Fig. 2.1.51, see also "Glass surfaces subjected to foot traffic", p. 99).

*Slope of the glazing*

Angles less than 7° should be avoided for glazing. This does not mean that shallower slopes are not possible but rather that users must be aware of the consequences and be prepared to deal with them. The degree of

Protective pane

Loadbearing laminated safety glass construction

2.1.51   Section through laminated safety glass for unrestricted foot traffic

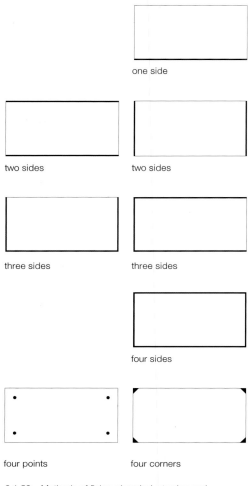

one side

two sides

two sides

three sides

three sides

four sides

four points

four corners

2.1.52    Methods of fixing glass balustrades and spandrel panels

180° swing door – opens in both directions

90° swing door – opens in one direction (here: DIN right)

90° swing door – opens in one direction (here: DIN left)

2.1.53    Possible door hinge arrangements

soiling increases with shallow angles. Leaves remain on the glass and even water, which cannot drain off because of the deflection of the panes, can lead to corrosion and leaching of the glass surface. Draining of the water via the drainage system of the construction must be guaranteed with shallow roof pitches because otherwise the edge seal of the insulating glass will be attacked, moisture can infiltrate the cavity and even the frame itself can suffer. If roof pitches < 7° are intended, then certain consequences, as outlined here, must be reckoned with.

**Types of glass**
*Single glazing*
When selecting the type of glass it should be ensured that, if broken, no glass fragments can fall and present a risk to persons underneath. The shallower the inclination of the pane, the greater is the effect of the self-weight of the glass on the fractured pane: fragments could drop off. Vertical panes which are broken remain in their frames (see also "Musterbauordnung").
Glasses which retain broken fragments satisfy this requirement. Laminated safety glass, e.g. with PVB interlayer or equivalent casting resin combinations, can be used in such situations. Wired glass is also possible but with restrictions.
In regions where frequent hailstorms are likely, this load should also be considered when selecting the glass. Laminated safety glass comprising two panes of heat-strengthened glass offers adequate safety in such circumstances. Once fractured the glass used must exhibit sufficient residual load-carrying capacity in order to prevent the glass falling into the room as it breaks – together with the snow.
These considerations also apply to roof windows where people live or work below (see also "Limit state design", p. 97).

*Insulating glazing*
In the case of insulating glazing, the outer pane should carry all the loads and the lower pane retain all the fragments upon fracture. The outer pane can be toughened safety glass in order to possess adequate stability during hailstorms. As only the strength to resist external loads is critical, the lower pane prevents the pieces from falling if the glass is fractured (see also "Special issues concerning residual load-carrying capacity", p. 98).

*Spandrel panels, balustrades*
These constructions serve to prevent persons from falling from a higher level to a lower one. If these are made of glass, then they have to fulfil the same requirements as other materials, i.e. the glass pane must be

able to withstand the impact of a person. The pendulum impact test to DIN 52337 (soft impact) is used to test this characteristic. The glass should not be completely shattered or penetrated by a 45 kg pendulum dropped from a height of 300, 700, 900 or 1200 mm. Owing to the very large splinters, float glass is unsuitable for such barriers. The draft European standard prEN 12600 will apply here in future.
For the glass to function properly it must be ensured that the supporting construction, in conjunction with the glass, fulfils the same criteria. The construction must be matched to the glass.
Toughened safety glass, laminated safety glass and laminated safety glass made from prestressed or heat-strengthened panes are conceivable here, depending on the fixings. The use of heat-strengthened glass alone is not adequate.
The fixings for balustrades fitted to the sides of stairs can move in relation to each other when the stairs are in use. This must not be allowed as it can induce additional stresses in the glass (Fig. 2.1.52). (See "Residual loadbearing capacity of safety barriers", p. 99.)

**Partitions**
Glass can be safely employed internally as storey-height partition walls. Such partitions should be, for safety reasons, sufficiently thick – at least 8 mm toughened safety glass, which can withstand the impact of a person owing to its high ultimate bending strength. If such panes do break, then the risk of injury is much lower than with normal glass because of the fracture pattern (small blunt dice). In certain circumstances it may be necessary for the partitions to comply with fire protection requirements and then the whole construction must fulfil these stipulations. Laminated safety glass of adequate thickness represents an alternative to toughened safety glass.

**All-glass doors/doorsets**
Owing to its high ultimate bending strength, toughened safety glass is ideal for self-supporting all-glass doorsets. Glass internal doors can be fitted to standard metal or timber frames to DIN 18101. The thickness of the individual glass leaves depends on the size but should not be less than 8 mm. The necessary door furniture is screwed to the glass pane with a resilient pad between metal and glass. In this case the glass is firmly joined to its furniture (Fig. 2.1.53). All-glass doors can be supplied with or without bottom rails.
In all-glass doorsets, consisting of door plus sidelight and fanlight, the necessary door furniture must be screwed to the panes of glass. Glass stiffening fins may also be

required in order to improve the stability of the construction and avoid deflections in the loadbearing glass elements. The hinge point of the door should be stabilized in the region of the fanlight.

Glass doors can be designed as revolving doors, sliding doors or 180° swing doors. Vestibules can be made entirely of glass. Variable room dividers many metres long are available in folding, rolling or concertina forms. With rolling systems without a bottom rail, care must be taken to ensure that the upper carriage is designed in such a way that when operating the system the panes of glass do not oscillate and injure the feet of the operator. When not in use, the individual glass leaves are stored in the space-saving position; when in use, they form a flat, transparent partition. The glass should be at least 10 mm thick (Fig. 2.1.54).

Glass doors can be made from float glass, clear, translucent, patterned or body-tinted glass, or glass with enamelled, acid-etched or printed patterns on one side. Doors made from clear glass should be rendered visible by acid-etching or other forms of treatment in order to prevent persons walking into them.

### Glass stair treads

Stair treads made of glass are subject to the same safety requirements as treads made from other materials. Stair treads must not only support the loads of persons walking on them but also heavy, hard objects, e.g. furniture, which is carried up and down them. Laminated safety glass must be used for glass stair treads.

If the treads are supported on all four sides, no large deflections are likely owing to the short spans involved. However, if they cantilever across the full width of the stair, the deflection caused by the maximum load must be kept small in order to avoid a trampoline effect. This deflection should be less than 2.5 mm. If necessary, the stability must be proved by way of suitable tests.

In the case of treads supported on two sides, fracture of the glass must not reduce the total loadbearing capacity to such an extent that the glass tread slips out of its fixings.

It is also important to provide a supporting construction which is sufficiently stable. If necessary, dynamic loads resulting from the use of the stair must be taken into account when designing glass and structure. The uppermost pane should be given a non-slip finish (e.g. by means of silk-screen printing).

### Glass for aquariums

The following points must be observed when providing glass for aquariums or designing all-glass aquariums (Fig. 2.1.55):

- The load of the water in an aquarium represents a permanent load for the glass and joints.
- The load of the water is distributed over the glass in the form of a triangle (increasing with depth). To simplify the analysis, a substitute load producing the same effect may be used (Fig. 2.1.55).
- The surface of the glass not in contact with the water is subjected to a tensile stress. Glass which is too thin and badly scratched can fail.
- The glass must be sufficiently thick and hence resistant to bending in order to avoid large deflections.
- For float glass, the maximum permissible bending strength (8 N/mm$^2$) should not be exceeded.

The glass thickness depends on the load of the water and the support conditions. Is the pane supported by a frame on all four sides, three sides or two? And if two, then top and bottom or at each end? This is critical because the high water load has a decisive influence on the glass thickness and the watertightness of the joints.

Laminated safety glass made from float glass is very suitable. Owing to the low maximum deflections permissible for such applications, glasses with higher permissible bending stresses are usually not necessary. Once broken, the residual strength of laminated safety glass made from float glass is higher than, for example, laminated safety glass made from thermally toughened glass. The same is true for the base plate if it is not supported across its full area on a flat surface. The permissible stress under permanent loading should be used to calculate the required thickness. The supports must be arranged so that the panes are held elastically but perfectly sealed. The width of the edge support should be roughly equal to the thickness of the glass.

In all-glass aquariums, both the glass thickness and the durability of the glued edges are critical (Fig. 2.1.56, p. 84). The forces due to the water load are transmitted from one pane via the adhesive joint to the next pane. Vertical butt-lap joints are to be avoided because in such cases the adhesive is subjected to either purely axial or purely shear stresses. Mitred joints are better because they are only subjected to 50% shear stresses. The materials used must be waterproof adhesives and not simply sealants. Such adhesive joints cannot accommodate pure shear forces but forces perpendicular to the joint.

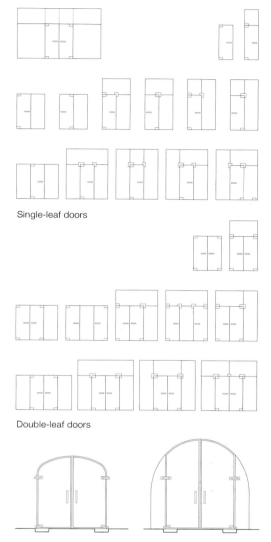

Single-leaf doors

Double-leaf doors

2.1.54  All-glass doors and doorsets

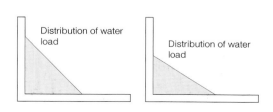

Distribution of water load

Distribution of water load

2.1.55  Water loads for different water depths

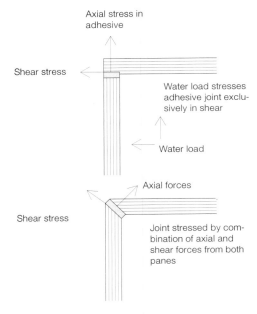

Axial stress in adhesive

Shear stress

Water load stresses adhesive joint exclusively in shear

Water load

Axial forces

Shear stress

Joint stressed by combination of axial and shear forces from both panes

2.1.56    Corner detail of an all-glass aquarium

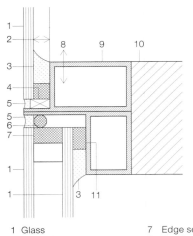

1 Glass
2 Width of rebate
3 Adhesion surface
4 Setting block
5 Weatherseal
6 Backer rod
7 Edge seal
8 Depth of rebate
9 Adapter frame
10 Structure
11 Spacer

2.1.57    Glass construction with loadbearing adhesive joints (structural sealant glazing), vertical section

[2] In the wake of the European standard, when obtaining approval in individual cases and a licence from the European Organization for Technical Approvals (EOTA) the basis for applications will be European standard prEN 1302 Parts 1 – 4. These define the fundamental methods of analysis and requirements for glass, the different types of glass and adhesive joints without referring to special methods of construction.

When used for aquariums, the edges of laminated safety glass are subjected to high amounts of moisture. Its effects on the edge zone can therefore not be ruled out (see "Laminated safety glass", pp. 68–70).

### Transparent thermal insulation

Transparent thermal insulation is often – despite its name – not clear but translucent. Besides acting as an insulator it also serves to improve energy gain – owing to its radiation permeability.

The simplest "transparent thermal insulation" is insulating glass with a U-value of approx. 3.0 $W/m^2K$. These units are used in windows because of their transparency.

Normally however, transparent thermal insulation is placed directly in front of a solid external wall. This is then heated up by solar radiation and this heat is dispersed into the rooms on the other side. Certain types of transparent thermal insulation can be used directly as façade infill panels, helping to contribute to the provision of daylight. Transparent thermal insulation can be formed by very thin plastic capillaries, thin-walled glass tubes or aerogels (foamed $SiO_2$ granulate), all placed between two panes of glass. Other elements have additional absorbers at the rear in order to absorb more solar energy. Transparent thermal insulation units should be shaded from the sun in summer.

### Structural sealant glazing

Structural sealant glazing (Fig. 2.1.57) is a system whereby the glass panes are not held mechanically in rebates but instead glued to an adapter frame which is then hung on the façade or fixed in some other mechanical way. This technique can be used for single or insulating glazing (see also "Linear supports", p. 156).

The edge seals of insulating glass units are made from a UV-resistant silicone specially developed for this purpose. The adherence to the glass must be specially tested and verified. In Germany an approval certificate is required for the complete glass/frame system in conjunction with independent monitoring during production.

The adhesive joint may only carry wind pressure and suction forces. The weight of the glass, if it induces shear forces in the joint, must always be carried by mechanical means so that the adhesive is not subjected to permanent shear. If long-term shear forces do occur at the joints, then the adhesive can fail. If these shear forces are to be taken into account, then a completely different safety concept must be devised, also in terms of the adhesive. Structural sealant glazing elements are manufactured in factories under controlled conditions. The processing directives of the adhesive supplier

must be adhered to. The glass elements should not be moved during the curing process; this is to avoid loading the joints. Production must take place in clean, uniform conditions.

In Germany structural sealant glazing installed at a height exceeding 8 m must be provided with additional retainers which ensure that, if the adhesive fails, the panes remain in their frames under load with a residual safety factor > 1. Approval by the building authorities must always be obtained. The required width and depth of the load-carrying adhesive joint must be calculated for each case; the size of the joint is limited by the necessary curing time and other material properties. The widths are predetermined by the spacer tapes which are sufficiently rigid and do not deform during production as a result of the weight of the glass (horizontal production with subsequent curing). The curing must take place free of stress, i.e. the adhesive joint may not be loaded before the curing process is complete. General building authority approvals or approval certificates for individual cases are always required for structural sealant glazing. At a European level, general approval provisions and test methods as well as a standard for glazing are being drawn up by the European Organization for Technical Approvals (EOTA). Façade applications must also consider fire protection requirements.[2]

## Physical phenomena

Glass is a transparent, absorbent and reflective building material. Therefore, normal, common, sometimes disturbing physical phenomena are frequently more readily visible and often wrongly attributed to the material, although the same effects also occur with other, non-transparent building materials.

### Bowing and dishing of insulating glass panes

The cavity of an insulating glass unit is hermetically sealed off from the outside air. The air pressure in the cavity corresponds to the air pressure at the time of manufacture. If the external barometric air pressure rises, the panes cave inwards, while low atmospheric pressure causes them to bulge outwards (Fig. 2.1.35, p. 70). This effect is more noticeable with large panes and wide cavities. Small panes, up to about 700 mm long, are very stiff and bend less; however, the bending stress in the glass increases. This bowing and dishing is most disturbing with reflective glasses because it leads to optical distortions. The glass thickness in such cases should not be selected merely on the basis of the structural analysis but instead should take into account the total physical behaviour. If the glass thickness is determined purely according to the non-linear method, the elasticity is fully used and larger deflections of the panes assumed.

### Interference

Under certain lighting conditions insulating glasses occasionally exhibit slightly shimmering, coloured, circular to elliptical areas. These interference phenomena are brought about by the superimposition of the light passing directly through and the light being reflected at the parallel glass surfaces. This effect cannot be avoided and is very much dependent on the angle of incidence of the light as well as the viewing angle.

### Condensation on inner panes

If the temperature of a surface is lower than the dew point temperature of the adjacent air, the dew condenses. This often happens when moist, warm internal air meets the cold surfaces of external wall components. The surface temperature of a pane is mainly dependent on the insulating efficiency of the glazing. With good thermal insulation the outer pane is very cold, the inner one hot – they take on the temperatures of their surroundings.

However, there are other conditions which are decisive, e.g. air circulation adjacent the pane and its edges. Projecting glazing bars, recesses or curtains can interrupt the flow of air locally and change the air circulation adjacent to the pane. If these framework conditions deviate briefly from the theoretical assumptions, condensation can temporarily appear on the inner panes of insulating glass units; this disappears, however, once the framework conditions have stabilized again.

### Condensation on outer panes

The good thermal insulation values of insulating glass also lead to large differences in the surface temperatures of the outer and inner panes when the internal and external temperatures differ. Temperature differences between objects always give rise to heat radiation. With a clear sky, the outer pane radiates energy into space, the temperature of which is extremely low (approx. -273 °C). Therefore, the pane cools down. If the relative humidity is high, then the temperature of the external air can drop below the dew point. This gives rise to condensation on the outer pane – a sign of good thermal insulation against outside influences. If a window is opened inwards when the outside temperature is low, condensation immediately appears on the outer surface of the insulating glass when the moisture content of the internal air is high and the outer pane is cold. Many other building

materials soak up such moisture and it is no longer visible, but with glass, condensation remains on the surface.

### Wettability

Moist glass surfaces – due to precipitation (outer surfaces in the case of insulating glass), rain or cleaning operations – can exhibit differing degrees of wettability across the surface. Wettability is the adherence of drops or films of moisture to the panes. With dry surfaces, e.g. as a result of roller pressure, this effect is not noticeable. This does not represent a change to the properties of the glass.

## Advice on glazing

A pane or a glass element is in principle one component in the whole construction. Therefore, the forces that act on the glass must always be acknowledged. This is especially important when the thickness and type of panes are to be optimized. For instance, a pane designed as having simple supports may not be installed with restrained supports since this gives rise to a stress distribution in the glass different from the one assumed during design, and this can lead to fracture. It is important to maintain all the framework conditions on which the analysis was based throughout the whole life of the glass. Besides structural considerations, the imperviousness of the whole construction and the lifetimes of the products must also be taken into account. Silicone sealant cannot on its own rectify mistakes in design and workmanship; it can at best only conceal them briefly.

### Protection for glass

Panes of glass must be protected from moisture stemming from wet concrete and plaster during the construction phase because although relatively tough, glass surfaces are not totally immune to damage. Alkaline solutions attacking the surface initiate a breakdown in the molecular structure of the glass. As the pH-value increases, so does the solubility of the glass. If alkaline solutions on the pane are dried out quickly by sunshine and the reaction products are not dissipated, subsequent moisture causes even more damage to the glass. The consequence is visible corrosion. This effect can also occur if stacks of glass panes are stored without protection on the building site for long periods. Capillary action causes condensation to infiltrate deep between the panes; this water then reacts with the glass. The reaction products are not dispersed and subsequent moisture exacerbates the damage. Stacks of panes should therefore not be stored for long periods without a

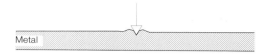
Permanent deformation in metal following a point load.

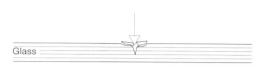
Splinters are ejected from the glass – a sign of its brittleness.

2.1.58   The mechanical properties of metal and glass

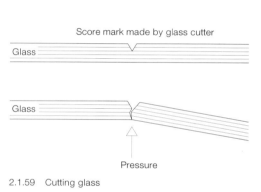
2.1.59   Cutting glass

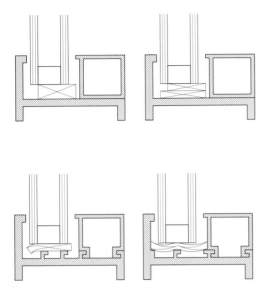

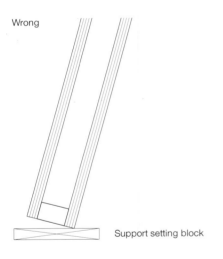

2.1.60  Incorrect positioning
of setting blocks

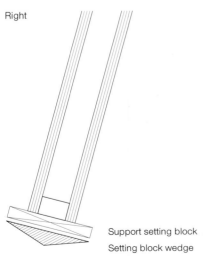

Wrong

Support setting block

Right

Support setting block

Setting block wedge

2.1.61  Right and wrong way of using setting blocks

good circulation of air.

Similar phenomena occur over time when the glass is in use, although the reaction products are washed away by rain or cleaning operations. Recessed window arrangements or flashings over the glazing can provide solutions for concrete or rendered façades.

Transport frames are seldom suitable for long-term storage over weeks or months. Therefore, in the open air, sometimes indoors too, the panes must be protected against the effects of moisture. However, airtight packaging too can lead to the build-up of condensation in the case of temperature fluctuations, and as the moisture cannot evaporate this will damage the glass. Transport frames or packagings are usually unsuitable for long-term storage, particularly outside.

**Setting blocks**

Setting blocks for glazing have to fix the position of the panes within their frames in such a way that the loads, e.g. self-weight, are carried via the anchorages or nodes of fixed frames or via leaf suspension points (four-hinge frames). Contact between metal and glass must be ruled out. The edge of the glass in the rebate must not touch the heads of any screws or other parts of the construction. The depth of the actual rebate must be defined. For normal float glass or insulating glazing made from float glass, the setting blocks must be positioned at least 20 mm from the corners and should be min. 80 – 100 mm long. The whole thickness of the pane must rest on the setting blocks; in practice the blocks are about 2 mm wider than the thickness of the glass unit. Impregnated hardwood or plastic setting blocks are favoured. The resistance of the blocks to the long-term compressive load as well as their compatibility with the other materials used must be verified.

Heavy units (> 100 kg) should be placed on setting blocks made of polyamide, chloroprenes, EPDM, polyethylene (no PVC) or silicone with a Shore A hardness of approx. 75 in order to reduce the pressure on the edges of the individual panes, e.g. in the case of laminated safety glass units on hard materials. In doing so it must be guaranteed that leaf and frame cannot distort or twist during use and that the leaf can be operated. This applies just as much to tilt-and-turn windows as it does to horizontal/vertical sliding windows. Furthermore, a normal-sized pane in a frame should not take on any loadbearing function for which it was not designed.

To work properly, the setting blocks must have a flat bearing. If the shape of the rebate does not allow this, then bridge setting blocks must be used which do not hin-

der the vapour-pressure equalization (Figs 2.1.60 and 2.1.61).

If setting blocks are omitted from the construction, permanent and verifiable substitutes must be found.

**Bearings for glass**

The choice of edge bearing for the glass is determined by the use. In vertical installations standard edge tapes can be laid between glass and frame as a prelude to the sealant. Some special glazing systems require elastic materials. For sloping installations bearings must be selected which are resilient enough to accommodate the long-term dead load of the glass and snow. These materials must have closed pores so that they do not absorb the moisture that can lead to damage over the long term. When selecting bearings it should not be forgotten that the whole construction must remain sealed. The contact pressure and the material must always be matched to the particular application. Here too, it is important to consider all physical aspects and not just isolated factors.

The bearing conditions of the different types of glass must also be taken into account, such as the constraints arising out of the particular application. For example, with insulating glass, limiting the deflection of the edge seal under load to l/300 of the glass edge so that with increasing deflections the edge seal is not subjected to too much shear, which can soon lead to leaks along the edge. The principal requirements for individual applications are explained on pp. 94–95.

**Vapour-pressure equalization, drainage**

Apart from float glass, the edges of the panes require a rebate with vapour-pressure equalization to the outside, i.e. an open rebate. This ensures that the vapour pressure does not rise too high and condense, and also that any moisture entering from the outside can be drained away and so does not attack and damage chemically the edge seal system of, for example, insulating glass, laminated (safety) glass or wired glass. As a 100% moisture seal along the entire rebate and its joints is not possible in practice, and as leakage water from outside can infiltrate, vapour-pressure equalization and the drainage of the open rebate are imperative.

In all types of construction, but especially sloping glazing, it should be ensured that the sealing level lies above the water run-off layer. Seals subjected to long-term water pressure may develop leaks.

### Butt joints

The general requirement for vapour-pressure equalization and drainage (see above) also applies to horizontal or vertical butt joints as well as frameless corner details. Therefore, butt joints in, for example, insulating glass, laminated (safety) glass and wired glass must be designed in such a way that permanent vapour-pressure equalization is guaranteed in order to allow moisture to escape from the rebate or cavity. Trying to fill the cavity completely with sealant always leads to defects in practice which then act as water traps and destroy the edge. (See "Joints at an unsupported edge", p. 161.)

### Eaves details for sloping glazing

To avoid thermal stresses and condensation, the edge zone of an insulating glass unit should be located internally and have contact with the air of the room (Fig. 2.1.62). The outer pane of the insulating glass unit may project beyond the actual edge seal. The projection should exceed 200 mm and the cantilevering pane should be made from thermally toughened safety glass. The edge seal must then be protected against solar radiation, in particular UV light, or the edge seal employed must be one suitable for use with structural sealant glazing.

### Cleaning and maintenance

Seen under the microscope, the surface of a glass pane is rough. Dirt and moisture which becomes trapped must be removed at regular intervals. Sloping panes require more frequent cleaning than vertical ones. The panes must be cleaned with liberal amounts of water to ensure that dust and dirt are not scraped dry across the glass and so damage it. Panes must be well wetted to loosen the particles of dirt. A broad, sharp blade should only be used very sparingly to remove stubborn patches of dirt from the surface. Scraping large areas is to be avoided at all costs as this can lead to projecting glass particles being torn out from the (microscopically) rough surface and carried along with the blade. As the blade is pulled back, these sharp, hard particles are rubbed across the surface leaving thin, parallel, shallow hairline scratches which are visible in direct light. In severe cases these can even impair the view through the glass. During cleaning, care must be taken to ensure that the wet cloth used does not push dry particles of dust and sand ahead of it and thus cause scratches. Wetting the glass well beforehand is therefore vital. The first cleaning on the building site must be carried out especially carefully to ensure that hardened splashes of plaster or concrete do not lead to scratches.

If damage occurs, the effect of the scratches should be assessed from a distance of 1 – 2 m, always looking from the inside to the outside under diffuse lighting conditions. Direct lighting and spotlights could reveal further optical defects and impairments which prevent the actual assessment of the scratches. The same applies to internal glazing.

Aggressive cleaning agents are often used for cleaning the frames. If these run onto the pane and are allowed to dry there, subsequent rainfall can reactivate the constituents which then attack the glass. Horizontal glass is more readily soiled than sloping or vertical glazing. In such cases standing water can cause leaching (Fig. 2.1.63). This chemical-physical effect must be taken into account when planning horizontal arrangements. The cleaning agents used must not attack seals and joints.

### Influence on functional data

All functional data is determined according to the stipulated dimensions given in the standards and subject to the defined ambient conditions, corresponding to the specified constructions. These values are used as the basis for product descriptions and so can be compared with the data of other building materials during the design procedure.

In practice the ambient conditions and dimensions differ from those in the standards. This leads to minor changes compared to the theoretical values. For example, the "pumping" action of insulating glass has an influence on the functional data, albeit temporary. These general observations apply to many building materials, not just glass. But these influences are, under certain circumstances, more readily noticeable in glass than they are in other, less complex, less versatile materials. "Super-accurate calculations" must be warned against. Many parameters help to consider the different influencing variables as a whole and to carry out case studies. Nevertheless, practical situations can deviate from these results – a fact which often only reveals itself much later.

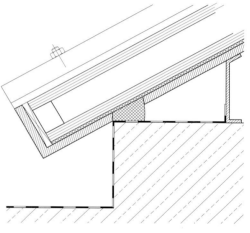

2.1.62  Incorrect eaves detail

Alkaline solution

Film of water on glass surface

Alkali as a reaction product in solution

Alkali diffusing out of glass surface into water (leaching)

Alkali as a reaction product in solution

Alkali reaction particles on the glass surface after drying

Sketch of glass cross-section reduced (corroded) by alkalines

2.1.63  Reactions caused by alkalines attacking glass

# Designing with glass – strength and loadbearing behaviour

Werner Sobek and Mathias Kutterer

2.2.1 The origin of a crack (microscopic fracture and fracture mirror) on a polished glass edge, 20x magnification.

2.2.2 Griffith flaws on a glass surface. Such cracks, which can be verified by way of sodium vapour-deposition, can be caused by, for example, abrasion of the surface

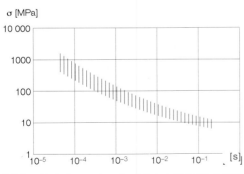

Relationship between strength of glass and depth of crack

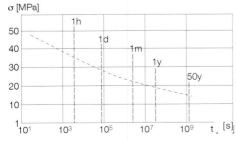

Relationship between strength of glass and duration of load

2.2.3 Reduction in the strength of glass

## Building with glass

### Designing with glass

The use of glass as a building material has grown in popularity in recent years. The reasons for this can be primarily found in developments in glass technology, which have led to higher mechanical strengths, an increase in the processing options and, crucially, considerable improvements to the properties relevant to building science, while at the same time maintaining the transparency. Hence, for the first time it is possible to utilize a high-quality and transparent building envelope material as a loadbearing element.

Designing with glass demands a detailed knowledge of the mechanical properties of this strong but, unfortunately, brittle material. As it behaves almost totally elastically and exhibits no reserves of plasticity, the maximum stress that a certain glass can accommodate is determined by local stress peaks which arise at flaws, chipped edges or at the tip of a crack. So the "strength" of glass only has limited applicability in terms of a material parameter. More importantly, the usable strength, the maximum stress, should be understood as a statistical variable dependent on the degree of inherent damage and hence, of course, the size of the element.

Recognition of this fact has led to the development of – in the construction industry – hitherto unknown methods for designing elements made from glass; and on the other hand to the drawing-up and observance of a whole series of design principles.

### Enclosing or loadbearing function?

As in other industries, e.g. automotive, tank fabrication and apparatus engineering, glass is employed in the construction industry in most cases as a transparent or merely translucent component, separating an interior space, defined in climatic, acoustic or other terms, from an exterior space. Here, the glazing forms a filtering function between the two volumes, permitting, blocking or reflecting certain physical flows. The glazing to the outer wall of a building protects against moisture and reduces both thermal flows as well as sound transmissions, but, for example, allows the passage of visible light.

Until a few years ago, glass was in most instances only accorded lowly, so-called tertiary, tasks in terms of structural functions. This was due, on the one hand, to the fact that glass as an engineering material had been virtually ignored for many years and as a result very little was known about its behaviour as a material; this lack of knowledge meant that its safe use as a primary or secondary element was simply out of the question. On the other hand, glass was classed as "too fragile" to undertake loadbearing functions. It was only with the increasing use of ever larger panes, combined with a constant expansion in the range of applications, right up to glass able to carry unrestricted foot traffic, that it became necessary to start detailed research into glass as a loadbearing material. At the same time it became necessary to analyse in what way glass, with its singular structural behaviour, could be exploited as a structural element or part of a structural system. We have come a very long way, although by no means all the relationships have been adequately researched.

## The material

### Microstructure and fracture behaviour

Owing to its strong atomic bonding forces, glass with an intact microstructure and perfectly smooth surface possesses a very high mechanical strength.

However, damage to the microstructure within the body of the glass and vents and scratches on the surface give rise to Griffith flaws (Fig. 2.2.1) with extremely high stress peaks upon applying mechanical loads to the element. In comparison to many other materials, these stresses cannot be dissipated by means of plastic deformation. As surface flaws can never be avoided at edges or around drilled holes, only a fraction of the real material strength can be exploited in a building component (Fig. 2.2.2).

Upon exceeding a "critical (tensile) stress", the crack begins to grow at the tip of a notch or crater. In some circumstances this growth only takes place in small steps, coming to a halt in between. In fracture mechanics this slow or "stable" crack growth is regarded as subcritical, and is primarily determined by the duration of the load. Short-term loads lead to higher allowable stresses than long-term loads. The subcritical crack growth is influenced by chemical reactions at the tip of the crack; for example, a high ambient humidity accelerates cracking, but other "crack-healing" effects have also been observed.

Once the critical crack growth velocity has been exceeded, a crack becomes "unstable", i.e. the widening process accelerates rapidly. This then leads to sudden failure of the glass element.

As the subcritical crack growth increases with long-term mechanical loads and as a result of chemical reactions taking place near the tip of the crack, it is necessary to substantially reduce the actual maximum stress of a component which has been in use for many years to a value well below that determined in short-term tests (Fig. 2.2.3).

References: Hlaváč 1983, Kerkhof 1991, Mecholsky 1974, Rawson 1980, Scholze 1988

**Surface structure**

Owing to the many different loads that can occur in construction, a glass element can be expected to suffer damage from a variety of mechanical sources, e.g. scratches, cleaning, wind erosion, during its long life (Fig. 2.2.4). Furthermore, mechanical or chemical treatments, e.g. cutting, grinding, sand-blasting, acid etching, coating or printing, affect the surface structure and hence the strength. More severe inherent damage is caused at edges and especially the sides of drilled holes; such damage cannot be rectified by subsequent polishing because the deep cracks responsible for failure, the ones where fracture of the pane originates, are not fully reached by the polishing operations.

The usable strength could be improved upon by giving a very carefully produced and processed glass element a surrounding protective layer, turning the element into a composite. The outer layers of the composite element would then act as wearing layers. Employing this concept, the inner glass surfaces of laminated safety or insulating glasses could, under certain conditions, be allocated higher maximum stresses than unprotected glasses. However, such a method must also take into account the fact that it is frequently the strength of the glass edges that is critical for the design. Regrettably, this aspect has not yet been explicitly dealt with in the design codes but instead has been allowed for in design by limiting the deflections.

References: Freimann 1980, Kutterer 1997, Mecholsky 1974

**Strength**

As already explained, the usable strength of a glass building component is not a pure material property but instead a variable dependent on the degree of damage to the surface of the glass (including edges and drilled holes). The probability that a local stress generated by a mechanical load coincides with critical inherent damage (crack depth) can only be allowed for in the design by way of statistical methods. A corresponding design method, based on the fracture probability, has been worked out by Blank and prepared for many practical cases to help users.

The size and distribution of microscopic cracks play key roles here. This is also made very clear by the evaluation of fracture tests. Even glass fresh from the production line exhibits a wide range of strengths, but relatively high on average. Up to the time of installation and throughout the life of the structure, damage to the surface of the glass "accumulates" so that the probability of a critical crack forming in a pane rises. Therefore, glasses with inherent damage have lower average strengths, but also considerably narrower statistical distributions, than those straight from the factory. The same relationship applies to the size of the (test) surfaces under observation: with a glazed area of 1000 m² the probability of one pane failing is 1000 times greater than with a pane of just 1 m².

Although brand-new panes are often used for the experimental determination of the strength of glass, it is, however, very much better to examine panes with inherent damage when assessing the reliability of the strength forecast. If the inherent damage is realistic, i.e. corresponds to the most unfavourable surface damage that can be expected, the tests will produce highly realistic strength figures. The average will then be low and the distribution narrow (Fig. 2.2.4). The reduction in strength of a glass element brought about by increasing surface damage over a long period must be clearly distinguished from the reduction in strength due to subcritical crack growth resulting from permanent loads as described above.

References: Blank 1990, Blank 1993, Richter 1980, Sedlacek 1995

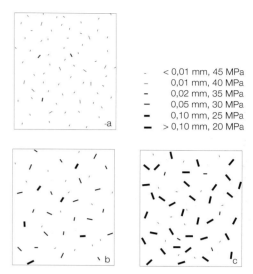

2.2.4 Statistical distribution of glass strength due to surface damage

- < 0,01 mm, 45 MPa
- 0,01 mm, 40 MPa
- 0,02 mm, 35 MPa
- 0,05 mm, 30 MPa
- 0,10 mm, 25 MPa
- > 0,10 mm, 20 MPa

Distribution of surface damage for a) new glass, b) weathered glass, c) glass with inherent damage.

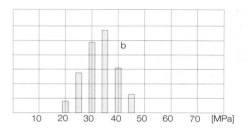

Distribution of strength determined in fracture tests

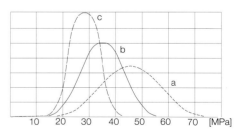

Normal distribution curves for a, b, c

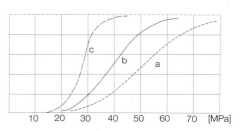

Cumulative frequency curves

2.2.5 Fracture patterns (not to scale) of
a) normal, b) heat-strengthened,
c) toughened safety glass

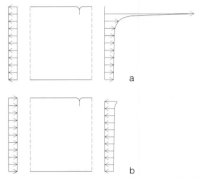

2.2.6 Stress distribution in a glass pane with shell and
vent in the case of a) tensile b) compressive load

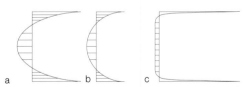

2.2.7 Stress distribution in prestressed glass:
a) toughened safety glass, b) heat-strengthened
glass, c) chemically strengthened glass

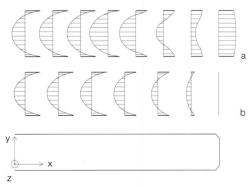

2.2.8 Stress distribution at the edge or the side of a
drilled hole: a) tangential (in z-direction), b) radial
(in x-direction)

## Prestressing

Vents and chips lead – of course only when the surface of the glass is subjected to tension – to the crack propagation mechanisms outlined above. Accordingly, panes subjected purely to compression need to be looked at less critically (Fig. 2.2.6). As soon as a tensile stress occurs at the glass surface, the useful strength or maximum stress of the glass element can only be enhanced by pre-compressing the surface beforehand.

The precompressive force brings about an overcompression of the surface cracks and damage. The upper edges of the cracks remain closed. So, with a precompressed pane, tensile stresses in the component or its surface initially lead to a decrease in the precompressive force. Only after the pre-compressive force has been fully neutralized on the tension face does a tensile stress occur in the glass. Therefore, the usable (tensile) strength of the glass component is increased by precisely the amount of the surface precompression.

With a so-called mechanical prestress the entire cross-section of the glass is overcompressed. This can be accomplished by compressing the pane by means of, for example, ballast (self-weight) or spring mechanisms. With a thermal or chemical prestress a compressive stress is generated on the surface of the pane while a tensile prestress is generated in its core. The tensile and compressive forces induced are in equilibrium (Figs 2.2.7, 2.2.8).

In the case of thermally toughened panes, the glass, already cut to its final size and drilled if required, is first heated to 620 °C and then quenched in blasts of cold air; in doing so the outer surfaces harden immediately but the inner core remains hot. In the course of the subsequent cooling the core tends to contract (like virtually all building materials upon cooling), but is prevented from doing so by the already solidified surfaces: the core wants to contract but cannot do so. The ensuing restraint means that the core assumes a tensile prestress, the surfaces a compressive prestress.

Production techniques lead to certain fluctuations in the level of internal stresses in toughened panes. The distribution is mainly influenced by the quantity, temperature and circulation of the cooling air. The maximum compressive stresses at the surface of the glass are 90 – 120 N/mm² in the case of toughened safety glass and 40 – 75 N/mm² for heat-strengthened glass. The scatter is much greater at the edges of such glasses. The transition from toughened safety glass to heat-strengthened glass, which takes place in the range 75 – 90 N/mm² and is not covered by any products, is characterized by a striking change in the fracture pattern. When broken, toughened safety glass

exhibits considerably smaller dice than heat-strengthened glass. Whether a glass product should be classed as toughened safety or heat-strengthened glass is also determined by counting the number of dice from a fractured pane within a defined area (see 2.1.26, p. 67).

The heat of the thermal prestressing process can lead to some existing microscopic cracks being "repaired" and hence a slight structural improvement and increase in the usable strength – but usually no more than 10 N/mm².

In the case of chemically strengthened glass, compressive stresses of up to 300 N/mm² can be reached at the surface. However, this is only in a very thin boundary layer which is easily penetrated by scratches.

References: Blank 1979 No. 1, Blank 1979 No. 2, Durchholz 1995

## Temperature stresses

The coefficient of thermal expansion of glass is $\alpha_T = 9 \times 10^{-6}$ [1/K] and so markedly lower than that of steel $\alpha_T = 12 \times 10^{-6}$ [1/K]). Rigid connections between glass panes and steel supporting constructions or inflexible glued joints between glass and steel cause internal stresses in the two materials upon a change in temperature. If the temperature rises, tensile stresses build up in the glass. Temperature stresses ensue when both materials are subjected to heating/cooling and also in the case of temperature differences, e.g. as a result of solar radiation warming up the steel components more than the glass. Moreover, temperature stresses in the glass can arise when too much solar radiation is absorbed or unevenly absorbed by the glass. This can happen when, for instance, the glass is printed or partly body-tinted. In addition, temperature stresses can be caused by the shading effects of other components.

The stresses occurring in the joined components brought about by a change in temperature can be estimated as follows:

$$\sigma = (\Delta\alpha \times T + \alpha \times \Delta T)E_1/[1+(E_1 A_1)/(E_2 A_2)]$$

or approximately, remaining on the safe side (for a large steel cross-section):

$$\sigma = (\Delta\alpha \times T + \alpha \times \Delta T)E$$

where

| | | |
|---|---|---|
| $\sigma$ | = | stress |
| $\alpha$ | = | coefficient of thermal expansion |
| T | = | temperature |
| $\Delta$ | = | difference |
| $E_1$, $E_2$ | = | modulus of elasticity of glass/steel |
| $A_1$, $A_2$ | = | cross-sectional area of glass/steel |

With a south elevation registering 50 °C, the difference with respect to an assumed installation temperature of 15 °C is already 35 K. If in addition a local heating of the steel components up to 65 °C also occurs, then the stresses in the glass are as follows:

$$\sigma = (0.000004 \times 35 \text{ K} + 0.000008 \times 15 \text{ K}) \, 70000 = 18 \text{ N/mm}^2$$

So the load induced by such a change in temperature leads to the "permissible stress" of float glass having been reached already.

### Durability

The soda-lime-silica glass customarily used in construction is highly resistant to the usual constituents found in the air. However, it is slightly soluble in water, which, in unfavourable circumstances, e.g. on horizontal panes on which rainwater can collect, may lead to "fogging". In the case of old glass which has been frequently subjected to moisture, slightly shimmering surfaces appear from time to time. This surface corrosion is caused by water infiltrating between the stacked panes by means of capillary action.

With standing water or permanent dampness it is above all the sodium ions that are leached out of the glass microstructure. This process is exacerbated by alkaline surroundings.

### Construction details

Like most building materials, glass elements can only be produced, delivered to site in prefabricated form and installed in situ in limited sizes. On site the glass elements are either individually fixed to a loadbearing construction or they are joined together to form a coherent, self-supporting structure. In doing so, the glass elements must be connected in such a way that the filtering or sealing functions are properly fulfilled. Owing to the transparency of the material, the discontinuity at joints is particularly noticeable; all construction details demand the utmost care.

### Transfer of stress

Fixings for glass and load-carrying connections between glass elements introduce forces into either the edge or the body of the glass. In order to avoid excessive stress peaks, a certain minimum size of stress transfer zone is always essential.

Local stress peaks, which occur as a result of unintentional contact with other components or twisting at the supports, must be avoided at all costs in glass construction. The mechanisms for transferring stresses in glass elements and the associated typical failure modes are explained below.

Reference: Techen 1997

#### Contact

Only compressive forces acting perpendicular to the contact face may be transmitted via contact (Fig. 2.2.9). A precompressed contact face accommodates external tensile forces up to the point of neutralization of the prestress.

The contact faces must be of such a size that the stresses occurring in the zone of stress transfer remain sufficiently low. With hard bearings (glass-steel or glass-glass contact) or when movements and constructional or geometric imperfections have to be absorbed, an intervening elastic pad is necessary.

A contact fixing can only fail if the materials in contact themselves fail as a result of the compressive load or if the contact faces are displaced in relation to each other as a result of vibrations or severe deformation, e.g. if a bent pane slips out of its glazing bead.

#### Friction

Forces in a glass element can be transferred by way of friction, i.e. the mechanical interlocking of the microscopic surface imperfections of both contact faces (Fig. 2.2.10). Besides the mechanical interlock, adhesive forces also occur at the contact face. The relationship between the axial force present and the thrust/shear force which may be transmitted to the glass element by way of friction is roughly linear. As glass cannot be placed directly on steel, the elasticity and fatigue strength of the intervening cushion are crucial to the quality of the friction joint. Intervening buffers may be made from soft metals (pure aluminium, soft-annealed), fibre-reinforced plastics (sealing materials from apparatus engineering) or natural materials processed to a limited extent (cork, leather, cardboard). All these materials must remain permanently within the elastic zone of the stress-strain curve when in use.

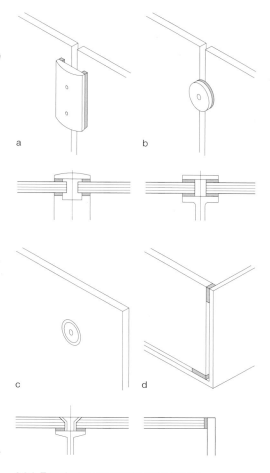

2.2.9 Transferring stresses by direct contact
a) clamping bar, b) clamping plate, c) screw fixing, d) setting blocks and spacer blocks

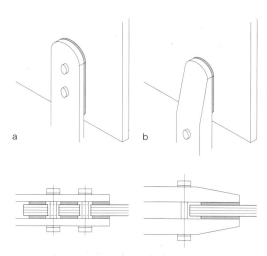

2.2.10 Transferring stresses by friction
a) with drilled hole, b) without drilled hole

Friction joints can fail for various reasons:

- Sliding of the contact faces due to changes in the friction characteristics, e.g. moisture infiltration.
- Sliding due to fading of the clamping forces, e.g. due to creep of the PVB interlayer in a laminated safety glass, creep in other intermediate layers or the occurrence of external tensile forces.
- Thermal expansion leading to glass fracture because the fixings are too rigid. (This problem has not yet been observed with the intervening cushioning materials mentioned above.)
- Glass fracture due to a prestress which is too high for clamping plates that are too soft, too stiff or unfavourably shaped.

*Material bonding*
Forces may also be transmitted by bonding two glass elements together.

This material bonding can be achieved by way of:

- welding (glass to glass), e.g. edge seal of insulating glasses;
- soldering, e.g. metal to glass;
- adhesives, e.g. using the "elastic" adhesives for laminated safety glass, insulating glass and structural sealant glazing, or the quasi-rigid adhesives like UV-curing, non-waterproof acrylic adhesive, or jointing cement.

Forces can be transmitted perpendicular or parallel to the face of the joint on the basis of adhesion or cohesion mechanisms. Welding and soldering have not been used up to now for loadbearing glass elements in buildings. This is because of the almost insurmountable problems which arise as a result of the unevenly distributed temperature stresses in the elements to be joined, both during fabrication and after installation. Adhesive joints for glass elements are widely used in construction. They always have relatively large contact faces and employ elastic adhesives. The forces to be transmitted are usually relatively small and are clearly dependent on temperature and duration of the load. The joint normally fails in a fire. In Germany loadbearing adhesive joints have up to now only been permitted when additional mechanical fixings prevent a pane from becoming completely detached. (One exception is façades up to 8 m high in which wind forces are carried by adhesives but the self-weight of the panes by mechanical fixings, e.g. via direct contact.)
The failure of a bonded joint is usually caused by inadequate preparation of the contact faces or the incompatibility of the materials employed; adhesive joints are par-

ticularly susceptible to both. For glasses which are to be attached to other components with a silicone adhesive, merely touching the glass surface with the hand is enough to reduce the bond of the adhesive. And thermal expansion can overload a joint made with a very stiff adhesive.

**Jointing**
The glazing elements must be joined together at their edges by way of adhesives, sealing gaskets, etc. Jointing means no more than producing a functional linkage, i.e. all the functions that have to be performed by the elements themselves must also be fulfilled at the joints necessitated by the construction. So the best glazing is one whose joints are equally as watertight, airtight and soundproof but at the same time as transparent as the glass itself. However, this is virtually impossible to achieve in practice; joints always represent weak spots, e.g. in terms of imperviousness, thermal transmission or the transfer of forces.

The following principles can be applied to sealed joints:

*Contact seals*
The seal to the glass surface is often accomplished by means of prefabricated sealing profiles made from permanently elastic materials (Fig. 2.2.11). We distinguish between solid profiles and ribbed profiles. The imperviousness of the contact face requires a certain contact pressure between glass and sealing profile as well as smooth glass surfaces. Generally, the sealing profile is shaped in such a way that contact is by way of straight blades and not over the complete face.
Deformations in the glass pane are accommodated by deformations in the blades or by the blades sliding on the surface of the glass. The blades must remain permanently elastic and also possess a certain resilience so that they can follow the deformations of the pane without at any time the sealing effect being impaired. The exact arrangement of the blades depends on the size of the pane and its thickness. Thicker panes have greater thickness tolerances which have to be accommodated by blades designed accordingly.

*Putty*
With the traditional fixing employing putty or jointing cement, the seal is achieved by contact across the complete putty/glass interface (Fig. 2.2.12). The joint is relatively stiff, meaning that in practice fine cracks appear in the putty which lead to absorption of moisture by capillary action. Assembly tolerances and construction inaccuracies

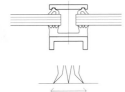

2.2.11 Contact seal: lips slide and deform in order to permit movement.

2.2.12 Putty: only limited movement possible.

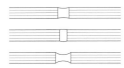

2.2.13 Adhesive joint with permanently elastic putty (silicone): material compresses or stretches in order to permit movement.

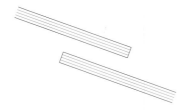

2.2.14 Overlap: unrestricted movement, limited sealing ability.

can be compensated for by filling with putty in situ. Compressive forces can be transmitted via the putty joint.
This type of joint can only accommodate very minor relative deformations.

*Adhesive seals*
Using adhesives across the full length and breadth of the joint creates a sealed connection without the need for external contact pressure (Fig. 2.2.13). The joint is based on adhesion and so also functions under the action of tensile loads. The adhesive can also be called upon to transmit forces.
The resilience of the joint can be controlled by selecting the elasticity of the adhesive and the width of the joint. Movements between the glass elements are taken up by the adhesive stretching along or across the joint. If larger relative deformations are expected, a suitably elastic profile should be glued over the joint.

*Overlaps*
Overlaps, e.g. as with glass shingles or labyrinth seals, can only keep out non-pressurized water or slow down air movements (Fig. 2.2.14). As no contact is required between the elements, even large relative movements can be accommodated. Therefore, this type of seal is ideal as protection against driving rain in flexible structures or as a movement joint between segments of a building.

**Glazing**
*Principles*
In glazing we distinguish between four principal functional components which are interrelated in different ways:

- $V$ = glazing element. The single pane, the insulating glass element, an enclosing element including frame with further integral functions such as shading, sound insulation, provision of privacy, transparent thermal insulation, photovoltaics, etc.
- $T$ = loadbearing structure. The supporting construction to which the glass panes and glazing elements are fixed and to which all loads are transferred.
- $B$ = fixing. Components transmitting the loads.
- $F$ = joint. Components comprising the seal.

The principal possibilities for combining these are:

Combined functions
– e.g. classic clamping bar arrangement
The two function chains are inextricably linked and cannot be installed or dismantled separately (Fig. 2.2.15).

Sealing function chain: V-F-B-F-V
Loadbearing function chain: V-F-B-T

Double function
– e.g. structural sealant glazing
The fixing and sealing components are one and the same, i.e. the silicone fulfils two functions (Fig. 2.2.16).

Sealing function chain: V-FB-T-FB-V
Loadbearing function chain: V-FB-T

Separate functions
– e.g. point fixings
The functions are separate and can be installed or dismantled separately (Fig. 2.2.17).

Sealing function chain: V-F-V
Loadbearing function chain: V-B-T

*Leaded glazing*
Leaded glazing represents the oldest technique for producing larger, coherent panes from smaller, hand-made pieces (Fig. 2.2.18). The individual pieces are inserted into H-section lead cames and tapped into place. The firmness of the glazing is due to the undercuts in the individual pieces as well as the sound bedding in the cames, which is sometimes improved by the subsequent addition of putty.

*Rebate with putty fillet*
Another traditional glazing technique employs glass panes embedded in an open rebate with the help of a putty fillet (Fig. 2.2.19). Here, the rebate is cut directly in the masonry or consists of a rebated timber or a cast/rolled metal frame; plastic or composite frames are also possible.
To install this glazing, the pane is first positioned and fixed; the rebate is then filled with a putty fillet. This method was used for many years for the glazing of simple, unsophisticated workshops and greenhouses; the infilling of small-format, thin panes was cheap and easily repaired. It should be pointed out that putty (like silicone by the way) must not be painted over!
This type of glazing is used for infill panels in which the putty joint holds the glass in place and also acts as a seal. Again and again, but always more or less empirically and intuitively, the glass panes are also called upon to brace the supporting sections.

*Rebate with glazing bead*
The next step in the development following leaded glazing and the rebate with putty fillet is distinguished by an ever greater differentiation between fixing and sealing functions (Fig. 2.2.20). Therefore, a glazing bead was introduced to ensure that the pane was

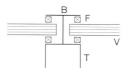

2.2.15 Combined functions with clamping bars.

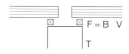

2.2.16 Double function of silicone joint in structural sealant glazing.

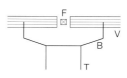

2.2.17 Separate functions with individual fixings.

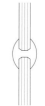

2.2.18 Leaded glazing

2.2.19 Rebate with putty fillet

**93**

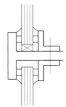

2.2.20 Rebate with glazing bead

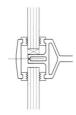

2.2.21 Patent glazing bar with clamping bar

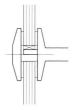

2.2.22 Individual fixings at the edge

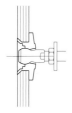

2.2.23 Individual drilled fixings

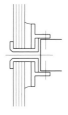

2.2.24 Adhesive fixing (structural sealant glazing)

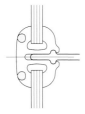

2.2.25 Integral profile

securely fixed to the supporting construction in order to cope with wind suction. This inevitably resulted in a difference between the internal and external sealing planes and hence the appearance of the covered rebate. We distinguish between rebates with and without sealing material. Filled rebates are nowadays only found in single glazing; unfilled rebates are the norm for all other types of glazing. These then always have a channel to allow any water in the rebate (rain, condensation) to drain away in a controlled manner (see "Vapour-pressure equalization, drainage", p. 86).

*Patent glazing bar with press-fit clamping bar*
As glass progressed from the classic window to the modern façade, i.e. from the perforated elevation to the curtain wall, so instead of frames (with glazing beads) let into the brickwork we find special, patented glazing bars mounted on the supporting construction (Fig. 2.2.21). These render possible huge areas of glass. To replace the glazing bead we now have a press-fit clamping bar which grips two adjoining panes.
Glazing with clamping bars generally employs preformed, permanently elastic profiles of silicone, EPDM (= ethylene-propylene-diene rubber) or some other suitable material for both sealing planes. The profiles are pressed against the glass by the clamping bar. Water is prevented from infiltrating by the lips or rows of blades incorporated in the seal design.
Such expanses of glazing make it necessary to differentiate between vertical and horizontal joints and combine them in a common drainage system which is open to the outside air and able to drain externally. In horizontal joints the panes must be supported on inverted bridge setting blocks to maintain the drainage channel. Corresponding junctions have to be fabricated at the corners and intersections.
Further differences occur with insulating glass: the clamping bar must be thermally isolated from the glazing bar. Opening lights with their moving parts, hinges and catches usually have to be incorporated in a fixed frame within the glazing system.

*Linear support without clamping bar*
In some horizontal or vertical glazing systems the panes are only supported on two sides. Here, the unsupported edges can be sealed flush with silicone. With laminated safety glass it must be ensured that only PVB-compatible silicone is used or that the PVB interlayer is isolated from the silicone by means of a suitable edge tape. If such a

tape is used, the air gap created by the tape must be drained, otherwise moisture can accumulate which may lead to "fogging" of the PVB interlayer along the edge and hence to a loss of adhesion between PVB and glass (delamination). Two sealing planes should be incorporated for insulating glass, with the silicone joint being applied to an edge tape on both sides. Again, the air gap created by the tape must be drained. In some types of construction the panes are continuously supported along all four sides but held down (against wind suction) at certain points by clamping bars or clamping plates, i.e. two structural systems are used, one for wind suction or other upward loads, another for wind pressure, self-weight or snow.

*Individual supports at the edge*
The system consisting of loadbearing profile and screwed clamping bar can be combined with unsupported edges and modified so that, in the extreme case, the glass pane is only supported and held at points along the edge (Fig. 2.2.22). This concept results in separate edge fixings with narrow bearing brackets for the setting blocks to take the in-plane forces and a clamping plate arrangement for the out-of-plane forces. No forces are transferred via the unsupported edges, but these edges must be sealed.

*Individual drilled fixings*
This involves fastening the glass panes by way of inserting bolts or screws in holes drilled through the glass itself (Fig. 2.2.23). The loadbearing function (fixing) is distinct from the sealing function in this case. The individual fixing is carried out in the plane of the glass, the sealing function on the unsupported edge. This intentional separation of the functions enables both to be substantially optimized and hence introduces even greater design freedom. Of course, the quality of the seal at the fixings must be equal to that along the unsupported edge.

*Adhesive fixing (structural sealant glazing)*
The fixing of glass panes to the supporting construction or frames by means of adhesive enables the intervening, intrusive clamping bars to be dispensed with (Fig. 2.2.24). The term "structural glazing" or (better still) "structural sealant glazing" refers to the loadbearing function of the adhesive joint. It must be stressed here that the structural glazing joint should only accommodate short-term loads, e.g. wind, earthquakes. The self-weight of the panes in structural glazing systems must be carried by – usually concealed – mechanical fixings.

## Integral profile

The glazing bar, the press-fit clamping bar and their associated sealing arrangements can be replaced by a single peripheral, preformed profile which surrounds the glazing unit and is interlocked with or glued to the supporting construction on site (Fig. 2.2.25). Such integral profiles are normally made from a permanently elastic synthetic material. This type of joint is well established and widely used in the automotive industry for the fixing of windscreens. In the construction industry this method is occasionally employed for façades. Compared to vehicles, the considerably longer periods of usage in buildings mean that good drainage of the profiles must be assured.

## Horizontal or near-horizontal glazing

We speak of horizontal glazing when the slope of the glass surface is so shallow that, owing to the need to drain rainwater, clamping bars can no longer be employed and the self-cleaning effect of draining water is limited. Completely horizontal glazing is only rarely used owing to the corrosive effect of standing water. A minimum pitch of 1 – 2° is recommended so that water can run off in a controlled manner. However, with such a shallow fall, dirt will generally remain in place.

Drainage of covered rebates with insulating glass is no longer guaranteed with slopes less than 10°.

The surface of the glazing should not present any barriers to the water run-off at any point. Cover strips transverse to the direction of flow should be flattened along their upper edges such that no significant build-up of water is possible (horizontal or sloping downwards). If this is not feasible, cover strips transverse to the direction of flow should be omitted. The recommended solution in this case is a pane supported continuously on two sides with cover strips parallel to the flow and silicone adhesive joints transverse. Individual fixings do not obstruct rainwater run-off.

Adequate self-cleaning effects cannot be guaranteed for glazing laid at a pitch less than 10° and subjected to normal weather conditions; dust and dirt, in autumn leaves, remain on the glass surface. With printing or a frosted and light-scattering glass surface, the negative impression of "dirty" panes can be considerably lessened.

The soiling behaviour can be substantially improved by treating the surface with dirt-repelling, hydrophobic or antistatic coatings. Appropriate products are currently undergoing development.

## Insulating glazing

UV resistance of edge seal

In insulating glazing, spacers and glass pane are normally glued together with "Thiokol", intensely impervious to gas diffusion and so also suitable for units with a noble gas filling. Thiokol is, however, not UV-resistant. Therefore, the edge seal must be covered with an opaque medium on the outside. In places where cover strips are not possible or undesirable for structural or aesthetic reasons, the edge seal can be protected against UV radiation by printing or similar.

Silicone edge seals are UV-resistant. They are however gas-permeable, meaning that an insulating glass unit with noble gas filling is not advisable.

## Flush joints

Adhesive silicone joints should be installed on a temporary backing or edge tape. If some of the panes of the insulating glazing are laminated safety glass, then it must be ensured that the silicone chosen is compatible with the PVB interlayer. If this is not possible, then a suitable edge tape is to be incorporated to prevent contact between PVB and silicone. When specifying silicone joints for insulating glazing it is important to remember that both the edge seal and the PVB interlayer (if present) must be protected against being damaged by condensation or rainwater in the joint. This is not easy to achieve in practice! Insulating glazing systems should employ two sealing planes with the silicone joint being applied to edge tapes on both sides. The air gap created by the tape must be drained.

When imperviousness is crucial, an open drainage arrangement below the joint is the best solution and is preferred to adhesive on both sides (Fig. 2.2.26).

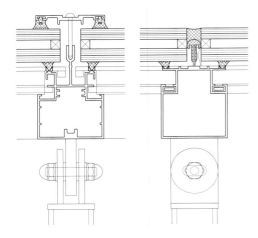

2.2.26 Horizontal glazing, administration building,
St Germain-en-Laye.
Architects: Brunet & Saunier, Paris

## Safety and design

### Determining deformations and stresses

Glass is a material that behaves entirely
elastically at the temperatures typical in
buildings. Although glass is often also
regarded as a supercooled liquid, its viscosity is so high that no flow takes place in
the periods relevant in practical building
terms. Consequently, glass exhibits no
creep and no relaxation.

The mechanical parameters of glass normally used for calculations using the elastic theory are:
- modulus of elasticity $E = 70\,000$ N/mm$^2$
- lateral strain $\nu = 0.23$ (0.22 is sometimes
  used)
- coefficient of thermal expansion
  $\alpha_T = 9 \times 10^{-6}$ [1/K]

As a comparison:

- modulus of elasticity, steel
  $E = 210\,000$ N/mm$^2$
- modulus of elasticity, aluminium
  $E = 70\,000$ N/mm$^2$

The theory of small deflections (first-order
analysis) is frequently used for calculating
the internal forces in a pane of glass subjected to external loads. Based on this theory it is common to determine the stresses
produced by external loads on rectangular
panes supported on two sides; for rectangular panes supported on four sides the
stresses are found from tables or the Bach
equation. Tables are also available for circular and triangular panes. These days, glass
panes are also frequently analysed with the
help of finite-element methods.

The stresses determined according to the
theory of small deflections (first-order analysis) are usually higher for larger panes than
those given by the theory of large deflections because when basing calculations on
the latter theory, membrane effects in the
pane – which usually go hand in hand with
lower bending stresses – are taken into
account. These effects are not considered in
the linear elastic theory and so this leads to
a greater glass thickness.

Owing to the complex bearing and stress
situations at load transfer positions, the
manual calculation of the stress distribution
at these points has become virtually impossible. Therefore, the use of finite-element
methods is both viable and customary in
order to examine force transfer issues but
also to analyse and design complete glass
elements. When applying FEM to glass
design there are a number of rules which
must be strictly observed; in particular,
areas of stress concentrations must be very
carefully modelled. Load transfer can be
simulated only by way of suitably detailed
modelling, and resilient intervening layers,
e.g. setting blocks, must always be included
in the model.
Tables of solutions, which provide at least a
rough idea of the size of the stress concentrations, are already available for a number
of standardized fixings, glass formats and
loads. Glass, like all non-plastic materials,
exhibits permanent stress peaks around
drilled holes equal to 2.5 to 3 times the
underlying stress.

### Design methods

There are various ways of describing the
mechanical behaviour of glass and deriving
a design method from these. The three
methods outlined below are each distinguished by a specific theoretical approach
but are not contradictory and so can be
combined.

*Permissible stress design*
The design is carried out on the basis of
permissible stresses. The advantage of this
approach is its similarity to existing methods
and its simplicity. However, this method
does not do justice to the material's behaviour and therefore in many situations leads
to results which are an inexact representa-
tion of the reality. To account for all probabilities and unknowns, and at the same time
achieve an adequate level of safety, relatively high safety factors are necessary. With
typical types of glass, these safety factors
are to 2.5 to 3 times higher than the characteristic strengths determined in bending
tests.

*Design according to probability of fracture*
This method, mainly based on the work of
Blank, uses fracture mechanics to appraise
and describe the statistical nature of the
usable strength and the influences of load
duration, area under stress and ambient
humidity. Here, the probabilities of fracture
for the glass under load and the duration of
the load are added for every loading case.
This approach correctly takes into account
the unfavourable influence of stresses acting on large areas over long periods of time.

The design method developed by Blank based on this notion has been briefly outlined earlier.

The behaviour of glass is very closely simulated in Blank's method. It is far more accurate than permissible stress design but is unfortunately also more complicated. For standard components, e.g. rectangular panes subjected to wind and snow loads, the method can be prepared in a user-friendly tabular form.

*Limit state design*
The limit state approach makes use of the different statistical distributions on the material side (strength) and the loading side (e.g. wind and snow). Furthermore, this method considers various limit states or modes of failure. In doing so, both the probability of a loading case occurring and the significance of the component for the stability of the structure as a whole, i.e. the effect of the component failing, are taken into account.

Because of its importance for glass construction, limit state design is dealt with in more detail below.

**Limit state design**
The design concepts for steel, timber or reinforced concrete used hitherto in building were all founded on the demand for an unconditional guarantee against failure for the individual member without considering the role of this member within the structure as a whole. The strict requirement of such a design philosophy, designated "safe-life concept" in the aircraft industry, that all members of a structure have a uniform level of safety actually no longer corresponds to the state of the art. Moreover, safe-life concepts for building components where, for example, spontaneous fracture is possible, are not realistic. Owing to the extreme distribution of glass strengths, the possibility of spontaneous fracture with thermally toughened glasses and the fact that accidental destruction of glass elements is comparatively simple, glass falls exactly into that group of building materials/components for which an unconditional safe-life guarantee is not possible. Accordingly, when building with glass, design strategies should be formulated which allow for the failure of individual glass elements; alternatively, the glass element should be designed in such a way that a safe-life guarantee is possible. An unconditional safe-life guarantee is however almost impossible with the means available at present (Fig. 2.2.27).

Design strategies which allow for the failure of individual components were virtually unknown in construction up to now. This made the development of a design concept suitable for glass rather difficult. In contrast,

the aircraft industry, in trying to save weight and hence costs, recognized at a relatively early date that it was necessary to divide components into those requiring an unconditional safe-life guarantee and those which may cause local failure but must not lead to a disproportionate failure of the whole construction (fail-safe concept).

A fail-safe concept requires an examination of the intact structural system but also a systematic analysis of the failure of individual glass elements within a structure in the form of so-called scenarios. Each scenario assumes the failure of one or more glass elements and the goal is to prove that the structure as a whole remains stable without this component, i.e. possesses a "residual stability". As a structure would only be placed in such a (damaged) situation temporarily, greater deformations, or rather a somewhat lower level of safety, can be accepted when analysing the residual stability.

It must always be ensured that a damaged glass element cannot become detached from the structure and, for example, fall out as a complete unit. This requirement applies to overhead glazing and façade elements. In both cases therefore, the individual glass element must itself possess a residual load-bearing capacity. This stipulation leads to, for example, laminated safety glass normally being specified for overhead glazing. The individual panes of laminated safety glass must be designed in such a way that each one can support the weight of the other, broken, pane as well as the external forces to which both are subjected. Greater deformations and a lower level of safety are acceptable in such instances. If both panes of laminated safety glass in an overhead system are broken, it must be proved that the damaged panes cannot become detached from their fixings.

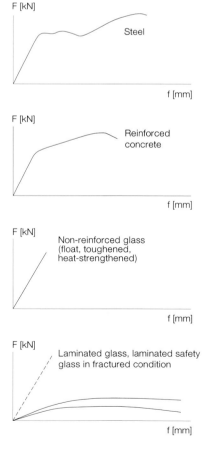

2.2.27 Strain behaviour of building materials in the non-linear zone

The limit state method includes the analyses customarily applied in construction for the serviceability limit state (all structural members intact):

· ability to accommodate all the stresses present in the member,
· limiting the deflections,

as well as analyses of the damaged condition (one or more glass elements broken):

· residual loadbearing capacity of damaged glass element itself, behaviour upon failing,
· residual stability of structure as a whole,
· toleration of large deformations in the damaged component and the structure as a whole.

The flow chart below (Fig. 2.2.28) shows a typical verification scheme for designing structural systems employing glass components.

**Special issues concerning residual loadbearing capacity**
*Residual loadbearing capacity of overhead glazing*
Glazing systems placed at an angle exceeding 10° from the vertical are classed as overhead glazing. As persons underneath such overhead glass units could be serious-

ly injured by falling fragments of glass, overhead glazing in the broken condition is required to be able to carry its own weight and a reduced snow load for a limited amount of time. "Technical rules for ... overhead glazing" stipulates appropriate requirements for continuously supported panes; observing these obviates the need for getting the arrangement approved for each individual project. Panes of glass in overhead glazing systems may only be comprised of laminated safety glass made from normal glass (in future also heat-strengthened glass or combinations of the two) or wired glass. The rules call for panes of laminated safety glass to be supported on all sides for spans > 1.20 m. The lower panes of insulating glass units must also fulfil these requirements; therefore, the upper pane may consist of simple float glass. Overhead glazing employing panes with point fixings is not covered by any codes of practice or building authority regulations and therefore every case must be approved or a general certificate relating to a specific form of construction must be obtained.

*Vertical glazing above circulation zones*
Vertical glazing above circulation zones, e.g. a multistorey façade directly adjacent a footpath, constitutes a similar risk to overhead glazing. However, the loads on the

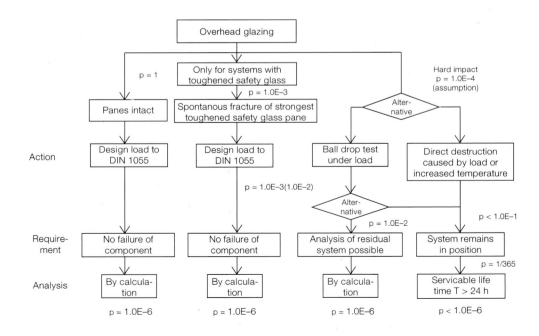

2.2.28  Flow chart for analysing failure scenarios and probabilities in overhead glazing
Reference: Wörner 1998

glass panes are less critical than those on overhead glazing because there is no permanent bending stress present due to self-weight. Therefore, accidental damage is usually the sole reason for spontaneous fracture. Advice and guidelines for the design and the types of glass that can be used are given in "Technical rules for the use of continuously supported vertical glazing" and DIN 18516 "External wall cladding, rear-vented – toughened safety glas". Glazing systems with drilled, glued, curved or stiffening panes are not covered by the regulations cited above; every individual case requires approval.

*Residual loadbearing capacity of safety barriers*
Façades, windows, doors, spandrel panels and partitions act as safety barriers when they separate a circulation zone from a lower level. For a change in height > 1 m between circulation zone and lower level, a precisely defined "safety barrier" function is prescribed for glass panes.
Glass elements acting as safety barriers are subjected to special rules regarding the choice of glass and the conducting of tests for "hard impact" and "soft impact". This is defined in "Requirements for glass in safety barriers".

This document distinguishes between three categories:
- A Safety barrier function provided by the glazing alone
- B Safety barrier function provided by glazing including continuous handrail
- C Safety barrier function provided by separate handrail

Category A requires laminated safety glass for single glazing and the inner pane (the stressed side) of insulating glass.
Categories B and C are satisfied by laminated safety, heat-strengthened or toughened safety glasses. The loadbearing capacity of the glass when subjected to the impact of a soft body or other realistic situation is to be verified by calculation for all three categories. This analysis may be omitted when, for category C, additional knee rails are incorporated.

*Glass surfaces subjected to foot traffic*
A distinction must be made between
- glass surfaces with access restricted to occasional authorized persons wearing suitable, clean footwear where a stated maximum load is not exceeded (all horizontal glass surfaces should be accessible for maintenance purposes),
and
- glass surfaces with generally unrestricted access and so subjected to greater loads

as well as soiling and scratches, e.g. glass floors, stairs, etc.

Means to prevent persons falling through the glass must be provided in both cases. Restricted access, i.e. access for maintenance purposes, must be ensured for all horizontal glazing. In both instances the imposed loads (maintenance only: depends on situation, e.g. 1 kN/m$^2$; unrestricted access: 5 kN/m$^2$) must be able to be safely carried. For the broken condition a residual loadbearing capacity for a limited length of time with reduced level of safety is to be proved.
Glass for unrestricted access should be checked for its slipperyness, in particular when wet or when worn. Therefore, the uppermost pane should always be given a non-slip printed finish or the surface should be roughened.
Elements made from glass for unrestricted access must consist of at least three panes of laminated safety glass. The uppermost pane – with non-slip finish and usually thinner than the others – can be considered to be loadbearing too.

## Structural systems

### Different structural systems
Every component within a building has the ability, and sometimes the task, to carry loads and transfer forces. A light partition carries its own weight and possibly light impact loads, a window pane transfers wind loads to its frame. The core of a building contributes substantially to carrying the wind loads imposed on the structure as well as a proportion of the self-weight. Hence, the sum of all loadbearing and interlinked individual structures forms a highly complex system.

*Hierarchical systems*
To render this complex system more comprehensible and easier to analyse, a complete structure is broken down into a hierarchy of substructures (Fig. 2.2.29, p. 100). The "primary structure" comprises all those parts required to carry all the forces acting on a building including its own weight. Failure of the primary structure is associated with collapse of the entire building. A number of secondary structures are integrated into or attached to the primary structure. Failure of one of these only results in local collapse, the structure as a whole remains stable. Larger or more complex buildings can even include tertiary structures in their hierarchy.

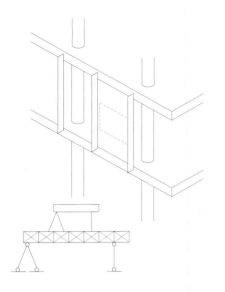

2.2.29  Hierarchical systems: e.g. primary, secondary, tertiary structure

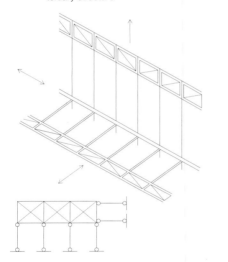

2.2.30  Discrete-work systems: e.g. separation of vertical loadbearing function and bracing

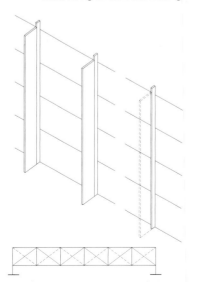

2.2.31  Redundant systems: e.g. glass constructions with residual loadbearing capacity

A typical building hierarchy follows this scheme:

Primary structure
Loadbearing core, all columns, walls, floors and bracing required to carry horizontal and vertical loads.

Secondary structures
Floors which are not part of the primary system; built-in items, partitions, roof structures and annexes; façade elements.

Tertiary structures
All constructions which are part of the secondary structures and whose stability is not critical to the stability of those secondary structures, e.g. a window within a façade element.

*Discrete-work systems*
Structural systems can be designed in such a way that certain members are only called upon to carry certain loads (Fig. 2.2.30). For example, in buildings vertical loads are carried by columns, horizontal loads by walls. In a suspended glass curtain wall with vertical fins the (vertical) self-weight is carried by the panes of glass, the (horizontal) wind loads by the fins.
Structural systems in which individual parts or substructures in each case only perform a clearly defined function are called discrete-work systems.
Such systems are frequently encountered in glass construction because this prevents total collapse following failure of a single component. Although after such a failure the construction can no longer carry all the loads, this is acceptable for a short time, for example, until repairs are effected, possibly in conjunction with restrictions placed on usage during that period.

*Redundant systems*
A system is considered redundant when it contains elements whose functions can be taken over by other elements if they fail (Fig. 2.2.31). So in this case the failure mechanism corresponds to the fail-safe principle, as discussed in detail on p. 97.
It is obvious that the intentional inclusion of redundancies or the deliberate creation of redundancy effects in the design is crucial to structures that incorporate glass elements.

*Other systems*
Generally, if neither a hierarchical nor a discrete-work arrangement of the substructures can be established, optimum design of the members is very awkward. Statically indeterminate structures are a good example of this: the stresses in the individual elements due to the various loading cases and failure modes can only be determined by time-consuming calculations. Furthermore, they are highly susceptible to restraint stresses caused by thermal and deformation loads. Owing to their high stiffness, however, glass elements attract restraint loads, only to suffer subsequent spontaneous fracture as a result. In statically indeterminate structures containing glass elements, therefore, it must be ensured that no restraint stresses can be transferred to the glass and that no unwanted or uncontrollable redundancy arises which leads to the glass elements being overloaded.
One exception to this rule is the delicate iron-and-glass palm houses of the 19th century. Their slender metal primary structures are braced by countless small glass panes. This produces a strong, complex structure with a high degree of static indeterminacy, and impossible to model in the computer. The individual panes of these constructions are embedded in a hard yet still slightly resilient putty and so form a myriad of interconnected load paths. Structures like these glasshouses appear rather foolhardy to us today because a metal rib is stabilized by glass and putty in a way which cannot be appraised in engineering terms. Notwithstanding, this certainly purposeful and, so far, successful form of construction can be justified if we consider the terms redundancy and residual stability. Redundancy is provided because failure of a single pane only results in a structurally insignificant defect in the shell. And the residual stability of such a structural system is immense because, if broken, the small panes adhere to the putty fillet and represent very little risk to persons underneath. However, trying to verify the effects of a chain reaction of fractures, whether by simulation or by experiment, would involve a huge amount of work.

**Loadbearing glass elements**
*Linear elements: bars, rods, columns*
Linear elements are components whose dimensions are small in two directions and large in the other, lengthwise, direction; they are subjected to purely axial loads, e.g. in a girder ties or struts subjected to tension or compression respectively. Compression members in cable-guyed structures are called props, vertical compression members columns; these are subjected to exclusively axial forces when they are connected to the

adjoining components, usually floor slabs, via articulated joints at both ends and when the axis of the member is perfectly straight. If columns are restrained at one or both ends, then the axial forces are combined with bending stresses.

In the case of a tie subjected to tension it is generally the strength of the material that is responsible for the design. In addition, the residual load-carrying capacity in the cracked condition must be examined; struts are mainly at risk of a stability problem.

### Straight glass members with a one-piece cross-section

Strips of float glass can be up to 19 mm thick, in special cases up to 25 mm. So with a maximum slenderness ratio of 1/50, the maximum height of a compression member made from a single sheet of float glass is only approx. 1 m. Therefore, glass tubes or solid, cast glass struts are more suitable as compression members.

### Straight glass members with a composite cross-section

Compared to glass members with a one-piece cross-section, combining individual glass strips or sections allows the creation of very interesting and strong compression members.

Joining individual glass strips to form a composite cross-section is carried out by means of:
- glueing glass to glass,
- glueing glass strips to metal connecting profiles,
- joining the strips via individual fixings.

Composite cross-sections can also be produced by joining standard tubes.

### Straight glass members in conjunction with other materials

Despite the progress in recent years, glass is still limited in its use for ties and struts. This can be attributed to the limited sizes of the semifinished product and the loss of loadbearing capacity upon fracture. Therefore, one alternative is to combine glass with plastic, metal or even timber and thereby overcome the specific disadvantages of a glass-only construction and render possible considerably stronger designs.

Using adhesive to attach the glass strips to metal connecting profiles has already been mentioned above. The concentric prestressing of monolithic glass tubes or those made from bent sheets is another elegant possibility to push back the application frontiers of this material. The concentric prestressing (Fig. 2.2.32) places the entire glass cross-section in compression, with the butt joints between the individual parts being realized

purely via direct contact. An axial tension load can be carried by neutralizing the in-built compressive (pre)stress.

### Slabs

Slabs are flat structures whose dimensions are large in two directions and small in the other, thickness, direction; they are subjected to forces acting perpendicular to the plane of the slab. Slabs thus have the same geometrical form as plates but are distinguished from these by way of the direction of the load action and, as a result, their considerably different loadbearing behaviour, characterized by bending stresses.

### Single-layer slabs

The single-layer slab, i.e. a single pane of float, toughened safety or heat-strengthened glass, represents the most widespread use of glass panes acting as slabs. Every window pane acts as a slab (and not a plate) under the action of wind loads. The pane carries the external (wind) loads via bending and transfers the forces to the continuous supports provided by the window frame. As bending members, however, glass panes are extraordinarily slender: a window pane of float glass, 1 x 1 m, with an average wind load of 0.8 kN/m², is just 6 mm thick – a span/depth ratio of 1:160.

Rectangular slabs supported continuously on all four sides and with a length/width ratio exceeding 1:2 still span in two directions. Beginning at a length/width ratio of about 1:2, the middle of the slab starts to span in one direction, with correspondingly higher stresses in the slab.

Accordingly, with linear supports on four sides, length/width ratios exceeding 1:2 are better from the structural point of view.

If the deflections of a slab supported on four sides become very large, i.e. greater than the thickness of the slab itself, then it starts to act like a membrane. The slab is then no longer subjected purely to bending but instead loads are increasingly carried as axial forces, like a stretched membrane or suspended fabric (Fig. 2.2.33, p. 101).

In this situation a peripheral compression zone forms in the glass pane. At the same time, the deflections increase less vigorously: the slab apparently becomes stiffer as soon as it begins to act like a membrane. For such slabs, calculations based on linear elastic slab theory deliver results which deviate too far – in the wrong direction – from the reality. Hess was the first person to demonstrate this in detail; he showed that using the theory of large deflections led to more slender dimensions and a very economic design, especially for larger, i.e. relatively thin, panes (Hess 1986).

The membrane effect cannot establish itself when there are only supports on two sides

2.2.32 Concentrically prestressed glass tube

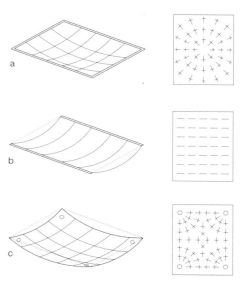

2.2.33 Deformation behaviour and main stress directions of slabs supported on a) four sides, b) two sides, c) four individual points.

unless both sides are held totally rigid, something that should be avoided because of thermal expansion. And as soon as a support permits movement, the slab is subjected exclusively to bending.

A slab supported at individual points will exhibit greater bending and shear stresses as well as greater deformations than one of the same size with linear supports. The large shear forces occur near the individual supports and are critical for the design of the fixings, among other things.

Generally speaking, individual supports lead to thicker glass when compared to linear supports.

Multilayer slabs

Multilayer or laminated slabs consist of single slabs laid loosely on top of each other or bonded together with adhesive across their entire surface (Fig. 2.2.34).

In the case of "multi-leaf" slabs, a cavity is formed by a continuous edge seal; this cavity is filled with a gaseous or liquid intermediate layer.

a) Without bond

If the slabs are laid loosely on top of each other, then each slab carries its share of the total load in proportion to its flexural strength. For instance, two slabs, thicknesses $t_1$ and $t_2$, spanning one way, would split an external load q in the ratio $(t_1/t_2)^3$. The maximum stress (symmetrical arrangement $t_1 = t_2 = t/2$) would then be $\sigma = 1.5$ q $(l/t)^2$ N/mm². Translucent or opalescent glasses are produced in this way (i.e. without bond) with a paper or gauze inlay laid loose between the panes and only the edges glued.

b) With bond

If we join two slabs together, one on top of the other, with a shear-resistant connection, then the loads can no longer be split in proportion to the strengths but instead are carried by a composite unit. The maximum stress would then be $\sigma = 0.75$ q $(l/t)^2$ N/mm², and the deflections reduced by a factor of 4 – an enormous increase in efficiency.

Like with other forms of composite construction (timber, sandwich members in lightweight construction), the mechanical behaviour of glass panes joined with a shear-resistant connection is fully dependent on the shear rigidity and shear strength of the intermediate layer. We meet a contradiction here: maximum rigidity favours the behaviour in bending, while if one or more panes are fractured, then a more viscous intermediate layer is advantageous for holding the fragments together.

We only speak of laminated safety glass when the laminated unit fulfils certain requirements concerning the adhesion and bonding of broken pieces. If this is not the case, then the glass is merely designated as laminated.

The properties of the (usually) transparent intermediate layers can be controlled to a great extent but normally high rigidity is coupled with a decrease in impact resistance and hence the bonding of glass fragments. The material most often used as the interlayer in laminated safety glass is polyvinyl butyral (PVB). As this is a thermoplastic, the loadbearing behaviour of this material, and hence that of the laminated unit, is very much dependent on the duration of the load and the temperature of the component.

The original thinking behind the introduction of laminated safety glass was to create a residual stability after the failure of a single pane. However, the bonding lends the glass an in-built loadbearing capacity as described above. In Germany taking such an effect into account is, in principle, not permitted, but a number of other countries, e.g. Canada, make good use of this scientifically proven fact – leading to more economical design. In particular, overhead glazing consisting of laminated safety glass – mandatory in Germany – would benefit from this effect (or by recognizing a shear transfer between the panes based on duration of load and temperature of component) as the thickness of the glass could be reduced.

c) With edge seal

Two mechanical effects are brought about by the edge seal. First, this creates a sort of flat hollow box, which reacts far more sensitively to deformation of the supporting construction, twist in particular, than a single slab. Second, the ensuing cushion of air acts structurally – an advantage and a disadvantage at the same time.

For example, in insulating glasses it is possible to combine the loadbearing ability by coupling the individual panes via the enclosed air or gas. This is called the catheter effect and is based on the Boyle-Mariotte Law, according to which the product of pressure x volume of the intervening gas remains constant so long as the temperature does not change. The catheter effect is not affected by the speed of the load application and so can be used for a whole series of design issues.

On the other hand, weather-related pressure and temperature fluctuations as well as differences in the geographical altitudes

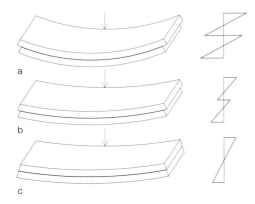

2.2.34 Deflection behaviour and stress distribution in
    a) panes laid loosely on top of each other,
    b) elastically bonded laminated safety glass,
    c) rigidly bonded or monolithic panes.

between factory and site cause consider-able imposed loads in hermetically sealed insulating glasses. The maximum isochore pressure difference can amount to more than 20 kN/m$^2$, although this pressure is reduced by the elasticity of the system. However, these climate loads are decisive when dealing with small panes, large glass thicknesses and large cavities. The situation is worse still with individual fixings because the panes are rigidly connected at these points and are subjected to large restraint stresses.

### Slabs with ribs and stiffeners

Longer spans (in turn limited by the pane sizes able to be manufactured of course) or more efficient constructions can be accomplished by combining flat slabs with ribs or stiffeners. The arrangement of the ribs increases the depth of the component and as the stresses in the slab are influenced by the reciprocal of the square of the depth and the deformations by the reciprocal of the cube of the depth this brings about a drastic reduction in the stresses in the component and its deformations. The type of joint between rib and slab is crucial to the loadbearing behaviour. If forces cannot be transferred across the joint, then we have a slab on beams. Only a continuous transfer of forces across the joint creates the integral loadbearing effect of a ribbed slab. The creation of a continuous force transfer, by way of adhesive, welding or soldering, is, however, relatively difficult.

One very successful variation is the channel shaped glass member in which ribs and slab are produced from one piece of flat glass by hot forming (Fig. 2.2.35).

The advantages of this type of construction

- long, uninterrupted spans,
- simple, additive assembly,
- multi-leaf insulating sections,

are primarily exploited for translucent glazing in industrial buildings. Up to now, transparent channel shaped glass members have not been used very frequently.

### Trussed slabs

In this type of construction the glass pane carries the compressive forces, the truss, provided in one or two axes, the tensile forces (Fig. 2.2.36). The truss is connected to the glass via props or glass webs. If the truss is placed on both sides of the glass pane, loads acting in either direction can be carried. An interesting solution for a one-sided trussed pane has been used by Robert Danz (Fig. 2.2.37 and example

pp. 298–299). Here, panes of laminated safety glass were used in conjunction with a truss of tension rods and compression posts along one axis. Both posts and truss are attached to the glass with individual fixings providing a self-anchored construction. The compressive stresses superimposed on the bending stresses is beneficial for the glass, provided no buckling problems are introduced.

### Supports

As glass panes are flat components, it is advisable to identify the loading effects and so decide whether the supports are effective in the plane of the glass or perpendicular to it (Fig. 2.2.38).

a) In the plane

Loads:
Self-weight is the primary loading in the plane of the glass. A certain proportion of snow or imposed loads can be induced tangentially, i.e. parallel to the surface, via friction.

Supports:
The most effective and simplest fixing is by way of contact at the edges of the panes; more or less elastic bearing strips made from hardwood, EPDM, silicone or similar material. These are the classic setting blocks. Individual fixings also transmit in-plane forces generally via contact with the sides of their holes. Only clamped connections function without edge contact (Fig. 2.2.39).

The statically determinate in-plane support of the pane is achieved, for an edge support, by two relatively stiff bearing strips (setting blocks) at the bottom edge. Lateral displacement is prevented by elastic spacer blocks at the sides (Fig. 2.2.40). The support must be incorporated absolutely free from any restraint because the pane is very stiff in its plane and deformations in the supporting construction cannot be allowed to lead to uncontrollable restraint stresses. The same applies to panes with individual fixings. Three supports are required for a statically determinate arrangement. The lines of action of their reactions should not be parallel and should not intersect at one point (Fig. 2.2.40).

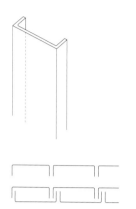
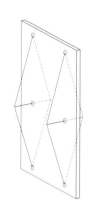

2.2.35 Channel shaped glass members

2.2.36 Pane trussed on both sides

2.2.37 Pane trussed on one side. Glass roof over castle ruins in the Southern Tyrol. Architect: Robert Danz

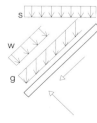

2.2.38 Loads and the directions in which they act, s = snow, w = wind, g = self-weight

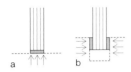

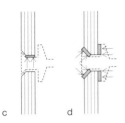

2.2.39 Supports for glass panes
　　a) c) in-plane, b) d) perpendicular
　　Transfer of forces
　　a) c) on edge or b) d) on side of drilled hole

2.2.40 In-plane supports

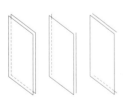

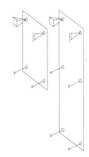

2.2.41 Supports perpendicular to the plane of the glass

b) Perpendicular to the plane

Loads:
Acting perpendicular to the glass we have distributed loads such as wind, snow, imposed loads and, for sloping panes, part of the self-weight as well. All have to be transferred to the supporting construction.

Supports:
The classic means of fixing holds the glass in place by way of a peripheral frame: a chase in the wall, a frame with rebate, a two-part glazing bar. The forces are transmitted via contact with the flanks of the frame. Point fixings, if used, follow exactly the same principle – via a frame encircling the hole. Countersunk fixings are no different (Fig. 2.2.39).
The support is either continuous, along at least two opposite edges of the pane, or, with point fixings, via at least three single supports. Four or more supports are also feasible because the panes are normally so flexible that deformations in the supporting construction perpendicular to the plane of the system can be absorbed by elastic deformations (Fig. 2.2.41).

*Plates*
Plates are understood to be flat structures whose dimensions are large in two directions and small in the other, thickness, direction. Plates are subjected to forces acting in the plane of the element itself. In geometric terms, they are exactly like slabs but are distinguished by the direction of the action of the loads and, consequently, by a considerably different loadbearing behaviour characterized by exclusively axial forces.
A large pane of glass in the form of a plate is relatively rare in buildings. Most of the panes in the internal and external fabric of the building are primarily loaded perpendicular to the glass and hence the slab effects are critical for the design. Larger members in which a pure plate effect is present are restricted to the longitudinal panes relegated to the role of glass beams. Even if a plate effect mainly occurs in conjunction with a slab effect, it is nevertheless important to discuss and understand the plate effect on its own. Plates subjected purely to tension are the easiest group to deal with. The residual stability requirement demands laminated safety glass consisting of at least two single panes in every case. The stress transfer in plates subjected to tension is of course troublesome because apart from adhesives only point fixings or friction-grip connections can be considered. Point fixings always lead to concentrations of stresses in the load transfer zone and hence

to a correspondingly inefficient use of materials. Therefore, friction-grip connections along the edges are particularly advantageous for plates subjected to tension in one or two axes.
Plates subjected to compression in one or two axes are easily supported; the forces are transferred via contact (setting blocks are sufficient for small loads). However, the compressive stresses lead to a stability problem in the plate. The pane sizes which may be used in these cases are severely restricted by this problem.
Of course, in the light of the residual stability required for a single pane, laminated safety glass consisting of at least two single panes should be employed, regardless of the type of support.

*Beams and girders*
In terms of their geometry, beams and, in their more massive form, girders correspond to the linear elements. In contrast to the latter, however, beams and girders are subjected to bending.
We distinguish between longitudinal and transverse bending, depending on the direction of the load, although both forms can of course occur simultaneously. When the load is applied eccentrically, the beam is also subjected to torsion.

Flat glass beams, glass fins
Glass beams are stressed similarly to the plates described above. However, bending about the major axis places most of the stress in the edges. In normal float glass the strength at the edge is generally lower than in the body of the glass. Therefore, toughened glass is usually employed. Although the tensile bending forces can be reduced by increasing the beam depth, at the same time this increases the risk of failure due to lateral buckling.
Very long glass fins must be made from several parts, e.g. connected by friction joints or point fixings. In both instances it is difficult to use laminated glass (Figs 2.2.44, 2.2.45).
A high residual stability can be achieved by initiating a likely redistribution of forces in the whole system, e.g. by combining a façade incorporating glass fins with slender steel sections. The "Façade ville" designed by RFR for the new terminal building at Charles de Gaulle Airport near Paris is held by glass fins 12 m high! Each of these comprises three panes of toughened safety glass each 19 mm thick spliced together with clamping plates. This primary structure is supplemented by an extremely delicate steel post-and-rail construction (Fig. 2.2.43). A fracture in the glass leads to severe deformations in the system but, nevertheless, the

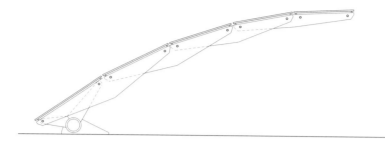

2.2.42 Glass roof cantilevering approx. 9 m,
Tokyo International Forum.
Architect: Rafael Viñoly
Engineers: Dewhurst Macfarlane

self-weight of the system plus an average wind load can still be carried. The external cantilevered edge is subjected to compression under the effects of wind pressure. The problem at this point is merely one of stability not of strength. Therefore, the glass fins are restrained via the horizontal crossbeams (rails), thereby leading to the characteristic wave buckling shape.

**Glass beams with a composite cross-section**
Combining individual monolithic glass sections can produce very effective and strong cross-sections.
Using this idea it is possible to fabricate I-sections or even box sections ideally suited to handling bending stresses (Fig. 2.2.42). Such cross-sections not only allocate considerably more material to the tensile zone but owing to their width and their substantially higher lateral bending strength,

or rather their much greater torsional rigidity, are far less susceptible to stability problems than the one-piece glass beam. Composite glass beams are supported on thrust bearings with contact via a durable elastic intermediate pad, by means of point fixings or friction-grip connections, especially in the webs.

**Glass beams combined with other materials**
If the brittle glass, strong in compression, is complemented by a ductile material with high tensile strength, then the tensile forces present in the beam – in the broken condition in particular – can be safely carried. It is only through this concept that many glass structures are possible at all. The glass essentially carries the compressive forces in the beam's compression zone as well as the tensile and compressive stresses in the webs. Prestressing the glass section

2.2.43 Glass curtain wall and fins with steel sections, Façade ville, terminal building, Charles de Gaulle Airport, Paris. Architects: ADP, Engineers: RFR

2.2.44 External glass fins, EU ministerial building, Brussels. Architects: Murphy/Jahn Engineers: Werner Sobek Ingenieure

2.2.45 Insulating glass façade with loadbearing glass fins, EU ministerial building, Brussels. Architects: Murphy/Jahn Engineers: Werner Sobek Ingenieure

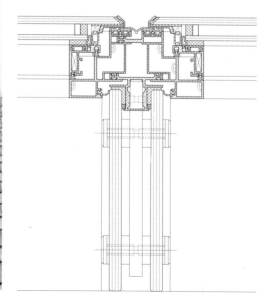

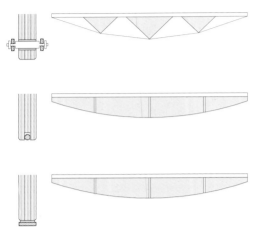

2.2.46  Reinforced glass beams: a) open,
b) tension member in groove,
c) strip-type tension member.

2.2.47  Panes of laminated safety glass, Skywalk,
Hanover. Architects: Schulitz & Partner
Engineers: RFR

2.2.48  Reinforced glass canopy, rue de Belleville, Paris.

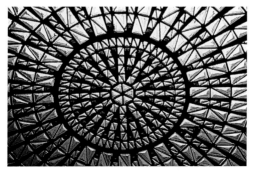

2.2.49  Self-supporting dome of glass bricks,
Champs Elysées, Paris.

enables it to retain loadbearing capacity even when cracked.

Numerous design forms are possible (Fig. 2.2.46). The most significant of these are:

- Open beams consisting of glass triangles connected by way of individual fixings with metal or fibre-reinforced plastic bottom chord.
- Beams made from three-ply laminated safety glass with a curved lower edge and a cable running in a groove.
- Beams with a curved lower edge and a strip of metal or CFRP – seated on an intermediate layer – as the tension member (as developed by the author).

In this third type the glass webs are not bonded to the tension member but simply laid on it. The tensile force is only anchored at the supports. Transferring these forces to the glass beam ("self-anchored beam") or into the support ("support-anchored beam") requires special care. The vertical forces at the supports are normally transmitted into the supporting construction via a thrust bearing (contact via an intermediate pad) prevented from overturning (forked bearing).

### Shells
Shell elements, like the preceding loadbearing glass elements, are primarily subjected to in-plane stresses. We distinguish between glass elements which are in themselves curved and those which are flat but are assembled to form a curved surface (faceted surface).

### Curved glass
Panes bent to form cylinders can in some instances carry much greater loads than flat panes, depending on the loading situation. One system of cylindrical panes on curved edge beams was employed in the glazing designed by RFR for the "Skywalk" at Hanover's Exhibition Grounds – the site of EXPO 2000. By taking account of the loadbearing shell effect, considerable savings were able to be made in the glass thickness. The glazing elements, 2.00 x 2.50 m, consist of laminated safety glass made from two panes of 6 mm float glass. In the tests to establish residual stability, the use of non-prestressed curved glass proved to be extremely advantageous. The loadbearing shell effect still remains fully effective even if the glass is cracked.
Panes bent in two planes are also possible, but only with large bending radii. The loadbearing effect is even more favourable than with panes bent in just one plane because in this case uneven loads can also be carried as axial forces without bending. Heinz Isler

has already postulated the one-piece glass dome. Investigations into the loadbearing capacity of "small domes" with cracks are being carried out at Stuttgart University under the direction of the author.

### Multipart glass shells
Larger shells made from glass elements have a radius of curvature which is very large in relation to the size of the elements. Therefore, these shells can consist of flat, faceted surfaces. The geometrical problem of the faceting is the same as in the lattice shells (see "Lattice shells", p. 109).
In glass-only shells the elements experience relatively high compressive stresses such that only glass bricks or relatively thick panes can be considered.
Domes of cast glass bricks, bonded together with mortar just like brickwork and only lightly reinforced, were common in the past but today have been largely forgotten. "Prism glass" may only be used for constructions in which the glass is not considered to carry compressive forces. Delicate shells like the wavy canopy in the "rue de Belleville" (Fig. 2.2.48) or the dome over an entrance foyer in the "Champs Elysées" (Fig. 2.2.49), both in Paris, are rarities today. Such shells have fallen victim to standardized glazing codes and, in the end, also disappeared from today's construction scene because of their labour-intensive production.
Instead of the full mortar beds, individual fixings can be used to connect the triangular facets, with glued clip-in brackets at the nodes. James Carpenter has also developed a similar solution.
Amazingly, shell constructions comprising thick glass elements are really quite advantageous when it comes to stability in the cracked condition or after suffering serious damage. However, we still have too little experience in this area. Tests on this aspect were first initiated by the authors and Bernhard Sill using an experimental arched girder. The compressive zone of the cable-trussed arch consists of a special three-ply laminate (Fig. 2.2.50).

### Membranes of glass
Membrane constructions made from glass are without doubt highly seductive in both architectural and engineering terms.
Apart from the special case of the flat pane subjected to tension, glass membranes are difficult in practice for the following reasons:

- Glass elements subject exclusively to uni-axial or biaxial tensile forces must always be treated very cautiously owing to the wide distribution of strengths.
- Transferring tensile forces between two

2.2.50 Trussed glass arch, Institute for Lightweight Structures, Stuttgart.

neighbouring panes is currently only feasible with individual fixings or clamping plates. This leads to stress concentrations in the individual panes local to the fixings.

- The residual loadbearing capacity of conventional glass products, e.g. laminated safety glass, is not adequate for high tensile stresses.

**Structural systems for glazing**
In the structural systems discussed below, the glass pane is no longer a primary component but instead integrated in a construction of a higher order. So the glass element only has a local loadbearing function. The actual loadbearing structure is made from steel, aluminium, timber, concrete or, indeed, another glass element. A multitude of different construction systems can be developed on this basis. Typical structural systems are presented in the following, classified depending on the loadbearing behaviour of the primary structure. The reader is referred to the preceding sections for details of the structural behaviour and the residual stability of secondary, or rather, subordinate, glazing elements or loadbearing glass components contributing to the system.

*Structural systems subject to bending*
Most façades and roof glazing systems have a structure consisting of members spanning vertically and/or horizontally and subjected to bending. The beams span from storey to storey, from floor to ceiling, between two wall plates or between two independent building segments – generally between two supports. These two supports are always somewhat resilient or movable. In addition, the beams elongate under the effects of temperature and so, if they are to remain free from the loads imposed by deformations in the supporting construction, they should not be restrained.

Only in rare instances are restrained supports possible for glass elements. In the normal situation, bearings are placed at one end which can move freely in the axis of the beam (Fig. 2.2.51).

*Self-supporting, spanning vertically*
In the simplest case of a short span, glass panes can support themselves across the opening. This is the case with standard storey heights and direct supports on the floors. The glazing units are either supported vertically (on setting blocks) or suspended from their upper edges by means of clamps or point fixings. The suspended variation is more involved but structurally better because it avoids the self-weight of the glass inducing compressive stresses and the ensuing stability problems. Gener-ally speaking, it must be remembered that adjacent floors deflect differently. Therefore, the glass must be provided with a sliding bearing top or bottom, depending on the type of fixing.

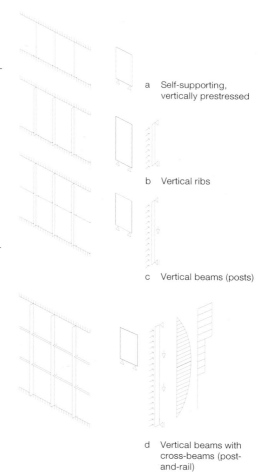

a   Self-supporting, vertically prestressed

b   Vertical ribs

c   Vertical beams (posts)

d   Vertical beams with cross-beams (post-and-rail)

2.2.51   Structural systems subject to bending

2.2.52 Cable trusses with and without compression chord, girder and rolled beam.

2.2.53 Cable truss with compression chord, Parc André Citroën, Paris. Architect: Patrik Berger Engineers: RFR

2.2.54 Horizontal beam

2.2.55 Self-supporting glass curtain wall, Av. Montaigne, Paris. Architects: Epstein, Glaiman, Vidal. Engineers: RFR

### Vertical ribs

Longer spans are backed up by vertical ribs. The ribs only carry loads perpendicular to the plane of the glass (wind). In-plane loads (self-weight and bracing loads) are carried by the glass panes themselves. The panes are now supported on four sides, with the acknowledged structural advantages. Consequently, longer glass formats can be incorporated without horizontal interruptions. Very tall panes are suspended.

### Vertical beams (posts)

If the glass panes are interrupted horizontally (butt joints), then the in-plane loads must also be carried by the vertical beams. So the self-weight of each pane is transferred into the suspended or freestanding beams.

Typical forms of construction for vertical beams are:

- Solid timber or concrete sections
- Hollow or rolled metal sections
- Girders
- Cable trusses spanning between the upper and lower supports (Fig. 2.2.52). Owing to the (normally) large forces which occur, particularly rigid support arrangements are required. Both a (wind) suction cable and a (wind) pressure cable are necessary, although these can be positioned almost at random in relation to each other in the plane of the truss. The suction and pressure cables are linked by perpendicular members which, depending on the configuration, can be loaded exclusively in tension or compression or alternate between the two.
- Cable trusses with integral compression chord. In this self-anchored construction the supports are not loaded by the pretensioning in the cables because this is neutralized by the integral compression chord (Fig. 2.2.53). The cables themselves are held clear of the compression chord by spreaders, which can be thin owing to their short length. Rotation about the truss axis, which could also be interpreted as lateral buckling, is to be prevented by tying into the plane of the glass, which must be designed accordingly, or other measures.

When the beams do not lie in the plane of the glass but instead are positioned in front or behind, as is frequently the case with the cable trusses above all, the self-weight of the glass is usually carried by an additional fixing (hanger). The wind loads are then transmitted from the pane to the beams via members capable of taking tension and compression.

The self-supporting glass curtain wall functions, in structural terms, exactly like the glass wall hung on cables. However, the glass here functions as a primary loadbearing component and must therefore be looked at differently with respect to safety aspects (Fig. 2.2.55).

### Vertical beams with cross-beams (post-and-rail)

Very wide pane formats require the insertion of transoms to support the setting blocks and sealing. This is the classic post-and-rail construction. The transoms lead to a horizontal coupling so that expansion joints need to be provided at larger spacings. The segments of tall façades also require in-plane bracing, particularly if lateral wind forces (acting on external ribs, wind friction etc.) or earthquake loads are expected.

### Horizontal beams

If the horizontal spans are so large that the panes need to be further subdivided, we no longer speak of transoms but instead of horizontal beams (Fig. 2.2.54). These have to carry not only wind loads but their own weight and that of the panes as well, and these beams deflect as a result. This problem of the beams deflecting about their minor axis can be avoided by suspending the beams at one or more points.
Apart from the effects just mentioned, beams spanning horizontally and vertically are otherwise identical. Therefore, all the forms of construction outlined above can also apply to horizontal beams.

### Props

Beams can be omitted from this type of construction. The horizontal forces from the panes are transmitted into other parts of the building, usually the floors, via props capable of taking tension and compression. The loadbearing components are now no longer the usual beams in the plane of the glazing but instead a core deep within the building, shear walls or similar. In this form of construction the self-weight of the panes is either carried by hangers or the panes themselves, suspended from above. Supporting the self-weight of the panes from below is not recommended owing to the associated compressive stresses in the panes.

### Arches

Arched structures are often used for roof glazing, sometimes for façades as well. Here too, the loadbearing elements span between two "banks" but have rigid supports, or abutments, on both sides. Movements in the supporting construction or thermal expansion in the glazing are catered for by the arched structure deforming slightly under load.

## Shell structures

Shells are thin-walled, curved structures which carry their own weight as well as external loads almost exclusively in the form of axial forces in the central axis of the shell. This leads to optimum use of the material. Bending stresses, which should always be avoided owing to their structural inefficiency, always crop up in the area of local force transfers, i.e. also at the supports. In the following discussion, a shell is to be understood as a structural system curved in three dimensions and subjected to compression. The "shells" carrying tensile forces are actually membranes and are dealt with in the next section.

Shells may be bent along a single axis (e.g. cylindrical) or two axes (e.g. spherical). The type and extent of curvature are usually described by specifying the Gaussian curvature $k = 1/(R_1 \times R_2)$ (where $R_1$ and $R_2$ are the main radii of curvature).

## Lattice shells

A lattice shell can be regarded as a shell with an acceptably high number of large openings but where the characteristic shell loadbearing behaviour is not impaired. If a lattice shell is fabricated from separate straight pieces, then it must be feasible to establish the shell loadbearing behaviour through the type of mesh and type of node joints. This normally leads to square-mesh systems with one diagonal brace in every bay capable of taking tension and compression, or X-bracing for tension only. If diagonal members are undesirable, then the nodes must be designed to resist bending. This leads to a more elaborate construction but at the same time a structure which is less effective then those with diagonal bracing. Such forms are thus more popular for shorter spans.

In recent decades a number of glazed domes have been built as frames with rigid joints, i.e. as shells without diagonal bracing. Most of these employed steel for the supporting construction. The glass retainers were made from aluminium, resulting in the "double-decker" form typical of these designs. Of course, this double-decker arrangement has the advantage that the aluminium sections can be manufactured to tighter tolerances than those usual for conventional steel fabrications. High-precision glass construction is thus possible on low-precision steelwork. But everything has its

price: in this case the ensuing structure is distinctly more massive in appearance.
It was not until the 1980s that the building industry believed itself capable of fabricating and erecting loadbearing steelwork with the accuracy necessary to carry the glazing directly via a plastic joint (Fig. 2.2.56). Jörg Schlaich in particular has pushed back the boundaries of glass construction. His net domes – lattice shells with articulated nodes and X-bracing made from thin cables – can be manufactured with such high precision that the glazing can be laid directly on the steelwork with just an EPDM bearing for the glass. The high degree of standardization (all the straight members are identical) and the simple erection led to inexpensive solutions for constructions with complex geometry. Slender straight members and thin cables became possible, and glazing bars, customary at that time, could also be omitted, leading to uncommonly delicate constructions.

Cylindrical lattice shells curved about one axis or those over long spans suffer from stability problems (buckling) which cannot be solved without additional measures. Cable-trussing or guying is one possible solution. As long ago as the first half of the 20th century Vladimir Šuchov was able to adequately brace unbelievably slender ring beams to glazed barrel-vault shells by means of cable guys (Fig. 2.2.58). In roofing-over an inner court in Hamburg, Jörg Schlaich was able to increase the loadbearing capacity of a barrel-vault shell in a similar fashion by using an arrangement of prestressed cable "spokes" (Fig. 2.2.59). Trussed or guyed configurations for shells curved about two axes are of course also possible.

Designs employing rotational or translational areas made from square facets are common. Even free geometrical surfaces can sometimes be described with square facets, although these are only computerized models at present. Otherwise, triangular facets must be used.

Very elegant architectural solutions – also without diagonal bracing – are feasible, especially for lattice shells with shorter spans, provided the nodes are designed as sufficiently rigid. The dome over the banking hall of a bank in Hanover is a good example (Fig. 2.2.60). The author designed this lattice shell in which all the components are made from spheroidal graphite iron and are joined merely by screwing together nodes and members – and erected without scaffolding. The insulating glass was laid directly on the iron with only an EPDM pad between. Retaining plates on the outside secure the panes against wind uplift.

Reference: Schlaich 1992

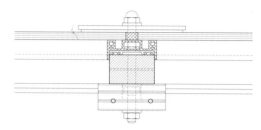

2.2.56 Glazing placed directly on the loadbearing construction, see pp. 316-319.

2.2.57 Glazed roof, Westfalenpark, Dortmund. Architects: LTK. Design and roof construction: Werner Sobek Ingenieure

2.2.58 Cable-guyed arch, Machinery Hall, All-Russia Exhibition, 1896, Vladimir Šuchov

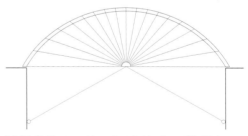

2.2.59 Cable-guyed barrel vault, Hamburg City History Museum, Hamburg. Architects: von Gerkan Marg & Partner Engineers: Schlaich, Bergermann & Partner

2.2.60 Dome over banking hall, Deutsche Bank, Hanover. Architects: LTK. Design and dome construction: Werner Sobek Ingenieure

*Membranes and nets*

Membranes are thin-walled structures normally curved in three dimensions which can support their own weight as well as external loads only by way of tensile stresses in the material. These tension-only structures are extremely efficient because all the extra mass required to deal with stability issues is no longer necessary. On the other hand, owing to their load-carrying behaviour, membranes cannot take on any arbitrarily curved shape. The membrane must always exhibit an equilibrium surface suitable for exclusively tensile forces. Therefore, the geometry of such membranes is developed with the help of special design aids, so-called shaping processes.

Nets can be considered as a special type of membrane. The material is no longer a thin-walled continuum but instead a net consisting of separate (discrete) elements – subject exclusively to tension as before. Nets vary considerably in their loadbearing behaviour, depending on the mesh configuration. The triangular mesh is the arrangement with a behaviour most similar to the thin-walled membrane continuum.

Glazed nets

In this form of construction a net made from (usually) steel cables takes on the primary loadbearing function. The glazing to the net could be called upon to stiffen the network but no-one has as yet made use of this feature in practice. The glass normally only has to fulfil the function of a covering and enclosing material.

Fabrication and erection requirements have led to virtually all cable nets being regular square meshes. Three-dimensional curvature and prestressing turns the squares of the mesh into rhomboids – with every rhomboid shape slightly different. If the mesh is to be fitted with glass panes, then each pane has to be different too. This is possible with modern computer-controlled production but on site would lead to an organizational problem par excellence!

The designs employed up to now have overcome or eased this problem as follows:

• Large panes, each of which covers a group of apertures in the mesh.

The advantage of this type of construction lies in the fact there are comparatively few individual panes with a special geometry which have to be cut to size and installed. On the other hand, the flat panes mean that this principle is limited to relatively large-radius nets. Furthermore, it must be ensured that the covering panes are fixed to the net in such a way that the net deformations caused by external loads do not lead to stresses in the glass. Consequently, floating mounts are required for the glazing; this can be achieved by using point fixings with, for example, appropriate intermediate pieces made from an elastomer. The best-known example of the use of large (albeit PMMA) panes are the roofs to the Munich Olympics structures built in 1972.

• Rotationally symmetric nets to reduce the number of different panes.

One example of this solution is the cable-net pavilion in the garden of the Diplomatic Club in Riyadh. This design by Bettina and Frei Otto used hand-painted glass panes as the covering.

2.2.61 A cable net glazed with glass shingles, hospital, Bad Neustadt.
Architects: Lamm, Weber, Donath
Engineers: Werner Sobek Ingenieure

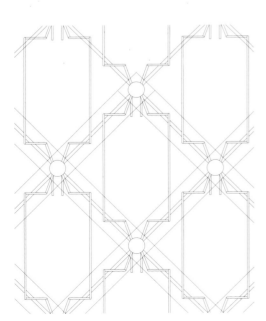

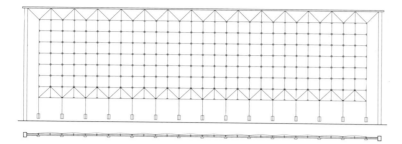

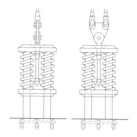

2.2.62 Cable-lattice façade prestressed with springs, **Hotel Esplanade**, Berlin.
Architects: Murphy/Jahn, Engineers: Werner Sobek Ingenieure

• Divorcing the pane geometry from the mesh geometry by introducing a shingling concept.

The principle was developed in 1996 by the author in collaboration with Viktor Wilhelm, and first employed for the cable nets with glass shingles over the inner courts of the Rhönklinik in Bad Neustadt (Fig. 2.2.61 and pp. 313–315). The cable nets have a mesh size of 400 mm but the geometry of each aperture differs owing to the three-dimensional curvature of the surface. They were covered with 22 000 square laminated-safety-glass shingles with edge lengths of 450 or 500 mm – all of which have the same geometry. They are clamped in stainless steel stirrups which in turn are attached to the nodes of the cable net. The shingles are installed one element at a time. The differences between the shingle geometry and the rhomboids of the mesh (every one unique) is compensated for by adjusting each stirrup at one of its fixing points on the net. While the upper fixing is rigidly clamped to a node, the lower fixing is provided with two stirrup ends approx. 150 mm long which must be threaded into the lower node. This allows the stirrups to span over different

length diagonals in the mesh.
Either individual fixings or clamping straps have been used up to now in order to attach the panes to the nets. Both should always be connected to the nodes of the mesh and not to additional fixing points on the cables. This achieves not only a better transfer of forces into the net but also a comprehensible form of construction normally associated with cost-savings.

Glazed cable or cable-lattice façades
These are variations on the glazed net. They are flat structural systems whose ability to carry loads perpendicular to the plane of the structure itself is only achieved by tolerating comparatively large deformations and correspondingly large forces in the cables. In order to control the deformation behaviour of these systems, the cables are prestressed accordingly. Despite the normally high prestress, deflections under wind load in the order of magnitude of l/50 to l/80 are easily possible. This means that the pane/net fixings must allow for movement because the initially flat and usually square mesh configurations deform such that they are no longer flat and, in elevation, frequently no longer square. Each individual mesh

2.2.63 Cable-lattice glass curtain wall, Hotel Kempinski, Munich.
Architects: Murphy/Jahn
Engineers: Schlaich, Bergermann & Partner

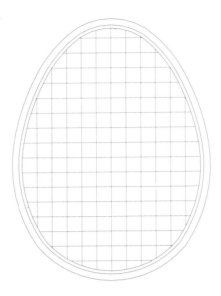

2.2.64  Flat cable-lattice roof, office building, Gniebel
Architects: Kaufmann Theilig & Partner
Engineers: Glasbau Seele

2.2.65  Trussed flat cable net, Rotonde Neuilly, Paris. Architect: D. Feichtinger. Engineers: RFR

aperture in the net undergoes distortion –
broken down into warping and racking – as
the whole net deforms. The glazing to such
a net must either distort in sympathy or be
held at its fixings in such a way that the net
can deform relative to the glass panes.
The fixing systems already employed in
practice are pocket-shaped retainers with a
soft lining fitted to the corners of the panes,
as used on Hotel Kempinski in Munich, or
drilled panes with point fixings which can
accommodate correspondingly large twists
and displacements, like on the roof of the
office building in Gniebel or the wall of Hotel
Esplanade in Berlin (Fig. 2.2.62).

The structural calculations for a glazed net
always proceed on the basis of determining
the warping and racking of each individual
pane for every loading case and comparing
these figures with permissible deformation
values. These permissible values of course
depend on the type and size of glass. Insulating glasses can only tolerate far less
severe deformations.
One of the first and certainly still most
remarkable examples of a flat, glazed cable
net is the atrium façade to Hotel Kempinski
in Munich (Fig. 2.2.63, p. 111).
A further advance on and minimization of
the flat net principle is achieved by omitting
one of the two groups of cables. The dis-
play-cabinet style of the glazing to the preserved remains of the Hotel Esplanade in
Berlin makes use of a façade 60 x 20 m consisting merely of cables spanning vertically
at a spacing of 2 m whose prestress is
maintained at a constant value by nests of
springs (Fig. 2.2.62). The forces in the
cables are almost constant thanks to the
spring prestressing, even under wind loads.
This leads to optimum design of the cables
and hence all adjoining elements. In particular, the spring prestressing is essentially
unaffected by temperature and allows deformation under wind loads. Thus, the typical
"softening" of the construction at high temperatures does not apply here. The 2 x 2 m
glass panes are fixed directly to the cables
via individual drilled fixings.
An interesting example of the use of a flat
net as roofing can be seen in the atrium roof
to the office building in Gniebel (Fig. 2.2.64).
This is a cable structure with a very flat span
situated in an oval steel ring, reminiscent of
the shape and loadbearing behaviour of a
tennis racket. The combination of the tennis-
racket principle with local trussing has resulted in a further refinement of the design
(Fig. 2.2.65).

# Glass and energy – construction physics

**Matthias Schuler**

Glass allows us to introduce radiation into a building but at the same time exclude climatic influences such as wind, rain or cold air. Owing to the selectivity of the radiation permeability, radiation can be gained for the purpose of heating the interior. Some short-wave solar radiation can pass through our layer of glass, while the long-wave heat radiation of the room in the sunlight is repelled by the, for this radiation, opaque glass and remains in the room. The famous "greenhouse effect" enables us to erect glasshouses for tropical plants in cold Central Europe; together with the evolution of structural engineering, this led to the great palm houses of the late 19th century.

Today, glass represents a high-quality building material whose physical properties are by no means inferior to other materials. This chapter explains the physical and energy-related aspects of glass in its various applications. Starting with the fundamental properties, the reader is subsequently introduced to energy gain, heat loss and daylight. A further section discusses and assesses specific uses and the effects of using glass as roofing and façade elements as well as system components.

## Glass properties relevant to energy issues and construction physics

To start our description of the principles and effects of using glass as a building material, a number of terms must be defined in order to guarantee clarity in the accounts.

### Transparency

According to the O.E.D. transparency is "the quality or condition of being transparent", which in turn is defined as "having the property of transmitting light... Allowing the passage of radiant heat or any other specified kind of radiation". However, this does not fully describe the physics of the passage of the radiation; the permeability is always associated with a certain radiation, a certain wavelength or wavelength spectrum. A transparent component permits an uninterrupted view, while a translucent component permits the passage of radiation but obstructs the view.

Transmission designates the radiation permeability irrespective of the quality of the

image of an object behind the component. For better clarity, the properties of radiation are explained first, before the properties of glass, because many effects are derived from the physical ambient conditions of heat and solar radiation.

### Radiation spectrum

For building purposes the radiation spectrum is normally divided into three wavelength groups: ultraviolet (UV) radiation (0 – 380 nm), visible light to which the human eye is sensitive (380 – 780 nm) and near infrared (IR) heat radiation (780 – 2800 nm). On a clear day the solar spectrum at the Earth's surface is distributed as shown in Fig. 2.3.1. This is made up mainly of visible light (47%) and heat radiation (46%). The relatively small ultraviolet portion (7%) comprises the biologically effective UV-B radiation (280 – 315 nm) and the long-wave UV-A radiation (315 – 380 nm). The integral of the sum of the radiation gives the solar constant of 1353 W/m$^2$ beyond the Earth's atmosphere. Besides the solar spectrum, the sensitivity of the human eye over the range of visible light plays a significant role in the use of glass (Fig. 2.3.2). On the other hand, it is only the shift in the wavelengths from short-wave solar radiation to long-wave heat radiation which permits the diode effect of glass, allowing the sun's warmth to penetrate but stopping heat radiation.

The spectral transmittance of a glass pane must first be known in order to be able to determine the solar radiation captured. Fig. 2.3.3 (p. 114) shows that float glass is virtually opaque to the biological UV radiation and that with a pane thickness > 5 mm the long-wave UV radiation is also completely absorbed. This effect manifests itself in the construction and operation of large greenhouses because the UV radiation, besides its biological influence, is also a natural opponent of pests. On the other hand, even just a small proportion of UV light behind the pane can bring about material changes like bleaching and embrittlement. One of the elements in the composition of glass which is responsible for the absorption and hence reduced transmission of solar radiation is iron oxide (Fe$_2$O$_3$); this gives glass its green tinge and is responsible, in particular, for the dip in transmittance around 1000 nm.

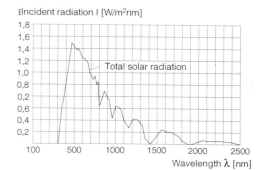

2.3.1 Standardized relative spectral distribution of total solar radiation to prEN 410

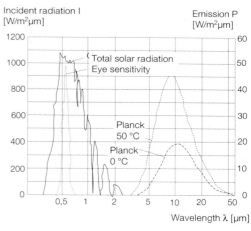

2.3.2 Eye sensitivity and heat radiation in comparison to the solar spectrum

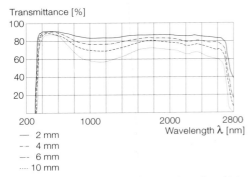

Transmittance [%]

— 2 mm
-- 4 mm
—- 6 mm
···· 10 mm

2.3.3   Spectral transmission for various float glass thicknesses with an average $Fe_2O_3$ content of 0.10%

The curves show the glass properties with high transmission in the visible range, reduced transmission in the near infrared range and opaqueness in the long-wave infrared range.
The radiation at the fall in transmission around 2800 nm corresponds to the heat radiation of a body at 800°C. This illustrates the fire problem of a glass partition, which can withstand a fire provided the temperature of the glass itself does not rise above 700°C although the heat radiated by the fire, generally in excess of 800°C, can pass through the glass and lead to spontaneous ignition on the other side.

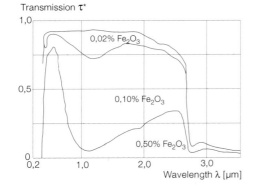

Transmission $\tau^*$

0,02% $Fe_2O_3$

0,10% $Fe_2O_3$

0,50% $Fe_2O_3$

Wavelength $\lambda$ [μm]

2.3.4   Spectra of various $Fe_2O_3$ contents

Reducing the proportion of $Fe_2O_3$ lowers the absorption in the glass and thus gives rise to a higher transmission. This is particularly noticeable in the range of visible light, which is why low-iron glass possesses a higher optical transparency. Fig. 2.3.4 shows the sum of the radiation permeability for the solar spectrum with different $Fe_2O_3$ contents. Glasses transparent to UV radiation for therapeutic purposes, e.g. in health resorts, can only be realized with float glass absolutely free from iron oxide or with quartz glass.

*Daylight transmission*
The transmission of visible radiation – called daylight – through the glass, with wavelengths from 380 to 780 nm, plays a decisive role in illuminating a room, in addition to the size of the windows. The arrangement of the window openings and the reflectivity of the interior surfaces are responsible for the distribution of the light. Light transmittance is the key value here. It should not be forgotten that even visible radiation is a form of energy and, when absorbed, is converted to heat radiation.

Light transmittance $\tau$ (to DIN 67507)
The light transmittance or optical transparency is a measure of the proportion of visible radiation directly penetrating the glass in the range of visible light (380 – 780 nm) and is related to the sensitivity of the human eye. Light transmittance is expressed as a percentage and is influenced by the thickness of the glass as well as other factors. The light transmittance should be chosen bearing in mind the building function and the internal environment in order to comply with DIN 5034 and the Places of Work Act. Increasing the area of the windows is an alternative. This value is especially important in the context of solar-control glass because glazing used as protection against the sun should exhibit a low g-value but a high light transmittance in order not to have to replace the sun's brightness with electricity for artificial lighting. Owing to these differences in the transmission of the total radiation spectrum and the part occupied by visible light, a distinction is made between the light transmittance and energy transmittance when describing a type of glass.

*Radiation transmittance*
The radiation transmittance $\sigma_e$, also known as energy transmittance, describes the proportion of solar radiation which passes directly through the glass and is related to the total solar spectrum. A simplification assumed here, which deviates from the actual relationships, is that the spectral distribution of the total solar radiation is unrelated to the solar altitude angle and the atmospheric conditions, e.g. dust, fumes, water-vapour content, and that the total solar radiation strikes the glass as a beam and almost perpendicular.

Total energy transmittance g (to DIN 67507)
The g-value is the total energy transmitted in the range of wavelengths from 300 to 2500 nm. This variable is important for HVAC calculations and is expressed as a percentage. The value is made up of the direct transmission of solar radiation and the heat emission from the radiation absorbed by the glass in the form of heat radiation and convection towards the inside.

*Radiation balance (transmittance, reflectance, absorptance)*
As no energy can be lost from the total system, the balance of the incident energy must be able to be resolved mathematically. Accordingly, all the energy incident on a pane of glass either passes through (transmittance), is turned back (reflectance) or is absorbed by the material and converted into heat (absorptance). The heated glass releases its energy again into its surroundings in the form of heat radiation and convection. Fig. 2.3.5 illustrates the balance for the two wavelength ranges, taking a 4 mm float glass pane as an example. It shows that transmittance varies over the spectrum, caused by varying absorptance and reflectance, and therefore, for float glass too, is different for the total range of solar radiation and the part occupied by visible light.

*The consequence: the "greenhouse effect"*
The consequence of the spectral dependency of the transmittance of float glass causes the greenhouse effect. High levels of short-wave solar radiation are able to enter the interior through the glass. Once inside, it is partly absorbed directly and partly reflected to be absorbed by other surfaces. Part of the radiation can also be reflected back through the glass and out of the room as short-wave radiation. The absorbed solar radiation is converted into heat at the surface of the body subjected to the radiation. However, the body reacts to this rise in temperature by emitting long-wave heat radiation, some of which also strikes the glass, where much is absorbed and some reflect-

ed. As a comparison, the heat flows excited by radiation entering the room are in the region of 500 W/m² of glass, whereas the heat losses out of the room for a 20 K difference are merely 120 W/m² of glass. This shows that the interior heats up under conditions of intense sunshine – the greenhouse effect (Fig. 2.3.6).

The increased amount of carbon dioxide in the atmosphere brought about by the burning of fossil fuels reduces, by way of absorption, the long-wave reradiation of heat from the Earth into space. This causes the greenhouse effect or global warming. Solar radiation heats up the Earth, fossil energy sources continue to be released, which heat up the Earth's surface even more and, simultaneously, transmission of long-wave radiation decreases so that the atmosphere becomes opaque to heat radiation.

In addition to those already mentioned, the following terms are also significant:

Selectivity
This is the ratio of the light transmittance to the total energy transmittance. For solar-control glass this figure indicates the success of the combination of desired high light transmittance with low total energy transmittance. A high selectivity, e.g. a ratio of 2:1, represents a good figure, i.e. plenty of light and little heat.

Shading coefficient b (to VDI 2078)
The shading coefficient or b-factor specifies the ratio of the g-value of a particular glazing to the g-value of a standard double glazing unit. The g-value of this insulating glass is taken to be a constant of 80%. This new reference replaced the old 3 mm single glazing standard (g-value 87%) in October 1994.

old b = g / 0.8   new b = g / 0.80

Colour rendering index $R_a$ (to DIN 6169)
Colour rendition is immensely important for physiological behaviour as well as psychological and aesthetic sensations. The colour of a room is influenced by the alteration of the spectral composition of the incoming daylight. Therefore, the $R_a$ D-value describes the colour recognition indoors under daylight conditions; the $R_a$ R-value assesses the colour rendition on the viewing side.

The colour rendition qualities of a glass are determined by the colour rendering index $R_a$ to DIN 6169. The $R_a$ scale reaches a maximum of 100, although the maximum figure possible with glass is 99. Normally, $R_a > 90$ represents excellent colour rendition; $R_a > 80$ is good. It should be noted that the real colour rendition depends on the viewing angle, while the definition above takes place

over an array of various radiation peaks. This can lead to colour distortion when viewing from the side, even when $R_a > 90$ is specified.

All the previous statements regarding transmission apply to radiation incident perpendicular to the surface; radiation striking the glass at an angle produces optical modifications.

Refraction
If a beam of light in a medium (e.g. air) strikes the boundary layer between that and another medium (e.g. glass) at a certain angle, then part of the beam is reflected at an equal angle and the remainder penetrates the other medium with a change in direction (refraction).

Upon passing from the optically thinner medium of air to the optically thicker medium of glass, the beam is refracted towards the perpendicular, i.e. the angle of refraction is less than the angle of incidence (Fig. 2.3.7, p. 116). Upon leaving the glass the exit angle is larger. The refractive index is a variable specific to the material. In line with this there is a critical angle for every pair of materials; beyond this angle the total beam is refracted to such an extent that, when passing from a thicker to a thinner material, the beam is prevented from leaving the material. This condition is known as total reflection. As a comparison, the refractive index of flat glass is 1.52, water 1.33 and diamond 2.42.

The relationship between transmission and the angle of incidence is shown in Fig. 2.3.8, p. 116, using the examples of single and multiple glazing.

Further parameters for uncoated glass:

Emissivity 0.85
This variable describes the ability of releasing energy in the form of radiation. In comparison, an ideal energy-emitting body, known as a black body, has an emissivity of 1.0. Glass is opaque to long-wave radiation, but a warm glass surface emits heat very efficiently. The upper layers in the glass surface, consisting of alkaline and earth alkaline oxides (electrical insulators), are responsible for the emissivity.

Thermal conductance 1 W/mK
(to CEN/TC 89, Annex B)
The thermal conductance λ specifies the heat flow which passes through a certain material thickness (in m) for a temperature difference of 1 K between inside and outside. If we compare the thermal conductance of glass with structural steel grade 38 (75 W/mK) or mineral wool (0.04 W/mK), then we see that although the value lies relatively low, seen in conjunction with the typi-

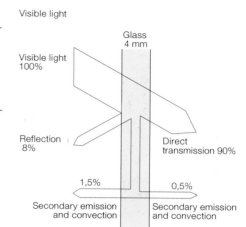

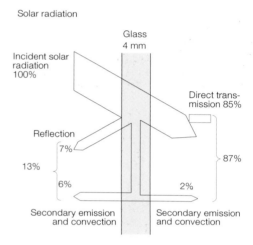

2.3.5   Energy and daylight balance for a 4 mm glass pane

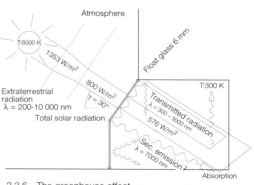

2.3.6   The greenhouse effect

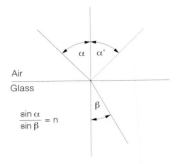

2.3.7 Refraction of a beam at a glass surface with the equation after Snellius

cal thicknesses used, e.g. 4 mm, we arrive at a very high specific heat flow of 250 W/mK. So glass cannot be called an insulating material. The insulating effect which occurs with single glazing is purely the outcome of the thermal resistances of the glass/air transitions on both sides; this results in a thermal transmittance value of 5.8 W/m²K.

Thermal expansion 9.0 x 10⁻⁶ 1/K
This is the change in length and volume of a body upon the application of heat. The thermal expansion is an important parameter when using glass in conditions of fluctuating temperatures. The average linear coefficient of expansion $\alpha$ is specified in 1/K and represents the change in size per unit length for a temperature rise of 1 K. The volumetric coefficient of thermal expansion $\beta$ can be roughly calculated from 3 x $\alpha$. A comparison with the thermal expansion behaviour of other building materials shows that steel (11 x 10⁻⁶ 1/K) and concrete (9 x 10⁻⁶ 1/K) are very similar, thus permitting composite constructions under conditions of fluctuating temperatures.

Specific heat capacity 840 J/kgK
This is the amount of heat required to raise the temperature of 1 kg of a substance by 1 K. As a mineral material, glass lies in the same region as steel (800 J/kgK) and concrete (880 J/kgK) but way behind water (4180 J/kgK). This value is interesting for larger pane thicknesses because in this case the inertia of the group of panes can come into play.

**Thermal insulation**
The thermal insulation function of glass as it separates two climates, e.g. inside and outside, is based, like an opaque wall, on the thermal resistance of the material and the resistances of the transfer at the surfaces. As glass conducts heat relatively efficiently, increased resistance must be achieved by introducing several layers with spaces between. Condensation and frost on single glazing are the signs of its low thermal resistance.

U-value (to prEN 693)
The thermal transmittance (U-value) is the key parameter for determining the heat loss through a component. The thermal transmittance specifies the amount of heat which passes through 1 m² of a component in 1 s for a temperature difference of 1 K between inside and outside air. The lower the U-value (W/m²K), the better is the thermal insulation effect.
For glazing, the thermal resistance and hence the heat flow through this component is determined by the thermal conductivity of the glass as well as the two external surface resistances. The sum of the individual resistances gives the thermal transmission resistance.[1]

*Heat loss via convection*
It is important here that the values calculated apply to a combined thermal transfer, i.e. include convection and radiation-related heat flows.[2]

Transmission as a function of the angle of incidence
Plotting transmission against angle of incidence gives the following curves for single and double glazing. Multiple reflections in the glass have been taken into account.

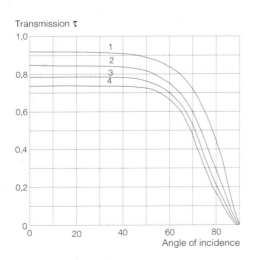

2.3.8 The relationship between transmission and angle of incidence for 1, 2, 3 and 4 panes of float glass

[1] Derivation of the equation:
DIN 4108 Part 4 and CEN/TC89, Annex B, are valid for the external surface resistances of glass panes installed at an angle between 60° and 90°.
$R_i$ = 0.13 m²K/W         $\alpha_i$ = 7.7 W/m²K
$R_a$ = 0.04 m²K/W         $\alpha_a$ = 25 W/m²K

Therefore, for 4 mm single glazing with internal surface resistance $R_g$:
$R_g = s/\lambda = 0.004$ m / 1 W/mK = 0.004 m²K/W
Hence $R_{tot} = R_i + R_g + R_a$
            = 0.13 + 0.004 + 0.04 = 0.174 m²K/W
Mit $U_{tot} = 1/R_{tot}$ = 5.75 W/m²K

[2] The pure thermal convection on the inside, i.e. a plate with perpendicular flows, can be shown to be 2 – 3 W/m²K. This indicates that in this case the heat flow exceeds the radiation exchange with approx. 5 W/m²K for an emissivity of 0.85. On the outside the external surface resistances very much depend on the wind speed, although the convection part can be correlated with the wind by means of the following equation (after Watmuff, 1977):
$\alpha_a = 2.8 + 3.0 \times v$ [W/m²K]        (v in m/s)

The equation applies to an uninterrupted area. Interruptions such as projections etc. can lead to local reductions in the flows but also to local turbulence. Near the edge of a window this can result in less heat transfer; the pane becomes colder because less heat is flowing from the inside to the outside and this can cause condensation.

[3] $T_{sky} = 0.0552 \times (T_{amb})^{1.5}$

(Temperature in K) Sky temperature after Swinbank
For example, this results in a sky temperature of 247.6 K (-24.4°C) for an ambient temperature of 0°C (272 K). This shows that, especially for horizontal glass surfaces facing only the sky, high radiation losses occur with clear skies. For a cloudy sky, an average temperature is found from $T_{sky}$ and the cloud or the dew point temperature of the external air; this depends on the degree of cloud cover.

*Heat loss via radiation*
The radiation portion on the outside very much depends on the heat radiation of the opposing emitter, in this case the sky. With clear skies this heat radiation can be defined via a fictitious sky temperature which, according to Swinbank, can be calculated from the ambient temperature with a clear sky.[3]
This results in an approximate heat flow of 4.8 $W/m^2K$ for radiation towards the sky. Therefore, on a clear night, i.e. in the absence of short-wave solar radiation, the heat flow into the sky can be 141 $W/m^2$ (ambient temperature 0 °C, pane surface temperature 5 °C). If we assume a wind speed of 1 m/s as well, then the convection heat flow is 29 $W/m^2$. If with a high U-value insufficient heat continues to be supplied from the inside, then the surface temperature drops. For well-insulated panes this can mean falling to below the ambient temperature, whereupon condensation or frost may form on the outer pane. Roof windows with low U-values can be permanently iced up during gloomy winter weather. On the other hand, higher wind speeds can in this situation lead to convection gains as the wind fans warmer air across the cold surfaces. The radiation losses can lead to condensation appearing on the insides of less well-insulated glazing when the surface temperature drops below the dew point temperature of the interior. This can often be seen in the roofs of single-glazed conservatories.

*Equivalent thermal transmittance $k_{eq}$*
In order to assess how glazing might contribute to supplementing the interior heating by solar radiation, Hauser and Rouvel introduced the notion of equivalent thermal transmittance $k_{eq}$. The reduction depends on the solar radiation available, and hence the orientation, and the total energy transmittance g of the glazing.[4]

[4]  $k_{eq} = k - (g \times S)$

where
k = U-value of glazing
g = total energy transmittance
S = radiation gain depending on orientation:
south          2.4 $W/m^2K$
east/west    1.8 $W/m^2K$
north          1.2 $W/m^2K$

The equation shows the close relationship between the balanced equivalent thermal transmittance and the material properties. However, a reduction in the U-value for a glazing unit does not necessarily lead to a lower equivalent thermal transmittance (Fig. 2.3.35).

*Improving thermal insulation – insulating glass*
Two or more single panes may be placed one behind the other in order to improve the thermal resistance of a glazing unit; this introduces insulating cushions of air between each pane. Fig. 2.3.9 shows the heat transfer mechanisms via pane and edge for an insulating glass unit. The heat flow is divided up into convection and conduction in the air gap and radiation exchange between the panes. The internal surface resistance of a layer of air depends on the spacing of the panes and position of the cavity, and for air reaches a minimum value at 15 mm. This represents an optimum compromise between suppressing convection, because convection increases as the gap widens, and conduction, which decreases as the gap widens. This value drops again at gaps exceeding 50 mm. This is why coupled windows exhibit slightly better thermal transmittance values. The edge seal of insulating glass – the static connection between the panes – represents a thermal bridge and contributes to heat transport by way of conduction. The U-value for glazing consisting of two panes of 4 mm float glass separated by a 15 mm cavity is 2.8 $W/m^2K$. The U-value of the very common countersash window with openable cavity is higher than the values for insulating glass owing to the non-airtight separating layer and air gaps of 25 mm or more which lead to increased convection.

*Consequences when using insulating glass*
In order to avoid condensation problems – and the resulting cleaning difficulties – in sealed cavities, the spacers in modern edge seals are provided with hygroscopic materials, e.g. zeolites, which absorb the moisture of the trapped, diffusing cavity air. Provided these moisture absorbers are not damaged, their capacity is adequate for the lifetime of the glazing – 30 – 35 years.
The airtight sealing of the cavity of insulating glass – it's not a vacuum! – means that differences in altitude exceeding 500 m between production plant and place of use must be taken into account. This is particularly relevant owing to the influence of air pressure and the "pumping" action of the group of panes (see "Bowing and dishing of insulating glass panes", p. 84). If, for exam-

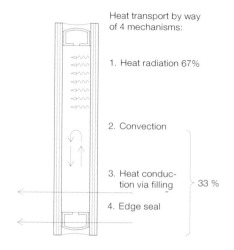

2.3.9   Heat transport in insulating glass

Heat transport by way of 4 mechanisms:

1. Heat radiation 67%

2. Convection

3. Heat conduction via filling    } 33 %

4. Edge seal

2.3.10   Designations for insulating glass

1  2  3  4

Outside                    Inside

2.3.11   Lighter test for determining the layers

2.3.12 Comparison of uncoated insulating and low-e glasses

| Type of glass | U-value [W/m²K] | g-value | Light transmittance [%] |
|---|---|---|---|
| Uncoated insulating glass | 2.8 | 73 | 81 |
| Low-e glass | 1.61 | 65 | 78 |

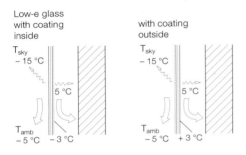

Low-e glass with coating inside

$T_{sky}$ − 15 °C

5 °C

$T_{amb}$ − 5 °C  − 3 °C

with coating outside

$T_{sky}$ − 15 °C

5 °C

$T_{amb}$ − 5 °C  + 3 °C

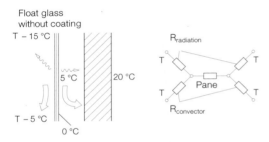

Float glass without coating

T − 15 °C

5 °C  20 °C

T − 5 °C

0 °C

$R_{radiation}$

T  T

Pane

T  T

$R_{convector}$

2.3.13 Radiation balance for single glazing

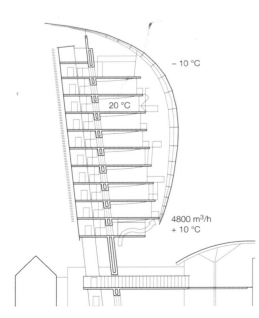

− 10 °C

20 °C

4800 m³/h
+ 10 °C

2.3.14 Building concept employing low-e single glazing for the outer envelope

ple, the location of the insulating glass production plant lies several hundred metres above the place of installation, then high-pressure weather could mean that large panes might actually come into contact (in the middle), and this must be allowed for. This reduces the insulation effect and spots of condensation can appear on the inner side of the pane under certain ambient conditions. Besides this thermal influence, deformations (bowing/dishing) caused by pressure differences also cause optical and acoustic changes. Thicker glass does reduce such deformations but places a greater load on the edge seal.

*Further improvements – several panes and coatings*
If we look at the proportions of the different heat transfer mechanisms (Fig. 2.3.9, p. 117), then it quickly becomes clear that to reduce the thermal transmittance further the radiation transport must be minimized. Triple glazing fulfils this requirement due to the decrease in the temperature difference between the opposing radiators. This is because the inner, warm pane only exchanges radiation with the central pane and not directly with the outer, cold pane. Triple glazing using float glass and two 15 mm cavities achieves a U-value of just below 2.0 W/m²K. The reduced losses mean that solar radiation causes the central pane to heat up quite considerably; to avoid fracture due to thermal expansion, this pane is normally made from toughened glass.

*Coated insulating glass for increased thermal insulation*
Surface coatings with thicknesses of 0.01 – 1 μm can improve the physical radiation properties of glass. The radiation transmission is reflected or absorbed, i.e. the emissivity is reduced, depending on the thickness and composition of the coating. The position of the coating is also important as this can bring about various refractive effects or release the absorption gains into the room or to the outside depending on the direction of the radiation. Possible coatings are sputtered noble metals, e.g. copper, silver, gold, or semiconductor or pyrolitically-sprayed semiconductor coatings, e.g. tin oxide. The silver- and gold-coloured low-e glasses of the 1970s have today been superseded by optically neutral coatings whose position is only disclosed by the lighter test (see Fig. 2.3.11, p. 117). The reflection with a different colour – compared to the other three – reveals the coating. Increased thermal insulation and maximum solar gain is provided by giving the inner pane of insulating glass an IR-reflecting

(low-e) coating at position 3. Fig. 2.3.10 (p. 117) shows the standard designations for insulating glass. A properly applied low-e coating lowers the radiation from the inside component to the cold outer pane. Simultaneously, the g-value is optimized via the usable secondary heat emission of the increased absorption in the coating on the inner pane. Another feature of this is that the total energy transmittance alters for the same glazing depending on the orientation of the installation. Accordingly, the g-value of a readily available low-e glass decreases from the 65% of the arrangement with low-e at position 3 to 56% when the coating is moved to position 2. This 9% in absolute terms is indeed 15% in relative terms, which is why low-e glass is given a stamp such as "This side inwards" at the factory.
The effect on the thermal transmittance of an insulating glass with air filling and low-e coating at position 3 is shown by an approximate calculation.[5]
The deviation between the real and theoretical U-values of an insulating glass with low-e coating (also known as heat-absorbing glass) is due to the insulation increasing temperature differences between the panes, although this does in turn increase the convection and the radiation exchange. These improvements can only be accomplished through reducing the total energy transmittance (Tab. 2.3.12). The low-e coating absorbs part of the solar radiation which can no longer by gained, even via secondary heat emission. The light transmittance is also diminished.

*Low-emissivity coatings on single glazing*
Scratch-resistant coatings, also known as hard coatings, are also available on single glazing. These are conceived for upgrading single-glazed windows or replacing single layers in countersash windows. Like with the considerations above, the U-values can be virtually halved if attention is paid to the sealing of the cavity.
Another application of this innovative single glazing is its use as such in rooms with minimal heating. The insulating effect thereby achieved is based on the radiation into the sky described above. On still, clear nights in

[5]  Insulating glass without coating:
U = 2.8 W/m²K    67 % radiation at e = 0.85
= 1.88 W/m²K
33 % via convection
= 0.92 W/m²K

Insulating glass with low-e coating:
7 % radiation at e = 0.1
= 0.2 W/m²K
33 % via convection
= 0.92 W/m²K

ideal U = 1.12 W/m²K
real  U = 1.61 W/m²K

particular, the thermal losses from the outside of a glazing unit are to a large extent based on radiation losses to the sky. Lowered pane temperatures and hence condensation on the inside and outside of single glazing is the outcome. If the outside is now given a low-e coating (e = 0.1), then the long-wave radiation is reduced to 10% of the value. The pane remains warmer due to its continuing good radiation exchange with its surroundings and the risk of condensation is greatly reduced. Despite its somewhat rougher outer surface, thanks to the reduced chance of condensation an external pane with a low-e coating does not attract dirt any more than an uncoated, smooth pane, as measurements in the Netherlands have shown.

*The effect of the coating position on single glazing*
If the low-e-coated single glazing is installed with its coating facing inwards, then the insulating effect is even greater because 50% of the heat transport always takes place on the inside. Consequently, the thermal transmittance of single glazing can be cut from the well-known 5.8 W/m²K to 4.0 W/m²K, as measurements undertaken at Stuttgart's Institute for Construction Physics have shown.
However, the reduced radiation exchange with the interior leads to a much lower pane temperature because the radiation link to the outside is still as good as before. Therefore, the risk of condensation on the inside is markedly higher, although a self-regulatory effect does come into play. If moisture condenses on the inner surface, i.e. on the coating, then this wetting leads to a loss in the reduced emissivity; the pane is heated up by the heat radiation from the interior and so dries. Once all the condensation is gone, the low-e coating is again fully effective. This effect, a disadvantage in winter, can be advantageous in other climates. For example, in the USA solar-control single glazing is provided with an internal low-e coating in order to obstruct heat radiation into the interior and improve thermal comfort. In our climate the optimization for winter conditions is preferred. This renders pos-

sible concepts for glass buffers with minimal heating, such as the one designed by the author in a study for an office building for Glasbau Seele (Figs 2.3.13 – 15).

*Gas fillings in insulating glass*
A further enhancement in thermal transmittance can be achieved by reducing the proportion of heat lost by convection and conduction. One good method is to use noble gases to fill the cavities of insulating glazing. The large atoms of these gases react much more sluggishly to the temperature differences between the panes and hence reduce the convection flows and the heat transport. In addition, their lower heat conductivities enable the cavity to be narrowed still further without having to pay for the savings in convection through increased conduction. In cavities > 12 mm the greater volume of gas enclosed may well lead to a higher load on the edge seal because of the larger pumping actions caused by temperature and air-pressure fluctuations. As outlined above, the thickness of the pane decides whether the gas expansion manifests itself in terms of glass deformation or increased load on the edge seal. Therefore, thicker glass, required for structural or safety reasons, leads to increased demands being placed on the edge seal; failure can cause cracks and lead to a breakdown of the airtight seal. Tab. 2.3.17 lists the specific properties of the gas fillings used in insulating glass. Sulphur hexafluor-ide ($SF_6$) exhibits characteristics similar to noble gases and is an excellent sound insulator but owing to its poor environmental properties is now hardly used for new glazing. Krypton has similar sound insulation qualities and may be used as a substitute. Owing to their different properties, each gas has an optimum cavity size. Fig. 2.3.16 illustrates the theoretical U-values for different cavities and gas fillings in vertical insulating glass. The optimum widths are also shown. Economic matters take precedence over technical ones when choosing a gas. The atmosphere contains approx. 1% argon, which is easily extracted and hence inexpensive. On the other hand, krypton and xenon are much harder to extract and so are

2.3.15 Comparison of coating variations on single glazing

|  | Uncoated float glass | low-e coating outside | low-e coating inside |
|---|---|---|---|
| Thickness [mm] | 4 | 4 | 4 |
| Radiation transmittance | 0.83 | 0.79 | 0.79 |
| g-value | 0.85 | 0.811 | 0.808 |
| Light transmittance | 0.89 | 0.84 | 0.88 |
| Light reflectance outside | 0.081 | 0.1 | 0.081 |
| Energy reflectance outside | 0.075 | 0.13 | 0.075 |
| Shading coefficient | 1.0 | 0.95 | 0.94 |
| U-value [W/m²K] | 5.63 | 5.34 | 3.8 |

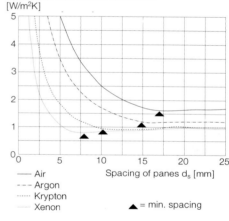

Convection heat transfer coeffficient [W/m²K]

— Air
--- Argon
...... Krypton
— Xenon

▲ = min. spacing

2.3.16 Convection thermal transmission between two panes plotted against gas filling and cavity width

2.3.17 Gas properties at 10°C

| Properties | Gas filling | | | | |
|---|---|---|---|---|---|
|  | Argon | Krypton | Xenon | $SF_6$ | Air |
| Thermal conductivity [W/mK] | $1.684 \times 10^{-2}$ | $0.900 \times 10^{-2}$ | $0.540 \times 10^{-2}$ | $1.275 \times 10^{-2}$ | $2.53 \times 10^{-2}$ |
| Density [kg/m³] | 1.699 | 3.56 | 5.897 | 6.36 | 1.23 |
| Dynamic viscosity [kg/ms] | $2.164 \times 10^{-5}$ | $2.34 \times 10^{-5}$ | $2.28 \times 10^{-5}$ | $1.459 \times 10^{-6}$ | $1.75 \times 10^{-5}$ |
| Spec. heat capacity [J/kgK] | 519 | 345 | 340 | 614 | 1007 |

2.3.18    Schematic diagram of vacuum glazing

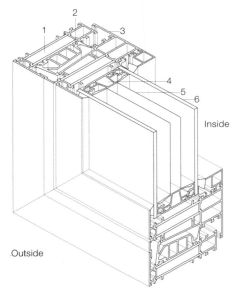

| | | | |
|---|---|---|---|
| 1 | Insulation | 4 | Desiccant |
| 2 | Opening light seal | 5 | Foil |
| 3 | Aluminium | 6 | Glass |

2.3.19    Section through a window with foil insulation

Coating substrate (foil)

2 cavities

Glass (coloured too, and with protection against injury, intruders and bullet penetration)

Special spacer

2.3.20    Section through heat-mirror superglazing

considerably more expensive and less readily available. A major increase in demand could have a positive influence on the price.

*Vacuum glazing*

In a vacuum, convection and conduction are reduced to zero. However, the atmospheric pressure ensures that even with a slight negative pressure in the cavity, the panes make contact or, if the deformation is too great, break. Therefore, vacuum glazing, as illustrated schematically in Fig. 2.3.18, is only possible in conjunction with support measures which enable the two panes to be linked structurally. For flat panes this mechanical propping leads either to isolated thermal bridges, e.g. in the form of individual spacers, or to large-scale supporting by a translucent, pressure-resistant insulating material that can be evacuated, e.g. aerogel. Vacuum glazing relies on an absolutely airtight edge seal, normally achieved by glass or solder glass. High thermal bridge losses occur at these points. Using spacer balls 0.5 mm diameter and two panes with low-e coatings, U-values of 0.6 W/m²K were measured at the Glazing Center in Colorado, USA.

As an alternative, vacuum glazing can be filled with a pressure-resistant insulating material called aerogel, a microporous silica lattice. This acts as the support and exhibits a very low thermal transmittance of 0.017 W/m²K in the non-evacuated state. Therefore, the thermal conduction between the panes is almost negligible, while the fine silica components with dimensions below the wavelength of light are only perceived by the human eye as a homogeneous, transparent material.

The geometric force transmission is carried out by the glass tube, which in the evacuated state is used as a single- or double-walled cylinder for thermal solar collectors (see "Active uses", pp. 148–150).

*Barriers to convection*

Besides reducing the convection by employing a gas, the heat transport by convection can be reduced by mechanical barriers. We distinguish between four groups here: parallel and vertical separation, chamber-type systems and virtually homogeneous fillings. At this point we shall only consider the parallel systems because these permit a view through and do not transform the glass into a translucent component.

Parallel convection barriers are usually made from glass or foil which need only comply with downgraded mechanical specifications and can carry additional coatings. These create extra cavities which act as brakes to convection but on the other hand maintain the resistance to thermal conductivity of the complete layer.

Products were developed aready years ago by a Swiss manufacturer of façades. A g-value between 0.1 and 0.5 and light transmittance value between 0.15 and 0.65 are possible. The U-value of the glazing is 0.4 – 0.6 W/m²K, depending on foil and coating. The disadvantage of the construction is the overall depth – about 130 mm for the glazing unit. Fig. 2.3.19 shows a window with foil.

Similar concepts were developed in the USA at the end of the 1980s; these were called "superglazing" and were subjected to intensive testing at the Lawrence Berkeley Laboratory. Today, low-e and solar-control glasses with one or two convection foils and coatings with emissivities as low as 0.09 are manufactured under licence worldwide. Therefore, in conjunction with a krypton or xenon filling, U-values of 0.4 W/m²K are feasible. The thin foils mean that the total thickness of the glazing is just 23 – 27 mm, and the g-value of the 0.4-glass is 0.43, with a daylight factor of 0.58. The fixing of the foil to the edge seal can be utilized as a thermal break. Fig. 2.3.20 is a section through the superglazing system.

The advantages of convection barriers over three- or four-ply glazing are the reduced weight, the absence of problems with overheated middle panes and the thinner overall width.

All the values quoted above refer to the centre of the pane, ignoring the effects of the pane edge. Therefore, Tab. 2.3.24 (p. 122), the types of glazing currently available and their properties, only relates to the centre of a pane. The effects of the edge seal – which cannot be ignored, especially on small panes – are dealt with later.

*The U-value as a function of the temperature difference – DIN values and reality*
The U-values listed are normally determined by the test method to DIN 52619 Part 2 "Thermal testing, determining the internal surface resistance and thermal transmittance of windows, measurements on the glazing". According to this, the glazing is measured in a twin-plate standard apparatus between a heating and a cooling plate with an average temperature difference of 10 K between the pane surfaces. This arrangement may be placed horizontally or vertically, whereby the influence of increased convection with wider cavities and low thermal transmittance should not be ignored. As a rule, three temperature ranges of the average temperature are measured for the specimen and then the internal surface resistance determined. The thermal transmittance is calculated from this using the standardized U-values 7.7 W/m²K for inside and 25 W/m²K for outside.
In our latitudes, however, temperature differences occur which by far exceed the reference 10 K figure, e.g. outside -14 °C, inside +22 °C; we can experience temperature differences of 20 – 35 K. At these greater temperature differences the convection processes in the cavity change and the internal surface resistance drops. Fig. 2.3.21 shows the relationship between thermal transmittance and temperature difference for different types of glazing. It can be seen that the double-glazed heat-protecting glass units are particularly sensitive to temperature difference and exhibit values up to 30% lower than the DIN value. The official U-value published in the *Bundesanzeiger* normally differs from the DIN value by 0.1 W/m²K upwards. A comparison of U-values for horizontal and vertical glazing is shown in Fig. 2.3.22.

*The influence of the edge seal on the energy parameters*
The spacer between the two panes in an insulating glazing unit is necessary for structural purposes but it introduces a classic thermal bridge. Usually made of metal, the thermal conductivity of, for example, an aluminium spacer without consideration of the thermal transmittance is, for example, 0.9 – 2.2 W/mK, depending on its shape. Because of the low thermal resistance in the edge seal, the pane temperatures here drop with respect to the centre of the pane. This leads to heat conduction parallel to the glass surface so that the reduction in the thermal resistance of the complete glazing has to be regarded as a two-dimensional issue.
In the *ASHRAE Handbook of Fundamentals*, the edge zone is defined as being 60 mm

wide and is assigned a uniform thermal transmittance $U_{edge}$. This value depends on the type of edge seal and spacer as well as the U-value of the glazing because only about 12 – 20 mm is directly covered by the spacer. Fig. 2.3.23 shows how the U-value is determined for the edge zone. The U-value in the edge zone of a certain glass can be read off via the U-value and the type of spacer.
A reduction of 25% in the glazing's thermal transmittance is evident. The equation illustrates the geometrical dependence, with the influence of the edge zone diminishing as the panes get larger[6] (Fig. 2.3.29, p. 123). In glass supported continuously along the edge, this effect is reduced by the insulating effect of the window frame, which overlaps the edge seal. With façades fixed at individual points, this aspect should not be disregarded in the glazing balance. Besides the increased heat losses, the local temperature drop at the spacer – which can lead to condensation appearing at the edge of the pane – must be taken into account. If the condensation that occurs cannot drain away easily, then there is a danger that this might infiltrate the edge seal. Once the drying capacity in the spacer is exhausted, fogging can occur (see "Internal condensation", p. 139).

[6] The U-value of a glazing unit is obtained from the non-influenced pane centre and the edge zone according to the geometrical weighting

$$U_{gl} = \frac{U_{PC} \times A_{PC} + U_{edge} \times A_{edge}}{A_{PC} + A_{edge}}$$

where
PC = pane centre, edge = edge zone

With, for example, a good low-e glass where $U_{PC}$ = 0.9 W/m²K, 1 x 1 m, i.e. a perimeter $U_{gl}$ of 4 m, this gives:

$A_{edge} = U_{gl} \times 0.06\,m = 0.24\,m^2$    $U_{edge} = 2.1\,W/m^2K$

$U_{edge} \times A_{edge} = 0.504\,W/K$

$A_{PC} = A_{gl} - A_{edge} = 0.76\,m^2$    $A_{gl} = 1.00\,m^2$

$U_{PC} = 0.9\,W/m^2K$    $U_{PC} \times A_{PC} = 0.684\,W/K$

$U_{gl} = 1.188\,W/m^2K$

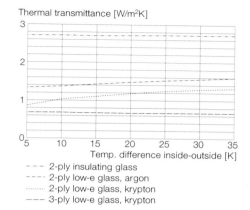
Thermal transmittance [W/m²K]

--- 2-ply insulating glass
---- 2-ply low-e glass, argon
····· 2-ply low-e glass, krypton
--- 3-ply low-e glass, krypton

2.3.21    The relationship between U-value and temperature difference

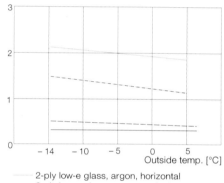
U-value dependent on temperature and position for a room temperature of 22°C

——— 2-ply low-e glass, argon, horizontal
---- 2-ply low-e glass, argon, vertical
--- 3-ply low-e glass, xenon, horizontal
——— 3-ply low-e glass, xenon, vertical

2.3.22    U-values for horizontal and vertical glazing plotted against external temperature

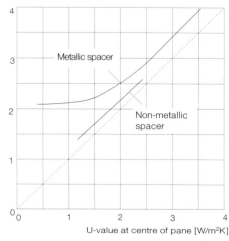
U-value in edge zone [W/m²K]

2.3.23    Thermal transmittance of edge zone

2.3.24 Available glazing types and their energy parameters for the centre of a pane

| | Type | $k_V$-value to DIN 52619 $\Delta\vartheta = 10$ K [W/m²K] | Radiation transmittance [%] | g-value [%] | Daylight transmittance [%] |
|---|---|---|---|---|---|
| Single | 1 No. 4 mm float | 5.2 | 80 | 87 | 90 |
| Double | 2 No. 4 mm float, air | 2.8 | 71 | 76 | 82 |
| | 1 No. 4 mm float + 1 No. IR-coated, air | 1.8 | 46 | 58 | 76 |
| | 1 No. 4 mm float + 1 No. IR-coated, argon | 1.3 | 46 | 58 | 76 |
| | 1 No. 4 mm float + 1 No. IR-coated, krypton | 1.0 | 46 | 58 | 76 |
| Triple | 1 No. 4 mm float + 1 No. IR-coated, krypton | 0.5 | 38 | 42 | 64 |

2.3.25 Influence of edge seal material on the U-value of glazing without frame overlap

| | | $U_{PC}$-value [W/m²K] | 1.3 | 0.9 | 0.4 |
|---|---|---|---|---|---|
| Dimensions | Spacer material | Actual U-value of glazing including edge seal | | | |
| 0.6 × 0.6 m | Aluminium | | 1.61 | 1.27 | 0.76 |
| | with thermal break | | 1.48 | 1.12 | 0.58 |
| 1.0 × 1.0 m | Aluminium | | 1.56 | 1.21 | 0.70 |
| | with thermal break | | 1.45 | 1.08 | 0.55 |
| 2.0 × 2.0 m | Aluminium | | 1.46 | 1.09 | 0.58 |
| | with thermal break | | 1.39 | 1.01 | 0.49 |
| 3.0 × 3.0 m | Aluminium | | 1.41 | 1.03 | 0.53 |
| | with thermal break | | 1.36 | 0.98 | 0.46 |

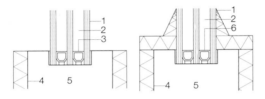

1  4 mm glass with selective coating internally
2  8 mm krypton
3  0.5 mm metal spacer
4  10 mm PU foam
5  Timber frame
6  30 mm cover to glazing above top of edge seal with PU integral foam wedge

2.3.26  Detail with and without insulating strips

In the case of glazing with better thermal insulation properties, e.g. 0.7 or 0.4 W/m²K, the provision of a thermal break or the use of an insulating material as the spacer should be considered. Even with a pane size of 2 x 2 m, an aluminium spacer in the edge seal downgrades the U-value from 0.4 W/m²K at the centre to 0.58 W/m²K for the whole pane – a reduction of 45%! A thermally isolated spacer with a U-value in the edge zone of 1.2 W/m²K limits the reduction to just 22% (0.49 W/m²K) (Fig. 2.3.26). The continuous thermal bridge along the spacer is responsible for the appearance of condensation. This is heated well or not so well by the inner pane, depending on the adjoining type of glass. Tab. 2.3.25 lists the actual U-values for different panes sizes and U-values at room temperatures of 20 °C and external temperatures of 0 °C in relation to the spacer material.

*The influence of frame and edge cover[7]*
The glass edge zone and the frame have a thermal influence on each other. The heat flow through the edge seal can be attenuated or augmented depending on the type of frame and edge cover (depth to which glass is inserted into rebate).
Fig. 2.3.27 shows the influence of the edge cover on the U-value of a window with aluminium spacer and timber frame. It can be seen that with this type of glass having a U-value at the centre of 1.55 W/m²K, a $U_{edge}$ value of 2.00 W/m²K for the given type of aluminium spacer and a timber frame with $U_F = 1.5$ W/m²K, the total thermal transmittance is 1.64 W/m²K when the edge cover coincides with the top of the edge seal. The decrease of the U-value by 6% compared to the middle can be reduced to 3% by increasing the overlap of the frame over the edge seal to 10 mm.

The frame effect is more pronounced for low-e glasses with very low U-values (0.4 – 0.7 W/m²K). Here, insulating strips are placed over the edge seal in addition to a deep rebate (Fig. 2.3.26). Wolfgang Feist made very detailed studies of this in the course of designing the Kranichstein passive-energy houses. Tab. 2.3.28 lists the U-values for edge and glazing of a window with respect to spacer material and edge length. Tab. 2.3.29 shows the influence of area and edge detail on the total thermal transmittance of a window.

2.3.27  Influence of edge cover on U-value of window with aluminium spacer and timber frame

$U_W$  Window
$U_F$  Frame
$U_{PC}$  Pane centre
$U_{PE}$  Pane edge (60 × 100 mm)

| Type of spacer | Aluminium | Aluminium | Aluminium |
|---|---|---|---|
| Glass edge cover [mm] | 20 | 25 | 30 |
| Air temperature difference [°C] | 20.4 | 20.4 | 20.4 |
| U-value [W/m²K] | $U_W$ $U_R$ $U_{PC}$ $U_{PE}$ | $U_W$ $U_R$ $U_{PC}$ $U_{PE}$ | $U_W$ $U_R$ $U_{PC}$ $U_{PE}$ |
| | 1.64  1.50  1.55  2.00 | 1.62  1.50  1.55  1.93 | 1.60  1.50  1.55  1.85 |

*Frame material and window parameters*
The material of the frame of course plays a role in the evaluation of a window. The influence of frame material and spacer on the U-value reduction from pane centre to overall window is shown in Tab. 2.3.30 for window sizes available on the market. Tab. 2.3.31 lists the differences in the thermal conductivities of various frame materials and their influence on the U-value of the window with glazing.

According to DIN 4108 "Thermal insulation in buildings" Part 4 "Heat and moisture protection parameters", the U-value of a window is calculated taking into account glass quality and thermal efficiency of edge seal (determined by the frame material group). Tab. 2.3.33 (p. 125) is an extract covering high-grade low-e glasses with differing frame qualities. This clearly demonstrates the need for a good frame, especially since the frame area is ineffective for concentrating energy.

*Summary of edge seal and frame*
All the above considerations illustrate that the edge seals and frames of low-e glass units reduce their thermal insulation properties. At the same time it can be seen that the edge seal and frame do not result in any energy gains for the window; instead, parts of the pane are shaded and so the solar gain area (aperture) of the component is reduced. Therefore, from an energy viewpoint it is desirable to install a few large panes with a minimal frame proportion instead of many small ones in order to minimize the heat losses and maximize the solar gains. As fixed leaves normally have a narrower frame width, the number of opening lights should be looked at critically. The lack of airtightness also plays a significant role in the case of wind pressure on the façade, defined by the joint permeability.

2.3.28  Average U-value of a window (example) (dark U-value, -10°C/20°C)

| Part | | Width | Height | Area | Length | U-value | TBc | Loss |
|---|---|---|---|---|---|---|---|---|
| | | [m] | [m] | [m²] | [m] | [W/m²K] | [W/mK] | [W/K] |
| Glass | 3 Ws Kr | 1.000 | 1.000 | 1.000 | | 0.700 | | 0.700 |
| Frame | 1 PU + 6 H + 1 PU | 0.120 | 0.120 | 0.538 | | 0.700 | | 0.376 |
| Edge | no Al | 1.000 | 1.000 | | 4.000 | | 0.115 | 0.460 |
| Window | total | 1.240 | 1.240 | 1.538 | | 0.999 | | 1.536 |

TBc = Thermal break coefficient

2.3.29  Parameter study: influence of area and edge detail on the total thermal transmittance of a window (without incident radiation). Based on a square window with given glass edge lengths.

| Edge seal | Edge | TBc | Glass edge length [m] | | | | | | | |
|---|---|---|---|---|---|---|---|---|---|---|
| | [mm] | [W/mK] | 0.6 | 0.8 | 1.0 | 1.2 | 1.4 | 1.6 | 1.8 | 2.0 |
| No aluminium | 0.5 | 0.115 | 1.091 | 1.040 | 0.999 | 0.966 | 0.939 | 0.917 | 0.899 | 0.883 |
| Steel | 0.5 | 0.112 | 1.081 | 1.031 | 0.991 | 0.959 | 0.933 | 0.912 | 0.894 | 0.879 |
| Stainless steel | 0.5 | 0.105 | 1.057 | 1.011 | 0.973 | 0.943 | 0.919 | 0.898 | 0.882 | 0.867 |
| Stainless steel 0.2 | 0.2 | 0.096 | 1.027 | 0.984 | 0.950 | 0.922 | 0.900 | 0.881 | 0.866 | 0.853 |
| No plastic | 1.0 | 0.068 | 0.931 | 0.901 | 0.877 | 0.857 | 0.842 | 0.829 | 0.818 | 0.808 |
| Aluminium PU1O | 0.5 | 0.056 | 0.890 | 0.866 | 0.846 | 0.830 | 0.817 | 0.806 | 0.797 | 0.789 |
| Stainless steel 0.2 PU1O | 0.2 | 0.049 | 0.867 | 0.845 | 0.827 | 0.813 | 0.802 | 0.793 | 0.785 | 0.778 |
| Aluminium PU30 | 0.5 | 0.035 | 0.819 | 0.804 | 0.791 | 0.781 | 0.773 | 0.766 | 0.761 | 0.756 |
| Stainless steel 0.2 PU3O | 0.2 | 0.031 | 0.805 | 0.792 | 0.781 | 0.772 | 0.765 | 0.759 | 0.754 | 0.749 |
| Plastic PU30 | 1.0 | 0.024 | 0.782 | 0.771 | 0.762 | 0.756 | 0.750 | 0.745 | 0.742 | 0.738 |

The thermal bridge coefficent (TBc) is related to the continuous length of the thermal bridge.

2.3.30  U-values for windows related to frame material, spacer and glazing parameters

| Frame $U_F$ [W/m²K] | Spacer | Glazing | | |
|---|---|---|---|---|
| | | Low-e 2, Ar $U_G$ = 1.8 W/m²K | Low-e 3, Ar $U_G$ = 1.2 W/m²K | Low-e 3, Kr $U_G$ = 0.8 W/m²K |
| Aluminium $U_F$ = 3.4 | Aluminium | 2.25 | 1.68 | 1.42 |
| | Alternative | 2.17 | 1.58 | 1.32 |
| PVC $U_F$ = 2.3 | Aluminium | 2.09 | 1.59 | 1.36 |
| | Alternative | 2.01 | 1.50 | 1.26 |
| Timber $U_F$ = 2.1 | Aluminium | 2.02 | 1.54 | 1.32 |
| | Alternative | 1.92 | 1.43 | 1.20 |

Window size: 1.2 × 1.2 m
Spacer: conventional aluminium as well as alternative with λ = 0.3 W/mK
Frame cross-sections vary; other frame constructions produce other absolute values, but the tendencies are similar.

[7]  In compliance with CEN/TC89/W67 "Thermal properties of doors and windows" and in accordance with ISO/TC160/SC2/WG2, the total thermal transmittance of a window $U_W$ is calculated as follows:

$$U_F = (A_g \times U_g + A_F \times U_F + P \times \psi) / (A_g + A_F)$$

where

$A_g$  area of glazing (m²)
$A_R$  area of frame (m²)
P  perimeter of glazing (m)
$U_g$  U-value at centre of pane (W/m²K)
$U_F$  U-value of frame (W/m²K)
ψ  linear internal surface resistance (W/mK) of edge seal

2.3.31  Differences in the thermal conductivity of frame materials and their influence on the U-value of the window with glazing

| Material | Thermal conductivity [W/mk] | U-value [W/m²K] Typical frame | U-value [W/m²K] Typical window |
|---|---|---|---|
| Timber | 0.12 | 2.1 to 3.1 | 1.5 to 2.8 |
| Aluminium | 220 | With thermal break 5.0 to 6.6 without thermal break 10 to 13 | 1.9 to 3.3 |
| PVC | 0.16 | 2.3 to 3.9 | 1.7 to 2.9 |

These values are derived from measurements of 200 window frames and one typical window (1.2 x 1.2 m) in the IEA research project Task 18, Advanced glazing and associated materials.

Joint permeability of windows
For openable façade elements in particular, heat losses caused by a lack of airtightness must also be considered in addition to those due to conduction through the component. Wind flows around a building give rise to regions of pressure and suction on the sides amounting to as much as 40 Pa; these can inject air into the building or suck it out. The airtightness of a façade component, or rather its joints, is expressed by the joint permeability and the joint permeability coefficient "a" of the component. This coefficient – in $m^3/(h \times m \times Pa^{2/3})$ – specifies how many cubic metres of air passes per hour and metre length of joint at a pressure difference of 1 Pa. The joint permeability of windows is regulated in DIN 18055.

Tab. 2.3.34 shows the joint permeability coefficients for windows to DIN 4701 Part 2. For example, for a window 1 x 1 m and hence a joint length of 4 m the joint permeability is 4 m x 0.6 $m^3/hmPa^{2/3}$ = 2.4 $m^3/h$ $Pa^{2/3}$. This means a flow rate of 3 $m^3/h$ through the joints of a window 1 x 1 m according to the design pressure in DIN 4701 for a one-room terraced house in a normal location in an area of low wind

speeds giving 1.6 Pa for the façades subjected to wind load. For a design temperature of, for example, -10 °C for the heating and a room temperature of 20 °C, this is 30 W and related to the temperature difference and the window size a loss of 1 $W/m^2K$. This demonstrates the importance of good joint imperviousness in preventing unwanted air flows. A minimum flow rate is desirable for interiors for reasons of hygiene and for removing the moisture that accumulates. The high imperviousness of modern façades can lead to the need for defined openings, e.g. permanent vents, being required to supply fresh air. A fresh-air supply rate that is too low, in conjunction with thermal bridges or components with low insulation value and high interior humidity, can lead to damage to the building. Mould and staining seen in refurbishment projects of the 1970s, in which new, sealed windows were installed but the thermal insulation not improved, are examples of this.

Fig. 2.3.32 shows the joint permeability per metre of joint related to the applied pressure difference (to DIN 18055).

*The effects of coupling thermal insulation with transmission of energy and daylight*
As we try to optimize the U-value, for example, the mutual interdependence of the energy parameters, e.g. total thermal transmittance U, total energy transmittance g and light transmittance τ, leads to non-optimized solar or daylight gains. Therefore, the glazing selected – depending on respective use, type of construction, geometry and orientation – will place one or other aspect in the foreground. The "effective U-value" was introduced as a simple means of assessing just the glazing itself, without taking specific details of the adjoining room into account. For the thermal balance, this parameter takes into account not only the transmission losses but also the solar gains which distinguish glazing from an opaque wall element. This definition (after Hauser) was incorporated into Germany's 3rd Thermal Insulation Act (1995). (See "Equivalent thermal transmittance $k_{eq}$", p. 117.) From the equation[4] (p. 117) it can be seen that a U-value reduction need not always produce a lower $k_{eq}$ when the g-value also decreases correspondingly. Tab. 2.3.35 makes this dilemma clear, one which applies particularly to an orientation with high solar gains, e.g. east/west and south.
Glazing with a high insulation value can compensate for the transmission losses via the solar gains during the heating period and, with proper orientation, become heat sources. For the south elevation in particular, upgrading the U-value from glass 3 to glass 4 (Tab. 2.3.35), which is linked to a severe drop in the g-value (brought about

Linear joint permeability
[V = V/in $m^3/hm$]

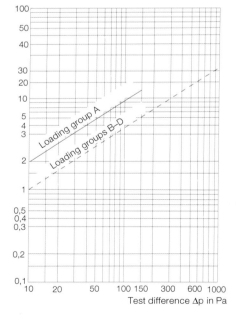

| Loading group | A | B | C | D |
|---|---|---|---|---|
| Height of building | 8 m | 20 m | 100 m | Special rule |

2.3.32  Joint permeability plotted against wind pressure on the façade (to DIN 18055)

by other coatings and more panes), has a negative effect on the overall balance. The lower heat losses do not outweigh the reduced radiation gains; the equivalent U-value rises. Even on the east and west sides, more marked on the north, the insulation effect outweighs the reduced solar gains, as would be expected with an improvement in the equivalent U-value from 3 to 4. These relationships must also be included in the discussions concerning sunspaces or double-leaf façades. Only when the savings in the transmission losses exceed the reduction in solar gains by way of the buffer effect can we reckon with a saving in the overall balance.
Similar observations have been noted for the

light transmittance/U-value relationship. However, there is no parameter like $k_{eq}$ here. It can be seen from Tab. 2.3.35, however, that improved insulation means less daylight. In office buildings with high internal heat gains, a severe reduction in daylight transmission can lead to the need for more artificial light, while in this case the heat losses play a subordinate role owing to the internal thermal loads. Nevertheless, the additional internal heat gains can lead to overheating in summer.
The balancing of the equivalent U-value can only provide a rough guide because it does not say anything about the usability of the solar gains nor glare problems. These depend very much on the usage, but also

on the relative area of the glazing. For residential accommodation with a standard design (medium construction) and standard glazing proportions (< 50% of the façade), the figures above can be used as an estimate. Deviations from this require detailed evaluation tools (see "Dynamic behaviour of rooms", p. 138).

2.3.33  Window U-values for low-e glass and various frame qualities to DIN 4108

| | Description of glazing | Glazing $U_g$ [W/m²K] | Windows and glazed doors including frame $U_F$ for frame material group [W/m²K] | | | | |
|---|---|---|---|---|---|---|---|
| | | | $U_F < 2.0$ 1 | $U_F < 2.8$ 2.1 | $U_F < 3.5$ 2.2 | $U_F < 4.5$ 2.3 | $U_f > 4.5$ 3 |
| 1 | | 1.8 | 1.8 | 2.0 | 2.2 | 2.5 | 3.0 |
| 2 | The thermal transmittance values $U_g$ for special glasses are taken from the test certificates of recognized test centres. | 1.7 | 1.7 | 2.0 | 2.2 | 2.4 | 2.9 |
| 3 | | 1.6 | 1.6 | 1.9 | 2.1 | 2.3 | 2.9 |
| 4 | | 1.5 | 1.6 | 1.8 | 2.0 | 2.3 | 2.8 |
| 5 | | 1.4 | 1.5 | 1.8 | 1.9 | 2.2 | 2.7 |
| 6 | | 1.3 | 1.4 | 1.7 | 1.9 | 2.1 | 2.7 |
| 7 | | 1.2 | 1.4 | 1.6 | 1.8 | 2.0 | 2.6 |
| 8 | | 1.1 | 1.3 | 1.6 | 1.7 | 2.0 | 2.5 |
| 9 | | 1.0 | 1.2 | 1.5 | 1.7 | 1.9 | 2.4 |

2.3.34  Computed values for joint permeability of components to DIN 4701 Part 2

| No. | Designation | | Category features | Joint permeability | |
|---|---|---|---|---|---|
| | | | | Joint permeability coefficent $m^3/(m \times h \times Pa^{2/3})$ | $a \times l$ |
| 1 | Window | opening | Loading groups B, C, D | 0.3 | - |
| 2 | | | Loading group A | 0.6 | - |
| 3 | | fixed | Normal | 0.1 | |

2.3.35  Equivalent $k_{eq}$ value [W/m²K] for various glazing types and orientations

| | U-value | Energy transmittance g | Light transmittance | South $k_{eq}$ | East/west $k_{eq}$ | North $k_{eq}$ |
|---|---|---|---|---|---|---|
| First glass | 1.8 | 0.7 | 0.81 | 0.12 | 0.54 | 0.96 |
| Second glass | 1.3 | 0.62 | 0.77 | -0.188 | 0.184 | 0.556 |
| Third glass | 1.1 | 0.58 | 0.76 | -0.292 | 0.056 | 0.404 |
| Fourth glass | 0.7 | 0.4 | 0.60 | -0.26 | -0.02 | -0.02 |

2.3.36 Total solar radiation and diffuse portion related to degree of cloud cover

|  | clear blue sky | bright, hazy partial cloud cover | over-cast sky |
|---|---|---|---|
| Total solar rad. [W/m²] | 600-1000 | 200-400 | 50-150 |
| Diffuse portion [%] | 10-20 | 20-80 | 80-100 |

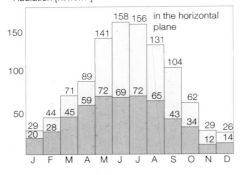

Radiation [kWh/m²]

Total solar radiation
Σ = 1040

Diffuse radiation
Σ = 533 (51%)

2.3.37 Monthly totals of total solar and diffuse radiation

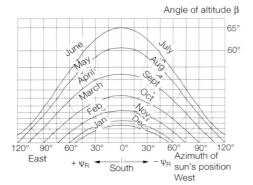

2.3.38 Solar trajectory (diagram for latitude 48° north)

## Gaining energy through glass – solar radiation, light

Besides forming the building envelope, the transparency and permeability of glass enables us to illuminate and heat interiors by means of the infiltration of light and solar radiation via openings in the façade. This is particularly important when the external temperature drops below 15 °C during the cold months of the year. Therefore, in examining the energy gain through glass we must first look at the climatic framework before discussing details of the order of magnitude and usefulness of these gains.

*Climatic framework*
The local weather data is indispensable for assessing the energy gains and losses through glass. This is true for both the total radiation spectrum as well as the special segment visible light. The available solar radiation reaching the ground, beam and diffuse, plays a crucial role with respect to energy gain. On the other hand, ambient temperature, wind speed, degree of cloud cover and internal temperature determine the thermal losses per square metre of glazing. The differing climate factors such as geographical latitude, altitude above sea level, sea and air streams enable us to distinguish between four primary climate zones in Central and Southern Europe:

- North European coastal climate
  Very cold winters with low levels of solar radiation, moderately warm summers.
- Central European coastal climate
  Cold winters with low levels of solar radiation, mild summers.
- Continental climate
  Relatively cold winters with high levels of solar radiation, warm summers.
- South European and Mediterranean climate
  Mild winters with high levels of solar radiation, hot summers.

Within these primary climate zones there are a number of regional ones which vary according to topography and vegetation and are influenced by factors such as high mountains, large expanses of water and forests, as well as population-related factors such as atmospheric pollution and density of development.
Apart from that, any specific location will also be subject to a microclimate which plays a decisive role in the evaluation of gains and losses. Orientation, existing neighbouring developments, topological features and also whether the site is exposed to or protected from the wind all influence the possibilities – via the glazing – for collecting solar radiation and daylight

and avoiding heat losses through wind effects. The following climate components have a significant effect on the energy evaluation:

- Solar radiation gain
  based on azimuth (compass direction) and zenith (angle of altitude) and depending on the time of year – divided into beam (i.e. direct) and diffuse radiation.
- Ambient temperature
  over the year, whereby the minimum temperature and the length of the cold period influences the glass specification by way of the total thermal transmittance.
- Wind speed
  with respect to cooling of the outer surface by reducing the external surface resistance and air infiltration caused by differential pressures.
- Moisture
  for the purpose of assessing the risk of condensation and degree of interior comfort.
- Long-wave radiation
  into the sky as an additional loss factor for the outer surface, determined by the degree of cloud cover.

*Solar radiation – distribution and energy levels*
The extraterrestrial solar spectrum is filtered by the Earth's atmosphere; the ozone in the stratosphere in particular cuts out the hazardous short-wave UV rays. On a clear day the radiation profile is as shown in Fig. 2.3.1 (p. 113); from a total of 1347 W/m² of extraterrestrial radiation, max. 1100 W/m² reaches the Earth's surface. Part of the solar radiation is reflected back into space and part is absorbed (and converted into heat) by the ozone, carbon dioxide and water vapour in the atmosphere, which determines the atmospheric counter-radiation. Some of the incoming radiation is scattered by particles and air molecules and reaches the surface as diffuse radiation. The part reaching the surface directly is designated beam radiation. The sum of the atmospheric counter-radiation plus the diffuse and beam radiation is called the total solar radiation. Although this radiation reaches a maximum value of 1100 W/m², which in one hour of sunshine is equal to the energy in 0.1 l of fuel oil, the available solar radiation striking the land surfaces of our planet is almost 2,500 times the world's annual energy requirement (1985 figure). The proportion of diffuse radiation is affected by the degree of cloud cover, the transparency of the sky and the length of the radiation's passage through the atmosphere. Tab. 2.3.36 lists the amounts of total and diffuse radiation for various degrees of cloud cover.

The absorption by particles in the air is defined by the turbidity factor, which is described by the number of successive clear days leading to an equal decrease in radiation. Turbidity factors vary between 2.1 and 5.0 over the year depending on location and use. The highest radiation densities are measured in spring in association with the solar altitude angle. Fig. 2.3.37 shows the annual distribution of the monthly totals for total solar and beam radiation on a horizontal surface in Stuttgart. Across Europe the annual sums of total solar radiation on a horizontal surface range from 980 kWh/m² p.a. (Hamburg) to 1780 kWh/m² p.a. (Almeria, Spain). The inclination and orientation (compass direction) of the collecting surface determine the maximum intensity and the quantity of energy behind the pane over the year; this is also affected by the angle of incidence of sunshine on a surface, and especially glazing in which the transmission changes with the angle of incidence. The reason for this is the solar trajectory, which in our latitudes varies quite considerably over the year. Although the sun is always due south at 12 noon, the maximum elevation in December is just 18° while in June it is 65°. The position of the sunrise also shifts from south-east to north-east and back again.

These seasonal changes are important for assessing the radiation gains but also for investigating the possibilities of employing fixed shading. Figs 2.3.38 and 2.3.39 can be used to determine altitude angle and compass direction during the year. The azimuth is defined in such a way that zero is due south, east +90 and west -90. The diagram can be used to read off, for example, that for a location with geographical latitude 48° (e.g. Stuttgart) the sun rises at 8 a.m. in the south-east in December, while at the same time in June it is almost due east and already exhibits an altitude angle of 35°.

A direct consequence for areas of glazing is the different daily distributions for the main compass directions in the case of both horizontal and vertical glazing. The two diagrams in Fig. 2.3.40 show the distribution of incident radiation on a sunny day in January (sun at min. altitude) and in June (sun at max. altitude) for five different orientations. We can see from this that in winter it is the south side that receives most of the radiation whereas in summer the radiation peaks are to be found on the east and west sides as well as a horizontal surface. Changing the inclination of the south façade produces various average daily radiation totals over the year, as Fig. 2.3.42 shows.

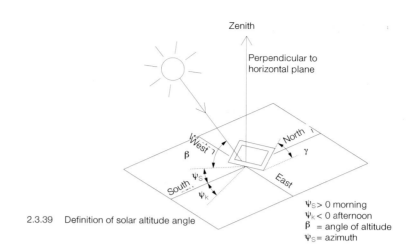

2.3.39    Definition of solar altitude angle

$\psi_S > 0$ morning
$\psi_k < 0$ afternoon
$\beta$ = angle of altitude
$\psi_S$ = azimuth

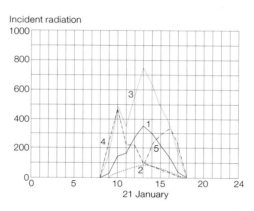

Incident radiation

21 January

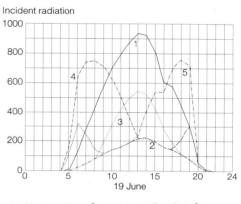

Incident radiation

19 June

| 1 | I-g-Horizontal [W/m²] | 4 | I-g-East [W/m²] |
| 2 | I-g-North [W/m²] | 5 | I-g-West [W/m²] |
| 3 | I-g-South [W/m²] | | |

2.3.40    Daily distributions of total solar radiation on sunny days in January and in June for various façade orientations

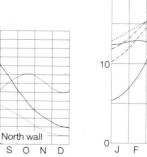

Energy [kWh/m²d]

Horizontal surface

South wall

East/West wall

North wall

2.3.41    Annual distribution of daily totals for various orientations

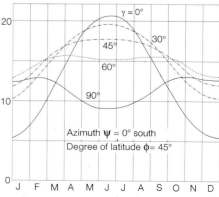

Average daily total solar radiation [MJ/m²d]

$\gamma = 0°$
30°
45°
60°
90°

Azimuth $\psi = 0°$ south
Degree of latitude $\phi = 45°$

2.3.42    Variation in radiation gain for different south-facing façades

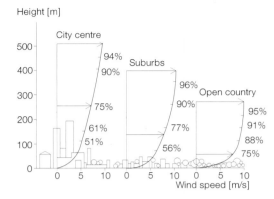

2.3.43    Wind profiles for different topography

2.3.44    Heating days $t_a$ and heating degree days $G_t$

| Location* | Heating limit 15°C | |
|---|---|---|
| | $t_a$ d | $Gt_{15}$ Kd |
| Berlin | 264.5 | 3748 |
| Dresden | 274.8 | 3898 |
| Frankfurt am Main | 265.6 | 3640 |
| Freiburg im Breisgau | 249.1 | 3309 |
| Hamburg | 293.3 | 3982 |
| Hof | 314.7 | 4856 |
| Mannheim | 254.6 | 3436 |
| Munich | 288.1 | 4246 |
| Nuremberg | 278.2 | 3983 |
| Passau | 284.4 | 4249 |
| Stuttgart | 278.6 | 3938 |
| Ulm | 290.7 | 4308 |
| Würzburg | 274.1 | 3861 |

\* The locations given here only represent a selection.

As a rule of thumb, the optimum angle of incidence for the annual radiation total is equal to the geographical latitude (for a south orientation at any location), e.g. 48° for Stuttgart. Surfaces optimized for winter conditions, e.g. conservatory, supply-air buffer, are best placed as steeply as possible, while those optimized for summer, e.g. swimming pool collectors, should be at a very shallow angle.

*External temperature, wind, degree days*
The annual distribution of the external air temperature follows the distribution of the total solar radiation. The degree of cloud cover acting as a shield against radiation, both for radiation gains as well as long-wave radiation losses, plays a crucial role here, analogous to a combined sunshade and temporary thermal insulation. Because of the shallow angle of the sun in winter, temperature fluctuations during the day are less than for when the sun is high in the sky in summer, meaning a higher radiation gain in summer. Large expanses of water attenuate severe temperature fluctuations; this explains the more modest annual fluctuations in coastal regions compared to the continental climate.
The density of development is another important factor for the microclimate. In winter the minimum temperature in inner cities is up to 4 K higher than in the open countryside, while in summer this effect coupled with surface sealing leads to peak temperature differences of up to 10 K. The wind is also partly responsible, providing desirable or undesirable cooling depending on the time of year. Besides the density of development, the regional topography also has an influence, affecting the direction and occurrence of the wind. Westerly winds prevail in Central Europe, while sea breezes are also involved on the coasts.
Apart from the influence on the external surface resistance, the wind must be considered when movable external sunshades are fitted to glazing. As wind speed increases

with height (corresponding to the degree of development), external sunshades must be moved to their parking positions above a certain wind speed to avoid damage. High or exposed buildings are particularly at risk. Fig. 2.3.43 illustrates wind profiles for different settlement densities.
The degree days figure can be used to obtain a rough estimate of the transmission heat losses through the glazing. This variable is derived from the average daily temperature at 6 a.m., 12 noon and 6 p.m. and the difference between these and the reference value of 20 °C, which corresponds to room temperature. In addition, a day is only classed as a heating day when this average daily temperature drops below 15 °C. Above this limit it is assumed that the heating requirement is covered by internal heat sources and solar gains. Tab. 2.3.44 shows a selection of German cities with their degree day figures[8] taken from DIN 4701. (Detailed calculations using these values can be found on pp. 139–140 "Glass as thermal insulation".)

*The solar gains behind the glazing*
As Fig. 2.3.8 (p. 116) illustrates, the transmission and hence the total energy transmittance through glazing depends on the angle of incidence on the glass as well as the material properties. We can see from the curves that reflections increase when the angle of incidence deviates by more than 60° from the perpendicular and that this

[8]    For example, if a location has a degree day figure of 3600 Kd (Kelvin days), then for the transmission losses through glazing with a thermal transmittance of 1 W/m²K this means:

$$QT = U \times A \times GT \times 24 \; \frac{W \times m^2 \times Kd \times h}{[m^2 Kd]} \; [Wh]$$

per 1 m²
= $1 \times 1 \times 3600 \times 24 = 86\,400$ Wh = 86.4 kWh

2.3.45    Monthly incident radiation totals for total solar radiation as well as transmission gains for various façade orientations for a low-e glass, g-value = 0.6, in Würzburg, E = incident radiation [kWh/m²], G = gains [kWh/m²].

| | | J | F | M | A | M | J | J | A | S | O | N | D | Year |
|---|---|---|---|---|---|---|---|---|---|---|---|---|---|---|
| South | E | 40 | 40 | 58 | 96 | 87 | 92 | 98 | 82 | 81 | 58 | 37 | 23 | 794 |
| | G | 16 | 15 | 22 | 32 | 28 | 29 | 31 | 27 | 28 | 22 | 15 | 9 | 274 |
| North | E | 9 | 15 | 26 | 46 | 61 | 73 | 74 | 51 | 34 | 24 | 13 | 7 | 434 |
| | G | 4 | 5 | 9 | 16 | 21 | 24 | 25 | 17 | 12 | 8 | 4 | 3 | 148 |
| East | E | 18 | 25 | 43 | 97 | 102 | 114 | 118 | 81 | 60 | 36 | 21 | 12 | 727 |
| | G | 6 | 9 | 16 | 36 | 38 | 42 | 44 | 30 | 22 | 13 | 7 | 4 | 267 |
| Year | E | 17 | 23 | 35 | 84 | 94 | 103 | 114 | 87 | 67 | 38 | 19 | 10 | 691 |
| | G | 6 | 8 | 13 | 31 | 34 | 38 | 42 | 32 | 24 | 13 | 7 | 3 | 252 |
| Horizontal | E | 24 | 35 | 61 | 137 | 157 | 184 | 190 | 133 | 97 | 56 | 28 | 16 | 1119 |
| | G | 7 | 11 | 21 | 49 | 58 | 68 | 69 | 48 | 34 | 18 | 9 | 5 | 397 |

reduces the transmission. The effects over the year vary depending on solar altitude angle (azimuth and zenith) as well as the orientation of the glazing.

Tab. 2.3.45 shows the monthly incident radiation totals for total solar radiation as well as total energy gains (transmission and secondary heat emission) for various façade orientations.

The figures prove that due to the incident angle of the transmission as well as the diffuse portion, assumed to have an average angle of incidence of 60° to the perpendicular, the annual distribution tends to intensify. It can be seen that for a conservatory a vertical southern façade is more important than a horizontal glass roof because the latter tends to produce overheating problems. To optimize the heating it is better to provide a solid roof or a glass one with sunshading. East and west elevations experience their maximum solar gains in summer because the shallow sun produces maximum transmission values. This fact should be taken into account when planning large areas of glass facing east and west, particularly as fixed shading in the form of overhanging eaves does not work.

*The usability of solar gains*

Not every kilowatt-hour of solar gain per square metre of window mentioned above can be put to use in lowering the heating requirement. Solar gains are influenced by the proportion of window area, orientation, type of construction, standard of insulation and function of the building. These effects lead to room temperatures which exceed the desired temperature and this must be compensated for by providing ventilation or a sunshade. The following calculations employ the room temperature as the key parameter in controlling ventilation and shading, but glare effects or temperatures experienced as too hot due to beam radiation are not considered.

The following statements are valid for the example described in Fig. 2.3.46. The four figures 2.3.47 to 2.3.50 illustrate the heating requirement based on proportion of glazing, orientation and type of construction. The curves for two types of building function are given.

The list[9] of all the heat flows into and out of the room with one external wall shows that the supplementary heating by no means covers all the losses; on the contrary, it brings about internal and solar gains. In this case the level of internal gains, different for residential and commercial applications, determines the amount of usable solar gains. Only these contribute to reducing the supplementary heating requirement, while the remaining solar gains have to be regulated through ventilation or they would lead

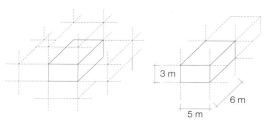

2.3.46    Example of an intermediate storey.
The section of the building considered here has only one external wall, the others border on rooms with identical temperatures. This increases the energy effects through the external wall.

[9]

| | |
|---|---|
| Usable area | 30 m² |
| Volume | 180 m³ |
| External surface | 90 m² |
| A/V ratio | 0.5 |
| Heating threshold | 20 °C air temperature |

External shading for room temperatures > 24 °C, degree of shading 80%

Ventilation:    3 air changes for room air > 26 °C

Construction:
• Lightweight: timber-stud walls clad in plasterboard, parquet flooring on air cushion, suspended ceiling.
• Medium: walls of hollow clay bricks, parquet flooring on screed with sound insulation, concrete slab with timber cladding.
• Heavy: walls of sand-lime bricks, tiles on screed with sound insulation, exposed concrete slab.

Standard of insulation (to 1995 Thermal Insulation Act):
| | | |
|---|---|---|
| U-value, walls | 0.5 | W/m²K |
| U-value, windows | 1.8 | W/m²K |
| U-value, roof | 0.3 | W/m²K |
| Ground floor | 0.5 | W/m²K |

"Low-energy house" standard:
| | | |
|---|---|---|
| U-value, walls | 0.3 | W/m²K |
| U-value, windows | 1.1 | W/m²K |
| U-value, roof | 0.2 | W/m²K |
| Ground floor | 0.35 | W/m²K |

"Passive-energy house" standard:
| | | |
|---|---|---|
| U-value, walls | 0.15 | W/m²K |
| U-value, windows | 0.7 | W/m²K |
| U-value, roof | 0.13 | W/m²K |
| Ground floor | 0.25 | W/m²K |
Ventilation with 65% heat recovery

Uses:
• Residential
1 person, present 6 p.m. to 7 a.m. weekdays, 24h weekends, heated from 6 a.m. to 10 p.m., otherwise reduced, internal heat gains 800 kWh p.a., basic ventilation 0.5 air changes/h.
• Commercial
1 person, present 8 a.m. to 6 p.m. weekdays, heated from 7 a.m. to 6 p.m. weekdays, otherwise reduced, internal heat gains 1 computer, lighting 10 W/m² when too dark, basic ventilation 0.5 air changes/h.

Heat gains/losses [kWh p.a.]

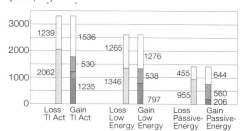

☐ Qtrans (transmission losses)
☐ Qinf (ventilation heat losses)
■ QHeiz (supplementary heating)
▨ QintGew (usable internal gains)
☐ Qsol (usable solar gains)

2.3.47    Heating requirement depending on insulation and influence of insulation standard for medium construction, 60% window ratio, south orientation, residential.

Heating requirement [kWh p.a.]

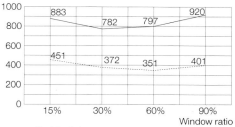

— Residential
···· Commercial

2.3.48    The usability of solar gains depending on proportion of glazing

Heating requirement [kWh p.a.]

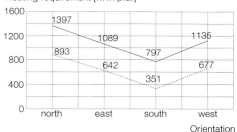

— Residential
···· Commercial

2.3.49    The usability of solar gains depending on orientation

Heating requirement [kWh p.a.]

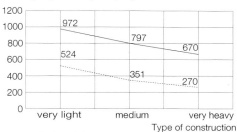

— Residential
···· Commercial

2.3.50    The usability of solar gains depending on type of construction

**129**

Heat gains/losses
[kWh p.a.]

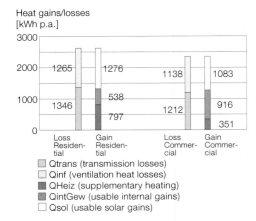

2.3.51   Heating requirement depending on type of use
          for medium construction, 60% window ratio,
          south orientation, "low-energy" standard of
          insulation.

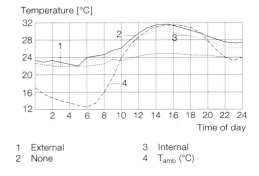

1   External          3   Internal
2   None              4   $T_{amb}$ (°C)

2.3.52   Comparison of summer temperatures for various
          types of sunshading

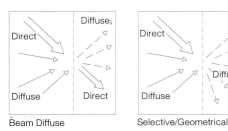

2.3.53   Different approaches to sunshade design

to an excessive room temperature. Incident solar radiation curtailed by temperature-controlled sunshading is not allowed for here. The figures given in Fig. 2.3.51 are evidence of how ineffective solar heat gains are for office buildings, owing to their high internal heat gains. The emphasis in such cases is on substituting artificial light for daylight in order to limit the internal heat sources.

Figs 2.3.48 to 2.3.50 (p. 129) no longer indicate the individual gains and losses in detail but instead the usefulness of solar gains for raising or lowering the heating requirement. Whereas the orientation is highly sensitive, due to the dissimilar amount of available solar radiation, the proportion of glazing in conjunction with the higher losses with large windows plays a lesser role owing to the relatively good glazing (1.1 W/m²K) of the "low-energy house" standard. This results in a generous degree of architectural freedom with respect to the areas of glazing; adequate sunshading, i.e. reducing the radiation to below 25% in the closed condition, must however be ensured. The standard of insulation cuts the losses and hence the requirements quite significantly. Therefore, the absolute usable solar gains decrease and so too the portion of total heat gain from supplementary heating, internal and solar gains because the solar gains can be cut out by the sunshades, while the internal heat gains cannot be switched off. The influence of the construction, whether light or heavy, increases the usability by way of the possible intermediate storage of solar gains in the mass of the structure.

As the incident radiation totals given in Tab. 2.3.45 (p. 128) indicate, vertical east, west and south elevations exhibit very high radiation gains in spring and summer. If these are not restricted, then they lead to problems of overheating. Fig. 2.3.52 shows the temperature distribution for no shading, internal sunshade and external sunshade; the necessity of sunshading is clearly evident.

The consequence of the preceding considerations is that the new Thermal Insulation Act prescribes a maximum energy transmission for summer thermal insulation in the case of large glazing ratios. According to this, the product of the g-value of the glazing (with shading) and the proportion of windows f on a façade may not exceed 0.25 if the interior is to be cooled or the glazing accounts for ≥ 50% of the area of the façade with this orientation. The northern orientation and windows shaded all day do not have to comply with this rule. DIN 4108 Part 2 also recommends a maximum value of g x f of 0.12 – 0.25, depending on type of construction and means of ventilation.

*Types of sunshades and their effects*
If we examine the make-up of the radiation incident on a horizontal plane on a sunny summer's day, then we see that the majority is beam radiation. Accordingly, the energy gain is mainly generated by beam radiation and hence could be controlled by eliminating this. The altitude angle of the sun, i.e. the angle between a horizontal plane and the current position of the sun, is thus very significant.
We distinguish between two types of sunshade (Fig. 2.3.53), categorized according to their shading function. Sunshading that "dilutes" the radiation, e.g. printing, coating or a translucent material, does not reduce the composition but instead the maximum intensity of the incident radiation. A selective or geometrical sunshade targets part of the radiation, usually the beam radiation, and reflects it and/or converts it to diffuse radiation. This difference is irrelevant for the pure energy considerations as long as the corresponding radiation quantities are reduced. However, it is important for assessing comfort criteria because, first, in terms of thermal comfort the beam radiation is weighted differently to the diffuse radiation and second, in terms of visual comfort the converted diffuse portion can lead to the occurrence of glare.

*The influence of the position of the sunshading*
As a lesser or greater part of the incident solar radiation is converted into heat, depending on the type of shade, the position of such shading plays a major role with respect to how it shades the interior. The greenhouse effect is a disadvantage here as the heat radiation generated in the room cannot be reflected outwards and so the inner surface of the pane heats up the internal walls via heat emission and the air in the room directly via heat convection. Whereas the by-product of this internal glare protection and sunshade is highly desirable during the heating period, it does lead to markedly higher room temperatures in the summer (Tab. 2.3.52). Therefore, an internal shade should be designed as highly reflective in order to repel as much short-wave solar radiation as possible, a certain proportion of it being able to escape outside again. This aspect should be given special attention when glazing with a high insulation value is being used because the total energy transmittance of such glass differs according to the direction of the radiation. Consequently, a low-e coating at position 3 (see Fig. 2.3.10, p. 117) contributes to an increased heating of the inner pane – welcome in winter but unwelcome in summer. Solar-control glasses exploit this effect (see "Coated insu-

lating glass for increased thermal insulation", p. 118).
Fig. 2.3.54 shows the energy balances related to the position of the sunshade.

*Evaluating various sunshading arrangements*
Reducing the radiation intensity by way of a sunshade also cuts down the amount of daylight entering the room. Since diffuse radiation is especially necessary for illuminating the interior, particular attention should be paid to the selectivity of a sunshade, i.e. the ratio of light transmittance to total energy transmittance. If a room is too dark when the sunshade is closed, then the artificial lighting must be switched on. Besides the inevitable electricity consumption, the extra thermal load must be allowed for due to the lower light output per unit of energy used (lm/W).
VDI 2078 defines the shading coefficient $t^b$ for thermal calculations. This factor specifies by what fraction a sunshade reduces the total energy transmittance compared to a clear insulating glass with a g-value of 0.8. If we wish to describe just the sunshade, then we use the reduction factor z to DIN 4108 Part 2 in which "1" is the factor for no shade. The table in the standard includes single and double glazing. Coated low-e and solar-control glasses behave totally differently, which is why the reduction factors must be used with care! An analysis to DIN 67507 "Light, radiation and total energy transmittance values for glazing" should be carried out if necessary. Tab. 2.3.55 summarises various types of shading and gives the corresponding z-factors.

If external sunshading is to function reliably, its susceptibility to the weather cannot be ignored. If certain wind speeds are exceeded, movable louvres or canopies must be able to be retracted to prevent them being ruined. However, this means that the sunshade is then not available for the room affected and this can easily lead to overheating. This aspect is particularly important in windy regions and on tall buildings.

*Glasses with variable total energy transmittance*
The dream of many architects and engineers is variable glazing whose total energy transmittance can be adapted or controlled to suit the current conditions or room temperatures. For instance, solar energy could be used for heating purposes in winter, while in the transitionary periods and in summer, protection against overheating would be automatically or manually controlled. The real goal is to incorporate this capability into the glass or glazing unit itself. This would overcome the problems of weather resistance, wind susceptibility and maintenance associated with traditional sunshading. We distinguish between two main groups depending on function: non-coloured, purely diffusing glasses (tropic) and coloured, non-diffusing glasses (chromic). The control signals are divided into temperature (thermo...) and radiation (photo...) – the weather-related methods – and the application of an electrical voltage (electro...) and the feeding of gas into the cavity (gaso...) – the user-controlled methods (Tab. 2.3.59, p. 132).

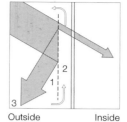 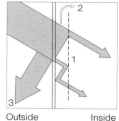

Outside     Inside     Outside     Inside

1   Sunshade
2   Convection
3   Reflection and absorption

2.3.54   Energy balance depending on the position of the sunshade

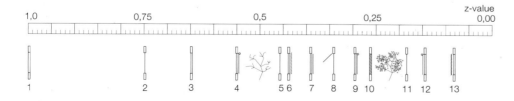

| 1,0 | 0,75 | 0,5 | 0,25 | z-value 0,00 |
|---|---|---|---|---|

1   Unglazed, unshaded window opening
2   6 mm single glazing
3   4-12-4 insulating glass
4   Internal dark roller blind, insulating glass

5   Tree without foliage, single glazing
6   Internal louvre blind, 45°, insulating glass
7   Internal reflective curtain, insulating glass

8   Awning, 45°, insulating glass
9   Internal roller blind, insulating glass
10   Internal louvre blind in cavity, 45°, counter-sash window

11   Tree with foliage, single glazing
12   External roller shutter, insulating glass
13   External louvre blind, insulating glass

2.3.55   Summary of various types of shading and their associated values

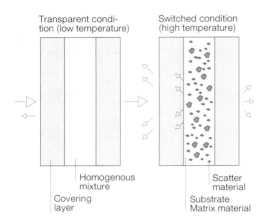

2.3.56    The composition of a thermotropic layer

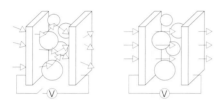

2.3.57    Microencapsulated liquid crystals

2.3.58    An example of glazing to a seminar room with
          and without a view through the glass

The composition of a thermotropic layer is illustrated in Fig. 2.3.56. Construction, method of operation and an example of electrotropic glazing are shown in Figs 2.3.57 and 2.3.60.

**Daylight**
Besides the thermal aspects, the relationship to the outside world and the admittance of daylight for illuminating interior spaces are also important factors in the use of glass. In addition to the subjective three-dimensional quality of a visual link to the outside (as required by the Places of Work Act), daylighting represents a saving in energy because of the reduced electricity consumption for artificial light while at the same time avoiding additional heating of the interior. This next section is intended to elucidate the principles of daylighting. The emphasis will be on outlining the geometrical effects of openings on the energy aspects because these can be measured and evaluated objectively. The influence of daylight on the atmosphere of a room or its occupants' well-being are undisputed; however, these effects are very difficult to assess in numerical terms. After a look at the concepts of daylighting, we shall examine the energy involved and how to plan for daylighting.

*Daylighting concepts, components and systems*
Building geometry concepts
The conventional use of daylight employs openings in the building envelope, i.e. in the sides or the roof (sidelighting, top lighting). Recent years have witnessed a growth in the popularity of atria, i.e. glazed internal courtyards, especially for office and commercial buildings. The main focus of interest is the vertical illuminance available at various levels in these internal courtyards. If there are no other components involved, then the illumination effects in these conventional cases are well known and relatively easy to predict (see "From glasshouse to atrium", p. 142).

Sidelighting
The quantity of daylight available in a room lit from the side is shown in Fig. 2.3.61 and the relevance of the window geometry, i.e. the height to the window sill, can be seen in Fig. 2.3.62, which shows that lowering the sill beyond a certain level does not lead to an increase in the amount of daylight in the room. This is due to the increased transparency, which must of course be shaded. The most significant aspect is that near the windows the illuminance is very high, frequently too high, and hence accompanied by problems of glare and overheating. By contrast, the illuminance is often already too low just a few metres into the room. Typical daylight factors – the ratio of the internal illuminance to the simultaneous external unobstructed illuminance on a horizontal plane under an overcast sky – for a point 3 m distant from a window 1 m high are 1% or less. Programs for calculating the exact figures for any specific situation with ease are now available for any standard PC. As daylight behaves independently of scale, models may be used for daylight studies (see "Planning for daylight", p. 136).
A common consequence of the inconsistent illuminance in sidelit rooms is that the sunshades are brought into use in order to reduce the high illuminance near the windows. This further deterioration of the already poor lighting conditions deeper inside the room leads to more lights being switched on despite the glorious sunshine! Therefore, new light-redirecting components have been developed with the aim of ensuring more even illuminance throughout the interior. Some of these will be described here. While overhanging eaves shade the entire window and provide protection against a sun high in the sky, i.e. protect against beam radiation and glare (Fig. 2.3.63), light shelves ensure a consistent lighting gradient farther back inside the room (Fig. 2.3.64)

2.3.59    The properties of switchable functional glasses

|  | g-value | Light transmittance | U-value of glazing system [W/m²K] | Optical impression |
|---|---|---|---|---|
| Thermotropic low-e window | 0.18-0.55 | 0.21-0.73 | 1.28 | white - clear |
| Electrochromic window | 0.12-0.36 | 0.2-0.64 | 1.1 | blue - neutral |
| Gasochromic low-e window | 0.15-0.53 | 0.15-0.64 | 1.05 | blue - neutral |

Phototropic, electrotropic (electro-optic) and thermochromic glasses are still undergoing trials and cannot yet be quantified. The figures quoted here may alter considerably in the course of further developments.

## Top lighting

The levels of illumination and daylight factors improve considerably as soon as openings in the ceiling are provided (Fig. 2.3.65). The effectiveness of top lighting as natural room illumination is clearly superior to that of sidelighting. The openings themselves are in the form of either rooflights or northlight roofs. Glare is not usually a problem. Nevertheless, it is advisable to screen off or reflect beam radiation in order to guarantee even illuminance and comfortable room temperatures.

## Atria

A section through a typical atrium and the associated illuminance distribution on the individual adjoining floors is shown in Fig. 2.3.66 (p. 134). As most atria are highly individual designs, the used of computer-assisted planning tools is recommended for ascertaining the illuminance distribution. The daylighting quality for a linear atrium, in relation to its size and construction, can be read off the graph in Fig. 2.3.108 (p. 144).

### Passive redirection of light

There is always sufficient daylight available to illuminate the interior of a building, even in poor weather. With, for example, 10 000 lux of vertical illuminance (roughly equal to 100 W/m² incident radiation), an opening having an area equal to 5% of the floor area would be enough to ensure 500 lx internally. Therefore, top-lighting concepts usually satisfy the lighting requirement. However, sidelit rooms are far more common and so components which direct the light from the outer walls into the interior are very appealing. A number of different configurations are possible and new ideas are constantly being developed and implemented.

Louvres are primarily designed to provide shade and are located in or in front of vertical windows. However, given a reflective surface and placed at the correct angle, they can be used to redirect the light. To avoid glare problems, light-redirecting louvres should only be used in overhead openings. Better redirection of the light is achieved when the louvres are installed with their curved sides (necessary for stability) facing downwards.

Another design employs specially shaped metallized louvres integrated in a glass/frame composite unit. These are manufactured for both façade and roof applications. They are shaped in such a way that the light from a low, winter sun is admitted virtually without hindrance and deflected up to the ceiling, whereas in summer the light is mainly reflected. Integrating these in pitched roofs reflects all the beam radiation. These units do not work on east or west elevations

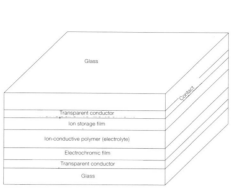

2.3.60   The structure of electrochromic glazing

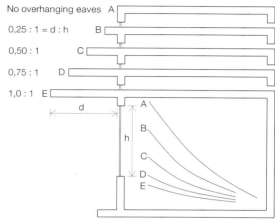

2.3.63   Daylight availability in a sidelit room with different eaves overhangs

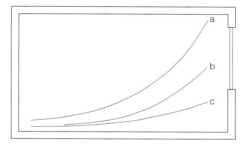

a  Window facing the sun, clear sky
b  Any orientation, overcast sky
c  Window not facing the sun, clear sky

2.3.61   Daylight availability in a sidelit room

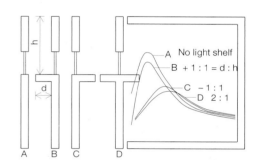

2.3.64   Daylight availability in a sidelit room with different light shelf geometries

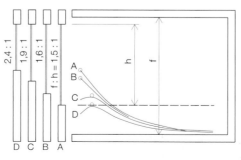

2.3.62   Daylight availability in a sidelit room with different sill heights (overcast sky)

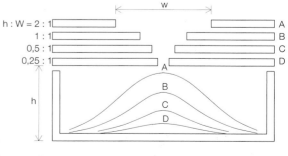

2.3.65   Daylight availability in a room with different widths of rooflights (overcast sky)

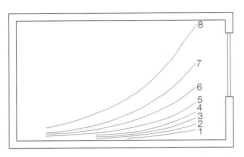

2.3.66    Average daylighting levels on the different floors

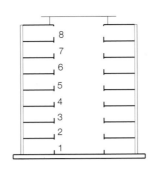

Section through building with atrium

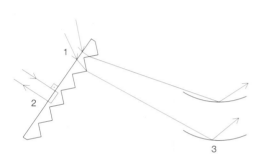

Transmission (1) of diffuse daylight and selective reflection (2) of direct sunlight through prismatic louvres. Redirecting (3) the diffuse light onto the ceiling and deeper into the interior by means of parabolic, partly perforated and metallized redirecting louvres.

2.3.67    Prism with solar-control function and redirection of zenith luminance

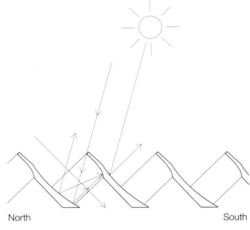

North                                    South

2.3.69    Section through a light grid

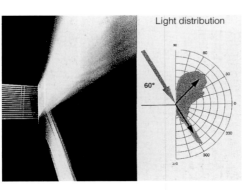

2.3.68    Schematic illustration of a glazing optimized for a particular application, with refractive panel and air inclusions.

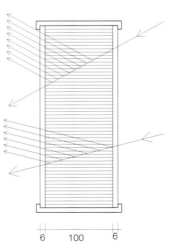

2.3.70    Schematic section through a transparent insulation element with honeycomb or capillary structure

and thermal problems can also occur due to the multiple reflections between the panes which lead to a certain amount of absorption and heating and hence higher glass temperatures.

Adjustable prism systems reflect the direct light back to the outside and deflect diffuse zenith luminance into a preferred direction, as Fig. 2.3.67 demonstrates. A view through is not possible.

Laser-cut and refractive panels are plexiglass panes with thin parallel incisions or parallel air inclusions. They redirect incident light by direct reflection but without impeding the view of the external surroundings. Thanks to flexible production methods, one principle of redirecting the light uses plates with variable angles and spacings (Fig. 2.3.68).

The linear systems described above all have the disadvantage that they are only matched to the altitude of the sun, not its direction. Two-dimensional systems can overcome this deficiency. These include reflective grids with optimized grid profiles as have been developed for roofs, where they can guarantee reflection of beam radiation at any time of day, any day of the year (Fig. 2.3.69). One well-known example is the Linz Exhibition and Congress Centre by Herzog + Partner (see p. 310).

Daylighting elements made from transparent thermal insulation combine excellent optical properties with low U-values. The hemispherical transmission of a typical honeycomb structure (Fig. 2.3.70) achieves approx. 75% of the glazing transmission and so is more than adequate for illumination purposes. Added to this is the light-redirecting effect of the structure. Direct observation of a double window (left half: insulating glass; right half: transparent insulation honeycomb) reveals that the illuminance of the transparent insulation element is about 35% higher than that of the insulating glass. Two systems are currently available: capillary or honeycomb structures made from PC or PMMA, sealed dust-tight between two panes (Fig. 2.3.70). All the reflections occurring in the structure are directed forwards and hence exhibit no losses. This explains the high transmission values. It should be noted that the light-redirecting property causes these surfaces to appear very bright under beam radiation, so they should be positioned carefully to avoid possible glare problems. Tab. 2.3.71 compares the physical parameters of transparent thermal insulation elements.

The number of hours of sunshine is relatively low in many regions, including Central Europe. Therefore, methods are required which redirect diffuse light in a preferred direction so that it can be treated like direct light. This works only at the expense of the total illuminance, although this disadvantage can be acceptable because, generally speaking, there is enough daylight available.

The most popular principle is the reverse use of non-imaging concentrators. The diagrams in Fig. 2.3.72 illustrate how this principle is implemented with conventional light shelves. This enables areas far away from the windows to be illuminated while excessive brightness adjacent the windows is reduced.

*Active redirection of light*
Single-axis tracking systems usually comprise large louvres or groups of louvres fitted in front of the building envelope (walls, roof). They can be rotated about one horizontal axis and, controlled by computer, track the altitude angle of the sun so that direct, distracting light is screened or redirected. Diffuse light passes through virtually unimpeded. Care is also taken to ensure that an adequate view out is maintained. A great many technical variations are possible: from single panes to prisms and transparent insulation to highly reflective metal tube structures. Opaque or diffuse reflective louvres are often employed overhead. Fig. 2.3.74 shows a single-axis tracking louvre system placed above a pitched glass roof and acting as a solar-control element and diffuser.

One intriguing new development can be seen on the check-in hall at Munich Airport (architect: Busso von Busse): three layers of grids consisting of parallel, white-coated aluminium tubes which can be slid back and forth in relation to each other. Fig. 2.3.73 shows a schematic section through such a tubular solar-control grid. The positions of the three layers are controlled by computer in such a way that direct light never enters the check-in hall. Instead, the direct light is scattered along the surfaces and reaches the interior as diffuse light.

Heliostats are double-axis tracking systems, normally with stationary mirrors as well. In the course of a day, direct light is reflected in a certain constant direction by rotating heliostats. As Fig. 2.3.75 (p. 136) shows, the light can be directed beneath and parallel to the floor slab, being deflected and spread above each individual work surface requiring illumination. Heliostats are interesting because sunlight can be focussed and redirected for illumination purposes. A heliostat surface the size of a postcard is sufficient to illuminate the whole surface of a desk with 500 lx. Furthermore, the almost parallel nature of sunlight permits a theoretically unlimited redirection of the light deep into the interior. However, the tracking accuracy does put a constraint on this. Fig. 2.3.77 (p. 136) shows a group of heliostats on the roof of a showroom in Munich.

Another way of supplying daylight to the inner zones of a building which cannot be served by top lighting or sidelighting is via tubes, so-called "light pipes", which are lined with a highly reflective material. The light is reflected into them from heliostats and fed to the respective place of use in diffuse or direct form (Fig. 2.3.76, p. 136).

*Daylighting and building energy requirement*
In most office and commercial buildings the energy required for lighting accounts for a considerable part of the total energy consumption. In addition, there is a close correlation between energy for lighting on the one hand and the thermal energy requirement for heating/cooling on the other.
Figs 2.3.78 and 2.3.79 (p. 137) indicate the qualitative dependence of a building's total energy requirement on the area of the windows. Starting with a completely impervious envelope, electricity consumption initially drops as the window area increases because less electricity is needed for the lighting. In winter (heating case) this means an increase in the heating requirement because fewer lights are producing less waste heat (Fig. 2.3.78, p. 137). And as the larger windows also generally lead to a higher average U-value for the building envelope, additional heat losses can be expected.

We can see that the thermal quality of the window areas is critical when deciding whether or not daylighting can save energy in the heating case. In summer the situation is reversed (Fig. 2.3.79, p. 137): the decline in the electricity required for the lighting means that the cooling demand also drops. The total energy requirement falls dramatically to the point where enlarging the windows still further no longer has any effect on the level of illumination. From this point on, every extra watt of incident radiation represents additional cooling load. Window areas with a high luminous efficacy are advantageous in summer. It is evident that daylighting can have negative effects on the energy balance. In extreme climatic regions, planning for daylighting is straightforward because either the heating or the cooling case dominates. Central Europe on the other hand often means a combination of the two has to be considered. Optimization is difficult because glare protection and sunshading also have to be matched to the daylighting.

| Type | TI thickness | U-value [mm] | g-value [W/m²K] | $\tau_e$ | $\tau_v$ |
|---|---|---|---|---|---|
| G-HC-G | 50 | 1.01 | 0.78 | 0.71 | 0.80 |
| G-HC-G | 70 | 0.85 | 0.78 | 0.70 | 0.79 |
| G-A-G | 20 | 0.96 | 0.49 | 0.48 | 0.40 |
| G-G | - | 2.93 | 0.79 | 0.74 | 0.82 |

2.3.71 Physical parameters of transparent thermal insulation (TI) elements (G = glass, HC = honeycomb structure, A = aerogel, g-value = total energy transmittance, $\tau$ = transmission, e = energy, v = visible)

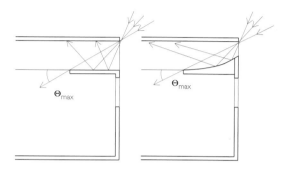

2.3.72 Conventional and anidolic light shelves

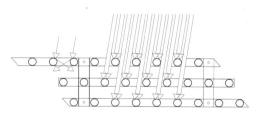

2.3.73 Schematic section through a tubular grid solar-control screen

2.3.74 "Single-axis" tracking louvres above a glass roof acting as solar-control element and diffuser

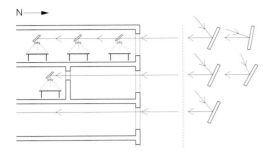

2.3.75 The principle of illuminating work surfaces by means of a heliostat system

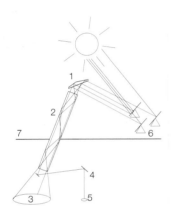

| | |
|---|---|
| 1 Focussing mirror | 5 Light spots |
| 2 Light pipe | 6 Heliostats |
| 3 Light cone | 7 Climate membrane |
| 4 Redirecting mirror | |

2.3.76 Light pipe: principle and application

### How daylighting influences energy and comfort in a building

The most effective form of lighting is the direct use of daylight, which has a better degree of illuminance (140 – 160 lm/W) than artificial light (20 – 100 lm/W).

### Visual comfort and limiting glare

Glare is a common phenomena in rooms with high illuminance among otherwise dark surroundings. It is usually caused by direct glare from light sources which are too bright, too large or inadequately screened. Numerous studies have been carried out into the effects of glare caused by lamps.[10] Windows also serve other purposes apart from providing light; a pleasant view might well partially compensate in psychological terms for unpleasant glare. The point at which glare becomes noticeable can be classed as the upper limit of tolerable illuminance. The lower limit is determined by the minimum level of illumination as prescribed by the relevant standards, e.g. DIN 5035 Part 2 "Illuminating internal rooms with artificial light; standard figures for places of work".

Perception-oriented lighting design is the key approach for the future. One of its pioneers, Richard Kelly, defined three forms of light: ambient light, the focal glow and the play of brilliance. "Ambient light" is defined by Kelly as quite simply the required illuminance. The provision of an adequate distribution of brightness enables us to organize the wealth of information in our surroundings; this is what Kelly means by "focal glow". The third variation, "play of brilliance", is the product of the realization that light itself represents information and a design element; "play of brilliance" invigorates interiors, furnishes them with an ambience. William Lam distinguishes between "activity needs" and "biological needs". The former is more or less identical with the

required illuminance; the latter, expressing the degree of visual comfort, embraces the requirements for orientation in time and space, the need to ease tension and the balance between humans' need to communicate and their need for a defined private sphere. Illumination can contribute much to fulfilling these demands.

### Planning for daylight

Methods of modelling under natural and artificial skies make use of the fact that daylight behaves independently of the scale. Using scale models of buildings is a widespread method of demonstrating and investigating architectural concepts. Such models can be placed in the open air or under an "artificial sky", a large hemispherical installation with computer-controlled lamps fitted to the inner surface to simulate various sky luminance conditions. A number of different versions can be found in practice. Cameras and endoscopes can be used to obtain an impression of and also measure the level of illumination in the interior. Daylighting elements made from new materials have to be scaled in order to gain a realistic impression of how they work in a room. Only clear or perfectly diffuse materials are excepted. The value of studying models under artificial sky conditions is limited, especially when employing innovative daylighting techniques. Fig. 2.3.81 shows daylight measurements on a scale model.

### Daylight availability

The luminous efficacy of daylight can also be interpreted as a mark of its quality: the higher the luminous efficacy of a light source, the lower is the energy required for generating a given luminous flux.[11] Tab. 2.3.80 lists the calculated values of $\eta$ for the AM 1.5 spectrum, its visible part and its extraterrestrial relationships (a black body emitter of 5777 K is assumed here).

[10] The degree of direct glare G can be expressed as follows:

$$G = \frac{L_s^m \times \omega^n}{L_b \times P^m}$$

where

L_s   the luminance of the glare source
L_b   the luminance of the background
ω    the solid angle subtended by the glare source as seen from the observer
P    the "position index", which basically contains the distance of the glare source, forwards and sideways, from the observer.

The exponents m and n vary from author to author (1.6 – 2.3 for m, 0.5 – 0.8 for n). Depending on the method, G is translated into a "glare index", a "visual comfort probability" (VCP) or a system consisting of luminance limit curves. The latter is mainly aimed at designers to help them avoid glare when positioning lamps.

[11] The luminous efficacy $\eta$ is calculated as follows:

$$\eta = \frac{M_v}{M_e} = \frac{K_m \int M_{e\lambda} V(\lambda) d\lambda}{\int M_{e\lambda} d\lambda}$$

where for daylight, the specific spectral emission of solar radiation must be used for $M_{e\lambda}$. $\eta$ depends on the limits of integration.

[12] http://eande.lbl.gov/BTP/WDG.html
[13] http://www.enermodal.com/framepls.html #vision4
[14] http://eande.lbl.gov/BTP/NFRCSPEC/ oder http://www.nfrc.org/
[15] http://erg.ucd.ie/wis/wis.html

2.3.77 Heliostats on the roof of the BMW pavilion in Munich

The luminous efficacy of daylight is comparable with that of high-pressure sodium discharge lamps and much higher than that of fluorescent tubes or incandescent bulbs. Filtering out all the non-visible parts from the solar spectrum can raise the luminous efficacy to 204 lm/W, a value not yet achieved by man-made lamps. The luminous efficacy is lower outside the earth's atmosphere than it is at sea level because of the absorption belts in the atmosphere, which lie mainly in the infrared range.

**Methods of calculating glass parameters and how glass influences interior climate and energy requirement**

*Glass parameters*
Typical glass parameters are published by the glass manufacturers in their sales literature. The values given apply to the centre of the pane and do not allow for edge zone effects. Apart from that, when it comes to U-values a distinction is made between the figures calculated according to DIN 52619 and those of the *Bundesanzeiger*. The latter quotes values which are, on average, 0.1 – 0.3 W/m²K higher than the DIN figures, and thus are more realistic for higher temperature differences. The total energy transmittance, the light transmittance and the details concerning reflectance and absorptance are valid for perpendicular incident radiation. The glass parameters should be corrected to allow for size of pane and frame area. But the values relevant to energy issues deteriorate for high-quality low-e glasses. One example from a manufacturer's catalogue is shown in Tab. 2.3.84 (p. 138).

*Methods of calculation, computer programs*
The introduction of glass coatings for modifying the U- and g-values as well as the use of various gas fillings in insulating glass led to such a vast number of combinations and hence chances of optimizing the glazing that the obvious way forward was to use a theoretical method of calculation. This gave birth to methods of calculation for determining the energy values for any combination of glasses and gas filling. Today, "Window 4.1" from the Lawrence Berkeley Laboratory (LBL) in California[12] and "Vision"[13] from the University of Waterloo in Canada represent computerized design aids which, on the American market, can even be used for analysing new types of glass without having to perform tests. This verifies the reliability of these methods of calculation compared to the problems encountered with measuring inaccuracies. The methods of calculation have now been extended into the spectral area and comprehensive details right up to

spectral parameters are available on the websites of many manufacturers.[14]
The following section shows excerpts from the parameter calculations for a specific window 1 x 1 m with low-e glass and argon filling. The frame is in this case merely the edge seal, which, taking into account a corner correction, raises the U-value from 1.49 to 1.66 W/m²K, i.e. by 11%. The optical parameters, e.g. daylight transmittance, g-value, are hardly affected by such a narrow edge seal. If this glazing is now placed in a 60 mm timber frame with a square cross-section, then the U-value climbs to 1.92 W/m²K, a decrease of almost 30% compared to the middle of the pane. At the same time, the shade provided by the frame (frame proportion 22%) reduces the parameters relevant to radiation with respect to the whole window: g-value now 0.51, daylight transmittance 57% (whole window figures 0.65 and 72% respectively). This reveals quite clearly that the frame must be taken into account when assessing the energy and daylight aspects of windows. Detailed values for complicated frame constructions with thermal breaks can only be computed via a two-dimensional thermal bridge calculation, like the one provided in the "Frame" program, the output of which may be transferred directly into "Window 4.1".
Other programs on the market are "GLAD" – optical and thermal properties of glazing materials (glass data bank GLAD-PC), concluding report, EMPA (Dübendorf, Switzerland, 1997) – and WIS, Windows Information System, the result of a European research programme.[15]

*Energy balances*
A comparison of the solar gains and the thermal losses must be carried out to balance the energy flows at a glazing unit. In doing so it must be remembered that not all the radiation penetrating the pane can be used because, in certain circumstances, it contributes to an overheating of the interior at that moment and not to supplementing the heating. Therefore, balances are only possible at an hourly interval. Balances covering longer periods must assess the usability of the solar gain, which depends on the construction, the heating controls, the inertia of the heating and the ventilation behaviour. Tab. 2.3.85 shows the method of balancing and its assessment of the solar usability, while Tab. 2.3.82 lists the usability of solar gains according to the 1995 Thermal Insulation Act.

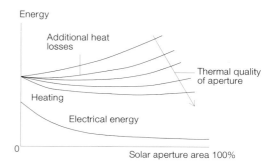
2.3.78 Qualitative correlation between total energy requirement of a building and area of windows (or openings) for the heating case

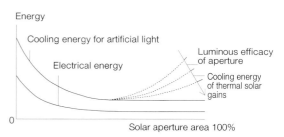
2.3.79 Qualitative correlation between total energy requirement of a building and area of windows (or openings) for the cooling case

22.3.80 Luminous efficacy of daylight under various spectral conditions

|   | AM 1.5 | AM 1.5 visible | Extraterrestrial |
|---|--------|----------------|------------------|
| η | 111 lm/W | 204 lm/W | 98 lm/W |

2.3.81 Measuring daylight on a scale model

2.3.82 Availability and usability of solar gains according to the Thermal Insulation Act
E = incident radiation, G = gain

| Orientation | | Year [kWh/m²] | To 1995 TI Act during heating period for g = 0.6 |
|---|---|---|---|
| South | E | 792 | 400 |
| | G | 274 | 110 |
| North | E | 433 | 160 |
| | G | 148 | 44 |
| East | E | 727 | 275 |
| | G | 267 | 76 |
| West | E | 691 | 275 |
| | G | 251 | 76 |
| Horizontal | E | 1118 | |
| | G | 397 | |

*Dynamic behaviour of rooms*
Since the internal climate of a room is not constant, i.e. not static, but instead reacts according to the changing external influences and the storage and discharge effects in the structure as the internal temperatures vary, i.e. reacts dynamically, then an accurate energy balance can only be drawn up by means of a dynamic method of calculation. To do this, the building must be modelled not only by way of the insulation values but by the materials and their dimensions too. On the other hand, the external climate with its changes by the hour, indeed by the minute, is treated as a framework. The calculation shows that heavy construction behaves very sluggishly when it receives solar radiation via a window. This means that, in contrast to the balancing

method, statements can be made concerning room temperatures and their distributions which, on the other hand, in turn permit a more exact assessment of the solar usability. Storage effects can also be described with this method; besides the use of solar and internal gains, these effects also permit an evaluation of the overheating behaviour of a building design and the drawing-up of ventilation strategies. Examples of dynamic building simulation programs are TRNSYS, DOE-2, ESP and TASS. The adaptation of VDI 2078 for the calculation of cooling loads (1995), from static to dynamic design, illustrates the response of the standards to such methods of calculation.
Fig. 2.3.83 shows the dynamic simulation of a temperature curve in a test room for heavy and lightweight construction.

Temperature [°C]

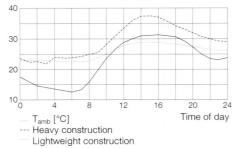

....... $T_{amb}$ [°C]
--- Heavy construction
........ Lightweight construction

2.3.83 Dynamic simulation of a south-facing office without sunshading

2.3.84 Example from a manufacturer's catalogue

Insulating glass

| Make-up outer/ cavity/ inner | $U_v$-value to DIN 52619 | $U_v$-value to *Bundesanzeiger* | Light transmittance Γ | Gen. colour rendering index $R_a$ in transparency | g-value | $R_w$ measured value | Light reflectance outwards | Shading coefficient b | Thickness | Weight | min. dimension (max. edge length) | min. dimension | max. surface | max. side ratio |
|---|---|---|---|---|---|---|---|---|---|---|---|---|---|---|
| mm | W/m²K | W/m²K | % | - | % | dB | % | - | mm | kg/m² | cm | m² | - | |
| .... .... | .... | .... | .... | .... | .... | .... | .... | .... | .... | | .... | .... | .... | .... |
| 4/16/4 | 1.1 | 1.2 | 76 | 98 | 58 | - | - | 0.67 | 24 | 20 | (240) | 24 × 24 | 2.83 | 1:6 |
| .... .... | .... | .... | .... | .... | .... | .... | .... | .... | | | .... | .... | .... | .... |

2.3.85 Balancing methods and their assessment of solar usability

| Method | Balance period | Solar use factor | Conditions |
|---|---|---|---|
| Thermal Insulation Act | Heating period | 0.46 | max. 60% glazing to façade |
| SIA 380/1, Hessen standard Energy pass | Month | 0.2–1 | Model of building, monthly climate totals |
| Dynamic simulation | Hour | 0–1 | Construction, controls, hourly climate values |

## Glass as thermal insulation

If we compare the thermal transmittance of single glazing (U-value 5.8 W/m²K) with that of a 175 mm single-leaf clay brick wall (U-value 1.6 W/m²K), then it is clear that glazing of this standard represents a major loss factor and the area of glazing in a façade is primarily determined by the amount of light required. High-quality low-e glasses these days reach U-values as low as 0.4 W/m²K, corresponding to 100 mm of mineral wool insulation of thermal conductance class 040. Taking solar gains into account, this turns glazing into heat sources and permits large expanses of glass. The reduced losses, particularly with lightweight construction, can however very quickly lead to problems of overheating. Therefore, some form of sunshading must be considered, since internal shading in conjunction with high-quality low-e glass has a severely restricted function and provides shading factors of 0.7 – 0.8. This means that 70 – 80% of the radiation gain still remains in the room. The Thermal Insulation Act therefore stipulates a maximum g-value[16] for glazing with shading of 0.25 for all orientations apart from north for the maximum summer temperature when the building incorporates mechanical cooling or has a window area exceeding 50% of the façade.

*Thermal energy balance at the glass pane*
Thermal energy balances for different orientations are listed in Tab. 2.3.86 for one typical and one exceptional low-e glass. A positive balance signifies an energy gain during the heating period, a negative one is an overall heat loss. The values must be seen in relation to the heating requirement over the heated area, which is max. 70 kWh/m² p.a. according to the 1995 Thermal Insulation Act and in the region of 35 kWh/m² p.a. for a low-energy house. Internal heat gains must be allowed for; these amount to 15 kWh/m² p.a. for residential property and 30 kWh/m² p.a. for office buildings.

*Temporary thermal insulation*
In the case of glazing with a U-value much higher than that of a wall, it is advisable to reduce the heat losses during the night – when solar gains are absent – by providing additional temporary thermal insulation. This can take the form of internal or external cov-

erings which utilize a captured volume of air or an additional thermal resistance to lower the U-value. Care should be exercised with an internal temporary insulator as the glass then no longer has a thermal link with the room and this can lead to condensation forming on the inner pane as it cools. Therefore, an airtight covering is important because otherwise the inner frame can suffer over the years. As the quality of the glass improves, so the potential savings offered by temporary insulation decrease dramatically. For U-values below 1.4 W/m²K this only appears advisable when all other loss factors have been minimized beforehand and, for example, mechanical ventilation with heat recovery is employed. The insulating effect of the very popular roller shutter is limited because the heat losses and the leakage paths via the shutter housing integrated within the wall often far exceed the savings.

*The problem of condensation on panes and edge seal*
If the surface temperature of the pane drops below the dew point, then the moisture in the air condenses on the surface. A distinction is made between internal and external condensation.

Internal condensation
Panes affected by condensation and frost are the signs of a condensation problem across the whole pane. The introduction of laminated and insulating glass substantially reduced this problem for the surface of the glass. However, the edge seal represents a thermal bridge which brings about a severe local reduction in the U-value, determined by the spacer and the covering by frame or cover strip.
If we take a low-e glass with a U-value of 1.4 W/m²K at the centre of the pane, then an edge seal incorporating an aluminium spacer gives us a U-value of 2.6 W/m²K in the edge zone. With internal and external temperatures of 20 °C and 0 °C respectively, the humidity limit for the centre of the pane drops from 77% to 65% relative humidity. An air humidity in the room which exceeds this means that condensation will appear in the edge zone. At this point the lowest edge zone temperatures are to be found along the bottom edge of the pane owing to the convection in the cavity. Using a stainless steel spacer raises the humidity limit of the edge zone to 70% and an insulated edge seal increases this still further to 77%. Fig. 2.3.87 shows the temperature curve for 20 °C room temperature and various humidities. The humidity limit decreases as the internal temperature drops in relation to the external temperature. The U-values for the centre of the pane and the edge zone at different

| 2.3.86 | Thermal balances of two low-e glasses according to the Thermal Insulation Act | | |
|---|---|---|---|
| Orientation | Solar gains to 1995 TI act during heating period [kWh/m²] | Heat losses [kWh/m²] | Thermal balance during heating period [kWh/m²] |
| g-value | g = 0.6; k = 1.4 W/m²K | | |
| South | 110 | 118 | - 8 |
| North | 44 | 118 | - 74 |
| East | 76 | 118 | - 42 |
| West | 76 | 118 | - 42 |
| g-value | g = 0.42; k = 0.4 W/m²K | | |
| South | 77 | 34 | + 43 |
| North | 31 | 34 | - 3 |
| East | 53 | 34 | + 19 |
| West | 53 | 34 | + 19 |

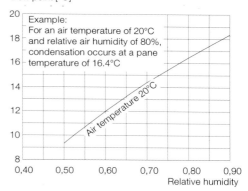

Dew point [°C]

Example:
For an air temperature of 20°C and relative air humidity of 80%, condensation occurs at a pane temperature of 16.4°C

Air temperature 20°C

Relative humidity

2.3.87 Dew point curve

[16] Calculating the g-value
$g_v = g_f \times z_v$
where
$g_v$ = shaded glazing
$g_f$ = g-value of window
$z_v$ = reduction factor for shading
(see also Fig. 2.3.55)

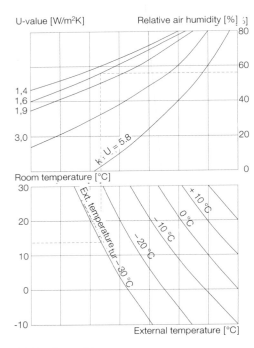

U-value [W/m²K]    Relative air humidity [%]

Room temperature [°C]

External temperature [°C]

2.3.88   Dew point nomogram

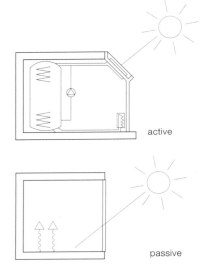

active

passive

2.3.89   The concepts of passive and active use
of solar radiation

2.3.90   Avoiding shading by ensuring appropriate
distances between buildings

room humidities can be read off the graph in
Fig. 2.3.88. The intersection of internal temperature and maximum external temperature
clearly shows at which point condensation
can be expected.

External condensation
This only occurs on glazing in rooms with
minimal heating or when using high-quality
low-e glass. It is caused by long-wave radiation from the outer pane into the sky when
this outweighs the incoming heat flow to the
glass, which happens with low room temperatures, e.g. in a car, or with very good insulation. The surface temperature of the outer
surface of the glass drops below the ambient temperature and can even fall below the
dew point temperature, leading to the formation of frost. This effect is particularly prevalent on roof windows employing high-quality
low-e glass; during dismal winter periods
such windows can remain covered in condensation or frost all day.

*Comfort effects due to "cold radiation" and
descending cold air*
If we compare the surface temperature of an
inner pane with the temperature in the room,
then we find it is 2 – 8 K lower, depending
on external temperature and the quality of
the glazing. The cold surface radiates into
the room and leads to discomfort in the
vicinity of large areas of glass. Accordingly,
the temperature as perceived by the occupants, made up of 50% room air temperature and 50% room surfaces temperatures,
drops rapidly.
The internal air cools at the surface of the
pane and, being heavier, descends. At a
certain height and with poor-quality glazing,
this descending cold air can lead to
draughts adjacent the façade, especially
near the floor because the deflected cold air
penetrates several metres into the room and
reaches velocities of up to 0.5 m/s.
In the past this was dealt with by placing
radiators under the windows. The ascending
hot air intercepted the descending cold air.
This is why finned heating pipes are often
positioned at regular intervals on tall
façades. If glasses with U-values of
1.0 W/m²K or better are used, then the radiators can be moved away from the windows
and the unsightly heating tubes dispensed
with.
Infrared-reflective coatings on the inside of
the pane do improve comfort by cutting
down on radiation but on the other hand iso-
late the pane from the room in thermal terms
and so lead to lower pane temperatures
and, possibly, increased cold air descending to the floor. A detailed study can only be
carried out by means of a computerized flow
simulation which demonstrates the distribution of temperatures and velocities.

## Glazing applications in buildings and systems

The applications of the properties and
effects described so far give rise to new
problems in the overall system, e.g. glare,
fire propagation, dense smoke. A number of
underlying concepts will be briefly outlined
in order to help understand the pros and
cons of the individual measures.

Function
The façade to a building serves as the cutoff
point for the weather, as the climate break.
In other words, it protects against rain and
wind, insulates against heat and cold, and
acts as a noise barrier. Variable apertures in
the façade permit a partial opening of this
boundary for the purpose of air exchange
and a relationship with the exterior. In addition, transparent and translucent façade
components enable the energy flow from
outside to inside in the form of short-wave
solar radiation, bringing heat and light with
it, and create a visual link with the outside
world for the user. The use of glass – transparent to solar radiation and opaque to heat
radiation – causes the glazed area to be
heated up – the greenhouse effect. These
heat gains are, on the one hand, appreci-
ated when the outside temperature is low
but, on the other hand, can very quickly
lead to overheating with higher external temperatures and/or high internal heat sources.
Sunshading may be required in such cases.
Further, daylighting is desirable for activities
near the windows but privacy and glare
must be considered, the latter particularly
so when VDUs are in use.

Basic concepts
There are two principal approaches to gaining solar energy: active and passive (Fig.
2.3.89). The critical factor is whether merely
building components are to be used (passive) or additional, moving elements are
employed for transport (active).

**Passive uses**

The simplest passive building component for exploiting solar radiation for illumination and for supplementary heating is the window, i.e. the use of direct gains. The unobstructed incidence of radiation on the window is decisive here, dependent on the surroundings, the solar altitude angle and the angle of incidence on the pane (Fig. 2.3.90). The solar altitude angle depends on the geographical latitude of the location; the minimum solar altitude angle at midday can be calculated.[17]

The solar gains in the rooms can be used to differing extents depending on the type of construction and use of the building (Figs 2.3.91 – 2.3.96). Moreover, the available solar radiation must be limited by way of

[17]  Minimum solar altitude angle
    = 90° - (degree of latitude + 23.45°)

According to this, the minimum distance between two rows of houses in Würzburg, 48.8° is 24 m, assuming a building height of 8 m, if the ground floor is to always remain outside the shadow of the neighbouring building. Suitable shaping of the top storeys can bring about an improvement.

suitable shading in order to protect the interior from overheating. As windows exhibit higher heat losses and compete with solid walls, other passive systems have been developed to overcome the disadvantages of the direct-gain window system.

*Translucent thermal insulation (TI)*
Whereas traditional thermal insulation attached to walls is opaque, i.e. impermeable to solar radiation, translucent thermal insulation (Fig. 2.3.97, p. 142) allows large amounts of solar radiation (up to 70%) to pass through. TI remains impervious to heat radiation and hot-air convection. This effect, frequently played out behind glass, is based on very thin capillaries which convey the sunlight to an absorber (dark-coloured solid wall) and capture the long-wave heat radiation from the wall but present a great obstacle to the convection between absorber and glazing and so lead to reduced losses. Consequently, the incidence of solar radiation causes the wall behind the translucent insulation to heat up and then transfer this warmth into the interior. The density and material of the wall play a crucial role here because it is these factors that allow the

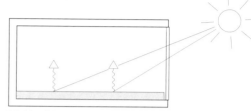

2.3.91    Direct gain

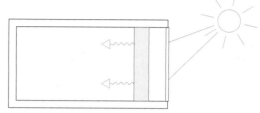

2.3.92    Trombe wall

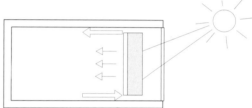

2.3.93    Vented solar wall

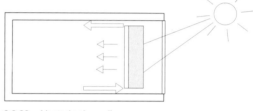

2.3.94    Glass extension (sunspace)

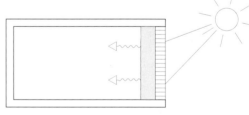

2.3.95    Translucent thermal insulation

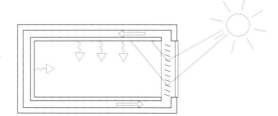

2.3.96    Window/Air collector

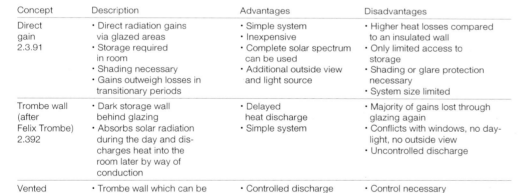

| Concept | Description | Advantages | Disadvantages |
|---|---|---|---|
| Direct gain 2.3.91 | • Direct radiation gains via glazed areas<br>• Storage required in room<br>• Shading necessary<br>• Gains outweigh losses in transitionary periods | • Simple system<br>• Inexpensive<br>• Complete solar spectrum can be used<br>• Additional outside view and light source | • Higher heat losses compared to an insulated wall<br>• Only limited access to storage<br>• Shading or glare protection necessary<br>• System size limited |
| Trombe wall (after Felix Trombe) 2.392 | • Dark storage wall behind glazing<br>• Absorbs solar radiation during the day and discharges heat into the room later by way of conduction | • Delayed heat discharge<br>• Simple system | • Majority of gains lost through glazing again<br>• Conflicts with windows, no daylight, no outside view<br>• Uncontrolled discharge |
| Vented solar wall 2.3.93 | • Trombe wall which can be specially discharged via rear vents<br>• Partly insulated on the room side | • Controlled discharge<br>• No overheating<br>• Reduced night-time losses | • Control necessary<br>• Non-return valve required<br>• Soiling |
| Glass extension (sunspace) 2.3.94 | • Projecting or integral section with large areas of glazing<br>• Only brings savings if not heated | • Temporary extra floor space<br>• Can be used as sun trap<br>• Buffer space with intermediate climate | • Can easily become an energy-guzzler<br>• Requires insulating glass because of condensation<br>• Sunshade necessary<br>• Not a frost-free planting area<br>• Less light in adjacent room |
| Translucent thermal insulation 2.3.95 | • Dark storage wall with translucent insulation<br>• Allows sunshine through but retains heat and discharges it into the room later by convection | • High gains, low losses<br>• Increased comfort due to warm wall<br>• Permits lower room air temperature | • Risk of overheating, must be shaded in summer<br>• Higher costs<br>• Conflicts with windows<br>• No daylight, no outside view |
| Window/ Air collector 2.3.96 | • Coupled window with integral sunshade and cavity with air circulation<br>• Driven by thermosyphon effect<br>• Heat transported to storage ceiling or wall | • Window and collector function<br>• Storage remote from room<br>• Natural control<br>• Low additional costs due to double function | • Higher temperatures in coupled window, also in summer<br>• Passive discharge cannot be controlled<br>• Air ducts required<br>• Additional storage required |

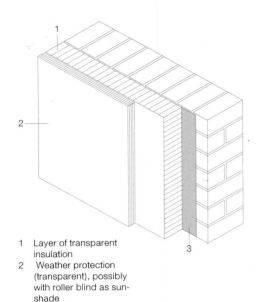

1 Layer of transparent insulation
2 Weather protection (transparent), possibly with roller blind as sunshade
3 Black paint (absorbent)

2.3.97   Typical TI wall

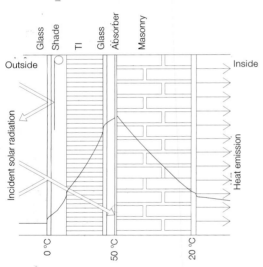

2.3.98   TI element with shading and temperature profile

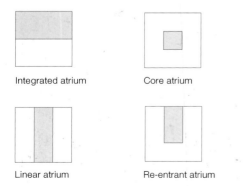

Integrated atrium

Core atrium

Linear atrium

Re-entrant atrium

2.3.99   Various arrangements of atria and heat buffers

heat gains to be passed on to the rooms after a certain delay. Hence, solar gains can be discharged up to six hours later into the rooms beyond the translucent insulation. If we balance the heat flows at the TI wall, then these reverse in the case of incident solar radiation: from a loss to the outside into a gain or excess for the inside.

To protect against overheating, TI façades must be fitted with a sunshade (Fig. 2.3.98). Motorized foil roller blinds are the most popular form, although fixed shades are conceivable for purely south-facing walls. An inexpensive alternative has been developed which uses a translucent plaster composed of glass balls and a bonding agent. Because of its reduced transmission, no shading is necessary. One interesting application is the use of translucent insulation in refurbishment projects to supplement inadequate thermal insulation and to solve many physical problems, e.g. humidity (Fig. 2.3.101).

*From glasshouse to atrium*
An important predecessor of today's glass architecture was London's Crystal Palace of 1851 (see p. 23). The new glazed trade fair hall in Leipzig (see pp. 300–303) continues this tradition.
Some glasshouses serve merely as weatherproof envelopes and are called "house-in-house" systems. These generate a local microclimate in which smaller, air-conditioned buildings are located (Fig. 2.3.102) One group represented in large numbers is the greenhouse for cultivated plants. Roof shape, heating, shading and type of glass are not chosen at random but instead matched to the plants underneath in order to achieve optimum economic results. We distinguish between four types of glasshouse according to their shape and relationship to the whole structure (Fig. 2.3.99).

Integrated atrium
In this variation the glasshouse is not separate but instead has at least one wall common with a solid part of the building. As a rule therefore, it usually possesses more storage capacity than a pure glasshouse.

Core atrium
In this classic arrangement it is only the glass roof that forms part of the external envelope. The internal climate is to a great extent determined by the walls enclosing the atrium, which in turn separate the surrounding spaces from the core atrium.

Linear atrium
This form (Fig. 2.3.103) links two parallel blocks. The ends are formed by glazed gables. It normally creates an intermediate climate which, for pure circulation zones, does not require additional heating.

Re-entrant atrium
In this variation on the core atrium, one wall of the atrium is at the same time an external wall.

Types of use
Glasshouses and atria can be categorized according to their uses:
• Weather protection
  The glasshouse serves to protect against rain and wind and only as a short-term space for people, e.g. unheated glass foyers, railway stations, indoor markets. Internal air temperatures < 0 °C are possible.
• Thoroughfare
  The atrium is a circulation zone and links heated parts of the building. It is only a short-term space for people. Internal air temperatures of 10 – 14 °C satisfy even higher demands of comfort.
• Active use
  People continually circulate in this space, e.g. sports halls, art exhibitions, hotel entrances. Internal air temperatures 12 – 18 °C.
• Full use, sedentary occupations
  People sitting for several hours, e.g. restaurants, offices. Internal air temperatures 20 – 22 °C.
• Indoor swimming pool
  Internal air temperatures 27 – 32 °C.
• Use for flora and fauna
  Growing and display of plants, keeping of exotic animals, e.g. garden centres and zoo facilities. Internal air temperature: min. 5 °C, max. 35 °C.

So, the internal climate in a glasshouse can vary from "virtually identical with the outside" with protection against precipitation (e.g. old railway stations) to the "moderate intermediate climate" of shopping malls to the tropical climates of palm houses.
The spectrum of the ensuing space heating requirement ranges from less than 0 kWh/m$^2$ p.a. (energy-savings due to unheated glass structures) to annual rates of 500 kWh per m$^2$ of floor area for single-glazed glasshouses permanently heated to 20 °C.
The provisions of the Thermal Insulation Act specify a maximum consumption of 55 – 100 kWh/m$^2$ p.a. depending on the building.

Energy functions
With appropriate planning, glasshouses not only do not require HVAC plant to maintain the desired conditions, on the contrary they can also fulfil HVAC functions:

## Heating

Provided the glasshouse is not heated to room temperature (20 – 22°C), it functions as a thermal buffer (Fig. 2.3.104, p. 144). It enables passive solar energy gains which can be transported via ventilation to the adjoining rooms. Therefore, the glazing should be designed as a vertical south-facing façade whenever possible. The effectiveness of the buffer function increases with better glazing. Heating energy can be saved by way of the following effects:
- Solar preheating of the fresh air required for the adjoining rooms.
- Limiting the transmission heat losses from the adjoining rooms.

## Cooling

The atrium can instigate the natural air circulation caused by temperature differences, above all in summer, and in this way disperse unwanted solar gains. Exploiting the air temperature stratification and arranging the openings properly can bring about high air change rates (50 – 80/h), especially at night when the atrium is initially warmer than the outside air.
Atria often have openings for cooling the building which may be left open at night without fear of unwanted intruders gaining access.

## Ventilation

The atrium can be used to distribute fresh air or act as a collection duct for exhaust air (Fig. 2.3.105, p. 144). Open, flowing areas of water can be employed as natural air humidifiers and, to a limited extent, for evaporative cooling.

## Lighting

An atrium can provide daylight for the adjacent rooms (Fig. 2.3.106, p. 144). The thermal buffer effect of the atrium enables larger windows to be incorporated without the heating energy consumption rising dramatically. In this way an atrium can introduce more daylight than the façade to an open, central courtyard. The provision of daylight in the adjoining rooms is primarily determined by the following parameters:
- shape of the atrium
- geometric height/width ratio
- colour of surfaces
- proportion of windows in partition walls
- quality of glass in the atrium and the partition walls.

## Energy considerations
### Heating energy consumption

Every atrium can be regarded as a thermal buffer for the rooms adjacent to it because their energy consumption is reduced in every case. If the atrium itself is unheated, then there is actually an energy gain. How-

ever, full use of the atrium with room temperatures of 20 – 22°C wastes energy because the transparent roof offers less thermal insulation than an insulated, opaque roof. The interaction of the heat losses from the solid core of the building and the energy gains of the glass atrium is sketched out in Fig. 2.3.108 (p. 144).
Three operating states can be recognized:
- Periods during which neither the atrium nor the main structure can make use of the atrium's energy gains.
- Periods during which the atrium supplies heat which can be used by the main structure (atrium as heat source).
- Periods during which the atrium requires heat energy in order to maintain the desired internal climate (atrium as additional heat consumer).

The length of time for which the atrium can supply heat and whether or not it is, in the end, a net supplier or consumer depend on many factors, e.g.
- type of atrium
- type of glass
- standard of thermal insulation
- external climatic conditions
- ventilation concept
- storage capacity
- required internal climate.

The effects of some key parameters are clarified below.

### Type of atrium

The stronger the link with the main structure, the better is the buffer effect and hence the potential to save energy. Core, re-entrant and linear atria have the best chances here. The "lean-to" glasshouse, with its limited thermal link to the main building, can at best be used for preheating the supply air by solar means.

### Type of glass and thermal insulation

Many unheated glass atria have only single glazing. Nevertheless, they are energy sources provided they remain unheated. This constraint is important because there have been cases where initially unheated atria have been converted to overcome a lack of space. This change to a superior function requires the area to be heated to 20°C – representing an enormous expenditure on energy.
Therefore, with atrium temperatures >15°C it is wise to use an insulating glass for the outer skin.
The influence of the quality of the glass is demonstrated excellently by Trondheim University, Norway (Fig. 2.3.103, p. 143). The atrium is heated to max. 5°C. The energy consumption of the whole building without atrium but with three-ply low-e glass on the façade to the central courtyard is 20% high-

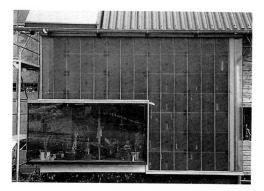
2.3.100    House with single TI glazing with capillary structure and cast glass covering

2.3.101    Refurbishment project with TI wall and translucent render

2.3.102    Tegut building, Fulda, Germany
Architects: LOG ID

2.3.103    Trondheim University, Norway
Architect: Per Knudsen

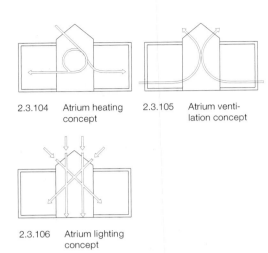

2.3.104    Atrium heating    2.3.105    Atrium venti-
           concept                      lation concept

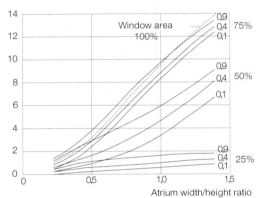

2.3.106    Atrium lighting
           concept

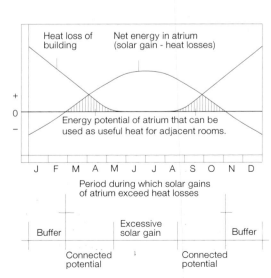

0.9/0.4/0.1            Reflectance characteristic
                      of walls
20%, 50%, 75%, 100%   Proportion of glazing in façade

2.3.107    Daylight factor of a linear atrium in relation to
           construction

2.3.108    Annual interaction in an atrium

er than the consumption with atrium in two-ply low-e glass and internal façade in standard insulating glass. Fig. 2.3.109 shows the heating requirement as a function of the atrium glazing.

Ventilation concept
An atrium is often an important component in the ventilation concept of a building. The following types of ventilation are among the standard concepts:
- common mechanical ventilation for atrium and main structure
- ventilation purely via windows
- no co-ventilation with the atrium
- atrium as exhaust-air collector
- atrium as supply-air distributor, possibly with upstream heat recovery from the exhaust air
- atrium distributes supply air and collects exhaust air
- solar preheating of supply air.

Internal temperature in atrium
The desired internal climate plays a crucial role for energy consumption if temperatures >10 °C are required.
Even with low-e glass, consumption rises drastically when the required temperature lies above 15 °C. For instance, the heating requirement of Trondheim University rose by about 30% when the atrium temperature was raised from 15 to 18 °C. (Fig. 2.3.110). The increased room temperatures were due to changing the use of the atrium. Originally planned as a circulation zone, lack of space in the university led to some areas being re-allocated as practice rooms requiring higher temperatures.

Cooling
It has been established that, on the whole, only glass atria in northern to temperate latitudes can be operated without mechanical cooling. As soon as a maritime climate is encountered, glass atria generate considerable cooling loads. In the USA the cooling energy requirement transcends by far the heating energy requirement. Therefore, the majority of American glass atria can be called "energy-guzzlers".
Although this may at first sound like a paradox, glass atria can be used to cool buildings in temperate climate zones. The cooling problem inherent in every atrium can be alleviated in the following ways:

Natural ventilation
Because of the natural stratification of air temperatures, atria can be readily ventilated without the need for mechanical installations. Guaranteeing the natural ventilation is the most important measure in order to limit overheating of the atrium. The correct layout of supply-air vents near the floor and

exhaust-air vents near the roof can ensure 3 – 5 air changes per hour in the atrium. To provide adequate cooling, the openings in the glasshouse should equal at least 5% of the floor area.

Shading
Another important measure is the provision of shade, which should in any case be movable in order to maintain an open path for light and heat during the seasons with no cooling problems. In atria, costs generally dictate the use of internal shading. As this causes a build-up of heat near the roof, considerably higher temperatures normally prevail in the top storey, as measurements in the atrium of Neuchâtel University, Switzerland, have confirmed (Fig. 2.3.111). Therefore, with internal shading it is advisable to raise the level of the roof in order to vent the solar gains naturally.

Cooling the building via the atrium
When the roof projection and the supply-air inlets in the main structure are correctly designed, the atrium can reinforce the ventilation of the building with relatively cool external air. Fig. 2.3.112 shows the summer night ventilation of the Gateway 2 building in London.

Daylight
Roofing-over a central, open courtyard or adding an atrium initially reduces the supply of daylight to the rooms beyond. This reduction in illumination is usually assumed to be 20% (provided clear glass is used and not solar-control glass). On the other hand, the buffer effect of the atrium enables the area of glass in the intermediate wall to be increased and hence admit more light into the interior of the main structure. The colour of the internal walls is significant: with 50% glazing, white walls in the atrium improve the daylighting by about 30% compared to dark surfaces.
Fig. 2.3.107 shows how the final daylight factor of a linear atrium is affected by the colour of the walls, the amount of glazing in the adjoining walls and the geometrical height/width ratio.

*Saving energy with glasshouses*
Glass atria can bring energy savings by observing the following points:
- Keep design room temperatures as low as possible.
- Only use clear glass in order to avoid a permanent reduction of the daylighting in adjacent rooms.
- Provide movable shading, preferably externally.
- Provide at least 5% in the form of opening lights for natural ventilation; this raises the chances of avoiding mechanical ventilation.
- Choose low U-values for the glazing because otherwise there is a risk that a change of use could result in inadequate thermal insulation.
- Use bright colours in the atrium.

## Double-leaf façades

Direct-gain systems rely on a sunshade and, owing to their manual control of ventilation, are readily accepted by users. However, external shading is susceptible to the rigors of the wind and sound insulation and security problems arise with open windows, leading to distinct limitations in terms of convenience (Fig. 2.3.113, p. 146). The problems of external shading, in conjunction with thoughts on how to influence the "outer" façade conditions, have led to the development of double-leaf concepts. This entails adding what is in essence a second skin, usually of glass, on the outside at a certain distance from the building. It improves the following parameters:
- thermal buffer
- wind and weather protection for the façade, sunshading, openings
- sound insulation
- security matters
- air flow
- installation space
- leisure space.

The functions of the former single-leaf façade are now shared between the two leaves. The outer leaf certainly acts as wind and weather protection. Energy evaluations reveal that, compared to a single-leaf façade with good glass, a double-leaf concept acting purely as a thermal buffer hardly contributes to saving heating energy – the decline in solar gains via the outer glazing is compensated for by the drop in transmission losses. But in terms of comfort and possible physical problems, e.g. condensation in rooms with higher humidities and temperatures, the increased surface temperature of the inner leaf is very beneficial. On the other hand, venting the buffer in summer must be allowed for in order to dissipate the solar gains linked to the sunshading.
The simplest method of incorporating the double-leaf façade in the ventilation concept (Fig. 2.3.116, p. 147) is to use opening lights in a buffer which is intentionally not airtight. If this permeability is fixed, then the ventilation cross-sections necessary for the summer lead to severe rear-ventilation in winter and cancel out much of the solar pre-heating or recovery of the transmission losses. If the ventilation openings are optimized for the winter, then, with mechanical cooling of the interior, the increased cooling requirement easily exceeds the savings in the heating requirement as compared to a single-leaf façade employing low-e glass. The function of the double-leaf façade diminishes to providing protection against weather and noise! With adjustable vents and window ventilation into the double-leaf façade, the danger of condensation forming on the outer leaf cannot be ruled out above a certain air-change rate as an arrangement with single glazing outside and insulating glass inside is recommended.
A similar system marketed under the name of "Twinface" (Fig. 2.3.114, p. 146) is available from several manufacturers and employs an exhaust-air chimney. It has been successfully used in several projects, e.g. refurbishment of the Deutsche Telekom building in Cologne (architects: Günter Müller and Horst Schlosser, Deutsche Telekom Building Dept). By arranging the supply-air and exhaust-air openings in the inner leaf at various levels, good ventilation can be guaranteed for the interior.

## Supply-air façade

A supply-air façade can only be accomplished in conjunction with mechanical air extraction from the offices. This enables solar preheating and partial recovery of the transmission losses into the double-leaf façade. Combining this with opening lights introduces manual control or influencing in order to bring about higher air-change rates locally. The savings in the heating requirement are about 30% of those made when using low-e glass and external ventilation. For reasons of interior comfort – surface temperature of inner pane – the glazing of the double-leaf façade should employ single glazing for the outer leaf, double glazing for the inner one. Increased rear-venting of the outer leaf in winter also plays a subordinate role here. In summer, exhaust-air vents in the outer leaf must be opened while maintaining the direction of venting in order to guarantee temperatures within the façade in the region of the ambient temperature. Here, the sunshading placed between the panes should be as reflective as possible. If the rear-venting is ignored, then simulation studies, checked by measurements on a test façade, show that, even compared to a version with internal shading, the cooling

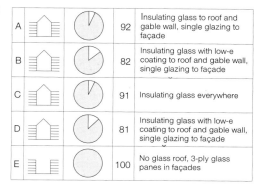

| | | | |
|---|---|---|---|
| A | | 92 | Insulating glass to roof and gable wall, single glazing to façade |
| B | | 82 | Insulating glass with low-e coating to roof and gable wall, single glazing to façade |
| C | | 91 | Insulating glass everywhere |
| D | | 81 | Insulating glass with low-e coating to roof and gable wall, single glazing to façade |
| E | | 100 | No glass roof, 3-ply glass panes in façades |

2.3.109   Heating requirement as a function of the atrium glazing

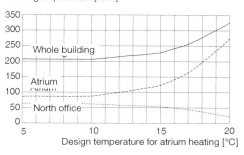

2.3.110   Heating requirement as a function of the desired temperature in the atrium

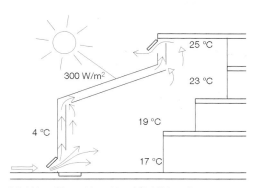

2.3.111   Glass atrium, Neuchâtel University, Architect: O. Gagnebloc

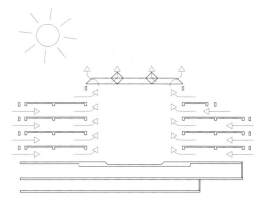

2.3.112   Gateway 2 building, London. Architects: Arup Associates

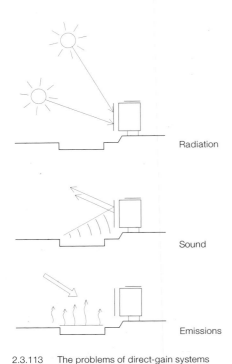

2.3.113    The problems of direct-gain systems

Radiation

Sound

Emissions

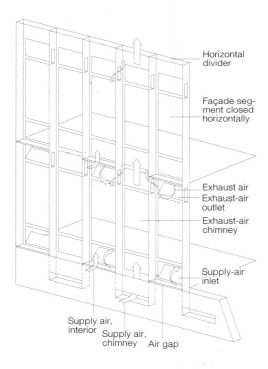

Horizontal divider

Façade segment closed horizontally

Exhaust air
Exhaust-air outlet

Exhaust-air chimney

Supply-air inlet

Supply air, interior
Supply air, chimney    Air gap

2.3.114    "Twinface" combination of window ventilation and ventilation chimney

requirement almost doubles and reaches the order of magnitude of the savings in the heating requirement. Another advantage of supply-air over window ventilation is the option of providing mechanically assisted night-time ventilation by means of the existing ventilation plant (see example, p. 274–277).

Exhaust-air façade
This is a reversal of the above venting direction. Here, the warm exhaust air in the double-leaf façade is compressed and hence called upon to reduce the transmission losses. If we retain the glazing arrangement of the supply-air façade, the savings drop to around 20% compared to our reference façade due to the lack of solar preheating. The outer leaf should comprise double glazing to avoid the appearance of condensation on this leaf, while the inner pane can be single glazing without having to worry about impairing comfort. This concept has been implemented on a small scale in Scandinavia and Switzerland in the form of exhaust-air windows, and in Germany this system is marketed in conjunction with decentral ventilation systems in the spandrel panels. The disadvantage of the exhaust-air façade, i.e. the fact that the solar gains in the façade cavity cannot be used directly like in the supply-air system, becomes an advantage in the summer because now the risk of overheating is overcome through an active venting of the double-leaf façade with internal air. Compared to the reference façade with internal sunshade, the cooling requirement can be significantly reduced – with increased night-time ventilation and thermally active building masses. However, the simple screening-off of the façade air gap leads to higher inner pane temperatures and hence a reduction in the standard of comfort. Fig. 2.3.117 (p. 148) shows the make-up of the double-leaf façade to the Volksbank in Pforzheim.
Compared to mechanical supply- and exhaust-air systems for offices using a single-leaf façade with heat recovery, a pure supply- or exhaust-air façade without heat recovery will increase the heating requirement by about 15%. However, a proper comparison should not ignore the higher electricity consumption for the supply- and exhaust-air plant, weighted to account for the primary energy source. Thus, integrating a double-leaf façade in a system with heat recovery would seem to favour the exhaust-air variation because in the supply-air version part of the recovered heat is lost again via the outer leaf.

Pure weather protection
One great dilemma when analysing the costs is the fact that these days most double-leaf façades consist of two external façades, one behind the other. The downgraded specification for the inner leaf is not "conspicuous" and so is not reflected in the price. For reasons of standardization, some façade suppliers prefer to offer two external façades at a reduced price. A simpler construction which fully exploits the fact that it is not exposed to wind and weather should be chosen for the inner, protected leaf, both to save capital investment and to take account of the grey energy – the en-ergy contained in the building materials. The façade to the vocational college in Bregenz (Fig. 2.3.119, p. 148) is a good example of this. The rainproof but ventilated glass louvres of the outer leaf protect the inexpensive timber construction of the inner leaf.

Integration in the mechanical ventilation
If we include the double-leaf façade as an air duct in a mechanical ventilation system, then we can save on supply- and/or exhaust-air ducting within the building. One good example of this is the refurbishment of the Martini Tower in Brussels carried out by Kohn Pedersen Fox, London, in collaboration with Battle McCarthy. In this project transferring the supply- and exhaust-air ducting to the double-leaf façade, necessary owing to the low clear headroom, approx. 30% more lettable space was gained. This example is designed with a open façade cavity extending over 30 storeys, used for ducting the exhaust-air, while the supply-air is fed via ducts in the cavity.

Multistorey or single storey?
Multistorey double-leaf façades should take account of the accumulation of radiation and ventilation gains with increasing height. The examples so far illustrate multistorey open double-leaf façades, in contrast to the façades designed for the Stadttor project, Düsseldorf (Fig. 2.3.120, p. 148), the RWE Tower, Essen (see pp. 266–273), and the Commerzbank headquarters, Frankfurt (architects: Sir Norman Foster & Partners). These three projects with their double-leaf façades arranged in storey heights and, in some instances, with vertical baffles on the grid lines, are based on similar concepts for using the double-leaf façade which for most of the time supply the offices behind them via window ventilation. The buildings are also equipped with mechanical supply and extract plant as well as cooling ceilings. Dividing the cavity floor by floor is intended to counter the problem of noise transmission

and fire protection. The propagation of sound in the double-leaf façade of the Stadttor project is illustrated in Fig. 2.3.118 (p. 148). Attention should be given to cleaning issues when designing double-leaf façades as instead of two there are now four glass surfaces to which access must be gained for cleaning. This necessitates a clear space of min. 400 – 500 mm – which exceeds the minimum value of 300 mm required for thermal and ventilation aspects.

### Double-leaf concept for renovating existing façades

Double-leaf façades are becoming increasingly favoured for refurbishment projects because they enable several problems to be solved. A glass skin placed in front of another façade protects it from the weather and also solves thermal and other problems. At the same time, the sound insulation achieved between buffer space and outside – 30 dB(A) for non-perforated external glazing and 10 – 15 dB(A) for external glazing with minimal openings – permits window ventilation and night-time ventilation without infringing security requirements. One example of this is the Zeppelin Block in Stuttgart, where the architects, Auer, Weber & Partner in association with Michel & Wolf, implemented this concept in the form of storey-height coupled windows (Figs 2.3.123 and 2.3.124, p. 149).

### Double-leaf glass roofs

The problem encountered in tall glass façades due to descending cold air with U-values > 1.4 W/m²K, which leads to the apparently "unavoidable" finned pipes, is amplified when it comes to glass roofs because now cold air bubbles, caused by adhesion, form under the roof. However, as cold air is heavier than hot air, gravity eventually takes over and a large bubble of cold air detaches itself and descends as a noticeable movement of the air. Afterwards, the process starts all over again. In addition, particularly in rooms with a large expanse of glazing, the lower temperature of the glass surface manifests itself as a lower operative temperature so that the same level of comfort can only be achieved by raising the air temperature. Therefore, glasshouses are best used as buffer spaces with minimal heating or none at all. Provided with good-quality glass, these rooms exhibit comfortable temperatures for almost 80% of the year.

If, nevertheless, a glasshouse is to be heated, then thermal improvements, particularly to the roof glazing, must be carried out to take account of the heating requirement. This apparently contradicts the demand for high transparency. Based on the idea of the double-leaf façade, a double-skin construction would seem to offer a solution here. The stationary layer of air can result in improvements in heat losses amounting to 25 – 50%, depending on the type of glass. Double-leaf glass roofs are difficult to clean; the usual answer is to provide fixed double glazing outside and movable single glazing inside. The overheating in summer demands shading for horizontal and shallow-pitched glass surfaces. External sunshading is more effective in thermal terms but must be weather-resistant, and if movable, needs extensive maintenance. Combining the shading function with the demand for two skins would seem to be a good solution. The adjustability of the sunshading can be combined with the movability of the inner leaf in the form of rotating glass louvres. The inner leaf may be shut to provide shade or to improve comfort levels in winter. As no descending cold air is to be expected when the sun shines, even during winter, and the glass heats up when exposed to sunshine, the glass louvres may be opened and the solar gains admitted directly into the room. The shading effect is achieved by printing on the glass louvres which still maintains the transparency.

The new entrance foyer to the Stuttgart Chamber of Trade and Industry (pp. 278–279) illustrates this concept in its almost horizontal glass roof. The printing to the louvres, black and also white, chosen for thermal reasons, leads to the printed areas providing good shade and the white covering layer good reflective properties, as expected. At the same time, the coverage density of 75% means that from underneath this does not appear solid, the eye complementing the image against the black pattern without difficulty, the transparency remains. The planned use of the solar gains in the buffer space, while shaded in the transitionary periods – the foyer has then exceeded the 23 °C room air temperature – was not carried out in the end. The louvres are closed in the summer (high solar altitude angle). The heat build-up in the buffer space is then mechanically dispersed by photovoltaic-powered fans, which possess a high potential owing to the PV modules incorporated at roof level, especially when the sun is high in the sky. In this way the temperature in the glasshouse can be lowered to below the ambient temperature, assisted by underground supply-air cooling. Fig. 2.3.125 compares the temperatures measured and shows the good correlation with a simulation using the simulation suite TRNSYS employed for the design. This keeps the room temperature below the ambient temperature, as

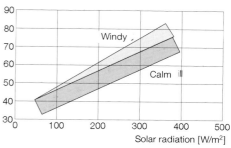

Air changes in façade cavity [1/h]

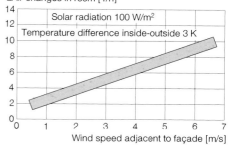

LAir changes in room [1/h]

2.3.115    Air-change rates for a double-leaf façade

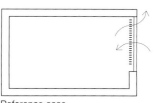

Reference case

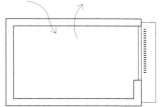

Buffer space

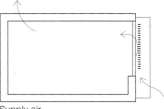

Supply air

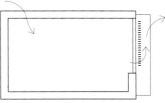

Exhaust air

2.3.116    Options for integrating a double-leaf façade in a ventilation concept

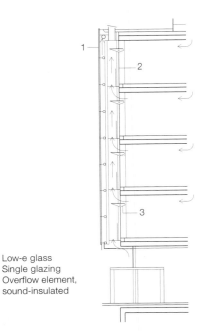

1  Low-e glass
2  Single glazing
3  Overflow element,
   sound-insulated

2.3.117    Exhaust-air façade: double-leaf façade to the
           Volksbank in Pforzheim
           Architects: Kauffmann Theilig & Partner

required by the brief. With a maximum external temperature of 31°C, the internal temperature just touches 28°C, as the concept function verifies.

This ventilation can also be backed up thermally in glass halls with internal sunshading if the glass roof can be raised above the level of the surrounding structure and ventilation openings incorporated there. Fig. 2.3.121 shows the raised double-leaf glass roof of the Bad Colberg Thermal Baths.

Solar chimney
One special form of the glasshouse or direct-gain system is the solar chimney. Here, in contrast to the rear-vented solar wall, we are not gaining heat for the interior but instead overheating the exhaust air by the trapped solar heat and so generating a supplementary stack effect. The aim of this concept is to maintain natural exhaust-air systems in summer too when internal-external temperature differences are low or even negative. One example of this arrangement is the entrance foyer to the Schleswig-Holstein Social Security Office in Lübeck (Fig. 2.3.122). The seven-storey glass hall with its generous expanse of pitched glazing facing south receives extra ventilation via a 15 m high solar chimney activated by solar radiation overheating the exhaust-air when incident radiation levels are high. For this, the glass chimney is fitted with absorbent surfaces which severely overheat the exhaust-air.

**Active uses**
In contrast to passive uses, active uses employ auxiliary motors and heat transport media in order to convey and store the energy gained from the sun.

*Solar collectors*
A solar collector exploits the same effects as a direct-gain system in that it converts short-wave solar radiation into heat radiation. The difference is that the collector space is not available for use but instead accommodates a heat exchanger which dissipates as much of the incident radiation as heat via air or water (Fig. 2.3.126, p. 150). A solar collector is designed to collect solar radiation and transfer the absorbed energy to a transport medium, e.g. water or air, with minimal losses. Therefore, a collector is specified by way of its capacity to absorb solar radiation and the magnitude of its heat losses. This "photothermic" way of generating heat via solar collectors is a different principle to the "photovoltaic" use for generating electricity from solar radiation via solar cells.
The optical properties of the collector covering – usually glass – and the surface of the absorber determine the ability of the solar collector to absorb solar radiation. A collector design that keeps the cover at a low temperature reduces the front-side heat losses. This can be achieved by reducing the heat transport between absorber and cover. The use of a "selective" absorber decreases the radiation portion of this heat transport from absorber to first cover layer.
The consequence of this surface treatment

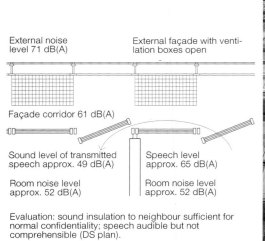

External noise
level 71 dB(A)          External façade with venti-
                        lation boxes open

Façade corridor 61 dB(A)

Sound level of transmitted      Speech level
speech approx. 49 dB(A)         approx. 65 dB(A)

Room noise level                Room noise level
approx. 52 dB(A)                approx. 52 dB(A)

Evaluation: sound insulation to neighbour sufficient for normal confidentiality; speech audible but not comprehensible (DS plan).

2.3.118    Sound propagation in double-leaf façade,
           Düsseldorf Stadttor

2.3.119    Vocational college, Bregenz
           Architects: Baumschlager Eberle

2.3.120    Düsseldorf Stadttor
           Architects: Petzinka, Pink & Partner

is a high absorption capacity of 90% in the solar radiation spectrum and a low emissions capacity of 15% in the long-wave heat radiation spectrum. Hence, the solar radiation is well intercepted and the radiation losses of the now warm absorber minimized. A cover with an infrared-reflective coating facing inwards works similarly and reduces the transmission losses to about 15%.

*Water collectors*
Fig. 2.3.127 (p. 150) illustrates various concepts for water-cooled collectors. Without covers and without thermal insulation at the rear they are designated absorbers and frequently used for heating swimming pools. As a heat exchanger to their surroundings they are used as a heat source for heat pumps.
These absorbers are made from metal or plastic and must be UV-resistant. In a flat-plate collector the absorber is provided with a transparent cover on the front and opaque insulation on all other sides – a sort of mini-greenhouse. The "evacuated collector" reduces the front-side losses between absorber and cover by introducing a vacuum to suppress the convection. Flat-plate collectors with albeit only slightly reduced internal pressures must support the cover with spacers to counteract the effects of atmospheric pressure.
Evacuated tube collectors (ETCs) (Fig. 2.3.128, p. 150) employ a high vacuum in order to suppress losses through heat conduction between air molecules. Some of these tube collectors make use of the heat exchanger tube principle to transfer heat from the absorber via the condenser to the

water. The thermal conductance of such a heat exchanger tube is 10 times higher than that of a plain copper pipe with the same dimensions. Heat transport takes place by the evaporation of water or a refrigerant in the absorber zone and via the condensation at the head of a heat exchanger tube which projects clear of the glass tube, exposed to the transport medium. This enables the construction to be reduced to a critical penetration.

*Air collectors*
Air collectors exhibit no corrosion and frost-protection problems and present fewer problems in terms of leakage.
Fig. 2.3.129 (p. 150) illustrates various concepts which all attempt to compensate for the disadvantage of poor heat transfer between the absorber and the transport medium, air, by enlarging the area of the heat exchanger. Contact between the heated air and the cover must be avoided. Air collectors for preheating the supply air or circulating air can be readily incorporated in HVAC plant. When doing so it should be remembered that the fans of air-cooled solar collectors, even with an optimized pressure drop, consume up to four times more energy than the pumps of water-cooled collectors. The choice of which collector to use is very much dependent on the process or temperature range in which the collector gains are to be used. Fig. 2.3.131 (p. 150) shows the various types of collectors with their degrees of efficiency at diverse temperature differences and their main applications. Tab. 2.3.133 (p. 150) lists the heat gains from collectors according to their uses.

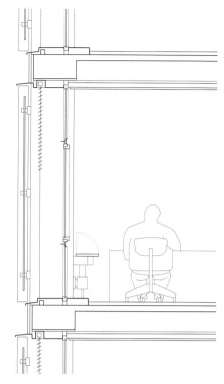

2.3.123    Façade construction, Zeppelin Block, Stuttgart
Architects: Auer, Weber & Partner

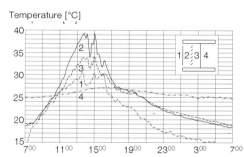

Temperature [°C]

1 Temperature at the window
2 Temperature between sunshade and inner pane    be
3 Ambient temperature
4 Room temperature

2.3.124    Temperatures measured in the coupled window of the Zeppelin Block

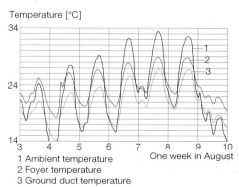

Temperature [°C]

One week in August
1 Ambient temperature
2 Foyer temperature
3 Ground duct temperature

2.3.125    Temperature curves in summer in the entrance foyer to the Stuttgart Chamber of Trade and Industry

2.3.121    Bad Colberg Thermal Baths
Architects: Kauffmann Theilig & Partner

2.3.122    Foyer, Social Security Office, Lübeck
Architects: Behnisch & Behnisch

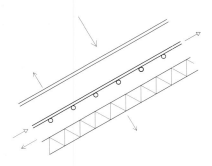

2.3.126    Schematic section through a solar collector

Absorber

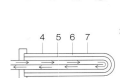

Aluminium roll-bond plate

Flat-plate evacuated collector (with supported cover)

2.3.127    Water collectors

1    Absorber
2    Glass tube
3    Reflector
4    Transparent surface
5    Selective surface
6    Vacuum
7    Evacuated twin-walled glass tube

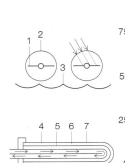

2.3.128    Evacuated tube collectors

2.3.130    Energy gained at various locations, heights and orientations

|  |  |  |  |  |  |  |
|---|---|---|---|---|---|---|
|  |  | ◓ | ◓ | ◓ | ◓ | ◓ |
|  | 1 | 1155 | 1155 | 1155 | 1155 | 1155 |
|  | 2 | 1368 | 1368 | 1368 | 1368 | 1368 |
|  | 3 | 1360 | 1360 | 1360 | 1360 | 1360 |
|  | 1 | 1072 | 1199 | 1250 | 1199 | 1072 |
|  | 2 | 1270 | 1475 | 1560 | 1475 | 1270 |
|  | 3 | 1260 | 1476 | 1562 | 1474 | 1260 |
|  | 1 | 987 | 1149 | 1213 | 1149 | 987 |
|  | 2 | 1170 | 1430 | 1545 | 1430 | 1170 |
|  | 3 | 1160 | 1435 | 1550 | 1435 | 1160 |
|  | 1 | 885 | 1055 | 1122 | 1055 | 885 |
|  | 2 | 1050 | 1334 | 1456 | 1334 | 1050 |
|  | 3 | 1040 | 1336 | 1462 | 1336 | 1040 |
|  | 1 | 650 | 771 | 808 | 771 | 650 |
|  | 2 | 773 | 995 | 1088 | 995 | 773 |
|  | 3 | 763 | 995 | 1090 | 995 | 763 |

1    440 m; north side of the Alps, 47° 30′
2    1560 m; Alps, 46° 50′
3    210 m; south side of the Alps, 46° 10′

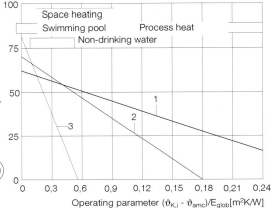

Degree of efficiency [%]

1    Evacuated tube collector
2    Flat-plate collector (n = 1, selective)
3    Absorber

2.3.131    Various types of collectors for different processes

Two-pass type (Satcunanthan)

Version with porous bed and glass cells for suppressing convection

8    Air ducts
9    Thermal insulation
10   Glass cells
11   Porous bed

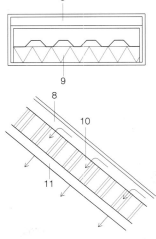

2.3.129    Air collectors

2.3.132    PV modules serving as fixed sunshading in a south-facing rooflight

## Photovoltaics or solar cells

In contrast to solar collectors, solar cells convert solar radiation not into heat but directly into electricity. The energy of the sun is employed to detach electrons from a semiconductor structure and distribute these by means of attached metal connections. Silicon is usually used for these semiconductors, the most common element on Earth apart from oxygen. To protect the skin-thin silicon wafers they are normally glued to a glass pane. We distinguish between amorphous, crystalline and poly-crystalline silicon and the corresponding solar cells, depending on the raw material used. A 100 x 100 mm solar cell produces approx. 1.5 W at full incident radiation and a voltage of 0.5 V.

Besides the inclination and orientation of the photovoltaic surface, the outputs of solar cells (Tab. 2.3.130) are also dependent on the type of cell. While monocrystalline cells achieve degrees of efficiency of 12 – 16%, the polycrystalline versions reach just 9 – 12%, and the amorphous a mere 3 – 6%. As the degree of efficiency of a solar cell decreases as the temperature rises, good ventilation or rear-venting of the photovoltaic modules should always be guaranteed. The individual cells can also be spaced within a laminated glass unit and in this form serve as fixed shading with integral energy source. Fig. 2.3.132 shows PV modules acting as fixed shading in a south-facing rooflight.

## Thin-film solar cells

The latest development in solar cell technology is the thin-film variety in which silicon is vacuum-sputtered directly onto a glass plate. By pure chance, the leading developer in this field, the "Solar Engineering and Hydrogen Centre", Stuttgart, discovered that the cells achieve better degrees of efficiency when coupled with normal float glass panes instead of the high-quality quartz glass panes used initially.

2.3.133   Energy outputs of collector systems

| System | Use | Operating period | Output |
|---|---|---|---|
| Water collector | Hot water provision | All year | 300 – 450 kW/m²a |
| Water collector | Supplementary heating | Heating period | 80 – 120 kW/m²a |
| Air collector | Preheating air in swimming pool | All year | 400 – 700 kW/m²a |
| Air collector | Preheating supply air for offices | Heating period | 40 – 100 kW/m²a |

# Part 3 · Construction details

## Contents

## Preliminary remarks

The following "Construction details" illustrate many different ways of fixing glass (section 3.1) and various treatments for openings (section 3.2). The subsequent section 3.3 shows key details for a glass façade, from ground to roof and including the adjacent construction, taking a post-and-rail façade as an example. For simplicity, the same aluminium glazing bar system has been used in all details. A great number of profiles are available on the market. They differ not only in terms of their appearance but also, in some instances, with regard to the way they solve various constructional details.

The solutions illustrated here are based on diverse structural and architectural conceptions. The prime objective is to show fundamental relationships and not the abundance of different approaches. The details in section 3.3 are not related to specific building tasks; on the contrary, together with the accompanying explanations they are intended to highlight particular troublespots and indicate potential answers.

The outer skin envelops the building like a "shell". It therefore involves many different trades and operations, which in turn demands accurate coordination in terms of detailing and scheduling. The façade is where the comparatively rough structural carcass, the internal fitting-out, the sunscreening and the precise glazing and metalwork meet.

The permissible conditions and tolerances of these various trades and operations must be coordinated at an early stage and taken into account at the interfaces.

It is recommended that specialists in façade design, construction physics, climate, structural engineering, etc. always be appointed for the draft and detailed design of complex façades.

A façade can be freestanding or – like the classic curtain wall – suspended from the floors. In every case, when detailing the fixing points it is important to ensure that movements originating in the primary structure or other components, and also the thermal expansion of metal constructions, can be accommodated without introducing restraint forces. The façade must be attached to its fixings such that adjustment is possible in three directions. Connections should be designed in such a way that they remain permanently airtight and diffusion-tight. An isolating material must be placed between aluminium and steel components in order to prevent galvanic corrosion.

This book describes glass in its role as a building material, and all its associated properties. These properties can be used correctly only when the glass and its supporting construction are harmonized. This means that forces transferred into the glass from the construction must be allowed for in the design. For example, temperature stresses can lead to movements which need to be acknowledged and treated accordingly.

Also critical is the durability of the materials used and their compatibility with each other. Organic building materials, which react with and influence each other, are being employed more than ever before. Great care must be exercised when selecting products and, if necessary, the respective manufacturers must be questioned about compatibility issues. This particularly applies to the sealants used in building.

The photographs accompanying the details are intended to illustrate basic architectural concepts and therefore do not always correspond with the drawings.

Some of the details in sections 3.1 and 3.2 are taken from actual structures; these and their architects are listed on page 328. The authors and publishers are indebted to the many colleagues and others who provided creative suggestions and assistance for the "Construction details" chapter. They are included in the list on page 328 as well as the many companies who kindly provided material for this part of the book.

## 3.1 Fixings for glass

**Glazing bead**
**Combined sealing and retaining function**
Linear support

3.1.1     Wood
3.1.2     Aluminium
3.1.3     Steel
3.1.4     Plastic
3.1.5 – 3.1.7     EPDM profiles

Horizontal and vertical sections, scale 1:2.5

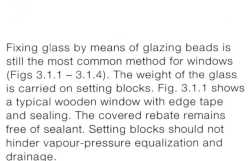

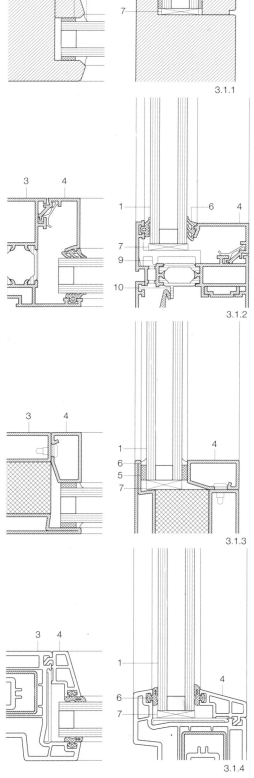

3.1.1

3.1.2

3.1.3

3.1.4

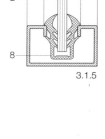

3.1.5

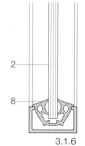

3.1.6

Fixing glass by means of glazing beads is still the most common method for windows (Figs 3.1.1 – 3.1.4). The weight of the glass is carried on setting blocks. Fig. 3.1.1 shows a typical wooden window with edge tape and sealing. The covered rebate remains free of sealant. Setting blocks should not hinder vapour-pressure equalization and drainage.

An aluminium frame with sealing profiles is shown in Fig 3.1.2. In this case the contact pressure exerted by the profile retains the pane and constitutes the seal. To allow for the uneven bearing caused by the thermal break, the setting blocks are carried on bridge setting blocks which guarantee an even bearing. Fig. 3.1.3 illustrates a steel window with integral thermal insulation, edge tape and sealing. Fig. 3.1.4 is a plastic frame with sealing profiles.

The examples shown in Figs 3.1.5 – 3.1.7 make use of EPDM profiles which both retain and seal the glass. These are mainly used for industrial glazing. In Fig. 3.1.7 the glass is first placed in the profile and then a continuous wedge inserted to stiffen the profile. In Figs 3.1.5 and 3.1.6 mechanical stability is achieved by inserting the profiles into metal frames. All the details of the glazing systems employing sealing profiles must be properly coordinated. The thickness tolerance of the glass pane is a crucial factor. All the examples shown here (Figs 3.1.1 – 3.1.7) have a glass pane which is free to rotate and thus introduces no restraint forces.

1 Double glazing
2 Single glazing
3 Window frame
4 Glazing bead
5 Edge tape
6 Seal
7 Setting block
8 Combined glass fixing/seal
9 Bridge setting block
10 Thermal break
11 Wedge insert

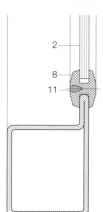

3.1.7

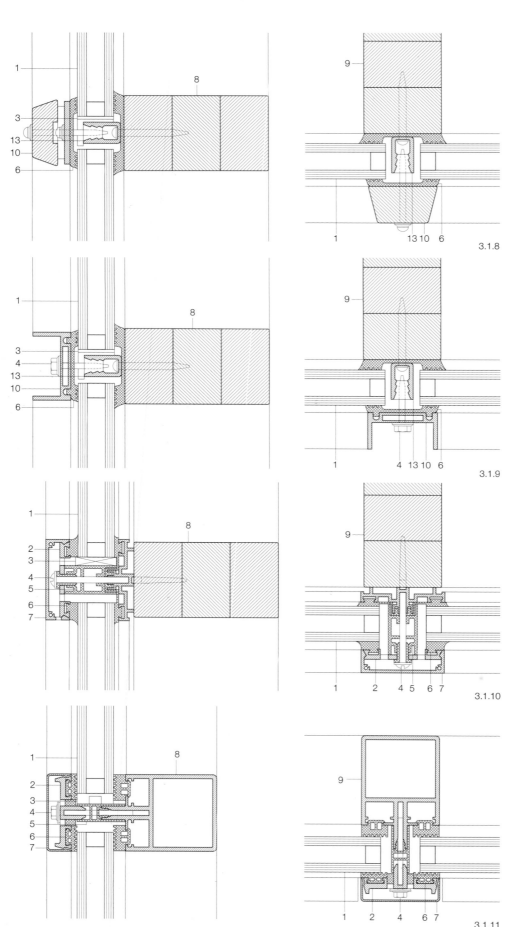

3.1.8

3.1.9

3.1.10

3.1.11

## Glazing bar
Linear support

3.1.8    Wood
3.1.9    Aluminium/wood
3.1.10   Aluminium/wood
3.1.11   Aluminium with cover strip
3.1.12   Steel with cover strip
3.1.13   Steel without cover strip
3.1.14   Aluminium with thermal insulation
3.1.15   EPDM integral profile

Horizontal and vertical sections, scale 1:2.5

Glazing with glazing bars uses an external aluminium, steel, timber or plastic profile to exert a contact pressure along the full length of the glass and supporting construction. Intermediate, permanently elastic pads of silicone or EPDM ensure a good seal and adequate elasticity of the fixing. The pressure applied is determined by the sealing profiles as well as by the edge seal of the insulating glass unit. In this system the load-bearing structure is located behind the glass, so the glazing bars visible externally can be relatively small. The width is derived from the rebate to be covered plus the width required for the fixing. As a rule, 50 mm is sufficient for insulating glass and metal glazing bars.

Setting blocks must be used in the frames of patent glazing. The gaps between individual glazing units must be left open to the outside to enable vapour-pressure equalization; condensation or rainwater must be able to drain to the outside. With large areas of glazing it is necessary to distinguish between vertical and horizontal joints and link them to form a common drainage system. If single glazing and non-insulated construction is called for, condensation collecting channels may be required.

In the case of insulating glass, the glazing bar must be thermally isolated from the supporting framework.

Glazing bars of steel and aluminium are characterized by their accurate profiles.

1 Double glazing
2 Pressure profile
3 Setting block
4 Screw
5 Insulating profile
6 Seal
7 Cover strip
8 Rail section

9 Post section
10 Glazing bar
11 Spacer sleeve
12 Clamping and sealing
   profile (integral profile)
13 Fixing and insulating
   profile

Clip-on cover strips to conceal the screws can be used with most systems (Figs 3.1.10, 3.1.11). Besides improving the overall appearance, these strips lessen the susceptibility to soiling. Fig. 3.1.12 shows a version in which the pressure and cover profiles are already assembled during production. To facilitate fixing to the building, the cover strip has holes that provide access to the screws. Metal glazing bars are available in a wide range of finishes. Aluminium has advantages over steel because of its corrosion resistance and, thanks to the extrusion process, a wide variety of profiles. The material of the glazing bar can be chosen independently of the material of the supporting construction.

A special type of glazing bar is shown in Fig. 3.1.15. Here, the permanently elastic (integral) plastic profile is clipped into the supporting construction and combines both clamping and sealing functions.

Aluminium or aluminium/wood glazing bars are often used in conjunction with a timber structure. These normally lead to slimmer profiles and also protect the timber from the weather (Figs 3.1.9, 3.1.10).

Auxiliary systems such as sunshading, safety harnesses, etc. should not be attached to glazing bars. This prevents the glass being subjected to any uncontrolled loads which might lead to fracture, and also prevents impairing the stability of the whole system.

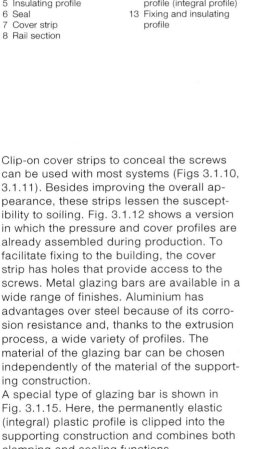

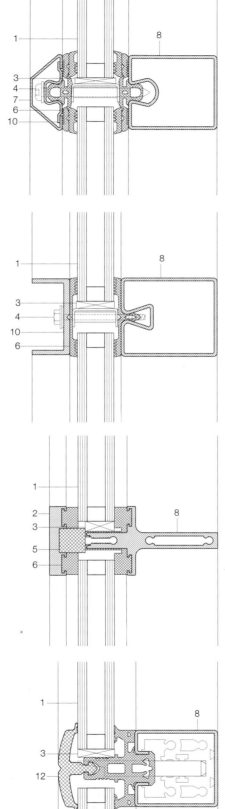

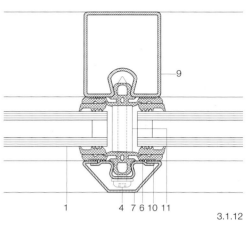

3.1.12

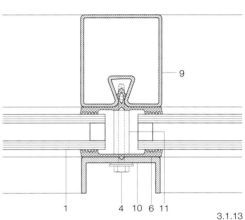

3.1.13

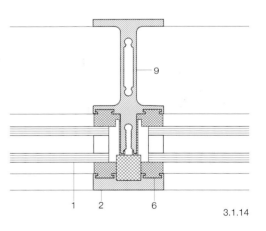

3.1.14

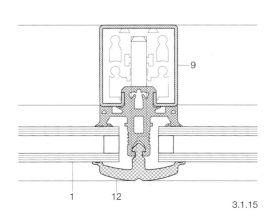

3.1.15

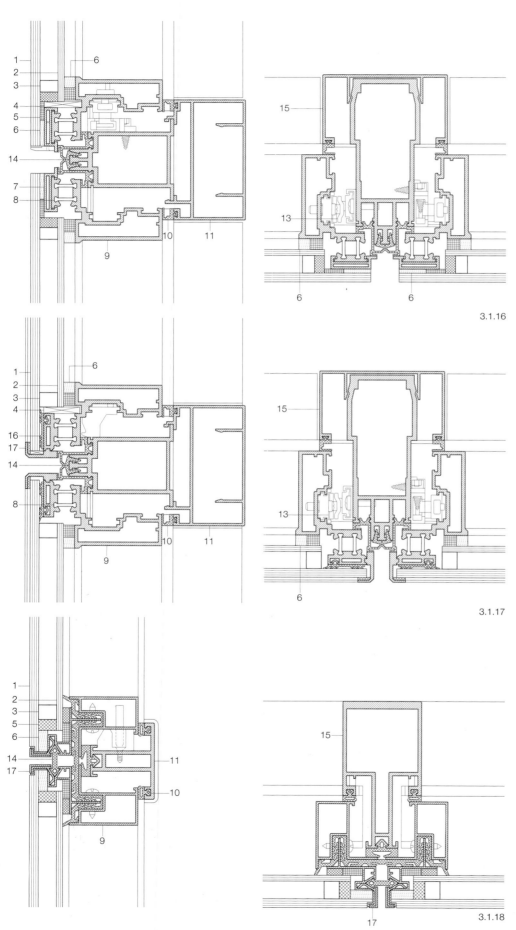

## Structural sealant glazing
Linear support

3.1.16   Without mechanical fixings
3.1.17 and 3.1.18
        Continuous mechanical fixings
3.1.19   Mechanical fixing and seal combined
        in one profile
3.1.20   Special solution for double-leaf
        façade with point mechanical fixings

Vertical and horizontal sections, scale 1:2.5

Glueing the glass elements directly to an adapter frame fitted to the supporting construction makes façades without frames or mechanical fixings possible. The peripheral glueing, besides providing an unrestrained mounting, can have a sound-insulating and, in some cases, a thermal break effect. The adhesive is always applied under precisely controlled factory conditions and must comply with very stringent specifications on its resistance to moisture, light, temperature and micro-organisms. Metal frames (adapter frames) and glass are supplied as complete elements and generally fixed to a post-and-rail construction on site. The frame is usually of steel or aluminium; however, steel must be protected against corrosion by means of galvanizing.
If both panes of a double glazing unit are glued to the frame, one of the adhesive joints must be softer than the other, otherwise shear stresses will occur in the edge seal as a result of glass movements caused by temperature fluctuations. Such stresses can lead to breakdown of the edge seal and leaks. In Germany the exclusive use of adhesive to fix panes is permitted only on elements no higher than 8 m above ground level (Fig. 3.1.16). For greater heights, an additional mechanical fixing is required to retain the panes. This mechanical retention

3.1.16

3.1.17

3.1.18

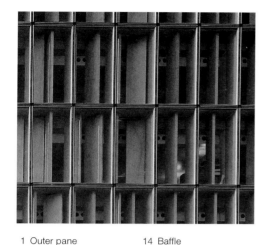

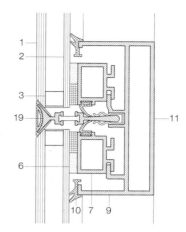

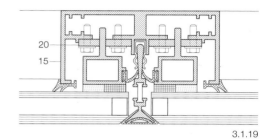

3.1.19

1 Outer pane
2 Inner pane
3 Edge seal of double glazing
4 Setting block
5 Edge tape
6 Silicone/Adhesive
7 "Corner angle"/ glueing profile
8 Thermal break
9 Modular frame system
10 Edge seal
11 Rail section
12 Cover profile
13 Folding scissors

14 Baffle
15 Post section
16 Back seal
17 Mechanical fixing, continuous
18 Mechanical fixing, discrete
19 Integral profile for mechanical fixing and seal
20 Retaining plate

function, which only comes into play if the adhesive fails, can be in the form of a perimeter frame (Figs 3.1.17, 3.1.18) or discrete fixings.

Fig. 3.1.19 shows a special version. A continuous integral profile positioned in the joints functions both as mechanical fixing and seal.

In Germany, structural sealant glazing systems always require certification or individual approval. Irrespective of the adhesive fixing, the self-weight of the glass must be transferred via setting blocks to the supporting construction; the adhesive may only carry wind suction loads. When using insulating glass it should be ensured that the edge seal is UV-resistant and suitable for structural sealant glazing.

The choice of the right type of glass is important. Coloured or mirrored glasses are often used for structural sealant glazing so that the supporting construction is not visible from the outside.

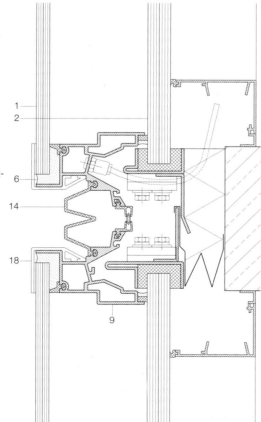

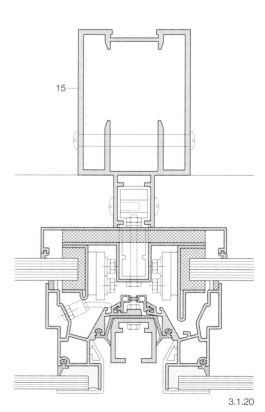

3.1.20

## Clamping plate
Linear/point support

3.1.21   Single glazing
3.1.22   Double glazing
3.1.23   Single glazing

Sections and elevations, scale 1:2.5

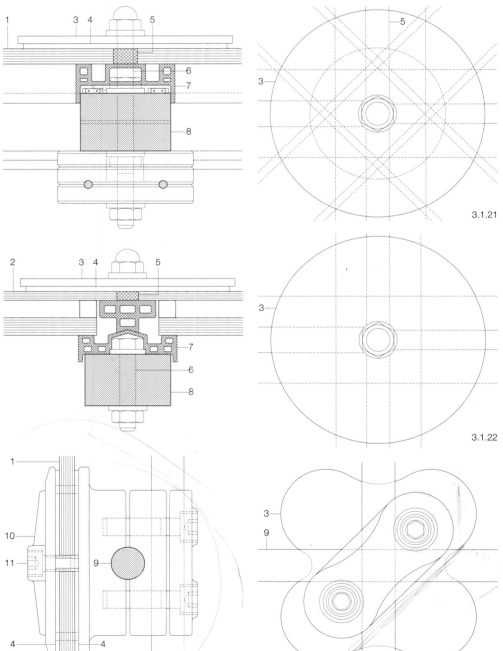

Fixing glass by means of clamping plates is
a simple method which requires a minimum
of material and enables the glass panes to
be installed without edge contact. The glass
can either be mounted on a linear support
but held by point fixings (Figs 3.1.21,
3.1.22) or supported and held by point fixings (Fig. 3.1.23). Clamping plates in the
form illustrated here are employed in, for
example, lattice-shell and cable-net structures.
It must be ensured that the panes are not
restrained; the glass should be able to follow its natural bending curve as the construction deflects under load. Any constraint
will lead to increased stresses in the glass.
As the pane deflects, the forces must be
transferred into the supporting construction
via the clamping plates. The position of the
plate fulcrum is important.

3.1.21

3.1.22

3.1.23

1  Single glazing
2  Double glazing
3  Clamping plate
4  Intermediate pad
5  Permanently elastic
   joint
6  Bolt
7  Sealing profile
8  Continuous metal sup-
   porting construction
9  Steel cable
10  Clamping plate
11  Screw

## Point fixing without penetrating the glass pane
Discrete support

3.1.24    Four-point clamp
3.1.25    Point fixing in the joint

Elevations and sections, scale 1:2.5

3.1.26    Fixing for shingle-type overlap

Plan and section, scale 1:5

Figs 3.1.24 – 3.1.26 show options for point fixings where the glass does not have to be drilled. With these details too it should be ensured that the glass is not restrained as the construction deflects under load, and that it can follow its natural bending curve. The cast aluminium clamp shown in Fig. 3.1.24 holds the corners of the panes. Fig. 3.1.25 illustrates one possible detail for point fixings in the joint. The self-weight of the glass is transferred via setting blocks to steel bolts (brackets) welded to the supporting construction. This method of point fixings in the joints is normally less expensive than point fixings through the panes because no expensive drilling (and provision of an edge seal around the holes in the case of insulating glass) is necessary. Fig. 3.1.26 is a detail of a stainless steel bracket which enables a shingle-type overlapping of the glass panes.

1 Single glazing
2 Double glazing
3 Clamping plate
4 Screw
5 Permanently elastic joint
6 Setting block
7 Welded bracket with internal thread
8 Edge tape
9 Four-point clamp
10 Adjusting bolt
11 Positioning angle, screwed on
12 Individual bracket
13 Silicone bearing profile, glued

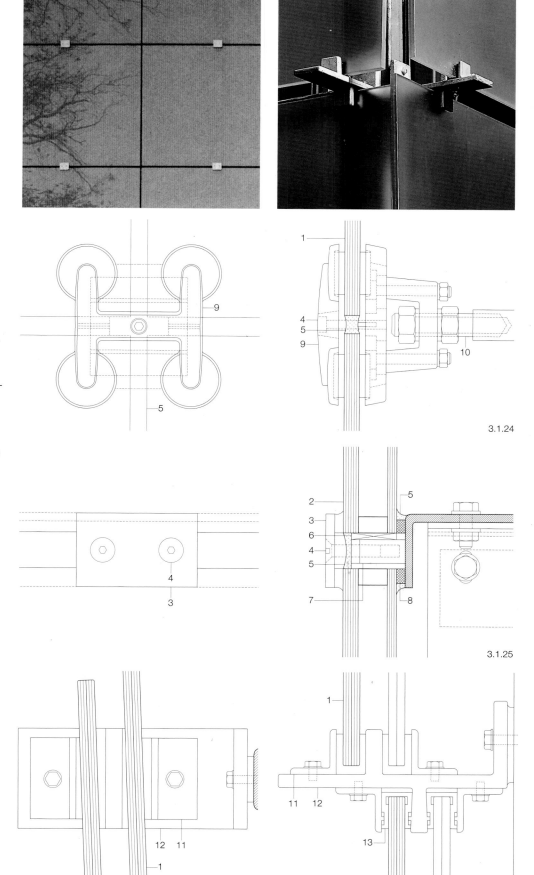

3.1.24

3.1.25

3.1.26

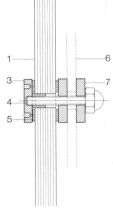

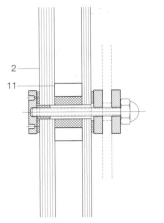

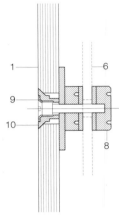

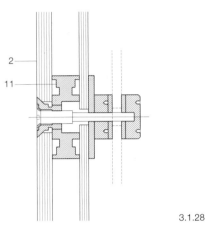

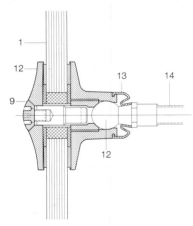

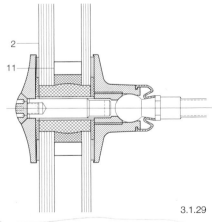

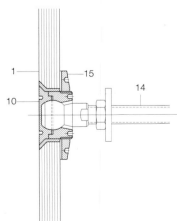

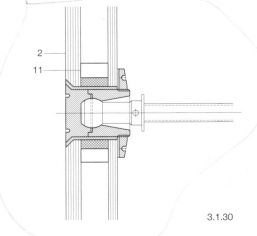

**Point fixing with drilled hole**
Discrete support

3.1.27 Non-flush, rigid
3.1.28 Flush, rigid
3.1.29 Non-flush, with articulated joint outside the glazing plane
3.1.30 Flush, with articulated joint in the glazing plane

Vertical sections for single and double glazing respectively, scale 1:2.5

Point fixings which carry the panes via holes drilled through the glass are available in a multitude of (mainly patented) versions. A distinction is made between those flush (Figs 3.1.28, 3.1.30) and those not flush (Figs 3.1.27, 3.1.29) with the glass, as well as rigid (Figs 3.1.27, 3.1.28) and articulated (Figs 3.1.29, 3.1.30) types.
Since panes supported by point fixings are subjected to greater bending and shear stresses than those of equal size but supported continuously, using point fixings leads to thicker glass being required.
Glazing employing point fixings demands greater accuracy during manufacture and installation than glazing with linear supports; this applies to both the supporting construction and the positions of the holes in the panes. The inevitable tolerances must be observed. Contact between metal and glass must be permanently and reliably prevented by suitable intermediate pads. When using point fixings it must be ensured that the glass is not restrained; it must be able to follow its natural bending curve. Articulated fixings are employed to avoid stresses in the glass. The fixing with the joint in the plane of the glass (Fig. 3.1.30) results in the lowest stresses in the glass. Due to the joint being located outside the glazing plane in Fig. 3.1.29, an additional lever arm is created between joint and glass. On the other hand, this fixing is relatively easy to combine with other components, e.g. tension rods in trussed arrangements.

3.1.27

3.1.28

3.1.29

3.1.30

1 Single glazing
2 Double glazing
3 Clamping disc
4 Bolt
5 Intermediate pad/seal
6 Supporting construction
7 Nut
8 Cover sleeve
9 Screw
10 Countersunk head
11 Edge seal
12 Ball joint
13 Sealing gaiter
14 Threaded bar
15 Threaded disc

**Joint at an unsupported edge**

3.1.31 Joint detail, single glazing
3.1.32 Joint detail, laminated safety glass
3.1.33 Joint detail, double glazing
3.1.34 Junction with partition, double glazing
3.1.35 Corner detail, double glazing

Horizontal sections, scale 1:1

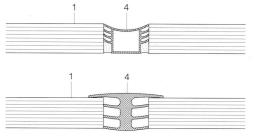

3.1.31

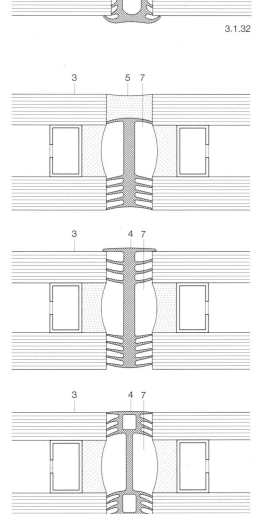

3.1.32

3.1.33

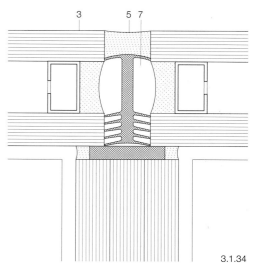

3.1.34

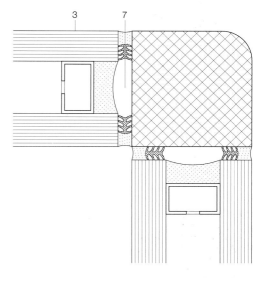

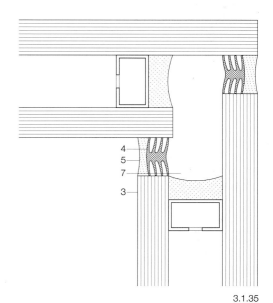

3.1.35

An essential characteristic of point fixings is the distinction between fixing and sealing. Figs 3.1.31 – 3.1.33 illustrate options for seals between glass elements without internal/external frames. The sealing profile – EPDM or silicone – is pressed into the joint; it should exhibit a certain prestress so that it fits tight. Such joints can be rapidly closed during installation; an injected sealant can be applied later. The covered rebates of insulating glass, laminated safety glass and wired glass must remain free of sealant so that vapour-pressure equalization and drainage are guaranteed. A backer rod must not be included here as this would block the open rebate and hinder the vapour-pressure equalization. Moisture escapes to the outside via the drainage system.

When using laminated safety glass, the sealing profile must cover the joint between panes so that, like with insulating glass, the edge seal and the exposed PVB interlayer or casting resin are in the area of the vapour-pressure equalization and hence no moisture builds up and remains trapped there over a longer period.

Fig. 3.1.34 shows a frameless connection between a glass partition and a double-glazed external wall.

Fig. 3.1.35 illustrates two different options for the corner detail of frameless double glazing. Here too, it must be ensured that the rebate remains free of sealant in order to guarantee the vapour-pressure equalization.

1 Single glazing
2 Laminated glass
3 Double glazing
4 Sealing profile
5 Permanently elastic joint
6 PVB interlayer
7 Drainage

**161**

## Suspended glazing
Discrete support

3.1.36   Glass suspended with clamping
          plates

Vertical section and elevation, scale 1:5

Instead of freestanding panes, a construction
may employ glazing suspended from above.
This method avoids the buckling of large
panes and so allows thinner glass to be used.
If the manufacturer's maximum pane size is
exceeded, several panes may be hung on
each other like a chain. When using suspended glazing it should be ensured that the
suspension system does not induce any extra
stresses in the panes. This can be avoided by
using, for example, an articulated joint. The
detail shown in Fig. 3.1.36 has the hangers
glued to the glass; another possibility is to
insert bolts in drilled holes. A suspension system involving vertical metal glazing bars is also
conceivable. The bottom edges of the panes
must be free to move; at this point they are
sealed in grooved profiles in such a way that
structural movement or deflections in the floor
slab can be compensated for.
If a pane is fractured, then the advantage of
suspended glazing is that the fragments do not
drop like a guillotine but instead continue to
hang from their supports.

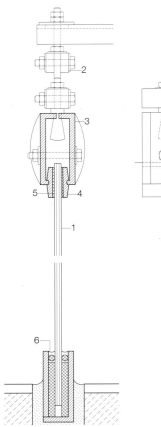
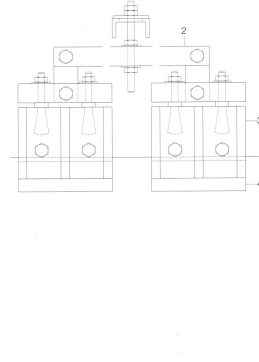

1 Glass
2 Articulated joint
3 Clamping plate
4 Glass fixing
5 Jointing cement
6 Permanently
  elastic joint

3.1.36

## Splices

3.1.37   Glass fin
3.1.38   Screwed splice connection

Elevations and plans, scale 1:5

In a splice, the glass elements cannot move
relative to each other. The screwed connections shown in 3.1.37 and 3.1.38 function as
though the individual glass components were
one piece. This is a rigid joint. The resulting
properties must be taken into account when
calculating the stresses in the glass. If an
expansion joint is required, it cannot be incorporated at a splice.

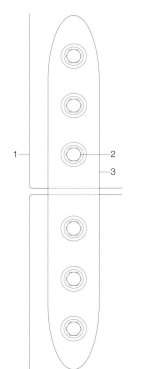
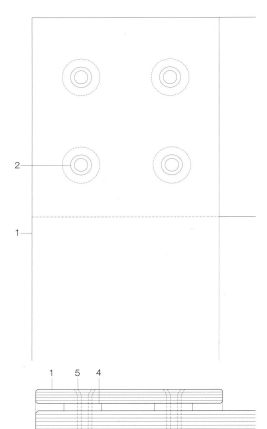

1 Glass
2 Bolt with locknut
3 Steel splice plate
4 Intermediate pad
5 Stainless steel fixing,
  rigid connection
  between beam and
  column

3.1.37        3.1.38

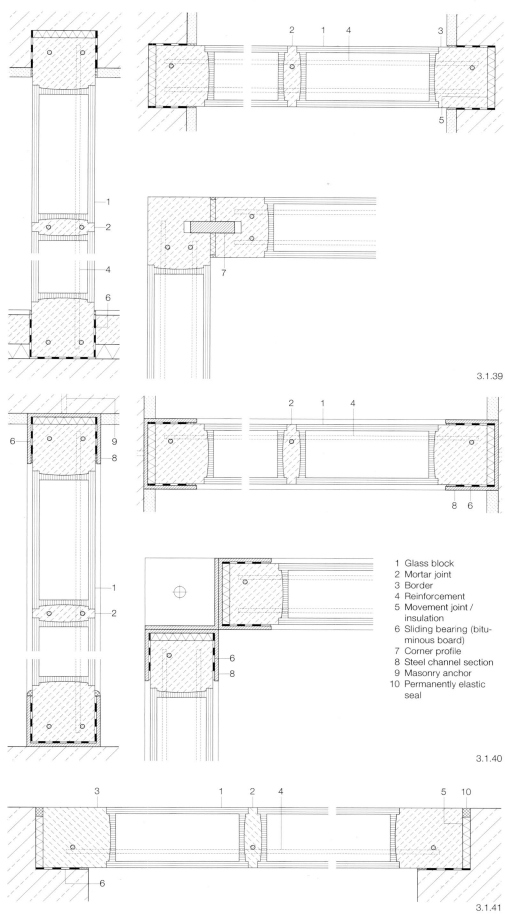

## Walls and floors of glass blocks

3.1.39   Glass block wall fitted into masonry
           chases
3.1.40   Glass block wall fitted into channel
           section
3.1.41   Glass floor made of hollow blocks

Vertical and horizontal sections, scale 1:5

1   Glass block
2   Mortar joint
3   Border
4   Reinforcement
5   Movement joint /
     insulation
6   Sliding bearing (bitu-
     minous board)
7   Corner profile
8   Steel channel section
9   Masonry anchor
10  Permanently elastic
     seal

Glass blocks must be built into a wall without restraint; no loads from the structure may be transferred to the glass blocks. Continuous expansion joints, filled with polystyrene or similar, are required at the sides and along the top. The bottom border should be laid on a sliding joint of plain bituminous board (Fig. 3.1.39). If fitted into channel sections (Fig. 3.1.40), then a sliding joint of oiled paper or plain bituminous board should be placed in the steel section. The lateral fixings to the building are to be designed as sliding anchors. The concrete between the glass blocks should not be too hard (max. grade B 25), so that the glass blocks are not compressed and damaged as a result of temperature fluctuations. The borders should be no wider than 100 mm to avoid thermal restraint. Reinforcement is to be calculated in line with structural requirements and should consist of galvanized or stainless steel bars. To reduce the restraint forces in glass block walls, expansion joints should be incorporated every 6 m; they should take account of the horizontal forces acting on the component. The coating to the sides of the individual blocks must remain intact – it ensures a good bond with the concrete. Joints must be sufficiently impervious to prevent the mortar ribs from becoming damp. Glazing with glass blocks can be erected to suit varying classes of fire protection.
Fig. 3.1.41 shows a hollow glass block floor. With appropriate detailing, both constructions can also be used for flat roofs. In the case of loadbearing glass block floors or glass and concrete floors, the interaction of the glass block, concrete and reinforcement causes the glass to be loaded as well. The glass block must therefore be bonded to the surrounding concrete so that it can accept the forces transferred from the total construction. The glass blocks used in such a case must be capable of carrying unrestricted foot traffic. Glass and concrete constructions are to be protected against restraint forces induced by the rest of the structure by means of expansion and sliding joints.

## 3.2 Openings

Window in solid wall

3.2.1 Wood
3.2.2 Aluminium
3.2.3 Steel
3.2.4 Plastic

Horizontal and vertical sections, scale 1:2.5

The options for fixing glass in window frames are shown in Fig. 3.1.1 "Glazing bead" on p. 153. Glazing beads are usually fitted to the inside. The junction with the wall must be provided with thermal insulation right around the perimeter and made vapour-tight internally. Externally, the seal must offer adequate weather protection, be able to withstand driving rain and be permanently resistant to UV radiation and other effects. The thermal expansion of aluminium, greater than that of wood or steel, must be taken into account.
Figs 3.2.1 and 3.2.2 illustrate examples with just one seal between subframe and

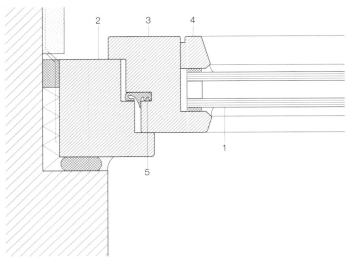

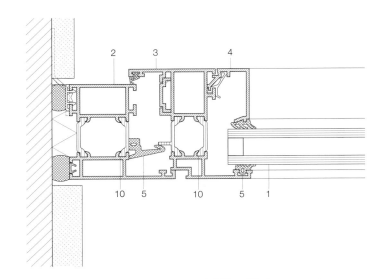

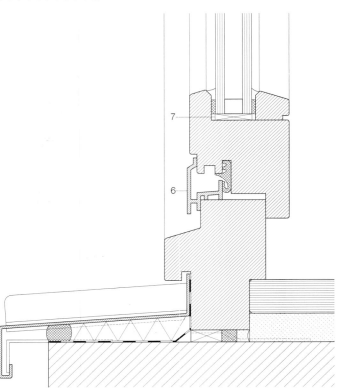

3.2.1

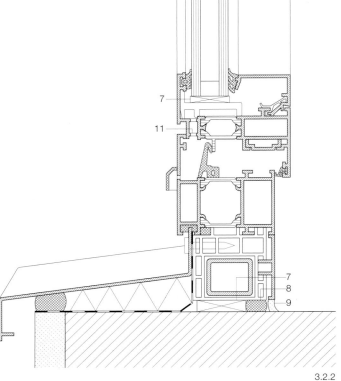

3.2.2

opening light. However, two seals are better for thermal insulation, as shown in Figs 3.2.3 and 3.2.4. An edge and a middle seal are incorporated in 3.2.3. In this case drainage and vapour-pressure equalization take place in front of the outer seal. Drainage in metal or plastic profiles is relatively easy to accomplish; in wooden windows this is best achieved via the mortise and tenon joint of the bottom rail.

1 Double glazing
2 Window frame
3 Sash framing
4 Glazing bead
5 Seal
6 Rainwater channel
7 Setting block
8 Edge tape
9 Permanently elastic joint
10 Thermal break
11 Weep hole
12 Drainage channel
13 Fixing

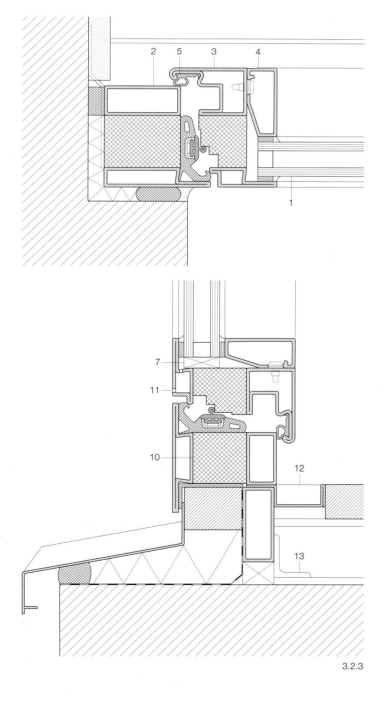

3.2.3

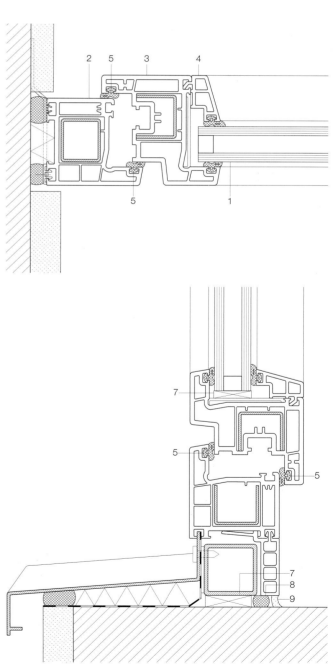

3.2.4

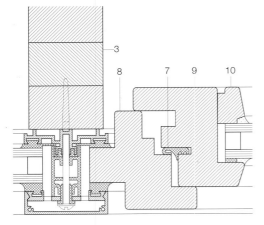

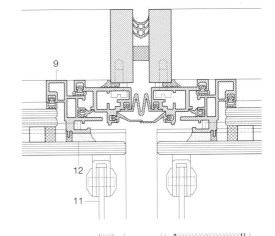

## Opening in patent glazing
## Opening in structural sealant glazing

3.2.5    Glazing bar, wooden window
         Horizontal and vertical sections
3.2.6    Glazing bar, aluminium window
         Vertical section
3.2.7    Structural sealant glazing
         Horizontal and vertical sections
3.2.8    Structural sealant glazing
         Vertical section

Scale 1:2.5

Figs 3.2.5 and 3.2.6 illustrate options for the junction of an opening light and post-and-rail construction with patent glazing. The subframe of the window in this case is inserted like an insulating glass unit between loadbearing section and glazing bar.
Fig. 3.2.5 shows a glazing bar connected directly to the insulating glass, without edge tape. A joint $\geq$ 5 mm must be provided here so that the pane is not restrained when attaching the glazing bar nor the edge of the glass damaged, which would inhibit the adhesion of the sealant on three flanks.
Figs 3.2.7 and 3.2.8 show possible openings in structural sealant glazing. In Fig. 3.2.7 a tilting window is combined with the metal sections of the sunshading.

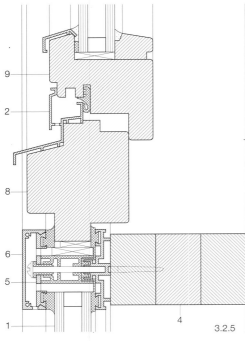

3.2.5

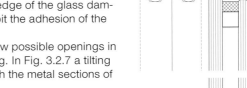

1  Double glazing
2  Rainwater channel
3  Post
4  Rail
5  Glazing bar with thermal break
6  Cover strip
7  Seal
8  Window frame
9  Sash framing / element frame / opening light
10 Glazing bead
11 Sunshading element
12 Adhesive
13 Mechanical fixing
14 Thermally insulated panel
15 Integral profile

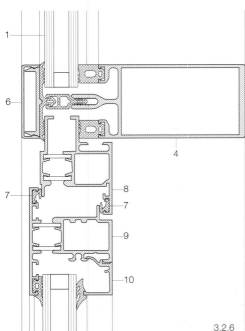

3.2.6

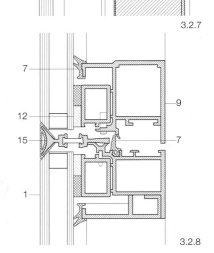

3.2.7

3.2.8

## Louvres

3.2.9     Single glazing, frameless
3.2.10   Double glazing with thermal break in
           frame

Vertical sections, scale 1:5

Louvre windows are suitable for fine regulation
of the venting of rooms or multi-skin façades.
They can also be used as smoke and heat
vents. Countless variations are available in
single or double glazing, with or without
frames. The basic structural considerations
apply like for a vertically pivoted window, for
example.

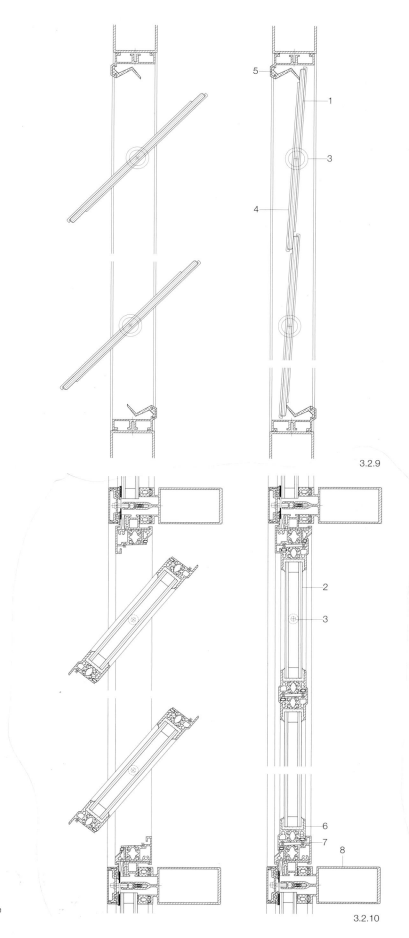

3.2.9

1 Single glazing
2 Double glazing
3 Pivot
4 Glass retainers at ends
5 Edge seal
6 Frame profile with
   thermal break
7 Brush type weatherstrip
8 Frame / installation frame

3.2.10

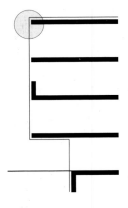

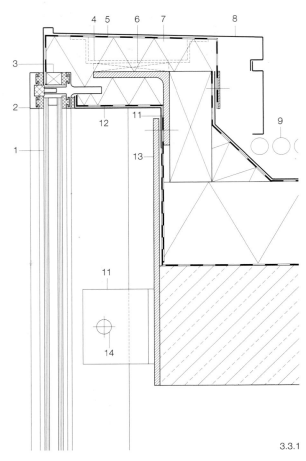

3.3.1

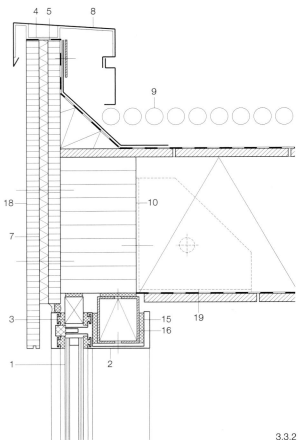

3.3.2

## 3.3 Architectural details

### Flat roof junction

| 3.3.1 | Concrete construction |
| 3.3.2 | Timber construction |
| 3.3.3 | Steel construction / penetration |
| 3.3.4 | Fascia plate / sunshade |

Vertical sections, scale 1:5

Fig. 3.3.1. The primary structure here is reinforced concrete. The edge of the slab and the overlying roof construction are clad with a steel plate anchored to the concrete. The posts are fixed to angles welded to this plate. The connection of the upper façade rail to the edge plate is diffusion-tight and airtight. The clearance between glazing and plate should be wide enough to allow cleaning of the glass. Heat reflected from the edge of the slab could lead to stresses in the glass caused by varying heating effects. A stationary layer of air can lead to condensation occurring; the inclusion of ventilation louvres is an advantage.

Fig. 3.3.2. The primary structure here is an insulated timber lattice; timber panels form the fascia. The junction with the façade is achieved two-fold: in the plane of the glass by a clamped plastic block, and in the structural plane by an insulated aluminium hollow section with thermal break. The connection must be able to accommodate movements in the façade as well as deformation of the primary structure caused by imposed loads, thermal expansion etc. It must also remain diffusion-tight and airtight and be thermally insulated.

Fig. 3.3.3. The primary structure here is steel. The façade posts are fixed to the main structure via steel angles. The steel beams penetrating the façade represent thermal bridges. Condensation may occur and this should be drained away in a controlled manner (e.g. condensation channel). The joint between external skin and beam must be able to accommodate the various movements of the façade and loadbearing structure (especially thermal expansion and wind loads). It must also be diffusion-tight and airtight. Such a joint is normally covered by a stainless steel sleeve fitted to the outside.

Fig. 3.3.4. The primary structure here is reinforced concrete. The façade posts are fixed to the main structure via a cast-in slotted channel. The connection of the upper façade panel is to be diffusion-tight. Sunshading in front of the façade should be fixed independently of the façade construction (warranty problems). A fascia panel conceals the sunshading installation.

1 Double glazing
2 Aluminium façade rail
3 Plastic spacer block
4 Sheet metal cleat
5 Vapour barrier
6 EPDM pad
7 Thermal insulation
8 Anodised aluminium sheet
9 Roof construction:
   chippings
   waterproofing
   thermal insulation
   vapour barrier
10 Glulam beam
11 Steel angle
12 Vapour barrier
13 Steel plate
14 Screw in elongated hole
15 Permanently elastic seal
16 Aluminium section, insulated, with thermal break
17 Movement joint
18 Plywood, with waterproof adhesive
19 Joist hanger
20 Aluminium angle fixed to supporting construction
21 Fabric sunshade
22 Steel bracket
23 Insulated façade panel
24 Cast-in slotted channel
25 Perforated steel beam
26 Stainless steel plate, screwed on
27 Steel tube
28 Steel trapezoidal sheeting

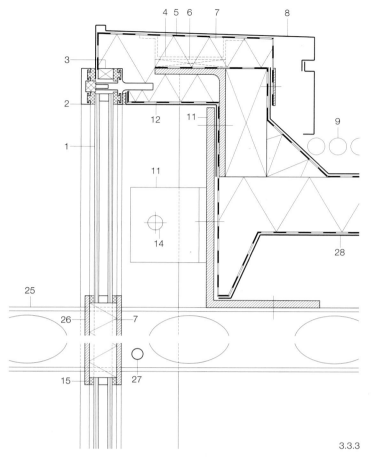

3.3.3

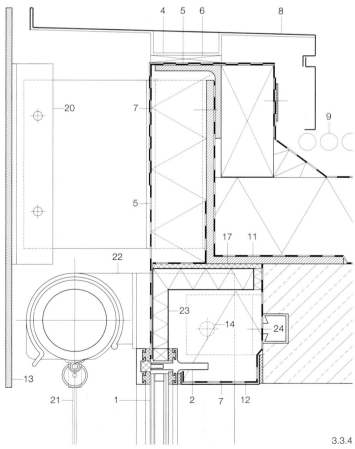

3.3.4

**169**

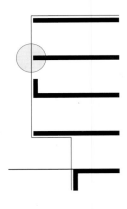

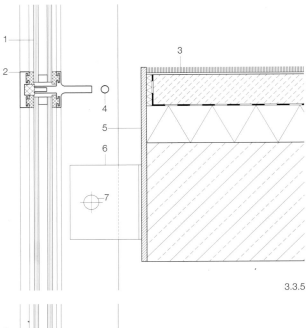

3.3.5

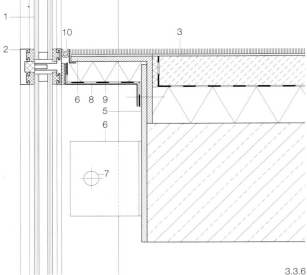

3.3.6

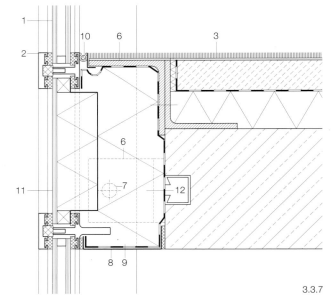

3.3.7

1 Double glazing
2 Aluminium façade rail
3 Floor construction:
  fabric floor covering
  screed
  isolating membrane
  thermal insulation
  floor structure
4 Safety grid, stainless steel tube
5 Steel plate, hot-dip galvanized
6 Steel angle, hot-dip galvanized
7 Screw in elongated hole
8 Aluminium sheet cover and vapour barrier
9 Thermal insulation
10 Movement joint, permanently elastic seal
11 Façade panel:
  toughened safety glass, printed
  insulation
  aluminium sheet
12 Cast-in slotted channel
13 Steel bracket, hot-dip galvanized
14 Timber lattice
15 Aluminium section, insulated, with thermal break
16 Plastic spacer block
17 EPDM pad
18 Façade panel:
  aluminium sheet
  thermal insulation
19 Wooden panelling
20 Horizontal louvre blind
21 Fabric sunshade
22 Vapour barrier

## Floor junction

3.3.5   Continuous façade
3.3.6   Floor covering extending to external skin
3.3.7   Smoke-tight junction
3.3.8   Smoke-tight junction, louvre blind
3.3.9   Smoke-tight junction, awning
3.3.10  Smoke-tight junction, lattice
3.3.11  Junction in timber construction

Vertical sections, scale 1:5

The floor junction details shown here differ in their specifications regarding fire protection, thermal insulation and sound insulation. If the glazing continues to the floor, then it must be remembered that cleaning equipment or other movable items could damage the glass and cause chips from which cracks can develop. If there is a risk of falling, inner panes must be made of safety glass with a thickness appropriate to the circumstances.
Fig. 3.3.5. The façade passes in front of the edge of the floor, which is covered by a steel plate. The joint between floor and façade is open. The post is fixed to the main structure by a welded plate. If the gap between floor and façade is ≥ 60 mm, a safety grid is normally required. The respective regional building authority stipulates what is necessary.
Fig. 3.3.6 corresponds to Fig. 3.3.5 but here the floor covering continues to meet the façade. Floor loads may not be transferred to the façade. The junction must include a permanently elastic seal but it is not smoke-tight and does not comply with the sound insulation requirements of DIN 4109.
Figs 3.3.7 – 3.3.10. The façade is interrupted at the floor. The connections are smoke-tight, diffusion-tight and airtight. The façade is to be checked for flanking sound transmissions in the case of a higher sound insulation specification (DIN 4109). Penetrations for the purpose of attaching sunshading (Figs 3.3.8 – 3.3.10) represent thermal bridges. Diffusion-tight and airtight connections and carefully designed insulation details are required. In addition, the joint in the glass panel must be capable of accommodating movements in the façade, the fascia and the primary structure, and must include a permanently elastic seal. If the vertical blind is fixed by means of a mounting fitted in the groove for the screw fixing, the outer skin is not penetrated. Such a detail demands exact coordination with façade and sunshade manufacturers (warranty).
Fig. 3.3.11. The primary structure is formed by an insulated timber lattice. The façade is interrupted at each floor by the timber beams. If the façade bears on the floor, then the upper joint must be able to accommodate movement.

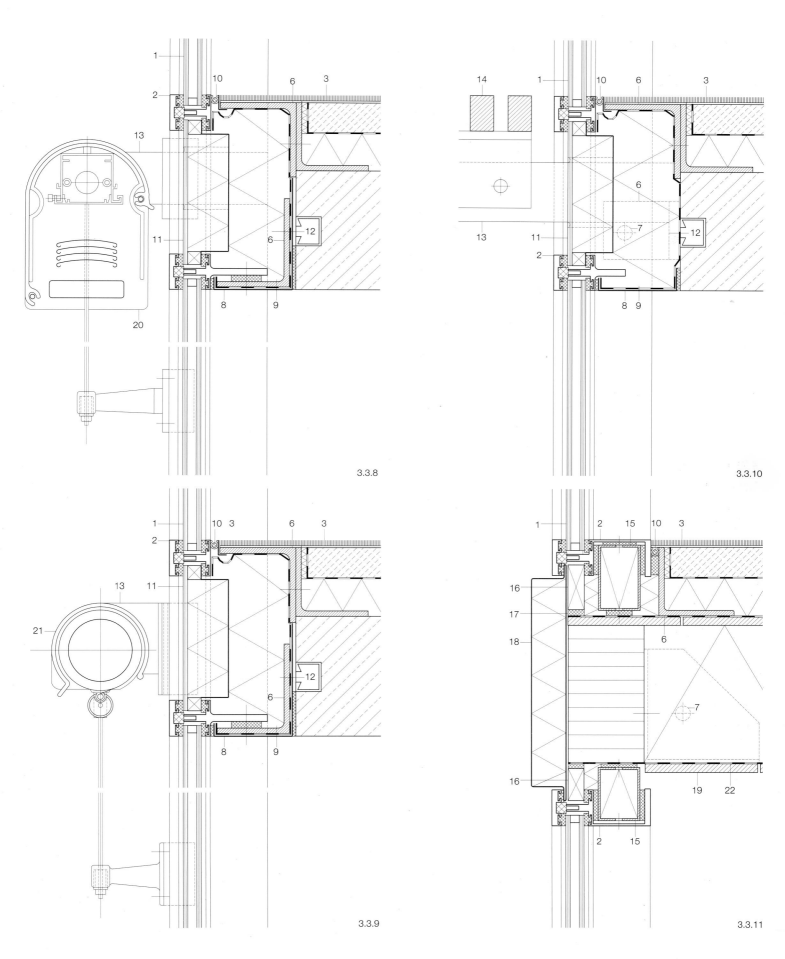

3.3.8

3.3.10

3.3.9

3.3.11

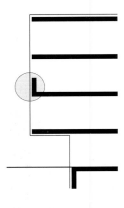

1 Double glazing
2 Aluminium façade rail
3 Plastic spacer block
4 Aluminium section, insulated, with thermal break
5 Vapour barrier
6 Anodised aluminium sheet
7 Steel angle
8 Thermal insulation
9 Air gap for ventilation
10 Vapour barrier
11 Aluminium sheet, 1.5 mm
12 Floor construction: fabric floor covering floating screed isolating membrane impact sound insulation
13 Cast-in slotted channel
14 Window sill on framing
15 Permanently elastic joint
16 Stainless steel fixed anchor
17 Reconstituted stone facing
18 Stainless steel movable anchor
19 Steel flat
20 Solid spandrel panel, concrete or masonry
21 Prefabricated reinforced concrete element

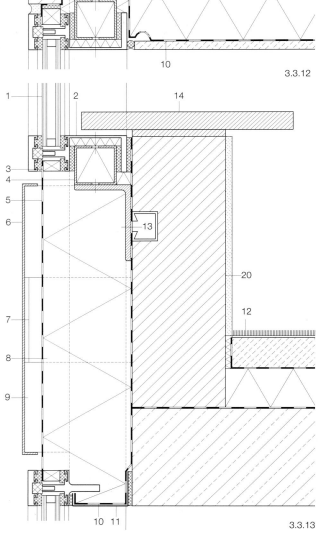

3.3.12

3.3.13

**Spandrel panel**

3.3.12   Prefabricated fair-face concrete spandrel panel
3.3.13   Metal spandrel panel
3.3.14   Reconstituted stone spandrel panel

Vertical sections, scale 1:5

Shown here are three examples of spandrel panels with varying architectural and constructional approaches, as well as different materials.
Fig. 3.3.12.  The primary structure here is reinforced concrete. The spandrel panel is made from a prefabricated fair-face concrete element and is thermally isolated from the reinforced concrete floor slab. It is connected by a special, thermally insulated reinforcing cage. The spandrel panel must be insulated on the inside and a vapour barrier – protected against damage – attached to the inner face. Consequently, the mass storage effect of the spandrel panel cannot be used for the internal climate. The surface finish of the spandrel panel is of fair-face quality. The façade bears on or is suspended from each floor. Connections are therefore either rigid or flexible. Fixing is by means of a façade rail fitted to an insulated aluminium hollow section with thermal break. Its position is adjusted by means of steel plates fitted underneath and it is fixed to the spandrel panel using stainless steel screws. To avoid galvanic corrosion, an intermediate pad (e.g. EPDM) must be placed between steel and aluminium. The connections must be permanently elastic, diffusion-tight and airtight.
Fig. 3.3.13.  The primary structure here is reinforced concrete. In this example the façade post continues past the spandrel panel and the façade is freestanding. Load transfer is at the top of the spandrel panel by an insulated aluminium hollow section with thermal break, steel angle and cast-in slotted channel in the solid spandrel panel. The upper connection fixes the façade horizontally and must be able to accommodate thermal expansion, movements due to wind load and structural movements; it must remain diffusion-tight and airtight. The façade is fixed to the main structure via an insulated steel angle integrated in the façade rail. Insulation is affixed to the outside of the spandrel panel. The vapour barrier must be correctly positioned and the insulation protected against dampness. There is an air gap behind the spandrel panel for ventilation.

A rigid aluminium sheet (larger ones require framing) is glued to aluminium angles independently of the actual façade. These angles penetrate the insulation and are fixed to the spandrel panel. The connections must be designed to be adjustable in three directions to compensate for the various tolerances in structural and façade works. In this example it is achieved via a cast-in slotted channel and elongated holes in the steel angles.

Fig. 3.3.14. The primary structure here is reinforced concrete. In this detail the outer skin is interrupted by the spandrel panels, and the façade is arranged between the floors. The fixing points are either rigid or flexible, depending on whether the façade is designed as freestanding or suspended. The rail is fixed to the main structure via an insulated aluminium hollow section (with thermal break) and discrete steel angles fixed to cast-in slotted channels. The fixing is adjustable in three directions to compensate for the various tolerances in structure and façade. The façade is fixed to the main structure by an insulated steel angle integrated in the rail. Insulation is affixed to the outside of the spandrel panel. The vapour barrier must be positioned correctly on the inside of the insulation, which must have a closed-cell structure so that it does not become saturated by driving rain. PE sheeting is also required to provide protection from the weather.

The rear-vented facing panel is a reconstituted stone element, e.g. prefabricated reinforced concrete. It is attached by stainless steel anchors which must be able to accommodate thermal movements in two directions. This is accomplished by means of plastic sleeves in the anchor holes and by allowing the lower anchor to move.

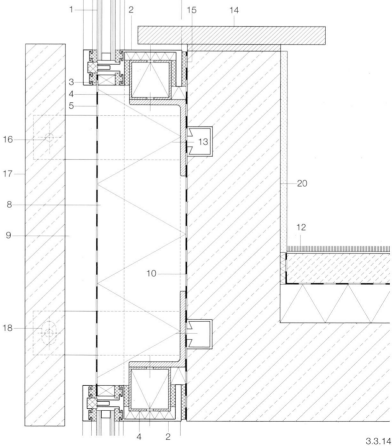

3.3.14

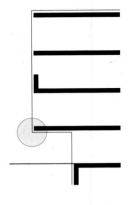

**Re-entrant façade**

3.3.15   Panel corner, with penetration
3.3.16   Panel corner, with penetration
3.3.17   Glazed corner

Vertical sections, scale 1:5

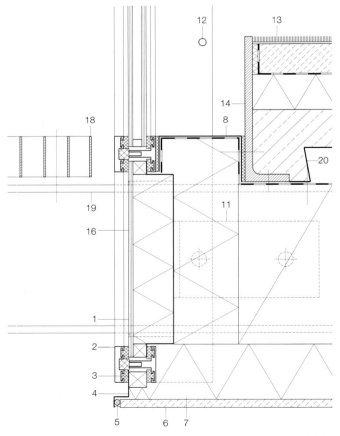

3.3.15

3.3.16

1   Double glazing
2   Aluminium façade rail
3   Plastic spacer block
4   Anodised aluminium
    sheet
5   Permanently elastic
    joint
6   Fibre-reinforced
    cement slabs on fram-
    ing
7   Thermal insulation
8   Aluminium sheet cover
    plus vapour barrier
9   Screw in elongated
    hole
10  Steel plate, hot-dip
    galvanized
11  Aluminium angle
12  Safety grid, stainless
    steel tube
13  Floor construction:
    fabric floor covering
    floating screed
    isolating membrane
    impact sound insula-
    tion
14  Steel angle, hot-dip
    galvanized
15  Cast-in slotted channel
16  Façade panel:
    toughened safety
    glass, printed
    thermal insulation
    aluminium sheet
17  Steel bracket with end
    plate, hot-dip galvan-
    ized
18  Open-grid flooring,
    hot-dip galvanized
19  Steel beam, hot-dip
    galvanized
20  Steel trapezoidal
    sheeting

Details in Figs 3.3.15 – 3.3.17 illustrate typical corner arrangements in post-and-rail construction for recessed or projecting sections in a vertical façade.

Façades may be designed as freestanding or suspended. In the freestanding case, the junction at the corner must be formed as a fixed support and be able to accommodate horizontal and vertical loads. For suspended façades, the junction need only accommodate horizontal loads. It must be able to slide vertically in order to enable movement caused by thermal expansion and wind loads; this is achieved by having elongated fixing holes.

Fig. 3.3.15. The primary structure here is reinforced concrete. The glass pane continues to finished floor level. The gap between façade and structure is bridged by a steel angle screwed on. The edge of the slab is covered by a glass panel with suitable insulation and permanently elastic, diffusion-tight and airtight sealing. The façade is firmly fixed to the structure via cast-in slotted channel and steel angles adjustable in three directions. The façade panel is penetrated at individual places by glass fins for attaching sunshades, escape balconies etc. This penetration must incorporate a permanently elastic seal to prevent the insulation from becoming damp.

Fig. 3.3.16. The primary structure here is steel. The construction consists of continuous steel beams and steel trapezoidal sheeting with concrete topping. The steel beam penetrates the outer skin. This point represents a thermal bridge which must be carefully detailed. The spaces between the beams are filled with glass panels. Joints must have permanently elastic seals and be able to accommodate movements caused by thermal expansion, different loading cases, etc. The junction between façade rail and steel beam must be able to accommodate the various tolerances in the façade and structural steelwork and also permit movements brought about by loads (wind, imposed etc.) and thermal stresses. The steel beam passes from cold outside air to heated interior and so constitutes a thermal bridge. It must therefore be completely insulated in order to prevent the occurrence of condensation. The inner face of the insulation is to be provided with a diffusion-tight and airtight vapour barrier.

Fig. 3.3.17. The primary structure here is reinforced concrete with a peripheral steel plate. The glass is extended downwards as far as possible. Thermal insulation is attached to the underside of the floor slab and faced with, for example, fibre-reinforced cement slabs. The façade is freestanding. Forces are transferred via the steel angle welded to the steel plate. The overlap of the façade and steelwork trades creates problems here (different tolerances, warranty issues). The façade rail is insulated in order to avoid thermal bridges. The inner face of the insulation must be provided with a permanently elastic seal and remain diffusion-tight and airtight. The gap between façade and structure is to be closed with a safety grid; in Germany the respective regional building authority stipulates what is necessary. Cleaning in this gap as well as the stationary layer of air – at a relatively poorly insulated spot – might lead to problems with this detail.

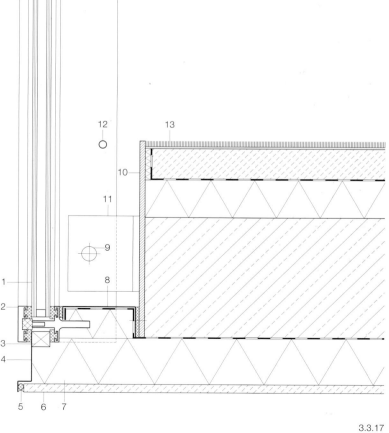

3.3.17

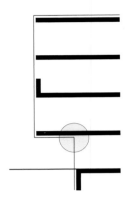

**Junction with underside of floor**

3.3.18   Junction with steel construction
3.3.19   Underside of timber construction
3.3.20   Underside of double-leaf construction
3.3.21   Underside of floor, external insulation
3.3.22   Underside of floor, with thermal break
3.3.23   Underside of floor, internal insulation

Vertical sections, scale 1:5

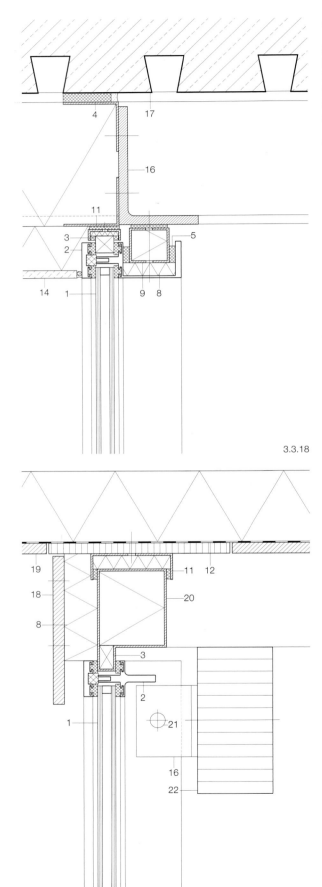

3.3.18

3.3.19

1   Double glazing
2   Aluminium façade rail
3   Plastic spacer block
4   Elastic sealing tape
5   Permanently elastic seal
6   Plastic angle
7   Anodised aluminium angle
8   Thermal insulation
9   Insulated aluminium section
10  Thermal break
11  Insulated aluminium section, with thermal break
12  Vapour barrier
13  Plasterboard ceiling on framing
14  Fibre-reinforced cement slabs on framing
15  Insulation-grade plaster
16  Steel angle, hot-dip galvanized
17  Steel trapezoidal sheeting
18  Timber fascia
19  Wooden panelling
20  Aluminium sheet façade panel
21  Screw in elongated hole
22  Glulam beam

Details in Figs 3.3.18 – 3.3.23 illustrate connections between a post-and-rail façade and various horizontal floor soffits which can occur, for example, with re-entrant façades.
Details in Figs 3.3.20 – 3.3.23 show different aesthetic intentions, e.g. whether the underside of a concrete slab is to be exposed, partly covered or fully concealed. In all cases the upper façade/floor connection must be designed in such a way that movements of the floor (caused by imposed loads, settlement etc.) do not induce any compression in the glass. A sliding joint must be incorporated if necessary.
Fig. 3.3.18.  The primary structure here is steel. The floor comprises steel trapezoidal sheeting with a concrete topping supported on I-beam sections. The beams and trapezoidal sheeting penetrate the outer skin. The entire steel construction is insulated externally in order to prevent internal condensation. The connection between façade and main structure is via a steel angle and allows for differential movement. Insulation is fitted between the beams. The external cladding should be removable. On the inside, the connection must be permanently elastic as well as diffusion-tight and airtight.
Fig. 3.3.19.  The primary structure here is timber. The façade is freestanding. The post is connected to the main structure via elongated holes to enable it to slide vertically. An insulated make-up piece, clamped in the upper façade rail and inserted via a channel section (as movement joint, with thermal break) so that it can move, connects the façade to the timber construction. A narrow fascia covers the joint. This should be removable so that the cover strip can be detached following breakage of the glass. The façade junction must be diffusion-tight and airtight on the inside.
Fig. 3.3.20.  The primary structure here is reinforced concrete. The façade is freestanding so the upper junction must be fixed horizontally

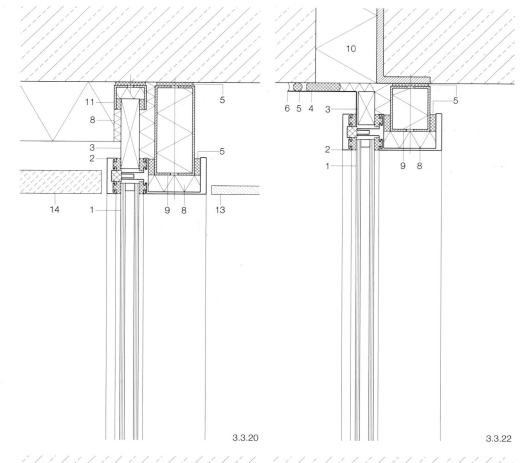

3.3.20

3.3.22

but free to slide vertically. The exposed under-side of the slab is covered with an insulation-grade plaster externally. The connection must be diffusion-tight and airtight on the inside.
Fig. 3.3.21. The primary structure here is rein-forced concrete. The junction with the under-side of the floor is, in principle, identical to that in Fig. 3.3.20, although in that detail the main structure is concealed internally and externally by a suspended ceiling. The junction must be permanently elastic as well as diffusion-tight and airtight. External cladding should be removable in the vicinity of the façade so that the cover strip can be detached following breakage of the glass.
Fig. 3.3.22. The primary structure here is rein-forced concrete. There is a thermal break in the floor slab above the façade. In contrast to Fig. 3.3.20, the junction is exposed on both sides. The façade is connected to the structure by an angle and elastic adhesive.
Fig. 3.3.23. The primary structure here is rein-forced concrete. The junction is basically the same as detail in Fig. 3.3.20 but in this case the underside of the floor slab is exposed externally. The slab must be insulated internally with strips of vapour retarders. The thickness and length of the vapour retarder strips are determined by the construction physics spe-cialist. Screw fixings for the façade are a prob-lem here because the screws are located in the cold area of the structure. Galvanic corrosion caused by condensation could occur at this point; stainless steel screws should therefore be used. The fixing must be diffusion-tight and airtight inside.

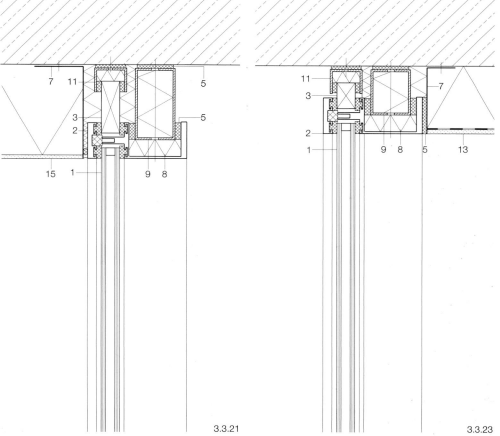

3.3.21

3.3.23

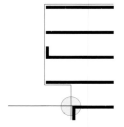

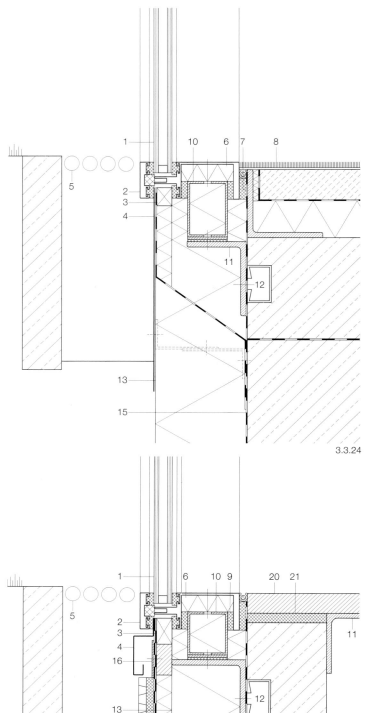

3.3.24

3.3.25

1 Double glazing
2 Aluminium façade rail
3 Plastic spacer block
4 Anodised aluminium
  sheet
5 Gravel-filled trench
6 Thermal insulation
7 Vapour barrier
8 Floor construction:
  fabric floor covering
  screed
  isolating membrane
  impact sound insulation
9 Permanently elastic seal
10 Insulated aluminium
  section
11 Steel angle, hot-dip
  galvanized
12 Cast-in slotted channel
13 Perimeter insulation
14 Raised timber grid
15 Lean-mix concrete
  blinding
16 Steel flat
17 Floor supports
18 Water bar
19 Drainage slab
20 Timber tread
21 Elastic sealing tape

## Base, level transition between inside and outside

3.3.24   Level transition to outside
3.3.25   Junction with grass-covered flat roof
3.3.26   Junction with terrace/balcony
3.3.27   Junction with grass-covered flat roof

Vertical sections, scale 1:5

Figs. 3.3.24 – 3.3.27 illustrate base details for a post-and-rail façade. These details could occur on flat roofs and terraces, but above all at ground floor level. This is where façade, structural, fitting-out and sealing trades all meet. Careful detailing is therefore required with respect to workmanship, scheduling and clarification of warranty issues. A permanent seal is essential at this transition. The min. 150 mm height difference between water run-off level and bottom seal on façade rail as laid down in the standards can be reduced or waived only in agreement with the owner/developer and contractor.

The inner or outer pane – depending on function – must be made from safety glass to prevent injury.

Figs. 3.3.24. The primary structure here is reinforced concrete. This a level transition between inside and outside. The façade is freestanding. The load is transferred via an insulated hollow section (with thermal break) which is fixed to the main structure by means of a steel angle and cast-in slotted channel. The connection can be adjusted in three directions. The floor construction is trimmed with a steel angle. The gap between façade and edge of slab is packed with suitable insulation, sealed permanently diffusion-tight on the inner face to prevent the insulation from becoming damp. The overlap of the façade and sealing trades is a problem. The façade erector clamps a sheeting overlap under the façade rail which is subsequently welded to the seal on the outer wall of the basement by the sealing crew. The offset in the sealing plane above the perimeter insulation is also critical. According to the relevant standards, the seal must be ≥ 150 mm above the water run-off level. The gap to the façade is filled with 16/32 filter gravel.

Fig. 3.3.25. The primary structure here is reinforced concrete. The different levels of the ground/floor constructions inside and outside are a problem here. A level transition is possible by means of a raised floor internally or by providing a step in the floor slab. In the example shown, there is a step on the inside. The freestanding façade is connected to the main structure via a thermally isolated and insulated hollow section, steel angle and cast-in slotted channel, which transfers the forces but still remains adjustable in three directions. The façade section is insulated with a permanent diffusion-tight and airtight seal to the inside. The concrete upstand is protected against water pressure with a water bar and has insulation attached externally. The overlap of the façade and sealing trades creates problems for the warranty. Movements in structure and façade must be allowed for by means of loops. Fig. 3.3.26. The primary structure here is reinforced concrete. The main structure near the façade is separated by way of a special, thermally insulated reinforcing element. A raised timber grid is provided outside in order to create a level transition. Movements can occur here which the façade/balcony (façade/terrace) seal must be able to accommodate (e.g. include loop). The point at which façade and sealing trades meet is critical; warranty issues must be clarified. The sealing sheet is protected against damage and UV radiation by a two-piece metal sheet cover. This freestanding façade is firmly fixed to the structural slab via a thermally isolated and insulated hollow section and a steel angle, adjustable in three directions. The section is insulated and provided with a diffusion-tight and airtight seal on the inside in order to prevent galvanic corrosion and the insulation becoming damp. The timber grid must be removable in order to permit access to the façade cover strip in the event of the glass being broken.

Fig. 3.3.27. This detail is similar to Fig. 3.3.25 but with a raised access floor inside (e.g. in an office building) to provide a level transition to the outside. The thermally isolated section is attached directly to the main structure from above by steel plates and is adjustable in three directions.

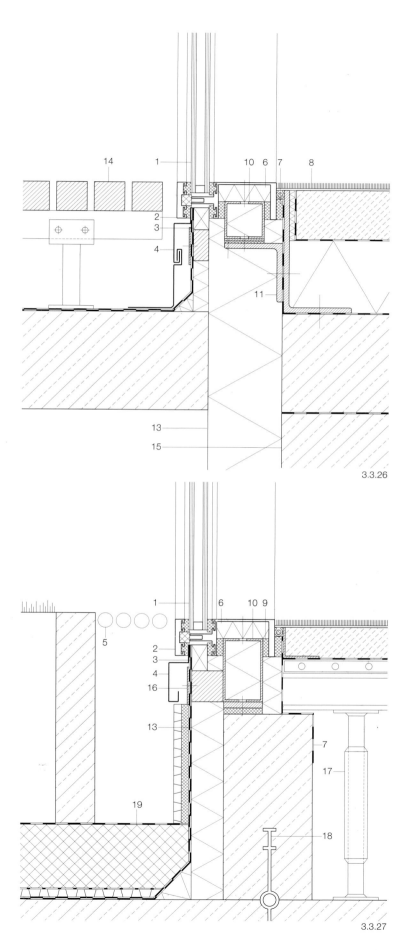

3.3.26

3.3.27

**179**

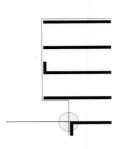

**Plinth**

3.3.28  Panel plinth
3.3.29  Reconstituted stone plinth
3.3.30  Recessed plinth

Vertical section, scale 1:5

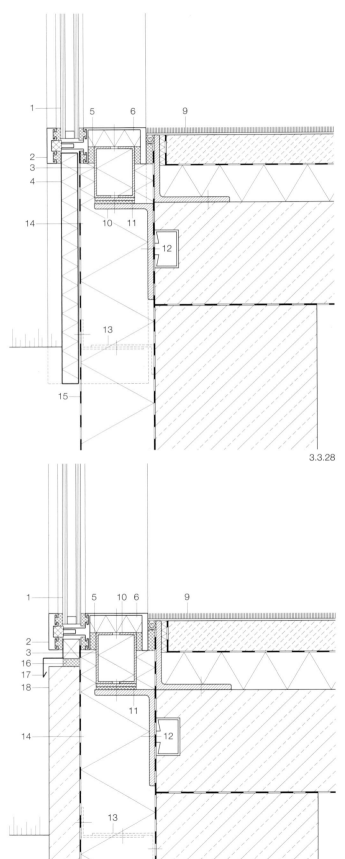

3.3.28

3.3.29

1 Double glazing
2 Aluminium façade rail
3 Insulated aluminium section, with thermal break
4 Insulated façade panel
5 Permanently elastic joint
6 Thermal insulation
7 Vapour barrier
8 Aluminium sheet
9 Floor construction: fabric floor covering screed isolating membrane impact sound insulation
10 Steel angle
11 EPDM pad
12 Cast-in slotted channel
13 Aluminium angle
14 Perimeter insulation
15 Filter fabric
16 Plastic spacer block
17 Anodised aluminium plate
18 Reconstituted stone plinth
19 Safety grid

The plinth details illustrated here could occur on flat roofs and terraces, but above all at ground floor level. This is where façade, structural, fitting-out and sealing trades all meet. If the glazing continues to the floor, then it must be remembered that cleaning equipment or other movable items could damage the glass and cause chips from which cracks can develop. If there is a risk of falling, then inner panes must be made of safety glass with a thickness appropriate to the circumstances. Fig. 3.3.28. The intention here is to continue the glazing to the floor. The plinth is formed by an insulated sheet metal panel fitted flush with the glass. The panel is clamped in the lower façade rail and joined to the main structure via an angle arrangement. The basement wall is sealed and insulated on the outside. The perimeter insulation runs uninterrupted up behind the panel right to the bottom edge of the façade. The façade is freestanding and fixed to the main structure via an insulated and thermally isolated aluminium hollow section, steel angles and cast-in slotted channel, adjustable in three directions. Steel and aluminium items must be separated by intermediate pads in order to prevent galvanic corrosion. Stainless steel screws should be used. The spaces in the construction should be completely filled with suitable insulation and the inner face completely covered with a vapour barrier to prevent the insulation becoming damp.
Fig. 3.3.29. This is similar to Fig. 3.3.28 but in this case the plinth is made from weather-resistant reconstituted stone (e.g. concrete). The façade is connected to the stone with a diffusion-tight, permanently elastic joint and plastic strip clamped in the lower façade rail. A rainwater drip is clamped in the façade rail to

cover and protect the silicone joint.
Fig. 3.3.30. Here, the plane of the façade is
positioned in front of the solid outer wall. It is
supported by steel angles which are fixed to
the main structure via a cast-in slotted channel
and elongated holes to permit adjustment in
three directions. A folded façade panel with
integral insulation is fitted to the lower façade
rail and attached to the external wall of the
basement by a plastic angle. This connection
must be permanently elastic as well as
diffusion-tight and airtight. The façade rail is
connected to the reinforced concrete floor by
an aluminium plate. The space that ensues
must be completely filled with suitable insulation and the inner face covered with a vapour
barrier to prevent the insulation becoming
damp. The gap between front edge of floor
construction and façade should be provided
with a safety grid (as stipulated by the regional
building authority). The outer wall of the basement has external perimeter insulation and is
protected against moisture by a suitable coating. A reconstituted stone panel is fitted in front
of the perimeter insulation; this is connected to
the façade panel by means of a permanently
elastic joint.

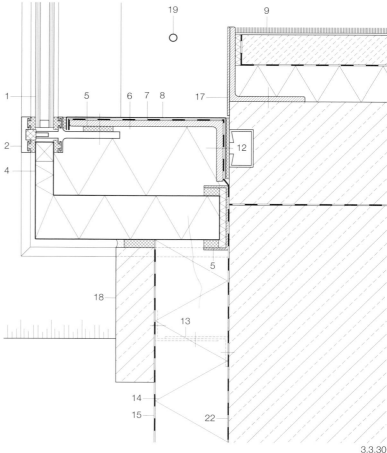

3.3.30

**181**

## Glass roofs

Vertical sections, scale 1:5

These details illustrate typical solutions for pitched glass roofs. In principle, the same materials may be used here as in vertical glazed façades. However, owing to the higher thermal and the different mechanical stresses compared to vertical glazing, special constructional measures are necessary. The sections used as posts and rails in the preceding façade details have been used again here for the longitudinal and transverse members. The connection to the main structure (steel) is by way of steel brackets that permit adjustment in three directions. The drainage system of the supporting construction should be modified to suit the sloping arrangement so that water can run off to the outside. Transverse clamping bars on the roof are flat and bevelled so that rainwater can drain properly. For overhead glazing in general, the lower pane should be a type which retains fragments upon fracture (e.g. laminated safety glass, or wired glass up to a certain size). For glazing subject to restricted/unrestricted foot traffic, the type of glass must be chosen accordingly. Gutters are required for larger roof areas.

Fig. 3.3.31. For reasons of appearance, the transverse rails should be located as near to the ridge as possible. The ridge is closed off with an insulated panel folded to the appropriate angle. The sloping rails have mitred joints and are connected together by the groove for screw fixings.

Fig. 3.3.32. The ridge is finished with a cover plate fitted into the screw groove of the ridge purlin.

Fig. 3.3.33. For reasons of appearance, the transverse rails are located as near to the corner as possible. The corner is closed off with an insulated panel bent to the appropriate angle. The façade posts and the pitched roof rails are mitred and joined together

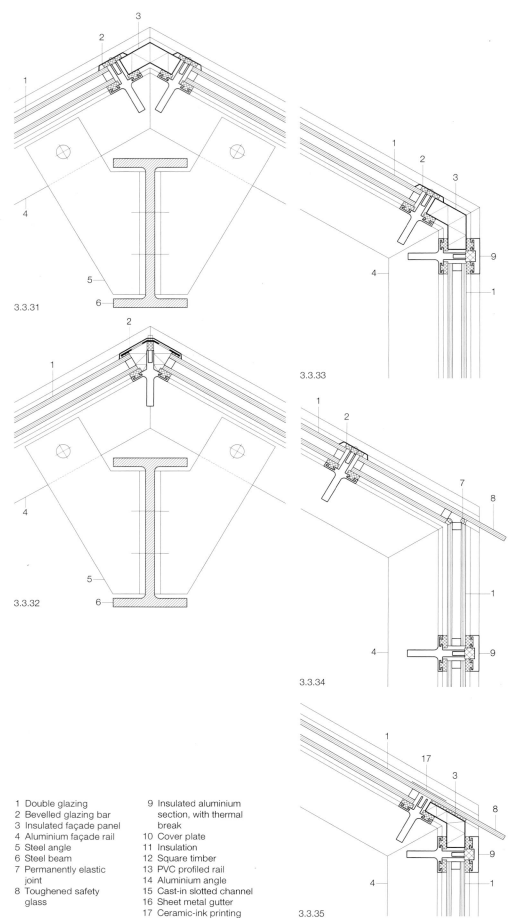

3.3.31

3.3.32

3.3.33

3.3.34

3.3.35

1 Double glazing
2 Bevelled glazing bar
3 Insulated façade panel
4 Aluminium façade rail
5 Steel angle
6 Steel beam
7 Permanently elastic joint
8 Toughened safety glass
9 Insulated aluminium section, with thermal break
10 Cover plate
11 Insulation
12 Square timber
13 PVC profiled rail
14 Aluminium angle
15 Cast-in slotted channel
16 Sheet metal gutter
17 Ceramic-ink printing

using steel angles or the screw. A channel for collecting the dirty condensate water is recommended for roofs without overhanging eaves.

Fig. 3.3.34. This shows a fully glazed corner. The uppermost sloping glass pane extends beyond the façade to form an eaves overhang. The joints between vertical glazing and roof are sealed with permanently elastic material. In this detail, chosen for reasons of appearance, the mounting for the upper pane must be properly executed and the drained joint tends to leak if the workmanship is not adequate. Only a silicone seal works here.

Fig. 3.3.35. This corner is closed with an insulated panel. The upper glass pane of the

inclined double glazing is glued to the panel and extends beyond the façade to form an eaves overhang. The exposed edge seal of the double glazing in Figs 3.3.34 and 3.3.35 must be suitably protected against UV radiation (e.g. printing).

Fig. 3.3.36 shows the upper junction of a pitched glass roof with a taller, insulated, reinforced concrete wall. The sloping rails are connected to the main structure via elongated holes, steel angles and a cast-in slotted channel, adjustable in three directions. The glass roof is joined to the structure using an insulated panel, PVC angle and sealing tapes, permanently elastic, diffusion-tight and airtight. In line with the standards, the flashing continues 150 mm

above the water run-off level.

Figs 3.3.37 and 3.3.38. The lateral junction with a sloping component can be realized with or without a gutter. The glass roof is joined to the structure using an insulated panel, a PVC angle and sealing tapes, permanently elastic, diffusion-tight and airtight. The gutter in Fig. 3.3.37 uses the depth of the inclined loadbearing rail. In the case of shallow pitches (< 10°), it may be necessary to heat the gutter in winter. Even on frost-free days, the gutter may become blocked (e.g. by leaves). The thermal transmittance of the adjacent insulation should match that of the insulating glass in order to avoid thermal bridges.

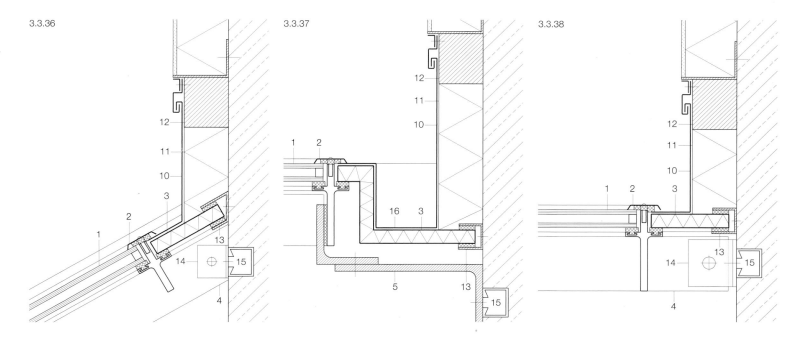

3.3.36

3.3.37

3.3.38

# Part 4 • Built examples and details

**Christian Schittich and Gerald Staib**

The buildings documented in the following section illustrate the wide range of applications that exist for glass in architecture - both internally and in the construction of façades and roofs. The selection of work included here was based in the first instance on design and architectural considerations. A further important aspect was the variety of constructional forms and the way glass can be combined with other materials - steel and aluminium, as well as timber, concrete and brickwork.

We consider topics such as the refurbishment of old buildings and the way glass can be used to create an appropriate contrast to historical fabric, as well as technical innovations and the application of this material in schemes with energy-conscious construction concepts. The examples included here are taken from various locations and are subject to quite different constraints in terms of climate, planning and building laws, technical regulations and standards. For this reason, the details documented on the following pages cannot simply be reproduced without certain reservations. They need to be adapted to the specific requirements of each individual situation. The details of the structures included here should not be regarded as standard recipes but as examples that may stimulate new conceptual ideas.

In order to provide a better understanding of the overall context, details of the projects are not shown in isolation. Basic information relating to the buildings is given in the form of site plans, layouts, sections etc. In only a few cases does the selection concentrate on individual façades or roof structures.

Example 1

**Suspended Pyramid in
the Louvre, Paris**

1993

Architects:
Ieoh Ming Pei & Partners, New York
Design, constructional and structural planning
of the pyramid:
RFR, Paris
Peter Rice, Henry Bardsley, Lionel Penisson,
Nicolas Prouvé

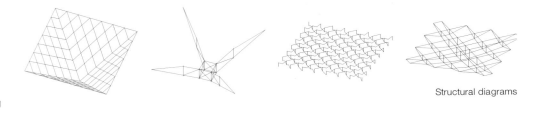

Structural diagrams

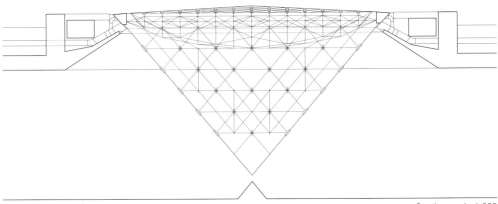

Section scale 1:200

The inverted pyramid is suspended like a huge
chandelier in the underground shopping
arcade beneath the Cour Caroussel in the
Louvre. Through its mirror-like sides, the structure allows daylight to enter this space and
functions as a luminous point of orientation, visible from a great distance at the intersection of
two newly created primary access routes. The
pyramid also resembles an independent sculpture that reflects and refracts light in a fascinating manner and divides it into the colours of
the spectrum.
The faces of the pyramid are like curtains hung
within an adjustable metal frame that is let into
the surrounding concrete structure. The individual sheets of glass, which bear the weight of
the panels below them, are joined together by
cruciform four-point connectors. The sloping
sides are stabilized by slender cables fixed in
the middle of the lozenge-shaped glazing panels and tensioned by the weight of the glass.
The cables are linked to the primary bracing
system, which consists of eight rocker arms
and the main cables. The tip of the pyramid
can be removed for cleaning and maintenance. The covering at the top is in the form of
a flattened pyramid, which facilitates the run-off
of rainwater. The glass panels of this structure,
which, for reasons of safety, was designed to
bear foot traffic, are supported at their four corners by cast stainless-steel elements. The roof
is supported by a double network of heavily
stressed cables which is independent of the
suspended pyramid. Loads from the roof are
transmitted to this cable network via compression rods.

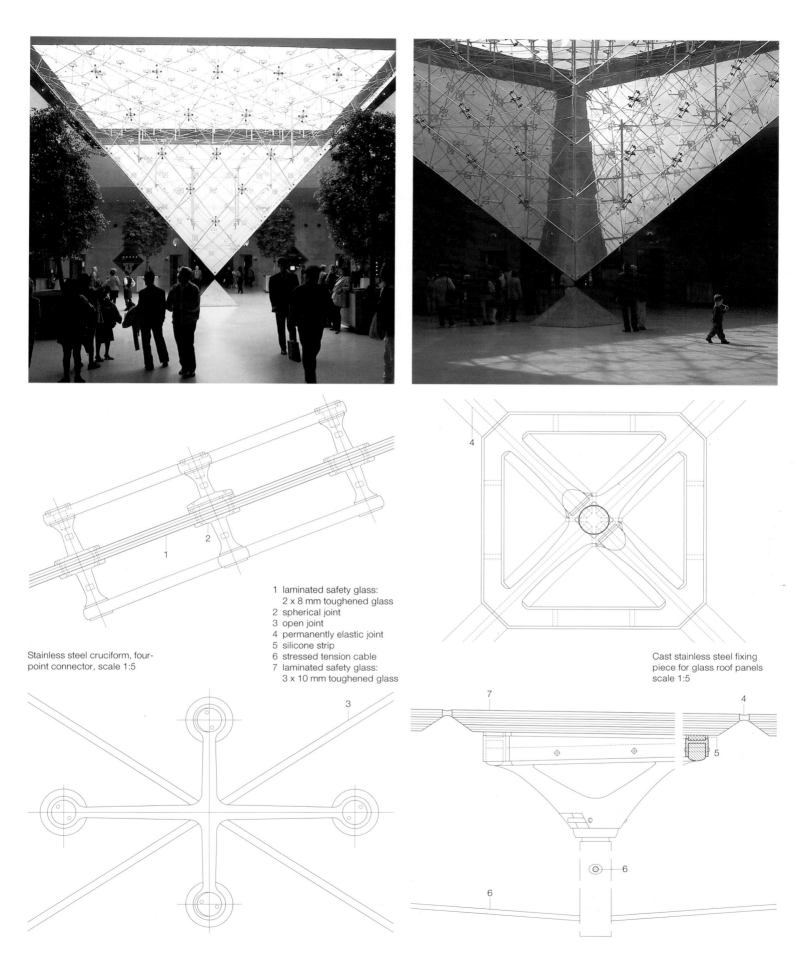

Stainless steel cruciform, four-point connector, scale 1:5

1 laminated safety glass:
  2 x 8 mm toughened glass
2 spherical joint
3 open joint
4 permanently elastic joint
5 silicone strip
6 stressed tension cable
7 laminated safety glass:
  3 x 10 mm toughened glass

Cast stainless steel fixing piece for glass roof panels scale 1:5

Example 2

## Administration Building in Berne, Switzerland

1994

Architect:
Rolf Mühlethaler, Berne
Assistants (Art Nouveau building):
Hansjürg Eggimann, Markus Studer
Assistants (extension):
Lukas Bögli, Hansjürg Eggimann,
Heinz Freiburghaus, Bernhard Leu,
Markus Studer
Structural engineers:
Hanspeter Stocker + Partner, Berne

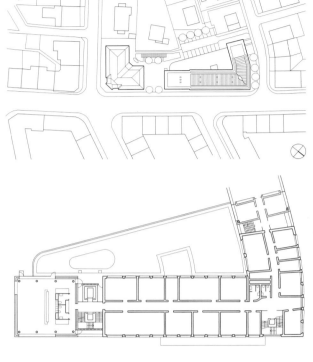

Site plan  scale 1:2500

Plan  scale  1:750

The Swiss Alcohol Administration in Berne was accommodated in two buildings: an Art Nouveau villa, which was in need of refurbishment, and an adjoining structure – a former post office building that dates from 1948. An overall concept was drawn up that led to the refurbishment of the villa and the extension of the adjoining structure, including the addition of a new attic storey to unify the diverse elements of this building. In both parts of the scheme, special attention was paid to the circulation zones. In the newer structure, the lift and staircase tract forms the link between the existing building and the extension. The space between these two sections was, therefore, not to be cluttered with new elements.

These constraints, together with the extremely tight spatial conditions, determined the design of the lift. The tubular framework supporting the frameless glazing is suspended from steel plate girders in the attic storey and fixed at the bottom with bolts. As a result, the steel structure is subject to purely tensile stresses, which allowed the required expression of slenderness to be achieved. Steel beams in the attic storey convey all loads to the solid walls at the sides. The steel frame is stabilized by stainless steel cables and is also fixed to the concrete floor slabs at the lift access landings. Each of the storey-height glass panels to the lift shaft is fixed between the tubular frame structure and the flights of stairs with four pipe clips. The fully glazed lift cars have a structural framework consisting of steel sections. Sheet-steel doors form a contrast to the material of the transparent outer skin.

In the Art Nouveau building, a completely transparent hydraulic lift was inserted in the cramped stairwell. Here, the lift shaft doors are also in glass, and the glazed enclosure, supported by vertical tubular members and stainless steel rods, is suspended from the side walls of the staircase. The reinforced guide track is fixed to the inner faces of the stairs. Horizontal loads are, therefore, tranmitted to the lift access landings. "Soft" connections permit a small degree of vertical movement.

A
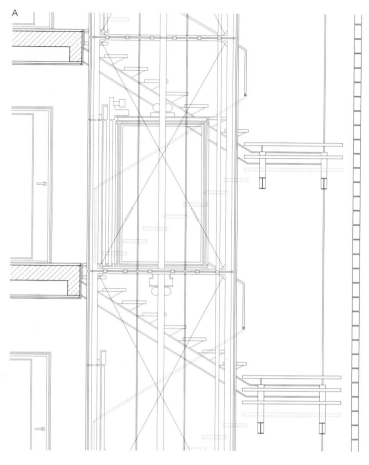

B
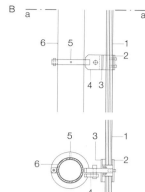

C
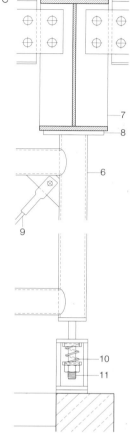

aa

A Passenger lift in
extension
Part elevation – plan
scale 1:50

B Fixing details for lift-
shaft glazing, scale
1:10

C Top and bottom details
of tubular framework
scale 1:10

1 laminated safety glass:
2 panes 8 mm tough-
ened glass
2 62x40x2 mm stainless
steel fixing plate
3 25x15x3 mm plug-
welded angle
4 steel flat welded to
pipe bracket
5 additional fixing with
grub screw

6 Ø 70.5x5 mm tube
7 steel girder: 8x330 mm
and 2 No. 12x180 mm
plates
8 160x160x12 mm head
plate
9 Ø 8 mm stainless steel
cable stay
10 spring
11 threaded rod with nut

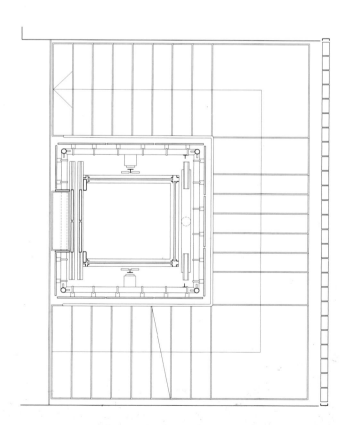

Example 2

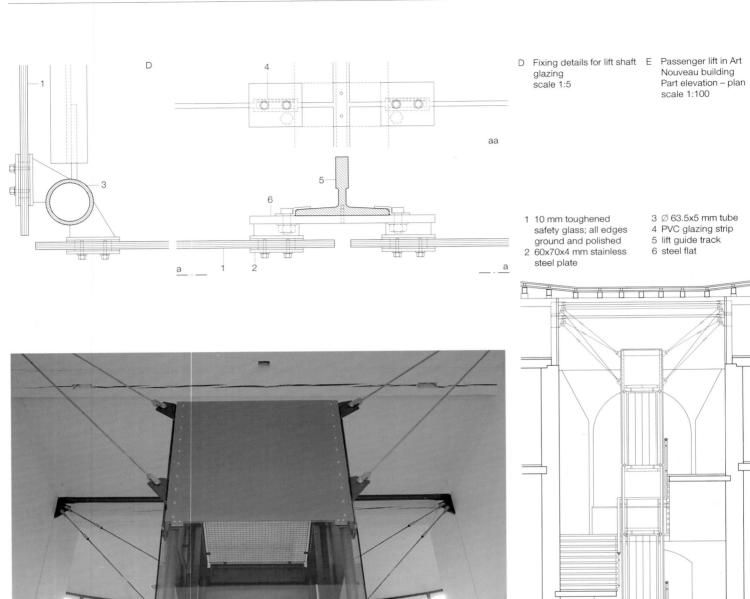

D  Fixing details for lift shaft
   glazing
   scale 1:5

E  Passenger lift in Art
   Nouveau building
   Part elevation – plan
   scale 1:100

1  10 mm toughened
   safety glass; all edges
   ground and polished
2  60x70x4 mm stainless
   steel plate

3  Ø 63.5x5 mm tube
4  PVC glazing strip
5  lift guide track
6  steel flat

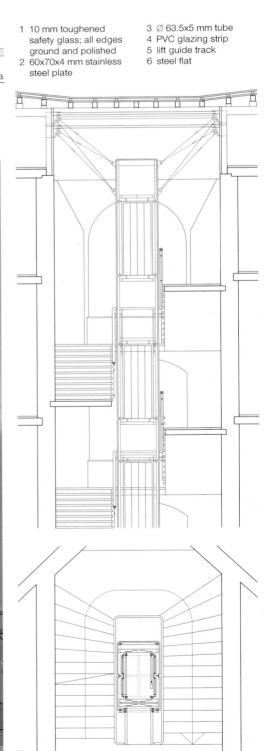

## Refurbishment and Conversion of a Museum in London

1991

Architects:
Foster and Partners, London
Structural engineers:
Anthony Hunt Associates, London

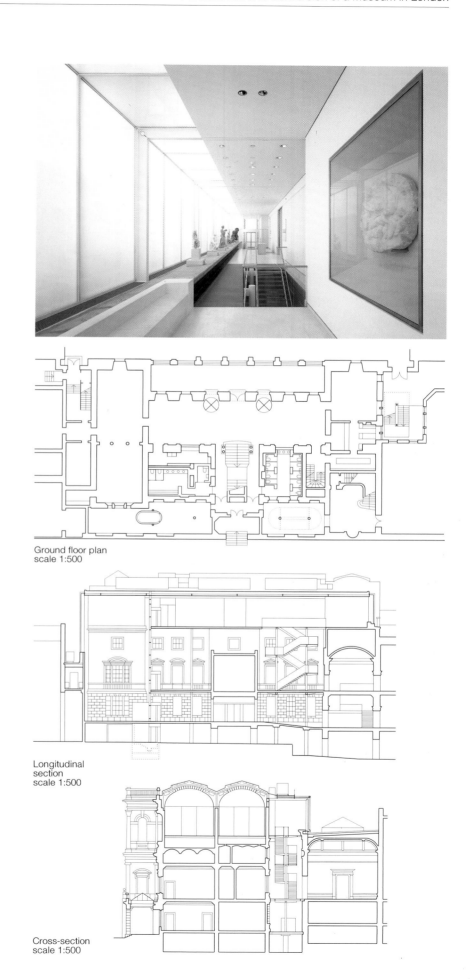

Ground floor plan
scale 1:500

Longitudinal
section
scale 1:500

Cross-section
scale 1:500

As a result of the refurbishment and conversion of the Victorian Diploma Galleries to form the Sackler Galleries, it was possible to introduce new and modern functions to this historic building. The refurbishment had been necessitated by the fact that the exhibition spaces – an annex of the Royal Academy of Arts – had remained unused for much of the time because of inadequate circulation and poor internal climate. The new galleries, housed within the old walls, are naturally lit from above via rooflights. An ingenious system of louvres in the ceiling regulates the ingress of light. The spaces are fully air-conditioned and now provide a fitting location for changing exhibitions of a demanding nature. The circulation problem was resolved by inserting a new staircase and glazed lift in the cramped existing lightwell between the old Burlington House and the Diploma Galleries. The new staircase, in a previously unused space, has become the central circulation route for both buildings of the Royal Academy. The Classical façade of Burlington House has been opened up again. All new fittings and finishings are extremely restrained in their detailing and are restricted to only a few materials. The staircase treads and the balustrades are of glass, so that light entering this narrow space from above can penetrate as far as the ground floor. On the top floor, a new foyer was created to serve the exhibition spaces. It also provides a fitting setting for the sculpture collection and for Michelangelo's famous *Tondo*. Wall glazing continued at right angles into the roof as well as a glazed floor strip allow natural lighting in this space and on the levels below. The careful conversion of the Sackler Galleries represents an outstanding example of the successful combination of old and new. In this respect, glass played a central role.

Example 3

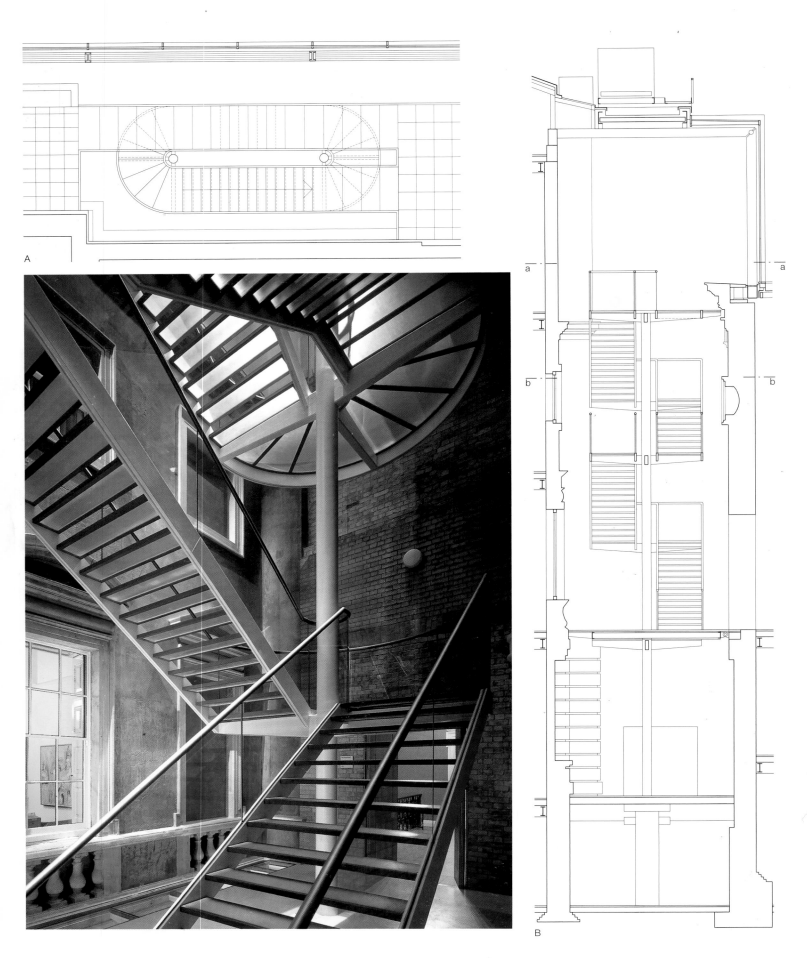

A

B

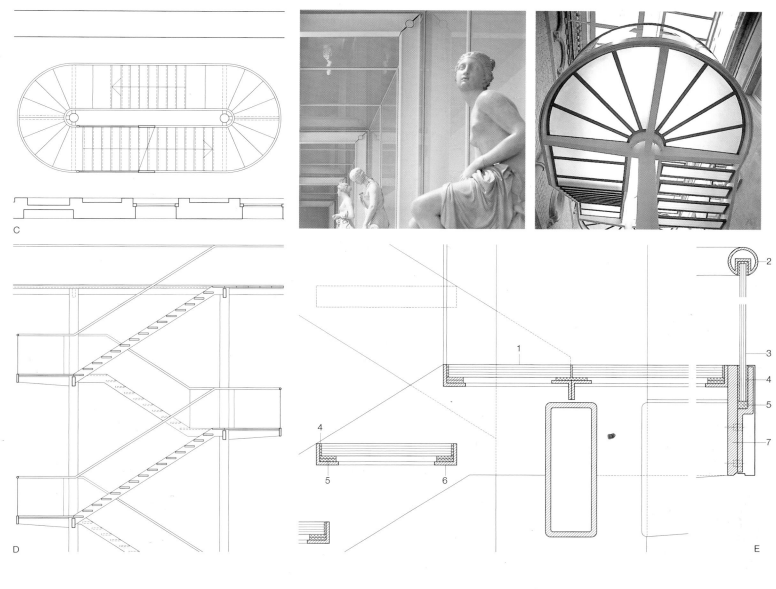

C

D

E

A   Section aa (part plan)
    Staircase at 2nd floor
    level
    scale 1:100
B   Cross-section through
    lightwell
    scale 1:100
C   Section bb (plan)
    scale 1:100
D   Longitudinal section
    through stairs
    scale 1:100

E   Detail of stairs
     scale 1:5

1   25 mm laminated
    safety glass with sand-
    blasted surface
2   ∅ 40 mm stainless
    steel handrail
3   16 mm toughened
    safety glass
4   silicone joint
5   EPDM bearing
6   40x40x5 mm stainless
    steel angle
7   220x22 mm steel stringer

Example 4

## Japanese Restaurant in Brussels

1997

Architect:
Moriko Kira, Amsterdam
Project architect:
Iwan Hameleers
Assistants:
H. Gladys, M. Hamashita. F. Nagasaka,
T. Omatsu, M. Reekers

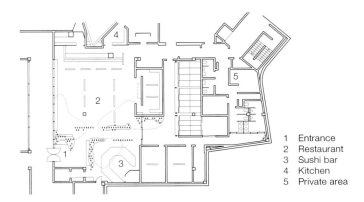

1 Entrance
2 Restaurant
3 Sushi bar
4 Kitchen
5 Private area

Plan    scale 1:500

After 20 years' service, one of the oldest and largest Japanese restaurants in Europe was in need of comprehensive refurbishment. The new design took as its model the traditional Japanese garden, which is distinguished by a free spatial layout and permits an informal interpretation of its design elements.
The restaurant space is articulated and divided into different areas by a combination of wood-sheet flooring, red-cedar vertical wall-screen elements and lightly curved bamboo soffit areas – all of which form an integral part of the "landscape".
On the one hand, the size of the space and the multifunctional quality it allows is a positive asset. On the other hand, guests have little privacy, since there are no secluded seating areas.
For that reason, design elements in the form of vertical wood strips were used to evoke an image of rows of trees. The strips are illuminated by floor and ceiling spots and can be adjusted by hand. By pivoting these elements individually, the division between the restaurant areas and the route leading to the ancillary spaces can be opened or closed to varying degrees. Other screening elements include sheets of glass used as divisions between tables, and room-height glazed partitions subdivided into horizontal strips. The strips are partly transparent and partly translucent with sand-blasted surfaces. The partitions consist of timber posts with laminated safety glass fixed between them in the areas of the walls and doors. Guests seated either on *tatami* mats or on chairs have a view through the transparent strips of glazing; but at the eye level of people walking past, the glass has a matt surface, thus obscuring direct visual contact. In this way, the partitions form a shield between the open public areas at the front and the business and private sectors to the rear.
On entering the restaurant, guests encounter a landscape of glass, timber and bamboo canes that allows glimpses through it, but also provides a sense of privacy.

A

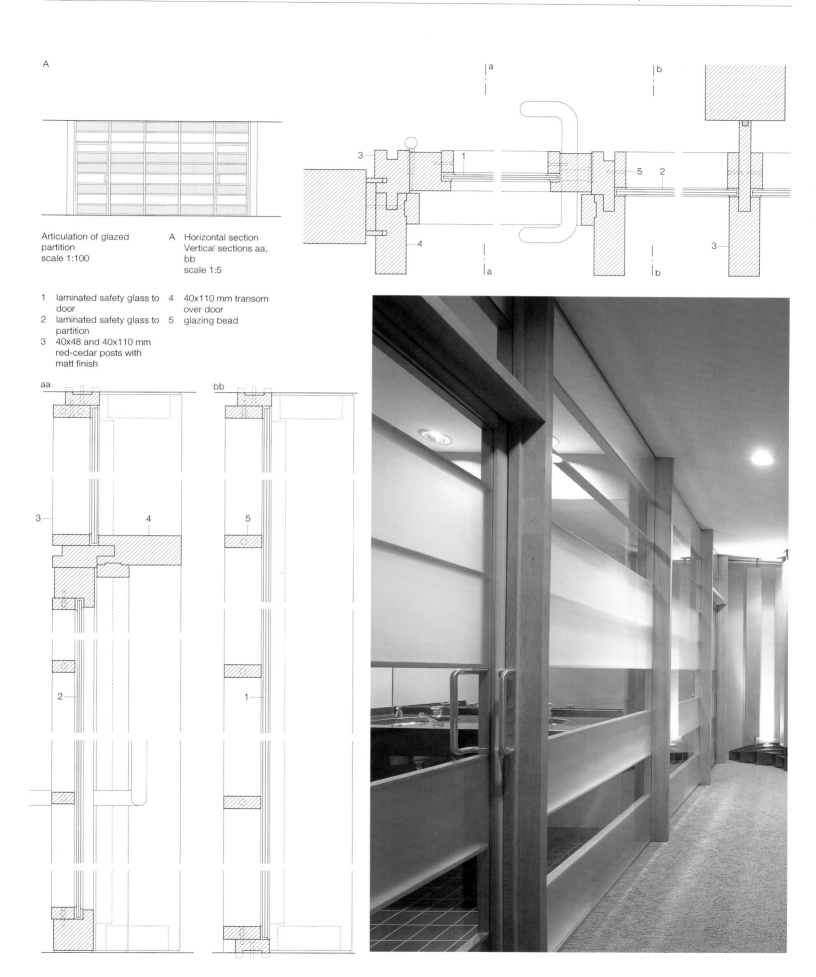

Articulation of glazed
partition
scale 1:100

A   Horizontal section
    Vertical sections aa,
    bb
    scale 1:5

1   laminated safety glass to
    door
2   laminated safety glass to
    partition
3   40x48 and 40x110 mm
    red-cedar posts with
    matt finish

4   40x110 mm transom
    over door
5   glazing bead

**197**

Example 5

**House near Bad Tölz, Germany**

1997

Architects:
Fink + Jocher, Munich
Dietrich Fink, Thomas Jocher
Assistants:
Nicole Hemminger, Thomas Pfeiffer
Structural engineers:
Toni Staudacher, Tegernsee

Section aa
scale 1:250

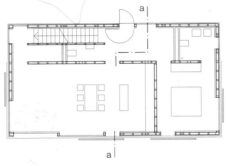

Ground floor plan
scale 1:250

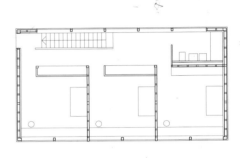

Upper floor plan
scale 1:250

Despite its modern form of construction, this two-storey low-energy house situated on the edge of a village in Upper Bavaria adopts the traditional formal canon of the surrounding farmhouses in its use of a few simple design elements. For energy-saving reasons, transparent areas in the outer skin were kept to a minimum in the north face. The structure consists largely of prefabricated timber units and was erected within the space of a few months. The façades are distinguished by a bold contrast between reddish-brown larch-strip cladding and areas of glass. The full-height ground floor windows in the south, west and east faces can be shaded by sliding shutter elements with louvres fixed at different angles. In addition to their sunshading function, these timber-slat units pleasantly filter the light that enters the house. The storey-height window frames are fixed to the façade in such a way that they are not visible from the inside, creating the impression of a complete area of glazing. Similarly, when the large sliding door is open, there is no raised threshold to impede the transition to the outdoor space. The windows on the upper floor, which were prefabricated in Norway, pivot outwards. For this reason, the glazing beads are fixed externally.

The house represents a successful synthesis of modern formal language and local tradition. It owes its unmistakable character not least to the generous areas of glazing.

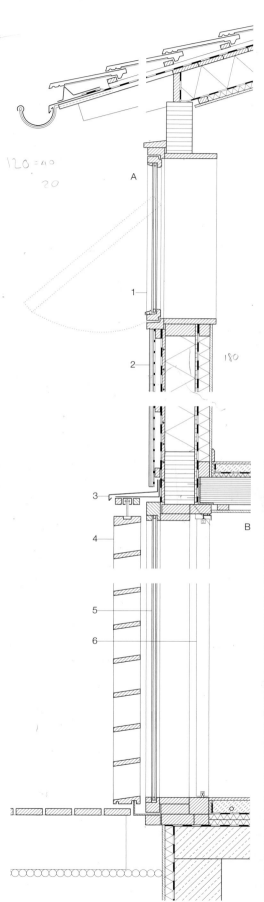

Section through façade
scale 1:20

A Detail of horizontally
  pivoted casement
B Detail of sliding door
  scale 1:5

1 horizontally pivoted
  wood casement, painted
  white; double glazed
  (6/12/6 mm)
2 wall construction:
  30x50 mm untreated
  larch strips
  insect screen
  30x50 mm battens
  windproof building
  paper
  24 mm softwood tongue-
  and-groove boarding
  160 mm thermal insu-
  lation between
  60x160 mm timber studs
  12 mm plywood con-
  struction board
  vapour barrier
  60 mm thermal insulation
  between
  60x60 mm timber
  battens
  12.5 mm plasterboard
3 0.7 mm sheet zinc
4 larch sliding element
5 fixed double glazing
  (6/12/6 mm)
6 wood sliding door with
  double glazing
  (6/12/6 mm)

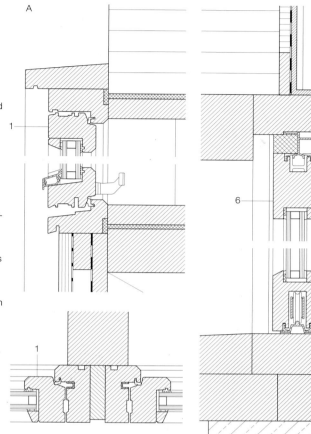

Example 6

## House in New South Wales, Australia

1994

Architects:
Glenn Murcutt & Associates, Mosman
Structural engineers:
James Taylor & Associates, Mosman

In the Blue Mountains, 150 km north-east of Sydney, a couple has had a retirement home built in a hilly, densely wooded landscape. The architect planned the building along the contour lines of the slope, parallel to a path, and divided the house into two pavilions separated by a pool of water.

The dwelling, the studio and the walkway that links them are raised on stilts above the rocky slope. The rear walls of the buildings, which face the hillside, are exposed to relatively cold winds and are, therefore, largely closed, with ancillary spaces laid out along this side. The solid walls are plastered internally and clad with shiny corrugated metal sheeting externally. The pavilions open out towards the east, an aspect of the design that is accentuated by the rising slope of the monopitch roofs. The generously glazed façade to the living areas affords a unique view of the landscape. The horizontal corrugated metal cladding to the walls facing the slope is continued round the end faces in part. The closed metal volumes are, therefore, contrasted with the open areas of fenestration and the louvred blinds to the main façade. At the lower level, this face is articulated into a number of sliding elements that extend over the full length of the living room. Above this is a separate strip of fixed glazing. The doors, the blinds and the textures of the insect screens create a multilayered façade, with the broad roof projection providing adequate sunshading. Only along the length of the sliding elements is additional screening necessary. The shiny, silvery trunks of the eucalyptus trees and the moving shadows cast by the leaves are reflected in the bright metal cladding. This play of light and shade is continued in the way the sunscreen louvres filter the light.

The house is simply detailed in accordance with the requirements of the Australian climate. It is a fine example of the kind of architecture that, using simple means and clear forms, creates a location with a specific character in the landscape.

Site plan
scale 1:1000

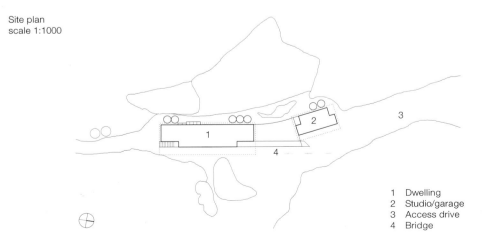

1 Dwelling
2 Studio/garage
3 Access drive
4 Bridge

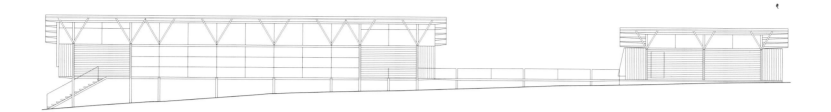

East elevation
scale 1:250

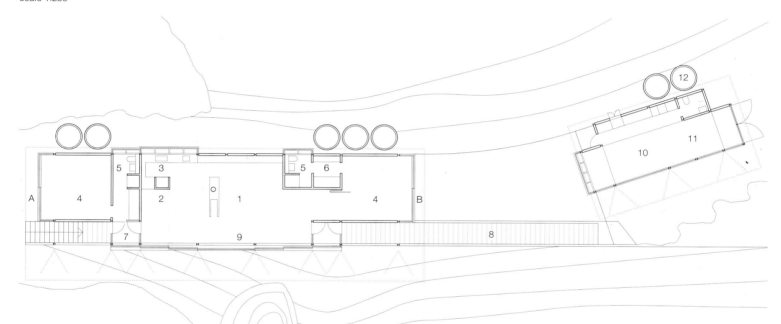

Ground floor plan
scale 1:250

1 Living area
2 Dining area
3 Kitchen
4 Bedroom
5 Bathroom
6 Dressing room
7 Entrance lobby
8 Bridge
9 Veranda
10 Pottery workshop
11 Garage
12 Water tank

Example 6

Sections through
façades
scale 1:20
A   South façade
B   North façade
    Section aa

1  1.6 mm sheet aluminium hood
2  aluminium louvre blind
3  6.4 mm single glazing
4  insect screen
5  stainless steel fin

6  corrugated aluminium
   sheeting
7  ventilated cavity
8  masonry wall
9  stainless steel angle
10 aluminium guide track

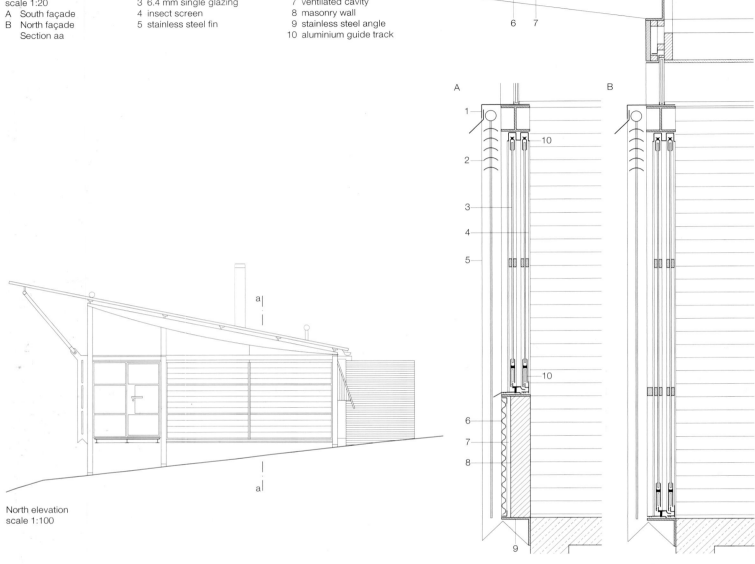

North elevation
scale 1:100

Example 7

**Old People's Home in Wesel, Germany**

1996

Architects:
HPP Hentrich – Petschnigg & Partner, Stuttgart
Partner responsible for project:
Wolfgang Vögele
Project architect:
Hans-Peter Bonasera
Assistants:
Kai von Scholley, Stefanie Sanner,
Christian Rothenhöfer, Stefan Ott, Eva Noller
Structural engineers:
Bovenkerk & Sack, Hamminkeln

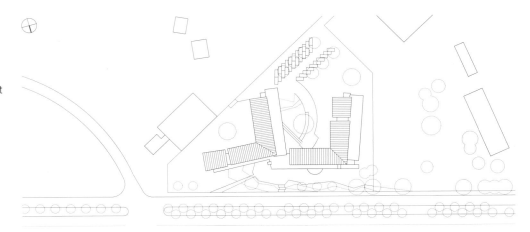

Site plan   scale  1:2500

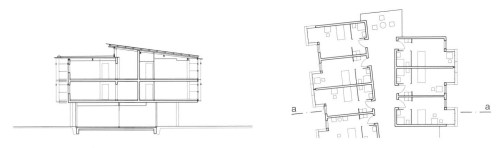

Section aa   scale  1:500

Part plan   scale  1:500

This home for senior citizens is situated on a road with heavy traffic. One of the main features of the planning is the way the development turns its back on the noisy highway and opens out on the garden face to the nearby river. The street fronts, built in the red bricks common to this area, have a solid appearance, whereas the courtyard faces seem light and almost dissolved in comparison. Areas of light-coloured rendering are punctuated by glazed oriels and other transparent elements. Each of the old people's dwellings has an oriel window. Arranged singly or in pairs, these bay-like projections form a transition and link between the rooms within and the external space. The slender dimension of these elements, with frameless glass joints at the corners and blind boxes that seem to float in the air, results in a transparent division between indoors and outdoors. The glazing is articulated by horizontal laminated-timber and metal rails, and in each room there is an opening light in a coloured frame, which forms a salient feature of the development. Structurally, the transparent corner detail of the oriels is made possible by internal stainless steel tubes which are scarcely visible. The steel sections fixed to the edges of the floor slabs and lined with fibre-cement sheets serve as a means of fire protection, preventing the spread of fire from floor to floor.

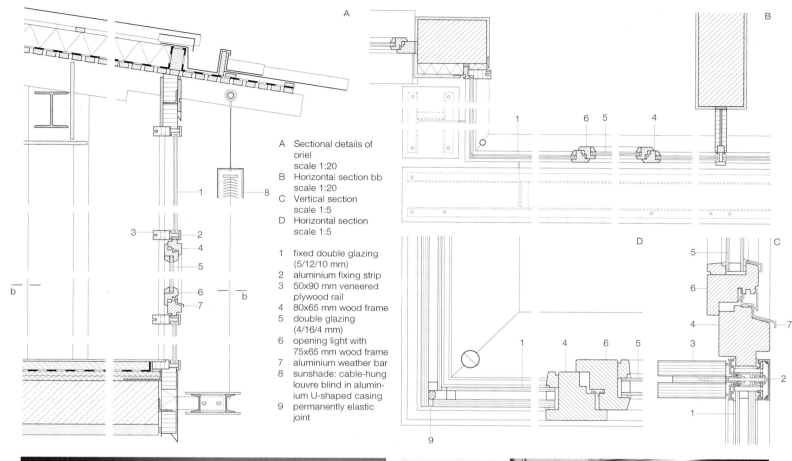

A  Sectional details of
   oriel
   scale 1:20
B  Horizontal section bb
   scale 1:20
C  Vertical section
   scale 1:5
D  Horizontal section
   scale 1:5

1  fixed double glazing
   (5/12/10 mm)
2  aluminium fixing strip
3  50x90 mm veneered
   plywood rail
4  80x65 mm wood frame
5  double glazing
   (4/16/4 mm)
6  opening light with
   75x65 mm wood frame
7  aluminium weather bar
8  sunshade: cable-hung
   louvre blind in aluminium U-shaped casing
9  permanently elastic
   joint

Example 8

## Housing in Amsterdam

1994

Architects:
Hans Kollhoff, Berlin, in collaboration with
Christian Rapp, Berlin/Amsterdam
Structural engineers:
Konstruktie-Bureau Heijckmann, Amsterdam

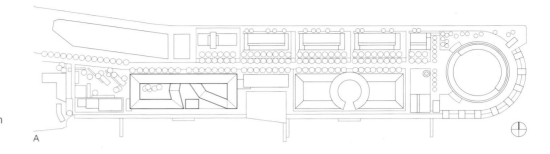

A

A Site plan
scale 1:7500
B Section and elevation
scale 1:1250
C Plan
scale 1:1250

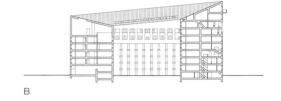

B

C

This 170 m long complex between four and nine storeys high was erected near the centre of Amsterdam on an island formerly used for the harbour and industry. The scheme comprises more than 300 dwelling units and forms part of a large-scale urban development planned jointly by a number of architects. The external appearance of the housing blocks is distinguished by the carefully detailed facing brickwork punctuated by rectangular openings, and by the conservatory windows along the south face, which from certain angles look like continuous strips. The living room casements in red cedar are recessed in the two-leaf outer wall construction by exactly the half-brick dimension of the outer skin. In terms of construction physics, therefore, they are sensibly aligned with the plane of the thermal insulation. The spandrel panels are finished at the top with a wood window sill internally and a stone sill externally. The single-glazed conservatory windows, with their small-scale divisions and frames consisting of simple powder-coated steel sections, make virtually no contribution in terms of construction physics. The glazing to the lower third is fixed. The area above this is divided in the middle and can be opened by "folding" the two halves together horizontally. The facade is thus enlivened by the many open casements projecting from the face of the building at different angles.

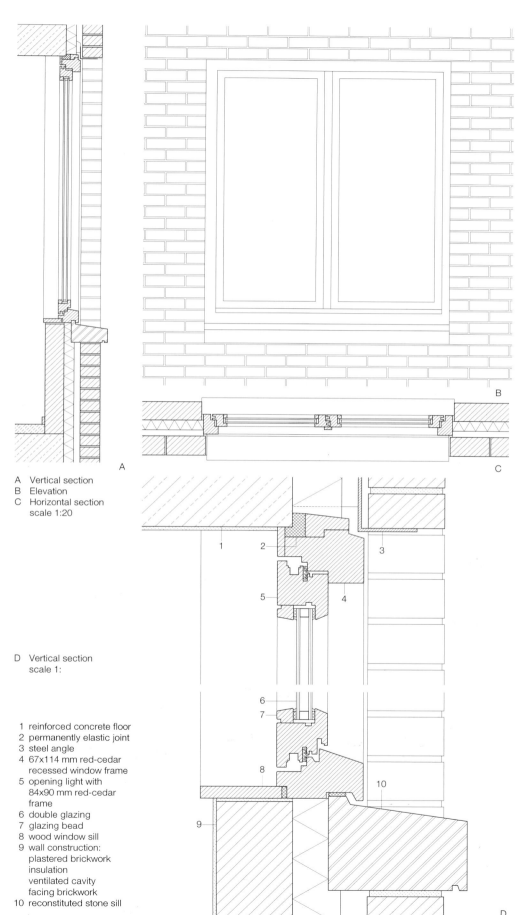

A Vertical section
B Elevation
C Horizontal section
  scale 1:20

D Vertical section
  scale 1:

1 reinforced concrete floor
2 permanently elastic joint
3 steel angle
4 67x114 mm red-cedar
  recessed window frame
5 opening light with
  84x90 mm red-cedar
  frame
6 double glazing
7 glazing bead
8 wood window sill
9 wall construction:
  plastered brickwork
  insulation
  ventilated cavity
  facing brickwork
10 reconstituted stone sill

207

Example 8

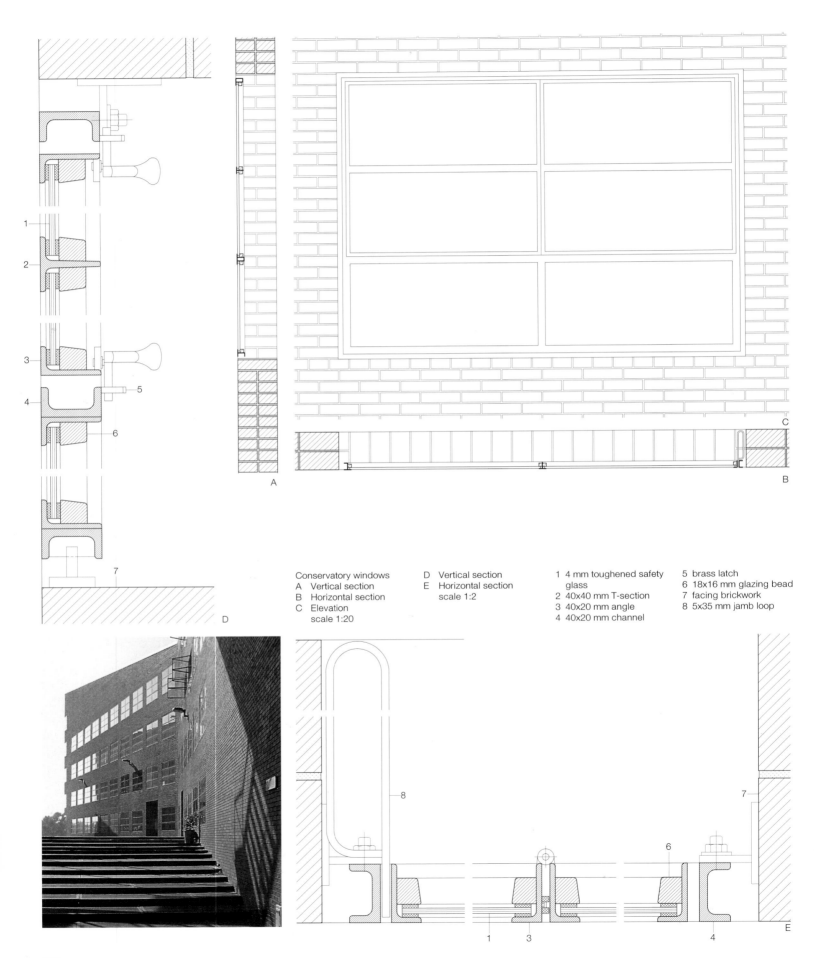

Conservatory windows
A Vertical section
B Horizontal section
C Elevation
   scale 1:20

D Vertical section
E Horizontal section
   scale 1:2

1 4 mm toughened safety
   glass
2 40x40 mm T-section
3 40x20 mm angle
4 40x20 mm channel

5 brass latch
6 18x16 mm glazing bead
7 facing brickwork
8 5x35 mm jamb loop

Example 9

## Conference Pavilion in Weil am Rhein, Germany

1993

Architect:
Tadao Ando & Associates, Osaka
Constructional planning and project
management:
Günter Pfeifer and Roland Mayer, Lörrach
Project architect:
Peter M. Bährle
Assistant:
Caroline Reich
Structural engineers:
Johannes C. Schuhmacher, Bad Krozingen

This two-storey conference and training centre for an office furniture manufacturer was built in an open field at the edge of the company site. The clearly defined volumes of the complex distinguish it from the heterogeneous surrounding buildings. Visitors approach the pavilion along a wall laid out to an L-shaped plan and enter a narrow rectangular tract that represents a continuation of the wall. This long access route is reminiscent of a Japanese path of meditation. The building has an ingenious layout. It consists of two rectilinear volumes that intersect at an angle. At the point of intersection the two tracts are penetrated by a cylindrical element, which accommodates the foyer and staircase. Integrated into this layout is the courtyard space, which is set below natural ground level. Viewed from the open field, only one storey of the building is visible, with the tops of the cherry trees rising above it. The internal spaces, of different sizes and laid out on two levels, include conference rooms, guest rooms, a lobby and library. As in almost all buildings by Tadao Ando, the character of this pavilion is strongly influenced by the carefully designed exposed concrete walls. Contrasted with these are the room-height windows, which appear as uniformly dark areas in the façades. The restrained detailing of the fenestration is consistent with the ascetic volumetric design of the building. All embellishments are deliberately avoided. The simple post-and-rail glazing construction in anthracite-grey anodized aluminium establishes a clear grid pattern that corresponds with the joints in the concrete surfaces. Ando's conference pavilion is a fine example of a successful combination of glass and concrete.

Section aa   scale 1:500

Section bb   scale 1:500

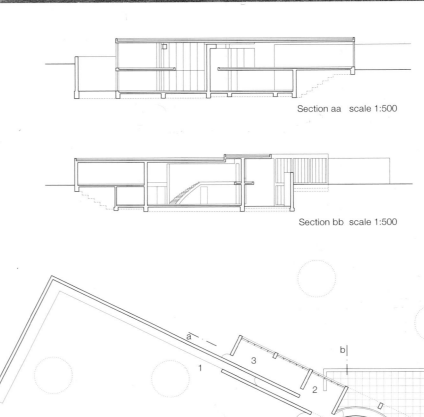

Site plan   scale  1:500

1 Access route
2 Entrance hall
3 Conference rooms
4 Void over foyer
5 Courtyard
6 Audio-visual space

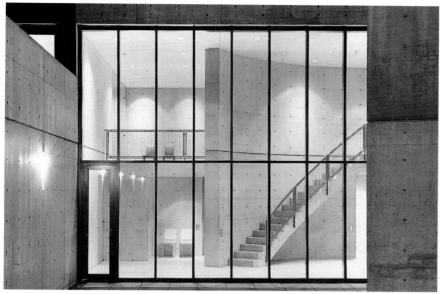

1 two-leaf exposed concrete wall with intermediate layer of insulation
2 aluminium post
3 aluminium rail
4 double glazing (6/12/6 mm)
5 aluminium glazing bar with cover strip
6 anodized stainless steel sheet bent to shape
7 raised concrete slab pavings
8 permanently elastic joint
9 parquet flooring
10 aluminium door frame
11 aluminium opening element

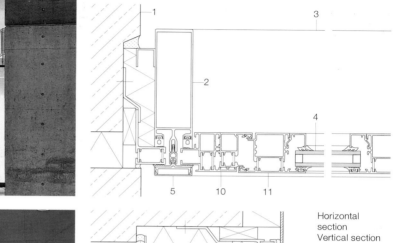

Horizontal section
Vertical section
scale 1:5

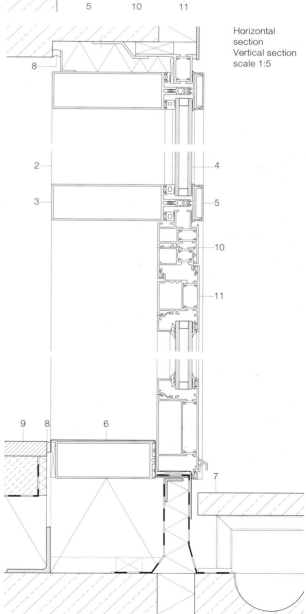

Example 9

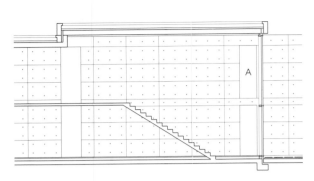

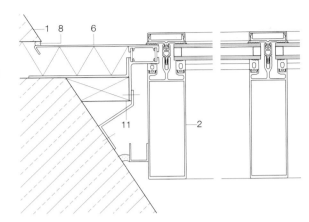

Horizontal section
Vertical section
scale 1:5

1 two-leaf exposed concrete wall
  with intermediate layer of insulation
2 aluminium post
3 aluminium rail
4 double glazing (6/12/6 mm)
5 aluminium glazing bar with
  cover strip
6 anodized stainless steel sheet
7 raised concrete slab pavings
8 permanently elastic joint
9 parquet flooring
10 stainless steel sheet
11 plastic strip

Section   scale 1:200

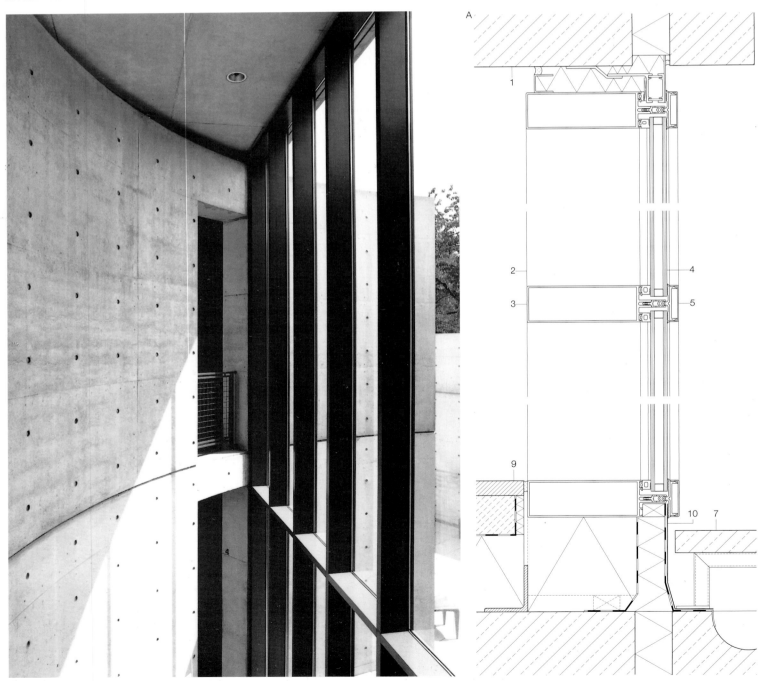

## Commercial Development in Lindau, Germany

1995

Architects:
Fink + Jocher, Munich
Dietrich Fink, Thomas Jocher
Assistants: Richard Waldmann,
Christof Wallner
Structual engineers:
Dr Becker + Partner, Lindau

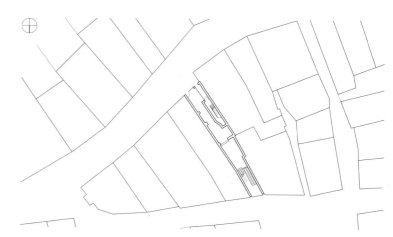

Site plan    scale  1:1000

The new structure closes a gap in the street development in the town centre of Lindau. At its narrowest point the site is only 2.90 m wide. In the course of the construction work the existing building to the rear of the new structure was refurbished with a minimum of interference to the fabric. The concept foresaw the use of the shop on the lower floors of the two buildings as a linking route between the narrow streets to front and rear.

To ensure maximum penetration of daylight with a shop depth of 35 m, the façade of the new structure was fully glazed. As a result, the internal structure of the building is visible from the street, in which the infill forms a kind of "urban joint". The layout of the shop on two levels reflects the topography of the site: the entrance level in the old building is one storey higher than the street level of the new structure. This is visible externally. The restrained detailing of the glass façade allowed the building to be inserted into the intact historical fabric of the street without conforming to the existing vocabulary. The reflection of the buildings opposite in its façade also indicates the multivalency of the situation: plane and relief, transparency and closed structure, old and new, interior and exterior, and the flowing boundaries between them. The panes of glass stretch across the full width of the façade and are secured at the sides by glazing bars. The horizontal joints, which are formally related to the façade banding of the adjoining building, are sealed with silicone. A system of openable glass louvres was used for the face of the second-floor loggia.

The entrance door forms an independent, non-transparent element in the façade. Here, the characteristic construction of the neighbouring buildings – with closed wall surfaces and transparent openings – is reversed, and the entrance is discreetly accentuated. In order not to contrast the building with its surroundings any further, the use of conspicuous materials in the façade was avoided. All metal components are painted with dark micaceous iron oxide. The exposed concrete walls represent the dominant feature of the interior of the shop.

Example 10

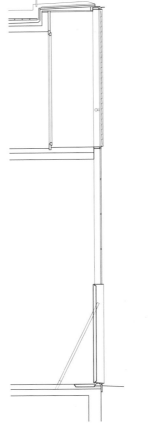
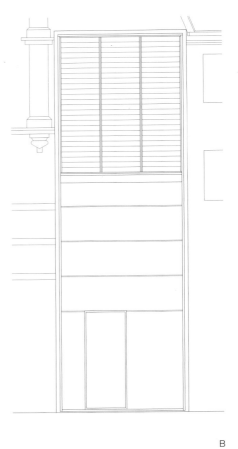

B

B  Section and elevation  scale 1:100
C  Horizontal section through façade  scale 1:5
D  Vertical sections through façade  scale 1:5

1  19 mm toughened safety glass
2  aluminium glazing bar
3  3 mm sheet aluminium
4  10 mm steel plate
5  40 mm chipboard door with tubular
   core: V 100 chipboard and 3 mm

fully bonded sheet-aluminium
cladding
6  10 mm steel-plate threshold with 2%
   slope to outside
7  50x6 mm steel flat
8  6 mm steel plate

9  10 mm hard rubber
10  140 mm steel channel
11  3 mm sheet aluminium
12  120x50 mm steel angle
13  adjustable glass louvres

14  composite wood board with sheet-steel
    cladding
15  metal grating
16  steel lining to floor convector
17  4 mm sheet-metal tray with coconut matting

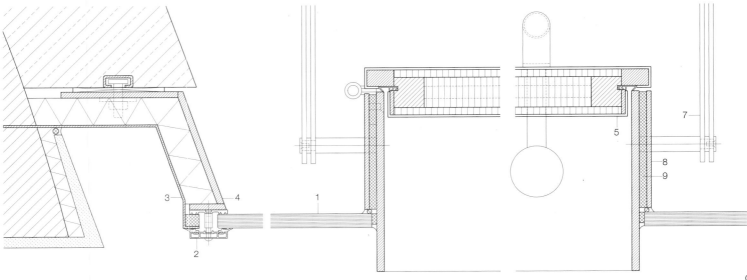

C

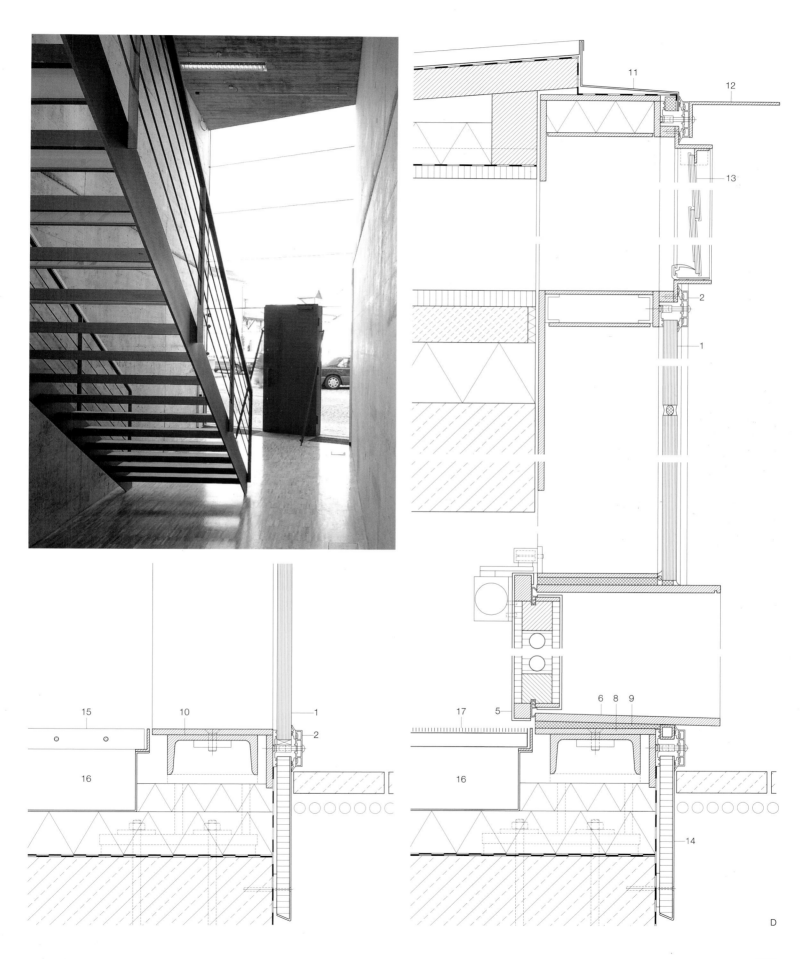

11

12

13

2

1

15    10    1

2

16

17    5    6  8  9

16

14

D

Example 11

## Caricature and Cartoon Museum in Basel

1996

Architects:
Herzog & de Meuron, Basel
Project architect: Yvonne Rudolf
Structural consultant: Mario Meier
Façade planning: Gerber-Vogt AG, Basel
Structural engineers: Helmut Pauli, Basel

Site plan
scale 1:3500

This small museum shows changing exhibitions of drawings, prints and photos from its own collection and from a stock of objects on loan. The museum comprises two separate buildings: an old and a new section, which stand on a narrow and extremely deep medieval site (6 x 25 m). The two sections are linked by a glazed corridor. The entrance to the museum, the curator's office, the library and a number of small exhibition spaces are housed in the older building. Each floor is different in its detailing, its wood flooring and wall finishings, since the building has undergone various conversions over the centuries. The new three-storey structure has a simple, homogeneous design. The concrete slabs forming the various exhibition levels are enclosed on the courtyard face by a glass wall. Each storey consists of an undivided 6 x 8 m area. The exhibits are displayed on the walls and in showcases. The glazed link between the old and new sections of the museum divides the courtyard into two narrow, stack-like spaces. The glass walls of the new building overlooking the courtyard intersect at an obtuse angle. As a result, the glazed yard resembles an illuminated volume and functions like a large lantern, bringing daylight into the interior of the exhibition spaces. By using two different kinds of reflecting glass, the kaleidoscopic spatial effect is heightened, with the outcome that the glazed courtyard appears even smaller and more intense. At first glance it is difficult for visitors to comprehend its spatial form. All glass panels are fixed without glazing sections. At the base, each panel is supported by two adjustable point fixings; at the top of the building, they are fixed in plane by steel angles. All joints are reduced to a minimum visually. For this reason, the horizontal joints between the panels of double glazing were detailed in such a way that the inner and outer panes of glass are vertically offset, the bottom edge of the outer pane overlapping the top edge of the inner pane. Viewed from within the confined spaces of the gallery, the glass, with its different surface coatings, appears reflective from certain angles and transparent from others.

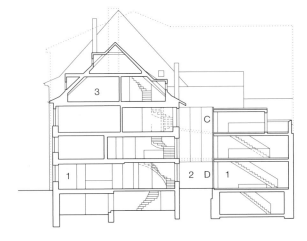

Longitudinal section aa
1 Exhibition space
2 Courtyard
3 Office/studio
scale 1:400

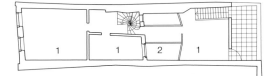

Second floor plan

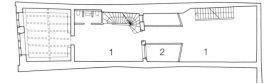

First floor plan

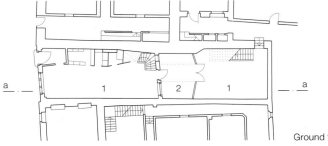

Ground floor plan

Example 11

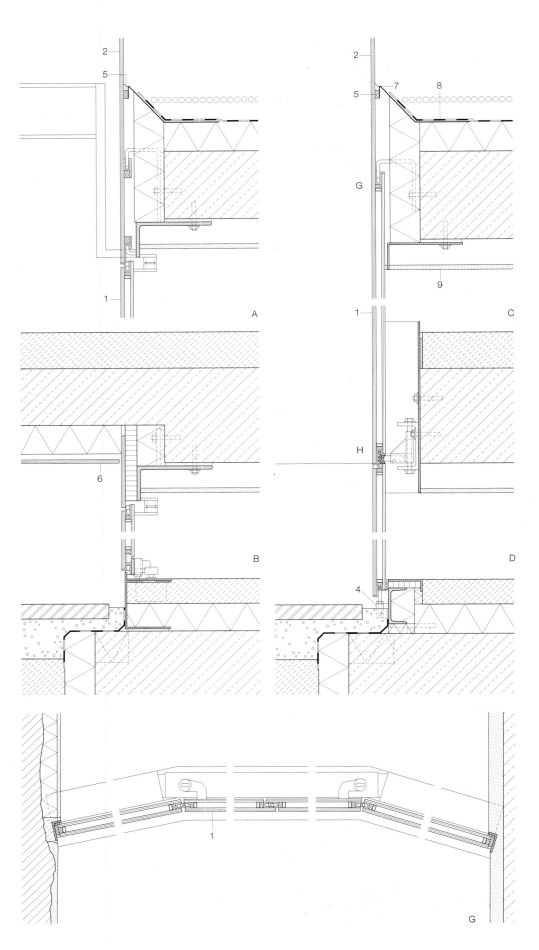

Vertical sections   scale  1:10
A   Glass door: second floor/roof terrace
B   Glass door: ground floor/bridge
C   Fixed glazing: second floor/roof
D   Fixed glazing: ground floor/first floor
E   Fixed glazing to bridge: second floor/roof
F   Fixed glazing to first floor bridge
Horizontal section   scale  1:10
G   Glass door: ground floor

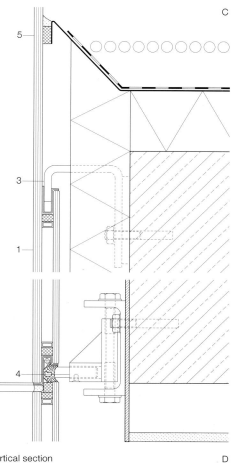

C

Vertical section
scale 1:5

D

1 toughened safety glass double glazing
2 toughened safety glass single glazing to roof
  upstand and at corners of façades
3 steel section for point fixing of glass
4 adjustable glass fixing
5 permanently elastic joint
6 mirrored glass
7 1 mm titanium-zinc sheeting
8 waterproof membrane
9 plasterboard suspended soffit
10 raised concrete slabs
11 2 mm titanium-zinc tray
12 rigid thermal insulation

Example 12

## Façade Refurbishment of Administration Building in Stuttgart

1996

Architects:
Behnisch & Sabatke, Stuttgart
Günter Behnisch, Manfred Sabatke,
Stefan Behnisch
Project architect: Carmen Lenz
Assistants: Holger Amft, Alexandra Burkard,
Ulrike Höhle, Andreas Ludwig
Indoor climate concept: Büro Langkau, Munich

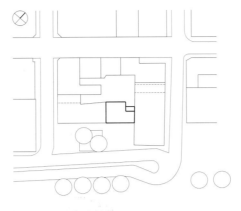

Site plan    scale  1:2000

The building was originally erected in 1969 by the same architects responsible for the redesign. As a means of sound insulation along the street front, a second skin of glass had been added over the the normal façade, which consisted of a layer of fixed glazing. This meant that the internal spaces had to be fully air-conditioned. When the Bayerische Vereins-bank took over the premises, the different demands made by the new owners could be met only through a complete conversion. In addition to workplaces that comply with mod-ern standards, the bank required a pleasant working environment with a minimum of techni-cal support. Other requirements included the provision of good daylight conditions and a façade with openable windows. In the mean-time, the road outside had been subject to traf-fic calming measures. To retain the character of the former façade – a glazed outer skin and a diffuse inner layer – the architects again designed a two-leaf construction. The outer skin now consists of all-glass louvres that can be controlled storey by storey. The existing precast concrete spandrel panels of the inner skin were insulated and clad with horizontal timber strips. Above the cladding are horizon-tal bands of vertically pivoting wood case-ments. Individually controlled louvre sunblinds were fixed in the intermediate space between the two façade layers, where they are protect-ed against the elements. The building is natu-rally ventilated via this buffer zone, which exploits the principle of a natural stack effect. In summer, the fresh air required for night-time cooling enters the intermediate space via the lower opening in the outer skin and flows through the windows into the offices. At night, the outer louvres are kept shut for security rea-sons. Slits in the corridor walls facilitate the necessary cross-ventilation. During the day, the louvres are opened wide to avoid any build-up of heat. In winter, even diffuse sunlight heats the cold external air within the buffer zone. The desired internal air conditions are achieved by a process of air exchange, by heat from conventional radiators and by a small extractor fan for peak loads.

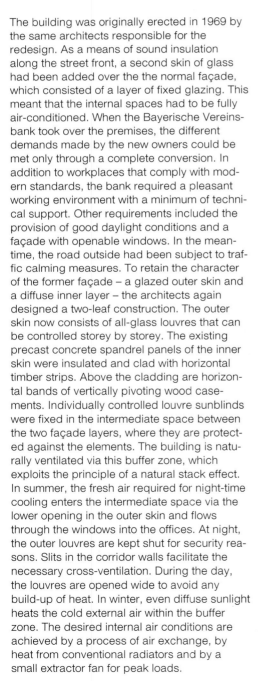

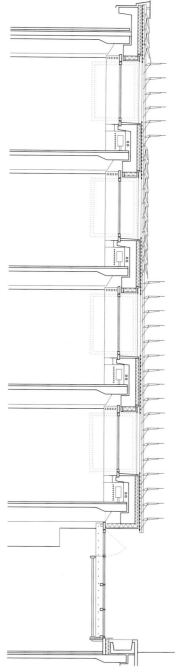

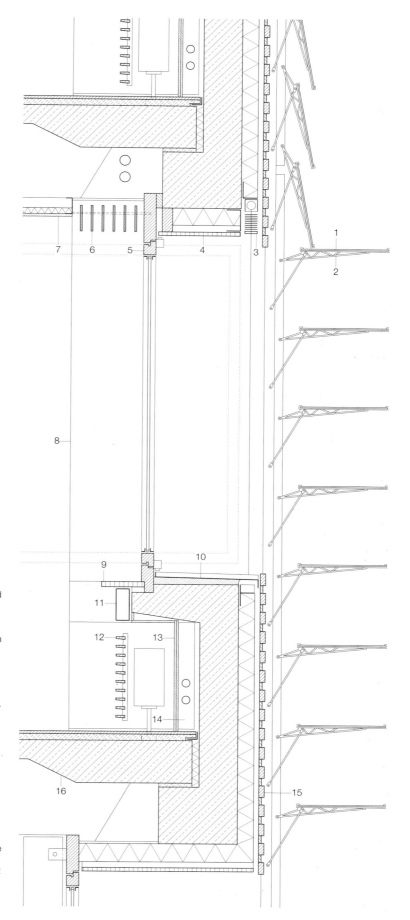

Section through façade
scale 1:100
Section through façade
scale 1:20

1 6 mm toughened
  safety glass
2 glass fixings con-
  nected to supporting
  structure
3 aluminium louvre blind
4 wood lining
5 vertically pivoting
  wood casement
6 10x140 mm aluminium
  fins
7 plasterboard suspen-
  ded soffit
8 14 mm toughened
  safety glass divider
9 200 mm veneered ply-
  wood sill
10 sheet aluminium win-
  dow sill
11 balustrade fascia
  conduit
12 wood grille
13 plasterboard lining
14 service duct
15 20x60 mm wood strip
  cladding on support-
  ing structure; 30 mm
  ventilated cavity;
  80 mm non-permeable
  insulation; precast
  concrete spandrel unit
16 precast concrete floor
  element

Example 13

**Glass Façade to an EU Ministerial Building
in Brussels**

1998

Architects:
Murphy/Jahn, Chicago
Structural engineers:
Werner Sobek Ingenieure, Stuttgart

In the course of an asbestos removal and refurbishment programme, the existing fabric of this
EU ministerial building in the centre of Brussels
was first demolished down to the reinforced
concrete frame structure and subsequently
rebuilt. The outer faces were clad with glass
elements and a special construction was
developed for the edges of the building. Horizontally, the façades are designed as a triple-
hinged structural system. Glass elements corresponding to those of the standard façades
are fixed in steel hollow-section framing members. These are braced against wind loading
by a tubular member fixed to the corners of the
building. Vertically, the dead load is transmitted by diagonal tension members over two
floors to the reinforced concrete structure. In
the plane of the roof there are two triangular
three-chord hollow-section trusses, which are
roughly 10 m high and span a distance of
approximately 45 m from the centre to the left-
and right-hand wings of the building respectively. Standard glass elements were fixed over
the entire height of these trusses, so the
façade continues over the "open" section of the
building as well.
Vertical glass fins, or "mullions", form a special
feature of the standard façade. These vertical
members are fixed on the outside of the building in front of all office spaces. As a result, the
surface of the façade acquires a structural
depth. The fins are connected to the window
glazing by aluminium sections that incorporate
a thermal break. The loadbearing function of
these vertical glass members enabled the
cross-sectional dimensions of the aluminium
frames to be reduced to a minimum. Structurally, they have no more than a residual stabiliz-
ing function in the event that a fin has to be
replaced or removed.

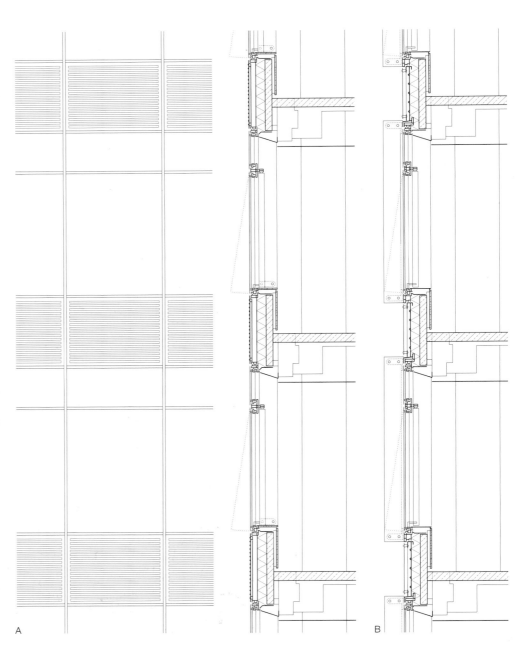

A

B

A Facade detail with internal
glass mullion
Elevation and vertical
section
scale 1:50
Horizontal section
scale 1:5
B Facade detail with external
glass mullion
Vertical section
scale 1:50
Horizontal section
scale 1:5

1 double glazing
(8/14/12 mm)
2 15 mm toughened
safety glass fin
3 two-part aluminium
structural-sealant glaz-
ing section
4 plastic sealing profile
5 point fixings for glass
6 15 mm steel fin

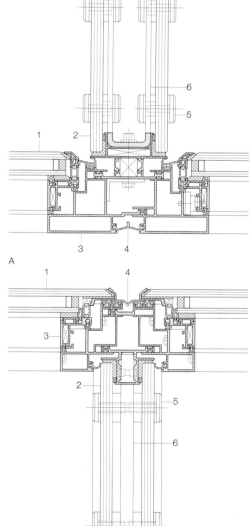

A

B

Example 14

## Office Building in Amsterdam

1991

Architects:
Hans van Heeswijk, Amsterdam
Assistants: Jan van den Berg, Geert Mol,
André de Ruiter
Structural engineers:
D3BN, The Hague
John Kraus, Gert Craanen, The Hague

The office complex on the Stadhouderskade in
Amsterdam adjoins the *Illustrierte Presse* building (1959) by Mart Stam. To preserve some
impression of the building as it looked in its
original state – a single, freestanding structure
– the architect linked the new and the existing
developments with a "glazed joint" in the form
of the recessed lift tower. As a further response
to the existing building, the new structure is
distinguished by the clarity and restraint of its
formal language. The transparency of the glass
façade places the office block in relation to its
surroundings and also reveals the internal
structure.
The building comprises seven floors of offices,
a set-back roof storey and a basement garage.
In contrast to the other storeys, the ground
floor extends over the full area of the site. The
entrance in the north face leads to a two-storey
foyer from where there is access to the lifts and
staircase.
Along the rear face of the building, the office
spaces have a standard depth of 5.40 m.
Those along the street face are 7.20 m deep.
In the 9.00 m wide intermediate zone is a lightwell that extends through all the storeys of the
building and brings daylight into the interior of
the ground floor.
In the articulation of the façade, emphasis was
placed on the horizontal lines. The outer skin is
in a post-and-rail form of construction suspended storey by storey from the face of the
building. On each floor, the façade is divided
into three horizontal strips with different types
of glass. The spandrel wall consists of enamelled glass panels. The middle band, with
opening lights, is in clear glass. The upper
strip is also in clear glass, but printed with a
grid of dots. The different degrees of transparency of the glazing serve to articulate the

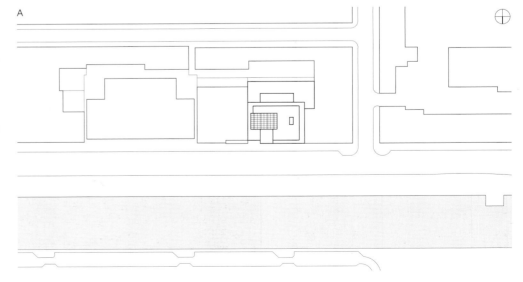

A

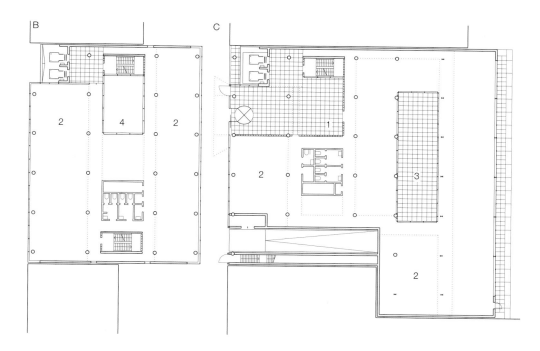

A Site plan
   scale 1:2000
B Upper floor plan
C Ground floor plan
D Cross-section
   scale 1:500

1 Foyer/hall
2 Offices
3 Patio
4 Lightwell/void over hall

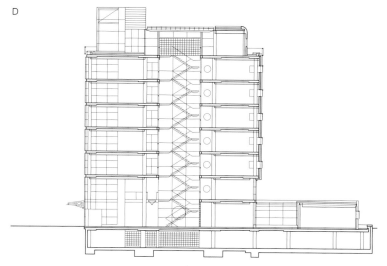

entire façade. Sheet-metal elements to the edges of the floor slabs accentuate the lines of the individual storeys.

In contrast, the glazed lift tower, the lift cars and the car doors are all completely transparent. Point fixings are used to attach the glass panels of the lift tower to the supporting structure, and the joints are simply sealed with silicone.

Glass was also used internally. The fully glazed staircase tower serves as an escape route, so that the façade had to provide 90 minutes fire resistance to prevent the spread of fire. Glass-block walls were used in the foyer, and there is a glazed pitched rooflight over the central hall.

Example 14

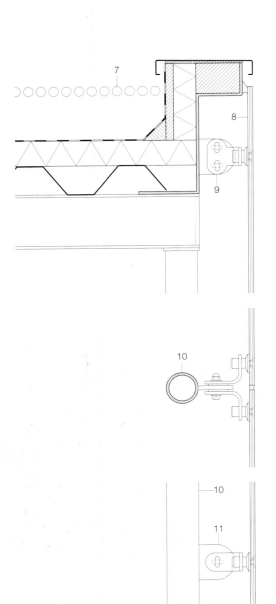

A  Vertical section through lift tower
B  Horizontal section through office façade
C  Vertical section through office façade
D  Vertical section through rooflight
   scale 1:10
 1  aluminium rail
 2  aluminium post
 3  double glazing printed with grid of dots
 4  plastic opening light
 5  insulating panel: toughened safety glass
    externally with enamelled surface
 6  steel section, adjustable in three directions,
    fixed to structure
 7  roof construction: gravel chippings
    elastomer-based bituminous sheeting,
    extruded foamed-glass insulation,
    trapezoidal-section steel sheeting
 8  14 mm toughened safety glass
 9  point glass fixing with metal lug welded on
10  ⌀ 85 mm (nom.) steel tube
11  point glass fixing with metal lug welded on
12  steel tube with metal lug welded on
13  rainwater gutter
14  steel I-beam 240 mm deep (IPE)
15  steel I-beam 140 mm deep (IPE)

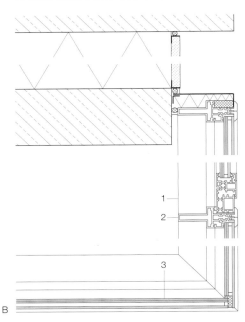

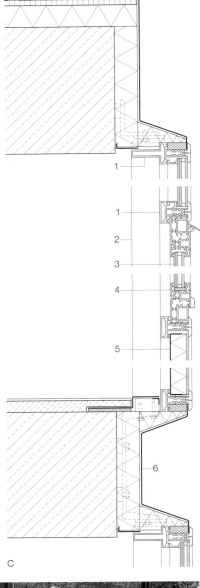

A

B

C

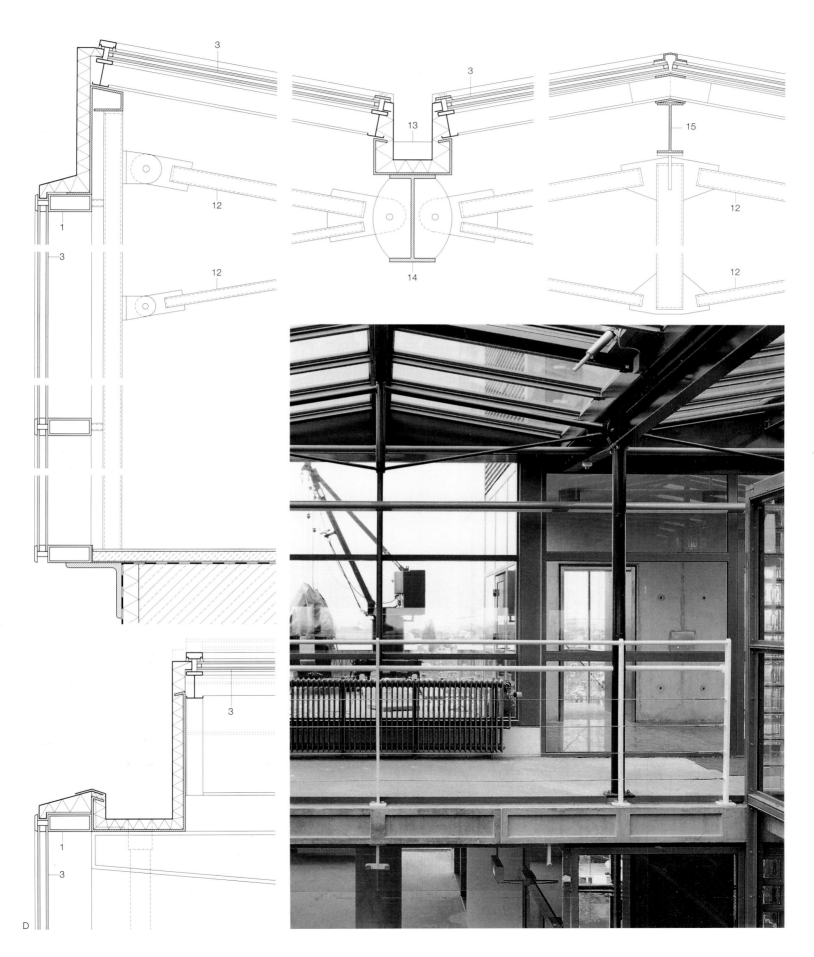

Example 15

## Finnish Embassy in Washington, D.C.

1994

Architects:
Mikko Heikkinen, Markku Komonen, Helsinki
Project architect:
Sarlotta Narjus
Partner office:
Angelos Demetriou & Associates,
Washington, D.C.
Project architect:
Eric Morrison
Structural engineers:
Smislova, Kehnemui & Associates,
Washington, D.C.
Matti Ollila, Finland

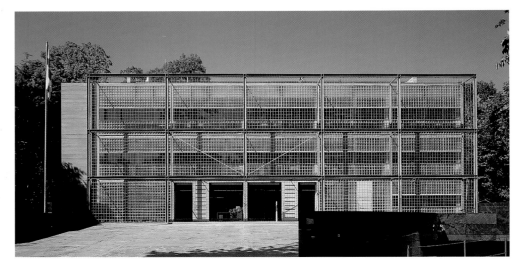

Finland's diplomatic mission is situated at the heart of Washington's embassy district in the immediate vicinity of the US vice-president's residence. The sloping site, covering nearly 5000 m², lies on the edge of a park and possesses a remarkable stock of mature trees of more than 20 species. In response to the constraints imposed by the natural environment, the building is intentionally restrained in its basic form and designed to occupy as small an area of the site as possible. It contains offices and conference rooms for a staff of about 50, plus a small library and a two-storey-high hall for receptions, seminars, exhibitions and concerts. Extending over the length of the building is a central circulation zone with stairs, ramps and galleries. The hall and corridors receive natural light through rooflights. The conference rooms, clad with copper panels on the sides facing the hall, are suspended in the dark blue continuous space in which the ventilation system is installed. The complex design of the interior is deliberately contrasted with the clear, restrained structure of the exterior. Great care was taken in the selection and combination of materials, with glass playing a special role. Used in many different ways, it makes a major contribution to the overall appearance of the embassy and allows links to be created at a number of points between internal spaces and the surrounding gardens. In addition to the use of glass, other striking features of the design include the varied application of copper panels, bronze sections and stone. The narrow faces of the building are clad with moss-green, polished granite, which corresponds in its coloration to the surrounding vegetation and the green-tinted glass of the adjoining transparent façades. The strict grid of the outer walls to the office tract in translucent glass blocks with narrow window strips creates an attractive atmosphere internally and allows an ample ingress of daylight, in spite of the dense vegetation. Below the office tract, on the outside of the hall, is a finely articulated single-glazed conservatory, the glass panes of which are held in posi-

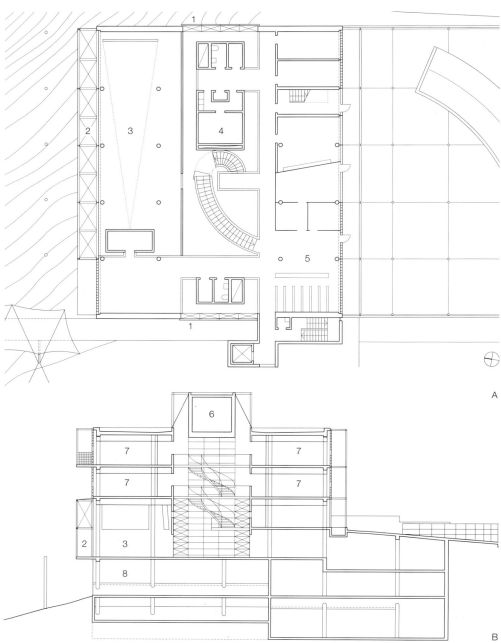

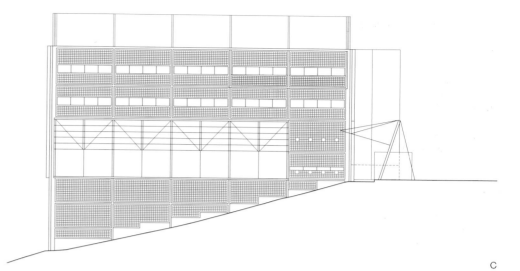

C

tion by stainless steel point fixings. The bullet-resistant façade required for embassy buildings was here set further inwards and forms the enclosing skin of the hall. In the case of the oriels to the end faces, with their cable-trussed glass construction, this inner layer is omitted. The heavy 36.5 mm thick double-glazed panels are, therefore, fixed with adhesive in solid-bronze angle frames.

The south face of the building is distinguished by a layering of the façade planes. A patinated bronze grating set in front of the outer skin forms a trelliswork for deciduous climbing plants, thus providing natural sunshading, the appearance of which changes with the seasons.

A   Plan with external areas
B   Section
C   North elevation
    scale 1:400

1   Glazed oriel
2   Conservatory
3   Finland Hall
4   Conference room
5   Foyer
6   Mechanical services
7   Office
8   Parking space

Example 15

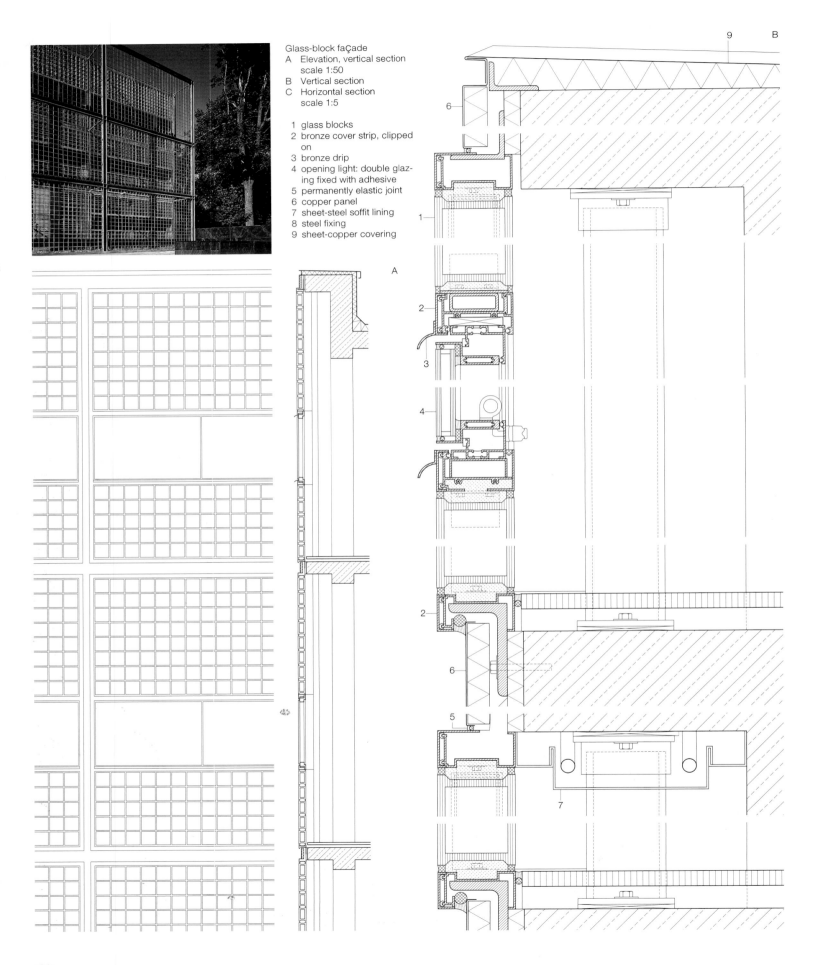

Glass-block faÇade
A   Elevation, vertical section
    scale 1:50
B   Vertical section
C   Horizontal section
    scale 1:5

1  glass blocks
2  bronze cover strip, clipped
   on
3  bronze drip
4  opening light: double glazing fixed with adhesive
5  permanently elastic joint
6  copper panel
7  sheet-steel soffit lining
8  steel fixing
9  sheet-copper covering

Example 15

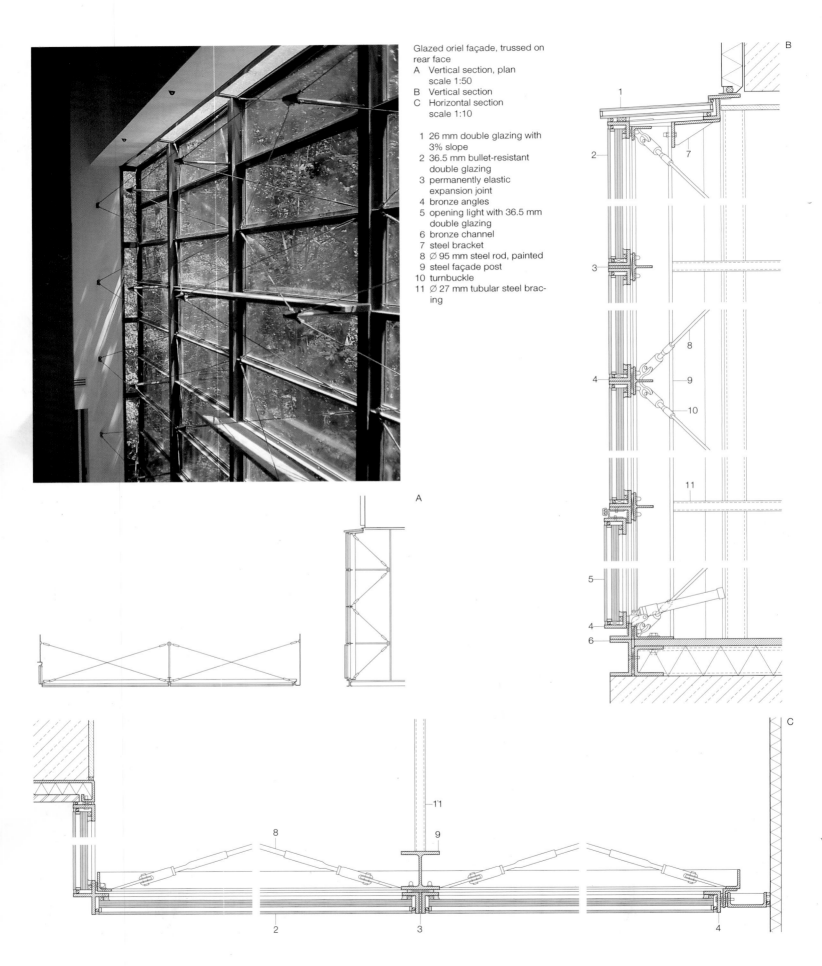

Glazed oriel façade, trussed on
rear face
A  Vertical section, plan
   scale 1:50
B  Vertical section
C  Horizontal section
   scale 1:10

1  26 mm double glazing with
   3% slope
2  36.5 mm bullet-resistant
   double glazing
3  permanently elastic
   expansion joint
4  bronze angles
5  opening light with 36.5 mm
   double glazing
6  bronze channel
7  steel bracket
8  ∅ 95 mm steel rod, painted
9  steel façade post
10 turnbuckle
11 ∅ 27 mm tubular steel bracing

D

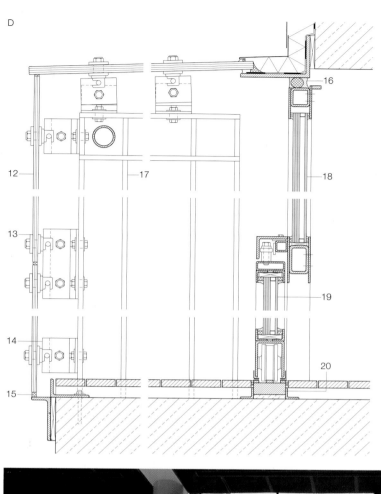

Conservatory façade
D  Vertical section
E  Horizontal section
   scale 1:10

12  12.7 mm laminated
    safety glass
13  point fixing
14  T-section
15  silicone joint
16  permanently elastic
    joint on joint profile
17  steel I-beam 140 mm
    deep (HEA)
18  double glazing
19  glass sliding door
20  steel plate

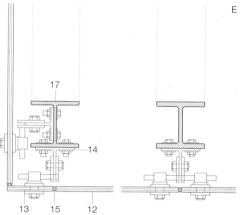

E

Example 16

## General Assembly and Annex of German Bundestag in Bonn

1992

Architects:
Behnisch + Partner, Stuttgart
Project partner and project architect:
Gerald Staib
Project architects:
Matthias Burkhart, Hubert Eilers, Eberhard
Pritzer, Alexander von Salmuth, Ernst-Ullrich
Tillmanns and many other assistants
With the collaboration of Christian Kandzia
Structural engineers:
Schlaich, Bergermann und Partner, Stuttgart
Façade consultants:
Berthold Mack, Rosengarten/Klecken
Lighting design:
Lichtdesign GmbH, Cologne
Christian Bartenbach, Aldrans, Austria

The inauguration of the new assembly complex
of the Bundestag in Bonn marked the conclusion of a planning period that had lasted
almost 20 years. It was a planning process that
had seen many committees and commissions
come and go and that was subject to all kinds
of conditions and statements of intent. The
concept as realized was based on the wish to
link the intrinsic nature of the new parliamentary areas with the characteristics and qualities
of the landscape along the Rhine – the
embankment terraces, the Siebengebirge and
the parks with the chancellery and presidential
tracts. In combining these two aspects, a
place with a special identity was to be created.
The assembly hall – the seat of parliament –
forms the centrepiece of the complex. It is
embedded in a hollow on the middle embankment terrace and is covered by an airy, light-
transmitting roof. The hall is surrounded by various other functional areas, including the
offices of the parliamentary president and
committees, press facilities, spaces for visitors'
and scientific services, as well as tiers of seating and the lounge and private areas for members of the Bundestag. These different zones
are not only volumetrically distinct; they are
also articulated by planes, lines, colours, light
and mood, and are in relation to other locations. The centre – the debating chamber – is,
therefore, defined by the arrangement of these
"individual elements" and the context they create, and it remains open on all sides.
In order to translate this concept into reality, an
ample loadbearing structure was necessary. A
steel frame was chosen for this purpose. The
low fire load, the clarity of the situation, the
relatively short escape routes and the installation of a sprinkler system enabled the fire-
resistance requirements to be reduced from 90
to 30 min. As a result, it was possible to leave

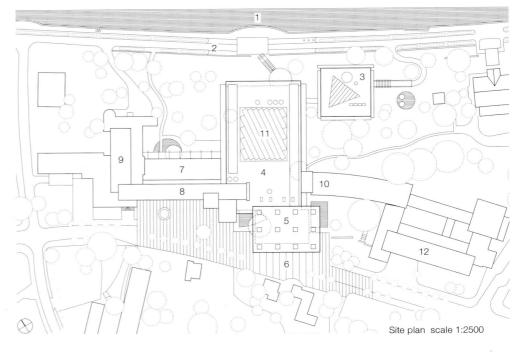

Site plan  scale 1:2500

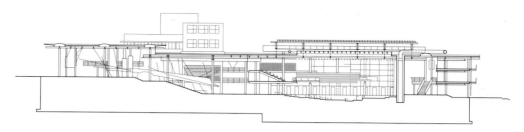

Section aa    scale 1:1000

1  River Rhine
2  Stresemann Embankment
3  Presidential annex
4  Lobby
5  Entrance hall
6  Parliament Square
7  Restaurant
8  Existing building
9  Bundesrat (second chamber)
10 South wing
11 Debating chamber
12 Former chamber of deputie

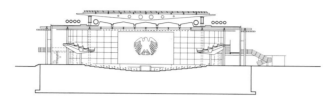

Section bb    scale  1:1000

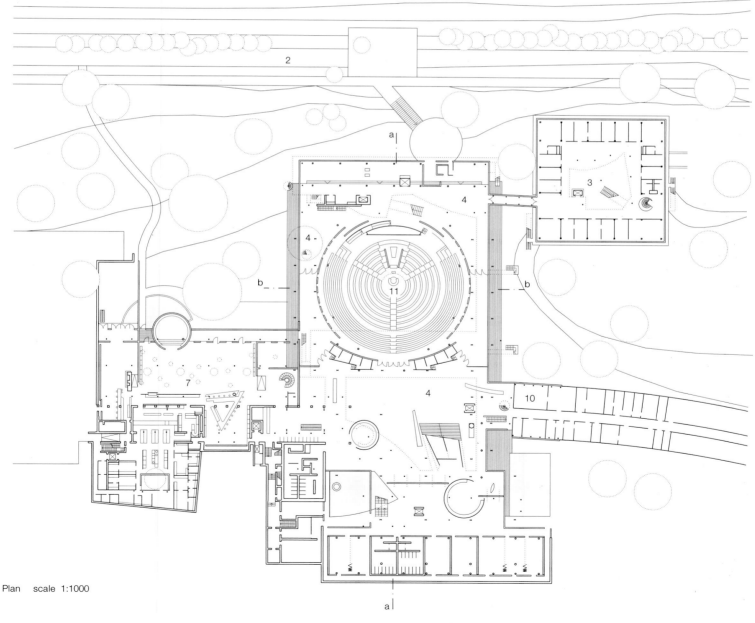

Plan    scale 1:1000

Example 16

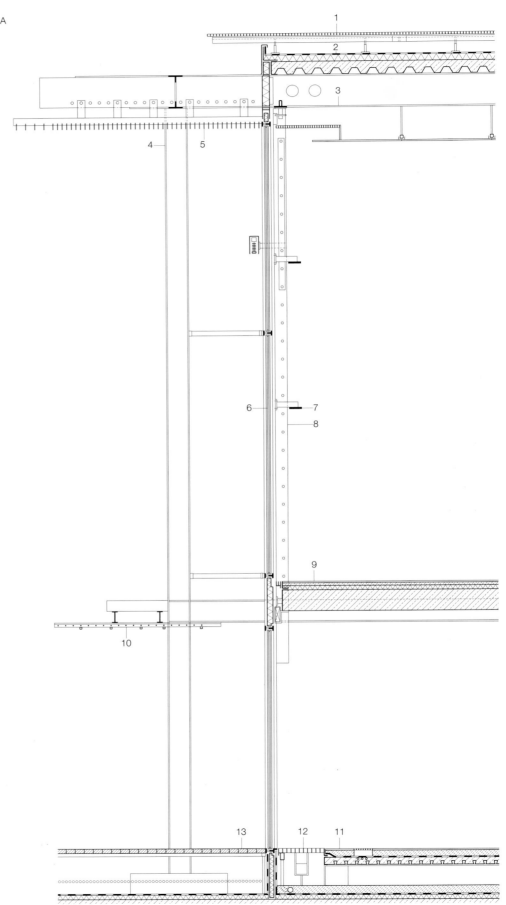

the steel structure unclad.

Sheet steel columns filled with concrete form a skeleton structure that supports the girder grids of the two roof layers and the "inserted" intermediate levels. The different spacings of the columns allow the structure to respond to individual situations.

The outer skin played a special role in realizing the design concept. The notion of individual locations laid out in a great open landscape required the "abolition" of the division between inside and outside in order to create an open, flowing space. The façade, therefore, had to be reduced to a minimum. This was achieved, on the one hand, through its broad articulation, and on the other hand, by dividing the façade construction into a number of layers. The basic elements of this construction are the extruded, multi-drawn steel posts and rails, which are dimensioned for storey-height (3.5 m) loading. In order to use this system for façades of up to 10 m height, the primary post-and-rail construction is reinforced by additional structural elements – by "load-distributing" and "load-collecting" members. The loads of the glass panes are conveyed via these intermediate elements to the structural carcass of the building and from there down to the foundations. This layering of the construction also facilitates individual responses to different situations. The division between inside and outside was overcome by allowing the elements in front of

A  Vertical section
   scale 1:50
B  Vertical section
   scale 1:5

1  steel grating
2  roof construction:
   waterproof membrane
   separating layer
   100 mm thermal insu-
   lation
   concrete topping layer
   trapezoidal-section
   metal sheeting
3  girder grid: rolled steel
   I-beams 450 mm deep
   (HEB)
4  300x350 mm double-
   web column filled with
   concrete
5  aluminium sunshade
   louvres
6  thermally insulating double glazing:
   2 panes 13 mm lamin-
   ated safety glass externally; 18 mm cavity;
   10 mm A3 intruder-
   resistant laminated
   safety glass internally
7  160x25 mm horizontal
   load-distributing mem-
   ber
8  vertical load-collecting
   member
9  ground floor construc-
   tion:
   22 mm parquet flooring
   30 mm mastic asphalt
   48 mm levelling layer
   300 mm concrete slab
10 horizontal timber trellis
11 floor construction:
   20 mm reconstituted
   stone
   80 mm screed
   two layers of polythene
   sheeting
   concrete on trapezoidal-
   section metal sheeting
   ventilation duct
12 6 mm metal grating
13 wood-strip paving
14 aluminium cover strip
15 60x45 mm extruded
   steel section
16 steel section with
   aluminium covering
17 ∅ 50 mm expansion
   tube
18 expansion joint

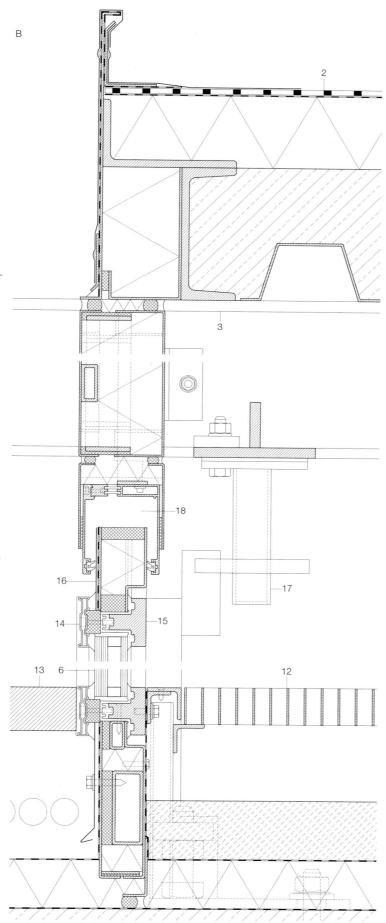

and behind the façade to enter into a spatial relationship with each other – the trees in the park, the grassed areas, the balconies, the pergolas, the sunscreen elements, the posts and beams in front of the façade, the sliding elements and timber structures, and the internal furnishings. A further factor in the dissolution of this division was the play of light and shade cast by the sun. In this way, the "outer skin" becomes a deep spatial zone, consisting of a large number of elements; at the same time, it is "reduced" to a thin glass plane that fulfils solely those functions that are related to construction physics and security technology. To reduce the hardness of the large areas of glazing, which are divided by widely spaced steel sections, an "internal façade" was created for the lounge and working areas. Consisting of vertical fabric blinds and translucent horizontal sliding elements in Scobalit and wood, it allows users to regulate the views in and out as well as the quantity of light entering the building. The internal façade elements are small in scale, soft in texture and more sensitive than those externally. They form part of the interior finishings and are, therefore, more carefully worked. The internal spaces can be naturally ventilated by means of large sliding doors and tall, narrow panel flaps.

Example 16

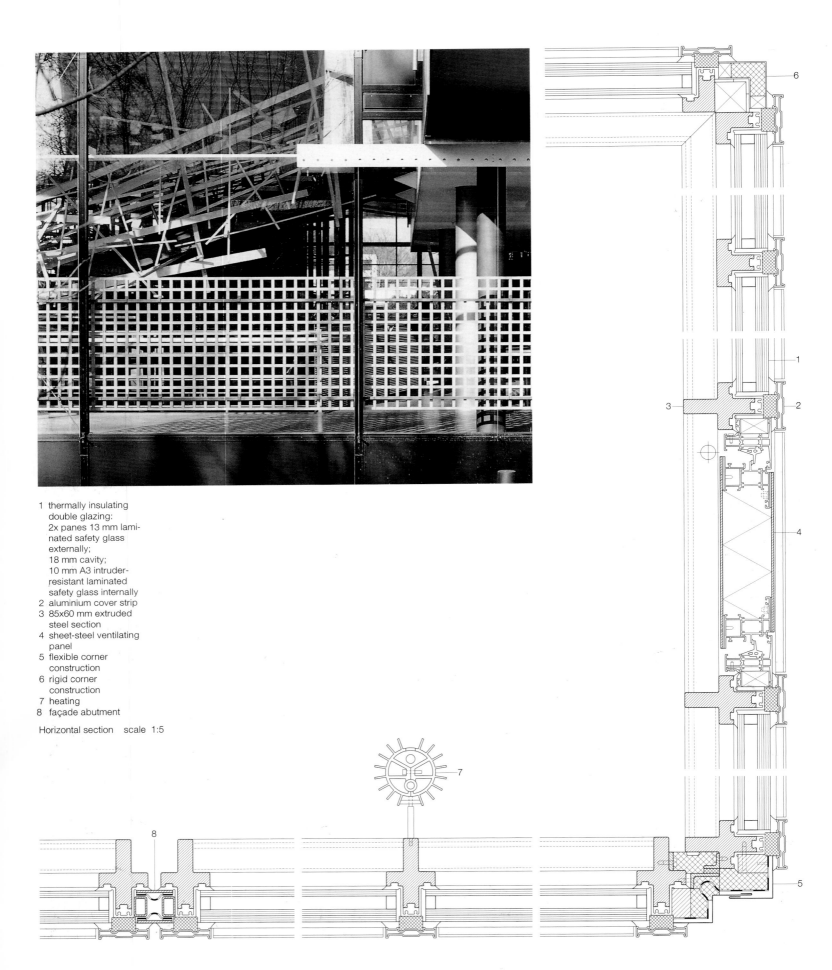

1 thermally insulating
   double glazing:
   2x panes 13 mm lami-
   nated safety glass
   externally;
   18 mm cavity;
   10 mm A3 intruder-
   resistant laminated
   safety glass internally
2 aluminium cover strip
3 85x60 mm extruded
   steel section
4 sheet-steel ventilating
   panel
5 flexible corner
   construction
6 rigid corner
   construction
7 heating
8 façade abutment

Horizontal section    scale  1:5

Example 16

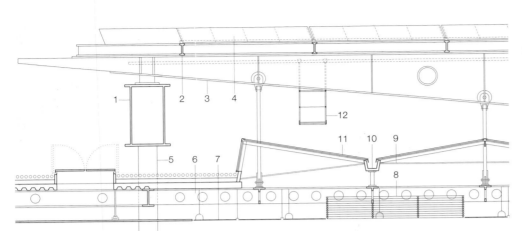

Vertical section   scale 1:100

1  1200x1700 mm welded steel main box girder
2  100x300 mm welded sheet-steel beam supporting light prisms, laid diagonally
3  550 mm tapering fish-belly girder
4  acrylic-glass, light-diffusing adjustable sunshade louvres
5  508x40 mm steel RHS stanchion supporting light-diffusing roof
6  girder grid: rolled steel I-beams 450 mm deep (HEB)
7  aluminium panel
8  luminaire-grid sus-pended ceiling: reflecting metal elements and prismatic cast glass (Fresnel lenses)
9  ∅ 16 mm tie rod
10 sheet-metal gutter
11 light-diffusing roof on I-beam 80 mm deep (IPE)
12 travelling cradle
13 ∅ 39 mm suspension member from fish-belly girder
14 silicone sealing collar with mineral wool insulation
15 aluminium sealing ring
16 33 mm double glazing
17 two-part sand-cast aluminium ring

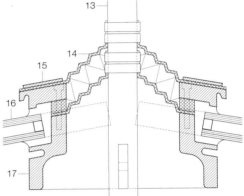

Roof suspension detail   scale 1:5

## Light-diffusing roof

It was the wish of the building commission that the assembly hall should be flooded with natural light entering from above. The architects' original idea was to create a large, circular opening in the roof, covered by a horizontal "glass disc". This was changed, for administrative reasons, into a pitched, folded, light-diffusing roof, supported on the underside by reflecting sheet-steel valley beams. Sunshading is provided on the outside by light-diffusing acrylic-glass prisms fixed over large fish-belly girders. The prisms are laid out in an east-west direction and are computer controlled to follow the path of the sun. In this way, direct sunlight falling on the prisms is reflected, and only indirect light is allowed to enter the hall through the opening in the roof. Various media installations, including the electrical services, sprinklers and the lighting and fire-alarm systems, are run beneath the light-diffusing roof. The underside of this multilayered roof zone is formed by a metal and cast-glass luminaire-grid soffit based on the principle of the Fresnel lens. In terms of lighting technology, these areas create a certain downward "lighting pressure", obviating any effect of glare for visitors and members of the Bundestag, and turning the roof into a play of light and materials, reality and illusion.

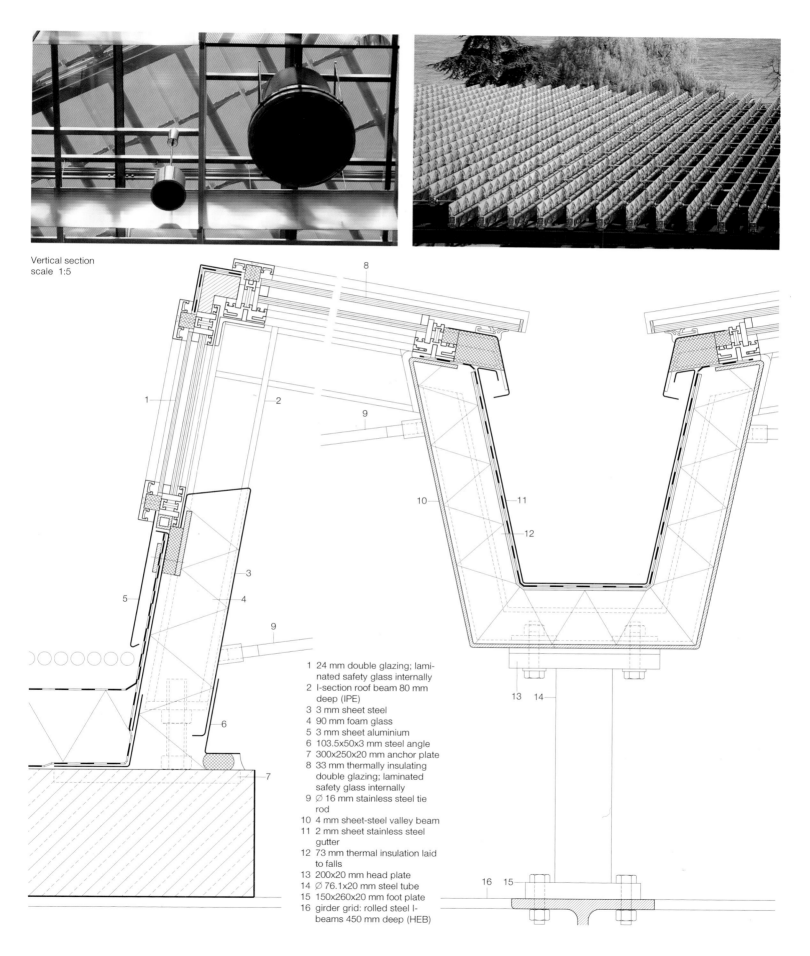

Vertical section
scale 1:5

1  24 mm double glazing; laminated safety glass internally
2  I-section roof beam 80 mm
   deep (IPE)
3  3 mm sheet steel
4  90 mm foam glass
5  3 mm sheet aluminium
6  103.5x50x3 mm steel angle
7  300x250x20 mm anchor plate
8  33 mm thermally insulating
   double glazing; laminated
   safety glass internally
9  Ø 16 mm stainless steel tie
   rod
10 4 mm sheet-steel valley beam
11 2 mm sheet stainless steel
   gutter
12 73 mm thermal insulation laid
   to falls
13 200x20 mm head plate
14 Ø 76.1x20 mm steel tube
15 150x260x20 mm foot plate
16 girder grid: rolled steel I-
   beams 450 mm deep (HEB)

Example 17

**Exhibition and Administration Building in Paris**

1994

Architects:
Jean Nouvel, Emmanuel Cattani & Associés, Paris
Project architect:
Didier Brault
Structural engineers:
Ove Arup & Partners, London
Façade engineer:
Arnauld de Bussiere, Paris

The Fondation Cartier building is located in the Boulevard Raspail in Montparnasse, Paris, where the American Cultural Center formerly stood. In redeveloping the site, the architects were faced with a number of constraints. To obtain building permission it was necessary to adhere to the building lines of the previous structure. Within these limits, adequate administrative accommodation had to be provided for the new company headquarters as well as a generous exhibition space for the Cartier Foundation of Modern Art. A further constraint was that the existing stock of trees that belonged to the old park, including a 100-year-old cedar, had to be retained.

The outcome is a glazed cube parallel to the road but set back from it. The boundary of the site along the pavement is marked by two 8 m high glazed walls, which define the main entrance and form a "frame" for the old cedar as well. The walls also continue the street line of the building immediately to the north. In order to extend the administration and exhibition building, which is relatively small in relation to the area of the site, the architects continued the front and rear façades at the ends beyond the actual building. These single-glazed extensions of the façade are supported by steel bracing at the narrow ends of the build-ing. Between the glass wall along the road and the building itself is a row of trees, which were planted in close symmetry to the large trees in the pavement outside.

The building is eight storeys high and extends seven storeys below ground. The ground floor and the first basement level are reserved for exhibition purposes. Above this are seven storeys of offices, with a reception area and roof garden on the eighth floor. The second to seventh basement levels are used mainly for parking, with access provided by a car lift. The

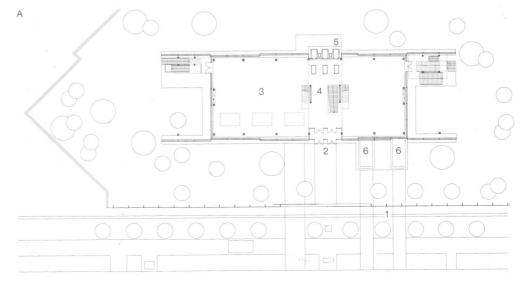

A Site plan
B Longitudinal section
C Cross-section
D Office storey
E Roof storey
  scale 1:750

B

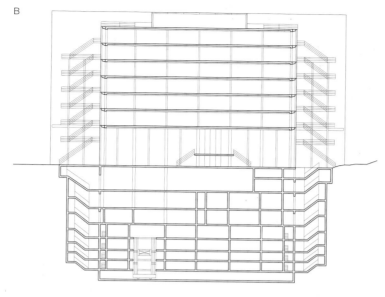

C

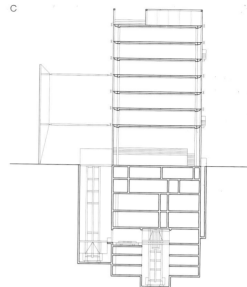

D

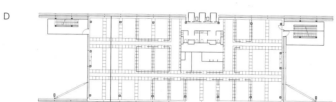

E

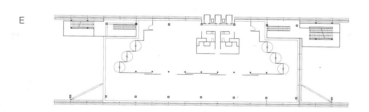

1 Freestanding glass
  façade
2 Entrance
3 Exhibitions
4 Gallery
5 Passenger lift
6 Car lift

exhibition halls on the ground floor are flooded
with light. The 8 m high glass walls to the long
faces can be slid aside as required to create a
flowing transition between inside and outside.
Glass panels let into the the ground floor slab
allow daylight to penetrate to the exhibition
spaces in the basement below.

The transparent façades are in a post-and-rail
construction. On the upper floors, the façades
consist of all-glass elements in a structural
sealant glazing system, articulated by a fine
network of stainless steel bars that provide a
mechanical means of securing the construction. The bars also serve to support the external fabric sunblinds, which are installed independently for each storey and are automatically retracted in the event of wind.

On the upper floors the internal partitions also
consist largely of glass. They are sand-blasted
up to eye level, with a gradual transition to
transparency at the top. To complete the
image of a house of glass, much of the office
furniture, which was designed by the architects
themselves, is in the same material.

By extending the external skin far beyond the
actual volume of the building, the architects
have to a large degree succeeded in creating
a dramatic urban and architectural effect. The
volume of the actual building recedes into the
background and is overlaid by an extensive
image of glass, with subtly superimposed layers of transparency and reflection, architecture
and nature.

Example 17

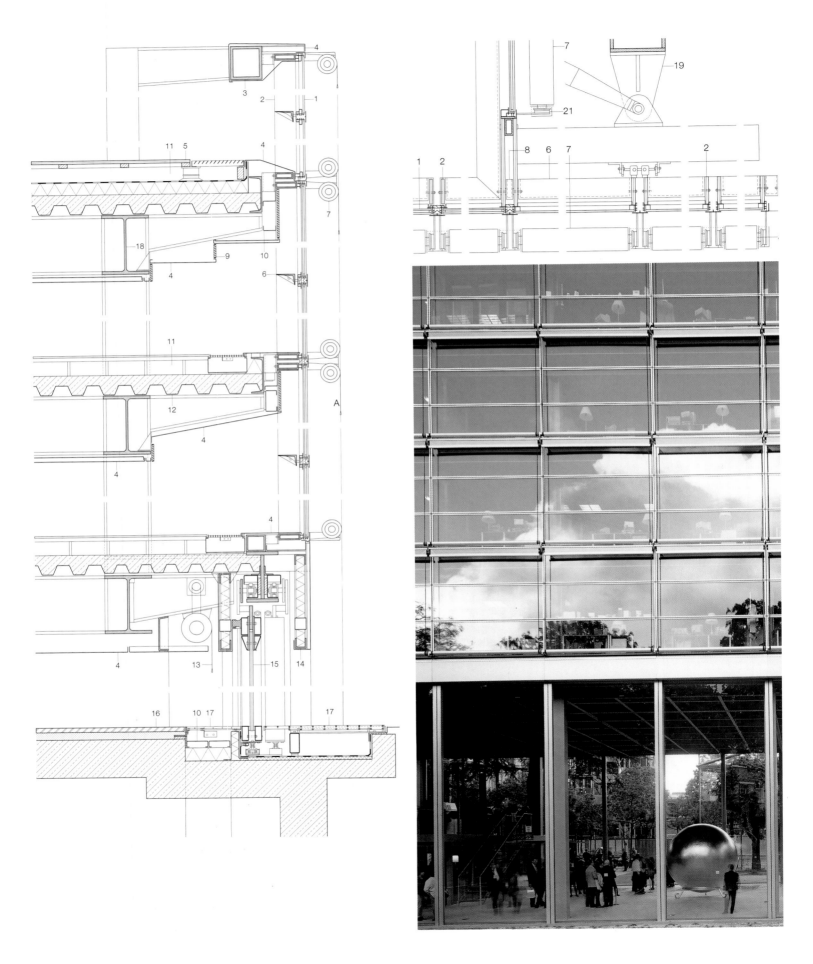

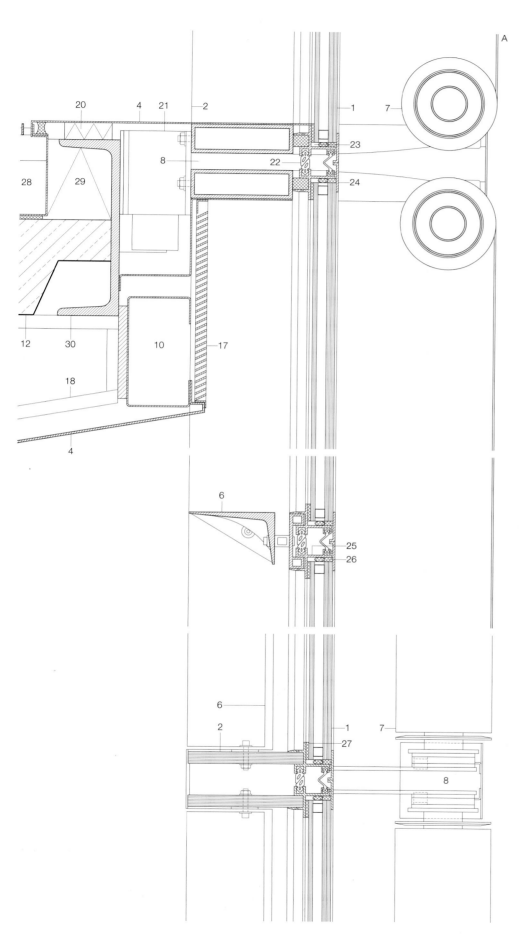

A

Vertical section through façade
Horizontal section through façade
scale 1:20
Vertical section
Horizontal section
scale 1:5

1 anti-reflection double glazing:
   12 mm laminated safety glass externally
   6 mm float glass internally in casement area
   6 mm toughened safety glass in apron wall area
   aluminium frame construction with external stainless
   steel glazing bars
2 19 mm suspended safety-glass fin
3 steel SHS supporting member
4 sheet metal covering
5 wood strip boarding
6 cast-aluminium transverse member
7 fabric sunshade, computer controlled; fixed with aluminium brackets
8 abutment between elements
9 aluminium grating
10 ventilation (air intake and extract)
11 cavity floor construction
12 trapezoidal section metal sheeting with concrete
   topping 130 mm deep
13 internal antiglare blind
14 insulating panel
15 glass sliding door with aluminium frame
16 granite slab pavings
17 steel grating
18 primary steel structure
19 steel supporting structure for freestanding glass wall
20 insulating block
21 steel angle for fixing façade
22 EPDM sealing lip
23 façade drainage
24 stainless steel cover strip
25 three-part aluminium façade rail
26 sealing strip
27 adhesive fixing of glass
28 130x250 mm service duct
29 100 mm insulation
30 240 mm steel channel (UPN)

Example 17

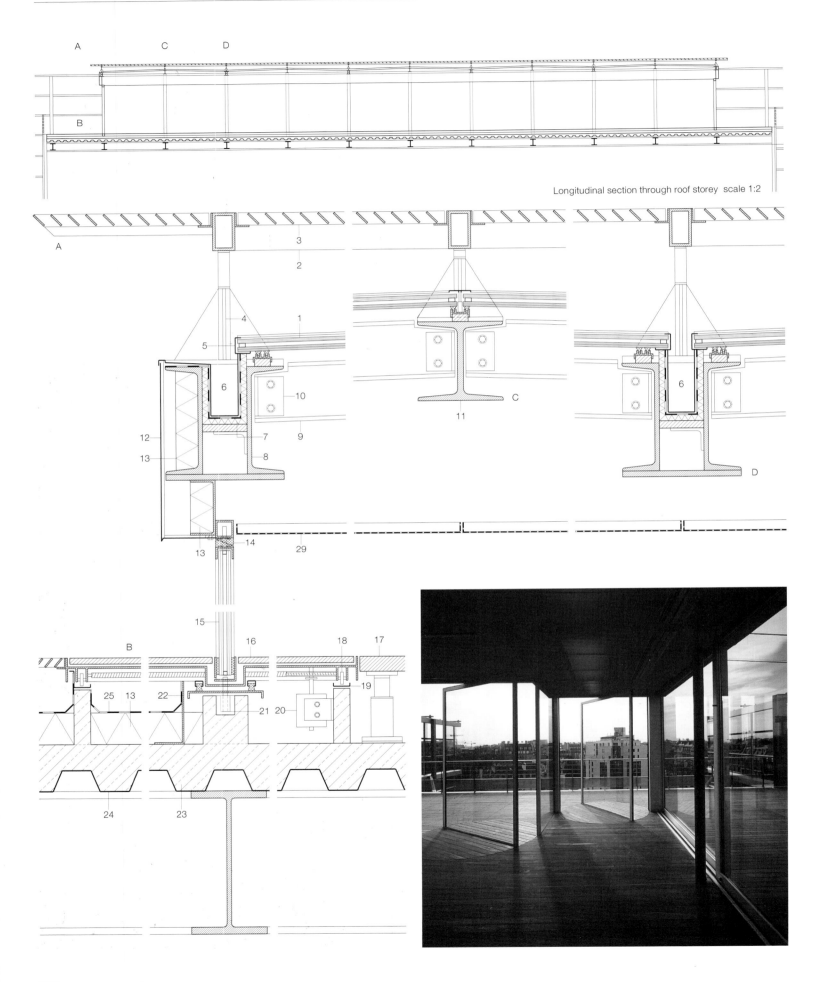

Longitudinal section through roof storey  scale 1:2

Longitudinal section
Cross-section
scale 1:10

1 anti-reflection double
  glazing:
  12 mm toughened
  safety glass externally
  10 mm cavity
  2 panes 6 mm lami-
  nated safety glass
  internally

2 framed grid: 100x60 mm
  galvanized steel RHS
3 external sunscreening:
  galvanized steel grating
4 galvanized steel fixing
  piece
5 aluminium angle
6 drainage channel
7 25 mm insulation
8 300x100 mm steel
  channel

9 steel I-beam 160 mm
  deep (IPE)
10 steel fixing angle
11 steel I-beam 220 mm
  deep (SIL)
12 aluminium fascia
  cladding
13 mineral-wool insulation
14 EPDM strip
15 glass revolving door
  with aluminium frame

and double glazing (12 +
10 + 12 mm)
16 25 mm wood covering
17 38 mm wood strip floor
18 running wheel for
  revolving door
19 galvanized steel angle
  fixing for revolving door
  track
20 electric motor for re-
  volving door

21 pivot for revolving door
22 stop angle
23 130 mm concrete top-
  ping
24 trapezoidal-section steel
  sheeting
25 elastomer-based bitu-
  minous membrane
26 frame drainage
27 19 mm toughened safety
  glass fin

28 80x80 mm steel sec-
  tion
29 perforated sheet-alu-
  minium suspended
  soffit
30 20 mm timber board-
  ing
31 flat-roof outlet
32 glass sliding door with
  aluminium frame
33 aluminium grating
34 steel I-beam 400 mm
  deep (HEA)

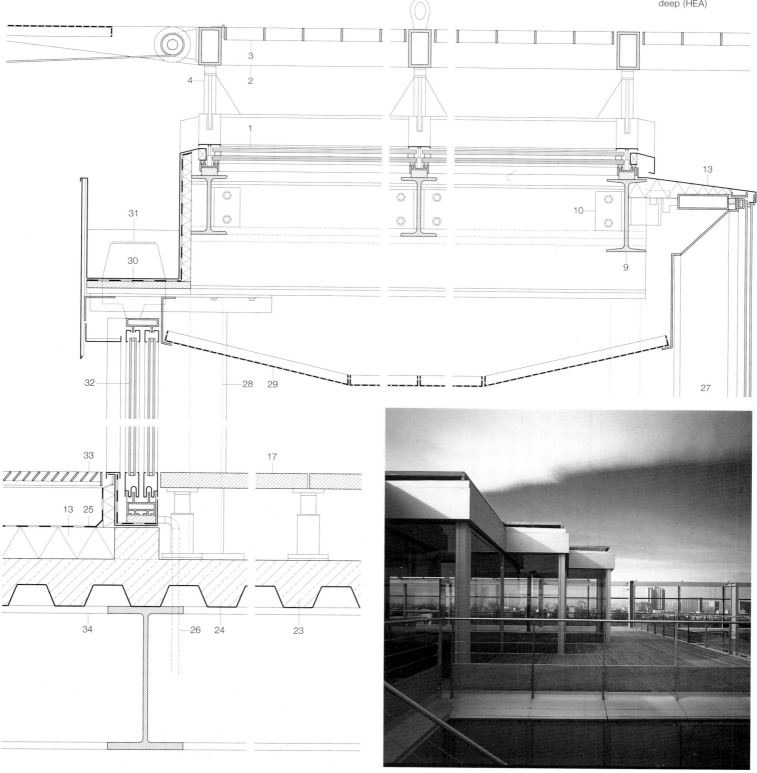

Example 17

## Faculty Building of University of Utrecht, The Netherlands

1996

Architects:
mecanoo architekten b.v., Delft
Erick van Egeraat, Francine Houben,
Chris de Weijer, Henk Döll
Structural engineers:
ABT, Delft

The building forms part of the new "Uithof" university complex east of Utrecht. The outline urban plan, drawn up by Rem Koolhaas, has as its theme: "The university and the landscape". It proposes a dense building structure that is meant to prevent further low-density sprawl and preserve the remaining landscape spaces from development. The plan is divided into a number of zones, each with its own specific character. The faculty building shown here is situated in the so-called "Kasbah Zone".

Adopting the characteristics of the traditional North African kasbah, the architects designed a three-storey, compact building structure laid out around three courtyards, each of which is distinguished by a specific theme. The courtyards form the centre of the faculty and, by virtue of their distinct forms, exert a great influence on the atmosphere of the development as a whole. The largest of these spaces is the Jungle Courtyard, which is planted with bamboo. It is also the only courtyard accessible via two steel bridges, which cross it at first floor level. The Zen Courtyard, inspired by Japanese gardens of meditation, is laid out with gravel. The Water Courtyard is occupied by a long, narrow pool and is separated from its surroundings by a glazed façade. Along the northern edge, these courtyards are enclosed by a transparent building tract that houses the "Conference Area", including lecture halls, a media library and a cafeteria. These spaces are inserted like discrete "boxes" in different materials into the entrance zone, which is fully visible from the outside. Corridors lead from this zone

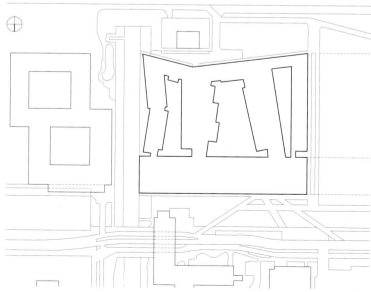

Site plan
scale 1:2500

Example 18

| | |
|---|---|
| 1 Main entrance | 9 Teaching rooms |
| 2 Reception | 10 Bamboo Courtyard |
| 3 Information centre | 11 Water Courtyard |
| 4 Shops | 12 Computer lab |
| 5 Kitchen | 13 Lecture halls |
| 6 Café | 14 Canteen |
| 7 Administration | 15 Media library |
| 8 Zen Courtyard | 16 Offices |

First floor plan  scale 1:1000

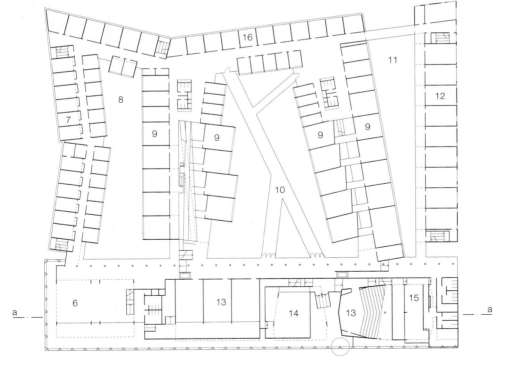

Ground floor plan  scale 1:1000

Section aa  scale 1:1000

to the lecture rooms and the offices in the various tracts of the building around the courtyards. The open spaces between the boxes in the conference area and the different forms of design of the corridors convey a sensation of openness and provide scope to use the building in a variety of ways.

The loadbearing structure for the roughly 7 m high upper area of glazing to the entrance front consists of room-height tubular columns from which pairs of T-section brackets are cantilevered. The façade rails are fixed to the underside of these brackets.

The horizontal lines of the façade are accentuated by glazing bars that hold the panes of glass in position. The vertical glazing abutments are jointed with silicone.

The horizontality of the post-and-rail façade construction to the ground floor area is equally pronounced. These two levels of glazing, horizontally staggered by half a module, are separated from each other by a 40 mm high "joint" in the form of a strip of ventilation louvres. The topmost rail of the ground floor façade zone is fixed to the lower pairs of cantilevered brackets.

To achieve a slender roof abutment detail, the roof drainage was placed behind the façade. In their contrasting design and use of materials, the façades to the three courtyards accentuate the individuality of these introverted spaces. The glazed wall to the south, the Water Courtyard, the narrowest of the three, affords a view of the surrounding polder landscape. The east façade adjoining this acquires its distinct texture from the aluminium louvres with which it is clad.

Large timber lattice elements are suspended in front of the internal spaces on the east and west sides of the Zen Courtyard. In the Jungle Courtyard, the cladding elements are in the form of steel gratings. The south faces of these two courtyards are finished with planar timber panels with incised window openings.

The complex is a model of university campus architecture: an open house with streets and public squares that are both interior and exterior space. It is a building of contrasts with the diversity of a small town; and it reveals a form of construction that, in continuation of the Dutch tradition of the 1970s and 80s, confirms the outstanding position this architecture enjoys.

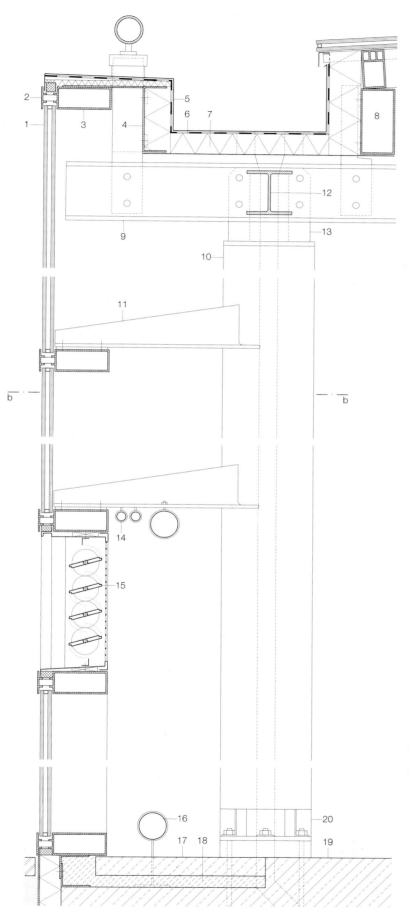

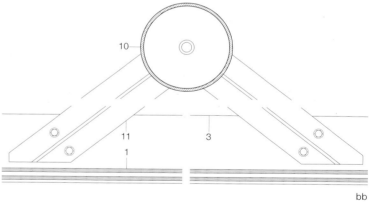

bb

Entrance façade
Vertical section
Horizontal section
scale 1:10

1 double glazing
  (10 + 12 + 8 mm)
2 aluminium glazing
  bars
3 aluminium façade rail
4 aluminium sheet bent
  to shape
5 2 mm sheet aluminium
  covering
6 plastic waterproof
  sheeting

7 thermal insulation
8 90x180x4 mm steel
  RHS
9 steel I-beam 140 mm
  deep (HEA)
10 Ø 240 mm (nom.) steel
  column
11 steel bracket
12 steel I-beam 120 mm
  deep (HEA)
13 steel head plate

14 services
15 ventilation element:
  electronically operated
  aluminium louvres
16 Ø 80 mm (nom.) stain-
  less steel tube
17 artificial stone
18 cement mortar
19 reinforced concrete
  floor
20 steel foot plate

Example 18

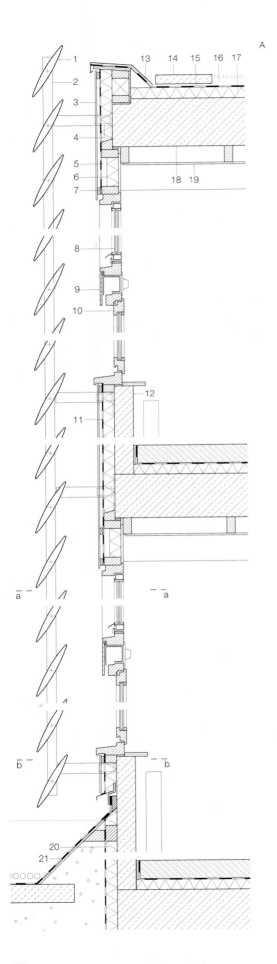

A

A Vertical section through
  façade to Water Courtyard
B Horizontal section
C Vertical section through
  façade to Zen Courtyard
  scale 1:20

1 adjustable aluminium
  louvre
2 30x30 mm aluminium SHS
3 8 mm fibre-cement fascia
4 stainless steel set bolt
5 ventilated cavity
6 mineral thermal insulation
7 timber rail
8 double glazing
9 10 mm composite wood
  board
10 wood casement
11 polythene film
12 precast concrete element
13 sheet aluminium capping
14 artificial stone
15 waterproof roofing membrane
16 roof planting
17 thermal insulation
18 reinforced concrete roof
   slab
19 suspended plasterboard
   soffit
20 insulation to outer wall
21 waterproof membrane
22 mortar joint
23 plasterboard
24 fine gravel chippings

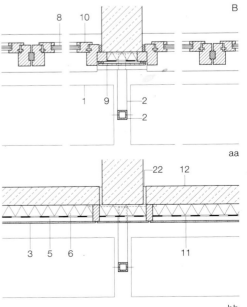

B

aa

bb

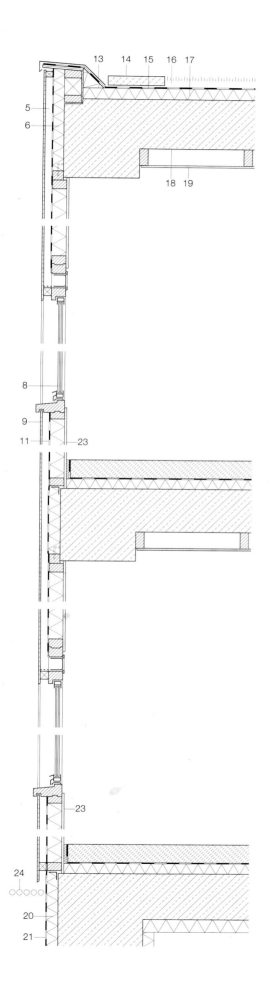

13  14  15  16  17

18  19

5
6

8
9
11        23

23

24

20
21

Example 19

## University Complex in Marne-la-Vallée, France

1996

Architects:
Chaix Morel & Partner, Paris
Philippe Chaix, Jean-Paul Morel,
Rémy Van Nieuwenhove
Assistants: Benoît Sigros, Walter Grasmug,
Nelly Breton, Dietmar Feichtinger, Sophie
Carré, Denis Germond, David McNulty, Olivier
Boiron, Laurent Bievelot, Franck Hughes, Paolo
Carrozzino
Structural engineers:
O. T. H. Bâtiments, Paris

The complex accommodates two universities:
the Ecole Nationale des Ponts et Chaussées
and the Ecole Nationale des Sciences Géo-
graphiques. The lecture halls, seminar rooms,
laboratories and offices are housed in three
parallel wings.

The suspended arched glass roofs between
these wings act as linking structures and mark
the line of the transverse atrium, which runs
through the entire complex. A number of larger
spaces such as the library and the dining hall
are also located beneath the arched roofs. The
atrium forms the division between the two universities, which are of different sizes; at the
same time it represents the common circulation
area for all users. The individual wings are also
linked by bridges both inside and outside the
building.

The suspended arched glass roofs are supported by a mixed form of construction, consisting
of steel columns and beams with prestressed
concrete hollow slab floors spanned between
them. Loads in the outer areas of the roof are
conducted via horizontal ties and raking compression members in front of the two long
faces to vertical tension cables. These are in
turn anchored in the ground by means of
powerful tension springs. Inside the building,
curving, tensioned rods beneath the arched
glass roofs act as wind bracing and counteract
uplift forces. All connections between the glass
roofs and the adjoining building tracts, the
facades and dividing walls are designed as flexible joints that can absorb movements of
several centimetres caused by snow or wind
loads. Metal louvres suspended beneath the
glass roofs prevent glare and also improve the
internal acoustics. The external fabric sunscreening is automatically retracted in the event of
strong winds.

The post-and-rail construction to the long faces
of the buildings continues in the same rhythm
along the front of the atrium and the office
wings. In the atrium, without floor slabs to provide bracing, the facades are trussed on their
rear faces with steel cables or rods. Spring
members keep the cable construction taut
while affording the necessary elasticity.

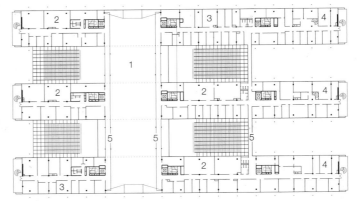

Upper floor plan   scale 1:1500

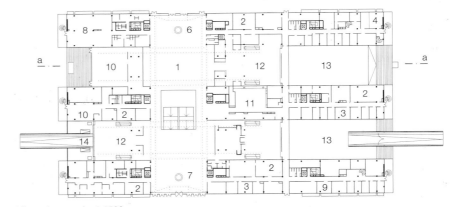

Ground floor plan   scale 1:1500

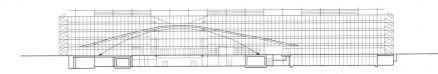

Section aa  scale 1:1500

| | |
|---|---|
| 1 Atrium | 8 Gymnasium |
| 2 Teaching rooms | 9 Laboratories |
| 3 Offices | 10 Cartography |
| 4 Research | 11 Small lecture hall |
| 5 Bridge/gallery | 12 Library |
| 6 Cafeteria | 13 Void |
| 7 Reception | 14 Basement garage ramp |

Example 19

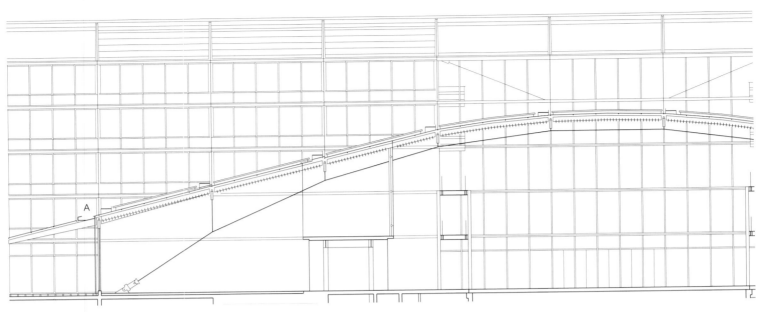

Section through glass roof   scale 1:250

1 double glazing: 8 mm
  toughened safety
  glass externally
  12 mm cavity
  2 panes 4.5 mm lami-
  nated safety glass
  internally
2 double glazing
  (6 + 10 + 4 mm)

3 ⌀ 36 mm steel
  suspension rod for
  glass roof
4 stainless steel rain-
  water gutter
5 fabric sunshade
6 maintenance catwalk

7 sliding window for
  smoke extract
8 fixed aluminium louvre,
  perforated and filled
  with mineral wool to
  improve acoustics
9 ⌀ 50 mm steel trussing
  rod

10 polycarbonate spacer
11 brush seal
12 extruded aluminium
   glazing bar
13 extruded aluminium
   facade post

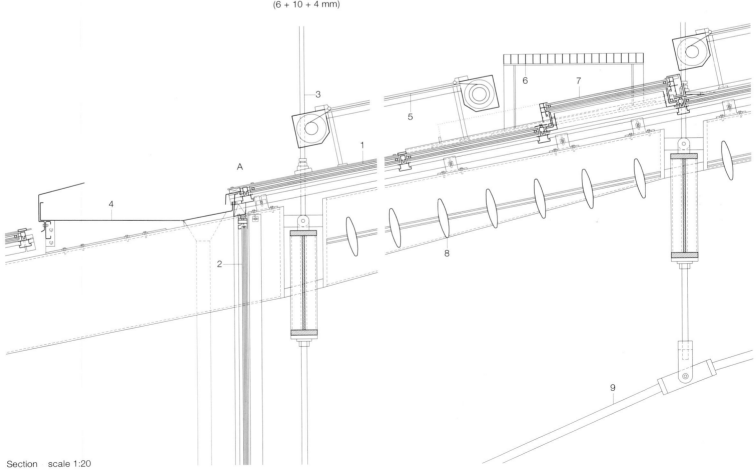

Section   scale 1:20

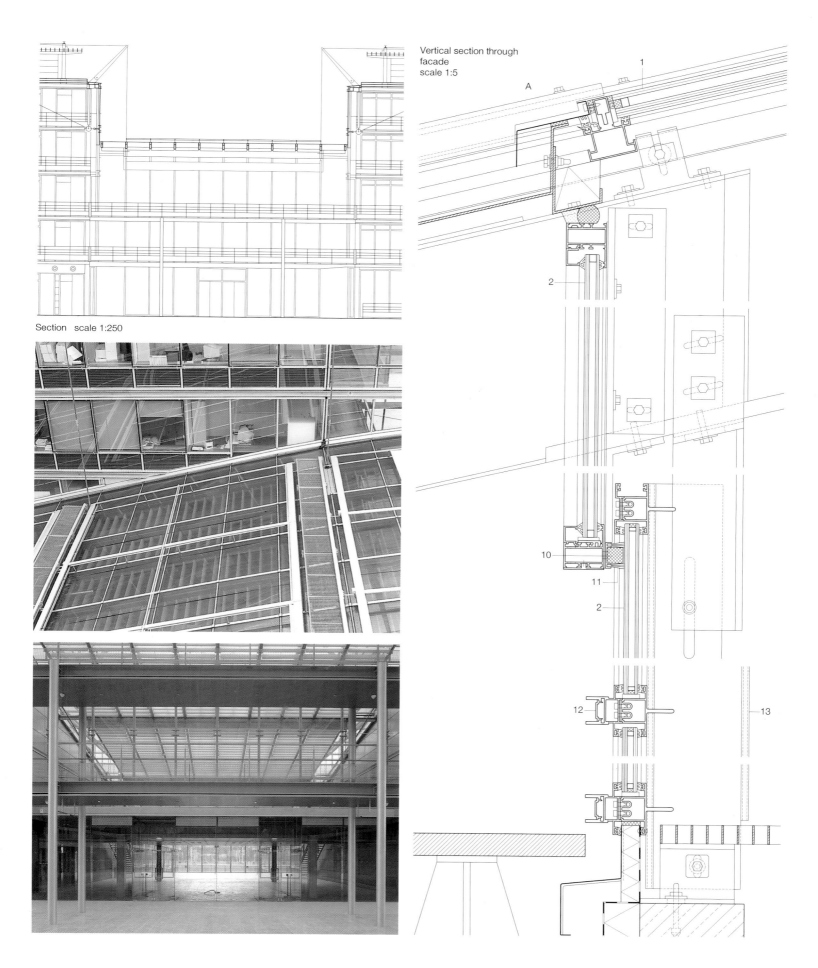

Vertical section through
facade
scale 1:5

A

1

2

10

11

2

12

13

Section   scale 1:250

Example 19

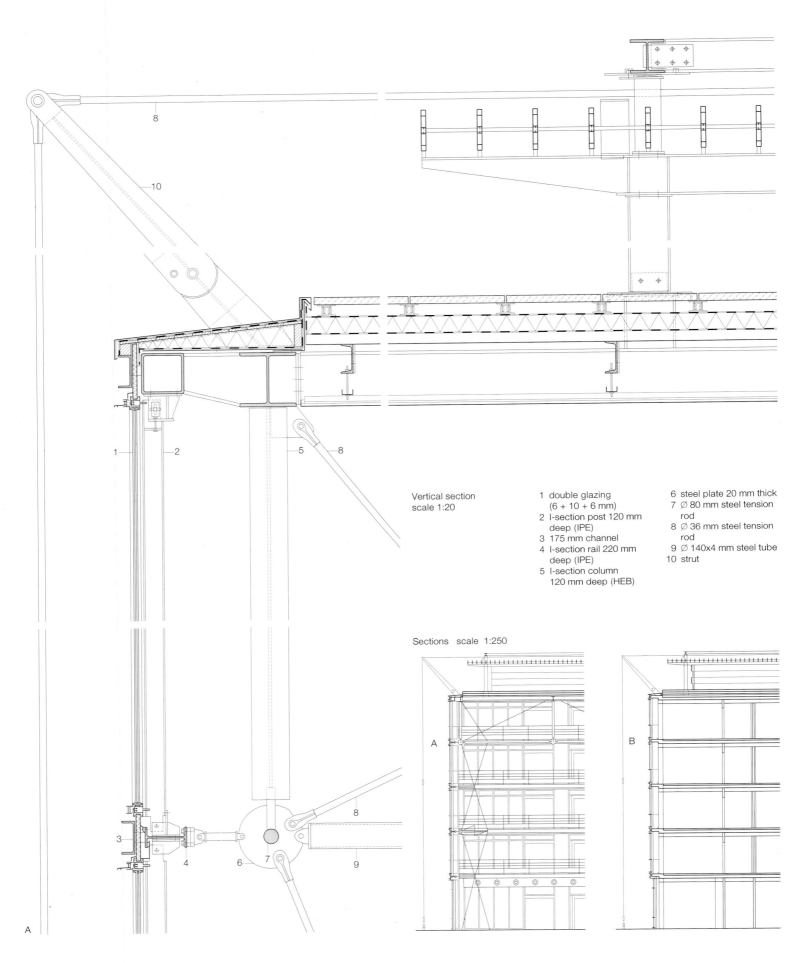

Vertical section
scale 1:20

1 double glazing
  (6 + 10 + 6 mm)
2 I-section post 120 mm
  deep (IPE)
3 175 mm channel
4 I-section rail 220 mm
  deep (IPE)
5 I-section column
  120 mm deep (HEB)

6 steel plate 20 mm thick
7 ∅ 80 mm steel tension
  rod
8 ∅ 36 mm steel tension
  rod
9 ∅ 140x4 mm steel tube
10 strut

Sections   scale  1:250

A

B

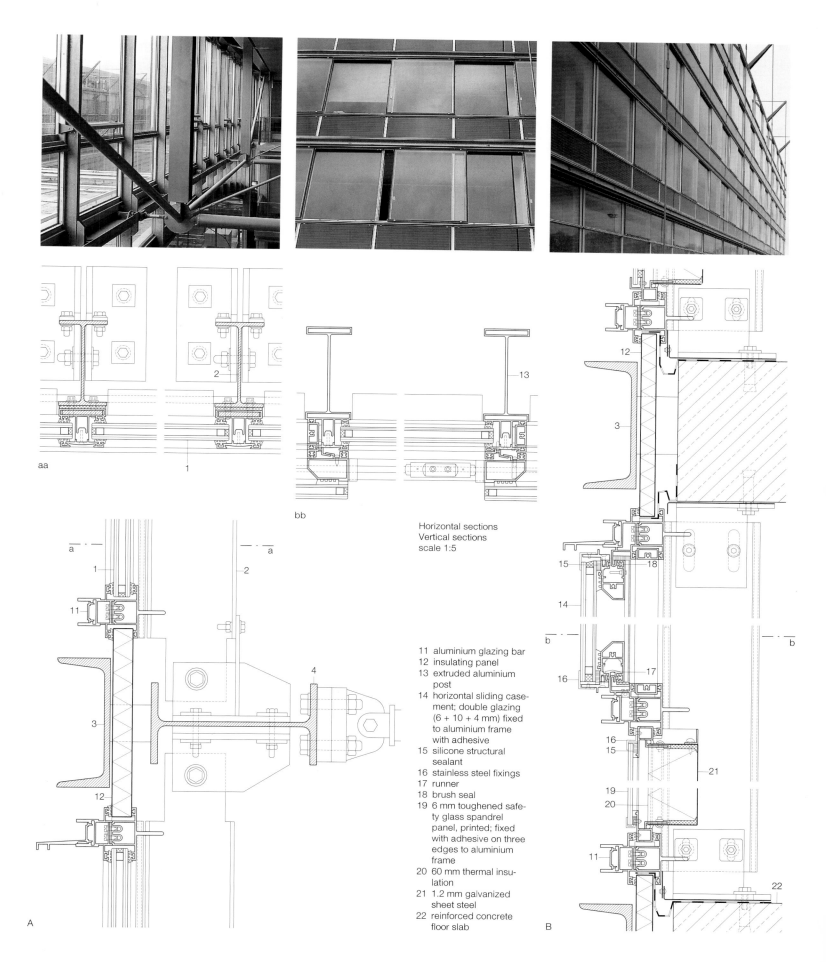

aa

1

2

bb

13

Horizontal sections
Vertical sections
scale 1:5

12

3

15    18

14

b                                                    b

16    17

16
15

21

19
20

11

22

a            a

1                                    2

11

3

4

12

11 aluminium glazing bar
12 insulating panel
13 extruded aluminium
   post
14 horizontal sliding casement; double glazing
   (6 + 10 + 4 mm) fixed
   to aluminium frame
   with adhesive
15 silicone structural
   sealant
16 stainless steel fixings
17 runner
18 brush seal
19 6 mm toughened safe-
   ty glass spandrel
   panel, printed; fixed
   with adhesive on three
   edges to aluminium
   frame
20 60 mm thermal insu-
   lation
21 1.2 mm galvanized
   sheet steel
22 reinforced concrete
   floor slab

A

B

Example 19

## Offices and Television Studios in London, England

1994

Architects:
Richard Rogers Partnership, London
Structural engineers:
Ove Arup & Partners, London,
RFR, Paris (curved entrance façade)

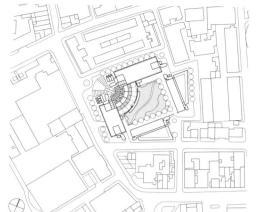

Site plan   scale 1:4000

The new headquarters of Channel 4 Television is well integrated into the scale of the surrounding urban fabric of its Westminster site. Only the lift and services tower, crowned by a mast and aerial, rises above the other buildings in the neighbourhood to mark the location. The L-shaped layout of the development closes the inner-city street block.

Visitors approach the building via a glazed bridge, over which a glass and steel canopy is suspended. The highlight of this effectively staged entrance is formed by the roughly 20 m high, concave, all-glass façade. At its points of abutment with the adjoining solid structure, the façade construction is angled on plan and thus visually separated from the rest of the building. The glass façade is suspended from cantilevered steel beams on the roof. Like a chain, each pane of glass supports the weight of all the panes below it. An internal double network of stressed stainless steel cables stabilizes the construction against wind loads. In the central section of the façade, wind pressure loads are restrained by horizontal cables, and suction forces by vertical cables. At the edges the arrangement is reversed. This system for the redistribution of loads led to the creation of a kind of planar network fixed at individual points, from where the glass panels are stabilized by short hinged rods.

All connections and glass fixings are in an articulated form of construction to ensure the predictability of the loading to which the individual elements are subjected and the transmission of external loads from the glass panels to the structure. The angled sections of the façade at the sides are in a rigid form of construction with structural silicone sealant.

The façades to the offices consist of storey-height panel elements. These are divided into four bands of glass set above each other and executed as structural sealant glazing with additional mechanical fixings. As a means of sunscreening, expanded metal mesh panels were placed in front of the uppermost and bottommost panes of glass. (On the north face the mesh is fixed only over the lowest panes.)

Example 20

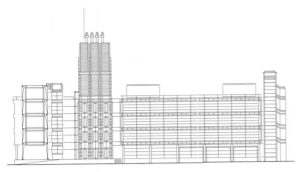

West elevation  scale 1:1000

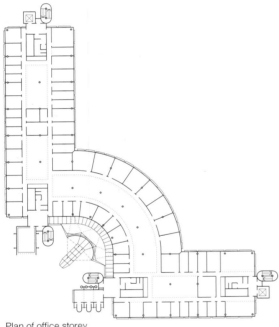

Plan of office storey

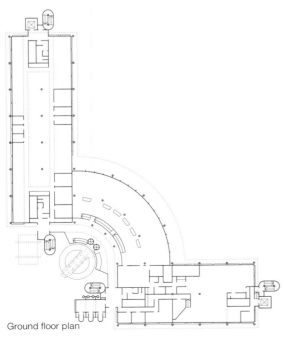

Ground floor plan

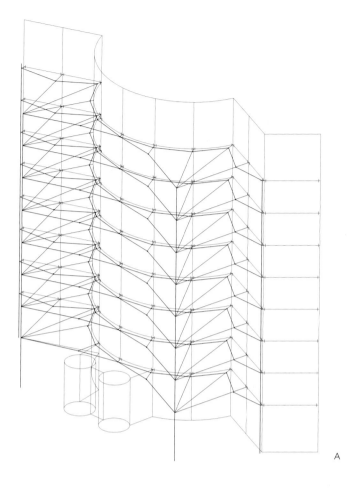

A Axonometric of entrance façade, showing horizontal bracing cables
B Section through entrance area scale 1:200
C Vertical section through façade mounting at top and glass fixing scale 1:10

1 12 mm laminated safety glass roof
2 12 mm curved laminated safety glass
3 stainless steel glass suspension element with spring
4 point fixings hinged in plane of glass
5 cast stainless steel four-point connector with two pivoting hinges
6 stainless steel hinged rod
7 silicone elastic jointing
8 Ø 34 mm stainless steel cable

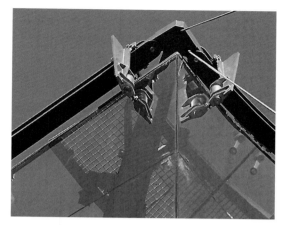

A

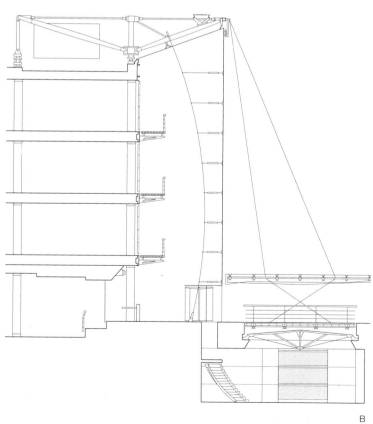

B

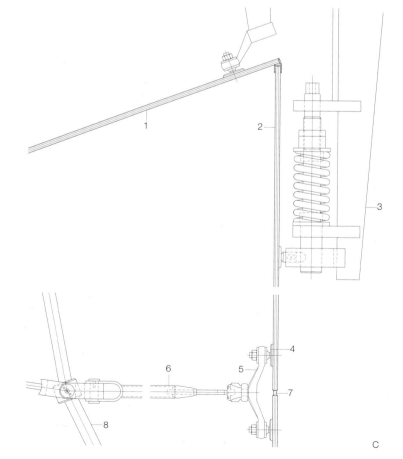

C

Example 20

Office façade
Vertical section
Horizontal section aa
scale 1:50

aa

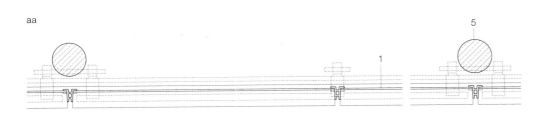

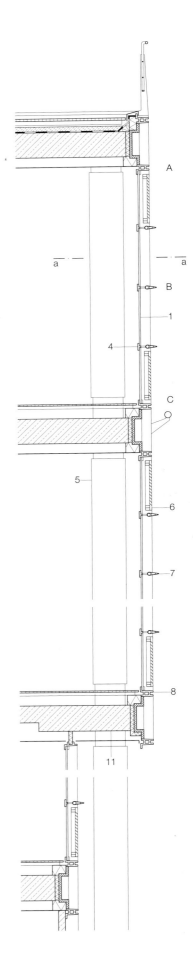

Office façade (upper floor)
Horizontal section, vertical section
scale 1:5
Aluminium members stove-
enamelled

1  double glazing
   (6 + 15 + 6 mm);
   toughened safety
   glass internally
2  structural silicone
   sealant
3  polythene thermal
   break

4  aluminium cover strip
5  reinforced concrete
   column
6  expanded aluminium
   mesh in aluminium
   frame
7  aluminium horizontal
   bracing section

8  aluminium panel
   frame
9  aluminium section
10 sheet aluminium
   bent to shape
11 reinforced con-
   crete floor slab

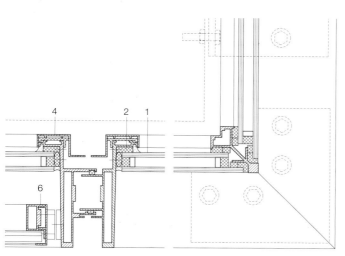

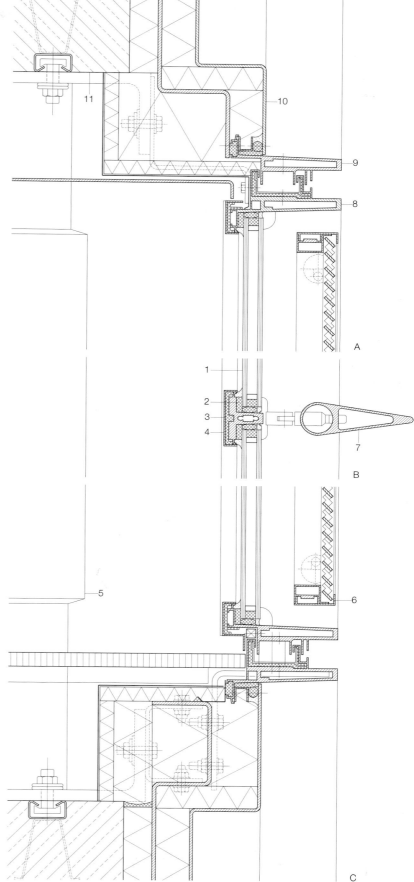

Example 21

## Company Headquarters Tower in Essen, Germany

1997

Architects:
Ingenhoven Overdiek Kahlen und Partner, Düsseldorf
Ch. Ingenhoven, A. Nagel, K. Frankenheim, K. J. Osterburg, E. Viera, M. Slawik, P. J. v. Ouwerkerk, C. de Bruyn, I. Halmai, R. Wuff, J. Dvorak, F. Reineke, M. Röhrig, S. Sahinbas, N. Siepmann
Structural engineers: Hochtief, Essen
HVAC engineers: HL-Technik, Munich, Ingenieurgemeinschaft Kruck, Mülheim/Ruhr

Plans of garden storey and ground floor
scale 1:1000

1 Lake
2 Terrace
3 Staff restaurant
4 Executive restaurant
5 Kitchen and pantry space
6 Dining rooms
7 Conference rooms
8 Cafeteria

9 Escape staircase
10 Entrance hall
11 Reception
12 Lift core/lift tower
13 Arrivals
14 Fire brigade lift
15 Meeting room
16 Stairs between individual floors
17 Conference room
18 Lift motor room

The cylindrical tower stands as an independent structure within a heterogeneous block development. By concentrating the volume of the building within a limited area it was possible to create an attractive landscaped park with a lake in the heart of the city. The concept of an energy-conscious tower design is reflected in the form and construction of the building. The circular plan ensures an ideal relationship between volume and surface area. The cylindrical form also results in an optimization of wind pressures, thermal losses, constructional resources and daylighting.

Despite the ubiquitous glazed skin to the building, the various functions remain legible: the entrance hall, the office storeys, the service storeys and the roof garden. Vertical circulation is housed in a satellite lift tower, which also serves as a point of orientation on each floor. The floor plans are divided into three zones: a core area used for common activities and communications (with internal staircases between some of the floors), a circular corridor zone and an outer ring of offices.

Special importance was attached to an optimum exploitation of daylight in all working areas. This was achieved by designing the façades with room-height glazing, by using extra-clear glass and by tapering the floor construction at the outer edge. Natural light is also brought into the core areas via clerestory strips at the tops of the internal partitions. The mechanical services are attuned to the personal needs of users. Members of staff can admit fresh air from outside periodically or constantly; they also have individual control over the lighting, temperature, sunshading and screening against glare in each room. When extreme weather conditions do not allow the windows to be opened, the rooms are ventilated by conventional means. To allow the thermal storage capacity of the concrete floor slabs to be exploited, they are clad on the underside with perforated metal sheeting. Integrated in the

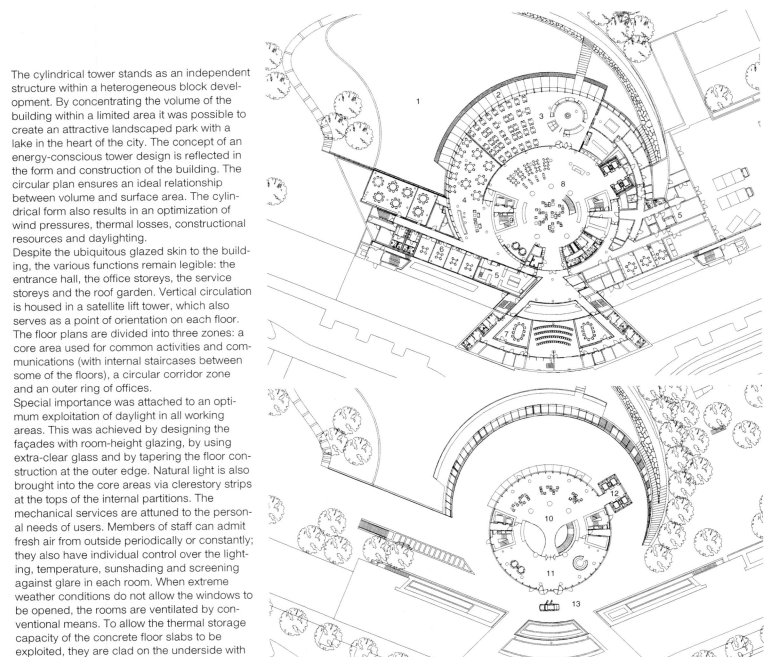

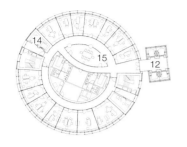

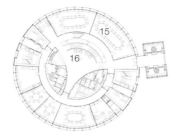

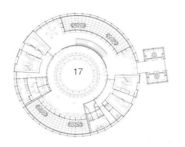

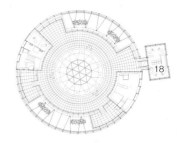

aa Standard floor

bb Meeting level

cc Conference hall

dd Roof garden

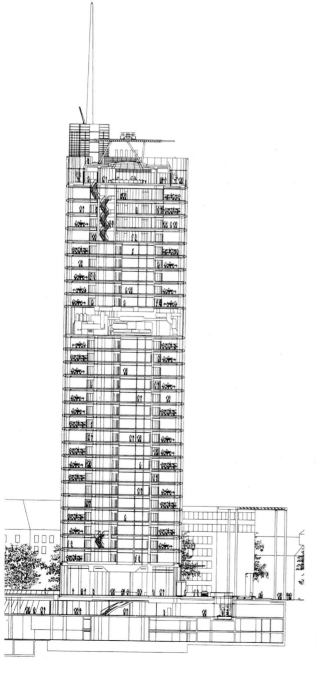

Example 21

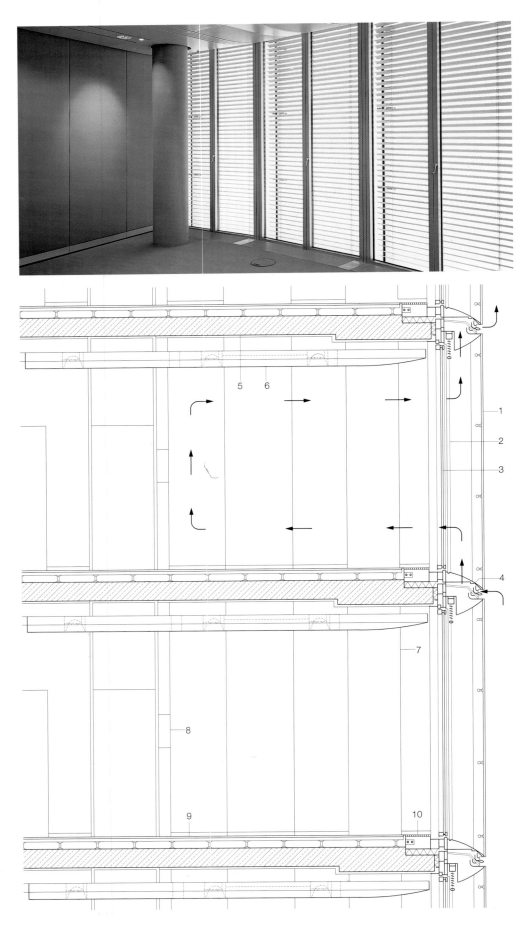

Section scale 1:50

1 outer facade layer
2 sunshading
3 inner facade layer
4 ventilation element
5 floor slab
6 multifunctional ceiling element
7 reinforced concrete column
8 control panel
9 hollow floor
10 convector duct

suspended ceiling elements are light fittings, smoke detectors, sprinklers and cold-water cooling pipes, which allow draughtproof cooling of the interior spaces.

The facade of the tower is in a ventilated double-leaf form of construction, a distinguishing feature of which is the continuous external layer of glass set in front of a conventional thermally insulated skin. The single-glazed outer layer extends up beyond the plane of the roof and protects the roof garden at 30th floor level against strong winds. The 500 mm wide intermediate space between the facade layers is divided into separate compartments along the vertical facade axes and at each floor level. The sunscreening within this space is thereby protected against the elements and is also positioned advantageously in terms of the energy concept. Under normal circumstances, the room-height sliding casements in the inner skin can be opened to a maximum width of 135 mm; for cleaning and maintenance purposes, they can be fully opened. Fresh air enters via 150 mm wide floor-level slits in the outer face and passes between sheet metal deflectors, which channel it into a convex air duct. The metal covering to these ducts is alternately perforated and unperforated from one facade element to the next, the layout being reversed at ceiling level. The diagonal ventilation route established in this way obviates the danger of a re-entry of exhaust-air from one storey to the next (see photo p. 269). The facade consists of a series of elements. All components of the inner and outer skins for each storey-height bay, including glass, opening lights and panels, are integrated in a single prefabricated element. The elements, 2 x 3.60 m (or 3.80 m) high, were transported to site on lorries and fixed to the construction foreseen for this purpose in the floor slabs. The dining rooms, conference rooms and lounges on the first basement level are separated from the park by storey-height sloping glazing. Computer-controlled manufacturing techniques facilitated the translation of this complex geometry into its finished constructional form, with metal sections and glazing of different dimensions. Three full-height sloping opening elements, operated by hydraulic rams, create a link between the internal spaces and the lakeside terrace.

Example 21

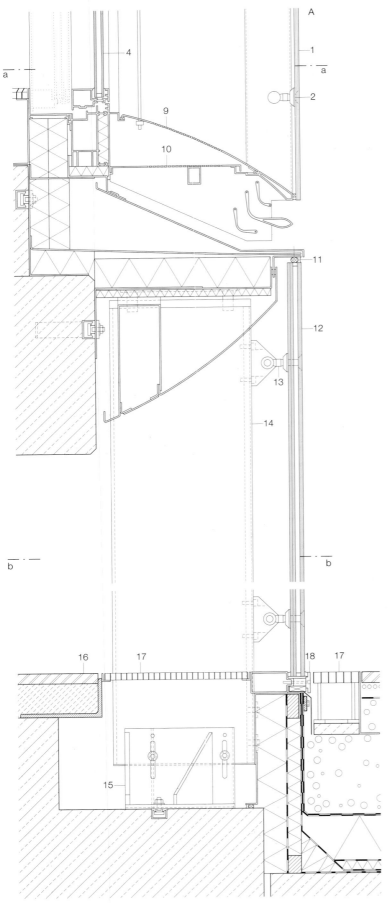

Façade details scale 1:10
A Vertical section through ground floor entrance hall
B Vertical section through top of façade (roof garden)
aa Horizontal section with abutment of partition
bb Horizontal section at ground floor level

1 outer façade: 10 mm toughened extra-clear safety glass
2 stainless steel point fixing
3 50x120 mm aluminium façade post
4 inner façade: thermally insulating double glazing: extra-clear glass in aluminium frame
5 sliding door element in alternate bays, with cranking handle for opening
6 toughened extra-clear safety glass dividing element
7 floor convector
8 175 mm office partition elements: perforated beech panels, matt varnish finish
9 4 mm natural anodized sheet aluminium hinged flap (perforated in alternate bays)
10 walkway for cleaning and inspection
11 silicone joint over backer rod
12 10 mm toughened safety glass externally; 14 mm cavity; 12 mm laminated safety glass internally
13 stainless steel point fixing for double glazing
14 aluminium façade post
15 adjustable foot to post

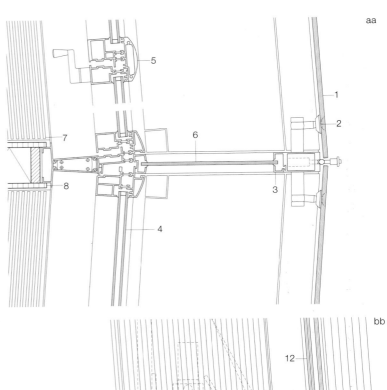

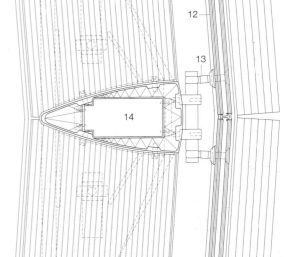

16 stone paving
17 metal grating
18 aluminium glazing bar
19 metal grating over drainage channel
20 balustrade: 12 mm toughened extra-clear safety
   glass fixed in ⌀ 100 mm aluminium handrail
21 fascia strip
22 50x280 mm stove-enamelled aluminium RHS post for
   two-storey glazing to roof garden
23 metal grating
24 4 mm sheet metal heated gutter with drainage outlets
   on façade axes within suspended soffit
25 fabric antiglare blind
26 stove-enamelled sheet metal multifunctional ceiling
   element, partly perforated
27 aluminium louvre sunshade blind
28 panel abutment; assembly joint
29 fixing head for travelling cradle
30 horizontal ventilation slit with natural anodized aluminium air deflectors
31 EPDM gasket
32 4 mm natural anodized sheet aluminium panel; perforated for ventilation in alternate bays

B

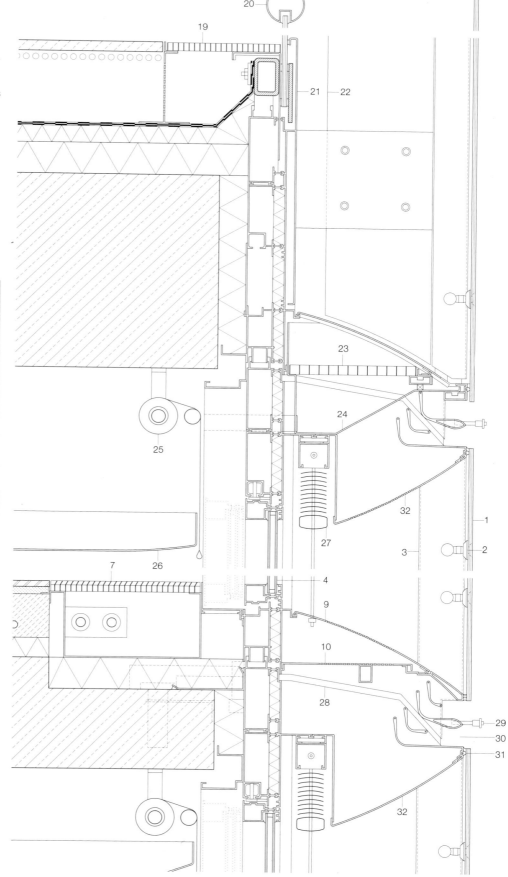

Example 21

A

B

C

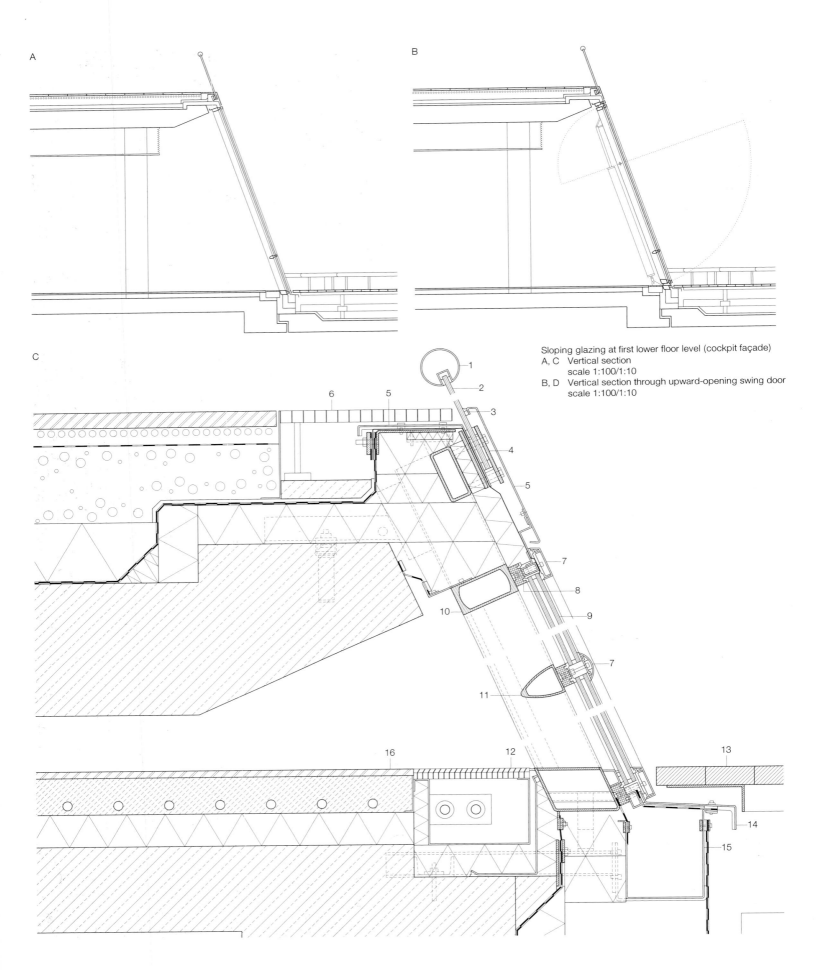

Sloping glazing at first lower floor level (cockpit façade)
A, C   Vertical section
          scale 1:100/1:10
B, D   Vertical section through upward-opening swing door
          scale 1:100/1:10

1 Ø 100 mm natural anodized aluminium handrail fixed with silicone to extra-clear glass
2 12 mm toughened extra-clear safety glass
3 silicone seal
4 steel fixing plate with EPDM underlay
5 natural anodized sheet aluminium
6 metal grating
7 aluminium glazing bar
8 EPDM strip
9 double glazing: 10 mm toughened safety glass externally; 12 mm cavity; 12 mm laminated safety glass internally
10 180x80x8 mm steel RHS with sharp arrises
11 steel rail
12 convector duct with grating cover
13 raised wood-strip flooring
14 3 mm sheet stainless steel with anti-drumming coating
15 2 mm stainless steel sheet drainage channel
16 stone paving
17 EPDM strip
18 swing door
19 hydraulic lifting mechanism
20 3 mm stainless steel sheeting

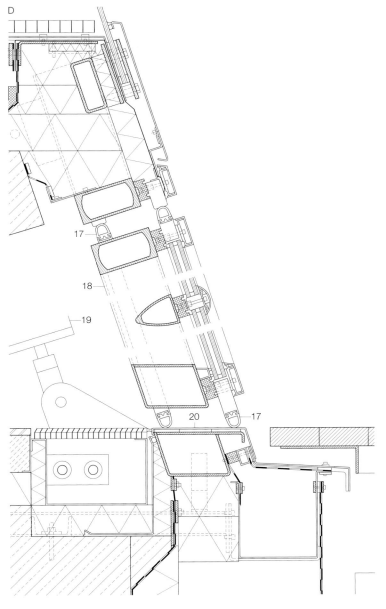

Example 22

## Administration Building in Würzburg, Germany

1995

Architects:
Webler + Geissler, Stuttgart
Martin Webler, Garnet Geissler
Assistants:
Markus Greif, Helmut Reifsteck
Structural engineers:
Rudi Wolff, Stuttgart
Planning of mechanical services:
Götz GmbH, Würzburg, Marcus Püttmer

An energy-saving building with high-quality workplaces, transparency and openness was required for the new administrative headquarters of a façade manufacturing company. The coordination of the building volume, the structure and the outer skin as well as the service installations and the control and instrumentation systems allowed the implementation of a holistic energy concept with an optimal exploitation of solar energy. The two storeys are relatively high (4.10 m) and are conceived as open-plan spaces. The partitions dividing up the few individual rooms are in a transparent frameless form of construction. They consist of 1.20 x 3.20 m laminated safety glass panels 16 mm thick which stand on the stone paving and are held in position at soffit level by metal sections on each side.

The centre and visual focus of the building is formed by the atrium. As a result of intensive planting, a pool of water and a sliding glass roof, this space makes an important contribution to the overall energy concept. The loadbearing structure is in the form of a steel frame laid out on a 12 x 12 m grid and braced around the atrium by a biaxial frame with cruciform-section columns (steel I-sections: HEB 550). The main beams spanning the width of the surrounding office zone are connected at one end to the bracing core and supported at the outer face of the building by slender tubular hinged columns with a dia-meter of 480 mm. The secondary beams – in the same plane as the main beams – are at 2.40 m centres in accordance with the finishings grid. To minimize the structural depth, the secondary beams and floors were executed in a steel and reinforced concrete composite form of construction. The trapezoidal-section metal sheeting that serves as permanent formwork assumes the function of tensile reinforcement to the concrete floor slabs.

One aim of the energy concept was to use fossil fuel only for peak loads. A major element in implementing this concept is the double-leaf façade, which functions as a climatic buffer zone around the building. It stands independently outside the loadbearing structure and is

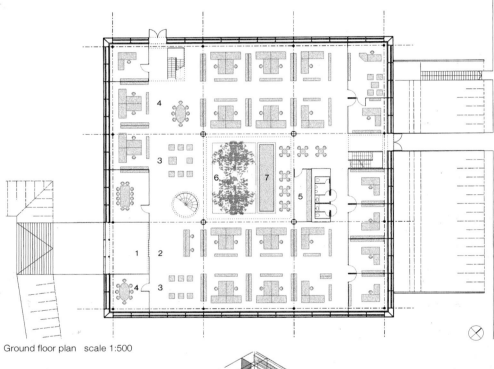

Ground floor plan   scale 1:500

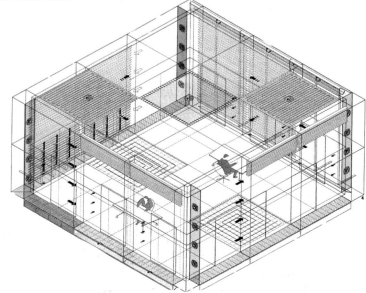

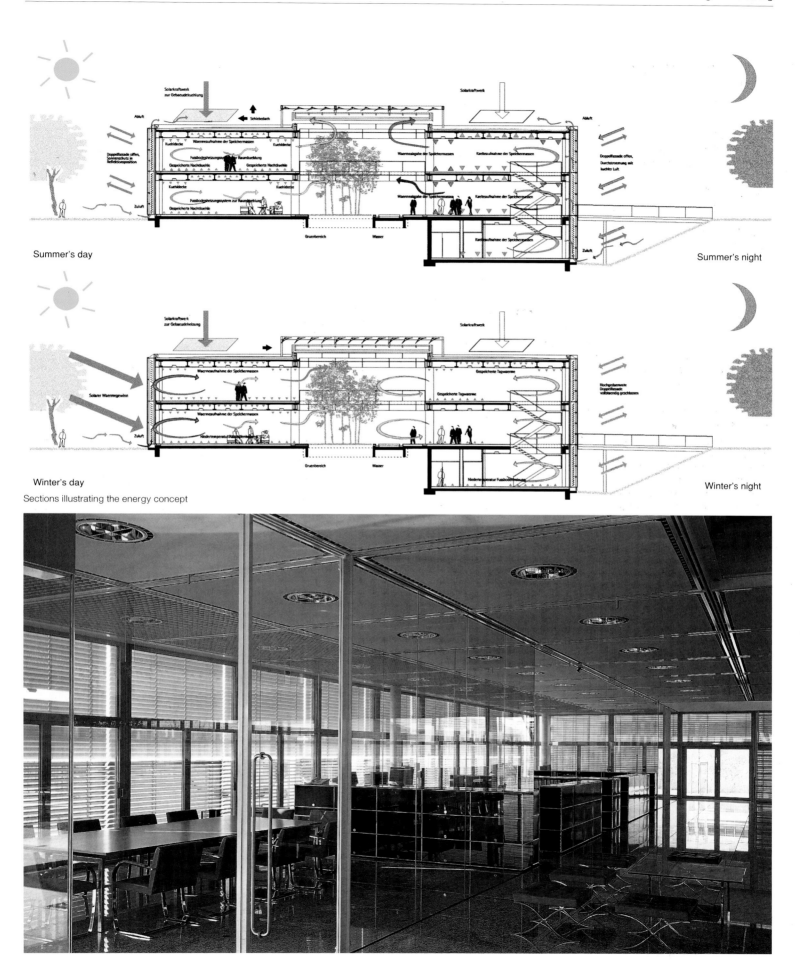

Summer's day

Summer's night

Winter's day

Winter's night

Sections illustrating the energy concept

Example 22

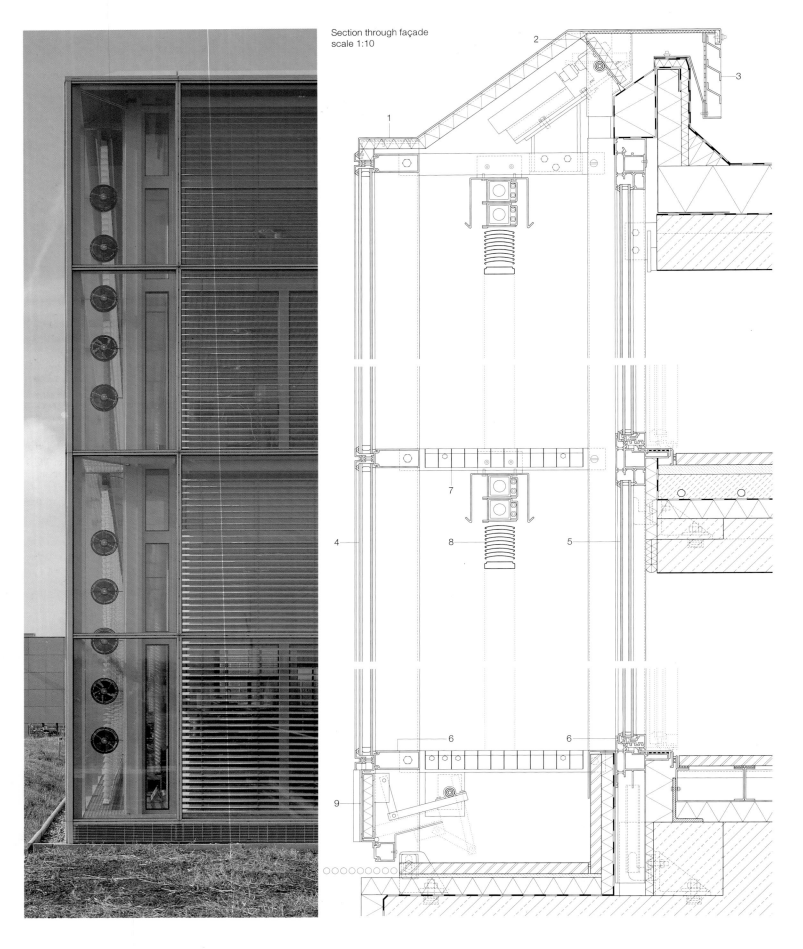

Section through façade
scale 1:10

Section through façade
scale 1:100

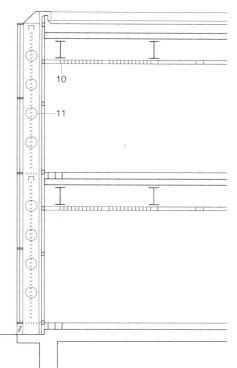

1 sheet aluminium with
  anti-drumming coating
2 upper ventilation flap
  with brush seals at
  sides
3 aluminium ventilating
  louvres with fly screen
4 outer façade glazing:
  8 mm safety glass
  externally; 22 mm cav-
  ity with inert-gas filling;
  6 mm low-e coated
  float glass
5 inner façade glazing:
  6 mm safety glass

externally; 16 mm cavity
  with inert-gas filling;
  6 mm low-e coated float
  glass
6 aluminium frame with
  thermal break
7 aluminium grating
8 blind with perforated
  lightweight metal louvres
9 lower ventilation flap
10 suspended soffit
11 axial fan

fixed solely to the floor slabs, to which horizontal loads are transmitted. The outer skin comprises a layer of fixed glazing with a post-and-rail supporting structure. Integrated in the inner façade elements are hand-operated sliding doors and motorized opening flaps, which serve as a means of ventilation. The fresh air supply is via the 600 mm intermediate space between the layers of glazing. Adjustable ventilation flaps in the outer skin in the plinth and-parapet zones allow the regulation of vertical natural convection currents. If required, axial flow fans at the corners can inject air horizontally into the façade space as a means of distributing pre-heated air. The sunshading is also installed in this space. Lightweight metal blinds either reflect direct sunlight away from the building or redirect it into the depth of the interior via the white, cotton-lined ceiling panels that serve to improve the internal acoustics. The blinds also act as a protection against glare. To the south and west faces, the lower sections of the louvres are dark-coated on one face. This considerably increases the thermal absorption capacity of the blinds if the louvres are set at the correct angle. Supply air can be heated as it passes through the intermediate space during the cold season. In summer, when the blinds are in a closed, reflecting position and the ventilation flaps are open, the building can be cooled by means of convection currents. Additional cooling is possible at night by opening the windows and the atrium roof. The thermal storage mass of the floor and roof slabs retards the heating up of the building on the following day. An adsorption heat pump can produce cold water for cooling when required, using solar energy from a 200 m$^2$ collector installation. This supplies special ceiling cooling panels along the glazed façades and in the atrium. If necessary, this installation can also supply energy for the underfloor heating, which can be regulated in separate zones. Should all this still prove inadequate, a district heating and generating plant provides the building with electricity and thermal energy. Since the cooling ceilings and the underfloor heating installation are both water-operated, the two systems can be used in reverse form. In other words, in winter, the cooling ceiling can be used for heating; and on very hot days the rooms can be cooled via the underfloor heating runs. The technical systems of the building are controlled by a computer in conjunction with a bus system, to which more than 250 indoor and outdoor sensors are connected for the meas-urement of relevant data. On the basis of this information, the control centre can react via more than 500 activators. This facilitates the operation of installations such as the solar collectors, the co-generation plant, cooling machinery, underfloor and ceiling heating, cooling ceilings and artificial lighting. In addition, there is scope for decentralized control by individual users via their computers.

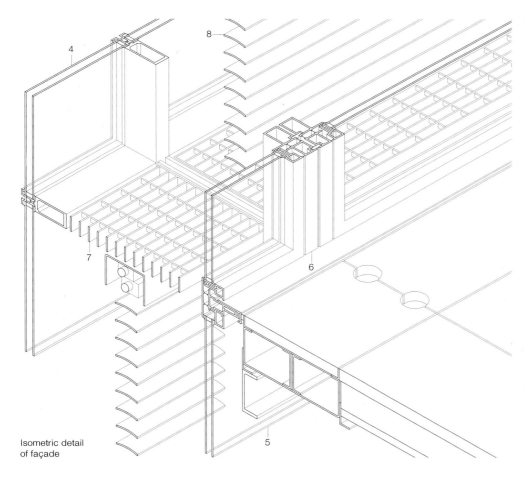

Isometric detail
of façade

Example 23

**Glass Roof to Chamber of Industry and Commerce in Stuttgart, Germany**

1996

Architects:
Kauffmann, Theilig & Partner, Stuttgart
Project architect:
Gerhard Feuerstein
Assistants:
Tanja Kampusch
Structural engineers:
Pfefferkorn & Partner, Stuttgart
Energy planning:
Transsolar, Stuttgart
Matthias Schuler, Volkmar Bleicher

So as not to obstruct the space between two existing 1950s buildings, the new entrance tract, containing reception and waiting areas, was to be as light and transparent as possible. The primary structure of the double-skin roof is formed by a grid of timber beams. The beams support the outer roof layer, which consists of thermally insulating glazed elements (U-value = 1.3 W/m²K). These elements are based on the same grid dimensions as the structure. 80% of this layer of glass is transparent. The other 20% is accounted for by closed panels and photovoltaic elements. Beneath the outer skin is a layer of glass louvres, which form the underside of the roof and which extend outside the building at the front to accentuate the entrance. The adjustable louvres act as a means of shading and daylight-redirection. They enable the roof to respond to changing seasonal and weather conditions, and allow a view out of the building even in a closed position. In winter, when the louvres are closed, a buffer zone is created, which improves the insulating value of the roof by up to 30%. On sunny winter days or during the transitional periods, the louvres can be opened, and solar energy heats the internal space. During the daytime in summer, the louvres are set at a slight angle. Solar-powered fans then extract the warm air in the roof space and at the same time draw in cool air in its wake from the existing air tunnel in the hillside. During summer nights the louvres are set in an open position so that the space can be more easily ventilated and warm air extracted. The stone floor and the side walls act as thermal storage masses. The entrance space is heated by an underfloor installation complemented by subfloor convectors. The need for finned heating tubes or radiators in front of the 8 m high façade was obviated by the use of high-quality glazing. Cooling in summer is effected by means of the air supply through the air tunnel. The length of the tunnel used for this purpose was dimensioned so that an internal temperature below 28°C can be guaranteed in the waiting areas of the hall, even in very hot periods in summer.

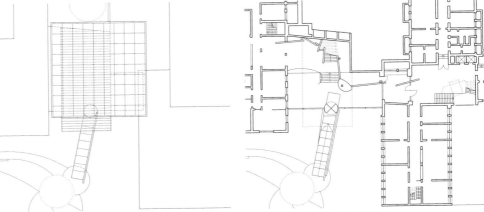

Plan of roof   scale 1:1000

Ground floor plan   scale 1:1000

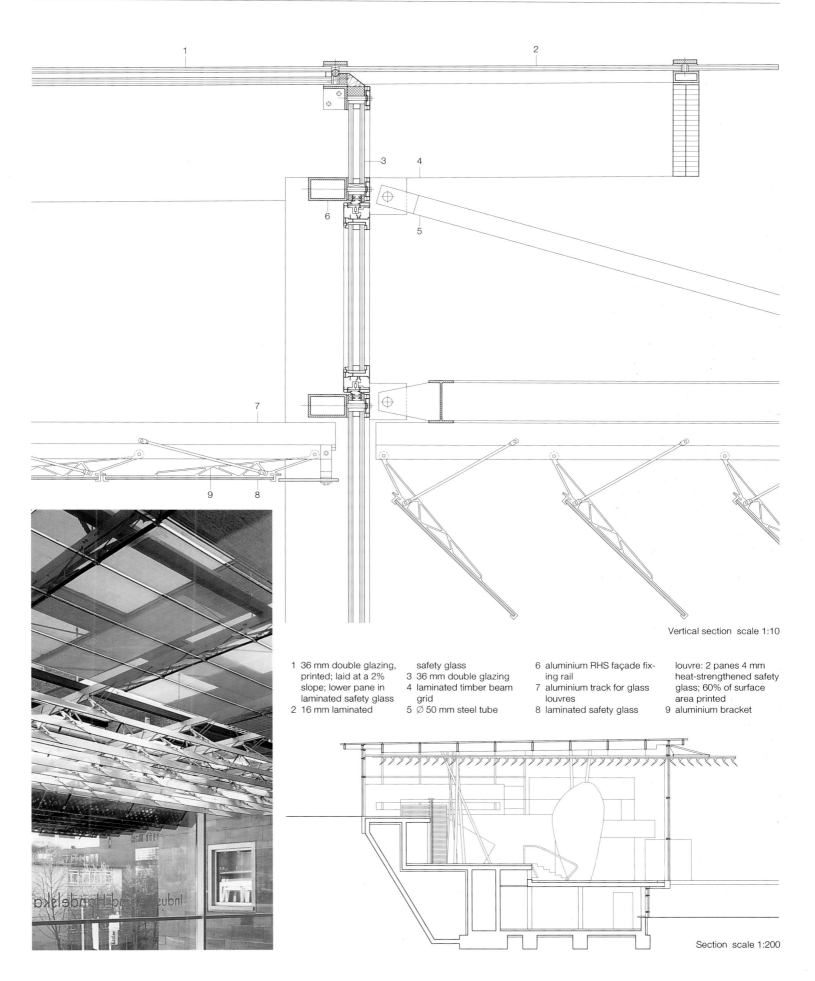

Vertical section  scale 1:10

1 36 mm double glazing,
printed; laid at a 2%
slope; lower pane in
laminated safety glass
2 16 mm laminated

safety glass
3 36 mm double glazing
4 laminated timber beam
grid
5 ⌀ 50 mm steel tube

6 aluminium RHS façade fixing rail
7 aluminium track for glass
louvres
8 laminated safety glass

louvre: 2 panes 4 mm
heat-strengthened safety
glass; 60% of surface
area printed
9 aluminium bracket

Section  scale 1:200

Example 24

## Glass Bridge in Rotterdam, The Netherlands

1994

Architects:
Dirk Jan Postel
Kraaijvanger · Urbis, Rotterdam
Structural engineers:
Rob Nijsse
ABT Velp, Arnheim

Exploded diagram

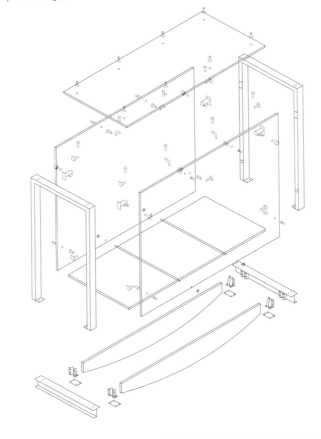

A Vertical section
B Horizontal section
scale 1:50

C Vertical section aa
D Vertical section bb:
abutment with wall
scale 1:5

1 laminated safety glass:
10 mm toughened glass
externally; 6 mm heat
strengthened glass internally
2 stainless steel point fixing
3 7 mm laser-cut stainless
steel plate
4 1.5 mm painted sheet-aluminium gutter on 18 mm
waterproof-bonded plywood
5 70x70x7 mm angle
6 80x120x6.3 mm steel RHS
7 2 panes 15 mm laminated
safety glass floor
8 3 mm sheet stainless steel
bent to shape; on 2 sheets
18 mm plywood
9 2 No. 90x90x9 mm angles
10 160 mm channel filled with
concrete
11 60x60x6 mm steel SHS
12 steel joist hanger
13 glass beam: 3 x 10 mm
laminated safety glass

This enclosed, all-glass bridge spans a distance of 3.20 m across a road and links the
rooms of the Kraaijvanger Urbis architectural practice. The architects took the brief as
the chance for an experiment to explore the
design and structural possibilities of glass
as a building material. Non-slip printing on
the floor sheet was deliberately omitted.
Walking out on to the bridge represents a
"step into the unknown"; a sense of fear has
to be overcome. On the other hand, there
are also a number of surprising, but less
breathtaking, experiences to be made.
These include lighting effects and the sensation that one's own shadow disappears
and then reappears several metres below in
the form of a silhouette on the pavement.
The floor consists of a sheet of laminated
safety glass. It is supported by two glass
beams, the form of which reflects the line of
the moment diagram. To make the system of
forces within the construction visible, the
minimally dimensioned metal connectors
are designed in different forms. They consist of standard point fixings with additional
stainless steel plates that reflect the flow of
forces at individual points. The complete
transparency of the bridge forms a striking
contrast to the solid buildings it links.

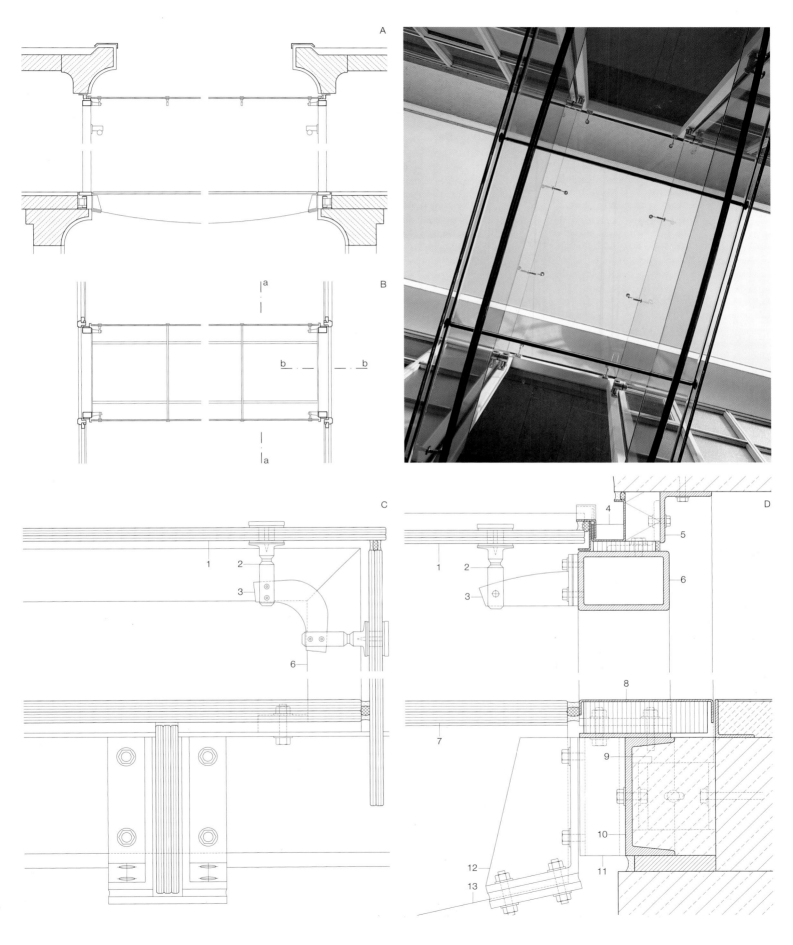

A

B

a

b b

a

C

1 2

3

6

D

4

5

6

1

2

3

7

8

9

10

11

12

13

Example 25

## Extension to Glass Museum in Kingswinford, England

1994

Architects:
Design Antenna, Richmond
Brent G. Richards, Robert Dabell
Structural engineers:
Dewhurst Macfarlane & Partners, London
Tim Macfarlane, Gary Elliot, David Wilde

The glass extension was the outcome of a refurbishment programme for the old museum building – a listed brick structure. The extension contains the new entrance to the museum and a sales area. Since the project involved a museum for glass – the collection on display contains mainly 17th- and 18th-century English glassware – it seemed appropriate to give a striking demonstration of the structural possibilities of this material. The use of glass also met conservational needs by leaving the existing structure almost wholly intact visually. The complete transparency of the extension means that the view of the old building remains virtually unimpaired.

The new glazed volume is a clear, simple structure 11 m long and 3.50 m high and is designed without visible metal connectors. The columns and beams at 1.10 m centres are in a three-ply laminated construction using resin adhesive. The 300 mm deep downstand beams span the entire 5.70 m width of the space and are fixed in steel joist hangers to the existing brick wall at the rear. At the front, along the glazed façade, the beams are connected to the columns by means of mortise and tenon joints to form a rigid frame. The lintel over the entrance is in the same form. The roof is covered with double-glazed panels 1.10 m wide laid at a 1% slope. It is designed to bear a snow load of 0.75 kN/m$^2$ and to support foot traffic for cleaning and maintenance.

The inner layer of the roof glazing is in laminated safety glass, since it is directly over the heads of visitors and staff. The outer layer, in colourless solar-control glass, is printed with a reflecting ceramic pattern as a further means of screening. These two measures meant that the transmittance of solar energy could be reduced to 37%. The façade is also clad with solar-control double glazing. Here, the energy transmittance is reduced to 59%, while the daylight illumination level is 61%.

Site plan
scale 1:2500

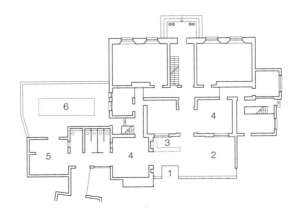

Ground floor plan
scale 1:500

1 Main entrance in new
   structure
2 Museum shop
3 Information counter

4 Exhibition spaces in
   existing building
5 Cafeteria
6 Sculpture garden

Example 25

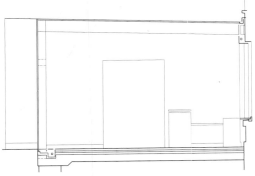

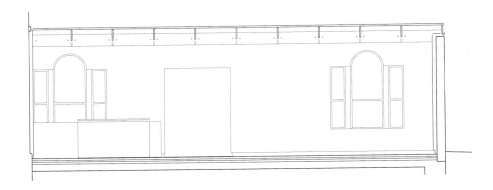

Cross-section and longitudinal section through
extension   scale 1:100

Axonometric (not to scale)

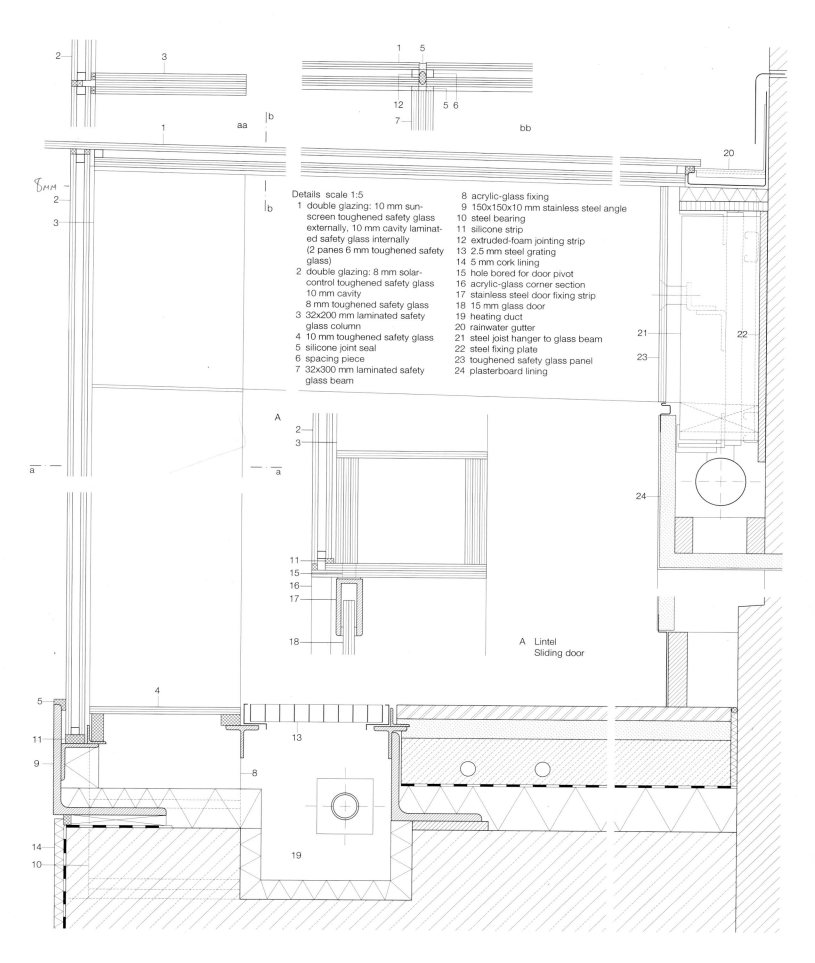

aa

bb

8MM

**Details  scale 1:5**

1  double glazing: 10 mm sun-screen toughened safety glass externally, 10 mm cavity laminated safety glass internally (2 panes 6 mm toughened safety glass)
2  double glazing: 8 mm solar-control toughened safety glass 10 mm cavity 8 mm toughened safety glass
3  32x200 mm laminated safety glass column
4  10 mm toughened safety glass
5  silicone joint seal
6  spacing piece
7  32x300 mm laminated safety glass beam

8  acrylic-glass fixing
9  150x150x10 mm stainless steel angle
10  steel bearing
11  silicone strip
12  extruded-foam jointing strip
13  2.5 mm steel grating
14  5 mm cork lining
15  hole bored for door pivot
16  acrylic-glass corner section
17  stainless steel door fixing strip
18  15 mm glass door
19  heating duct
20  rainwater gutter
21  steel joist hanger to glass beam
22  steel fixing plate
23  toughened safety glass panel
24  plasterboard lining

A  Lintel
   Sliding door

Example 26

## Museum of Art in Lille, France

1997

Architects:
Jean-Marc Ibos and Myrto Vitart, Paris
Assistants:
Pierre Cantacuzène, Sophie Nguyen
Structural engineers:
Kephren Ingénierie, Paris

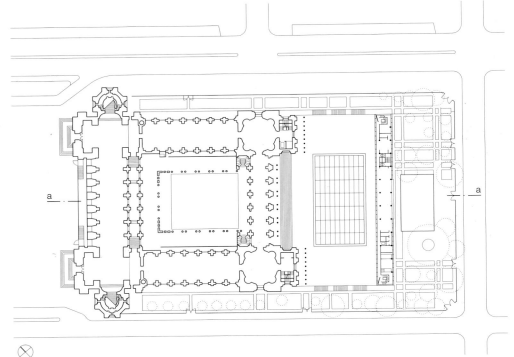

Ground floor plan   scale 1:1500

Built in 1892, the Musée des Beaux-Arts in the city of Lille in northern France contains one of the most important art collections in that country. The purpose of the refurbishment scheme was to give the old palace a new and grander appearance as a means of redressing the numerous changes and extensions it has undergone in the course of its life. Additional exhibition space was also needed. In order to open up the building towards the city without impairing the visual quality of the existing structure, the offices were moved to a separate, largely transparent tract. New gallery spaces are housed in the basement and are naturally lit via a 720 m$^2$ horizontal glass roof laid to just a 1% slope. The roof surface is at precisely the same level as the pavings to the surrounding square, in which it resembles a reflecting area of water. Although the roof is surrounded by a strip of water, designed to prevent direct access to the glass, the construction had to be able to bear foot traffic. The six aluminium-clad main beams accommodate the air-conditioning and lighting installations. A grid of channel sections assembled above the steel beams supports the 5.45 x 1.90 m glass roof panels and also drains off any water that may penetrate the outer construction. The ingress of daylight is controlled by adjustable aluminium louvres.

The façade of the office tract facing the historical building is clad with 416 panels of double glazing, the outer panes of which are in mirror glass printed on the inner face with a silver-coloured grid. As a result, the old palace is reflected in an impressionistically alienated form, and the new structure acquires an immaterial quality. To heighten the visual effect of an all-glass wall, the edge of the flat roof is detailed in a very concise form and slopes down to the rear.

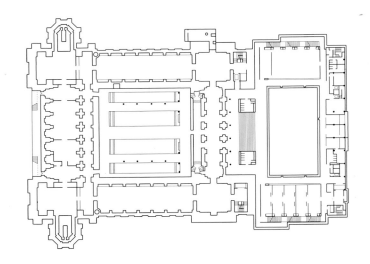

Basement plan   scale 1:1500

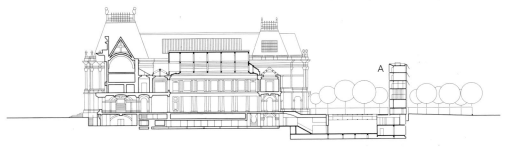

Section aa  scale 1:1500

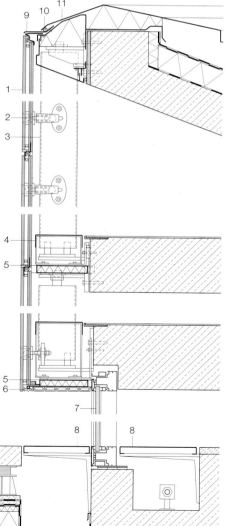

A  Section through
   façade
   scale 1:20

1 double glazing:
  12 mm toughened
  safety glass externally
  with mirrored outer
  face and ceramic
  printing on inner face
  15 mm cavity
  12 mm laminated safe-
  ty glass internally
2 cast stainless steel
  point fixings hinged in
  plane of glass
3 stainless steel post
4 perforated sheet stain-
  less steel
5 stainless steel panel
6 EPDM peripheral
  jointing section
7 laminated safety glass
  in aluminium frame
8 stainless steel grating
9 polished sheet alu-
  minium
10 silicone joint
11 aluminium sheet cov-
   ering, bent to shape

Example 26

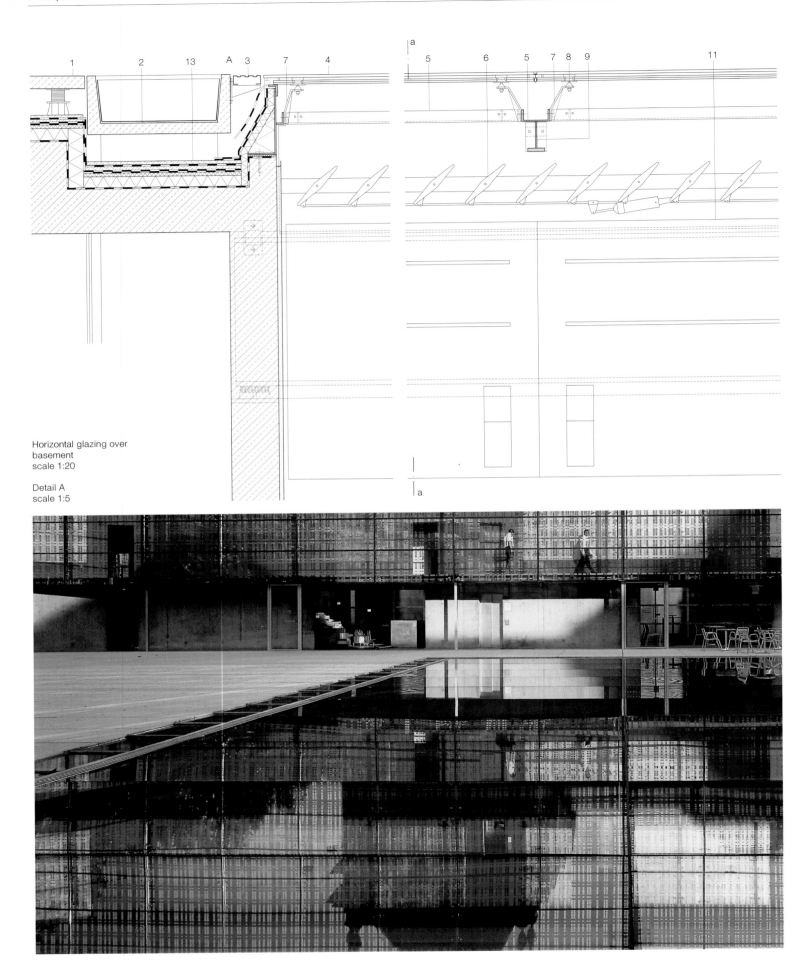

Horizontal glazing over
basement
scale 1:20

Detail A
scale 1:5

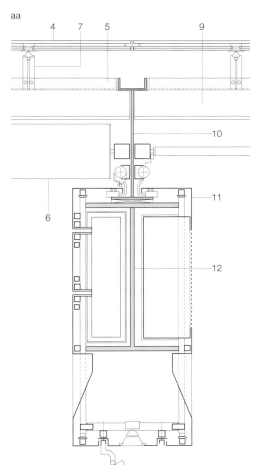

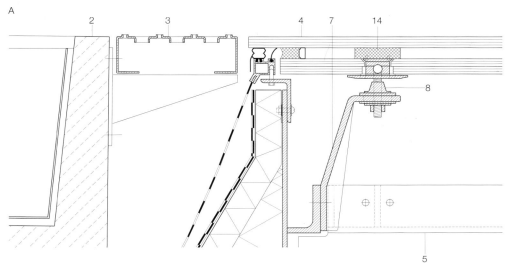

1 fine-aggregate concrete slabs on adjustable plastic
   supports
2 peripheral water channel
3 2 mm sheet stainless steel grating
4 15 mm toughened mirror glass
   black silicone joint seal
   15 mm cavity
   20 mm laminated safety glass
5 grid of 150 mm steel channels (UAP sections)
6 aluminium sunscreen louvres
7 cast-steel member bolted to steel channel grid
8 cast-steel point fixing, hinged in plane of glass
9 steel secondary beam

10 steel suspension piece for fixing louvres
11 3 mm sheet metal cladding on 30x30x2 mm
   steel SHS construction
12 steel main beam
13 2 coats 20 mm mastic asphalt
   glass-fibre mat
   plastic waterproof sheeting
   20 mm expanded clay insulation
   polythene insulation
   vapour barrier
   concrete
14 EPDM bearing

Example 27

**Research Laboratory and Architectural
Practice in Genoa, Italy**

1991

Architects:
Renzo Piano Building Workshop, Genoa
Design team: R. Piano, M. Cattaneo,
F. Marano, S. Ishida, M. Lusetti, M. Nouvion
with the support of:
M. Carroll, O. Di Blasi, R. V. Truffelli,
M. Varratta
Structural engineers:
P. Costa, Genoa

Site plan  scale 1:2000

Situated on a steep, terraced slope overlooking the Gulf of Genoa, the building accommodates the offices of the Renzo Piano Building Workshop and a laboratory financed by the UNESCO for research into the constructional principles of natural materials. The large glass roof, which follows the slope of the site, covers what is more or less a single, large continuous space. The floor is stepped down parallel to the hillside terraces. Even the entrance to the building is a dramatically staged situation. Access is via a fully glazed diagonal lift, which affords fantastic views of the sea along its route. Within the building, the glass roof and the fully glazed walls allow further views of the landscape and the sky.

The structure of the building and the materials used are extremely restrained and combine local traditions with modern state-of-the-art technology. The formal language makes reference to the greenhouses of the area. The roof is borne by laminated timber beams supported by steel columns. The individual panes of glass are fixed with adhesive to timber frames and jointed with silicone. Depending on the degree of incident solar radiation, the sun-screen louvres – operated by solar cells – are automatically closed. The dimensions of the timber beams obviate virtually any deflection, so that it was possible to construct the all-glass façade to abut the roof without slip joints. The walls are braced by slender glass fins that project from both faces.

The building not only accommodates research facilities; it was conceived as a research project in itself. Therefore, it was possible to experiment with the glass roof construction and with the indoor climate. Experience gained in the first few years shows that the internal spaces are subject to overheating on hot summer days, despite the air-conditioning and sunshading. This was partly the outcome of a lack of thermal storage mass. This deficiency was accepted in view of the high design quality and the successful use of glass and timber in combination with each other.

Plan   scale 1:500

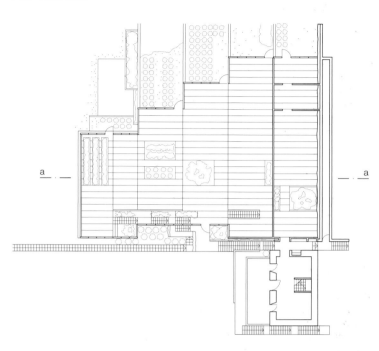

a ―  ·―                                                                      a ― ·―

Section aa   scale 1:500

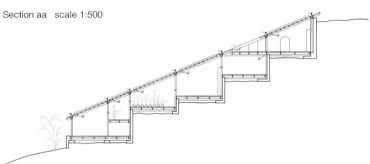

Example 27

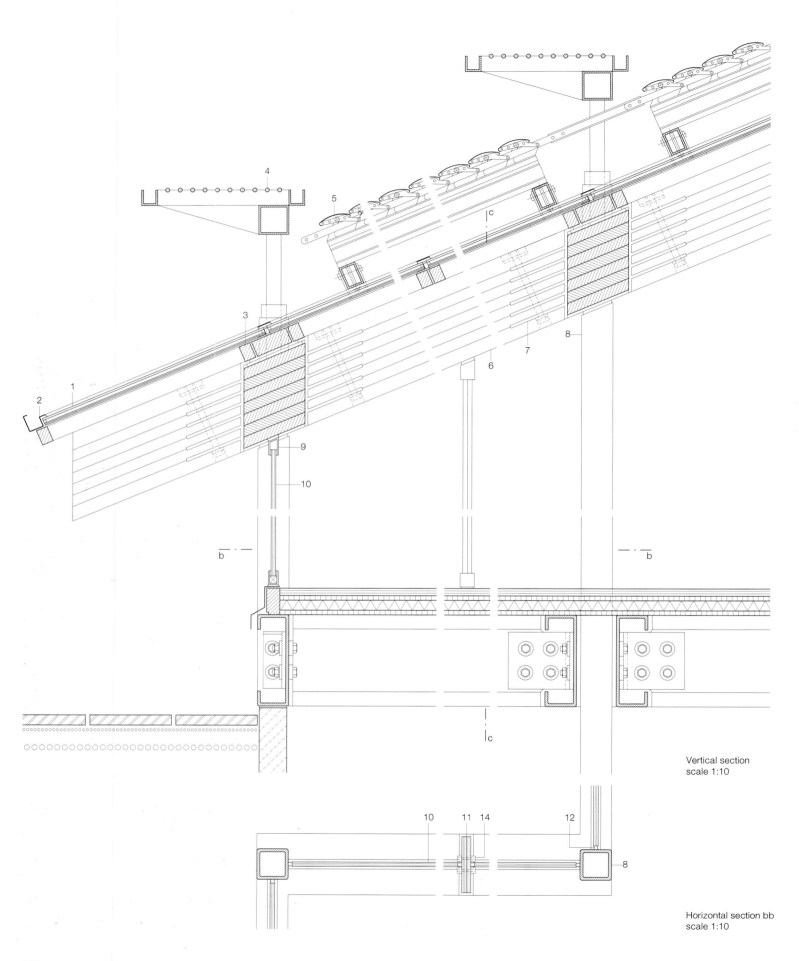

Vertical section
scale 1:10

Horizontal section bb
scale 1:10

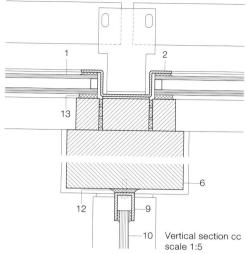

1 double glazing (6 + 15 + 6 mm); lower pane in laminated safety glass
2 sheet stainless steel rainwater gutter
3 34x45 mm wood frame
4 galvanized steel maintenance catwalk
5 adjustable aluminium sunscreen louvre
6 160x240 mm laminated timber beam
7 node connector: welded steel plates
8 85x85 mm steel SHS column
9 aluminium section
10 10 mm toughened safety glass
11 2 panes 10 mm laminated safety glass fin
12 elastic seal
13 silicone adhesive joint
14 acrylic-glass fixing piece, screwed to both faces of glass fin

Vertical section cc
scale 1:5

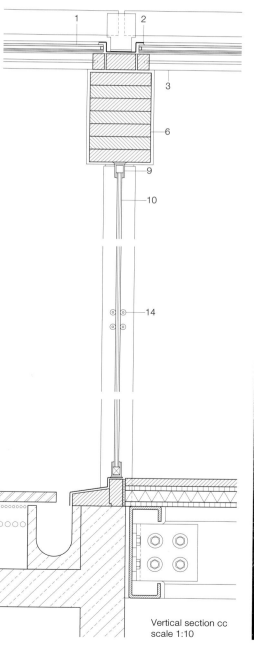

Vertical section cc
scale 1:10

Example 28

**Secondary School in Flöha, Germany**

1996

Architects:
Markus Allmann, Amandus Sattler, Ludwig
Wappner, Munich
Assistants: Karin Hengher, Robinson Pourroy,
Detlev Böwing, Katharina Duer, Kilian Jokisch,
Astrid Jung, Anita Moum, Susanne Rath, Jan
Schabert, Dominikus Stark
Structural engineers:
Obermeyer Albis Bauplan, Chemnitz
Ingenieurgesellschaft Hagl, Munich
Façade consultants:
Richard Fuchs, Munich

The new school is situated in a virtually
untouched meadow landscape on the outskirts
of a small town. In order to impinge as little as
possible on the natural surroundings, the ring-
shaped building is raised 4 m above the
ground for most of its area and seems to hover
over the site. The circular form is also an
expression of the community of pupils. The
organization of the school building is quite simple. The southern section of the two-storey ring
houses the classrooms. Course rooms and
specialist classrooms are accommodated in
the northern part. On the ground floor are
rooms for teachers and the administration. The
structure within the ring, covered by an
inclined roof, contains the indoor recreation
hall used during school breaks as well as
spaces for special uses. The façades to the
raised tracts are in a metal and glass form of
construction suspended from the face of the
building. The outer façade of the ring is boldly
articulated by broad cantilevered sunshading
elements and escape balconies. The elevation
overlooking the courtyard was designed in a
more planar form, without cover strips and vertical sections. Here, the boundary between
inside and outside is dissolved. The pressure
and suction loads to which the panes of glass
are subjected are borne by internal flat steel
sections. A special feature of the complex is
the finely articulated glazed roof – with a slope
of 4.5% – over the recreation hall. Narrow panels of double glazing are suspended from the
external steel structure by hinged point fixings.
The slim glazing construction goes almost to
the bounds of technical feasibility, since the
additional loads acting on the panes of glass
and caused by atmospheric changes of pressure in the cavity between the layers of double
glazing are quite considerable. This loading
had to be taken into account in the structural
calculations. To ensure a means of ventilation
at the edges of the double glazing, the joints
were sealed with silicone only in the topmost
layer. Sunshading is provided by the external
steel structure and by ceramic printing on the
glass surfaces.

Site plan   scale 1:2500

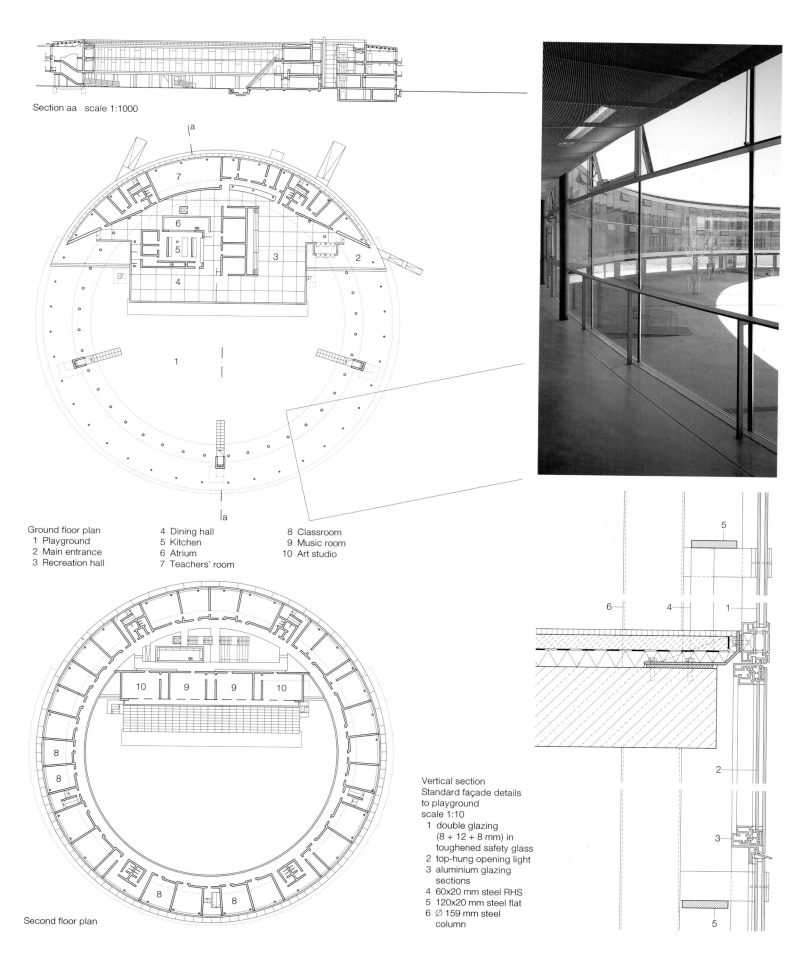

Section aa   scale 1:1000

Ground floor plan
1 Playground
2 Main entrance
3 Recreation hall
4 Dining hall
5 Kitchen
6 Atrium
7 Teachers' room
8 Classroom
9 Music room
10 Art studio

Second floor plan

Vertical section
Standard façade details
to playground
scale 1:10
1 double glazing
  (8 + 12 + 8 mm) in
  toughened safety glass
2 top-hung opening light
3 aluminium glazing
  sections
4 60x20 mm steel RHS
5 120x20 mm steel flat
6 Ø 159 mm steel
  column

Example 28

Section
scale 1:250

A    B         C

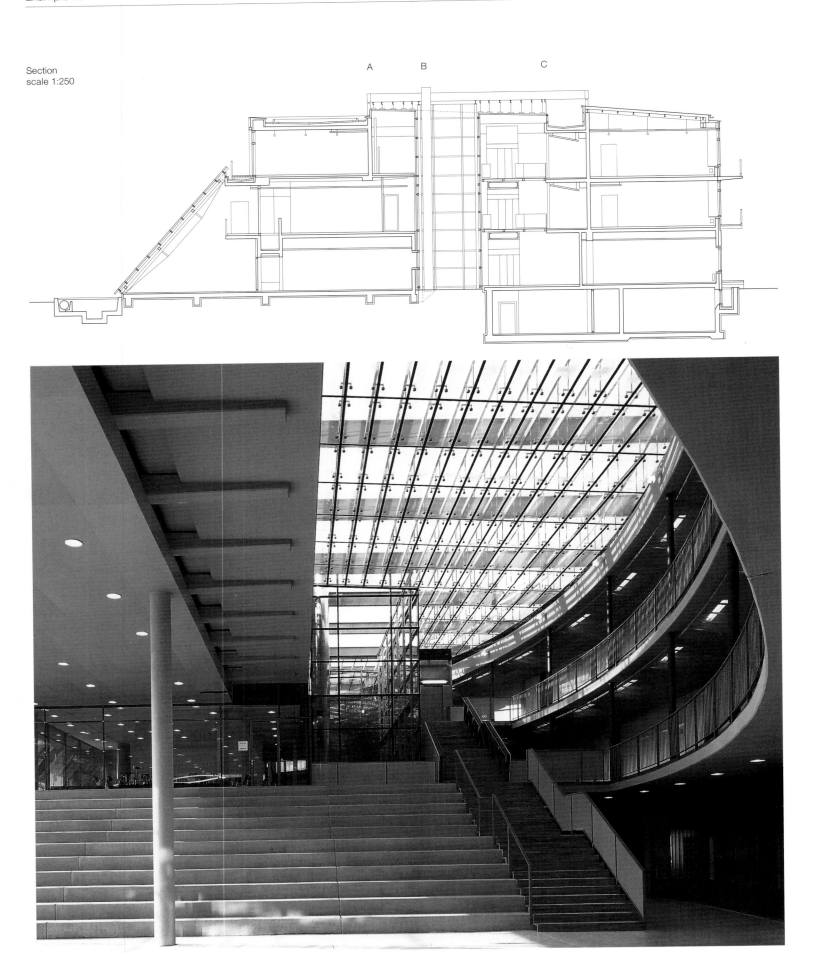

296

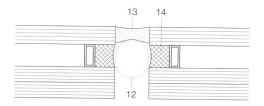

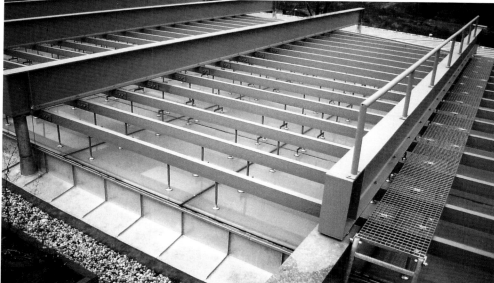

Glass joint, scale 1:2.5
Sectional details through
glass roof with 4.5% slope
scale 1:10

1 double glazing:
   12 mm toughened
   safety glass externally
   12 mm cavity
   16 mm laminated safe-
   ty glass: 2 panes
   8 mm heat-strength-
   ened glass
2 stainless steel point
   fixing
3 ⌀ 16 mm steel suspen-
   sion tube

4 steel channel beam
   140 mm deep
5 steel channel edge
   beam 180 mm deep
6 360x600 mm steel
   I-beam (IPE)
7 ⌀ 165 mm steel column
8 double glazing
9 aluminium glazing bar
10 panel
11 smoke-extract flap
12 assembly tube
13 silicone joint
14 UV-resistant silicone
   edge seal

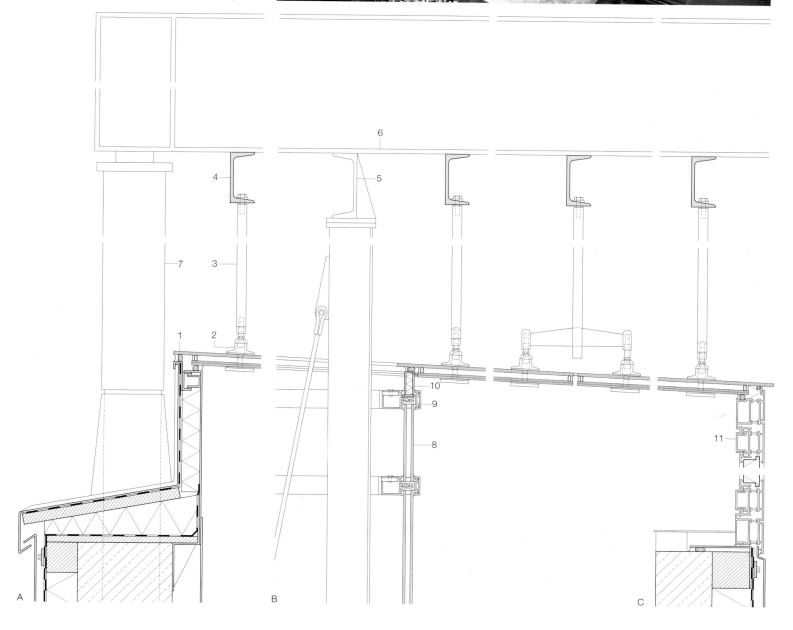

A                    B                    C

Example 29

**Glass Roof over a Castle Ruin in Alto Adige, Italy**

1996

Architect:
Robert Danz, Schönaich
Site management:
Konrad Bergmeister, Bressanone
Structural engineers:
Delta-X, Stuttgart
Albrecht Burmeister, E. Ramm, Stuttgart

A Plan
B Section aa
C North-east elevation
scale 1:400

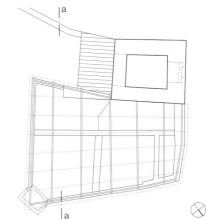

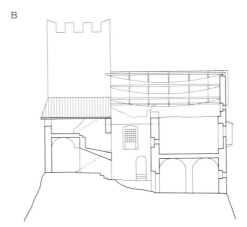

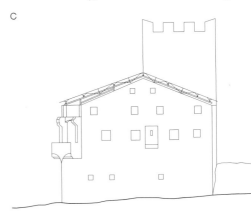

In the Middle Ages, Juval Castle, situated on an outcrop of rock nearly 1,000 metres above sea level, guarded the entrance to the Schnals Valley in the Vintschgau region. After changing hands many times it was acquired in 1983 by the mountaineer Reinhold Messner and underwent a gradual process of renovation. The erection of the roof over the ruined area next to the keep marked the conclusion of the construction work. This measure was designed to preserve the walls from further decay and to make the internal space available for sculpture exhibitions. A glass structure was chosen for conservational reasons. In its form, the roof follows the lines of the original construction. Fixed at only a few points to the existing walls and extending beyond them by between 250 and 400 mm at the edges, it seems to hover above the historic ruins. To strengthen the impression of a spatial enclosure, the lower layer of the laminated glazing is in green-tinted glass. The panes of glass are trussed on the underside in the direction of the slope and connected to the main beams – which run parallel to the ridge – by means of hinged point fixings and balance arms. The structural calculations assumed a loading of 1.85 kN/m$^2$ for snow and dead loads. The trapezoidal plan form of the building resulted in a radial layout, which meant that all the glass panes have different dimensions. The process of cutting the panes to size and drilling them was performed electronically.

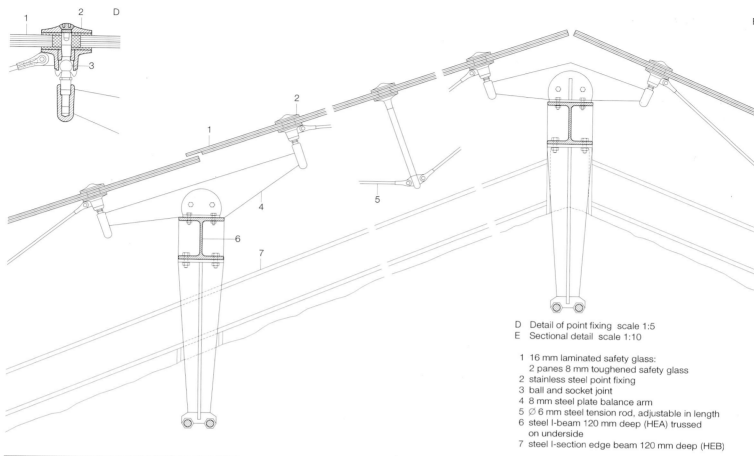

D   Detail of point fixing  scale 1:5
E   Sectional detail  scale 1:10

1   16 mm laminated safety glass:
    2 panes 8 mm toughened safety glass
2   stainless steel point fixing
3   ball and socket joint
4   8 mm steel plate balance arm
5   Ø 6 mm steel tension rod, adjustable in length
6   steel I-beam 120 mm deep (HEA) trussed
    on underside
7   steel I-section edge beam 120 mm deep (HEB)

Example 30

## New Trade Fair Hall in Leipzig, Germany

1996

Architects:
von Gerkan, Marg + Partner, Aachen/Leipzig
Design: Volkwin Marg
Partner in charge of project: Hubert Nienhoff
Structural engineers: Polónyi + Partner,
Cologne
Steel and glass structures in central hall:
von Gerkan, Marg + Partner, Leipzig,
in collaboration with Ian Ritchie Architects,
London

The New Trade Fair in Leipzig was erected on the northern outskirts of the city in an area spoiled by indiscriminate developments. The centrepiece of the complex is the large glazed hall, which is flooded with light. It serves as the reception and circulation area for the fair and as a means of orientation on the site. Its formal language reveals the influence of the large railway stations of the 19th century with their broad arched trusses. As in those structures, one of the special features of the Leipzig Fair hall is the combination of glass and steel.
The loadbearing structure consists of ten large tubular lattice girders at 25 m centres, which stabilize the tubular grid barrel vault.
Attached to the transverse arched members of this grid are cast-steel fixing arms from which the glazed enclosing skin of the hall is suspended. To reduce the loads on the vaulted structure, the two end faces of the hall were designed as self-supporting elements. The glazed skin with its point fixings represented the main challenge of the scheme, however. In order to counteract potential deformation in the outer structure and deflection in the individual panes of glass, a system had to be devised

Site plan  scale 1:8000

 1  Trade fair arrivals
 2  Pool of water
 3  Western entrance hall
 4  Pocket Park
 5  Eastern entrance hall
 6  Eastern park
 7  Fair tower
 8  Administration
 9  Trade centre
10  Forum
11  High hall
12  Hall restaurant
13  Exhibition hall
14  Conferences
15  Open-air exhibition area
16  Parking

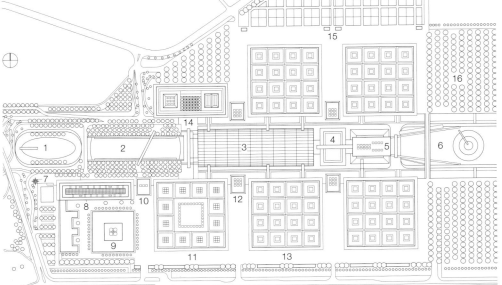

that guaranteed a concordant (non-constricting) form of glass support. A system of ball-and-socket joints in the plane of the glass was not adequate in this case. A decision was made, therefore, to use three different kinds of glass fixings, which would allow different degrees of latitude. The first type is rigidly fixed in the plane of the glass panels. The second permits deflection in the plane of the glass in a single direction. Flexibility is provided in this case by a simple axial hinge. The third type of fixing allows deflection in all directions; in other words, the panes of glass are fixed only along the vertical axis. In this case, a ball-and-socket joint is used to achieve the necessary flexibility.

The laminated safety glass panels are 1524 x 3105 mm in size. The upper sheet is inset from the lower pane by 10 mm on all edges. The flexible jointing loops between panels are fixed with adhesive in the rebate thus created. They serve to close the joints, which have a mean width of 20 mm, and they can accommodate calculated movements of ± 8 mm. The points of intersection between the jointing loops are covered with purpose-made overlapping pieces fixed with adhesive. The joints to the glass are sealed with injected silicone.

The problem of overheating in summer is overcome by natural ventilation. Fresh air enters the hall between glass louvres that extend in a continuous band up to a height of 2.5 m above the base of the outer skin. The intake of cool air forces the warm air within the building upwards to the glass flaps along the crest of the roof where it can escape. These flaps also serve as smoke-extract openings in the event of fire. Ceramic printing on the surface of the glass reduces solar gains in critical areas, and the external loadbearing structure shades roughly 15% of the surface exposed to solar radiation. On very hot days, the areas of glazing can be sprayed with decalcified water from an external washing installation. This leads to a process of evaporative cooling.

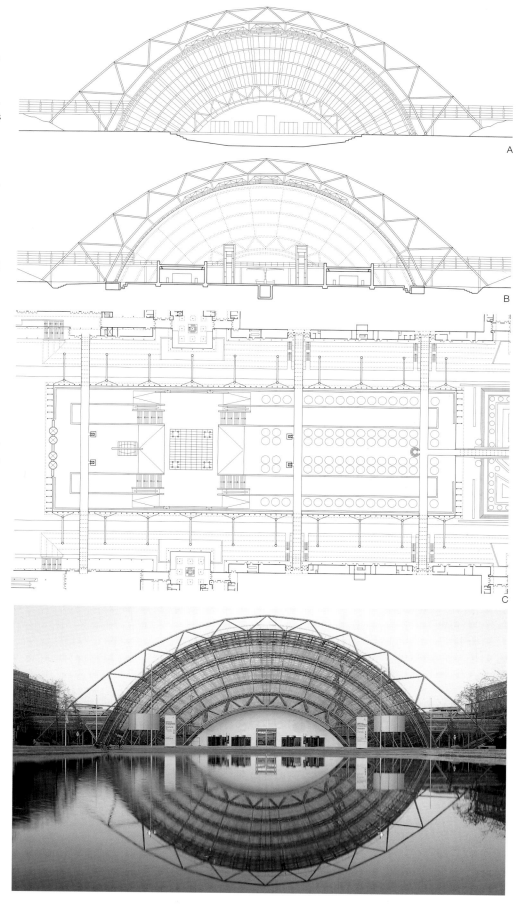

A   Elevation
B   Section
    scale 1:1000
C   Plan
    scale 1:2500

Example 30

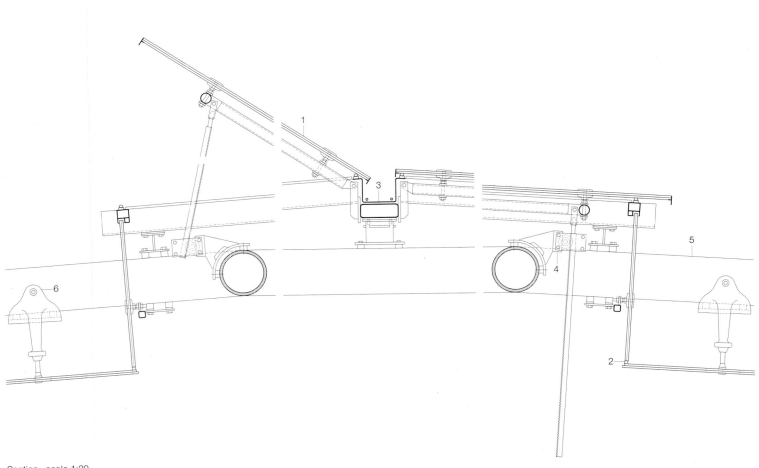

Section   scale 1:20

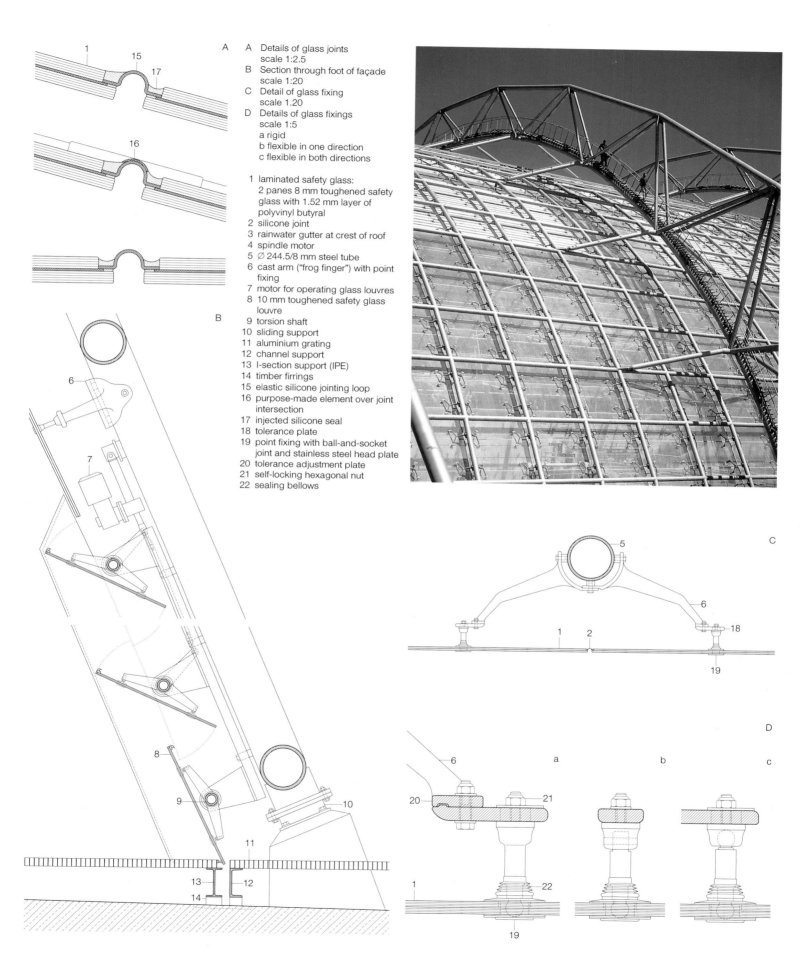

A
A  Details of glass joints
   scale 1:2.5
B  Section through foot of façade
   scale 1:20
C  Detail of glass fixing
   scale 1.20
D  Details of glass fixings
   scale 1:5
   a rigid
   b flexible in one direction
   c flexible in both directions

1  laminated safety glass:
   2 panes 8 mm toughened safety
   glass with 1.52 mm layer of
   polyvinyl butyral
2  silicone joint
3  rainwater gutter at crest of roof
4  spindle motor
5  ⌀ 244.5/8 mm steel tube
6  cast arm ("frog finger") with point
   fixing
7  motor for operating glass louvres
8  10 mm toughened safety glass
   louvre
9  torsion shaft
10 sliding support
11 aluminium grating
12 channel support
13 I-section support (IPE)
14 timber firrings
15 elastic silicone jointing loop
16 purpose-made element over joint
   intersection
17 injected silicone seal
18 tolerance plate
19 point fixing with ball-and-socket
   joint and stainless steel head plate
20 tolerance adjustment plate
21 self-locking hexagonal nut
22 sealing bellows

Example 31

## Station in London

1994

Architects:
Nicholas Grimshaw and Partners, London
Nick Grimshaw, Neven Sidor, David Kirkland,
Ursula Heinemann
Structural engineers:
Anthony Hunt Associates, Cirencester
Tony Hunt, Alan Jones, Mike Otlet,
David Dexter

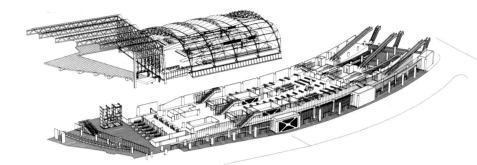

Isometric view of layout

Waterloo International Terminal is the British
point of access to the Channel Tunnel rail link,
which connects London with Paris and Brussels in only three hours' travelling time. The
structure echoes the tradition of the English
station halls of the 19th century. At the same
time, it is a symbol of a new age of rail travel.
The most distinctive feature of the scheme is
the curving glazed roof, which results in a station flooded with light. The whole appearance
is dominated by the use of glass, a material
that is also used innovatively in the suspended
partitions and façades of this development.
The main problem to be overcome in designing
the terminal was posed by the confined inner-
city site at the edge of the old main-line station.
The architects solved this by allowing the
400 m long structure to follow the meandering
lines of the tracks. The span of the roof varies
from about 32 m to 48 m.
The functional organization of the station is
comparable to that of an airport. Platforms,
arrival and departure areas are clearly separated and are located on different floor levels.
The platforms, which are on the same level as
the existing Waterloo Station, are covered by
the single-span glass roof. On the floor below
this are the departure areas. After proceeding
through the zone for ticket and security
checks, passengers enter a waiting area, from
where escalators convey them up to the trains.
Conversely, arriving passengers are conducted down from the platforms to passport and
customs controls. The spaces on the lower levels, which are naturally lit through the frameless glazing to the west face, are accessible to
the general public and contain waiting areas,
shops and offices.
The filigree roof structure consists of pairs of
bowstring trusses joined off-centre to form flattened triple-hinged arches, which are resolved
into tension and compression members. The
subtlety of the roof lies in its asymmetric form.
The reason for this is a track on the western
edge of the terminal, where the line of the roof
has to rise more steeply in order to provide
adequate headroom for trains. In this area, the
loadbearing structure is located outside the
roof skin.

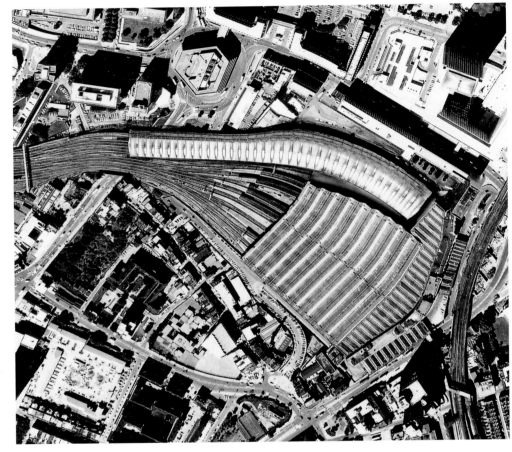

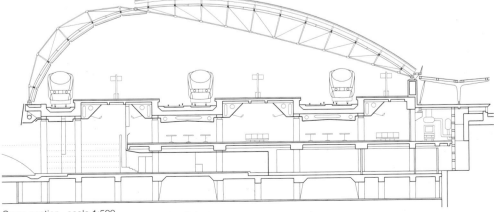

Cross-section   scale 1:500

Example 31

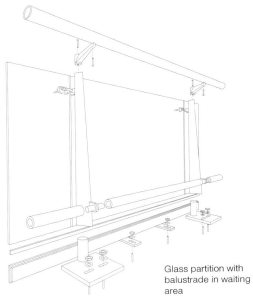

Glass partition with balustrade in waiting area

To ensure an economic use of materials, the cross-section of each transverse compression chord of the trusses varies in accordance with the forces to which it is subjected. The difference between the two parts of the arched trusses is reflected in the form of the roof skin. The flatter side adjoining the old station hall consists of closed bays of roofing alternating with glazed strips. The steeper side, in contrast, is completely transparent.

The scale-like glazing to this complex form, which is curved in two directions, was executed with standard, rectangular, single-sized glass panes. The glazing sections are fixed to stainless steel hinged connecting pieces that allow the roof skin to move. The panes of safety glass are fixed at the sides with neoprene strips designed to fit different joint spacings and absorb movement in the skin. Bracing between the main trusses is provided by diagonal tension rods.

The two-storey public space along the west face is divided from the waiting rooms by a frameless, suspended glass partition. Like the street façade, which is in a similar form, this glazed partition has to accommodate different degrees of movement, which at times may be quite considerable. Thermal expansion over the entire length of the reinforced concrete structure, for example, can be as much as 55 mm; and the deflection to which the coffered ceiling is subjected is roughly 11 mm with each arriving train.

Flexible stainless steel bolts in the four-point cast-steel glass connectors permit movement between the individual panes. The uppermost panes of glass are each suspended from the ceiling from a single point in the middle. Via the four-point connectors, they bear the weight of all the panes below them. The glazed wall is braced by suspended glass fins. The joints are elastically sealed with injected black silicone.

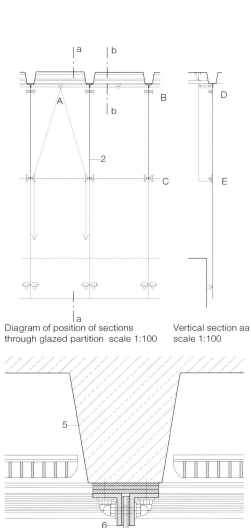

Diagram of position of sections
through glazed partition scale 1:100

Vertical section aa
scale 1:100

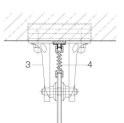

Vertical section bb
scale 1:10

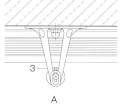

A

Vertical section
section 1:10

1 12 mm toughened
   safety glass
2 12 mm toughened
   safety glass fin
3 cast stainless steel
   glass suspension ele-
   ment
4 flexible EPDM seal
5 reinforced concrete
   coffered ceiling

6 65x85x12 mm stain-
   less steel angles for
   suspending glass fin
7 cast stainless steel
   four-point connector
8 stainless steel flex-
   ible bolt
9 flush point fixing

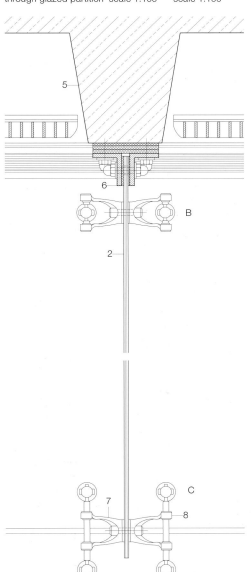

Vertical section cc
scale 1:10

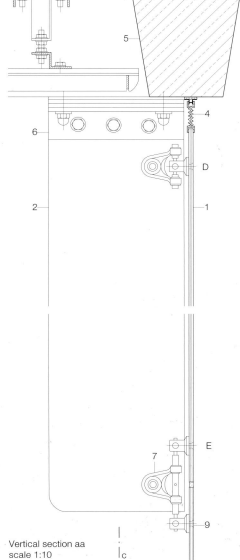

Vertical section aa
scale 1:10

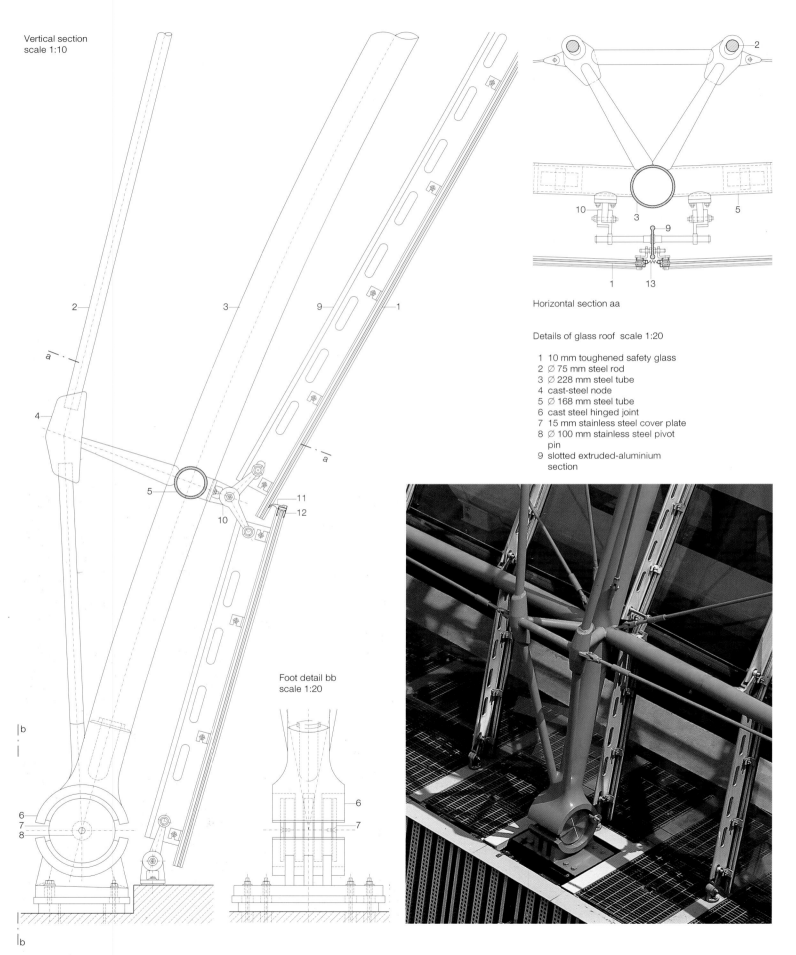

Example 31

Vertical section
scale 1:10

a

2

3 9 1

a

4

5

10

11
12

6
7
8

b

Foot detail bb
scale 1:20

6

7

b

2

10 5

3

1 13

Horizontal section aa

Details of glass roof  scale 1:20

1  10 mm toughened safety glass
2  ∅ 75 mm steel rod
3  ∅ 228 mm steel tube
4  cast-steel node
5  ∅ 168 mm steel tube
6  cast steel hinged joint
7  15 mm stainless steel cover plate
8  ∅ 100 mm stainless steel pivot
   pin
9  slotted extruded-aluminium
   section

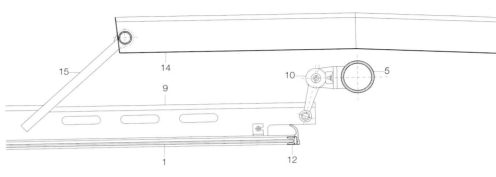

Longitudinal section through gutter   scale 1:20

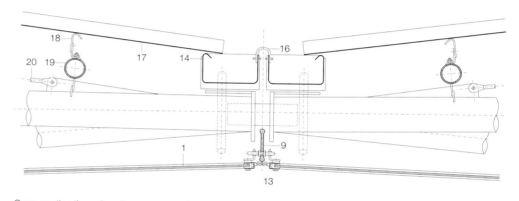

10 cast stainless steel hinge
11 EPDM sealing strip
12 aluminium glazing section
13 EPDM jointing strip
14 2 mm sheet stainless steel rainwater gutter
15 stainless steel drainpipe
16 EPDM joint cover strip
17 stainless steel trapezoidal-section sheeting
18 stainless steel rail, adjustable in height
19 ⌀ 114 mm steel tube
20 ⌀ 23 mm steel rod

Cross-section through gutter over expansion joint   scale 1:20

Example 32

## Exhibition and Congress Building in Linz, Austria

1994

Architects (design and planning):
Herzog + Partner, Munich
Thomas Herzog and Hanns Jörg Schrade
Project supervision/technical management:
Heinz Stögmüller, Linz
Structural engineers:
Sailer + Stepan, Munich
Daylight technology:
Christian Bartenbach, Aldrans

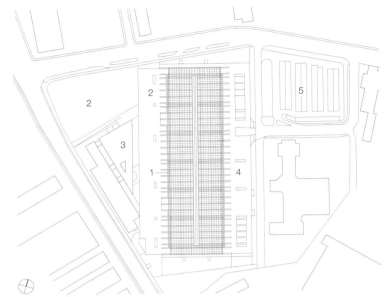

Site plan
scale 1:4000

1 Congress and exhibition hall
2 Open-air exhibition area
3 Hotel with restaurant
4 Deliveries
5 Parking area

The congress and exhibition hall in Linz city centre represents a reinterpretation of the "Crystal Palace" concept. The full glazing to this large clear-span structure allows daylight qualities to be achieved internally that one might expect in the open air. Here, however, the quality of light entering the building is controlled and improved, and greater thermal losses are avoided. The arched cross-section of the hall allows an optimum use of space, providing different room heights from area to area; it also reduces the volume of air to be heated. The maximum room height is limited to that required for staging trade fairs. The loadbearing structure of the hall consists of 34 steel box girders at 7.20 m (and 2.40 m) centres. The trusses span a distance of 73 m. The crest of the roof was designed in a form that facilitates the natural ventilation of the building. Horizontal forces resulting from the thrust of the arches are resisted by tension cables spanned between the anchor points at the feet of the girders. Secondary beams along the length of the hall, fixed at 2.70 m centres between the main girders, form the supporting structure for the coated, thermally insulating, laminated glazing panels to the roof. Between the two layers of glazing is a new type of grid – only 16 mm deep and coated with a thin layer of pure aluminium. These units allow daylight to enter indirectly via closely spaced rows of tiny "light shafts"; at the same time, they prevent the ingress of direct solar radiation. The geometry of these grids varies, depending on their position on the arched roof. In this way, an optimum exploitation of daylight is achieved without glare or overheating.

The hall in Linz shows that when daylight-redirection and energy-control functions are added to the traditional protective role of a roof, the skins of buildings are subject to technical and constructional changes that also have an influence on the aesthetic effect.

A View from above
B Lateral abutment
C Longitudinal abutment
 scale 1:5

D Functional principle of
 sunshading grid

1 double glazing:
 6 mm toughened safe-
 ty glass externally
 lighting grid
 laminated safety glass
 internally: 2 panes
 6 mm toughened safe-
 ty glass
2 stainless steel glazing
 bar
3 EPDM seal
4 steel I-beam 100 mm
 deep (IPE)

a 6 mm toughened safe-
 ty glass externally
b laminated safety glass
 internally: 2 panes
 6 mm toughened safe-
 ty glass
c grid strips barring
 direct ingress of sun-
 light
d secondary bars at right
 angles to reflecting
 strips
e surface reflecting solar
 radiation

B

C

A

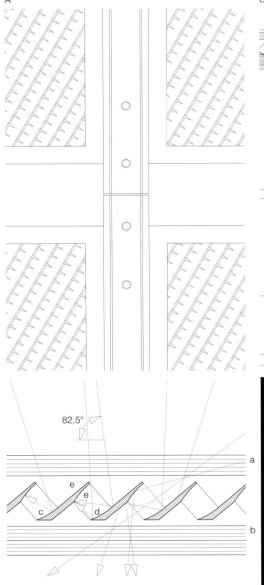

82,5°

D

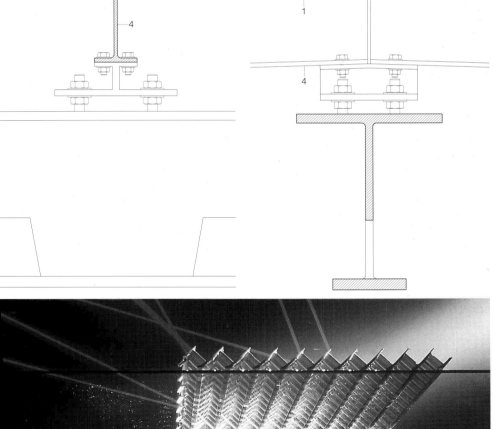

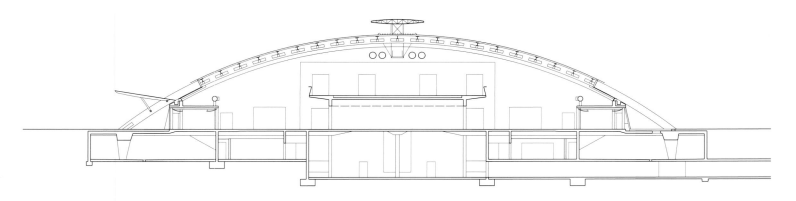

Cross-section   scale 1:500

## Glazed Cable Net for Clinic in Bad Neustadt, Germany

1997

Architects:
Lamm, Weber, Donath und Partner, Stuttgart
Structural design and planning:
Sobek und Rieger, Stuttgart
Werner Sobek, Josef Linder, Theodor Angelopoulos, Eduard Ganz, Harald Meckelburg, Alfred Rein, Jürgen Schreiber, Viktor Wilhelm

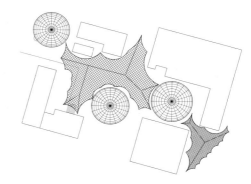

Site plan   scale 1:3000

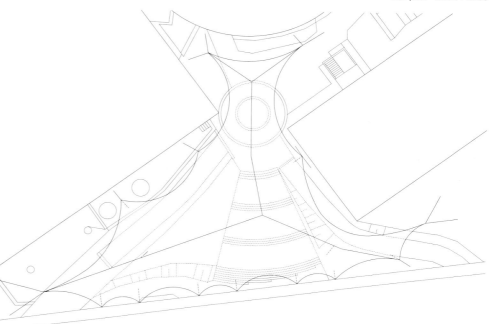

Roof plan   scale 1:500

This tent-like pavilion spanning between brick buildings is the first glass-covered cable-net structure in the world. It is based on a system developed by the engineers, in which glass sheets of identical size are assembled on a cable net in a lapped, shingle-like manner and fixed with standard stainless steel stirrups. The quadrilaterals of the network all have different geometries.

The curved form of the cable structure was determined by computer-aided design calculations. The net consists of high-strength galvanized steel cables, with additional cables at the edges. The latter transmit the loads from the structure to compression columns and tensile cable stays. The columns – up to 12 m in length – are in laminated timber cut to shape. The optimized form of the columns, which taper towards the ends, reflects the needs of buckling stability. Conical cast-steel shoes at the ends transmit the loads from the timber columns to the foundations via steel ball-and-socket joints, which guarantee the flexibility of the structure.

The laminated safety glass shingles are fixed with metal stirrups, which were clipped round the individual panes on the ground before the units were connected to the nodes of the cable net. The ridge coverings and the rainwater gutters at the edges consist of transparent polycarbonate elements.

Example 33

1 laminated safety glass:
  2 panes 4 mm heat-
  strengthened glass
2 stainless steel stirrup for
  fixing glass
3 fixing node

4 Ø 10 mm steel cable
5 Ø 28 mm edge cable
6 polycarbonate gutter
7 polycarbonate ridge
  covering
8 elastic cover strip

9 Ø 46 mm ridge cable
10 nut and bolt (M8) with
   plastic washers

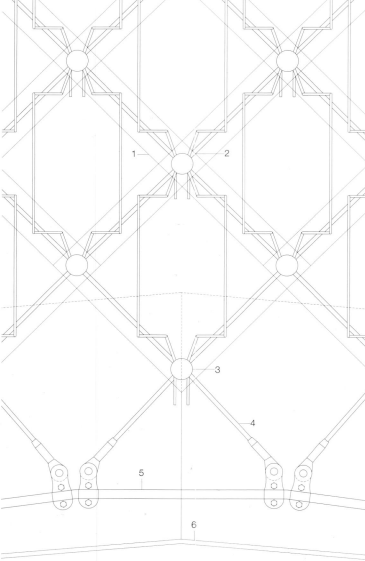

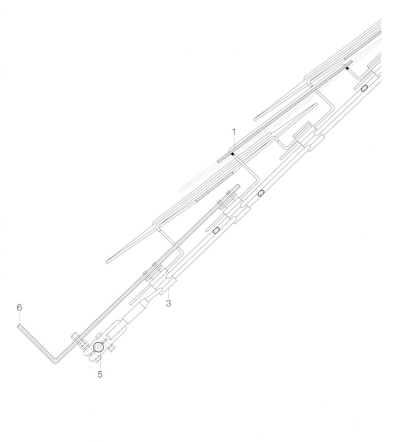

View from above   scale 1:10

Vertical section through eaves   scale 1:10

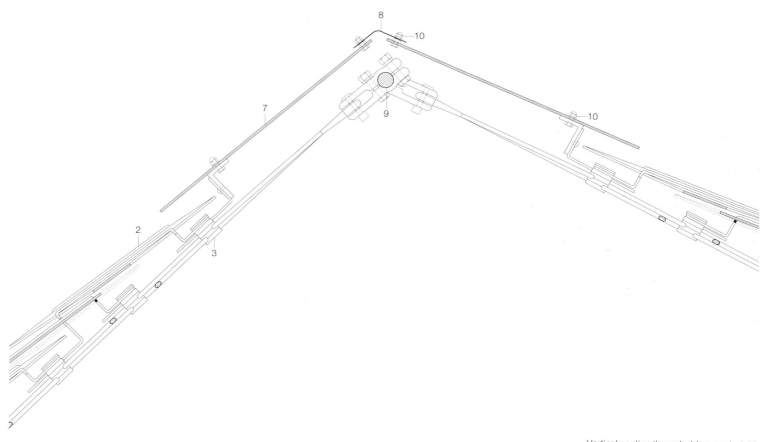

Vertical section through ridge  scale 1:10

Example 34

## Covering for Museum Courtyard in Hamburg

1989

Architects:
von Gerkan, Marg + Partner, Hamburg
Assistant: Klaus Lübbert
Structural engineers:
Schlaich, Bergermann + Partner, Stuttgart
Assistant: Karl Friedrich
Design: Volkwin Marg, Jörg Schlaich

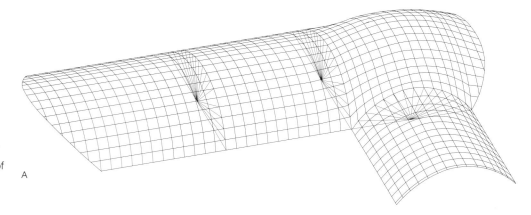

A

To allow fuller use of the L-shaped courtyard of the Hamburg City History Museum, built by Fritz Schumacher between 1914 and 1926, a proposal was made to cover it with a glazed roof. The museum is a listed building, so that an extremely light, transparent type of construction was required. The structure consists of a lattice shell in the form of two arched vaults linked at their point of intersection by a dome-like element. The constructional geometry, with flowing transitions between the three main sections, was the outcome of a process of optimization in which roof loads were to be transmitted to the ground largely in the form of membrane-shell compression forces – thereby avoiding bending stresses.

By restricting the nature of the forces in this way, it was possible to reduce the cross-sectional dimensions of the shell members. The loadbearing structure consists of 60 x 40 mm flat steel sections, which are the minimum dimensions required to support the glass covering. These sections were assembled to form an orthogonal loadbearing network with constant mesh dimensions and with pivoting bolts at the nodes. Since this would have allowed a distortion of the rectangular mesh layout into a series of rhombuses, diagonal members were necessary to divide the rectangles into triangles and create a rigid shell structure. To ensure a maximum degree of slenderness, the diagonals were formed with cables, which run in two directions so that one of the diagonals is always in tension. The glazing consists of sheets of 10 mm toughened safety glass laid on the flat steel sections and held in position by point fixings in the form of flat plates over the nodes. This is the first example of a roof structure with direct glazing; i.e. without additional glazing bars. Around the edge of the roof is a continuous rigid steel I-beam, to which the glazing sections are fixed. The I-beam is set roughly 70 – 90 mm above the existing roof and is point-fixed through it to the reinforced concrete slabs and walls within. To prevent the formation of condensation, a heating wire was inserted between the edge bearing of the glazing and the supporting bars. Air heated by solar radiation can escape via the edge of the roof and ventilation flaps.

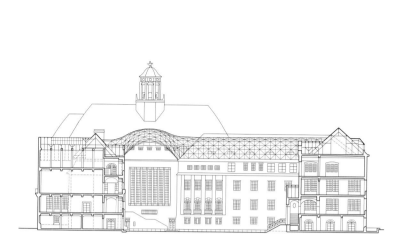

B

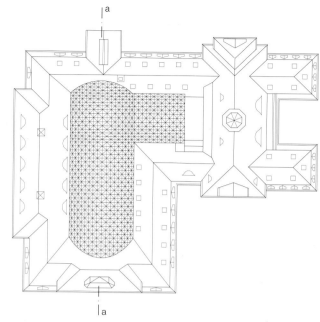

C

A  3D view of lattice shell structure
B  Section aa and part elevation
scale 1:1000
C  Plan of roof
scale 1:1000
D  Lattice shell structure with section through "hub"
E  Detail of hub
scale 1:10

1  ⌀ 16 mm stainless steel spokes
2  left-handed thread (M16) 50 mm long
3  20 mm node plate
4  ⌀ 16 mm stainless steel tension cable
5  40x4 mm clamping piece

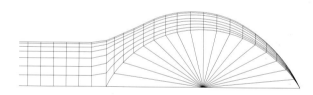

D

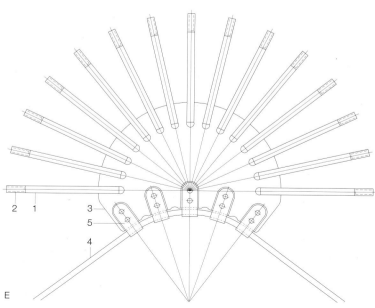

E

Example 34

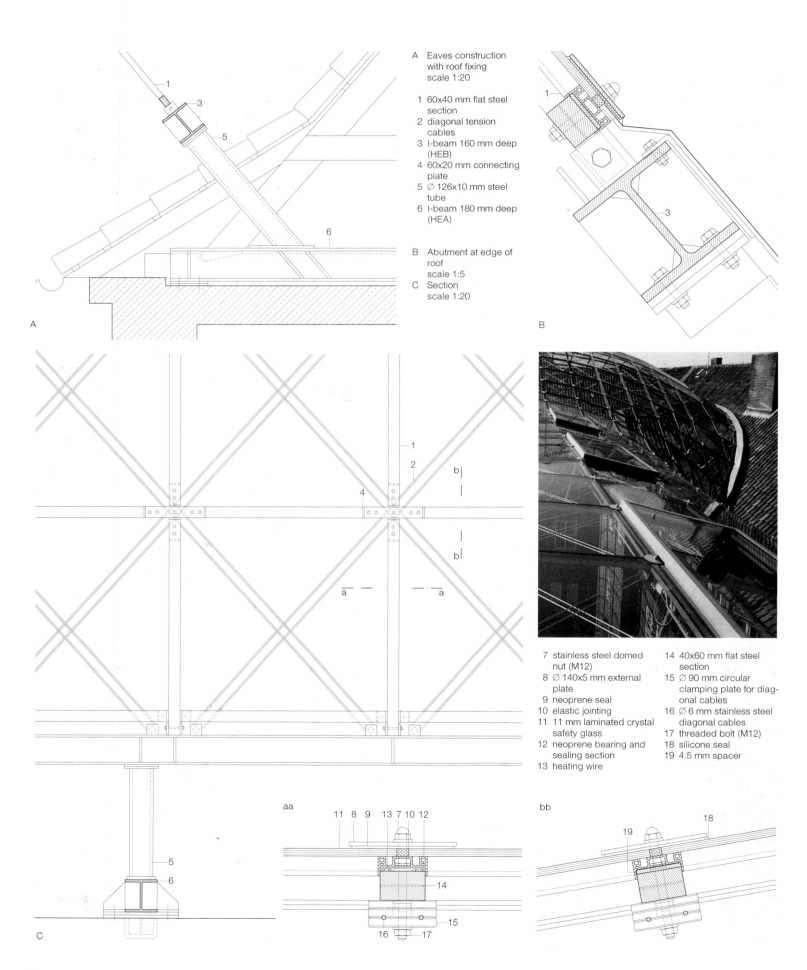

A Eaves construction
   with roof fixing
   scale 1:20

1 60x40 mm flat steel
  section
2 diagonal tension
  cables
3 I-beam 160 mm deep
  (HEB)
4 60x20 mm connecting
  plate
5 Ø 126x10 mm steel
  tube
6 I-beam 180 mm deep
  (HEA)

B Abutment at edge of
   roof
   scale 1:5
C Section
   scale 1:20

7 stainless steel domed
  nut (M12)
8 Ø 140x5 mm external
  plate
9 neoprene seal
10 elastic jointing
11 11 mm laminated crystal
   safety glass
12 neoprene bearing and
   sealing section
13 heating wire

14 40x60 mm flat steel
   section
15 Ø 90 mm circular
   clamping plate for diagonal cables
16 Ø 6 mm stainless steel
   diagonal cables
17 threaded bolt (M12)
18 silicone seal
19 4.5 mm spacer

A

B

C

aa

11 8 9 13 7 10 12

14

15

16 17

bb

19

18

# Statutory instruments, directives and standards

## Requirements of construction law

Technical standards, statutory instruments and directives serve to create a framework and set standards for the construction industry. They are the product of experience and should be constantly updated.

Standards and directives, which are components of construction law, must be adhered to. Divergence from these is only permitted if appropriate verification of the serviceability can be furnished; the same level of safety must be maintained.

Technical rules provide users with advice on methods of design and construction which experience has shown to be successful. Therefore, the same success can be achieved with other methods and materials complying with the requirements. This opens up the way for new designs.

Voluntary agreements on the strict adherence to standards not required by law, as well as supplementary properties and requirements, must be stipulated in the contract. Simply including a note in the contract that all standards are to be observed is nonsense and will not be acceptable in the future. Prescribing which standards are to be observed and which features of those standards apply, in the case of differing levels of requirements, is the only way to avoid disputes.

The following list is intended to help optimize the planning of specific projects. It cannot be exhaustive nor final. The latest edition of each standard is valid. The new European standards will replace the national standards in the foreseeable future. A clear distinction should be made between product, application and testing standards. When comparing materials care should be taken to ensure that the numerical results are based on the same methods of testing or calculation. For glass it is especially the physical data of radiation and the U-values that are critical.

In Germany, the "Ü" designation signifies the conformity of products for which building authority requirements or standards included in construction law exist. The corresponding standards are included in the list. The "CE" symbol will later replace the "Ü" designation. The procedure is similar in other countries. The final "CE" symbol will signal the conformity of products with the respective, harmonized European CEN standards. This is an ongoing process and depends on when the CE standards are introduced in the individual countries.

## Thermal insulation

In Germany, the requirements of the *Wärmeschutzverordnung* (Thermal Insulation Act) apply. Requirements for heat losses are specified for the entire building envelope depending on type of construction, use and geometrical form. Minimum *k-Werte* (= U-values) have to be achieved for the individual components of the construction.

For glass, this act takes into account a solar gain dependent on compass direction. This is the purpose of the "equivalent U-value". The total U-value of a window is a combination of the effects of glass and frame. DIN 4108 Part 4 contains the applicable U-values.

Some European countries have similar requirements and rules which must be observed. The national building authorities should be consulted during planning or when changing or replacing glass.

## Sound insulation

The sound insulation required for buildings is covered by DIN 4109. Examples for windows are listed in the amendment. If local sound insulation requirements apply, e.g. near airports and on through-roads, then these must be investigated and adhered to. Simple glass combinations selected to provide thermal insulation can also insulate against sound as well. The thickness of the glass is crucial for determining the sound insulation. The thickness should be chosen not only to comply with structural requirements but also to suit acoustic aspects.

Some European countries have similar requirements and rules which must be observed. The national building authorities should be consulted during planning or when changing or replacing glass.

## Safety, security

Glazing which has to provide protection against falling must consist of toughened or laminated safety glass, with the thickness being calculated using the appropriate loads and conditions. If necessary, tests in line with DIN 52337 – pendulum impact test, soft body – should be carried out.

In the UK for example, BS 6206 (1981) applies but differs from the German DIN in that an impact body with a peripheral tape is used. European standard prEN 12600 is being drawn up to harmonize these variations.

Overhead glazing to areas permanently occupied must include a pane of laminated safety glass on the underside. The same applies to horizontal dustproof ceilings.

Fire protection requirements must be clarified and maintained in every case. Special conditions apply to escape routes and rooms with high fire loads. A change of use may mean that a higher specification applies. Spread of fire to adjoining properties must be considered when designing façades.

Some European countries have similar requirements and rules which must be observed. The national building authorities should be consulted during planning or when changing or replacing glass.

## Requirements of civil law

Further contractual requirements may be agreed in addition to the provisions of construction law. This is particularly important for the radiation, mechanical and optical properties of glasses. The finishes to exposed edges must be defined.

It is also recommended to relate tolerances for dimensions and functional data to standards. For special glasses chosen for reasons of appearance it is important to have samples produced in order to establish the anticipated range of tolerances. This especially applies to colours and patterns because every production run exhibits tolerances which can be minimized but must be stipulated.

In some countries reference is made to various standards in the tender documentation. These may be national, European (EN) or international (ISO) standards. It should be remembered that requirements and tests vary. Materials can only be compared if the relevant data has been determined in the same manner. The framework conditions for measurements and calculations and the associated parameters must be studied closely. "Mixing" different sets of standards is not recommended.

The European standards covering the various products and tests are either already published or are in the final phases of drafting. Therefore, the numbering cannot be complete. It is strongly recommended that conformity with national standards be ensured during design and realization. The European and international standards can be called up via the following Internet addresses: http://www.nssn.org./search.html and http://www.iso.ch.sdis

## The material glass

| | | |
|---|---|---|
| DIN 1249 | 1 | Glass in building; sheet glass, concepts, dimensions |
| | 3 | Plate glass, concepts, dimensions |
| | 4 | Cast glass, concepts, dimensions |
| | 5 | Cast glass – U-shaped building elements; concepts, dimensions |
| | 10 | Chemical and physical properties |
| | 11 | Glass edges |
| | 12 | Thermally toughened glass |
| EN 572 | | Basic soda lime silicate glass products |
| | 1 | Definitions and general physical and mechanical properties |
| | 2 | Float glass |
| | 3 | Polished wired glass |
| | 4 | Drawn sheet glass |
| | 5 | Patterned glass |
| | 6 | Wired patterned glass |
| | 7 | Wired or unwired channel-shaped glass |
| prEN 1096 | | Glass in building — coated glass |
| | 1 | Definition and classification |
| | 2 | Test methods for durability of A, B and S coatings |
| | 3 | Test methods for durability of C and D coatings |
| | 4 | Factory production control and evaluation of conformity |

| | | |
|---|---|---|
| DIN 1238 | | Mirror of silver-coated plate glass |
| prEN 1036 | | Glass in building – mirrors from silver-coated float glass for internal use |
| DIN 11525 | | Horticultural sheet glass |
| DIN 11526 | | Horticultural cast glass |
| DIN 1259 | | Terminology relating to glass products |
| DIN 52333 | | Testing of glass; Knoop hardness |
| DIN 52322 | | Testing of glass; alkali resistance |
| DIN 12116 | | Testing of glass; determination of the acid resistance and classification of glass into acid classes |
| DIN 12111 | | Testing of glass; hydrolytic classes |
| prEN 12150 | | Glass in Building – thermally toughened safety glass |
| prEN 12024 | | Thermally toughened borosilicate safety glass |
| prEN 1863 | | Glass in Building – heat-strengthened soda lime silicate glass |
| prEN 12337 | | Glass in Building – chemically strengthened soda lime silicate glass |
| ISO 12543 | | Glass in Building – laminated glass and laminated safety glass |
| | 1 | Definitions and description of component parts |
| | 2 | Laminated safety glass |
| | 3 | Laminated glass |
| | 4 | Test methods for durability |
| | 5 | Dimensions and edge finishing |
| | 6 | Appearance |
| prEN 1748 | | Glass in Building – special basic products |
| | 1 | Borosilicate glasses |
| | 2 | Glass ceramics |
| prEN 1279 | 1 - 6 | Glass in Building – insulating glass units |

## Thermal insulation

| | | |
|---|---|---|
| Energy-savings Act of 22 July 1976 | | |
| Thermal Insulation Act of 16 August 1994 | | |
| DIN 4108 | 2, 4 | Thermal insulation in buildings |
| DIN 52612 | | Determination of thermal conductivity by the guarded hot-plate apparatus |
| prEN 673 | | Determination of thermal transmittance (U-value) – calculation method |
| prEN 674 | | Determination of thermal transmittance (U-value) – guarded hot-plate method |
| prEN 675 | | Determination of thermal transmittance (U-value) – heat flow meter method |
| prEN 12898 | | Determination of the emissivity |

## Sound insulation

| | | |
|---|---|---|
| VDI dir. 2719 | | Sound insulation with windows |
| DIN 4109 | | Sound insulation in buildings; amendments 1 and 2 |
| DIN 52210 | | Tests in building acoustics |
| prEN 12758 | | Glass in building – glazing and airborne sound insulation |
| | 1 | Definitions and determination of properties |
| EN 20717 | 1 | Rating of sound insulation in buildings and of building elements Airborne sound insulation (ISO/DIS 717-1: 1993) |
| ISO 140/1 - 1978 and ISO/DIS 140/9 | | Tests in building acoustics; airborne and impact sound insulation; laboratories for measuring the sound reduction of building elements |

## Sunshading, physical properties of radiation

| | | |
|---|---|---|
| DIN 67507 | | Light transmittance; radiant transmittance and total energy transmittance of glazings |
| prEN 410 | | Glass in building – determination of light transmittance, solar direct transmittance, total solar energy transmittance and ultraviolet transmittance, and related glazing characteristics |
| 4108 | 2 | Thermal insulation in buildings |

## Safety, security

| | | |
|---|---|---|
| DIN 52290 | 1 - 5 | Security glazing |
| DIN 52349 | | Structure after fracture of glass used in buildings |
| DIN 52337 | | Pendulum impact tests |
| DIN 52338 | | Ball drop test for laminated glass |
| CEN/TC 129/WG3 N7 | | |
| ISO/TC 160/SC1/WG3 N7 | | |
| prEN 12600 | | Glass in building – pendulum test – impact test; method for flat glass and performance requirements |
| DIN 18103 | | Burglar-resistant windows, doors and shutters |
| DIN 18038 | | Sport halls; halls for squash, rules for planning and construction |
| EN 10204/ DIN 50049 | | Inspection documents for the delivery of metallic products |
| DIN V19054 | | Windows, burglar-resistant windows; terms, requirements and tests |
| prEN 356 | | Glass in building – security glazing; testing and classification of resistance against manual attack |
| prEN 12603 | | Glass in building – determination of the bending strength of glass; procedures for goodness of fit confidence intervals for Weibull distributed data |
| ISO/DIS 14439 | | Glass in building – glazing requirements – glazing blocks |
| ISO/DIS 14440 | | Specification for security glazing – explosion-pressure-resistant glazing – classification and test method |

## Fire protection

| | | |
|---|---|---|
| DIN 4102 | | Fire behaviour of building materials and building components |
| DIN 18095 | | Doors; smoke-control doors; definitions and requirements |

## Structural issues, strength

| | | |
|---|---|---|
| MBO | | *Musterbauordnung* |
| LBO | | *Landesbauordnung* |
| DIBt | | *Deutsches Institut für Bautechnik*, Berlin Technical rules for the use of continuously supported vertical glazing (draft) |
| | • | Main requirements for vertical glazing subject to approval, Feb 1998 |
| | • | Main requirements for overhead glazing subject to approval, Feb 1998 |
| | • | Main requirements for glazing subject to foot traffic and requiring approval for each individual case, Feb 1998 |
| EOTA | | Guideline for European Technical Approval for Structural Sealant Glazing Systems (SSGS), Oct 1997 (draft) |
| ENV 1991-1 EC 1 | | Basis of design and actions on structures – 1: basis of design |
| ENV 1991 2.1 EC | | Unit loads, self-weight |
| ENV 1991 2.3 EC | | Wind actions |
| ENV 1991 2.4 EC | | Snow actions |
| DIN 52292 | 1 | Testing of glass and glass ceramic; determination of bending strength; coaxial double-ring bending test on a flat test piece with small test area |
| DIN 52292 | 2 | Determination of bending strength; coaxial double-ring bending test on a flat test piece with large test area |
| DIN 52299 | | Testing of glass; measurement of compressive surface stresses of tempered flat glass |
| DIN 52300 | 1 | Glass in building; determination of bending strength of glass; introduction to testing of glass |
| DIN 52303 | 1 | Test methods for flat glass in buildings; determination of bending strength; testing with resting on two supports |
| DIN 52338 | | Test methods for flat glass in buildings; ball drop test for laminated glass |

| | | |
|---|---|---|
| DIN 18055 | | Windows |
| DIN 18056 | | Window walls, design and construction |
| DIN 18516 | 1 | Cladding for external walls, ventilated at rear; requirements, principles of testing |
| | 4 | Tempered safety glass; requirements, design, testing |
| DIN 32622 | | Aquariums of glass |
| DIN 1055 | | Design loads for buildings |
| DIN 11535 | | Greenhouses |

## Other aspects

| | | |
|---|---|---|
| DIN 1286 | | Insulating glass units |
| DIN 1259 | 1 | Glass; terminology relating to glass types and groups |
| | 2 | Terminology relating to glass products |
| DIN 51110 | 1 | Testing of advanced technical ceramics; 4-point bending test at room temperature (draft) |
| | 3 | 4-point bending test; statistical evaluation, determination of the Weibull parameters |
| DIN 52294 | | Testing of glass; determination of the loading of desiccants in multiple-walled insulating glass units |
| DIN 18545 | | Sealing of glazings with sealants |
| DIN 18055 | | Windows; air permeability of joints, water-tightness and mechanical strain, requirements and testing |
| EN 1026 | | Windows and doors; air permeability of joints, methods of testing |
| DIN 18175 | | Glass building bricks and blocks |
| DIN 7863 | | Non-cellular elastomer glazing and panel gaskets |
| DIN 4242 | | Glass block walls |
| DIN 4243 | | Glasses for floors of reinforced concrete |
| DIN 18360 | | Metal construction works (Contract Procedures for Building Works Part C), June 1996 |
| DIN 18361 | | Glazing works (Contract Procedures for Building Works Part C), Sept 1988 |
| DIN 68121 | | Timber profiles for windows and window-doors |
| DIN 52293 | | Testing the gas-tightness of gas-filled insulating units |
| DIN 52460 | | Sealing and glazing – terms |
| DIN 52454 | | No-sag properties of sealants |
| DIN 52455 | | Testing of sealing compounds in building constructions; adhesion and expansion test |
| DIN 52452 | | Compatibility of sealants |
| DIN 52344 | | Weathering test for insulating glass units |
| DIN 52345 | | Determination of dew-point temperature of insulating glass units |
| DIN 52328 | | Testing of glass; determination of coefficient of longitudinal expansion |
| DIN 52313 | | Determination of the resistance of glass products to thermal shock |
| DIN 5034 | | Daylight in interiors |
| | 1 | General requirements |
| | 2 | Principles |
| | 3 | Calculation |
| | 4 | Simplified determination of minimum window sizes for dwellings |
| | 5 | Measurement |
| | 6 | Simplified determination of suitable dimensions for rooflights |
| prEN 32573 | | Thermal bridges in building construction - heat flows and surface temperatures - general calculation methods |

## References

### General glass literature and history

Banham, Reyner, Die Revolution der Architektur, Hamburg 1964
Banham, Reyner, The Architecture of the Well-tempered Environment, Chicago 1969
Bartetzko, Dieter, Die Konsequenz der Moderne, in: Der Architekt 5/98
Bauen mit Glas – 13 Statements, in: Detail 1998/3
Behling, Sophia and Stefan, Sol Power, Munich 1996
Behne, Adolf, Die Wiederkehr der Kunst, Leipzig 1919
Behnisch/Hartung, Eisenkonstruktionen des 19. Jahrhunderts in Paris, Darmstadt 1984
Behnisch/Hartung, Glas- und Eisenkonstruktionen des 19. Jahrhunderts in Großbritannien, Darmstadt 1984
Benevolo, Leonardo, Geschichte der Architektur des 19. und 20. Jahrhunderts, vols 1 & 2, Munich 1978
Binding, G.; Mainzer, U.; Wiedenau, A., Kleine Kunstgeschichte des deutschen Fachwerkbaus, Darmstadt 1989
Blaser, Werner, Chicago Architecture – Holabird & Root 1880–1992, Basel 1992
Blaser, Werner, Ludwig Mies van der Rohe – Less is more, Zurich 1986
Blondel, Nicole, Le Vitrail, Paris 1993
Bluestone, Daniel, Constructing Chicago, New Haven/London 1991
Boissière, Olivier, Jean Nouvel, Basel 1996
Borsi, Franco; Goddi, Ezio, Pariser Bauten der Jahrhundertwende – Architektur und Design der französischen Metropole um 1900, Stuttgart 1990
Breukelmann, Alfred, Tendenzen der Glasarchitektur: Glasfassadenkonzepte aus England, in: glasforum 3/1989
Cali, François, Das Gesetz der Gotik, Munich 1965
Camesasca, Ettore (ed.), Geschichte des Hauses, Berlin 1986
Camille, Michele, Die Kunst der Gotik, Cologne 1996
Chadwick, George F., The Works of Sir Joseph Paxton, London 1961
Cohen, Jean-Louis, Ludwig Mies van der Rohe, Basel 1995
Compagnie de Saint-Gobain 1665–1965, pub. by Compagnie de Saint-Gobain, Paris 1965
Compagno, Andrea, Die intelligente Glashaut, in: Bauwelt 1994/26
Condit, Carl W., The Chicago School of Architecture, Chicago 1964
Condit, Carl W., American Building, Chicago 1982
Curtis, William J.R., Modern Architecture since 1900, London 1996
Davies, Mike, A Wall for all Seasons, in: RIBA Journal, February 1981
Davies, Mike, Eine Wand für alle Jahreszeiten, in: Arch+ 104, Juli 1990
Der Westdeutsche Impuls. Die Deutsche Werkbund-Ausstellung Cöln 1914, exhibition catalogue Kölnischer Kunstverein, Cologne 1984
Duby, Georges, Die Zeit der Kathedralen, Frankfurt/M. 1991
Dupré, Judith, Wolkenkratzer, Cologne 1996
Elliot, L.W., Structural News: USA, in: The Architectural Review, April 1953
Engel, Heinrich, Measure and Construction of the Japanese House, Rutland/Vermont 1985
Fischer, Wend, Geborgenheit und Freiheit, Krefeld 1970
Ford, Edward R., Das Detail in der Architektur der Moderne, Basel 1994
Forter, Franziska, Die Kraft des Unsichtbaren, in: Fassade 2/98
Foster, Norman, Buildings and Projects of Foster Associates – Volume 2, 1971–1978, Volume 3, 1978–1985, Berlin 1989
Foster, Norman, Buildings and Projects of Team 4 and Foster Associates – Volume 1, 1964–1973, Berlin 1991
Frampton, Kenneth, Die Architektur der Moderne, Stuttgart 1983
Frampton, Kenneth, Grundlagen der Architektur – Studien zur Kultur des Tektonischen, Munich/Stuttgart 1995

Frampton, Kenneth, Villen in Amerika, Stuttgart 1995
Friemert, Chup, Die gläserne Arche. Kristallpalast London 1851 und 1854, Munich 1984
Glass – History, Manufacture and its Universal Application, pub. by Pittsburgh Plate Glass Company, Pittsburgh 1923
Geist, Johann Friedrich, Passagen. Ein Bautyp des 19. Jahrhunderts, Munich 1978
Giedion, Sigfried, Bauen in Frankreich. Bauen in Eisen. Bauen in Eisenbeton, Berlin/Leipzig 1928
Giedion, Sigfried, Raum, Zeit, Architektur, Zurich 1978
Ginsburger, Roger, Neues Bauen in der Welt, Vienna 1930
Glockner, Winfrid, Glastechnik, Munich 1992
Gössel, Peter; Leuthäuser, Gabriele, Architektur des 20. Jahrhunderts, Cologne 1990
Graefe, Rainer (ed.), Zur Geschichte des Konstruierens, Stuttgart 1989
Handbuch der Architektur, part 4, half-volume 2, issue 2 (Geschäfts- und Kaufhäuser, Warenhäuser und Meßplätze, Passagen und Galerien), Stuttgart 1902
Hannay, Patrick, Gläserne Amöbe – Hauptverwaltung von Willis Faber Dumas in Ipswich, in: Deutsche Bauzeitung 1997/4
Heinz, Thomas A., Frank Lloyd Wright – Glass Art, London/Berlin 1994
Hennig-Schefold, Monica; Schmidt-Thomsen, Helga, Transparenz und Masse, Cologne 1972
Hildebrand, Grant, The Wright Space, Washington 1991
Hitchcock, Henry-Russell, In the Nature of Materials, New York 1942
Hix, John, The Glasshouse, London 1996
Hofrichter, Hartmut (ed.), Fenster und Türen in historischen Wehr- und Wohnbauten, Marksburg/Braubach 1995
Hütsch, Volker, Der Münchner Glaspalast 1854–1931, Berlin 1985
Interpane (ed.), Gestalten mit Glas, Lauenförde 1997
Jaeggi, Annemarie, Adolf Meyer, Berlin 1994
Jelles, E. J., Duiker 1890–1935, Amsterdam 1976
Jencks, Charles, Die Sprache der Postmodernen Architektur, Stuttgart 1980
Joedicke, J.; Plath, Ch., Die Weissenhofsiedlung, Stuttgart 1977
Joedicke, Jürgen, Geschichte der modernen Architektur, Stuttgart 1958
Kimpel, Dieter; Suckale, Robert, Die gotische Architektur in Frankreich 1130–1270, Munich 1985
Kohlmaier, Georg; Sartory, Barna von, Das Glashaus, Munich 1988
Koppelkamm, Stefan, Künstliche Paradiese – Gewächshäuser und Wintergärten des 19. Jahrhunderts, Berlin 1988
Korn, Arthur, Glas im Bau und als Gebrauchsgegenstand, Berlin 1929
Krewinkel, Heinz W., Der Baustoff Glas – Stand der Entwicklung, 1. Fachkongreß Innovatives Bauen mit Glas, Munich 1993, Conference proceedings, Munich 1993
Krewinkel, Heinz W., Glas – Energieeinsparung und Energiegewinnung, 4. Fachkongreß Innovatives Bauen mit Glas, Munich 1996, Conference proceedings, Munich 1996
Krewinkel, Heinz W., Glasarchitektur, Basel 1998
Kuhnert, Nikolaus; Oswalt, Philipp, Medienfassaden, in: Arch+ 108, August 1991
Lerner, Franz, Geschichte des Deutschen Glaserhandwerks, Schorndorf 1981
Male, Emile, Die Gotik, Stuttgart 1994
Marrey, Bernard, Le Fer à Paris – Architectures, Paris 1989
Marrey, Bernard; Ferrier, Jacques, Paris sous Verre, Paris 1997
Martin Wagner 1885–1957, Exhibition catalogue Akademie der Künste Berlin, Berlin 1985
McCarter, Robert (ed.), Frank Lloyd Wright – A Primer on Architectural Principles, New York 1991
McGrath, Raymond; Frost, A.C., Glass in Architecture and Decoration, London 1961
McKean, John, Crystal Palace, London 1994
Meyer, Alfred Gotthold, Eisenbauten. Ihre Geschichte und Ästhetik, Esslingen 1907

Neuhart, Marilyn and John, Eames House, Berlin 1994
Neumann, Dietrich, Prismatisches Glas, in: Detail 1995/1
Norberg-Schulz, Christian, Vom Sinn des Bauens, Stuttgart 1979
Norberg-Schulz, Christian, Roots of Modern Architecture, Tokyo 1988
Ogg, Alan, Architecture in Steel. The Australian Context, Australia 1989
Patterson, Terry L., Frank Lloyd Wright and the Meaning of Materials, New York 1994
Pehnt, Wolfgang, Die Architektur des Expressionismus, Stuttgart 1998
Perrault Dominique, Bibliothèque nationale de France 1989–1995, Basel 1998
Petzold, Armin; Marusch, Hubert; Schramm, Barbara Der Baustoff Glas, Schorndorf 1990
Pevsner, Nikolaus, Europäische Architektur, Munich 1994
Phleps, Hermann, Deutsche Fachwerkbauten, Königstein i.T. 1951
Phleps, Hermann, Holzbaukunst. Der Blockbau, Karlsruhe 1981
Piano, Renzo, Renzo Piano 1987–1994, Basel 1995
Platz, Gustav Adolf, Die Baukunst der neuesten Zeit, Berlin 1930
Posener, Jukius, Aufsätze und Vorträge 1931–1980, Braunschweig 1981
Rice, Peter; Dutton, Hugh, Transparente Architektur, Basel 1995
Rice, Peter, An Engineer Imagines, London 1994
Ritchie, Ian, Architektur mit (guten) Verbindungen, London/Berlin 1994
Ronner, Heinz, Öffnungen. Baukonstruktion im Kontext des architektonischen Entwerfens, Basel 1991
Rowe, Colin; Slutzky, Robert; Hoesli, Bernhard, Transparenz, Basel 1989
Scheerbart, Paul, Glasarchitektur, Berlin 1914
Schild, Erich, Zwischen Glaspalast und Palais des Illusions, Braunschweig 1983
Schittich, Christian, Glas in Paris, in: Detail 1995/1
Schmidt-Brümmer, Horst, Alternative Architektur, Cologne 1983
Schneck, Adolf, Fenster aus Holz und Metall, Stuttgart 1942
Schulze, Franz, Ludwig Mies van der Rohe, Berlin 1986
Schulze, Konrad Werner, Glas in der Architektur, Stuttgart 1929
Singer, Charles; Holmyard, E. J.; Hall, A. R.; Williams, T. I., A History of Technology, Oxford, Vol. II 1956, Vol. III 1957, Vol. IV 1958
Strike, James, Construction into Design, Oxford 1991
Taut, Bruno, Die Stadtkrone, Jena 1919
Taut, Bruno, Die neue Wohnung, Leipzig 1924
Taut, Bruno, Die neue Baukunst in Europa und Amerika, Stuttgart 1929
Taylor, Brian Brace, Pierre Chareau – Designer and Architect, Cologne 1992
Tegethoff, Wolf, Ludwig Mies van der Rohe – Die Villen und Landhausprojekte, Essen 1981
The Contribution of the Curtain Wall to a New Vernacular, in: The Architectural Review, May 1957
Thiekötter, Angelika u.a., Kristallisationen, Splitterungen, Bruno Tauts Glashaus, Basel 1993
Ullrich, Ruth-Maria, Glas-Eisenarchitektur – Pflanzenhäuser des 19. Jahrhunderts, Worms 1989
Vavra, J. R., Das Glas und die Jahrtausende, Prague 1954
Völckers, Otto, Glas und Fenster, Berlin 1939
Völckers, Otto, Glas als Baustoff, Eberswalde/Berlin/Leipzig 1944
Völckers, Otto, Bauen mit Glas, Stuttgart 1948
Von der Waldhütte zum Konzern, pub. by Flachglas AG, Schorndorf 1987
Welsh, John, Das moderne Haus, Berlin 1995
Wigginton, Michael, Glass in Architecture, London 1996
Yoshida, Tetsuro, Das Japanische Wohnhaus, Tübingen 1969
Zukowsky, John (ed.), Chicago Architecture 1872–1922, Munich 1987
Zwischen Innen und Außen, Daidalos 13/1984

**Technical glass literature**

Balkow, Dieter; Bock, Klaus von; Krewinkel, Heinz W.; Rinkens, Robert, Technischer Leitfaden Glas am Bau, Stuttgart 1990

Beckmann, William A.; Duffie, John A., Solar Engineering of the Thermal Processes, New York 1991

Blank, Kurt, Thermisch vorgespanntes Glas, Glastechn. Ber. 52 (1979) No. 1

Blank, Kurt, Thermisch vorgespanntes Glas, Teil 2, Glastechn. Ber. 52 (1979) No. 2

Blank, Kurt, Dickenbemessung von rechteckigen Glasscheiben unter gleichförmiger Flächenlast, in: Bauingenieur 68 (1993)

Blank, Kurt; Grüters, Hugo; Hackl, Klaus, Contribution to the size effect on the strength of float glass, in: Glastechn. Ber. 63 (1990), No. 5

Bosshard, Walter, Tragendes Glas?, in: Schweizer Ingenieur und Architekt, No. 27/28, 3 July 1995

Braun, Peter; Merko, Armin, Thermische Solarenergie an Gebäuden, ISE Frauenhofer Institut Solare Energie-systeme, Berlin 1997

Brookes, Alan J.; Grech, Chris, Das Detail in der High-Tech-Architektur, Basel 1991

Button, David; Pye, Brian (ed.), Glass in building, Oxford 1993

Charlier, Hermann, Bauaufsichtliche Anforderungen an Glaskonstruktionen, in: Der Prüfingenieur, 11 Oct. 1997, pp. 44–54

Compagno, Andrea, Intelligente Glasfassaden. Material, Anwendung, Gestaltung, Zürich 1995

Compagno, Andrea, Tragende Transparenz, in: Fassade 2/1998

Daniels, Klaus, Technologie des ökologischen Bauens, Basel/Boston/Berlin 1995

DIN-Taschenbuch 217, Raumlufttechnik 1, Berlin/Cologne 1994

DIN-Taschenbuch 99, Verglasungsarbeiten VOB/StLB, Berlin/Cologne 1993

Durchholz, Michael; Goer, Bernhard; Helmich, Gerd, Method of reproducibly predamaging float glass as a basis to determine the bending strength, in: Glastechn. Ber., Glass Sci. Technol. 68 (1995), No. 8

Ehm, H., Wärmeschutzverordnung '95. Grundlagen, Erläuterungen und Anwendungshinweise. Der Weg zu Niedrigenergiehäusern, Wiesbaden/Berlin 1995

Fahrenkrog, Hans-Hermann, Mehrscheiben-Isolierglas. Geschichte und Entwicklung, in: Deutsches Architektenblatt 1995/9

Feist, Wolfgang, Passivhäuser in Mitteleuropa, thesis, University of Kassel 1993, Darmstadt 1993

Feldmeier, Franz, Zur Berücksichtigung der Klimabelastung bei der Bemessung von Isolierglas bei Überkopfverglasung, in: Stahlbau 65 1996/8

Fisch, M. Norbert, Solartechnik I, Universität Stuttgart, Institut für Thermodynamik und Wärmetechnik, Abt. Rationelle Energienutzung, Stuttgart 1990

Freiman, S.W., Fracture mechanics of glass, in: Glass. Science and Technology, Vol. 5, pub. by D.R. Uhlmann, N.J. Kreidel, New York 1980

Führer, Wilfried; Knaack, Ulrich, Konstruktiver Glasbau 1, Aachen 1995

Glas am Bau, Technisches Handbuch, pub. by Vegla Vereinigte Glaswerke GmbH, Aachen 1998/99

Glas im Bauwesen, OTTI Technologiekolleg, pub. by Ostbayerisches Technologie Transfer Insitut e.V. Regensburg, Regensburg 1997

Glas und Praxis, Kompetentes Bauen und Konstruieren mit Glas 1994, pub. by Glas Trösch AG, Bützberg 1994

Glashandbuch 1997, pub. by Pilkington Flachglas, Gelsenkirchen 1997

Hess, Rudolf, Bemessung von Einfach- und Isolier-verglasungen unter Anwendung der Membranwirkung bei Rechteckplatten großer Durchbiegung, HBT Report No.13, Institut für Hochbautechnik, ETH Zürich 1986

Hess, Rudolf, Stahl und Glas – Bemessung, Konstruktion und Anwendungsgebiete, in: Baukultur 1/2–95

Hlaváč, Jan, Glass Science and Technology. The Technology of Glass and Ceramics. An Introduction, Amsterdam / Oxford / New York 1983

Humm, Othmar, Niedrigenergiehäuser. Innovative Bauweisen und neue Standards, Staufen 1997

Humm, Othmar; Toggweiler, Peter, Photovoltaik und Architektur. Photovoltaics in Architecture, Basel/Boston/Berlin 1993

IEA Passiv Solar Commercial and Institutional Buildings, A Sourcebook of Examples and Design Insights, Task 18, Chichester 1994

IEA Solar Heating and Cooling Programme, Frame and Edge Seal Technology, A State of the Art Survey, Task, 18 Advanced Glazing and Assoziated Materials for Solar and Building Applications, 1994

Kerkhof, F.; Richter, H.; Stahn, D., Festigkeit von Glas in Abhängigkeit von der Belastungsdauer und -verlauf, in: Glastechn. Ber., Nov. 1991

Klimke, Herbert; Walochnik, Wolfgang, Wann trägt Glas?, in: glasforum 2/1993

Kutterer, M.; Görzig, R., Glasfestigkeit im Bohrungs-bereich, IL-Forschungsbericht FB 01/97

Lehmann, Raimund, Auslegung punktgehaltener Gläser, in: Stahlbau 1998/4

Lotz, Stefan, Untersuchungen zur Festigkeit und Lang-zeitbeständigkeit adhäsiver Verbindungen zwischen Fügepartnern aus Floatglas, thesis, Kaiserslautern 1995

Marusch, H.; Petzold, A.; Schramm, B., Der Baustoff Glas. Grundlagen, Eigenschaften, Erzeugnisse, Glas-bauelemente, Anwendungen, Berlin/Schorndorf 1990

Mecholsky, J. J.; Rice, R. W.; Freiman, S. W., Prediction of fracture energy and flaw size in glasses from mea-surements of mirror size, in: J. Am. Ceram. Soc. 57 (1974), pp. 440–443

Minor, Joseph E.; Reznik, Patrick L., Failure Strengths of Laminated glass, in: J. of Structural Engineering 116 (4)/1990

Oswalt, Philipp, Wohltemperierte Architektur. Neue Techniken des energiesparenden Bauens, Cologne 1994

Produkt Information Handbook, pub. by Transsolar and National Observatory of Athens, The European Com-mission – Directorate General for Energy 1997

Rathert, Peter, Wärmeschutzverordnung und Heizungs-anlagen-Verordnung, Cologne 1995

Rawson, Harold, Glass Science and Technology 3 – Properties and Applications of Glass, Amsterdam 1980

Recknagel, Hermann; Schramek, Rudolf; Sprenger, Eberhard, Taschenbuch für Heizung und Klimatech-nik, Munich/Vienna 1995

Rice, P.; Dutton, H., Transparente Architektur, Basel/Boston/Berlin 1995

Richter, H., Langsame Rißausbreitung und Lebensdauer-bestimmung. Vergleich zwischen Rechnung und Experiment, in: Bericht Deutsche Keramische Gesellschaft 57 (1980) No. 1, pp. 10–12

Robbins, Claude I., Daylighting Design and Analysis, New York 1986

Schlaich, J.; Schober, H., Verglaste Netzkuppeln, in: Bautechnik 69 (1992), issue 1, pp. 3–10

Scholze, H., Glas: Natur, Struktur und Eigenschaften, Berlin/Heidelberg 1988

Schulz, Christina; Seger, Peter, Großflächige Ver-glasungen, in: Detail 1991/1

Schulz, Christina; Seger, Peter, Glas am Bau 1+2 – Konstruktion von Glasfassaden, in: Deutsches Architektenblatt 3/1993 and 5/1993

Sedlacek, G.; Blank, K.; Güsgen, J., Glass in Structural Engineering, in: The Structural Engineer, Vol. 73, No. 2/17 January 1995

Techen, H., Fügetechnik für den konstruktiven Glasbau, thesis, Bericht Nr. 11 – TU Darmstadt, Institut für Statik 1997

Treberspurg, Martin, Neues Bauen mit der Sonne, Vienna/New York 1994

Witte, Friedrich, Recycling von Flachglas, in: Glastechn. Ber., Glass Sci. Technol. 68 (1995) No. 8, 107

Wörner, J.-D.; Shen, X., Sicherheitskonzept für Glas-fassaden, Bauingenieur 69 (1994) pp. 33–36

Wörner, J. D.; Pfeiffer, Rupert; Schneider, Jens; Shen, Xiaofeng, Konstruktiver Glasbau, in: Bautechnik 75 (1998), issue 5

## Picture credits

The authors and publishers would like to express their sincere thanks to all those who provided visual material, gave us permission to reproduce details or provided information and so contributed to the production of this book. All the drawings and diagrams were specially commissioned. Photographs not specifically acknowledged were supplied by the architects named in the index of persons or from the archives of the journal *DETAIL*. The numbers refer to the figures (parts 1 and 2) or the page numbers (parts 3 and 4).

### From photographers and picture archives

Akademie der Künste, Berlin: 1.1.47
Archiv Herzog, Munich: 1.2.57
Archiv Institut für Leichte Flächentragwerke, Stuttgart: 2.2.1, 2.2.50
Arizona State University, USA: 1.2.59
Art Institute of Chicago/The Hilbersheimer Collection, Stiftung George Danforth: 1.1.42, 1.1.43, 1.2.43
av Studios GmbH, Stuttgart: p. 211 bottom
Bartenbach, Peter, Munich: p. 311 top right and bottom, 312
Bednorz, Achim, Cologne: 1.1.31
Bergeret, Gaston, Saint-Mandé: 2.2.43
Blaser, Werner, Basel: 1.1.19
Bonfig, Peter, Munich: pp. 213–215
Brandl, Sonja, Munich: p. 263 centre, 307 top, centre
Bryant, Richard/Arcaid, Surrey: 1.2.67, p. 265
Buckminster Fuller Institute, Los Angeles, California: 1.2.69
Cannon Architects, Engineers, Planners, Buffalo/New York: 1.2.65
Carpenter, James, Design Associates, New York: 1.2.22, 1.2.23
Charles, Martin, Isleworth: 1.2.26
Cook, Jeffrey, Arizona State University: 1.2.58
Cook, Peter/View, London: p. 175, p. 262 bottom, 264
Couturier, Stéphane/Archipress, Paris: 1.2.50
Denancé, Michel/Archipress, Paris: 1.2.20
Dyer, Michael, London: p. 304
Esch, Hans Georg, Cologne: 1.2.18, pp.151, 167 top, 280, 281, 300–302, 316, 317 bottom, 319
Fessy, Georges, Paris: pp. 157, 287–289
FLC/VG Bild-Kunst, Bonn, 1989: 1.2.16
Fogg Art Museum, Harvard University Art Museums, Cambridge, Massachusetts: 1.1.22
Fotoarchiv Hirmer Verlag, Munich: 1.1.11
Frahm, Klaus/Contur, Cologne: 1.1.44, pp. 303, 317 top
Fregoso & Basalto, Genoa: pp. 290, 291
Gascoigne, Chris/Arcaid, Surrey: 1.2.51
Gassner, Jochen, Egenhofen: p. 311 top left
Gilbert, Dennis/View, London: 1.2.46, 1.2.47, pp. 59, 193, 194, 195 bottom and top left, 282–284
Gordon, J.E., University of Reading, England: 2.2.2
Halbe, Roland/Contur, Cologne: 2.3.121
Hanisch, Manfred, Mettmann-Metzhausen: p. 204
Heinz, Thomas A.: 1.1.34
Helfenstein, Heinrich, Adliswil (CH): p. 164
INGLAS, Friedrichshafen: 2.3.68
Iseli, Daphné, Bern: pp. 190–192
Jäger, Helmut, Frankenmarkt (A): p. 310
Jocher, Thomas, Munich: pp. 198, 199
Kandzia, Christian, Stuttgart: pp. 169, 220 top, 234, 236, 237, 239, 241
Kaunat, Angelo, Graz: pp. 294, 295
Keller, Andreas, Kirchentellinsfurt: 2.2.64
Kik, Friedemann, Stuttgart: 2.3.11
Kinold, Klaus, Munich: 1.2.24, 1.1.49, pp. 173, 185, 211 top
Kirkwood, Ken, Northamptonshire: 1.2.42
Knauf, Holger, Düsseldorf: pp. 268, 269, 271, 273
Koppelkamm, Stefan, Berlin: 1.1.20

Krewinkel, Heinz W., Böblingen: 2.2.37, p. 299
Kutterer, Mathias, Stuttgart: 2.2.47, 2.2.48, 2.2.49. 2.2.55, 2.2.65
Linden, John Edward, London: p. 306 top
McGrath, Norman, New York: 1.2.12
Morency, Eric, Paris: p. 254
Müller-Naumann, Stefan, Munich: p. 296
Municipal Archive Utrecht/E.A. van Blitz: 1.1.39
Narjus, Sarlotta, Helsinki: p. 232
Nederlands Architectuurinstituut, Rotterdam: 1.1.53
Neuhart, Andrew, El Segundo, California: 1.2.6
Ouwerkerk, Erik-Jan, Berlin: pp. 206–209
Prokschi, Werner, Munich: pp. 200–203
Reichel-Vossen, Johanna, Munich: 2.3.119
Reid, Jo & Peck, John, Newport: p. 305
Richter, Ralf/Architekturphoto, Düsseldorf: pp. 167 bottom, 220 bottom, 221, 278 bottom, 279
Richters, Christian, Münster: pp. 159 left, 181, 196, 197, 249, 251–253, 255, 257 bottom, 259 right, 260
Riehle, Thomas/CONTUR, Cologne: 2.3.120
Rietveld Schröder Archive, Utrecht: 1.2.28
Rijksmuseum, Amsterdam: 1.1.17
Rocheleau, Paul/Freeman, Michael: 1.2.3, 1.2.4
Roth, Lukas, Cologne: pp. 242, 243, 248
Ruault, Philippe, Nantes: pp. 166, 244
Schittich, Christian, Munich: 1.1.7, 1.1.8, 1.1.9, 1.1.30, 1.2.1, 1.2.13, 1.2.14, 1.2.15, 1.2.17, 1.2.19, 1.2.21, 1.2.27, 1.2.30, 1.2.33, 1.2.48, 1.2.49, 1.2.66, 2.2.37, 2.2.53, pp. 153, 159 right, 183, 188, 189, 195 top right, 210, 212, 216, 240, 245, 257 top, 259 left and centre, 261, 262 top, 263 top, 278 top, 293, 298, 306 bottom right, 308, 309
Schmidt-Brümmer, H./Vista Point Verlag, Cologne: 1.2.63
Schuster, Oliver, Stuttgart: p. 205
Sick, Friedrich, Stuttgart: 2.3.74, 2.3.77
Sobek, Werner, Stuttgart: 2.2.57, 2.2.60, pp. 313–315
Spiluttini, Margherita, Vienna: pp. 217, 219
Staatliche Galerie Moritzburg, Halle, Landeskunstmuseum Sachsen-Anhalt, Sammlung Photographie, Hans Finsler Nachlaß: 1.1.51
Staib, Gerald, Stuttgart: 1.1.10, 1.1.21, 1.1.23, 1.1.52, p. 238
Stedeldijk Museum, Amsterdam: 1.1.41
Stoller, Ezra/Esto, New York: 1.2.9, 1.2.38
Suzuki, Hisao, Barcelona: 1.2.31, pp. 246, 247
Tiainen, Jussi, Helsinki: pp. 228–230, 233
Tölle, Frank/Architekton, Mainz: p. 267
Transsolar, Stuttgart: 2.3.81, 2.3.100
van der Vlugt, Ger, Amsterdam: pp. 224, 227
VEGLA-Bildarchiv, Alsdorf: 2.3.58
Voeten, Sybolt, Breda: p. 225
Voithenberg, G. and E. von, Munich: 1.1.1
Walser, Peter, Stuttgart: 1.1.12

### From books and journals

Arne Jacobsen, in: 2 G, 1997/IV, Revista Internacional de Arquitectura, Barcelona, p. 54: 1.2.35, 1.2.36
Benevolo, Leonardo, Die Geschichte der Stadt, Frankfurt/New York 1983, p. 762: 1.1.16
Compagnie de Saint-Gobain 1665-1965, pub. by Compagnie de Saint-Gobain, Paris 1965: 1.1.5
Daidalos, No. 66, 1997, p. 85: 1.1.26
Elliott, Cecil D., Technics and Architecture, The development of Materials and Systems for Buildings, MIT Press, Cambridge, Massachusetts, 1992, p. 114: 1.1.3
Ford, Edward R., Details of Modern Architecture, Cambridge Massachusetts 1990, p. 342, 1.1.35
Frank Lloyd Wright Monograph 1924-1936, Tokyo 1985, (Fotos: Futagawa, Yukio), p. 278; p. 190: 1.1.36, 1.1.40
Futagawa, Yukio (pub./photos); Bauchet, Bernard; Vellay, Marc, La Maison de Verre. Pierre Chareau. Tokyo 1988, p. 31: 1.1.54
Hennig-Schefold, Monica; Schmidt-Thomsen, Helga, Transparenz und Masse, Passagen und Hallen aus Eisen und Glas 1800–1880, Cologne 1972, p. 56: p. 7
Humm, Othmar; Toggweiler, Peter, Photovoltaik und Architektur, Photovoltaics and Architecture, Birkhäuser Verlag Basel/Boston/Berlin: 2.3.132
IEA Passive solar commercial and institutional buildings,

John Wiley & Sons Ltd, Battins Lane, Chichester, England: 2.3.102, 2.3.103
Kiraly, Josef, Architektur mit der Sonne, Heidelberg 1996, p. 48: 1.2.59
Klotz, Heinrich, Von der Urhütte zum Wolkenkratzer, Munich 1991, p. 207: 1.1.27
Martin Wagner 1885–1957, exhibition catalogue Akademie der Künste, Berlin 1985, p. 21: 1.2.58
Mies van der Rohe, Vorbild und Vermächtnis, DAM, Frankfurt/Main, Stuttgart 1986, p. 86/2, p. 88/7, p. 36/1: 1.1.42, 1.1.43, 1.1.48
Riley, Terence; Reed, Peter, Frank Lloyd Wright, Architect, New York 1994, p. 235; p. 134: 1.1.37, 1.1.38
Singer, Charles; Holmyard, E. J., A History of Technology, Volume III, Oxford 1957, p. 209: 1.1.2
Speidel, Manfred, Bruno Taut. Natur und Fantasie 1880–1938, Berlin 1995, p. 131: 1.1.45
Sumi, Christian, Immeuble Clarté 1932, Zurich 1989, p. 36: 1.1.50
Taut, Bruno, Die Neue Baukunst in Europa und Amerika, Stuttgart o. J., p. 25: 1.1.46
umweltforum BAU e.V., Niedrigenergiehäuser, KBK Druck + Verlag Karl Braun GmbH, Karlsruhe 1997, p. 43: 2.3.101
Völckers, Otto, Glas und Fenster, Berlin 1939: 1.1.6, 1.1.14, 1.1.15
Yoshida, Tetsuro, Das Japanische Wohnhaus, Berlin 1935, p. 118: 1.1.18

### Full-page illustrations
Page 7    Dome of the Bourse de Commerce, Paris, 1811, Henri Blondel
Page 59   Offices of Willis, Faber & Dumas, Ipswich, 1971-75, Norman Foster
Page 151  New Trade Fair, Leipzig, GMP
Page 185  Art Gallery, Bregenz, Peter Zumthor

The following illustrations in Part 3 "Construction details" were taken from projects actually built:

**Photos**

| | |
|---|---|
| Page 153 | Private house, Ulm, Karl Josef Schattner |
| Page 155 | Montessori School, Ingolstadt, Behnisch & Sabatke |
| Page 157 | Nationalbibliothek François Mitterand, Paris, Dominique Perrault |
| Page 158 | Hotel Kempinski, Munich, Murphy/Jahn, Schlaich Bergermann + Partner |
| Page 159 right | Extension to a theatre, Vidy-Lausanne, Rodolphe Luscher |
| Page 159 left | Art Gallery, Bregenz, Peter Zumthor |
| Page 164 | Forestry works centre, Turbenthal, Marianne Burkhalter, Christian Sumi |
| Page 165 | Finnish Embassy, Washington, Heikkinen + Komonen |
| Page 166 | Court building, Nanterre, François Deslaugiers |
| Page 167 top | New Trade Fair, Leipzig, GMP |
| Page 167 bottom | Facade, Vereinsbank Stuttgart, Behnisch & Sabatke |
| Page 169 | Bundestag, Bonn, Behnisch |
| Page 173 | Museum of Arts & Crafts, Frankfurt, Richard Meier |
| Page 175 | Television station headquarters, London, Richard Rogers |
| Page 181 | Office building, Hamburg, Hilde Léon and Konrad Wohlhage |
| Page 183 | Private house, Ulm, Karl Josef Schattner |

**Drawings**

| | |
|---|---|
| p. 157, 3.1.20 | Nationalbibliothek François Mitterand, Paris, Dominique Perrault |
| p. 158, 3.1.21 | Hamburg City History Museum, GMP, Schlaich Bergermann + Partner |
| p. 158, 3.1.22 | Aquatoll glass dome, Neckarsulm, Schlaich Bergermann + Partner |
| p. 158, 3.1.23 | Hotel Kempinski, Munich, Murphy/Jahn, Schlaich Bergermann und Partner |
| p. 159, 3.1.24 | Component testing shop, State Materials Testing Institute, Stuttgart, Friedrich Wagner |
| p. 159, 3.1.25 | Extension to a theatre, Vidy-Lausanne, Rodolphe Luscher |
| p. 159, 3.1.26 | Art Gallery, Bregenz, Peter Zumthor |
| p. 162, 3.1.37 | Charles de Gaulle airport terminal, Paris, Paul Andrea, RFR |
| p. 162, 3.1.38 | Bus shelter, Paris, Helmut Jahn, Werner Sobek |
| p. 166, 3.2.5 | Senior citizens' residence, Wesel, HPP |
| p. 166, 3.2.6 | Conference pavilion, Weil am Rhein, Tadao Ando, Günter Pfeifer |
| p. 166, 3.2.7 | Court building, Nanterre, François Deslaugiers |

The authors and publishers would like to thank the following manufacturers and companies for providing information and drawings:

BGT Bischoff Glastechnik, Bretten
Bouwmag GmbH, Düsseldorf
BSP Silikonprofile GmbH, Wiesbaden
Eduard Hueck GmbH & Co. KG, Lüdenscheid
EuroLam GmbH, Weimar
Fenster Werner fw Fassadensysteme, Darmstadt
Flachglas AG, Gelsenkirchen
Geilinger Tür- und Fenstersysteme AG, Winterthur, Switzerland
Glas Marte GmbH & CoKG, Bregenz
Glasbau Hahn, Frankfurt/Main
Götz GmbH, Würzburg
Hartmann & Co., Munich
Helmut Fischer GmbH, Thalheim
Hermann Forster AG, Arbon, Switzerland
Hutchinson Industrie-Produkte GmbH, Mannheim
Interpane Glas Industrie AG, Lauenförde
Josef Gartner & Co., Gundelfingen
L. B. Profile GmbH, Herbstein
MBM Metallbau Möckmühl GmbH, Möckmühl
MERK-Holzbau GmbH & Co., Aichach
Oberland Glas AG, Wirges
PHP-Glastec-Systeme, Landsberg am Lech
Riesterer Metallbau GmbH, Weil am Rhein
Rodan Danz GmbH, Schönaich
Sälzle GmbH & Co.KG, Illertissen
Schüco International KG, Wertingen
Seufert-Niklaus GmbH, Bastheim
STABA Wuppermann GmbH, Leverkusen
Trube & Kings Metallbaugesellschaft mbH, Uersfeld
Vegla Vereinigte Glaswerke GmbH, Aachen
Weck GmbH & Co., Wehr

The authors would also like to thank the following for their advice and suggestions concerning Part 3 "Construction details":

Gerhard Häberle / Ingenieurbüro Brecht, Stuttgart
Prof. Hans-Busso von Busse, Munich
Dipl. Arch. Andrea Compagno, Zurich
Dipl.-Ing. Dietrich Fink, Munich
Dr. Winfried Heusler / Gartner, Gundelfingen
Dipl.-Ing. Lutz Liebold, Remshalden-Grunbach
Prof. Eberhard Schunck, Munich
Dipl.-Ing. Peter Seger, Stuttgart